Lecture Notes in Computer Science   10855

Commenced Publication in 1973
Founding and Former Series Editors:
Gerhard Goos, Juris Hartmanis, and Jan van Leeuwen

More information about this series at http://www.springer.com/series/7407

Fabio Fioravanti · John P. Gallagher (Eds.)

Logic-Based Program Synthesis and Transformation

27th International Symposium, LOPSTR 2017
Namur, Belgium, October 10–12, 2017
Revised Selected Papers

 Springer

Editors
Fabio Fioravanti (iD)
University of Chieti-Pescara
Pescara
Italy

John P. Gallagher (iD)
Roskilde University
Roskilde
Denmark

ISSN 0302-9743   ISSN 1611-3349 (electronic)
Lecture Notes in Computer Science
ISBN 978-3-319-94459-3   ISBN 978-3-319-94460-9 (eBook)
https://doi.org/10.1007/978-3-319-94460-9

Library of Congress Control Number: 2018947448

LNCS Sublibrary: SL1 – Theoretical Computer Science and General Issues

Printed on acid-free paper

This Springer imprint is published by the registered company Springer Nature Switzerland AG
The registered company address is: Gewerbestrasse 11, 6330 Cham, Switzerland

Preface

This volume contains a selection of the papers presented at LOPSTR 2017, the 27th International Symposium on Logic-Based Program Synthesis and Transformation held during October 10–12, 2017, at the University of Namur, Belgium. It was co-located with PPDP 2017, the 19th International ACM SIGPLAN Symposium on Principles and Practice of Declarative Programming. The co-location of these two related conferences has occurred several times and has been stimulating and cross-fertilizing.

Previous LOPSTR symposia were held in Edinburgh (2016), Siena (2015), Canterbury (2014), Madrid (2013 and 2002), Leuven (2012 and 1997), Odense (2011), Hagenberg (2010), Coimbra (2009), Valencia (2008), Lyngby (2007), Venice (2006 and 1999), London (2005 and 2000), Verona (2004), Uppsala (2003), Paphos (2001), Manchester (1998, 1992 and 1991), Stockholm (1996), Arnhem (1995), Pisa (1994), and Louvain-la-Neuve (1993). More information about the symposium can be found at: https://www.sci.unich.it/lopstr17/.

The aim of the LOPSTR series is to stimulate and promote international research and collaboration in logic-based program development. LOPSTR is open to contributions on all aspects of logic-based program development, all stages of the software life cycle, and issues of both programming-in-the-small and programming-in-the-large. LOPSTR traditionally solicits contributions, in any language paradigm, in the areas of synthesis, specification, transformation, analysis and verification, specialization, testing and certification, composition, program/model manipulation, optimization, transformational techniques in software engineering, inversion, applications, and tools. LOPSTR has a reputation for being a lively, friendly forum that allows for the presentation and discussion of both finished work and work in progress. Formal proceedings are produced only after the symposium so that authors can incorporate the feedback from the conference presentation and discussion.

In response to the call for papers, 29 contributions were submitted from 13 different countries. The Program Committee accepted five full papers for immediate inclusion in the formal proceedings, and 14 more papers presented at the symposium were accepted after a revision and another round of reviewing. Each submission was reviewed by three Program Committee members or external referees. The paper "Context Generation from Formal Specifications for C Analysis Tools" by Michele Alberti and Julien Signoles won the best paper award, sponsored by Springer. In addition to the 19 contributed papers, this volume includes the abstracts of the invited talks by three outstanding speakers: Sumit Gulwani (Microsoft Research, USA) and Marieke Huisman (University of Twente, The Netherlands), whose talks were shared with PPDP, and Grigore Roşu (University of Illinois at Urbana-Champaign, USA).

We want to thank the Program Committee members, who worked diligently to produce high-quality reviews for the submitted papers, as well as all the external reviewers involved in the paper selection. We are very grateful to the LOPSTR 2017 Symposium Chair, Wim Vanhoof, and the local organizers for the great job they did in managing the symposium. Many thanks also to Brigitte Pientka, the Program Committee chair of PPDP, with whom we often interacted for coordinating the two events. We would also like to thank Andrei Voronkov for his excellent EasyChair system that automates many of the tasks involved in chairing a conference. Special thanks go to the invited speakers and to all the authors who submitted and presented their papers at LOPSTR 2017.

We also thank our sponsors, the University of Namur, le Fonds de la Recherche Scientifique (FNRS), the GRASCOMP Doctoral School, the FOCUS Research Group, Microsoft Research, and Springer for their cooperation and support in the organization of the symposium. Finally, Fabio Fioravanti gratefully acknowledges financial support from the Italian INdAM Research group GNCS.

April 2018   Fabio Fioravanti
                                                         John P. Gallagher

Organization

Program Chairs

Fabio Fioravanti   G. d'Annunzio University of Chieti-Pescara, Italy
John P. Gallagher   Roskilde University, Denmark and IMDEA Software
         Institute, Madrid, Spain

Program Committee

Roberto Bagnara	University of Parma and BUGSENG, Italy
Sabine Broda	University of Porto, Portugal
Henning Christiansen	Roskilde University, Denmark
Emanuele De Angelis	G. d'Annunzio University of Chieti-Pescara, Italy
Daniel De Schreye	Katholieke Universiteit Leuven, Belgium
Maribel Fernández	King's College London, UK
Miguel Gómez-Zamalloa	Complutense University of Madrid, Spain
Arie Gurfinkel	University of Waterloo, Canada
Geoff Hamilton	Dublin City University, Ireland
Gerda Janssens	Katholieke Universiteit Leuven, Belgium
Bishoksan Kafle	University of Melbourne, Australia
Andy King	University of Kent, UK
Fribourg Laurent	CNRS, ENS Paris-Saclay, France
Jacopo Mauro	University of Oslo, Norway
José F. Morales	IMDEA Software Institute, Spain
Jorge A. Navas	SRI International, USA
Corneliu Popeea	CQSE GmbH, Germany
Francesca Scozzari	G. d'Annunzio University of Chieti-Pescara, Italy
Theresa Swift	NOVALINKS, Universidade Nova de Lisboa, Portugal
Alicia Villanueva	Universitat Politècnica de València, Spain

Organizing Committee Chair

Wim Vanhoof   University of Namur, Belgium

Additional Reviewers

Alpuente, María	Alves, Sandra	Baruzzo, Andrea
Bournez, Olivier	De Angelis, Guglielmo	Dominguez, Jesus
Gordillo, Pablo	Isabel, Miguel	Jaber, Guilhem
Lescanne, Pierre	Paramonov, Sergey	Pettorossi, Alberto
Stulova, Nataliia	Tamarit, Salvador	Tveito, Lars
Varga, Janos	Vidal, German	

Abstracts of Invited Talks

Programming by Examples: Applications, Algorithms, and Ambiguity Resolution

Sumit Gulwani

Microsoft Research, USA
sumitg@microsoft.com

Abstract. 99% of computer users do not know programming and hence struggle with repetitive tasks. Programming by Examples (PBE) can revolutionize this landscape by enabling users to synthesize intended programs from example based specifications. A key technical challenge in PBE is to search for programs that are consistent with the examples provided by the user. Our efficient search methodology is based on two key ideas: (i) Restriction of the search space to an appropriate domain-specific language; (ii) A divide-and-conquer based search paradigm that inductively reduces the problem of synthesizing a program with a certain top-level operator to simpler synthesis problems over its sub-programs by leveraging the operator's inverse semantics. Another challenge in PBE is to resolve the ambiguity in the example based specification. Our ambiguity resolution methodology leverages two complementary approaches: (a) machine learning based ranking techniques that can pick an intended program from among those that satisfy the specification, and (b) active-learning based user interaction models. I will illustrate these various concepts using Flash Fill, FlashExtract, and FlashRelate—PBE technologies for data manipulation domains. These technologies, which have been released inside various Microsoft products, are useful for data scientists who spend 80% of their time wrangling with data. The Microsoft PROSE SDK allows easy construction of such technologies.

A Verification Technique for Deterministic Parallel Programs

Marieke Huisman

University of Twente, The Netherlands
m.huisman@utwente.nl

Abstract. A commonly used approach to develop parallel programs is to augment a sequential program with compiler directives that indicate which program blocks may potentially be executed in parallel. This talk presents how we use our verification technique for concurrent software, as supported by the VerCors tool set, to prove correctness of compiler directives combined with functional correctness of the program. We propose syntax and semantics for a simple core language, capturing the main forms of deterministic parallel programs. This language distinguishes three kinds of basic blocks: parallel, vectorized and sequential blocks, which can be composed using three different composition operators: sequential, parallel and fusion composition. We show that it is sufficient to have contracts for the basic blocks to prove correctness of the compiler directives, and moreover that functional correctness of the sequential program implies correctness of the parallelized program. We also show how a widely-used subset of OpenMP can be encoded into our core language, thus effectively enabling the verification of OpenMP compiler directives, and we discuss automated tool support for this verification process.

K: A Logic-Based Framework for Program Semantics and Analysis

Grigore Roșu

University of Illinois at Urbana-Champaign, USA
grosu@illinois.edu

Abstract. K (kframework.org) is a logic-based executable semantic framework in which programming languages, type systems and formal analysis tools can be defined using special rewrite rules. The K (rewrite) rules make it explicit which parts of the term they read-only, write-only, read-write, or do not care about. Several real languages have been defined in K, such as C (ISO C11 standard), Java (1.4), JavaScript (ES5), Ethereum Virtual Machine (EVM), Python, Scheme, Verilog, and dozens of prototypical or classroom languages.

The ISO C11 semantics and a fast OCAML backend for K power RV-Match (runtimeverification.com/match), one of the most advanced commercial automated analysis tools for C. K is a best-effort implementation of matching logic, a logic which uniformly generalizes several logical frameworks important for program analysis, such as: propositional logic, algebraic specification, FOL with equality, modal logic, and separation logic.

Contents

Theory

Verification

Analysis

Generation of Initial Contexts
for Effective Deadlock Detection

Elvira Albert, Miguel Gómez-Zamalloa, and Miguel Isabel[✉]

Complutense University of Madrid (UCM), Madrid, Spain
{elvira,mzamalloa}@fdi.ucm.es, miguelis@ucm.es

Abstract. It has been recently proposed that testing based on symbolic execution can be used in conjunction with static deadlock analysis to define a deadlock detection framework that: (i) can show deadlock presence, in that case a concrete test-case and trace are obtained, and (ii) can also prove deadlock freedom. Such symbolic execution starts from an *initial distributed context*, i.e., a set of locations and their initial tasks. Considering all possibilities results in a combinatorial explosion on the different distributed contexts that must be considered. This paper proposes a technique to effectively generate initial contexts that can lead to deadlock, using the possible conflicting task interactions identified by static analysis, discarding other distributed contexts that cannot lead to deadlock. The proposed technique has been integrated in the above-mentioned deadlock detection framework hence enabling it to analyze systems without the need of any user supplied initial context.

1 Motivation

Deadlocks are one of the most common programming errors and they are therefore one of the main targets of verification and testing tools. We consider a distributed programming model with explicit *locations* (or distributed nodes) and *asynchronous* tasks that may be spawned and awaited among locations. Each location represents a processor with a procedure stack and an unordered queue of pending tasks. Initially all processors are idle. When an idle processor's task queue is non-empty, some task is selected for execution, this selection is non-deterministic. Let us see now our motivating example in Fig. 1 which simulates a simple communication protocol between a database location and a worker location. Our implementation has the main method, and two classes Worker and DB implementing the worker and the database, respectively. The main method creates two distributed locations: the database and the worker, and (asynchronously) invokes methods register and work on each of them, respectively. The work method of a worker simply accesses the database (invoking asynchronously method getData) and then *blocks* until it gets the result, which

This work was funded partially by the Spanish MINECO project TIN2015-69175-C4-2-R, and by the CM project S2013/ICE-3006.

```
 1 main(){                          22  int connect(){
 2     DB db = new DB();            23      connected = 3;
 3     Worker w = new Worker();     24      return connected;
 4     db!register(w);              25  }
 5     w!work(db);}                 26  int register(Worker w){
 6                                  27      connected = 5;
 7 class Worker{                    28      Future⟨Data⟩ g;
 8   Data data;                     29      g = this!getData(w);
 9   int work(DB db){               30      await g?;
10     Future⟨Data⟩ f;             31      if (connected > 0){
11     f = db!getData(this);        32          connected = connected − 1;
12     data = f.get;                33          Future⟨int⟩ f = w!ping(5);
13     return 0;                    34          if (f.get == 5) client = w;
14   }                              35      }
15   int ping(int n){return n;}     36      return 0;
16 }// end of class Worker          37  }
17                                  38  Data getData(Worker w){
18 class DB{                        39      if (client == w) return data;
19   Data data = ...;               40      else return null;
20   Worker client = null;          41  }
21   int connected = 1;             42 }// end of class DB
```

Fig. 1. Working example. Communication protocol between a DB and a worker

is assigned to its data field. The instruction get blocks the execution in the current location until the awaited task has terminated. We use future variables [7,8] to detect the termination of asynchronous tasks. The register method of the database makes a call to getData and waits for its execution. Once it has finished, it checks if the number of possible connections is bigger than 0. In that case connected is decreased by one, and the database makes sure that the worker is online. This is done by invoking asynchronously method ping with a concrete value and blocking until it gets the result with the same value. Then, the database registers the provided worker reference storing it in its client field. Method getData of the database returns its data field if the caller worker is registered, otherwise it returns null. Finally, method connect sets the field connected to 3. Depending on the sequence of interleavings, the execution of this program can finish: (1) as one would expect, i.e., with worker.data = db.data, (2) with w.data = null if getData is executed before the assignment at line 34, or, (3) in a deadlock.

We have recently proposed a deadlock detection framework [2,3] that combines static analysis and symbolic execution based testing [1,3,6,14]. The deadlock analysis (for example, [9]) is first used to obtain descriptions of potential deadlock cycles which are then used to guide the testing process. The resulting deadlock detection framework hence can: (i) show deadlock presence, in which case a concrete test-case and trace are obtained, and (ii) prove deadlock freedom (up to the symbolic execution exploration limit). However, the symbolic execution phase needs to start from a concrete initial distributed context, i.e., a set of locations and their initial tasks. In our example, such an initial context is provided by the main method, which creates a Database and a Worker location, and schedules a work task on the worker with the database as parameter, and, a register task on the database with the worker as parameter. This is however only one out of the possible contexts, and, of course, it could be the case that it does not expose an error that occurs in other contexts (for example, it does not manifest any deadlock). This clearly limits the framework potential.

A fundamental challenge for a symbolic execution framework of distributed programs is to automatically and systematically generate *relevant* distributed contexts for the type of error that it aims at detecting. This would allow for instance applying symbolic execution for system and integration testing. The generation of relevant contexts involves two challenging aspects: (1) A first challenge is related to the elimination of redundant (useless) contexts. Observe that there is a combinatorial explosion on the different possible distributed contexts that can be generated when one considers all possible types and number of distributed locations and tasks within them. Therefore, it is crucial to provide the *minimal* set of initial contexts that contains only one representative of equivalent contexts. (2) For the particular type of error that one aims at detecting, an additional challenge is to be able to only generate initial contexts in which the error can occur. In the case of generating initial contexts for deadlock detection in our working example, this would mean generating for instance, a context with a database location and some worker location with a scheduled work task and a register task on the database for it, i.e., the context created by the main method. For instance, contexts that do not include both tasks would be useless for deadlock detection. Let us observe that if the assignment at Line 23 is changed to assign 0, then the initial contexts must also include a connect task, otherwise no deadlock will be produced. Interestingly, deadlock analyses provide [9, 11, 12] potential *deadlock cycles* which contain the possibly conflicting task interactions that can lead to deadlock. This information will be used to help our framework anticipate this information and discard initial distributed contexts that cannot lead to deadlock from the beginning. Briefly, the main contributions of this paper are the following:

- We introduce the concept of *minimal* set of initial contexts and extend a static testing framework to automatically and systematically generate them.
- We present a deadlock-guided approach to effectively generate initial contexts for deadlock detection and prove its soundness.
- We have implemented our proposal within the aPET/SYCO system [4] and performed an experimental evaluation to show its efficiency and effectiveness.

2   Asynchronous Programs

A program consists of a set of classes that define the types of locations, each of them defines a set of fields and methods of the form $M::=T\ m(\bar{T}\ \bar{x})\{s\}$, where statements s take the form s::=s; s | x=e |if e then s else s | while e do s | **return** x; |

b=new $T(\bar{z})$ | f = x ! $m(\bar{z})$ | **await** f? | x = f.**get**. Syntactically, a location will therefore be similar to a *concurrent object* that can be dynamically created using the instruction new $T(\bar{z})$. The declaration of a future variable is as follows Future$\langle T \rangle$ f, where T is the type of the result r, it adds a new future variable to the state. Instruction f = x ! $m(\bar{z})$ spawns a new task (instance of method m) and it is set to the future f in the state. Instruction **await** f? allows non-blocking synchronization. If the future variable f we are awaiting for points to a finished task, then the **await** can be completed. Otherwise the task yields the lock so that any other task of the same location can take it. On the other hand, instruction f.get allows blocking synchronization. It waits for the future variable without yielding the lock, i.e., it blocks the execution of the location until the task that is awaiting is finished. Then, when the future is ready, it retrieves the result and allows continuing the execution. This instruction introduces possible deadlocks in the program, as two tasks can be awaiting for termination of tasks on each other's locations. Finally, instruction **return** x; releases the lock that will never be taken again by that task. Consequently, that task is *finished* and removed from the task queue. All statements of a task takes place serially (without interleaving with any other task) until it gets to a **return** or **await** f? instruction. Then, the processor becomes idle again, chooses non-deterministically the next pending task, and so on.

A *program state* or *configuration* is a set of locations $\{loc_0, ..., loc_n\}$. A *location* is a term $loc(o, tk, h, \mathcal{Q})$ where o is the location identifier, tk is the identifier of the *active task* that holds the location's lock or $\perp$ if the location's lock is free, h is its local heap, and $\mathcal{Q}$ is the set of tasks in the location. A *task* is a term $tsk(tk, m, l, s)$ where tk is a unique task identifier, m is the method name executing in the task, l is a mapping from local variables to their values, and s is the sequence of instructions to be executed. We assume that the execution starts from a *main* method without parameters. The initial state is $S=\{loc(0, 0, \perp, \{tsk(0, main, l, body(main))\}$ with an initial location with identifier 0 executing task 0, maps local variables to their initial values, and $body(m)$ is the sequence of instructions in method m and $ini(main)$ is the initial program point in method m. From now on, we represent the state as a Prolog list, and we write $[x \mapsto v]$ to denote $h(x) = v$ (resp. $l(x) = v$), that is, field x in the heap h (resp. local variable x in the mapping l) takes the value v.

In what follows, a *derivation* or *execution* [20] is a sequence of states $S_0 \xrightarrow{o_1.t_1} ... \xrightarrow{o_n.t_n} S_n$, where $S_i \xrightarrow{o_i.t_i} S_{i+1}$ denotes the execution of task t_i in location $o_i \in S_i$. The derivation is *complete* if S_0 is the initial state and $\nexists \, loc(o, \_, \_, \{tk\} \cup \mathcal{Q}) \in S_n$ such that $S_n \xrightarrow{o.tk} S_{n+1}$ and $S_n \neq S_{n+1}$. Given a state S, $exec(S)$ denotes the set of all possible complete executions starting at S.

3   Specifying and Generating Initial Contexts

In our asynchronous programs, the most *general* initial contexts consist of sets of locations with *free* variables in their fields, and initial tasks in each location queue with *free* variables as parameters, i.e., neither the fields nor the parameters have concrete values. A first approach to systematically generate initial contexts could consist in generating, on backtracking, all possible multisets of initial tasks (method names), and for each one, generate all aliasing combinations with the locations of the tasks belonging to the same type of location. They are multisets because there can be multiple occurrences of the same task. To guarantee termination of this process we need to impose some limit in the generation of the multisets. For this, we could simply set a limit on the multiset global size. However it would be more reasonable and useful to set a limit on the maximum cardinality of each element in the multiset. To allow further flexibility, let us also set a limit on the minimum cardinality of each element. For instance, if we have a program with just one location type A with just one method m, and we set 1 and 2 as the minimum and maximum cardinalities respectively, then there are two possible multisets, namely, $\{m\}$ and $\{m, m\}$. The first one leads to one initial context with one location of type A with an instance of task m in its queue. The second one leads to two contexts, one with one location of type A with two instances of task m in its queue, and the other one with two different locations, each with an instance of task m in its queue.

On the other hand, it makes sense to allow specifying which tasks should be considered as initial tasks and which should not. A typical scenario is that the user knows which are the main tasks of the application and does not want to consider auxiliary or internal tasks as initial tasks. Another scenario is in the context of integration testing, where the tester might want to try out together different groups of tasks to observe how they interfere with each other. Also, the use of static analysis can help determine a subset of tasks of interest to detect some specific property. This is the case of our deadlock-guided approach of Sect. 4. With all this, the input to our automatic generation of initial contexts is: a set of tuples $(C.M, C^{min}, C^{max})$, where C.M is an *abstract task*, i.e., a task name, being C and M the class and method name resp., and, C^{min} resp. C^{max} is the associated minimum resp. maximum cardinality. Note that this does not limit the approach in any way since one could just include in $\mathcal{T}_{ini}$ all methods in the program and set $C^{min} = 0$ and a sufficiently large C^{max}.

Example 1. Let us consider the set $\mathcal{T}_{ini} = \{(\text{DB.register}, 1, 1), (\text{DB.connect}, 0, 1)\}$. The corresponding multisets are $\{\text{register}\}$ and $\{\text{register}, \text{connect}\}$. All contexts must contain exactly one instance of task register and at most one instance of task connect. This leads to three possible contexts: (1) a DB location instance with a task register in its queue, (2) a DB location instance with tasks register and connect in its queue, and, (3) two different DB location instances, one of them with an instance of task register and the other one with an instance of task connect. For instance, the state corresponding to the latter context would be:

$$S = [\text{loc}(\text{DB1}, \text{bot}, [\text{data} \mapsto \text{D1}, \text{clients} \mapsto \text{Cl1}, \text{checkOn} \mapsto \text{B1}],$$
$$[\text{tsk}(1, \text{register}, [\text{this} \mapsto \text{r}(\text{DB1}), \text{m} \mapsto \text{W1}], \text{body}(\text{register}))])$$
$$\text{loc}(\text{DB2}, \text{bot}, [\text{data} \mapsto \text{D2}, \text{clients} \mapsto \text{Cl2}, \text{checkOn} \mapsto \text{B2}],$$
$$[\text{tsk}(2, \text{connect}, [\text{this} \mapsto \text{r}(\text{DB2})], \text{body}(\text{connect}))])],$$

where D1, Cl1, and B1 (resp. D2, Cl2, and B2) are the fields data, clients, and checkOn of location DB1 (resp. DB2), and W1 resp. W2 the parameter of the task register resp. connect, and body(m) is the sequence of instructions in method m. Note that both fields and task parameters are fresh variables so that the context is the most general possible. Note that the first parameter of a task is always the location this and it is therefore fixed.   □

In the following, we formally define the contexts that must be produced from a set of abstract tasks $\mathcal{T}_{ini}$ with associated cardinalities. We use the notation $\{[m_1, ..., m_n]_{o_i}\}$ for an initial context where there exists a location $loc(o_i, \bot, h, \{tk(tk_1, m_1, l_1, body(m_1))\} \cup ... \cup \{tk(tk_n, m_n, l_n, body(m_n))\})$. Note that we can have $m_i = m_j$ with $i \neq j$. For instance, the three contexts in Example 1 are written as $\{[\mathsf{register}]_{\mathsf{db}_1}\}$, $\{[\mathsf{register}, \mathsf{connect}]_{\mathsf{db}_1}\}$ and $\{[\mathsf{register}]_{\mathsf{db}_1}, [\mathsf{connect}]_{\mathsf{db}_2}\}$, respectively. Let us first define the set of initial contexts from a given $\mathcal{T}_{ini}$ when all tasks belong to the same class.

Definition 1 (Superset of initial contexts (same class C_i)). *Let* $\mathcal{T}_{ini} = \{(C_i.m_1, C_1^{min}, C_1^{max}), \ldots, (C_i.m_n, C_n^{min}, C_n^{max})\}$ *be the set of abstract tasks with associated cardinalities. Let us have* $\sum_{i=1}^{n} C_i^{max}$ *different identifiers:*

$o_{1,1}, \ldots, o_{1,C_1^{max}}, \ldots, o_{n,1}, \ldots, o_{n,C_n^{max}}$. *We can find at most* $\sum_{i=1}^{n} C_i^{max}$ *instances of class C_i, that is, each abstract task m_i ($i \in [1, n]$) has at most C_i^{max} instances and each of them can be inside a different instance of class C_i. Let $u_{i,j}^{m_k}$ be an integer variable that denotes the number of instances of task m_k inside the location $o_{i,j}$ and let us consider the following integer system:*

$$\begin{cases} C_1^{min} \leq u_{1,1}^{m_1} + \ldots + u_{1,C_1^{max}}^{m_1} + \ldots + u_{n,1}^{m_1} + \ldots + u_{n,C_n^{max}}^{m_1} \leq C_1^{max} \\ \ldots \\ C_n^{min} \leq u_{1,1}^{m_n} + \ldots + u_{1,C_1^{max}}^{m_n} + \ldots + u_{n,1}^{m_n} + \ldots + u_{n,C_n^{max}}^{m_n} \leq C_n^{max} \end{cases}$$

Each formula requires at least C_k^{min} and at most C_k^{max} instances of task m_k. Each solution to this system corresponds to an initial context. Let $(d_{1,1}^{m_1}, \ldots, d_{n,C_n^{max}}^{m_1}, \ldots, d_{1,1}^{m_n}, \ldots, d_{n,C_n^{max}}^{m_n})$ be a solution, then the corresponding initial context contains:

- $loc(o_{i,j}, \bot, h, \mathcal{Q})$, *that is, a location $o_{i,j}$ whose lock is free, the fields in h are mapped to fresh variables, and the queue $\mathcal{Q}$ contains: $d_{i,j}^{m_1}$ instances of abstract task m_1,..., and $d_{i,j}^{m_n}$ instances of m_n, if $i \in [1, n]$, $j \in [1, C_i^{max}]$ and $\exists d_{i,j}^{m_k} > 0, k \in [1, n]$, where each instance of m_i is $tsk(tk, m_i, l, body(m_i))$ and every argument in l is mapped to a fresh variable.*

Example 2. Let us consider the example $\mathcal{T}_{ini} = \{(\mathsf{DB.register}, 0, 1), (\mathsf{DB.connect}, 1, 1)\}$. The identifiers are $o_{1,1}$ and $o_{2,1}$, and the variables of the system are $u_{1,1}^{reg}$, $u_{2,1}^{reg}$, $u_{1,1}^{get}$ and $u_{2,1}^{get}$. Finally, we obtain the next system:

$$\begin{cases} 0 \leq u_{1,1}^{reg} + u_{2,1}^{reg} \leq 1 \\ 1 \leq u_{1,1}^{get} + u_{2,1}^{get} \leq 1 \end{cases}$$

We obtain 6 solutions: $(0, 0, 1, 0), (0, 0, 0, 1), (1, 0, 1, 0), (1, 0, 0, 1), (0, 1, 1, 0)$ and $(0, 1, 0, 1)$. Then, the superset of initial contexts is

$$\{\{[\text{connect}]_{o_{1,1}}\}, \{[\text{connect}]_{o_{2,1}}\}, \{[\text{register}, \text{connect}]_{o_{1,1}}\}, \{[\text{register}, \text{connect}]_{o_{2,1}}\},$$

$$\{[\text{register}]_{o_{2,1}}, [\text{connect}]_{o_{1,1}}\}, \{[\text{register}]_{o_{1,1}}, [\text{connect}]_{o_{2,1}}\}\}$$

□

Let us observe that the two last contexts are equivalent since they are both composed of two instances of DB with tasks register and connect respectively. Therefore, we only need to consider one of these two contexts for symbolic execution. Considering both would lead to *redundancy*. The notion of minimal set of initial contexts below eliminates redundant contexts, hence avoiding useless executions.

Definition 2 (Equivalence relation $\sim$). *Two contexts C_1 and C_2 are equivalent, written $C_1 \sim C_2$, if $C_1 = C_2 = \emptyset$ or $C_1 = \{loc(o_1, \bot, h_1, \mathcal{Q}_1)\} \cup C_1'$, and $\exists\, o_2 \in C_2$ such that:*

1. $C_2 = \{loc(o_2, \bot, h_2, \mathcal{Q}_2)\} \cup C_2'$,
2. $\mathcal{Q}_1$ and $\mathcal{Q}_2$ contain the same number of instances of each task, and
3. $C_1' \sim C_2'$.

Example 3. The superset in Example 2 contains 3 equivalence classes induced by the relation $\sim$: (1) the class $\{\{[\text{connect}]_{o_{1,1}}\}, \{[\text{connect}]_{o_{2,1}}\}\}$, where both contexts are composed of a location with a task connect, (2) the class $\{\{[\text{register}, \text{connect}]_{o_{1,1}}\}, \{[register, connect]_{o_{2,1}}\}\}$, whose locations have two tasks register and connect. and, finally, (3) the class $\{\{[\text{register}]_{o_{2,1}}, [\text{connect}]_{o_{1,1}}\}, \{[\text{register}]_{o_{1,1}}, [\text{connect}]_{o_{2,1}}\}\}$, where both contexts have two locations with a task register and a task connect, respectively. □

Definition 3 (Minimal set of initial contexts $\mathcal{I}^{C_i}$ (same class Cl_i)). *Let $\mathcal{T}_{ini}$ be the set of abstract tasks, then the minimal set of initial contexts $\mathcal{I}^{Cl_i}$ is composed of a representative of each equivalence class induced by the relation $\sim$ over the superset of initial contexts for the input $\mathcal{T}_{ini}$.*

Example 4. As we have seen in the previous example, there are three different equivalence classes. So, the minimal set of initial contexts is composed of a representative of each class (we have renamed the identifiers for the sake of clarity):

$$\mathcal{I}^{DB} = \{\{[\text{connect}]_{db_1}\}, \{[\text{register}, \text{connect}]_{db_1}\}, \{[\text{register}]_{db_1}, [\text{connect}]_{db_2}\}\}$$

□

Let us now define the set of initial contexts $\mathcal{I}$ when the input set $\mathcal{T}_{ini}$ contains tasks of different types of locations.

Definition 4 (Minimal set of initial contexts $\mathcal{I}$ (Different classes)). *Let* $\mathcal{T}_{ini} = \{(C_1.m_1, C_1^{min}, C_1^{max}), \ldots, (C_n.m_n, C_n^{min}, C_n^{max})\}$ *be the set of abstract tasks with associated cardinalities, and let us consider a partition of this set where every equivalence class is composed of abstract tasks of the same class. Hence, we have:* $\mathcal{T}_{ini}^{C_1} = \{C_1.m'_1, \ldots, C_1.m'_{j_1}\}, \ldots, \mathcal{T}_{ini}^{C_n} = \{C_n.m''_1, \ldots, C_n.m''_{j_n}\}$ *where* $C_i \neq C_j, \forall i, j \in [1, n], i \neq j$.
Then, let $\mathcal{I}^{C_i}$ *be the minimal set of initial contexts for the input* $\mathcal{T}_{ini}^{C_i}$, $i \in [1, n]$ *and* $U : \mathcal{I}^{C_1} \times \ldots \times \mathcal{I}^{C_n} \to \mathcal{I}$, *defined by* $U(s_1, \ldots, s_n) = s_1 \cup \ldots \cup s_n$. *The set* $\mathcal{I}$ *is defined by the image set of application* U.

Example 5. Let us consider the set $\mathcal{T}_{ini} = \{(\mathsf{DB.register}, 1, 1), (\mathsf{DB.connect}, 1, 1), (\mathsf{Worker.work}, 1, 1)\}$ from which we get the initial contexts $\mathcal{I}^{Worker} = \{\{[\mathsf{work}]_{w_1}\}\}$ and $\mathcal{I}^{DB} = \{\{[\mathsf{register}, \mathsf{connect}]_{db,1}\}, \{[register]_{db_1}, [connect]_{db_2}\}\}$. Then, by Definition 4,

$$\mathcal{I} = \{\{[\mathsf{register}, \mathsf{connect}]_{db_1}, [\mathsf{work}]_{w_1}\}, \{[\mathsf{register}]_{db_1}, [\mathsf{connect}]_{db_2}, [\mathsf{work}]_{w_1}\}\}$$

□

It is straightforward to implement a function that generates the minimal set of initial contexts from a provided set of initial tasks (for instance [5]). Such a function is denoted as *generate_contexts*($\mathcal{T}_{ini}$). The main complication is to avoid the generation of equivalent contexts (Definition 2) as soon as possible during the process. For this aim one can rely on the definition of a normal form according to the number of tasks inside each location.

4   On Automatically Inferring Deadlock-Interfering Tasks

The systematic generation of initial contexts produces a combinatorial explosion and therefore it should be used with small sets of abstract tasks (and low cardinalities). However, in the context of deadlock detection, in order not to miss any deadlock situation, one has to consider in principle all methods in the program, hence producing scalability problems. Interestingly, it can happen that many of the tasks in the generated initial contexts do not affect in any way deadlock executions. Our challenge is to only generate initial contexts from which a deadlock can show up. For this, the deadlock analysis provides the possibly conflicting task interactions that can lead to deadlock. We propose to use this information to help our framework discard initial contexts that cannot lead to deadlock from the beginning. Section 4.1 summarizes the concepts of the deadlock analysis used to obtain the deadlock cycles, and Sect. 4.2 presents the algorithm to generate the set of initial tasks $\mathcal{T}_{ini}$.

4.1   Deadlock Analysis and Abstract Deadlock Cycles

The deadlock analysis of [9] returns a set of abstract deadlock cycles of the form $e_1 \xrightarrow{p_1:tk_1} e_2 \xrightarrow{p_2:tk_2} \ldots \xrightarrow{p_n:tk_n} e_1$, where $p_1, \ldots, p_n$ are program points,

$tk_1, \ldots, tk_n$ are *task abstractions*, and nodes $e_1, \ldots, e_n$ are either *location abstractions* or task abstractions. The abstractions for tasks and locations can be performed at different levels of accuracy during the analysis: the simple abstraction that we will use for our formalization abstracts each concrete location o by the program point at which it is created o_{pp}, and each task by the method name executing (as in Sect. 3). They are abstractions since there could be many locations created at the same program point and many tasks executing the same method. Points-to analysis [9,18] can be used to infer such abstractions with more precision, for instance, by distinguishing the actions performed by different location abstractions. Each arrow $e \xrightarrow{p:tk} e'$ should be interpreted like "abstract location or task e is waiting for the termination of abstract location or task e' due to the synchronization instruction at program point p of abstract task tk". Three kinds of arrows can be distinguished, namely, *task-task* (an abstract task is awaiting for the termination of another one), *task-location* (an abstract task is awaiting for an abstract location to be idle) and *location-task* (the abstract location is blocked due the abstract task). *Location-location* arrows cannot happen.

Example 6. In our working example there are two abstract locations, o_2, corresponding to location **database** created at line 2 and o_3, corresponding to the n locations **worker**, created inside the loop at line 3; and four abstract tasks, $register$, $getD$, $work$ and $ping$. The following cycle is inferred by the deadlock analysis: $o_2 \xrightarrow{34:register} ping \xrightarrow{15:ping} o_3 \xrightarrow{12:work} getD \xrightarrow{38:getD} o_2$. The first arrow captures that the location created at Line 2 is blocked waiting for the termination of task **ping** because of the synchronization at L34 of task **register**. Also, a dependency between a task and a location (for instance, **ping** and o_3) captures that the task is trying to execute on that (possibly) blocked location. Abstract deadlock cycles can be provided by the analyzer to the user. But, as it can be observed, it is complex to figure out from them why these dependencies arise, and more importantly the interleavings scheduled to lead to this situation. □

4.2   Generation of Initial Tasks

The underlying idea is as follows: we select an abstract cycle detected by the deadlock analysis, and extract a set of potential abstract tasks which can be involved in a deadlock. In a naive approximation, we could take those abstract tasks that are inside the cycle and contain a blocking instruction. We also need to set the maximum cardinality for each task to ensure finiteness (by default 1) and require at least one instance for each task (minimum cardinality).

This approach is valid as long as we only have blocking synchronization primitives, i.e., when the location state stays unchanged until the resumption of a suspended execution. However, this kind of concurrent/distributed languages usually include some sort of non-blocking synchronization primitive. When a location stops its execution due to an **await** instruction, another task can interleave its execution with it, i.e., start to execute and, thus, modify the location state (i.e., the location *fields*). Then, if a call or a blocking instruction involved in a deadlock depends on the value of one of these fields, and we do not consider all the possible values, a deadlock could be missed. As a consequence, we need to consider at release points, all possible interleavings with tasks that modify the fields in order to capture all deadlocks.

Let us consider now a simple modification of our working example. Line 27 is replaced by connected = 0. Now it is easy to see that if we only consider register and work as input, deadlocks are lost: once register is executed and the instruction at line 30 is reached, the location's queue only contains task getData but no connect and, therefore, when task register is resumed, field connected stays unchanged and the body of the condition is not executed, so we cannot have a deadlock situation.

In the following we define the *deadlock-interfering* tasks for a given abstract deadlock cycle, i.e., an *over-approximation* of the set of tasks that need to be considered in initial contexts so that we cannot miss a representative of the given deadlock cycle. In our extended example, those would be, register and work but also connect.

Definition 5 (initialTasks(C)). *Let C an abstract deadlock cycle. Then,*

$$initialTasks(C) := \bigcup_{i_{call} \in t \in C} initialTasks(t, i_{call}, C) \cup \bigcup_{i_{sync} \in t \in C} initialTasks(t, i_{sync}, C)$$

where:

- $initialTasks(t, i, C) = \emptyset$ *if* $o \xrightarrow{t} t_2 \notin C$ *and* $i \neq i_{mod}$ *and* $\nexists\, i_{await} \in [t_0, i]$
- $initialTasks(t, i, C) = \{t\}$ *if* $(o \xrightarrow{t} t_2 \in C$ *or* $i = i_{mod}$) *and* $\nexists\, i_{await} \in [t_0, i]$
- $initialTasks(t, i, C)$

$$= \{t\} \cup \bigcup_{f \in fields(i)} \left(\bigcup_{(i_{mod}, t_{mod}) \in mods(f)} initialTasks(t_{mod}, i_{mod}, C) \right)$$
if $\exists\, i_{await} \in [t_0, i]$

The definition relies on function fields(l) which, given an instruction l, returns the set of class fields that have been read or written until the execution of instruction l. Let mods(f) be the set of pairs (instruction,task) that modify field f. We can observe that *initialTasks(C)* is the union of the initial tasks for each relevant instruction inside the cycle C, i.e., asynchronous calls and synchronization primitives. We can also observe in the auxiliary function *initialTasks(t,i,C)* that: (1) if the instruction i is not producing a *location-task edge* and it is not an instruction modifying a field, then t does not need to be added as initial task, (2) if i produces a *location-task edge* or is modifying a field, and we do not have any await instruction between the beginning of the task and i, then i is going to be executed under the most general context, so we do not need to add more initial tasks but t, and (3) on the other hand, if there exists an await instruction between the beginning of task t, namely t_0, and instruction i, each field f inside the set fields(i) could be changed before the resumption of the await by any task modifying f. Thus, tasks containing any of the possible f-modifying instructions must be considered and, recursively, their initial tasks.

It is important to highlight that this definition could be non-terminating depending on the program we are working with. For instance, if we apply the

Data: An abstract cycle C and a maximum cardinality M
Result: A list with the interfering tasks for C
$Q = \emptyset; L = \emptyset$;
forall the $t \in C$ **do**
    i_{call} = receiveCall(t,C); enqueue(Q,(i_{call},t));
    i_{await} = receiveSync(t,C); enqueue(Q,(i_{await},t));
    i_{get} = receiveSync(t,C); enqueue(Q,(i_{get},t));
    if $\exists \in o \xrightarrow{t} t_2 \in C$ **then**
       | insert(L,(i_{get},t));
    end
end
while *!empty(Q)* **do**
    (i,t) = dequeue(Q);
    if $\exists i_{await} \in t$ *between the beginning of t and i* **then**
       forall the $f \in fields(i)$ **do**
          forall the $(i_{mod}, t_{mod}) \in mods(f)$ **do**
             if *!member(L,(i_{mod}, t_{mod}))* **then**
                insert(L,(i_{mod}, t_{mod}));
                enqueue(Q,(i_{mod}, t_{mod}));
             end
          end
       end
    end
end
return [(m,1,M) : m $\in$ set(project$_y$(L))];

Algorithm 1. Algorithm to infer interfering tasks for a given deadlock cycle

definition to the abstract cycle C in Example 6, $initialTasks$(db.register, $32, C$) will be evaluated. It fits well with the conditions on the third clause, as there exists an **await** instruction, fields(32) = {connected} and then again 32 is a modifier instruction of field connected, so $initialTasks$(db.register, $32, C$) will be evaluated again recursively.

Algorithm 1 shows how to finitely infer the interfering-tasks for a given deadlock cycle as defined by Definition 5. Function $receiveCall(t, C)$ ($receiveSync(t, C)$) receives the asynchronous call (synchronization instruction) of a task t inside the cycle C. Q is the queue of pending pairs {instruction, task}, and L is the list containing all such pairs whose tasks we have to consider. Finiteness is guaranteed because each instruction is added to Q and L at most once, and the number of instructions is finite. For each task in the cycle, we take the call and the corresponding synchronization instruction, and we add them to Q. Instructions **get** producing a *location-task edge*, are also added to L, as they have to be inside the initial context. The other tasks included in the initial context are the ones which could affect the conditions of the aforementioned instructions.

In the second loop, we take a pending instruction inside Q and we check if there exists an **await** instruction where the field values could be changed (third clause in Definition 5). In case it does, we need to include all tasks which contain instructions modifying such field. However, this change could be inside an if-else body and we also need to consider the fields inside such condition. Therefore, we add the modifier instruction to the pending instructions queue Q. The algorithm finishes when Q is empty and L is the list of pairs with all interfering instructions and their container tasks. Finally, we only take the tasks, i.e., the second component of each pair (project$_y$), remove duplicates (set) and set their minimum and maximum cardinalities. From now on, we denote $initial\_tasks(c,M)$, the set of initial tasks inferred for the abstract deadlock cycle c and the maximum cardinality M.

Example 7. Let us show how the algorithm works for our modified example and the maximum cardinality $M = 1$. For the sake of clarity, instructions are identified by their line numbers. After executing the first **forall** loop, the value of Q and L is $\{(33, \mathsf{DB.register}), (34, \mathsf{DB.register}), (11, \mathsf{Worker.work}), (12, \mathsf{Worker.work})\}$ and $[(34, \mathsf{DB.register}), (12, \mathsf{Worker.work})]$, respectively. Let us assume Q uses a LIFO policy, hence $(12, \mathsf{Worker.work})$ is taken first. Since fields(12) $= \emptyset$, L stays unchanged. The same happens with $(11, \mathsf{Worker.work})$. At the beginning of the third loop, Q is $\{(33, \mathsf{DB.register}), (34, \mathsf{DB.register})\}$ and $(34, \mathsf{DB.register})$ is taken. Now, fields(34) $=$ $\{\mathsf{connected}\}$ and $\exists inst_{await}$ (line 30) between lines 26 and 34. We find three pairs modifying the field connected: (23,DB.connect), (27,DB.register) and (32,DB.register). None of them is a member of L and hence they are added to both queues. Now, Q is $\{(33, \mathsf{DB.register}), (27, \mathsf{DB.register}), (32, \mathsf{DB.register}), (23, \mathsf{DB.connect})\}$ but again fields(32) $=$ fields(23) $= \emptyset$ and, thus, L stays unchanged. Finally, both $(33, \mathsf{DB.register})$ and $(27, \mathsf{DB.register})$ are taken and fields(33)= fields(27)={connected}, but the modifier instructions have been previously added to L, hence L remains unchanged. At the end of **while**, L is $\{(34, \mathsf{DB.register})$, $(12, \mathsf{Worker.work}), (27, \mathsf{DB.register}), (32, \mathsf{DB.register}), (23, \mathsf{DB.connect})\}$. Finally, the algorithm projects over the second component of each pair in the list, removes duplicates and returns the set $\mathcal{T}_{ini}=\{(\mathsf{DB.register}, 1, 1),$ $(\mathsf{Worker.work}, 1, 1), (\mathsf{DB.connect}, 1, 1)\}$. Our generation of initial contexts for this set (see Example 5) produces

$$\mathcal{I} = \{ \{[\mathsf{register}, \mathsf{connect}]_{\mathsf{db}_1} [\mathsf{work}]_{\mathsf{w}_1}\},$$
$$\{[\mathsf{register}]_{\mathsf{db}_1}, [\mathsf{connect}]_{\mathsf{db}_2}, [\mathsf{work}]_{\mathsf{w}_1}\}\},$$

where both initial contexts are composed of a worker location with a task work. However, the former context contains a database location with tasks register and connect, whereas the latter one contains two locations with a task register and a task connect, respectively.   □

The next theorem establishes the soundness of our approach. Intuitively, soundness states that, for a given deadlock cycle c and maximum cardinality M, if there is an initial context, fulfilling M, from which a deadlock representative of c can be obtained, then our approach will generate a context (possibly different from the above) from which a deadlock representative of c is obtained.

Theorem 1 (Soundness). *Given a program P, an abstract deadlock cycle c and a maximum cardinality M, if there exists a derivation starting at a state S_{ini} and ending at S_{end} such that the cardinality of each task in S_{ini} is less than M and S_{end} is a representative of the cycle c, then there exists an initial context $St_0 \in generate\_contexts(initial\_tasks(c, M))$ such that $S_{end_2} \in exec(St_0)$ and S_{end_2} is also a representative of the cycle c.*

Proof. (Sketch) Let us define a task t as necessary in S_{ini} for the deadlock cycle c if and only if $\nexists S_{e'}$ such that $S_{ini}\backslash\{t\} \xrightarrow{*} S_{e'}$ and $S_{e'}$ is a representative of c, where $S\backslash\{t\}$ denotes the context S without the task t. Let us define now an initial context $nec(S)$ as the initial context that only contains the necessary tasks in S for c. In order to prove soundness, we need to prove that $nec(S_{ini}) \in generate\_contexts(initial\_tasks(M, c))$. We reason by contradiction. Assume that there exists a necessary task $t \in nec(S_{ini})$, instance of method m, which is not in any initial context generated. This is equivalent to assume that method m is not inferred by Algorithm 1. We can distinguish two different roles which task t plays in the deadlock situation:

- If task t gets blocked, then t contains an instruction pp:**get** where pp is the program point, and, by the soundness of the deadlock analysis (Theorem 1 of [9]), pp:**get** is the tag of an edge inside the deadlock cycle c. So, the pair (pp, m) is added to L in the first loop of Algorithm 1 and m is finally inferred. Thus, we have a contradiction.
- If task t modifies a field f at program point pp that appears in a condition of another task r, then we cannot get a deadlock if t is not executed before the evaluation of condition in task r (t is necessary). Here, we need to notice that if task r does not contain any **await**, symbolic execution explores all possible execution paths and t would be unnecessary. But we have supposed that t is necessary, then r contains an **await**. Then, (pp, m) will be added to L because of the third forall in Algorithm 1 and m is inferred, what contradicts our assumption.   □

5   Experimental Evaluation

We have implemented the proposed techniques within the aPET/SYCO tool [4], a testing tool for the ABS [13] *concurrent objects* language. The tool is available for online use at http://costa.ls.fi.upm.es/syco, where the benchmarks below can also be found. This section summarizes our experimental evaluation whose objectives are the following:

1. Show the effectiveness of our approach in Sect. 4 to generate initial contexts for deadlock detection w.r.t the full systematic generation of Sect. 3.
2. Demonstrate the potential of the technique when being applied in practice within our deadlock detection framework.

The benchmarks we have used include classical concurrency patterns containing deadlocks, namely: *DBProt* is an extension of the database communication protocol of our working example; *Barber* is an extension of the *sleeping barber* problem, *Fact* is a distributed and recursive implementation of a factorial function, *Loop* is a loop that creates asynchronous tasks and locations, and, *Pairing* is the pairing problem.

Effectiveness of generation of initial contexts for deadlock detection: Table 1 shows, for each benchmark: the number of generated initial contexts using the full systematic generation of contexts of Sect. 3 (column *Syst.*), the number of contexts generated using our deadlock-guided generation of Sect. 4 (column *G*), and, the number of contexts among those generated that lead to a deadlock (column *D*). This is done for three different values of maximum cardinality, namely, $M = 1$, $M = 2$ and $M = 3$. The rest of the columns are explained in the next paragraph. A timeout of 30 s is used and, when reached, we write $>X$ to indicate that we encountered X contexts up to that point. The reductions of our deadlock guided generation of contexts w.r.t the full systematic generation are huge. As expected the full systematic generation blows up fast for most examples. We can also observe that our deadlock guided generation of contexts is very precise, producing no false positives, i.e., contexts that do not lead to deadlock, except for *DBProt*. The reason of the loss of precision in the *DPProt* example is that task register only gets blocked if task connect changes the value of field connected. Therefore, contexts in which these two tasks do not belong to the same location will not lead to deadlock. This can be observed in Example 7. Improving our method to capture this situation is left for future work.

Table 1. Evaluating generation of initial contexts: Systematic vs. deadlock-guided

Bench.	T_A/C	M = 1				M = 2				M = 3			
		Syst.	G	D	T	Syst.	G	D	T	Syst.	G	D	T
DBProt	5/1	30	2	1	35	>12960	57	30	101s*	>6308	576	156	974s*
Barber	5/1	8	1	1	35	6859	9	9	57	>8310	36	36	309
Fact	6/2	15	2	2	11	2419	6	6	14	>4771	12	12	16
Loop	20/1	3375	1	1	30	>13433	27	27	495	>4771	216	216	77s*
Pairing	4/2	2	2	2	9	57	12	12	37	576	42	42	162

Application within our deadlock detection framework: Our deadlock-guided generation of initial contexts has been integrated within the deadlock detection feature of the testing system aPET/SYCO as follows: After running the static deadlock analysis, and only in case it outputs a non-empty set of potential abstract cycles (i.e. if the program is not already proven deadlock-free), we run our deadlock guided generation of initial contexts for each of the cycles inferred by the analysis. For each generated initial context, we start (possibly in parallel) a deadlock-guided symbolic execution [2,3] that stops as soon as it finds a deadlock. As a result, we obtain a concrete test-case with its associated trace and sequence of interleavings. A local timeout for each symbolic execution is set so that it does not degrade the overall process in case a blowup is produced before finding a deadlock. This is relatively frequent with false-positive contexts (see paragraph above). Table 1 shows, for each benchmark, the time of the static deadlock analysis and the number of generated deadlock cycles (column T_A/C), and, the overall time of the rest of the process (column T), which includes both the time of the generation of contexts and the symbolic executions. Times are in milliseconds except where indicated and are obtained on an Intel(R) Core(TM) i7 CPU at 2.5 GHz with 8 GB of RAM, running Ubuntu 5.4.0. A timeout of 5s is set for each symbolic execution and an asterisk in the time indicates the timeout has been reached at least once.

Overall, our deadlock guided generation of initial contexts hence enables our deadlock detection framework to analyze systems without the need of any user supplied initial context. Also, it allows generating concrete test cases that lead to deadlock for integration and system testing.

6   Conclusions and Related Work

We have proposed a framework for the automatic generation of initial contexts for deadlock-guided symbolic execution. Such initial contexts are composed of the interfering tasks which, according to a static deadlock analyzer, might lead to deadlock. Given the initial contexts, we can drive symbolic execution towards paths that are more likely to manifest a deadlock, discarding safe contexts. There is a large body of work on deadlock detection including both dynamic and static approaches. Much of the existing work, both for asynchronous programs [9,10] and thread-based programs [17,19], is based on static analysis techniques. Although we have used the static analysis of [9], the information provided by other deadlock analyzers could be used in an analogous way. Deadlock detection has been also studied in the context of dynamic testing and model checking [6,15,16], where sometimes has been combined with static information [1,14]. The initial contexts generated by our framework are of interest also in these approaches. As regards the application in a thread-based concurrency model, the fundamental difference is that our whole approach is defined at the level of atomic tasks that execute concurrently using non-preemptive scheduling, unlike thread-based preemption. However, our approach would be adaptable to thread-based applications that rely on synchronized blocks of code (such as in monitors or concurrent objects). As future work, we plan to investigate how our framework could be adapted to this model.

References

1. Agarwal, R., Wang, L., Stoller, S.D.: Detecting potential deadlocks with static analysis and run-time monitoring. In: Ur, S., Bin, E., Wolfsthal, Y. (eds.) HVC 2005. LNCS, vol. 3875, pp. 191–207. Springer, Heidelberg (2006). https://doi.org/10.1007/11678779_14
2. Albert, E., Gómez-Zamalloa, M., Isabel, M.: Deadlock Guided Testing in CLP. Technical report (2017). http://costa.ls.fi.upm.es/papers/costa/AlbertGI17tr.pdf
3. Albert, E., Gómez-Zamalloa, M., Isabel, M.: Combining static analysis and testing for deadlock detection. In: Ábrahám, E., Huisman, M. (eds.) IFM 2016. LNCS, vol. 9681, pp. 409–424. Springer, Cham (2016). https://doi.org/10.1007/978-3-319-33693-0_26
4. Albert, E., Gómez-Zamalloa, M., Isabel, M.: SYCO: a systematic testing tool for concurrent objects. In: Proceedings of CC 2016. ACM (2016)
5. Albert, E., Gómez-Zamalloa, M., Isabel, M.: On the generation of initial contexts for effective deadlock detection. Technical report, October 2017. https://arxiv.org/abs/1709.04255
6. Christakis, M., Gotovos, A., Sagonas, K.F.: Systematic testing for detecting concurrency errors in erlang programs. In: Sixth IEEE International Conference on Software Testing, Verification and Validation, ICST 2013, Luxembourg, Luxembourg, 18–22 March 2013. IEEE Computer Society (2013)
7. de Boer, F.S., Clarke, D., Johnsen, E.B.: A complete guide to the future. In: De Nicola, R. (ed.) ESOP 2007. LNCS, vol. 4421, pp. 316–330. Springer, Heidelberg (2007). https://doi.org/10.1007/978-3-540-71316-6_22
8. Flanagan, C., Felleisen, M.: The semantics of future and its use in program optimization. In: 22nd ACM SIGPLAN-SIGACT Symposium on Principles of Programming Languages (1995)
9. Flores-Montoya, A.E., Albert, E., Genaim, S.: May-happen-in-parallel based deadlock analysis for concurrent objects. In: Beyer, D., Boreale, M. (eds.) FMOODS/-FORTE -2013. LNCS, vol. 7892, pp. 273–288. Springer, Heidelberg (2013). https://doi.org/10.1007/978-3-642-38592-6_19
10. Giachino, E., Grazia, C.A., Laneve, C., Lienhardt, M., Wong, P.Y.H.: Deadlock analysis of concurrent objects: theory and practice. In: Johnsen, E.B., Petre, L. (eds.) IFM 2013. LNCS, vol. 7940, pp. 394–411. Springer, Heidelberg (2013). https://doi.org/10.1007/978-3-642-38613-8_27
11. Giachino, E., Kobayashi, N., Laneve, C.: Deadlock analysis of unbounded process networks. In: Baldan, P., Gorla, D. (eds.) CONCUR 2014. LNCS, vol. 8704, pp. 63–77. Springer, Heidelberg (2014). https://doi.org/10.1007/978-3-662-44584-6_6
12. Laneve, C., Giachino, E., Lienhardt, M.: A framework for deadlock detection in core ABS. Softw. Syst. Model. 15(4), 1013–1048 (2016)
13. Johnsen, E.B., Hähnle, R., Schäfer, J., Schlatte, R., Steffen, M.: ABS: a core language for abstract behavioral specification. In: Aichernig, B.K., de Boer, F.S., Bonsangue, M.M. (eds.) FMCO 2010. LNCS, vol. 6957, pp. 142–164. Springer, Heidelberg (2011). https://doi.org/10.1007/978-3-642-25271-6_8
14. Joshi, P., Naik, M., Sen, K., Gay, D.: An effective dynamic analysis for detecting generalized deadlocks. In: Proceedings of FSE 2010. ACM (2010)
15. Joshi, P., Park, C., Sen, K., Naik, M.: A randomized dynamic program analysis technique for detecting real deadlocks. In: Proceedings of PLDI 2009. ACM (2009)
16. Kheradmand, A., Kasikci, B., Candea, G.: Lockout: Efficient Testing for Deadlock Bugs. Technical report (2013). http://dslab.epfl.ch/pubs/lockout.pdf

17. Masticola, S.P., Ryder, B.G.: A model of Ada programs for static deadlock detection in polynomial time. In: Parallel and Distributed Debugging, pp. 97–107. ACM (1991)
18. Milanova, A., Rountev, A., Ryder, B.G.: Parameterized object sensitivity for points-to analysis for java. ACM Trans. Softw. Eng. Methodol. **14**, 1–41 (2005)
19. Savage, S., Burrows, M., Nelson, G., Sobalvarro, P., Anderson, T.E.: Eraser: a dynamic data race detector for multithreaded programs. ACM Trans. Comput. Syst. **15**(4), 391–411 (1997)
20. Sen, K., Agha, G.: Automated systematic testing of open distributed programs. In: Baresi, L., Heckel, R. (eds.) FASE 2006. LNCS, vol. 3922, pp. 339–356. Springer, Heidelberg (2006). https://doi.org/10.1007/11693017_25

A Rule-Based Approach to Analyzing Database Schema Objects with Datalog

Christiane Engels[1]([⊠]), Andreas Behrend[1], and Stefan Brass[2]

[1] Institut für Informatik III, Rheinische Friedrich-Wilhelms-Universität Bonn,
Endenicher Allee 19A, 53115 Bonn, Germany
{engelsc,behrend}@cs.uni-bonn.de
[2] Institut für Informatik, Martin-Luther-Universität Halle-Wittenberg,
Von-Seckendorff-Platz 1, 06099 Halle, Germany
brass@informatik.uni-halle.de

Abstract. Database schema elements such as tables, views, triggers and functions are typically defined with many interrelations. In order to support database users in understanding a given schema, a rule-based approach for analyzing the respective dependencies is proposed using Datalog expressions. We show that many interesting properties of schema elements can be systematically determined this way. The expressiveness of the proposed analysis is exemplarily shown with the problem of computing induced functional dependencies for derived relations. The propagation of functional dependencies plays an important role in data integration and query optimization but represents an undecidable problem in general. And yet, our rule-based analysis covers all relational operators as well as linear recursive expressions in a systematic way showing the depth of analysis possible by our proposal. The analysis of functional dependencies is well-integrated in a uniform approach to analyzing dependencies between schema elements in general.

Keywords: Schema analysis · Functional dependencies
Dependency propagation · Datalog

1 Introduction

The analysis of database schema elements such as tables, views, triggers, user-defined functions and constraints provides valuable information for database users for understanding, maintaining and managing a database application and its evolution. In the literature, schema analysis has been investigated for improving the quality of SQL/program code or detecting program errors [5], for detecting the consequences of schema changes [18], for versioning [13], and matching [19]. In addition, the analysis of schema objects plays an important role for tuning resp. refactoring database applications [4]. All these approaches rely on exploring dependencies between schema objects and an in-depth analysis of their components and interactions. A comprehensive and flexible analysis of schema

© Springer International Publishing AG, part of Springer Nature 2018
F. Fioravanti and J. P. Gallagher (Eds.): LOPSTR 2017, LNCS 10855, pp. 20–36, 2018.
https://doi.org/10.1007/978-3-319-94460-9_2

elements, however, is not provided as these approaches are typically restricted to some subparts of a given schema. The same is true for analysis features provided by commercial systems where approaches such as integrity checking, executing referential actions or query change notification (as provided by Oracle) already use schema object dependencies but in an implicit and nontransparent way, only. That is, no access to the underlying meta-data is provided to the user nor can be freely analyzed by means of user-defined queries. Even the meta-data about tables and SQL views which are sometimes provided by system tables cover only certain information of the respective schema elements. This makes it difficult for database users to understand a given schema, explain specific derivations or oversee the consequences of intended schema modifications.

In this paper, we propose a uniform approach for analyzing schema elements in a comprehensive way. To this end, the schema objects are compiled and their meta-data is stored into a Datalog program which employs queries for deriving interesting properties of the schema. This way, indirect dependencies between tables, views and user-defined functions can be determined which is important for understanding follow-up changes. In order to show the expressiveness of the proposed analysis, our rule-based approach is applied to the problem of deducing functional dependencies (FDs) for derived relations, i.e., views, based on FDs defined for base relations. This so-called *FD propagation* or *FD-FD implication* problem has been studied since the 80s [7,12,15,16,21,22] and has applications in data exchange [11], data integration [8], data cleaning [12], data transformations [9], and semantic query optimization [20].

Functional dependencies describe relationships between attributes of a database relation and are the most widely used uni-relational dependencies [10]. They arise naturally in many ways, for instance when modeling key constraints, one-to-one or one-to-many relationships. The problem of FD propagation is undecidable in the general setting and coNP-complete for many special cases [12]. Consequently, the task of finding induced FDs is rather complex and needs to be flexible in order to allow for further refinements. We show that our rule-based approach to schema analysis is well-suited for realizing techniques for FD propagation in a declarative way indicating the expressiveness of the proposed analysis. In particular, our contributions are as follows:

- We propose a rule-based approach for analyzing the properties of views, tables, triggers and functions in a uniform way.
- Our declarative approach in Datalog can be easily extended for refining the analysis by user-defined queries and transferred into corresponding SQL views for an in-database analysis.
- In order to show the expressiveness of our approach, the implication problem for functional dependencies is investigated using our approach.
- As a proof-of-concept a PROLOG-based implementation of the proposed Datalog solution is presented showing the solution of small technical issues arising from our proposed declarative solution.

The paper is organized as follows: First, we introduce the rule-based framework for analyzing schema objects in Sect. 2. Afterwards, the problem of FD

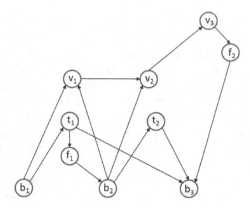

Fig. 1. Dependency graph induced by views, triggers and functions

propagation is investigated serving as a use case in Sect. 3. In this section, a systematic way for deriving FD propagation rules is developed (Subsect. 3.3) before the most difficult operations 'union' and 'recursion' are investigated in more detail in Subsect. 3.4. Finally, we draw a conclusion in Sect. 4.

2   Rule-Based Schema Analysis

A database schema describes the structure of the data stored in a database system but also contains views, triggers, integrity constraints and user defined functions for data analysis. Functions and these different rule types, namely deductive, active and normative rules, are typically defined with various inter-dependencies. For example, views are defined with respect to base relations and/or some other views inducing a hierarchy of derived queries. In particular, the expression CREATE VIEW q AS SELECT ... FROM $p_1, p_2, \ldots, p_n$ leads to the set $\{p_1 \to q, \ldots, p_n \to q\}$ of direct dependencies where q is a derived relation and p_i denote either a derived or a base relation. These direct dependencies are typically represented by means of a predicate dependency graph which allows for analyzing indirect dependencies, too. Those indirect dependencies allow for understanding the consequences of changes made to the instances of the given database schema (referred to as update propagation in the literature) or to its structure. Understanding the consequences of structural changes of a base table, for example, is important if a database user wants to know all view definitions potentially affected by these changes.

Various dependencies are provided by the rules and functions in a database schema such as table-to-table dependencies induced by triggers or views-to-table dependencies which can be induced by functions. A sample dependency graph is given in Fig. 1 depicting dependencies between the base relations $\{b_1, b_2, b_3\}$, the derived relations $\{v_1, v_2, v_3\}$, the triggers $\{t_1, t_2\}$, and the functions $\{f_1, f_2\}$. For example, trigger t_2 fires upon changes in b_2 and refers in its action part to b_3 whereas function f_2 is called from v_3 and executes operations affecting b_3.

The transitive closure allows for detecting indirect dependencies such as the one between b_2 and b_3 due to the path $b_2 \rightarrow v_2 \rightarrow v_3 \rightarrow f_2 \rightarrow b_3$.

This analysis can be further refined by structural details (e.g., negative vs. positive dependencies as needed in approaches for update propagation) as well as by considering the syntactical components of schema objects such as column names (attributes) or operator types (sum, avg, insert, delete, etc.). To this end, the definitions of schema objects need to be parsed and the obtained tokens stored as queryable facts. This kind of analysis is well-known from meta-programming in Prolog which led to the famous vanilla interpreter [14]. For readability reasons we use Datalog instead of Prolog or SQL. Datalog facts of the form

```
dep(To,From)   % dependency relation (path/2 its transitive closure)
base(R,A)      % base relation R with arity A
derived(V,A)   % view V with arity A
call(V,I,O,F)  % input I and output O of function F in view V
attr(R,P,N)    % position P of attribute named N in relation R
```

are used (amongst others) for representing meta-information about different schema objects. Based on these facts, the analysis of schema elements can be simply realized by means of Datalog queries like

```
attr_dups(R1,R2,N) ← attr(R1,_,N),attr(R2,_,N),R1<>R2.
idb_func_pred(V)   ← derived(V,_),call(V,_,_,_).
base_changes(B)    ← path(B,f₁),base(B,_),func(f₁,_).
tbl_dep(A,B)       ← base(A,_),base(B,_),path(A,F),path(F,B),func(F,_).
```

for determining reused attribute names, views calling a function, base tables possibly changed by function f_1, and cyclic dependencies between two base tables through a function. In doing so, many interesting properties of schema elements can be systematically determined which supports users in understanding the interrelations of schema elements. Most database systems already allow for storing and querying meta-data about schema elements in a simple way but a comprehensive (and in particular user-driven) analysis is missing. In contrast, the proposed Datalog program can be easily extended by user-defined rules and the respective program can be directly transferred into a given database using SQL. This way, the schema analysis becomes a natural part of a database application.

3   Functional Dependency Propagation

In order to show the expressiveness of our approach, we investigate the possibility to compute induced FDs for derived relations using the deductive rules introduced above. FDs form special constraints which are assumed to hold for any possible valid database instance. The FD propagation problem analyzes how FDs are propagated through the dependency graph of a database. The problem is undecidable in the general setting for arbitrary relational expressions [15] and even restricted to SC views, i.e., relational expressions allowing selection and cross product only, it turns out to be coNP-complete.[1] In favor of addressing the general setting, we drop the ambition of achieving completeness by considering a special case, only. Instead, we allow for arbitrary expressions over all relational operators, multiple propagation steps and possibly finite domains[2] in order to cover the majority of practical cases. Due to the inherent complexity of the necessary reasoning process, the FD propagation problem is well-suited for showing the expressiveness of using deductive rules for schema analysis.

After giving some preliminaries in Subsect. 3.1, we present our FD propagation approach in Subsects. 3.2, 3.3 and 3.4 and discuss implementation details of our proof-of-concept implementation in Subsect. 3.5. We conclude this section with a discussion (Subsect. 3.6) and related work (Subsect. 3.7).

3.1 Preliminaries

A functional dependency $\alpha \to B$ states that the attribute values of α determine those of B. The restriction to univariate right sides can be done without loss of generality as multivariate right sides can be composed using Armstrong's composition axiom [2]. We allow $\alpha = \emptyset$ which means that the attribute values of B are constant and restrict the represented FDs to those satisfying $B \notin \alpha$ (omitted FDs can be retrieved via Armstrong's augmentation axiom).

For our FD propagation rules, we employ a Datalog variant with special data types for finite, one-leveled sets denoted by Greek letters (with corresponding set operations union $\cup$, intersection $\cap$, set minus $-$, as well as the check for empty sets $\alpha \neq \emptyset$) and finite, possibly nested lists denoted by squared brackets (with comparison and manipulation functionality). For example, the expression

$$\mathtt{p(L[1,2],\varepsilon)} \leftarrow \mathtt{b(L[1,2],\alpha,Y)}, \ \mathtt{c(Y,\gamma,Z)}, \ \varepsilon = \alpha \cup (\gamma - \{\mathtt{Z}\}).$$

defines a join between two predicates b and c where the first attribute of p is a list comprising two elements 1 and 2, and the second attribute of p is the union of the sets α and γ without the value in Z.

In our approach we use the extended transitivity axiom

$$\alpha \to B, \ \gamma \to D, \ B \in \gamma, \ D \notin \alpha \ \Rightarrow \ \alpha \cup (\gamma - B) \to D \tag{1}$$

to derive transitive FDs. Note that if $B \notin \alpha$ and $D \notin \gamma$, then the derived FD also satisfies $D \notin \alpha \cup (\gamma - B)$.

Rule Normalization. In order to provide a systematic approach for FD propagation, we need the input rules to be in a so-called normal form, where each rule corresponds to exactly one relational operator. Any set of Datalog rules can be transformed into an equivalent set of normalized rules while properties of the original rule set like being stratifiable are preserved [3]:

---

[1] An in-depth discussion on the complexity can be found in [12].
[2] Finite domains cause troubles as FDs can occur due to the fact of limited possible value combinations without being induced by another FD (cf. [12]).

Example 1. The rule p(W,Z) ← s(W,X), t(X,Y,Z), Y = 2. can be normalized as

$$p(W,Z) \quad\quad \leftarrow \quad q(W,X,Y,Z).$$
$$q(W,X,Y,Z) \leftarrow r(W,X,Y,Z), Y = 2.$$
$$r(W,X,Y,Z) \leftarrow s(W,X), t(X,Y,Z).$$

where the first rule corresponds to the projection operator π, the second is a selection σ with constraint Y = 2, and the third represents the join $\bowtie$ of s and t.

In the following, we assume that the Datalog rules defining views are transformed into normal form for further analysis. That is, each Datalog rule corresponds to exactly one of the following relational algebra operators ($\{X_h\}$, $\{Y_i\}$, $\{Z_j\}$ denote sets of pairwise distinct variables):

Projection π: p(X_1, ...,X_k) ← q(Y_1, ...,Y_n). for $\{X_1,\ldots,X_k\} \subseteq \{Y_1,\ldots,Y_n\}$
Extension π': p($X_1,\ldots,X_k,Y_1,\ldots,Y_n$) ← q($X_1,\ldots,X_k$), $Y_1 = t_1,\ldots,Y_n = t_n$.
     where each t_i is a variable X_{j_i} or a constant c_i
Selection σ: p($X_1,\ldots,X_k$) ← q($X_1,\ldots,X_k$), <Condition($X_1,\ldots,X_k$)>.
Cross product $\times$: p($X_1,\ldots,X_k$) ← q($Y_1,\ldots,Y_n$), r($Z_1,\ldots,Z_m$).
     for $\{X_1,\ldots,X_k\} = \{Y_1,\ldots,Y_n\} \cup \{Z_1,\ldots,Z_m\}$
Union $\cup$: p($X_1,\ldots,X_k$) ← p_i($X_1,\ldots,X_k$). for $1 \le i \le 2$
Intersection $\cap$: p($X_1,\ldots,X_k$) ← q($X_1,\ldots,X_k$), r($X_1,\ldots,X_k$).
Negation $-$: p($X_1,\ldots,X_k$) ← q($X_1,\ldots,X_k$), not r($X_1,\ldots,X_k$).

Join $\bowtie$: p($X_1,\ldots,X_k$) ← q($Y_1,\ldots,Y_n$), r($Z_1,\ldots,Z_m$).
    for $\{X_1,\ldots,X_k\} = \{Y_1,\ldots,Y_n\} \cup \{Z_1,\ldots,Z_m\}$
Renaming ρ: p($X_1,\ldots,X_k$) ← q($X_1,\ldots,X_k$).

In order to simplify the FD propagation, we will not allow for self joins or cross products (i.e., q = r) which can always be achieved by applying renaming of one of the respective relations first.

3.2   Representation of FDs and Normalized Rules

We assume that functional dependencies for EDB predicates are given in a relation edb_fd(p, α, B, ID). Here α and B are (sets of) column numbers of the relation p. The fact represents the functional dependency $\alpha \to B$ for the relation p. The ID is of type list and used to identify the dependency in later steps, e.g., in case of union. The derived functional dependencies will be represented in the same way in an IDB predicate fd(p, α, B, ID'). Here ID' is related to the dependency's ID where the FD is derived from for propagated FDs or to a newly created ID for FDs that arise during the propagation process.

As in normal form every rule corresponds to exactly one operator, we can refine the above defined dependency relation dep/2 to rel/3 by adding the respective operator. A fact rel(p,q,op) indicates that a relation p depends (positively) on a relation q via a relational operator op which is one of 'projection', 'extension', 'selection' 'product', 'union', 'intersection', 'negation', 'join', and 'renaming'.

We further introduce an EDB predicate pos(head, body, pos_head, pos_body) for storing information on how the positions of non position preserving operators (cf. Table 1) transform from rule body to head (since FDs are represented via column numbers). For the rules of Example 1 these are:

p(W,Z) ← q(W,X,Y,Z)   → pos(p,q,1,1). pos(p,q,2,4).
r(W,X,Y,Z) ← s(W,X),t(X,Y,Z) → pos(r,s,1,1). pos(r,s,2,2).
                                                        pos(r,t,2,1). pos(r,t,3,2).
                                                        pos(r,t,4,3).

Remembering that each relation is defined via one operator only and that we exclude self joins for simplicity (cf. Sect. 3.1), the above defined relation pos/4 is non-ambiguous. Finally, we have two EDB predicates eq(pred, pos1, pos2) and const(pred, pos, val) for information on equality conditions (e.g., X = Y or X = const resp.) in extension and selection rules.

3.3   Propagation Rules

In this section, we present three different types of propagation rules for (a) propagating FDs to the next step, (b) introducing additional FDs arising from equality constraints, and (c) calculating transitive FDs.

Example 2. Consider again the rule set introduced in Example 1. If we assume two FDs fd(s, {1}, 2, ID_1) and fd(t, {1,2}, 3, ID_2) for the base relations s and t we obtain the following propagation process (omitting IDs). First, both FDs are propagated to r resulting in fd(r, {1}, 2) and fd(r, {2,3}, 4) (with the appropriate column renaming for the latter FD). By transitivity we have fd(r, {1,3}, 4) as a combination of the two. All three FDs are propagated to q together with fd(q, ∅, 3) resulting from the equality constraint Y = 2. Applying transitivity results in three more FDs for q, but only fd(q, {1}, 4) is propagated further to p as fd(p, {1}, 2). The complete list of propagated FDs including IDs is given in Example 3.

Table 1 summarizes the properties of how FDs are propagated via the different relational operators which form the basis for the propagation rules. (Note that in the first two rows attention has to be paid for *no/−*, whereas in the last three rows special attention has to be paid for *yes/×*.) In most cases, the FDs are propagated as they are (with adjustments on the positions for π, $\times$, and $\bowtie$). If there is a single rule defining a derived relation, the source FDs transform to FDs for the derived relation (restricted to the attributes in use). Union forms an exception where even common FDs are only propagated in special cases and is therefore treated separately (cf. Sect. 3.4). For extensions and selections where additional FDs can occur due to equality conditions as well as for joins transitive FDs may appear so that taking the transitive closure becomes necessary. In cases where the number of tuples is reduced (i.e., σ, $\cap$, $\bowtie$, and $-$) it is possible that new FDs appear as there are less tuples for which the FD constraint must be satisfied. But as we are working on schema and not on instance level, this FD

Table 1. Properties of FD propagation categorized by operator

Properties	π	π'	σ	$\times$	$\cup$	$\cap$	$-$	$\bowtie$	ρ
FDs are preserved	$\times$*1	$\times$	$\times$	$\times$	$-$	$\times$	$\times$*2	$\times$	$\times$
Positions are preserved	$-$	$\times$	$\times$	$-$	$\times$	$\times$	$\times$	$-$	$\times$
Transitive FDs can appear	$-$	$\times$	$\times$	$-$	$-$	$\times$	$-$	$\times$	$-$
Additional FDs from equality conditions (variables and constants)	$-$	$\times$	$\times$	$-$	$-$	$-$	$-$	$-$	$-$
Additional FDs caused by instance reduction may appear	$-$	$-$	$\times$	$-$	$-$	$\times$	$\times$	$\times$	$-$

$\times \,\hat{=}\,$ yes, $- \,\hat{=}\,$ no
*1: those where all contained variables are maintained, *2: those of the minuend

had to be present in a specific part of the parent relations. The only case, where a FD is propagated to just a part of the derived relation is union.

The different propagation rules for the relational operators except union, additional FDs due to equality conditions, and transitive FDs are specified in the following. The definition and usage of IDs and how they are propagated is deferred to Sect. 3.4.

(a) Induced FDs. For direct propagation of FDs from one level to the next, we distinguish between *position preserving* and *non position preserving* operators. In the first case FDs can be directly propagated (2), whereas in the latter adjustments on the column numbers are necessary (3). The EDB predicates pos_pres and non_pos_pres comprise the respective operators as listed in Fig. 2.

$$\text{fd}(P,\alpha,B) \leftarrow \text{fd}(Q,\alpha,B)\,,\ \text{rel}(P,Q,Op)\,,\ \text{pos\_pres}(Op)\,. \tag{2}$$

$$\text{fd}(P,\{X_1,\ldots,X_n\},Y) \leftarrow \text{fd}(Q,\{A_1,\ldots,A_n\},B),$$
$$\text{pos}(P,Q,X_1,A_1),\ldots,\text{pos}(P,Q,X_n,A_n),\text{pos}(P,Q,Y,B), \tag{3}$$
$$\text{rel}(P,Q,Op),\ \text{non\_pos\_pres}(Op).$$

pos_pres	non_pos_pres	
'selection'	'projection'	
'extension'	'product'	
'negation'	'join'	
'intersection'		
'renaming'		

```
trans(R) ← base(R,_).
trans(R) ← rel(R,_,'intersection').
trans(R) ← rel(R,_,'join').
trans(R) ← eq(R,_,_).
trans(R) ← const(R,_,_).
```

Fig. 2. Position preserving (left) and non position preserving (middle) operators, and relations where transitive FDs may occur (right).

(b) Additional FDs. For any equality constraint $X = Y$ we can deduce the dependencies $X \rightarrow Y$ and $Y \rightarrow X$ as after the application of the constraint the values of X and Y coincide. Similar, a constant constraint $X = \mathtt{const}$ induces the dependency $\emptyset \rightarrow X$. Translated to our approach that is for any fact $\mathtt{eq(R,Pos1,Pos2)}$ and $\mathtt{const(R,Pos,Val)}$ respectively we derive the following FDs:

$$\mathtt{fd(R,\{Pos1\},Pos2)} \leftarrow \mathtt{eq(R,Pos1,Pos2)}. \tag{4}$$

$$\mathtt{fd(R,\{Pos2\},Pos1)} \leftarrow \mathtt{eq(R,Pos1,Pos2)}. \tag{5}$$

$$\mathtt{fd(R,\emptyset,Pos)} \leftarrow \mathtt{const(R,Pos,Val)}. \tag{6}$$

(c) Transitive FDs. Since transitive FDs can only arise for certain operators it is sufficient to deduce transitive FDs in those cases (cf. Table 1). For the computation we use the following two rules:

$$\mathtt{fd(P,\varepsilon,D)} \leftarrow \mathtt{fd(P,\alpha,B)}, \ \mathtt{fd(P,\gamma,D)},$$
$$\mathtt{B} \in \gamma, \mathtt{D} \notin \alpha, \varepsilon = \alpha \cup (\gamma - \{\mathtt{B}\}), \mathtt{trans(P)}. \tag{7}$$

$$\mathtt{fd(P,\{X\},Y)} \leftarrow \mathtt{fd(P,\alpha,X,ID)}, \ \mathtt{fd(P,\alpha,Y,ID)}, \ \mathtt{trans(P)}. \tag{8}$$

The first rule implements the extended transitivity axiom (1) and the second equates the right sides of two identical FDs (identified by matching IDs, cf. Sect. 3.4). The IDB predicate $\mathtt{trans/1}$ defined in Fig. 2 comprises those relations where transitive FDs may occur. Base relations are included to start with a complete set of representatives.

3.4   Union and Recursion

In case of union $p = p_1 \cup p_2$ even common FDs of p_1 and p_2 are only propagated in special cases. Consider the following example of student IDs. For each university, the student ID uniquely identify the student associated with it. But the same student ID can be used by different universities for different students. So although we have the FD *student ID* → student name in the relations $\mathtt{Bonn\_students}$ and $\mathtt{Cologne\_students}$, it is not a valid FD in the union of both. A common FD of p_1 and p_2 is only propagated to p if the domains of the FD are disjoint, or if they match on common instances. The first case can only be handled safely on schema level if constants are involved. The latter is the case if the FDs have the same origin and are propagated in a similar way. Whether two FDs have the same origin can be easily checked with the $\mathtt{path}$ relation of Sect. 2. This criteria is not yet enough as the FDs might have been manipulated during the propagation process (e.g., changes in the ordering, equality constraints, etc.). So we employ a system of identifiers to track those changes made to a certain FD. For the IDs we use a list structure that adopts the tree structure of [15] who represents FDs as trees with source domains as leaves and the target domain as the tree's root. As the target is already handled in the FD itself, we keep track of the source domains and transitively composed FDs, only.

At the beginning, each FD $\alpha \rightarrow B$ gets a unique identifier ID_i. The idea is to propagate this ID together with the FD and to keep track of the modifications made to that FD. For this purpose we attach an ordered tuple, a (possibly nested) list to the ID, i.e., $ID_i[A_1, \ldots, A_n]$ for the above base FD with $\alpha = \{A_1, \ldots, A_n\}$. For the position preserving operators (that in particular do not change the FD's structure) the ID is identically propagated in (2). For the non position preserving operators the positions are updated (using a UDF) similarly to the position adjustments of the FD itself in (3). The difference is that the ID maintains an ordering and that the cardinality stays invariant. For constant constraints, we set the constant value as ID in (6), equality constraints in (4), (5) and (8) get the (column number of the) left side as ID. In (7) we replace the occurrences of the column number B in the ID of $fd(X, \gamma, D, -)$ by the ID of $fd(X, \alpha, B, -)$. Note that this corresponds to a column number replacement for equality constraints.

Example 3. For the FD propagation in Example 2 we have the following IDs:

```
fd(s,  {1},    2, ID₁[1]).          fd(q,  {1},    2, ID₁[1]).
fd(t, {1,2},   3, ID₂[1,2]).        fd(q, {2,3},   4, ID₂[2,3]).
                                    fd(q, {1,3},   4, ID₂[ID₁[1],3]).
fd(r,  {1},    2, ID₁[1]).          fd(q,   ∅,     3, '2').
fd(r, {2,3},   4, ID₂[2,3]).        fd(q,  {2},    4, ID₂[2,'2']).
fd(r, {1,3},   4, ID₂[ID₁[1],3]).   fd(q,  {1},    4, ID₂[ID₁[1],'2']).

                   fd(p,  {1},    2, ID₂[ID₁[1],'2']).
```

A common ID implies that the same modifications (not counting column number shifts due to joins, projections and equality constraints) have been made to a common base FD. This means that the FD is preserved in the case of union. So the final propagation rule for union reduces to a check for similar IDs:

$$fd(P, \alpha, B, ID) \leftarrow fd(P_1, \alpha, B, ID), fd(P_2, \alpha, B, ID), P_1 \neq P_2, \qquad (9)$$
$$rel(P, P_1, 'union'), \ rel(P, P_2, 'union').$$

Common FDs resulting from equality and constant constraints are propagated in any case. Due to the choice of IDs this case is captured in the above ID comparison rule. Note that there are FDs with different IDs for with the common FD is maintained in the union. Examples of such cases which are not covered by our approach can be found in [15].

Recursion. Recursion forms another special case. Consider the following recursive example modeling the ancestor relationship of a tree. We have the following two rules recursively defining the relation p:

```
p(Child, Parent, Parent) ← q(Child, Parent).
p(Child, Parent, Ancestor) ← p(Child, Parent, X), q(X, Ancestor).
```

Or equivalently transformed into the normal form:

$$
\begin{aligned}
\text{p(C, P, A)} &\leftarrow \text{p}_1\text{(C, P, A)}. \\
\text{p(C, P, A)} &\leftarrow \text{p}_2\text{(C, P, A)}. \\
\text{p}_1\text{(C, P, Y)} &\leftarrow \text{q(C, P)}, \text{ Y=P}. \\
\text{p}_2\text{(C, P, A)} &\leftarrow \text{p}_3\text{(C, P, X, A)}. \\
\text{p}_3\text{(C, P, X, A)} &\leftarrow \text{p(C, P, X)}, \text{q(X, A)}.
\end{aligned}
$$

Each vertex has a unique parent, so we assume the FD *Child → Parent* for q, i.e., fd(q, {1}, 2, *[1]). With the rules defined above we cannot compute any FD for p although the FD *Child → Parent* is propagated from q. This is because the FD is propagated to the recursion's base case and survives the recursion step. The rules above cannot detect this FDs as it is only propagated to p_1 but not derivable for p_2 or p_3.

Our solution is to take the *potential* FDs propagated to the recursion's base case and feed them into the recursion step(s). If they *survive* the recursion step, i.e., if they are propagated with the above defined rules (2)–(9), then they are propagated as FD for the whole relation.

Since we limited the union rule in the definition of the normal form to two operands (cf. Sect. 3.1) the rule defining a linear recursive relation P has only two components, which are w.l.o.g. a base case Q and a recursive component R. We maintain this information in an EDB predicate rec(P, Q, R). As potential FDs we introduce those that are propagated from the base case Q to the base part of the recursive relation P.

$$\text{pfd(P, } \alpha \text{,B,ID)} \leftarrow \text{fd(Q, } \alpha \text{,B,ID)}, \text{ rec(P,Q,R)}.$$

Finally after propagating them through the dependency graph, we can deduce those FDs present in the recursive relation by ID comparison:

$$\text{fd(P, } \alpha \text{,B,ID)} \leftarrow \text{fd(Q, } \alpha \text{,B,ID)}, \text{ pfd(R, } \alpha \text{,B,ID)}, \text{ rec(P,Q,R)}.$$

Applied to the ancestor example this results in the following facts correctly deriving the FD $1 \rightarrow 2$, i.e., *Child → Parent*, for relation p:

fd(q,1,2,*[1]).	pfd(p,1,2,*[1]).	fd(p₃,3,4,*(3)).	pfd(p₂,1,2,*[1]).
	pfd(p,2,3,3).	pfd(p₃,1,2,*[1]).	pfd(p₂,2,3,*[2]).
fd(p₁,1,2,*[1]).	pfd(p,3,2,3).	pfd(p₃,2,3,2).	pfd(p₂,1,3,*[*[1]]).
fd(p₁,2,3,2).	pfd(p,1,3,*[1]).	pfd(p₃,3,2,3).	
fd(p₁,3,2,3).		pfd(p₃,1,3,*[1]).	fd(p,1,2,*[1]).
fd(p₁,1,3,*[1]).		pfd(p₃,2,4,*[2]).	
		pfd(p₃,1,4,*[*[1]]).	

In addition to the case of union it is not only important that the FD's ID is maintained to keep the FD property through the recursion's union, but also the propagation process has to be tracked to ensure the propagated FD as the following example shows.

Example 4. Consider the following rule set defining the recursive relation r:

$$r(W, X, Y, Z) \quad\quad \leftarrow \quad r_1(W, X, Y, Z).$$
$$r(W, X, Y, Z) \quad\quad \leftarrow \quad r_2(W, X, Y, Z).$$
$$r_1(A, B, A_2, B_2) \quad \leftarrow \quad e(A, B),\; A_2 = A,\; B_2 = B.$$
$$r_2(Y, Y_2, W, X) \quad\quad \leftarrow \quad r_3(W, X, Y, Z, Y_2).$$
$$r_3(W, X, Y, Z, Y_2) \quad \leftarrow \quad r(W, X, Y, Z),\; Y_2 = Y.$$

If we assume a FD fd(e, {1}, 2, *[1]) for the base relation e, the approach would calculate the FD fd(r, {3}, 4, *[3]) for r as the pfd(r, {3}, 4, *[3]) survives the recursion step. But this is not correct as the fact e(1, 2) yields p(1, 2, 1, 2), p(1, 1, 1, 2), and p(1, 1, 1, 1). The problem is that pfd(r, {3}, 4, *[3]) is propagated from pfd(r, {1}, 2, *[1]) which does not survive the recursion step and therefore causes the violation of the first in the second recursion step. So the IDs have to be slightly updated to keep track of the used FDs during the propagation.

3.5   Implementation

We developed an implementation that can execute the above Datalog meta rules. It is available from the following web page:

http://www.informatik.uni-halle.de/~brass/fd/

It reads an input file consisting of

- declarations of base predicates and their functional dependencies, and
- Datalog rules in normal form defining derived predicates (views).

These definitions are transformed into the facts of the meta program described above, i.e. facts of the predicates base, base_fd, rel, pos, const, and eq. The parser actually produces the lower level representation of Datalog rules presented in [6]. We used Datalog to check for the rule normal forms and compute the meta-level facts that encode the input rules.

For representing the left-hand side of an FD we use sets of integers with the following built-in predicates as an extension of standard Datalog:

- set_one(A, α) produces a singleton set from an element, i.e. $\alpha = \{A\}$.
- set_elem(A, α) checks whether $A \in \alpha$.
- set_minus(α, A, β) removes an element from a set, i.e. $\beta = \alpha - \{A\}$.
- set_plus(α, A, β) adds an element to a set, i.e. $\beta = \alpha \cup \{A\}$.
- set_split(α, A, β) permits to iterate over all elements of a set. For a given set α it returns an element $A \in \alpha$ and the rest of the set $\beta = \alpha - \{A\}$. In our implementation, A is always the smallest element of α.
- set_union(α, β, γ) computes the union of two sets, i.e. $\gamma = \alpha \cup \beta$.

Our Datalog implementation also uses an aggregation function to compute sets from single facts, which is used to compute the base_fd facts that are considered given here.

Nested sets are excluded, thus sets can contain only the finitely many constants of the given input, which ensures termination. Furthermore, sets of small numbers as used here could be represented internally as short bit strings.

The situation with the IDs is more difficult. IDs encode how functions corresponding to the FDs in the base tables were composed. An ID for an FD $\alpha \to B$ is a term consisting of function symbols for base table FDs, and the column numbers from α (plus constants from the program). Note that column numbers and constants must be distinguished. Our special data type for IDs comprises the following built-in predicates:

- `id_gen(`R`, FdNo, {`$A_1, \ldots, A_n$`}, `B`, ID)` generates an ID $f(A_1, \ldots, A_n)$ for a base relation, where the function symbol f uniquely identifies the FD $A_1, \ldots, A_n \to B$ in the base relation R.
- `id_col(`B`, ID)` is used for equality conditions and generates an ID that consists only of the column number B.
- `id_const(`c`, ID)` is used for conditions of the form $X = c$ and constructs an ID that consists of c specially marked as constant.
- `id_subst(IdIn, `B`, IdSubst, IdOut)` is used for computing the ID of an FD that was derived by transitivity. It walks through `IdIn`, and replaces every leaf node that is column number B by `IdSubst`.
- `id_map_start(IDin, IDout)` is needed together with the following predicate for mapping column numbers for non position preserving operators. Since the rules must walk through each input-output column pair, we must avoid that after e.g. column 1 was replaced by 2, it is replaced again, when column 2 is mapped. This predicate marks all column numbers in the ID. The next predicate replaces only marked columns, and removes this mark, so the resulting column will not be touched again in this mapping.
- `id_map(IdIn, `A`, `B`, IdOut)` replaces marked occurrences of A by B.

Note that an unrestricted application of the transitivity rule could lead to non-termination by building larger and larger terms due to ID composition. This could happen already for a base relation $R(A, B, C)$ with FDs $A \to B$, $B \to A$, and $B \to C$. As the following example illustrates, it is not a feasible solution to restrict an FD to one ID only. Consider the case with two base predicates `r(A, B)` and `s(A, B)` each with FD $A \to B$ and the following rules

```
t(X,Y) ← r(X,Y), s(X,Y).
p(X,Y) ← r(X,Y).          q(X,Y) ← s(X,Y).
p(X,Y) ← t(X,Y).          q(X,Y) ← t(X,Y).
```

The FD $1 \to 2$ derived for t needs two IDs, namely the IDs of the given FDs in r and s. Only then we can derive the FD for the union predicates p and q.

So our solution to the termination problem is as follows. If the transitivity rule was applied to $\alpha \to B$ and $\gamma \to D$ with result $\varepsilon \to D$, then no further application of the transitivity rule (directly or indirectly) to ε can re-introduce B. If this would happen, we could remove $\alpha \to B$ from the sequence of FDs that are transitively composed (and also FDs that replace attributes introduced by α), and get the same or a stronger FD (with a subset on the left hand side). Since the set of "forbidden columns" (which cannot appear in α) grows for each application of the transitivity rule (B is added), this ensures termination for each predicate. When we derive an FD for another predicate, the set of forbidden columns is initialized to $\emptyset$. Since recursion can never introduce new FDs and new IDs, also global termination is ensured.

3.6   Discussion

In Sect. 3.3 we introduced our propagation rules for propagating functional dependencies. To compute the set of propagated FDs these rules are simultaneously applied to the input Datalog program in normal form including specified base FDs and the extracted meta-data tokens. (Note that the relation fd comprising the propagated functional dependencies is recursively defined.) The rules are based on the observations in Table 1 which can be easily verified. For example an equality constraint $X = Y$ introduces two FDs between the attributes X and Y as the attribute values of one determine the identical attribute values of the other. Due to a new FD a transitive deduction of FDs inside the view may become possible, e.g., $X = Y$, $Y \rightarrow Z \Rightarrow X \rightarrow Z$. If there is a functional dependency $\alpha \rightarrow B$ for which not all attributes of $\alpha \cup \{B\}$ are present in the projected relation p, then either one of the source domains or the target domain is missing, so the FD cannot be propagated to p. If A is missing in p and $\alpha - \{A\} \rightarrow B$ is a valid FD in p, then the FD has a matching FD in the parent relation and is propagated to p via this FD.

The propagated functional dependencies of our approach are not complete as the problem is undecidable in the general setting. Also limited to a less expressive subset of the relational operators (e.g., restricted operator order SPC views) one has to assume the absence of finite domains to achieve completeness. Nevertheless we are able to deal with many cases appearing in real world applications and the provided rules can be directly used for an implementation (as indicated in the previous Subsection). The implementation shows that a schema analyzer tool can be realized in any expressive rule-based language such as Prolog or SQL. Note the performance of the implementation is not a critical issue even though the number of propagated FDs may grow exponentially in the number of considered attributes per relation[3]. This is due the fact that a typical relation does not contain a multitude of attributes and the analysis has no real-time requirements.

The FD propagation approach can be further generalized to allow user-defined functions $Y_i = f(X_{i_1}, \ldots, X_{i_n})$ in the extension operator π'. As the EDB predicate call/4 already maintains the information which function F is called in a view V with input I and output O, we just can use the propagation rule

$$\texttt{fd(V,I,O,F[I])} \leftarrow \texttt{call(V,I,O,F)}.$$

to include this case as well. After a function call, the output of the UDF is functionally determined by the input, i.e., $\texttt{I} \rightarrow \texttt{O}$.

---

[3] A subsumption step could be added for avoiding redundant FD representations.

3.7 Related Work

The work of [15] was the first addressing the FD propagation problem. In his paper, Klug considers relational algebra expressions and defines a set of rules which iteratively compute the set of induced FDs. The rules are sound and – limited to restricted operator order which is as powerful as relational algebra without set difference – complete, assuming the absence of finite domains. The propagation with this approach is not complete anymore when considering more than one propagation step as in this case the restricted operator order might be violated which can cause the loss of FDs that reappear in later steps. In any rule based approach, special attention has to be paid to the union operator. In [15] this difficulty is addressed with an algorithm systematically testing possible value combinations using formal values.

The authors of [12] use the concept of *conditional FDs* to handle union. The idea is that the dependencies are not propagated to the whole view but are still maintained in its subsets. In the student ID example above, the IDs are still unique restricted to one university. So on the condition that the university is University of Bonn (Cologne), the FD *student ID → student name* can be propagated.

Besides the mentioned rule based approaches, *the chase* is an established algorithm for FD implication. Originally developed as lossless join test [1], the chase has been used to infer dependencies inside one relation [17] and for FD-FD implication [7]. Related to the approach of [15] the idea is to equate formal values following and applying functional dependencies. In [21] the chase is used to deal with FD propagation in linear recursive Datalog programs.

4 Conclusion

In this paper, we discussed a uniform framework for analyzing schema objects using deductive rules. In doing so, many interesting schema object properties as well as relationships can be systematically deduced. These form valuable information for database users. Our approach can be easily extended for refining the analysis by user-defined queries and is suitable for SQL systems due to the choice of Datalog. The expressiveness of the underlying reasoning process has been demonstrated by the analysis of induced functional dependencies. The respective FD propagation problem is known to be undecidable and intricate in detail. And yet, the proposed deductive rules supplemented by a proof-of-concept implementation allow for covering known approaches to solving the FD propagation problem proposed so far. This includes multiple propagation steps, union and linear recursion showing the depth of analysis which can be achieved for schema analysis in this way. Identifying how other FD propagation approaches can be integrated into our rule based approach as well as the experimental evaluation of our proposal is part of further research.

References

1. Aho, A.V., Beeri, C., Ullman, J.D.: The theory of joins in relational databases. TODS **4**(3), 297–314 (1979)
2. Armstrong, W.W.: Dependency structures of data base relationships. In: IFIP Congress 1974, pp. 580–583 (1974)
3. Behrend, A., Manthey, R.: A transformation-based approach to view updating in stratifiable deductive databases. In: Hartmann, S., Kern-Isberner, G. (eds.) FoIKS 2008. LNCS, vol. 4932, pp. 253–271. Springer, Heidelberg (2008). https://doi.org/10.1007/978-3-540-77684-0_18
4. Boehm, A.M., Seipel, D., Sickmann, A., Wetzka, M.: Squash: a tool for analyzing, tuning and refactoring relational database applications. In: Seipel, D., Hanus, M., Wolf, A. (eds.) INAP/WLP 2007. LNCS (LNAI), vol. 5437, pp. 82–98. Springer, Heidelberg (2009). https://doi.org/10.1007/978-3-642-00675-3_6
5. Brass, S., Goldberg, C.: Proving the safety of SQL queries. In: QSIC 2005, pp. 197–204 (2005)
6. Brass, S.: Language constructs for a datalog compiler. In: Benslimane, D., Damiani, E., Grosky, W.I., Hameurlain, A., Sheth, A., Wagner, R.R. (eds.) DEXA 2017. LNCS, vol. 10438, pp. 130–140. Springer, Cham (2017). https://doi.org/10.1007/978-3-319-64468-4_10
7. Brisaboa, N.R., González, A., Hernández, H.J., Paramá, J.R.: The chase of datalog programs. In: Embury, S.M., Fiddian, N.J., Gray, W.A., Jones, A.C. (eds.) BNCOD 1998. LNCS, vol. 1405, pp. 165–166. Springer, Heidelberg (1998). https://doi.org/10.1007/BFb0053479
8. Calì, A., Calvanese, D., De Giacomo, G., Lenzerini, M.: Data integration under integrity constraints. Inf. Syst. **29**(2), 147–163 (2004)
9. Davidson, S.B., Fan, W., Hara, C.S., Qin, J.: Propagating XML constraints to relations. In: ICDE 2003, pp. 543–554 (2003)
10. Delobel, C., Adiba, M.: Relational Database Systems. Elsevier, New York (1985)
11. Fagin, R., Kolaitis, P.G., Popa, L., Tan, W.C.: Reverse data exchange: coping with nulls. In: PODS 2009, pp. 23–32 (2009)
12. Fan, W., Ma, S., Hu, Y., Liu, J., Wu, Y.: Propagating functional dependencies with conditions. PVLDB **1**(1), 391–407 (2008)
13. Herrmann, K., Voigt, H., Behrend, A., Rausch, J., Lehner, W.: Living in parallel realities - co-existing schema versions with a bidirectional database evolution language. In: SIGMOD 2017, pp. 1101–1116 (2017)
14. Hill, P.M., Lloyd, J.W.: Analysis of meta-programs. In: Meta-Programming in Logic Programming, pp. 23–51 (1989)
15. Klug, A.C.: Calculating constraints on relational expressions. TODS **5**(3), 260–290 (1980)
16. Klug, A.C., Price, R.: Determining view dependencies using tableaux. TODS **7**(3), 361–380 (1982)
17. Maier, D., Mendelzon, A.O., Sagiv, Y.: Testing implications of data dependencies. TODS **4**(4), 455–469 (1979)
18. Maule, A., Emmerich, W., Rosenblum, D.S.: Impact analysis of database schema changes. In: ICSE 2008, pp. 451–460 (2008)
19. Milo, T., Zohar, S.: Using schema matching to simplify heterogeneous data translation. In: VLDB 1998, pp. 122–133 (1998)

20. Paramá, J.R., Brisaboa, N.R., Penabad, M.R., Places, Á.S.: A semantic query optimization approach to optimize linear datalog programs. In: Manolopoulos, Y., Návrat, P. (eds.) ADBIS 2002. LNCS, vol. 2435, pp. 277–290. Springer, Heidelberg (2002). https://doi.org/10.1007/3-540-45710-0_22

21. Paramá, J.R., Brisaboa, N.R., Penabad, M.R., Places, Á.S.: Implication of functional dependencies for recursive queries. In: Broy, M., Zamulin, A.V. (eds.) PSI 2003. LNCS, vol. 2890, pp. 509–519. Springer, Heidelberg (2004). https://doi.org/10.1007/978-3-540-39866-0_49

22. Wang, K., Yuan, L.: Preservation of integrity constraints in definite DATALOG programs. Inf. Process. Lett. **44**(4), 185–193 (1992)

Deadlock Detection of Java Bytecode

Cosimo Laneve[(✉)] and Abel Garcia

Department of Computer Science and Engineering,
University of Bologna – Inria Focus, Bologna, Italy
cosimo.laneve@unibo.it

Abstract. This paper presents a technique for deadlock detection of Java programs. The technique uses typing rules for extracting infinite-state abstract models of the dependencies among the components of the Java intermediate language – the Java bytecode. Models are subsequently analysed by means of an extension of a solver that we have defined for detecting deadlocks in process calculi. Our technique is complemented by a prototype verifier that also covers most of the Java features.

1 Introduction

Deadlocks are common flaws of concurrent programs that occur when a set of threads are blocked because each one is attempting to acquire a lock held by another one. Such errors are difficult to detect or anticipate, since they may not happen during every execution, and may have catastrophic effects for the overall functionality of the software system. At the time of writing this paper, the *Oracle Bug Database*[1] reports more than 40 unresolved bugs due to deadlocks, while the *Apache Issue Tracker*[2] reports around 400 unresolved deadlock bugs. These two databases refer to programs written in Java, a mainstream programming language in a lot of domains, such as web and cloud applications, user applications and mobile applications.

The objective of our research is to design and implement a technique capable of detecting potential deadlock bugs of Java programs *at static time*. This objective is difficult because Java has a complex concurrency model: it uses threads that may perform read/write operations over shared variables and whose execution depends on the scheduling strategy implemented in the Java Virtual Machine (JVM). In addition, Java, being a full-fledged programming language, includes an extensive standard library with lots of features implemented in native language.

To reduce the complexity of our work, we decided to address the Java bytecode, namely 198 instructions that are the compilation target of every Java application and have a reference semantics that is defined by the JVM behaviour. Therefore, it is possible to deliver correctness results without narrowing/oversimplifying our original goal. In this paper, we present our technique on a subset of

---

[1] http://bugs.java.com/.

[2] https://issues.apache.org/jira.

© Springer International Publishing AG, part of Springer Nature 2018
F. Fioravanti and J. P. Gallagher (Eds.): LOPSTR 2017, LNCS 10855, pp. 37–53, 2018.
https://doi.org/10.1007/978-3-319-94460-9_3

Java bytecode, called JVML_d, which includes basic instructions for concurrency, such as thread creations, synchronizations, and creations of new objects. The language is defined in Sect. 3.

The technique consists of two stages. The first stage defines a type system that reconstructs the concurrent behaviour of methods. The key principles are the following ones. Each method has an associated type that depends on the type of the arguments (the object "this" is one argument) and that expresses the *concurrent behaviour*. This "concurrent behaviour" reports (*i*) the *sequence of locks* that has been acquired/released by the method, (*ii*) the *threads created*, and (*iii*) the *methods that have been invoked*. The type also includes the analysis of aliases that traces the creation of new objects and their copies (because JVML_d instructions may create and copy objects). The alias analysis is performed in a *symbolic way* by using a *finite set of names*: this is a critical part of our technique because methods may create threads and, when methods are either recursive or iterative, the set of created threads may be infinite. Therefore, we had to devise finite representatives of (infinite sets of) thread names that are sound with respect to the (deadlock) analysis. Section 2 reports a code that can be written in (a simple extension of) JVML_d and that is problematic as regards deadlock detection. Section 4 is a gentle introduction to the type system and Sect. 6 overviews the typing of complex features of JVML.

The second stage of our technique defines the analysis of the behavioural model. In fact, the three reports above – (*i*), (*ii*), and (*iii*) – are terms in a modelling language that extend so-called *lams* [7,8,10]. Lams, which are introduced in Sect. 5, are conjunctions and disjunctions of object dependencies and method invocations and the extension has been necessary for modelling Java *reentrant locks*. In particular, our dependencies also carry thread names – $(a, b)_t$ means that the thread t, which owns the lock of a, is going to lock b. In Java, the lam $(a, a)_t$ is not a circular dependency because it means that t is acquiring the same lock *twice*. Because of this extension, the algorithm for detecting circularities in lams is different than the one in [7,10]. In Sect. 5 we also address this issue.

Our deadlock detection technique has been prototyped and the verifier is called JaDA. While the type system in this paper simply checks static information, JaDA infers the behavioural types from the bytecode. Inference is important in practice because it lightens the analysis but checking is crucial for type safety[3]. JaDA includes several features of JVML; this has made possible to deliver initial assessments of the tool, which are discussed in Sect. 7. Section 8 discusses related work and reports our concluding remarks.

2   Overview of JVML and of our technique

Figure 1 reports a Java class called Network and some of its JVML_d representation. The corresponding main method creates a network of n threads – the philosophers – by invoking buildNetwork – say $t_1, \cdots, t_n$ – that are all potentially running in parallel with the caller – say t_0. Every two adjacent philosophers

---

[3] The technical details of type safety appear in [12].

```
class Network{                          public void buildNetwork(int n, Object x, Object y)
                                         0  iload_1         //n
  public void main(int n){               1  ifne 13
    Object x = new Object();             4  aload_0         //this
    Object y = new Object();             5  aload_2         //x
    buildNetwork(n, x, y); //no deadlock 6  aload_3         //y
    buildNetwork(n, x, x); // deadlock   7  invokevirtual 24 //takeForks(x, y):void
  }                                     10  goto 50
                                        13  new 3
  public void buildNetwork(int n,       16  dup
                Object x, Object y){     17  invokespecial 8  //Object()
    if (n==0) {                         20  astore 4         //z
      takeForks(x,y) ;                  22  new 26
    } else {                            25  dup
      final Object z = new Object() ;   26  aload_0          //this
      Thread t = new Thread(){          27  aload_2          //x
        public void run(){              28  aload 4          //z
          takeForks(x,z) ;              30  invokespecial 28 //Network$1(this, x, z)
      }} ;                              33  astore 5         //thr
      t.start();                        35  aload 5          //thr
      this.buildNetwork(n-1,z,y) ;      37  invokevirtual 31 //start():void
    }                                   40  aload_0          //this
  }                                     41  iload_1          //n
                                        42  iconst_1
  public void takeForks(Object x,       43  isub
                Object y){              44  aload 4          //z
    synchronized(x){ synchronized(y){ } } 46 aload_3         //y
  }                                     47  invokevirtual 36 //buildNetwork(n-1, z, y):void
}                                       50  return
```

Fig. 1. Java Network program and corresponding bytecode (only the buildNetwork method).

share an object – the fork –, which is also created by buildNetwork. Every thread t_i locks the two adjacent forks, that are passed as (implicit) arguments of the thread, and terminates – this is performed by the method takeForks. It is well-known that when the network is a table (it is circular – the thread t_n is sharing one of its forks with t_0) and all the threads have a symmetric strategy of locking objects then a deadlock may occur. On the contrary, when either the network is not circular or one thread has an anti-symmetric strategy, no deadlock will ever occur. Therefore buildNetwork(n,x,y) is deadlock free, while buildNetwork(n,x,x) is deadlocked (when n > 0).

The problematic issue of Network is that the number of threads is not known statically because n is an argument of main. This is displayed in the bytecode of buildNetwork in Fig. 1 by the instruction at address 30 where a new thread is created and by the instruction at address 37 where the thread is started. The recursive invocation that causes the (static) unboundedness is found at instruction 47. Our technique is powerful enough to cope with such problems and to predict the correct behaviour of the code of Fig. 1 and the faulty one if we comment buildNetwork(n,x,y) and de-comment buildNetwork(n,x,x). The technique works as follows. It infers abstract methods' behaviors by computing types, called *lams*, of their bytecode bodies. These lams abstract each bytecode instruction by dropping the *non-relevant* information for the deadlock analysis (e.g. operations on integer variables). In practice, the relevant operations for deadlock analysis are: locking operations (monitorenter and monitorexit instructions), thread spawning operations, function invocations and objects' structures. Thereafter the abstract model is analysed by a solver.

3   The Language JVML$_d$

JVML$_d$ is a restriction of JVML that includes basic constructs and instructions for concurrency[4]. In JVML$_d$, a program is a collection of *class files* whose methods have bodies written in JVML$_d$ bytecode. This bytecode is a partial map from *addresses* ADDR to instructions. Addresses, ranged over by L, L', $\cdots$, are intended to be natural numbers and we use the function $L + 1$ that returns the least address that is strictly greater than L. When P is a program, we write $dom(P)$ to refer to its domain (the set of addresses) and we assume that $0 \in dom(P)$ for every bytecode P.

We use a number of *names*: for classes, ranged over by C, D, $\cdots$, for fields, ranged over by f, f', $\cdots$, for methods, ranged over by m, m', $\cdots$, and for local variables, ranged over by x, y, $\cdots$. A possible empty sequence of names or syntactic categories of the following grammar is written by over-lining the name or the syntactic category, respectively. For instance a sequence of local variables is written $\overline{x}$. However, when we need to access to the elements of a sequence, we use the notation $x_1, \cdots, x_n$. Class files *CF* are defined by the grammar:

$$CF ::= class\ C\ \{fields : \overline{FD}\ \ methods : \overline{MD}\} \qquad MD ::= T\ m\ (C, \overline{T})\ P$$
$$FD ::= C.f : T \qquad\qquad\qquad\qquad\qquad T\ \ \ ::= \top\ |\ int\ |\ C$$

where "*fields :*" and "*methods :*" are keywords and $\top$ is a special type that include all the other types (any value of any type has also type $\top$). This type will represent values that are unusable in our static semantics. The type name C represents a class type, *which is never recursive* in JVML$_d$.

Instructions *Instr* of JVML$_d$ bytecode are of the following form:

$$Instr ::= inc\ |\ pop\ |\ push\ |\ load\ x\ |\ store\ x\ |\ if\ L\ |\ goto\ L$$
$$|\ new\ C\ |\ putfield\ C.f : T\ |\ getfield\ C.f : T\ |\ monitorenter\ |\ monitorexit$$
$$|\ invokevirtual\ C.m(\overline{T})\ |\ start\ C\ |\ return$$

The informal meaning of these instructions is as follows:

- inc increments the content of the stack; pop and push, respectively, pops an element from the stack and pushes the integer 0 on the stack; load x and store x respectively loads the value of x on the stack and pops the top value of the stack by storing it in x; if L pops the top value of the stack and either jumps to the instruction at address L, if it is nonzero, or goes to the next instruction; goto L is the unconditional jump;
- new C allocates a new object of type C, initializes it and pushes it on top of the stack; putfield C.f : T pops the value on the stack and the underlying object value, and assigns the former to the field f of the latter; getfield C.f : T pops the object on the stack and pushes the value in the field f of that object;

---

[4] Actually, JVML$_d$ has a minor difference with respect to JVML: in JVML, local variables are addressed by non-negative integers instead of names.

- `monitorenter`, `monitorexit` are the synchronization primitives that pop the object on the stack and lock and unlock it, respectively;
- `invokevirtual` $C.m(T_1, \cdots, T_n)$ pops n values from the stack (the arguments of the invocation) and dispatches the method `m` on the object on top of the stack; when the method terminates, the returned value is pushed on the stack;
- `start C` creates and starts a new thread for the object on top of the stack. This operation corresponds to `invokevirtual java/lang/Thread/start()` on a thread of class `C` in JVML. We separate it from `invokevirtual` in order to provide more structure to our semantics (because it has an effect on the set of threads – see the operational semantics in the Appendix, where we also consider the instruction `join`);
- `return` terminates program execution.

The bytecode in Fig. 1 is written in a sugared extension of JVML_d. In particular, `aload` and `iload` correspond to our `load` instruction (when the argument is an object or an integer, respectively), `ifne` corresponds to `if`, `dup` duplicates the top of the stack, `sub` subtracts the element on top of the stack from the last-by-one, `invokespecial` is the method invocation of the constructor of the class.

In order to simplify the presentation, in this paper we assume that fields are read-only as they cannot be modified after the initialisation (which is done by constructors that, in turn, are sequential). The full paper [12] reports the complete analysis that also addresses race conditions.

4   The Type System

The purpose of the type system is to associate lams to JVML_d bytecodes. Since JVML_d is the target (of large part) of Java, the association is complex because we must deal with objects and aliasing, object creation and updates performed by constructors, and the concurrent operations – creation of new threads, lock and unlock operations. Therefore the details are pretty technical.

In this paper we adopt a didactic approach by discussing features that are of increasing difficulty. In particular, we focus on one typing rule – that of `invokevirtual` – and we will study the basic, sequential case, the case of invocation of constructors, and the case of invocation of a concurrent thread. The complete set of rules appears in [12].

Typing rules associate types, which are *lams*, to JVML_d instructions by means of *judgments* that are usually abstractions of the machine states. In case of JVM, the state is a memory, called *heap* and the set of running *threads*. In turn, every thread is a stack of activation records – each one containing the address of the instruction to be performed, a stack, and a local memory – plus the sequence of locks owned.

A possible judgment for the instruction at address i of the JVML_d program P is

$$\Gamma, F, S, Z, i \vdash_t P : \ell$$

where Γ, called *environment*, is the abstraction of the heap, F and S are the abstraction of the local memory and the stack, respectively, and Z is the sequence of locks acquired by the thread. The term ℓ is the *lam* of the instruction i and t is a symbolic name identifying the thread that is executing the instruction. (At static time it is not possible to model the stack of activation records).

Environments Γ, memories F, stacks S, and sequences of locks Z are defined by means of *types*, which are more descriptive than those in JVML$_d$ syntax. In particular object types are not just classes C, that is records $[\mathbf{f}_1 : \mathbf{T}_1, \cdots, \mathbf{f}_n : \mathbf{T}_n]$, where $\mathbf{f}_i$ are the fields of the class, because this notation is not adequate for dealing with aliasing. For example, let C be a class with two fields $\mathbf{f}_1$ and $\mathbf{f}_2$ that store objects of class D. If C-objects are represented by $[\mathbf{f}_1 : \mathsf{D}, \mathbf{f}_2 : \mathsf{D}]$ then it is not possible to recover the identities of the values of $\mathbf{f}_1$ and $\mathbf{f}_2$; therefore we cannot distinguish the cases when $\mathbf{f}_1$ and $\mathbf{f}_2$ store the same object or two different objects, which is important when we compute object dependencies.

Therefore we decided to use *symbolic names*, ranged over by a, b, $\cdots$, which also include *void* and *thread names* (threads are objects in Java; we use t, t', $\cdots$ when a name addresses a thread). Symbolic names allow us to define *flattened types* such as $[\mathbf{f}_1 : b, \mathbf{f}_2 : b]$ and $[\mathbf{f}_1 : b, \mathbf{f}_2 : c]$, thus separating the two foregoing cases. Actually, in order to avoid ambiguities with different classes having same field names, the flattened types also carry the class name, e.g. $([\mathbf{f}_1 : b, \mathbf{f}_2 : b], \mathsf{C})$. The binding of symbolic names and flattened types is defined by the *environments*, ranged over by $\Gamma, \Gamma_i, \cdots$. For example $[a \mapsto ([\mathbf{f} : b], \mathsf{C}), b \mapsto ([\mathbf{g} : \mathtt{int}], \mathsf{D})]$ is an environment that defines the names a and b. The function $typeof(\Gamma, a)$ returns the type of a in Γ.

In the type system Γ, F, S, Z are *vectors* that are indexed by the addresses in $dom(P)$. The elements of these vectors are

- Γ_i is the environment at address i;
- the map F_i maps local variables to type values;
- S_i is a sequence of type values;
- Z_i is the *sequence of symbolic names* locked at address i.

Simple Methods. We begin with the rule for `invokevirtual` of a method that has no argument, does not modify the carrier and returns *void*. Operationally, `invokevirtual` (without arguments) takes the element on the stack, which is the invoked object, and executes the first instruction of the corresponding method. In this case, the typing rule is

$$\frac{\begin{array}{c} P[i] = \mathtt{invokevirtual}\ \mathsf{C.m}\ (\ ) \qquad i+1 \in dom(P) \\ S_i = a \cdot S' \quad typeof(\Gamma_i, a) = \mathsf{C} \\ \Gamma_{i+1} = \Gamma_i \quad S_{i+1} = void \cdot S' \quad F_{i+1} = F_i \quad Z_{i+1} = Z_i \end{array}}{\Gamma, F, S, Z, i \vdash_t P : \mathsf{C.m}(a, t, \lceil Z_i \rceil)}$$

The rule verifies that the top element of the stack is of type C and constraints the stack S_{i+1} to be the same as S_i, except for the top element, which is replaced by *void*. The lam of the instruction i indicates that the instruction is a method invocation: we will discuss this term later; we just notice that $\lceil Z_i \rceil$ is the first name in the sequence Z_i (that represents the last object locked by t).

Constructors. We next discuss what happens when methods update the carrier, such as constructors, and return an object. In Java, the returned object is usually a new object (in the JVM it is a fresh run time name) and it is possible to create infinitely many objects by means of iterations or recursions. In the type system, since objects are represented by symbolic names, which must be finitely many, we admit that one symbolic name may represent infinitely many instances of objects. Technically, we use a function $names(i)$ that takes an address i and returns a tuple of names whose length is finite and depends on the address. This function returns a name that may occur already in the judgment when the instruction is not executed once.

The above rule for `invokevirtual` has no element specifying (i) the type of the returned object (because, in that case, it was *void*) and (ii) the symbolic names created by the invocation (because, in that case, there was no one). We discuss the extension of the rule for `invokevirtual` to manage these issues.

First of all, we need a map associating methods to types. Again, types cannot be simple types because we need to trace the identity of objects. For example, let C.m be a method that returns an object of class C; we must distinguish the cases when C.m is the identity or returns a new object with the same fields of the carrier, or with the two fields storing a same object, etc. Instead of using environments for defining this association we decided to use a further map – the *behavioural class table*, noted BCT. This because the BCT is an invariant of the system – it does not change from one instruction to another – and the separation highlights this fact.

The types used in the BCT are a variation of flattened types that completely specifies the tree structure of the object. These types are called *structured types* and are ranged over by $\rho, \rho', \cdots$. For example

$$(a[\mathtt{f}_1 : (b[\mathtt{g} : \mathtt{int}], \mathtt{D}), \mathtt{f}_2 : (c[\mathtt{g} : \mathtt{int}], \mathtt{D})], \mathtt{C})$$

is an object of class C whose symbolic name is a and that stores two different objects of class D in the fields. There is a simple way to transform a symbolic name and an environment into a structured type and conversely, to get an environment out of a structured type. We call these functions $mk\_tree(\Gamma, a)$ and $env(\rho)$, respectively, and we leave their definitions as an exercise.

Let us discuss two examples of method types in the behavioural class table:

– C.m is the identity; hence it returns the carrier and the type also specifies that the carrier has not been modified. The method type is

$$\textsc{bct}(\mathtt{C.m}) = (X, t, b) \to \langle X, X, \ell \rangle.$$

We notice that the type uses *variable names*, ranged over by $X, Y, \cdots$, when the structure of the argument is not relevant. Additionally, the arguments of C.m are three: the first element is the structured type of the carrier, the second and the third arguments are two symbolic names. The name t is the thread that performed the invocation and b is the last object name whose lock has been acquired by t. These two informations are used by the analyser to build the right dependencies between callers and callees and appear in the lam ℓ of the return type.

In the above method type, the carrier is addressed by X. This means that the symbolic name of the carrier is not used in the dependencies of ℓ. When this name is used, we write BCT(C.m) as

$$((a[\mathtt{f}_1 : X, \mathtt{f}_2 : Y], \mathtt{C}), t, b) \rightarrow \langle (a[\mathtt{f}_1 : X, \mathtt{f}_2 : Y], \mathtt{C}), (a[\mathtt{f}_1 : X, \mathtt{f}_2 : Y], \mathtt{C}), \ell \rangle,$$

which binds the occurrences of a in the return type.

- C.p is the constructor of the class C that returns the carrier where the two fields have been initialised with the same new object of class D (we assume D has no field and we shorten $c[\ ]$ into c). In this case, BCT(C.p) is

$$((a[\mathtt{f}_1 : X, \mathtt{f}_2 : Y], \mathtt{C}), t, b) \rightarrow$$
$$(\nu\, c)\langle (a[\mathtt{f}_1 : (c, \mathtt{D}), \mathtt{f}_2 : (c, \mathtt{D})], \mathtt{C}), (a[\mathtt{f}_1 : (c, \mathtt{D}), \mathtt{f}_2 : (c, \mathtt{D})], \mathtt{C}), \ell \rangle$$

We notice that the return type has a binding $(\nu\, c)$. This binding specifies that the name c is *new*, namely it does not occur in the arguments $(a[\mathtt{f}_1 : X, \mathtt{f}_2 : Y], \mathtt{C}), t, b$.

The last concept we need for presenting the new rule for invokevirtual is that of *instance* of a method type. Let BCT(C.p) be

$$((a[\mathtt{f}_1 : X, \mathtt{f}_2 : Y], \mathtt{C}), t, b) \rightarrow$$
$$(\nu\, c)\langle (a[\mathtt{f}_1 : (c, \mathtt{D}), \mathtt{f}_2 : (c, \mathtt{D})], \mathtt{C}), (a[\mathtt{f}_1 : (c, \mathtt{D}), \mathtt{f}_2 : (c, \mathtt{D})], \mathtt{C}), \ell \rangle$$

When C.p is invoked with $(a'[\mathtt{f}_1 : \top, \mathtt{f}_2 : \top], \mathtt{C}), t', b')$ (e.g. a' has been created without initialising the fields) then the return type is

$$\langle (a'[\mathtt{f}_1 : (c', \mathtt{D}), \mathtt{f}_2 : (c', \mathtt{D})], \mathtt{C}), (a'[\mathtt{f}_1 : (c', \mathtt{D}), \mathtt{f}_2 : (c', \mathtt{D})], \mathtt{C}), \ell\{a', t', b', c'/a, t, b, c\} \rangle$$

that will be written as $\text{BCT}(\mathtt{C.p})((a'[\mathtt{f}_1 : \top, \mathtt{f}_2 : \top], \mathtt{C}), t', b')(c')$.

The type rule of a constructor C.m without arguments that returns the updated carrier (by creating one object and storing it in the two fields of its) is

$$P[i] = \mathtt{invokevirtual}\ \mathtt{C.m}\ (\ )\qquad i+1 \in dom(P)$$
$$S_i = a \cdot S'\quad typeof(\Gamma_i, a) = \mathtt{C}$$
$$\rho = mk\_tree(\Gamma_i, a)\quad b = names(i)\quad \text{BCT}(\mathtt{C.m})(\rho, t, \lceil Z_i \rceil)(b) = \langle \rho', \rho'', \ell \rangle$$
$$\Gamma_{i+1} = \Gamma_i + env(\rho') + env(\rho'')\quad S_{i+1} = root(\rho') \cdot S'\quad F_{i+1} = F_i\quad Z_{i+1} = Z_i$$

$$\overline{\text{BCT}, \Gamma, F, S, Z, i \vdash_t P : \mathtt{C.m}(\rho, t, \lceil Z_i \rceil) \rightarrow \rho'}$$

The third line in the premise is the new part of the rule. In particular, in order to compute the instance of $\text{BCT}(\mathtt{C}.m)$, we construct $mk\_tree(\Gamma_i, a)$. The instance of the return type $\langle \rho', \rho'', \ell \rangle$ is used to update Γ_i (in this case $\rho' = \rho''$, therefore $env(\rho') = env(\rho'')$). The function $root(\rho)$ returns the root of the structured type ρ.

Concurrent Methods. The last feature we discuss is concurrency. Let C.m be a constructor that creates and starts a new thread, say t' (and returns it as a field of the carrier). Since t' runs in parallel with the current thread, say t, the *conjunctive* effects of t and t' must be analysed by our tool (the second stage of our technique). In order to delegate the analyser to check the consistency of these conjunctive effects, the type system must record the threads that are created. We therefore extend the judgments with a set collecting such thread names. Actually, we use *two sets* because the set of threads may be infinite (when the method is recursive or iterative). In order to have a more precise analysis, we distinguish the cases when the thread creation is executed once from those when the thread creation is executed several times. In the first case, the analyser will spawn exactly one thread; in the second case the analyser will spawn infinitely many threads (see the last part of Sect. 5). The two sets of tread names are called T, for the names created once, and R for the names that will be spawned infinitely many times, each time with a fresh name. Therefore the judgment becomes

$$\text{BCT}, \Gamma, F, S, Z, T, R, i \vdash_t P : \ell$$

Let "i *is executed once*" be the predicate that is true whenever the method containing the instruction i is not (mutual) recursive or the instruction i is not inside an iteration (this predicate can be easily computed in our type system).

The type rule for a method C.m that creates two threads – t' executed once, t'' spawned several times – is

$$P[i] = \text{invokevirtual } \text{C.m ( )} \qquad i+1 \in dom(P)$$
$$S_i = a \cdot S' \quad typeof(\Gamma_i, a) = \text{C}$$
$$\rho = mk\_tree(\Gamma_i, a) \quad t', t'' = names(i) \quad \text{BCT}(\text{C.m})(\rho, t, \lceil Z_i \rceil)(t', t'') = \langle \rho', \{t'\}, \{t''\}, \rho'', \ell \rangle$$
$$\Gamma_{i+1} = \Gamma_i + env(\rho') + env(\rho'') \quad S_{i+1} = root(\rho') \cdot S' \quad F_{i+1} = F_i \quad Z_{i+1} = Z_i$$
$$T_{i+1}, R_{i+1} = \begin{cases} T_i \cup \{t'\}, \ R_i \sqcup \{t''\} & \text{if } i \text{ is executed once} \\ T_i, \ R_i \cup \{t', t''\} & \text{otherwise} \end{cases}$$

$$\overline{\text{BCT}, \Gamma, F, S, Z, T, R, i \vdash_t P : \text{C.m}(\rho, t, \lceil Z_i \rceil) \to \rho'}$$

In this case, the last premise defines the values of T_{i+1} and R_{i+1} according to the instruction i is executed once or not.

5   Lams and the Analysis of Circularities

In our technique, the dependencies between symbolic names are expressed by means of *lams* [7], noted ℓ, whose syntax is

$$\ell ::= 0 \ \mid \ (a, b)_t \ \mid \ \text{C.m}(\overline{\rho}) \to \rho' \ \mid \ (\nu a)\ell \ \mid \ \ell \& \ell \ \mid \ \ell + \ell$$

The term 0 is the empty type; $(a, b)_t$ specifies a dependency between the object a and the object b that has been created by the thread t. The term $\text{C.m}(\overline{\rho}) \to \rho'$ defines the invocation of C.m with arguments $\overline{\rho}$ and with returned type ρ'. The argument sequence $\overline{\rho}$ has always at least three elements in our case: the first element is the carrier, while the last two elements are the thread that performed the invocation and the last object name whose lock has been acquired by it. The operation $(\nu\, a)\ell$ creates a new name a whose scope is the type ℓ; the operations $\ell \,\&\, \ell'$ and $\ell + \ell'$ define the conjunction and disjunction of the dependencies in ℓ and ℓ', respectively. The operators $+$ and $\&$ are associative and commutative.

A *lam program* is a pair $(\mathscr{L}, \ell)$, where $\mathscr{L}$ is a *finite set* of *function definitions*

$$\text{C.m}(\overline{\rho}) \to \rho' = \ell_{\text{C.m}}$$

with $\ell_{\text{C.m}}$ being the *body* of C.m, and ℓ is the *main lam*. We notice that the type ρ' is considered an argument of the lam function as well. When $\rho' = void$, the function definitions are shortened into $\text{C.m}(\overline{\rho}) = \ell_{\text{C.m}}$ and the invocations into $\text{C.m}(\overline{\rho})$.

```
Main(this,t,u) = (ν x,y)( Object.init(x,t,u)->x + Object.init(y,t,u)->y
        + buildNetwork(this,_,x,y,t,u) )

takeForks(this,x,y,t,u) = (u,x)_t & (x,y)_t

buildNetwork(this,_,x,y,t,u) = (ν z,t1,u1)(
      takeForks(this,x,y,t,u)
    + Object.init(z,t,u) -> z
    + Network$1.init(t1[this$0:T,val$x:T,val$z:T],this,x,z,t,z) ->
        t1[this$0:this,val$x:x,val$z:z]
    + Network$1.run(t1[this$0:this,val$x:x,val$z:z],t1,u1) &
        buildNetwork(this,_,z,y,t,u) )

Object.init(this,t,u) -> this =   0

Network$1.init(this[this$0:X,val$x:Y,val$z:Z],x1,x2,x3,t,u) ->
    this[this$0:x1,val$x:x2,val$z:x3] = 0

Network$1.run(this[this$0:x1,val$x:x2,val$z:x3],t,u) = takeForks(x1,x2,x3,t,u)
```

Fig. 2. Network's lams (the _ is a place holder for an integer)

As an example, the lams of the Network's code in Fig. 1 is reported in Fig. 2 (lams have been simplified for easing the readability). We discuss the methods takeForks and buildNetwork. The method takeForks has arguments this, x, y, t and u, where t and u are as discussed above. This method acquires the locks of x and y in order; therefore its lam is quite simple: there is a dependency between u and x and a dependency between x and y, namely $(u,x)_t$ & $(x,y)_t$. The lam of buildNetwork is more complex. The first line corresponds to the then-branch (lines 0–10), namely the invocation to takeForks. The other lines correspond to the else-branch. Here we have the creation of the object z and the invocation of the corresponding constructor (second line of the body of the lam function and line 17 of the bytecode), the invocation to the constructor of Network, that is called Network$1, which returns a new thread that we call t1. The last line of the lam of buildNetwork contains the invocation of t1.start and the recursive invocation to buildNetwork. These invocations are *in conjunction* because they are in parallel.

It is important to notice that the dependencies specified by the judgment

$$\text{BCT}, \Gamma, F, S, Z, T, R, i \vdash_t P : \ell$$

are actually those defined by ℓ *and* those defined by Z_i, T_i, and R_i. In particular, let $Z_i = a \cdot a'$, $T_i = \{t'\}$, and $R_i = \{t''\}$. Then the dependencies of the instruction i are $(mk\_tree(\Gamma_i, t') = (t'[\overline{\mathtt{f} : \rho'}], \mathtt{C})$ and $mk\_tree(\Gamma_i, t'') = (t''[\overline{\mathtt{f} : \rho''}], \mathtt{C}))$:

$$\ell \ \& \ (a', a)_t \ \& \ \mathtt{C.run}((t'[\overline{\mathtt{f} : \rho'}], \mathtt{C}), t', lock_{t'}) \ \& \ \text{RUN}(t''[\overline{\mathtt{f} : \rho''}], \mathtt{C})$$

where $\mathtt{C}$ is a subclass of $\mathtt{Thread}$, $lock_{t'}$ is a (fake) name associated to t' and representing a default object locked by t', and RUN is a lam function defined by

$$\text{RUN}(a[\overline{\mathtt{f} : \rho}], \mathtt{C}) = \mathtt{C.run}((a[\overline{\mathtt{f} : \rho}], \mathtt{C}), a, lock_a) \ \& \ (\nu\, a') \, \text{RUN}(a'[\overline{\mathtt{f} : \rho}], \mathtt{C})$$

The difference between T and R is exactly the fact that RUN is recursive. This means that every name in R corresponds to the parallel composition of infinitely many threads with different root names. The following analyser verifies whether this composition is consistent or not (with respect to deadlocks).

Operational Semantics of lams. The semantics of lams is very simple: it is the unfolding of function invocations. Since the unfolding may create new fresh names and the function definitions may be recursive, the model may have infinite states. To formalise the semantics, take a lam program $(\mathscr{L}, \ell)$ such that every $\mathtt{C.m}(\overline{p}) \to \rho' = \ell_{\mathtt{C.m}}$ in $\mathscr{L}$ has $\ell_{\mathtt{C.m}} = (\nu\, \overline{a})\ell'_{\mathtt{C.m}}$ and $\ell'_{\mathtt{C.m}}$ without ν-binder. We also assume that ℓ does not contain any ν-binder (the lam functions in Fig. 2 satisfy these constraints). Let a *lam context*, noted $\mathsf{L}[\,]$, be a term derived by the following syntax:

$$\mathsf{L}[\,] \quad ::= \quad [\,] \quad | \quad \ell \& \mathsf{L}[\,] \quad | \quad \ell + \mathsf{L}[\,]$$

As usual $\mathsf{L}[\ell]$ is the lam where the hole of $\mathsf{L}[\,]$ is replaced by ℓ. According to the syntax, lam contexts have no ν-binder; that is, the hassle of name captures is avoided. The operational semantics of a program $(\mathscr{L}, \ell)$ is a transition system where *states* are lams, the *transition relation* is the least one satisfying the rule

$$\frac{\mathtt{m}(\overline{p}) \to \rho' = (\nu\, \overline{c})\ell_\mathtt{m} \in \mathscr{L} \quad (\overline{p} \to \rho')\sigma = \overline{p}'' \to \rho''' \quad \overline{c}' \text{ fresh} \quad (\ell_\mathtt{m}\{\overline{c}'/\overline{c}\})\sigma = \ell'_\mathtt{m}}{\mathsf{L}[\mathtt{m}(\overline{p}'')] \to \overline{p}'''] \to \mathsf{L}[\ell'_\mathtt{m}]}.$$

The initial state of $(\mathscr{L}, \ell)$ is ℓ. (The class name in the names of lam functions has been dropped, for simplicity.) We write $\to^*$ for the reflexive and transitive closure of $\to$.

Definition 1. The *flattening* of a lam ℓ, noted $(\ell)^\flat$, is the lam ℓ where every function invocation has been replaced by 0.

For example, let $\ell = \mathtt{m}(a, b, c, t) + (a, b)_t \& \mathtt{m}'(b, c, t') \& \mathtt{m}(d, b, c, t)$ (we assume that return types of lam functions are empty). Then $(\ell)^\flat = 0 + (a, b)_t \& 0 \& 0$.

Let V ranges over lams that do not contain function invocations and let $\equiv$ be the least congruence containing the axioms:

$$\mathtt{V} \& \mathtt{V} = \mathtt{V} \qquad \mathtt{V} + \mathtt{V} = \mathtt{V} \qquad \mathtt{V} \& (\ell' + \ell'') = \mathtt{V} \& \ell' + \mathtt{V} \& \ell'' \qquad (1)$$

We notice that these axioms permit to rewrite a lam *without function invocations* as a *collection* (operation $+$) *of relations* (elements of a relation are gathered by the operation $\&$).

Definition 2. Let ℓ be a conjunction of dependencies. The *transitive closure* of ℓ, noted ℓ^+, is the least conjunction that contains ℓ and such that if $(a, b)_t \& (b, c)_{t'}$ is a subterm of ℓ^+ then (i) if $t \neq t'$ implies $(a, c)_\checkmark$ is a subterm of ℓ^+, (ii) if $t = t'$ implies $(a, c)_t$ is a subterm of ℓ^+.

A lam ℓ has a *circularity* if $(\ell)^\flat \equiv \sum_{i \in I} \ell_i$, where every ℓ_i is a conjunction of dependencies, and, for some a and i, $(a, a)_\checkmark$ is a subterm of ℓ_i^+.

A lam program $(\mathscr{L}, \ell)$ *has a circularity* if there exists ℓ' such that $\ell \to {}^* \ell'$ and ℓ' has a circularity.

For example $\ell = (a, b)_t \& (b, a)_t \& (b, c)_{t'}$ has no circularity because $\ell^+ = (a, b)_t \& (b, a)_t \& (a, a)_t \& (b, b)_t \& (b, c)_{t'} \& (a, c)_\checkmark$ does not contain any pair $(a, a)_\checkmark$.

The Analysis Algorithm and the Correctness of the Type System. Our analysis relies on an algorithm that we have studied in [11]. In particular, the algorithm computes an interpretation function $I_{\mathscr{L}}$ that is a fixpoint on the set $\mathscr{P}(\mathscr{P}(A \times A \times A \cup \{\checkmark, \bullet\}))$ where ($\checkmark$ has been discussed above)

- $\bullet$ is a special name that indicates an unknown thread (because it is created during the evaluation). In particular, the transitivity of $(a, b)_\bullet, (b, c)_\bullet$ is $(a, c)_\checkmark$ because the two $\bullet$ might correspond to two different (thread) names.

We omit the definition of $I_{\mathscr{L}}$ and refer to [11] for the details. What is relevant for this paper is that the computation of $I_{\mathscr{L}}$ terminates because the domain $\mathscr{P}(\mathscr{P}(A \times A \times A \cup \{\checkmark, \bullet\}))$ is finite. The main result about extended lams is the following:

Theorem 1 ([11]). *Let $(\mathscr{L}, \ell)$ be a lam program and $\ell \to^* \ell'$. If $I_{\mathscr{L}}(\ell')$ has a circularity then $I_{\mathscr{L}}(\ell)$ has also a circularity.*

The proof of correctness of our technique is a consequence of Theorem 1 and a subject reduction theorem (we state it informally and we refer to [12] for the formal statement).

Theorem 2. *If a JVM configuration cn has lam ℓ and cn reduces to a configuration cn' then (i) cn' is also well-typed and (ii) if ℓ' is the type of cn' then $\ell \to^* \ell'$.*

Since our algorithm uses a saturation technique on names based on a power-set construction, it has a computational complexity that is *exponential* on the number of names. We remind that the names we consider are the *arguments* of lam functions (which corresponds to methods' arguments), which is usually not big. In fact, the algorithm is quite efficient in practice (see Table 1).

6   More About Typing and JaDA

The type system overviewed in Sect. 4 has been prototyped. It also covers features such as constructors, arrays, exceptions, static members, interfaces, inheritance, recursive data types. The overall system is called JaDA. Here we overview two relevant extensions – inheritance and recursive data types –, the details of these two extensions and the other ones can be found in Garcia's PhD thesis [6].

Inheritance. JVML$_d$ does not admit to derive classes from other classes. As a consequence, when a method is invoked, it is possible to uniquely locate the method definition (the output of $typeof(\Gamma_i, a)$ in Sect. 4 *is always a single element*. Therefore we cannot type

```
C w ;  {  if (z) w = new D ; else w = new E ;  } w.foo();
```

which is a correct Java program, assuming that D and E are subclasses of C. In this case, if D and E have different implementations of foo, we do not know how the invocation w.foo() will be dispatched at run-time. Our solution consists of relaxing the relation between consecutive environments Γ_i and Γ_{i+1} in such a way that the type of $\Gamma_{i+1}(\mathtt{w})$ may be the one of $\Gamma_i(\mathtt{w})$ *plus a set of subclasses therein.* Henceforth, the lam corresponding to the invokevirtual of w.foo() is $\sum_{C' \in typeof(\Gamma_i, \mathtt{w})} C'.\mathtt{foo}(\mathtt{w}, t, a)$, namely $C.\mathtt{foo}(\mathtt{w}, t, a) + D.\mathtt{foo}(\mathtt{w}, t, a) + E.\mathtt{foo}(\mathtt{w}, t, a)$.

Recursive Types. Recursive types are managed by using finite representations. Object names of recursive types are *special names* indexed by \$. A flattened *recursive* record type is built by unfolding the recursive types (exactly) up to those nodes containing a name of a class already present in the tree. Nodes inside the tree are labelled by new names, nodes in the leaves are labelled either (for non recursive types) with $\top$ or int or with names already present in the environment or (for recursive types) with names subscribed by a \$ that correspond to the nodes of the classes that are already present in the tree. By construction, these structures are finite. For instance, if C is a class whose type is [val : Thread, next : C] (a list of threads) then, in correspondence of a new C instruction, we produce an environment $r_\$ \mapsto [\mathtt{val} : (a[\,], \mathtt{Thread}), \mathtt{next} : r_\$]$.

Lists like the foregoing one are managed in ad-hoc ways. In particular we can deliver a precise analysis as long as *the nodes of the list are all equal*, otherwise we return false positives. We observe that this technique is more precise than one would think. For instance, assume to create a list of threads, where the field val of each node contains a new thread. This list is created by an iteration and the instruction creating the thread is always the same – say i. Hence, by definition of the function $names(i)$, the nodes of the list always contain the same name and can be represented as described above. Finally, in order to have a sound analysis, we also modify our definition of circularity in lams. In particular, if the types of $r_\$$ and of $r'_\$$ are the same, a term like $(r_\$, c)_t \& (c, r'_\$)_{t'}$ is a circularity because $r_\$$ may be replaced by *every name of the same type*, including $r'_\$$.

7   Assessment of JaDA

Since JaDA covers many features of Java, it has been possible to deliver an initial assessment of it with respect to existing deadlock analysis tools. In particular, we have considered tools using different techniques: Chord for static analysis [13], Sherlock for dynamic analysis [3], and GoodLock for hybrid analysis [2]. We have also considered a commercial tool, ThreadSafe[5] [1]. Out of these tools, we were able to install and effectively test only two of them: Chord and ThreadSafe; the results corresponding to GoodLock and Sherlock come from [3]. We also had problems in testing Chord with some of the examples in the benchmarks, perhaps due to some misconfigurations, that we were not able to solve because Chord has been discontinued.

Table 1. Comparison with different deadlock detection tools. The inner cells show the number of deadlocks detected by each tool. The output labelled "(*)" are related to modified versions of the original programs: see the text.

			Static			Hybrid	Dynamic	Commercial
benchmarks	LOC, #Threads	deadlock	JaDA[tm]		Chord[tm]	GoodLock[tm]	Sherlock[tm]	ThreadSafe[tm]
Sor	1274, 5	Yes	1	[135 s]	1 [210 s]	7 [4 s]	1 [39 s]	4 [435 s]
RayTracer(*)	1292, 5	No	0	[155 s]	0 [223 s]	8 [2 s]	2 [30 s]	0 [502 s]
MolDyn (*)	1351, 5	No	0	[110 s]	0 [191 s]	6 [5 s]	1 [49 s]	0 [423 s]
MonteCarlo (*)	3619, 4	No	0	[231 s]	0 [342 s]	23 [5 s]	2 [102 s]	0 [821 s]
BuildNetworkN	40, N+1	Yes	3	[8 s]	0 [50 s]			0 [50 s]
PhilosophersN	60, N+1	Yes	3	[12 s]	0 [51 s]			0 [51 s]
ThreadArraysN	23, N+1	Yes	1	[6 s]	1 [40 s]			1 [40 s]
ThreadArraysJoinsN	37, N+1	Yes	1	[6 s]	1 [41 s]			0 [41 s]
ScalaSimpleDeadlock	39, 2	Yes	1	[3 s]				
ScalaPhilosophersN	62, N+1	Yes	3	[4 s]				

We have analysed a number of programs that exhibit a variety of sharing patterns. The source of all benchmarks in Table 1 is available either at [3,13] or in the JaDA-deadlocks repository[6]. Since the current release of JaDA does not completely cover the JVML, in order to gain preliminary experience, we modified the Java libraries and the multithreaded server programs of RayTracer, MolDyn and MonteCarlo (labelled with "(*)" in the Table 1) and implemented them in our system. This required little programming overhead; in particular, we removed volatile variables, avoided the use of Runnable interfaces for creating threads, and reduced the invocations of native methods involved in I/O

---

[5] http://www.contemplateltd.com/threadsafe.
[6] https://github.com/abelunibo/Java-Deadlocks.

operations. For every program, we give the lines of code (LOC), the number #Threads of threads explicitly created (in the second and third block this number depends on the argument N). We also state whether the program under examination has a deadlock or not and the time in seconds (tm) each tool took to perform the analysis. The times for GoodLock and Sherlock were taken from the literature [3].

Here are our remarks. The first block of programs belongs to a well known group used as benchmarks for several Java analysis tools; the second block corresponds to examples designed to test JaDA against complex deadlock scenarios. First of all JaDA is the unique tool that never returns false positives or false negatives. Chord and ThreadSafe are unsound because they return false negative (see the second block). The execution time of the tools are similar (JaDA appears more efficient), except for GoodLock and Sherlock, which appear however much less precise (they return a lot of false positives). As regards the second block, we observe that JaDA returns few deadlocks, which do not depend from N. This is because our analysis is symbolic and does not consider numeric values (most of the deadlock are considered "to be similar").

The third group reports the analysis of two examples of Scala programs [14] (the Scala compiler 2.11 produces Java bytecode). To the best of our knowledge, there is no static deadlock analysis tool for Scala (for this reason the entries corresponding to the other tools are empty).

We have also analyzed the whole Java library. The overall analysis took 5 h and 40 min. We have considered as entry points the public static parameterless methods and we have run the analyzer with the following limitations: native codes are not analyzed (their behavioural type is 0) and concurrency dependencies caused by wait/notify patterns are not verified. The analysis has not reported any deadlock.

8   Related Work and Conclusions

We do not have space to discuss in detail the related work; therefore we focus on the tools used in the assessment of Sect. 7 and their theories. ThreadSafe uses a data-flow analysis that constructs an execution flow graph and searches for cycles within this graph. Some heuristics are used to remove likely false positives. No alias analysis to resolve object identity across method calls is attempted. This analysis is performed in Chord [3,13], which can detect re-entrance on restricted cases, such as when lock expressions concern local variables (it is not possible to use fields). GoodLock [2] and its refinement Sherlock [3] use a theory that is based on monitors. Therefore the technique is a runtime technique that tags each segment of the program reached by the execution flow and specifies the exact order of lock acquisitions. Thereafter, these segments are analyzed for detecting potential deadlocks that might occur because of different scheduler choices (than the current one). This kind of technique is partial because one might overlook sensible patterns of methods' arguments (cf. BuildNetwork, for instance). Two powerful static tools that are based on abstract interpretation are Checkmate [4] and SACO [5]. The former one does not seem to be available, therefore we haven't been able to compare JaDA with it. SACO has been developed for ABS, an object-oriented language with a concurrent model different from Java. A comparison between SACO and a tool using a technique similar to the one in this paper can be found in [9].

In this paper we have defined a new technique for detecting deadlocks in Java programs by analysing the Java intermediate language JVML. The technique has been specified by focusing on a subset of JVML featuring thread creations and synchronizations, called $JVML_d$. We have also developed a prototype, called JaDA, which also covers complex features of Java, such as static members, arrays, recursive data types, exception handling, inheritance and dynamic dispatch. These extensions have made possible to deliver an initial assessment of JaDA with respect to existing deadlock analysis tools for Java.

Our future work includes the analysis of features of Java that have not yet been studied. One relevant feature is thread coordination, which is expressed by the methods wait, notify and notifyAll. Another extension addresses *native methods*, namely methods that are not implemented within the language and that are used when it is necessary to interact with the Operating System or for meta-programming purposes. Our current solution is to manually insert in the BCT the behavioural types of native methods. We are investigating testing mechanisms that may help in writing the types of such methods.

Acknowledgments. We thank Elena Giachino for the fruitful discussions and useful comments, in particular for the help in the proof of Theorem 2.

References

1. Atkey, R., Sannella, D.: ThreadSafe: static analysis for Java concurrency. In: ECE-ASST, vol. 72 (2015). http://journal.ub.tu-berlin.de/eceasst/article/view/1025
2. Bensalem, S., Havelund, K.: Dynamic deadlock analysis of multi-threaded programs. In: Ur, S., Bin, E., Wolfsthal, Y. (eds.) HVC 2005. LNCS, vol. 3875, pp. 208–223. Springer, Heidelberg (2006). https://doi.org/10.1007/11678779_15
3. Eslamimehr, M., Palsberg, J.: Sherlock: scalable deadlock detection for concurrent programs. In Proceedings of the 22nd International Symposium on Foundations of Software Engineering (FSE-22), pp. 353–365. ACM (2014)
4. Ferrara, P.: Checkmate: a generic static analyzer of java multithreaded programs. In: Proceedings of 7th IEEE International Conference on Software Engineering and Formal Methods, SEFM 2009, pp. 169–178. IEEE Computer Society (2009)
5. Flores-Montoya, A.E., Albert, E., Genaim, S.: May-happen-in-parallel based deadlock analysis for concurrent objects. In: Beyer, D., Boreale, M. (eds.) FMOODS/FORTE -2013. LNCS, vol. 7892, pp. 273–288. Springer, Heidelberg (2013). https://doi.org/10.1007/978-3-642-38592-6_19
6. Garcia, A.: Static analysis of concurrent programs based on behavioral type systems. Ph.D. thesis, School in Computer Science and Engineering (2017). JaDA.cs.unibo.it
7. Giachino, E., Kobayashi, N., Laneve, C.: Deadlock analysis of unbounded process networks. In: Baldan, P., Gorla, D. (eds.) CONCUR 2014. LNCS, vol. 8704, pp. 63–77. Springer, Heidelberg (2014). https://doi.org/10.1007/978-3-662-44584-6_6

8. Giachino, E., Laneve, C.: Deadlock detection in linear recursive programs. In: Bernardo, M., Damiani, F., Hähnle, R., Johnsen, E.B., Schaefer, I. (eds.) SFM 2014. LNCS, vol. 8483, pp. 26–64. Springer, Cham (2014). https://doi.org/10.1007/978-3-319-07317-0_2
9. Giachino, E., Laneve, C., Lienhardt, M.: A framework for deadlock detection in core ABS. Softw. Syst. Model. **15**(4), 1013–1048 (2016)
10. Kobayashi, N., Laneve, C.: Deadlock analysis of unbounded process networks. Inf. Comput. **252**, 48–70 (2017)
11. Laneve, C.: A lightweight deadlock analysis technique of object-oriented programs, January 2018. Submitted for publication
12. Laneve, C., Garcia, A.: Deadlock detection of Java Bytecode (full version), November 2017. cs.unibo.it/ laneve/papers/ddJB.pdf
13. Naik, M., Park, C.-S., Sen, K., Gay, D.: Effective static deadlock detection. In: 31st International Conference on Software Engineering (ICSE 2009), pp. 386–396. ACM (2009)
14. Odersky, M., et al.: An overview of the scala programming language. Technical report IC/2004/64, EPFL, Lausanne, Switzerland (2004)

Inferring Energy Bounds via Static Program Analysis and Evolutionary Modeling of Basic Blocks

Umer Liqat[1,3], Zorana Banković[1], Pedro Lopez-Garcia[1,2]([⊠]),
and Manuel V. Hermenegildo[1,3]

[1] IMDEA Software Institute, Madrid, Spain
{umer.liqat,zorana.bankovic,pedro.lopez,manuel.hermenegildo}@imdea.org
[2] Spanish Council for Scientific Research (CSIC), Madrid, Spain
[3] Universidad Politécnica de Madrid, Madrid, Spain

Abstract. The ever increasing number and complexity of energy-bound devices (such as the ones used in *Internet of Things* applications, smart phones, and mission critical systems) pose an important challenge on techniques to optimize their energy consumption and to verify that they will perform their function within the available energy budget. In this work we address this challenge from the software point of view and propose a novel approach to estimating accurate parametric bounds on the energy consumed by program executions that are practical for their application to energy verification and optimization. Our approach divides a program into basic (branchless) blocks and performs a *best effort* modeling to estimate upper and lower bounds on the energy consumption for each block using an evolutionary algorithm. Then it combines the obtained values according to the program control flow, using a *safe* static analysis, to infer functions that give both upper and lower bounds on the energy consumption of the whole program and its procedures as functions on input data sizes. We have tested our approach on (C-like) embedded programs running on the XMOS hardware platform. However, our method is general enough to be applied to other microprocessor architectures and programming languages. The bounds obtained by our prototype implementation on a set of benchmarks were always safe and quite accurate. This supports our hypothesis that our approach offers a good compromise between safety and accuracy, and can be applied in practice for energy verification and optimization.

Keywords: Energy modeling · Evolutionary algorithms
Static analysis · Energy consumption analysis and verification
Resource analysis and verification

1 Introduction

Reducing and controlling the energy consumption and the environmental impact of computing technologies has become a challenging problem worldwide. It is a

© Springer International Publishing AG, part of Springer Nature 2018
F. Fioravanti and J. P. Gallagher (Eds.): LOPSTR 2017, LNCS 10855, pp. 54–72, 2018.
https://doi.org/10.1007/978-3-319-94460-9_4

significant issue in systems ranging from large data centers and high-performance computing systems down to small *Internet of Things (IoT)* devices, sensors, smart watches, smart phones, portable/implantable medical devices, wearables, etc. Such devices often rely on small batteries or energy harvested from the environment, and may have to operate and intercommunicate continuously for long periods of time, which implies that their energy consumption should be very low. Although there have been improvements in battery and energy harvesting technology, they alone are often not enough to achieve the required level of energy consumption to fully support *IoT* and other energy-bound applications. In addition, for many of these IoT applications (as well as others, such as, e.g., space systems or implantable/portable medical devices), beyond optimizing energy consumption, it is actually crucial to guarantee that execution will complete within a specified energy budget, i.e., before the available system energy runs out, or that the system will function for a given period of time.

In spite of the recent rapid advances in energy-efficient hardware, it is software that controls the hardware, so that far more energy savings remain to be tapped by improving the software that runs on these devices. In this work we address these challenges from the software point of view, focusing on the *static* estimation of the energy consumed by program executions (i.e., at compile time, without actually running the programs with concrete data), as a basis for energy optimization and verification. Such estimations are given as functions on input data sizes, since data sizes typically influence the energy consumed by a program, but are not known at compile time. This approach allows abstracting away such sizes and inferring energy consumption in a way that is parametric on them.

Different types of resource usage estimations are possible, such as, e.g., probabilistic, average, or safe bounds. However, not all types of estimations are valid or useful for a given application. For example, in order to verify/certify energy budgets, *safe upper and lower bounds* on energy consumption are required [14,15] Unfortunately, current approaches that guarantee that the bounds are always safe tend to compromise their accuracy with overly conservative bounds, which may not be useful in practice. With this safety/accuracy trade-off in mind, we propose an approach that combines a *best effort* modeling with a *safe* static analysis, to infer accurate bounds that are on the safe side in most cases, in order to be practical for verification applications, in addition to energy optimization.

Describing how energy *verification* is performed is out of the scope of this paper, and we refer the reader to [13,14] for a description on how upper and lower bounds on resource usage in general can be used for verification within the CiaoPP system [6], and to [15] for a specialization to energy consumption verification. Herein we focus instead on the *inference* of energy bounds. Nevertheless, in the following we provide the intuition on how these bounds are used in our system for verification and certification: assume that E_l and E_u are (strict) safe lower and upper bounds (respectively) on the energy consumption of a program, and that E_b is an energy budget expressed by a program specification, e.g., defined by the capacity of the battery. Then:

1. If $E_u \leq E_b$, then the given program can be safely executed within the existing energy budget.

2. If $E_l \leq E_b \leq E_u$, it might be possible to complete the execution of the program, but we cannot claim it for certain.

3. If $E_b < E_l$, then it is not possible to execute the program (the system will run out of batteries before program execution is completed).

Of the small number of static energy analyses proposed to date, only a few [11,12,20] use resource analysis frameworks that are aimed at inferring safe upper and lower bounds on the resources used by program executions. A crucial component in order for such frameworks to infer information regarding hardware-dependent resources, and, in particular, energy, is a low-level resource usage model, such as, e.g., a model of the energy consumption of individual instructions. Examples of such instruction-level models are [10], at the Java bytecode level, or [9], at the Instruction Set Architecture (ISA) level.

Clearly, the safety of the bounds inferred by analysis depends on the safety of the low-level models. Unfortunately, instruction-level models such as [9,10] provide *average* energy consumption values or functions, which are not really suitable for safe upper- or lower-bounds analysis. Furthermore, trying to obtain instruction-level models that provide strict safe energy bounds would result in very conservative bounds. Although when supplied with such models the static analysis would infer high-level energy consumption functions providing strictly safe bounds, these bounds would not be useful in general because of their large inaccuracy. For this reason, the analyses in [11,12,20] used instead the already mentioned instruction level average energy models [9,10]. However, this meant that the energy functions inferred for the whole program were not strict bounds, but rather approximations of the actual bounds, and could possibly be below or above. This trade-off between safety and accuracy is a major challenge in energy analysis. In this paper we address this challenge by finding a good compromise and providing a *best effort* technique for the generation of lower-level energy models which are useful and effective in practice for verification-type applications.

The main source of inaccuracy in current instruction-level energy models is inter-instruction dependence (including also data dependence), which is not captured by most models. On the other hand, the concrete sequences of instructions that appear in programs exhibit worst cases that are not as pessimistic as considering the worst case for each of the individual intervening instructions. Based on this, we decided to use *branchless blocks* of ISA instructions as the modeling unit instead of individual instructions. We divide the (ISA) program into such *basic blocks*, each a straight-line code sequence with exactly one entry to the block (the first instruction) and one exit from the block (the last instruction). We then measure the energy consumption of these basic blocks, and determine an upper (resp. lower) bound on the energy consumption of each block. In this way the inter-instruction data dependence discussed above and other factors are accounted for within each block. The inter-instruction dependencies between blocks are still modeled in a conservative way, and hence can be one of the sources of inaccuracy. However, such modeling does not affect the safety of the energy bounds. The energy values obtained for each block are supplied to our (safe) static resource analysis, which combines them according to the program control flow and produces functions that give both (practical) upper and lower bounds on the energy consumption of the whole program and its procedures, as functions on input data sizes.

In order to find bounds on the energy consumption of each basic block we use an evolutionary algorithm (EA), varying the basic block's input values and taking energy measurements directly from the hardware for each input combination. This way, we take advantage of the fast search space exploration provided by EAs. The approach in [22] also uses EAs for estimating worst case energy consumption. However, it is applied to *whole* programs, rather than at the basic block level. A major disadvantage of such an approach is that, if there are data-dependent branches in the programs, as is often the case, the EA quickly loses accuracy, and does not converge since different input combinations can trigger different sets of instructions [22]. This can make the problem intractable. In contrast, our approach combines EAs and static analysis techniques in order to get the best of both worlds. Our approach takes out the treatment of data-dependent branches from the EA, so that the same sequence of instructions is always executed in each basic block. This way, the EA converges and estimates the worst (resp. best) case energy of the basic blocks with higher accuracy. We take care of the program control flow dependencies by using static analysis instead.

For concreteness, in our experiments we focus on the energy analysis of programs written in XC [25], running on the XS1-L architecture [17], designed by XMOS.[1] However, our approach is general enough to be applied as well to the analysis of other architectures and other programming languages and their associated lower-level program representations. XC is a high-level, C-based programming language that includes extensions for concurrency, communication, input/output operations, and real-time behavior. Our experimental setup infers energy consumption information by processing the ISA (Instruction Set Architecture) code compiled from XC, and reflects it up to the source code level. Such information is provided in the form of *functions on input data sizes*, and is expressed by means of *assertions* [7].

The results of our experiments suggest that our *best effort* approach is quite accurate, in the sense that the inferred energy bounds are close to the actual upper and lower bounds. Furthermore, the energy estimations produced by our approach were always safe, in the sense that they over-approximated the actual bounds (i.e., the inferred upper bounds were above the actual highest energy consumptions and the inferred lower bounds below the actual lowest energy consumptions). We argue thus that our analysis provides a good practical compromise.

In summary, the main contributions of this paper are:

– A novel approach that combines dynamic and static analysis techniques for inferring more accurate upper and lower bounds on the energy consumption of program executions as functions of input data sizes. The dynamic part is based on EAs, and produces low-level energy models that contain *(best effort)*

---

[1] http://www.xmos.com/.

upper and lower bounds on the cost of the elementary operations, as opposed to just average values.

- The proposal of a new abstraction level at which to perform the energy modeling of program components, namely at the level of basic (branchless) blocks of ISA instructions, and a method based on EAs to dynamically obtain upper and lower bounds on the energy of such basic blocks with a good safety/accuracy compromise.
- A prototype implementation and experimental study that supports our claims.

In the rest of the paper, Sect. 2 explains our *best effort* technique for energy modeling of program basic blocks. Section 3 shows how these models are used by the safe static analysis to infer (practical) upper and lower bounds on the energy consumed by programs as functions of their input data sizes. Section 4 reports on an experimental evaluation of our approach. Related work is discussed in Sect. 5, and finally Sect. 6 summarizes our conclusions.

2   Modeling the Energy Consumption of Blocks

As mentioned before, the first step of our energy bounds analysis is to determine upper and lower bounds on the energy consumption of each basic (branchless) program block. We perform the modeling at this level rather than at the instruction level in order to cater for inter-instruction dependencies. We first identify all the basic blocks of the program, and then perform a *best effort* profiling of the energy consumption of each basic block for different input data using an EA. These steps are explained in the following sections.

2.1   Identifying the Basic Blocks to Be Modeled

A *basic block* over an inter-procedural control flow graph (CFG) is a maximal sequence of distinct instructions, S_1 through S_n, such that all instructions $S_k, 1 < k < n$ have exactly one in-edge and one out-edge (excluding call/return edges), S_1 has one out-edge, and S_n has one in-edge. A basic block therefore has exactly one entry point at S_1 and one exit point at S_n.

In order to divide a program into such basic blocks, the program is first compiled to a lower-level representation, ISA in our case. A dataflow analysis of the ISA representation yields an inter-procedural control flow graph (CFG). A final control flow analysis is carried out to infer basic blocks from the CFG. These basic blocks are further modified so that they can be run and their energy consumption measured independently by the EA. Modifications for each basic block include:

1. A basic block with k function call instructions is divided into $k + 1$ basic blocks without the function call instructions.
2. A number of special ISA instructions (e.g., *return, call, entsp*) are omitted from the block. The cost of such instructions is measured separately and added to the cost of the block or the function.

3. The harness function that runs the blocks in isolation provides the context to each block needed for the results to be applicable to the original program. For example the memory accesses in each block are transformed into accesses to a fixed address in the local memory of the harness function. The initial values placed in this local memory are the inputs to the block that the EA explores.

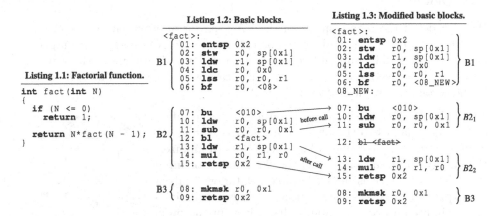

Fig. 1. Example: basic block modifications

An example of modifications 1 and 2 above is shown in Fig. 1. Listing 1.2 shows an ISA representation of a recursive factorial program where the instructions are grouped together into 3 basic blocks $B1$, $B2$, and $B3$. Consider basic block $B2$. Since it has a (recursive) function call to *fact* at address 12, it is divided further into two blocks in Listing 1.3, such that the instructions before and after the function call form two blocks $B2_1$ and $B2_2$ respectively, and the call instruction (*bl*) is omitted. The energy consumption of these two blocks is maximized (minimized) by providing values to the input arguments to the block (see below) using the EA. The energy consumption of $B2$ can then be characterized as:

$$B2_e^A = B2_{1e}^A + B2_{2e}^A + bl_e^A$$

where $B2_{1e}^A$, $B2_{2e}^A$, and bl_e^A denote the energy consumption of the $B2_1$, and $B2_2$ blocks, and the *bl* ISA instruction respectively, with approximation A (where $A =$ upper or $A =$ lower).

For each modified basic block, a set of input arguments is inferred. This set is used for an individual representation to drive the EA algorithm to maximize (minimize) the energy consumption of the block. For the entry block, the input arguments are derived from the signature of the function. The set $gen(B)$ characterizes the set of variables read without being previously defined in block B. It is defined as:

$$gen(b) = \bigcup_{k=1}^{n} \{v \mid v \in ref(k) \land \forall(j < k).v \notin def(j)\}$$

where $ref(n)$ and $def(n)$ denote the variables referred to and defined/updated at a node n in block b, respectively. For the basic blocks in Listing 1.2 (Fig. 1), the input arguments are $gen(B1) = \{r0\}$, $gen(B2_1) = \{sp[0x1]\}$, $gen(B2_2) = \{sp[0x1], r0\}$, and $gen(B3) = \emptyset$.

2.2 Evolutionary Algorithm for Finding Energy Bounds for Basic Blocks

We now detail the main aspects of the EA used for approximating the upper-bound (i.e., worst case) and lower-bound (i.e., best case) energy consumption of a basic block. The only difference between the two algorithms is the way we interpret the objective function: in the first case we want to maximize it, while in the second one we want to minimize it.

Individual. The search space dimensions are the different input variables to the blocks. Our goal is to find the combination of input values which maximizes (minimizes) the energy consumption of each block. The set of input variables to a block is inferred using a dataflow analysis (as explained in the previous section). Thus, an individual is simply an array of input values given in the order of their appearance in the block. In the initial population, the input values to an individual are randomly assigned to 32-bit numbers. In addition, some corner cases that are known to cause high or low energy consumption for particular instructions are included.[2]

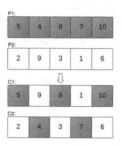

Fig. 2. Crossover

Crossover. The crossover operation is implemented as an even-odd crossover, since it provides more variability than a standard n-point crossover. The process is depicted in Fig. 2, where $P1$ and $P2$ are the parents, and $C1$ and $C2$ are their children created by the crossover operation.

32 bits	32 bits	32 bits
0...0101	0...01101	...
0...0111	0...00011	...
0..0010	0...01110	...

Fig. 3. Mutation

Mutation. For the purpose of this work we have created a custom mutation operator. Since the energy consumption in digital circuits is mainly the result of bit flipping, we believe that the best way to explore the search space is by performing some bit flipping in the mutation operation. This is implemented as follows. For each gene component (i.e., for each input value to the basic block):

1. We create a random 32-bit integer (a random mask).
2. Then we perform the XOR operation of that integer and the corresponding gene. This results in a random flipping of the bits of each gene: only the bits of the gene at positions where the value of the random mask is 1 are flipped.

---

[2] For example, all 1s for high energy consumption, or all 0s for low energy consumption as operands to a multiply ISA instruction.

The process is depicted in Fig. 3, where the input values are given as binary numbers.

In the ISA representation of the program, the type structure is implicit and each operand (e.g., register) of an ISA instruction is a 32-bit value that either represents data or a memory address holding data. Since the input variables to a block holds data (memory accesses are transformed as described in the previous section), the mutation and crossover operators could generate data that such input variables would never take if the block were to run as part of the whole program. Thus, this conservative modeling of inter-block data dependencies could be one source of inaccuracy.

Objective function. The objective function that we want to maximize/minimize is the energy of a basic block, which is measured directly from the chip. The concrete measurement setting will be explained in Sect. 4.

The XMOS XS1 architecture used in our experiments is a *cache-less, by design-predictable architecture*, and it does not exhibit pipeline effects such as stalls (to resolve pipeline hazards), since exactly one instruction per thread is executed in a 4-stage pipeline. However, in general, pipeline effects, which depend on the state of the processor at the start of the execution of a basic block, can affect the upper/lower bound estimated on the energy consumption of such a block, and have to be taken into account. Intra-block pipeline effects are accounted for by our approach just because the dependencies among the instructions within a block are captured. The inter-block pipeline effects could be modeled in a conservative way by assuming a maximum stall penalty for the upper bound estimation of each block (e.g., by adding a stall penalty to the execution time of the block). Similarly, for the lower bound estimation a zero stall penalty could be used. To approximate these effects, in [2], the authors characterize each block through pairwise executions with all of its possible predecessors. Each basic block pair is characterized by executing it on an Instruction Set Simulation (ISS) to collect cycle counts. A similar reasoning would apply to cache effects due to module boundaries. These effects could also be bounded using cache and pipeline analysis techniques [16].

3   Static Analysis of the Program Energy Consumption

Once (best effort) energy models are obtained for each basic block of the program, the energy consumption of the whole program is bounded by a (safe) static analyzer that takes into account the control flow of the program and infers (practical) upper/lower bounds on its energy consumption. We have implemented such an analyzer by specializing the generic resource analysis framework provided by CiaoPP [3,4,21,23], for programs written in the XC programming language [25] and running on the XMOS XS1-L architecture. This includes the use of a transformation [11,12] of the ISA code into an intermediate representation for analysis which is a series of connected code blocks, represented as Horn Clauses (HC IR). Such a transformation is shown in Fig. 4 where the ISA representation of the factorial function from Listing 1.2 (Fig. 1) is shown. It transforms the blocks into clauses and instructions into clause literals. Conditional branching is modeled by predicates with two clauses, one with the condition true and the other false. The input/output arguments of each block are inferred via a dataflow analysis. The final step transforms the blocks into Static Single Assignment (SSA) form where each variable is assigned exactly once. The analyzer deals with this HC IR always in the same way, independently of where it originates from. We have also written the necessary code (i.e., assertions [7]) to feed such analyzer with the block-level upper/lower bound energy model obtained by using the technique explained in Sect. 2. The analyzer enables a programmer to symbolically bound the energy consumption of a program P on input data $\bar{x}$ without actually running $P(\bar{x})$. It automatically sets up a system of recurrence (cost) equations that capture the cost (energy consumption) of P as a function of the sizes of its input arguments $\bar{x}$. Typical metrics used for data sizes in this context are the actual value of a number, the length of a list or array, etc. [21,23].

```
1  <fact>:
2  01: entsp 0x2
3  02: stw   r0,  sp[0x1]
4  03: ldw   r1,  sp[0x1]
5  04: ldc   r0,  0x0
6  05: lss   r0,  r0, r1
7  06: bf    r0,  <008>

11 07: bu    <010>
12 10: ldw   r0,  sp[0x1]
13 11: sub   r0,  r0, 0x1
14 12: bl    <fact>

16 13: ldw   r1,  sp[0x1]
17 14: mul   r0,  r1, r0
18 15: retsp 0x2

21 08: mkmsk r0,  0x1
22 09: retsp 0x2
```

```
1   fact(R0,R0_3):-
2     entsp(0x2),
3     stw(R0,Sp0x1),
4     ldw(R1,Sp0x1),
5     ldc(R0_1,0x0),
6     lss(R0_2,R0_1,R1),
7a    bf(R0_2,0x8),
7b    fact_aux(R0_2,Sp0x1,R0_3,R1_1).

10  fact_aux(1,Sp0x1,R0_4,R1):-
11    bu(0x0A),
12    ldw(R0_1,Sp0x1),
13    sub(R0_2,R0_1,0x1),
14a   bl(fact),
14b   fact(R0_2,R0_3),
16    ldw(R1,Sp0x1),
17    mul(R0_4,R1,R0_3),
18    retsp(0x2).

20  fact_aux(0,Sp0x1,R0,R1):-
21    mkmsk(R0,0x1),
22    retsp(0x2).
```

Fig. 4. An ISA (factorial) program (left) and its Horn-clause representation (right)

Consider the example in Fig. 4 (right). The following cost equations are set up over the function *fact* that characterize the energy consumption of the whole function using the approximation A (e.g., upper/lower) of each block inferred by the EA, as a function of its input data size $R0$ (in this case the metric is the actual value of $R0$):

$$fact_e^A(R0) = B1_e^A + fact\_aux_e^A(0 \le R0, R0)$$

$$fact\_aux_e^A(B, R0) = \begin{cases} B2_e^A + fact_e^A(R0 - 1) & \text{if } B \text{ is true} \\ B3_e^A & \text{if } B \text{ is false} \end{cases}$$

These inferred recurrence relations/equations are then passed on to a computer algebra system (e.g., CiaoPP's internal solver or an external solver such as Mathematica, both used for the results presented in this paper) in order to obtain a closed form function for them. If we assume (for simplicity of exposition) that each basic block has unitary cost in terms of energy consumption, i.e., $Bi_e = 1$ for all i, we obtain the energy consumed by fact as a function of its input data size $R0$ as: $fact_e(R0) = R0 + 1$.

The functions inferred by the static analysis are arithmetic (including polynomial, exponential, logarithmic, etc.), and their arguments (the input data sizes) are natural numbers. The generic resource analyzer ensures that the inferred bounds are strict/safe if it is supplied with energy models which provide safe bounds.

4   Experimental Assessment

The main goal of our experimental assessment is to perform a first comparison of the actual upper and lower bounds on energy consumption measured on the hardware against the respective bounds obtained by evaluating the functions inferred by our proposed approach (which depend on input data sizes), for each program considered and for a range of input data sizes. As mentioned before, the experiments have been performed with XC programs running on the XMOS XS1-L architecture [17]. The particular (development) hardware for which we derive the branchless-block-level model is a dual-tile board that contains an XS1-A16-128-FB217 processor.

In order to take power measurements during execution on real hardware, record and/or display them in real time, we use the hardware and software harness designed by XMOS, as an extension of the XMOS toolchain, which includes:

- A (hardware) debug adapter (xTAG v3.0) that enables power to be measured.[3] The basic principle consists in placing a small shunt resistor of R_{shunt} ohm in series within the supply line. By measuring the voltage drop on the shunt V_{shunt}, the current is calculated as $I_{shunt} = V_{shunt}/R_{shunt}$ (Ohm's law), which is also the current of the power supply $I_{sup} = I_{shunt}$. Then the power consumption is estimated as $V_{sup} \times I_{sup}$, where V_{sup} is the voltage of the power supply. The xTAG v3.0 adapter has an extra connector that carries the analog signals required to estimate the power consumption, as explained above. The measurements regarding these signals are transported to the host computer over USB using the xSCOPE interface.[4]

- A (software) tool (xgdb, the debugger), which collects data from the xTAG to be used by the analysis, by connecting to it over a USB interface (using libusb), and reading both ordinary xSCOPE traffic and voltage/current measurements.

The selected benchmarks, shown in Table 1, are either iterative or recursive. For conciseness, the first column only shows the names of the programs and

---

[3] https://www.xmos.com/download/private/xTAG-3-Hardware-Manual.pdf.

[4] https://www.xmos.com/download/private/Trace-data-with-XScope(X9923H).pdf.

Table 1. Accuracy of upper- and lower-bound estimations

Program	DDBr	Upper/Lower bounds (nJ) $\times 10^3$	vs. HW
$fact(N)$	n	$ub = 5.1\ N + 4.2$	+7%
		$lb = 4.1\ N + 3.8$	−11.7%
$fibonacci(N)$	n	$ub^a = 5.2\ lucas(N) + 6\ fib(N) - 6.6$	+8.71%
		$lb = 4.5\ lucas(N) + 5\ fib(N) - 4.2$	−4.69%
$reverse(A)$	n	$ub = 3.7\ N + 13.3$ (N = length of array A)	+8%
		$lb = 3\ N + 12.5$	−8.8%
$findMax(A)$	y	$ub = 5\ N + 6.9$ (N = length of array A)	+8.7%
		$lb = 3.3\ N + 5.6$	−9.1%
$selectionSort(A)$	y	$ub = 30\ N^2 + 41.4\ N + 10$ (N = length of array A)	+8.7%
		$lb = 16.8\ N^2 + 28.5\ N + 8$	−9.1%
$fir(N)$	y	$ub = 6\ N + 26.4$	+8.9%
		$lb = 4.8\ N + 22.9$	−9.7%
$biquad(N)$	y	$ub = 29.6\ N + 10$	+9.8%
		$lb = 23.5\ N + 9$	−11.9%

[a]The mathematical function $lucas(n)$ satisfies the recurrence relation $lucas(n) = lucas(n-1) + lucas(n-2)$ with $lucas(1) = 1$ and $lucas(2) = 3$.

the arguments that are relevant for their energy-bound functions. The first two benchmarks are small arithmetic programs, and the third one reverses elements of an input array A of size N ($reverse(A)$). A sorting algorithm ($selectionsort$) and a simple program for finding the maximum number in an array ($findMax$) are also included. The latter, which is also part of the former, is a program where data-dependent branching can bring significant variations in the worst- and best-case energy consumption for a given input data size. We have also studied two audio signal processing benchmarks, $biquad$ and fir (Finite Impulse Response), provided by XMOS as representatives of XS1 application kernels. Both programs perform filtering tasks that attenuate or amplify specific frequency ranges of a given input signal. The **DDBr** column expresses whether a benchmark has data-dependent branching or not (y/n). The third column shows the upper- and lower-bound energy functions (on input data sizes) estimated by our approach, as well as the size metric used. When an input argument (in the first column) is numeric, its size metric is its actual value (and is omitted in the third column). Column **vs. HW** shows the average deviation of the energy estimations obtained by evaluating such functions, with respect to the actual bounds measured on the hardware as explained above. A deviation is positive (resp. negative) if the estimated value is over (resp. under) the actual measurement. For a given input data size n the actual upper and lower bounds measured on the hardware are obtained by using data of size n that exhibit the worst and best cases respectively.

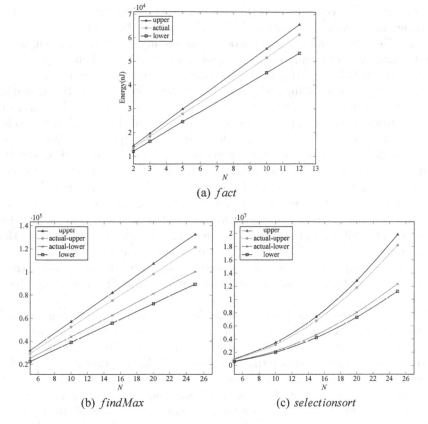

Fig. 5. Estimated energy upper/lower bounds vs. actual measurements (Color figure online)

Figure 5(a) depicts the upper- and lower-bound energy functions estimated by the analysis, as well as the actual bounds measured on the hardware for the $fact(N)$ program (taking different values of N). In this case, both the actual upper- and lower-bounds coincide, as shown by the middle curve (in red), which plots the actual measurements on the hardware. It can be observed that the values of the upper-bound function estimated by the static analysis supplied with the model obtained by the EA always over-approximate the actual hardware measurements (by 7%, as given by Table 1), whereas the lower-bound values under-approximate them (by 11.7%).

Similarly, the $findMax$ benchmark is shown in Fig. 5(b). Unlike $fact$, the actual upper- and lower-bound functions of $findMax$, depending on input arrays of length N, do not coincide, due to the data-dependent branching. The actual energy consumption of $findMax$ not only depends on the length of the input array, but also on its contents, and thus cannot be captured exactly by a function that depends on data sizes only (i.e., by abstracting the data by their sizes). A call to $findMax$ with a sorted array in ascending order (of a given length N) will discover a new max element in each iteration, and hence update the current max variable, resulting in the actual upper bound (i.e., worst case of the algorithm). In contrast, if the array is sorted in descending order, the algorithm will find the max element in the first iteration, and the rest of the iterations will never update the current max variable, resulting in the actual lower bound (i.e., best case). Thus, Fig. 5(b) depicts four curves: the upper- and lower-bound energy functions estimated by our approach for $findMax$, as well as the two actual energy bound curves measured on the hardware. The former are obtained by evaluating the energy functions in Table 1 for different array-lengths N, as before. The latter are obtained with actual arrays of length N that give the worst and best cases, as explained above. Note that it is not always trivial to find data that exhibit program worst and best case behaviors. Table 1 shows that the estimated upper- (resp. lower-) bounds over- (resp. under-) approximate the actual upper- (resp. lower-) bounds measured on the hardware by 8.7% (resp. 9.1%). Figure 5(c) for $selectionsort$ shows a similar behavior but with quadratic bounds.

The inaccuracies in the energy estimations of our technique come mainly from two sources: the modeling, which assigns an energy value to each basic block as described in Sect. 2, and the static analysis, described in Sect. 3, which estimates the number of times that the basic blocks are executed depending on the input data sizes, and hence, the energy consumption of the whole program. Table 2 shows part of the results of our study in order to quantify the inaccuracy originating from those sources. Different executions of the $findMax$ benchmark are shown for different input arrays of length **N** (Column **N**). The table is divided into two parts. The first part uses randomly generated input arrays of length **N**, while the second part (three lower rows) uses input arrays that cause the worst- and best-case energy consumption. Column **Cost App** indicates the type of approximation of the automatically inferred energy functions: upper bound (**ub**) and lower bound (**lb**). Such energy functions are shown in Table 1. We have then compared the energy consumption estimations obtained by evaluating the energy function (Column **Est**) with the observed energy consumption of the hardware measurements (Column **Obs**). Column **D%** shows the relative harmonic difference between the estimated and the observed energy consumption, given by the formula:

$$rel\_harmonic\_diff(Est, Obs) = \frac{(Est - Obs) \times (\frac{1}{Est} + \frac{1}{Obs})}{2}$$

Column **Prof** shows the result of estimating the energy consumption using the energy model and assuming that the static analysis was perfect and estimated the exact number of times that the basic blocks were executed. This obviously represents the case in which all loss of accuracy must be attributed to the energy model. The values in Column **Prof** have been obtained by profiling actual executions of the program with the concrete input arrays, where the profiler has been instrumented to record the number of times each basic block is executed. The energy consumption of the program is then obtained by multiplying such numbers by the values provided by the energy model for each basic block, and adding all of them. Col-

Table 2. Source of inaccuracies in *findMax*: analysis vs. modeling

N	Cost App	Energy(nJ) $\times 10^3$			D%	PrD%
		Est	Prof	Obs		
Random array data						
5	lb	22.3	24.9	27.3	−20.1	−9.2
	ub	31.9	30.2		15.6	10
15	lb	55.9	61.8	69.1	−17	−11
	ub	82.1	75.1		21	8.3
25	lb	89.4	99.6	110.9	−17.6	−10.7
	ub	132.2	120.8		21.7	8.5
Actual worst- and best-case array data						
5	lb	22.3	22.3	25.2	−12.2	−12.2
	ub	31.9	31.9	29.4	8.1	8.1
15	lb	55.9	55.9	62.6	−11.3	−11.3
	ub	82.1	82.1	75.5	8.3	8.3
25	lb	89.4	89.4	100.2	−11.4	−11.4
	ub	132.2	132.2	121.5	8.4	8.4

umn **PrD%** represents the inaccuracy due to the energy modeling of basic blocks using the EA, which has been quantified as the relative harmonic difference between **Prof** and the observed energy consumption **Obs**. The difference between **D%** and **PrD%** represents the inaccuracy due to the static analysis.

Although the first part of the table, using random data, may give the impression that both the static analysis and the energy modeling contribute to the inaccuracy of the energy estimation of the whole program, the second (lower) part of the table indicates that the inaccuracy only comes from the energy modeling. This is because in the lower part the comparison was performed with input arrays that make *findMax* exhibit its actual upper- and lower-bounds (depending on the length of the array). In this case, Columns **Est** and **Prof** show the same values, which means that there was no inaccuracy due to the static analysis (regarding the inference of the *actual upper- and lower-bound functions*), and that the overall inaccuracy is due to the over- and under-approximation in the EA to model energy consumption of each basic block.

Table 3 shows a similar experiment for the *reverse* program, which has no data-dependent branching. Since the number of operations performed by *reverse* is actually a function of the length of its input array (not of its contents), Columns **Est** and **Prof** show the same values for random data (unlike for *findMax*), which means that no inaccuracy comes from the static analysis part.

Regarding the time taken by the EA, it can vary depending on the parameters it is initialized with, as well as the initial population. This population is different every time the EA is initiated, except for a fixed number of individuals that represent corner cases. In the experiments, the EA is run for up to a maximum of 20 generations, and is stopped when the fitness value does not improve for four consecutive generations. In

Table 3. Source of inaccuracies in *reverse*: analysis vs. modeling

N	Cost	Energy(nJ) $\times 10^3$			D%	PrD%
	App	Est	Prof	Obs		
Random array data						
5	lb	28	28	29	−3.5	−3.5
	ub	31.8	31.8		9.2	9.2
15	lb	59	59	64	−8.1	−8.1
	ub	68.8	68.8		7.2	7.2
25	lb	90	90	98	−8.5	−8.5
	ub	105.8	105.8		7.7	7.7

all the experiments the *biquad* benchmark took the most time (a maximum time of 230 min) for maximizing the energy consumption. In contrast, the *fact* benchmark took the least time (a maximum time of 121 min). The times remained within the 150–200 min range on average. Time speed-ups were also achieved by reusing the EA results for sequences of instructions that were already processed in a previous benchmark (e.g., return blocks, loop header blocks, etc.). This makes us believe that our approach could be used in practice in an iterative development process, where the developer gets feedback from our tool and modifies the program in order to reduce its energy consumption. The first time the EA is run would take the highest time, since it would have to determine the energy consumption of all the program blocks. After a focused modification of the program that only affects a small number of blocks, most of the results from the previous run could be reused, so that the EA would run much faster during this development process. In other words, the EA processing can easily be made incremental.

The static analysis, on the other hand, is quite efficient, with analysis times of about 4 to 5 s on average, despite the naive implementation of the interface with external recurrence equation solvers, which can be improved significantly.

5   Related Work

Static analysis of the energy consumed by program executions has received relatively little attention until recently. An analysis of Java bytecode programs that estimated upper-bounds on energy consumption as functions on input data sizes was proposed in [20], where the Jimple (a typed three-address code) representation of Java bytecode was transformed into Horn Clauses [18], and a simple energy model at the Java bytecode level [10] was used. However the energy model for the Java opcodes used *average* estimations, which are not suitable for verification applications. Also, the results were not compared with actual, measured energy consumption. A similar approach was proposed in [12] for XC programs, using an ISA-level model. This work did compare to actual energy consumptions, obtaining promising results, but the ISA-level model also provided average energy values, which implied the same problem for verification.

Other approaches to static analysis based on the transformation of the analyzed code into another representation have been proposed for analyzing low-level languages [5] and Java bytecode [1]. In [1], cost relations are inferred directly for these bytecode programs, whereas in [20] the bytecode is first transformed into Horn Clauses [18].

Other work is based on techniques referred to generally as *WCET* (Worst Case Execution Time Analyses), which have been applied, usually for imperative languages, in different application domains (see e.g., [26] and its references). These techniques generally require the programmer to bound the number of iterations of loops, and then apply an Implicit Path Enumeration technique to identify the path of maximal consumption in the control flow graph of the resulting loop-less program. This approach has inspired some worst case energy analyses, such as [8]. It distinguishes instruction-specific (proportional to data) from pipeline-specific (proportional to time) energy consumption, and also takes into account branch prediction and cache misses. However, it requires the user to identify the input which will trigger the maximal energy consumption. In [24] the approach is refined for estimating *hard* (i.e., over-approximated) energy bounds using *relative* energy models (at the LLVM level), where the energy of instructions is given *in relation to each other* (e.g., if all instructions have relative energy 1, then they all consume the same absolute energy), which does not depend on the specific hardware, but can be applied if a mapping between LLVM and low-level ISA instructions exists. If the energy bounds are not *hard* (i.e., the application allows their violation) a genetic algorithm is used to obtain an under-approximation of the energy bounds. However, this approach loses accuracy when there are data-dependent branches present in the program, since different inputs can lead to the execution of different sets of instructions. A similar approach is used in [22] to find the worst-case energy consumption of two benchmarks using a genetic algorithm. In contrast to our approach, the evolutionary algorithm is applied to whole programs, which are required to not have any data-dependent branching. The authors further introduce probability distributions for the transition costs among pairs of independent instructions, which can then be convolved to give a probability distribution of the energy for a sequence of instructions.

In contrast to the work presented here and in [19], all these WCET-style methods (either for execution time or energy) do not infer cost functions on input data sizes but rather absolute maximum values, and, as mentioned before, they generally require the manual annotation of all loops to express an upper bound on the number of iterations, which can be tedious (or impossible). Loop bound inference techniques can also be applied but require that all loop counts can be resolved. All of this essentially reduces the case to that of programs with no loops.

6   Conclusions

We have proposed a combined static/dynamic approach for estimating parametric upper and lower bounds on the energy consumption of a program.

The dynamic part, based on an evolutionary algorithm, is a *best effort* approach to approximating the maximum/minimum energy consumption of the basic blocks in the program. Such blocks contain multiple instructions, which allows this phase to capture inter-instruction dependencies. Moreover, the basic blocks are branchless, which makes the evolutionary algorithm approach quite practical and efficient, and the energy values inferred by it are accurate, since no control flow-related variations occur. A safe static analysis is then used to combine the energy values obtained for the blocks according to the program control flow, and estimate energy consumption bounds of the whole program that depend on input data sizes. In the experiments we performed on a set of benchmarks, the upper and lower bounds obtained were always safe and quite accurate. Such results suggest that our approach offers a good safety/accuracy compromise, estimating bounds that are practical for its application to energy verification and optimization.

Acknowledgments. This research has received funding from the European Union 7th Framework Program agreement no 318337, ENTRA, Spanish MINECO TIN2015-67522-C3-1-R *TRACES* project, and the Madrid M141047003 *N-GREENS* program. We also thank Henk Muller, Principal Technologist, XMOS, for his help with the measurement boards, evaluation platform, benchmarks, and overall support.

References

1. Albert, E., Arenas, P., Genaim, S., Puebla, G., Zanardini, D.: Cost analysis of Java bytecode. In: De Nicola, R. (ed.) ESOP 2007. LNCS, vol. 4421, pp. 157–172. Springer, Heidelberg (2007). https://doi.org/10.1007/978-3-540-71316-6_12
2. Chakravarty, S., Zhao, Z., Gerstlauer, A.: Automated, retargetable back-annotation for host compiled performance and power modeling. In: Proceedings of CODES+ISSS 2013, pp. 36:1–36:10. IEEE Press, USA (2013). http://dl.acm.org/citation.cfm?id=2555692.2555728
3. Debray, S.K., Lin, N.W., Hermenegildo, M.V.: Task granularity analysis in logic programs. In: Proceedings of PLDI 1990, pp. 174–188. ACM, June 1990
4. Debray, S.K., López-García, P., Hermenegildo, M.V., Lin, N.W.: Lower bound cost estimation for logic programs. In: ILPS 1997, pp. 291–305. MIT Press (1997)
5. Henriksen, K.S., Gallagher, J.P.: Abstract interpretation of PIC programs through logic programming. In: Proceedings of SCAM 2006, pp. 184–196. IEEE Computer Society (2006)
6. Hermenegildo, M., Puebla, G., Bueno, F., García, P.L.: Integrated program debugging, verification, and optimization using abstract interpretation (and The Ciao System Preprocessor). Sci. Comput. Program. **58**(1–2), 115–140 (2005)
7. Hermenegildo, M.V., Bueno, F., Carro, M., López, P., Mera, E., Morales, J., Puebla, G.: An overview of Ciao and its design philosophy. TPLP **12**(1–2), 219–252 (2012). http://arxiv.org/abs/1102.5497
8. Jayaseelan, R., Mitra, T., Li, X.: Estimating the worst-case energy consumption of embedded software. In: Proceedings of IEEE RTAS, pp. 81–90. IEEE Computer Society (2006). http://dx.doi.org/10.1109/RTAS.2006.17
9. Kerrison, S., Eder, K.: Energy modeling of software for a hardware multithreaded embedded microprocessor. ACM TECS **14**(3), 1–25 (2015). http://doi.acm.org/10.1145/2700104

10. Lafond, S., Lilius, J.: Energy consumption analysis for two embedded Java virtual machines. J. Syst. Archit. **53**(5–6), 328–337 (2007)
11. Liqat, U., Georgiou, K., Kerrison, S., Lopez-Garcia, P., Hermenegildo, M.V., Gallagher, J.P., Eder, K.: Inferring parametric energy consumption functions at different software levels: ISA vs. LLVM IR. In: van Eekelen, M., Dal Lago, U. (eds.) Proceedings of FOPARA. LNCS, vol. 9964, pp. 81–100. Springer, Heidelberg (2016)
12. Liqat, U., Kerrison, S., Serrano, A., Georgiou, K., Lopez-Garcia, P., Grech, N., Hermenegildo, M.V., Eder, K.: Energy consumption analysis of programs based on XMOS ISA-level models. In: Gupta, G., Peña, R. (eds.) LOPSTR 2013. LNCS, vol. 8901, pp. 72–90. Springer, Cham (2014). https://doi.org/10.1007/978-3-319-14125-1_5
13. López-García, P., Darmawan, L., Bueno, F.: A framework for verification and debugging of resource usage properties. In: Technical Communications of ICLP. LIPIcs, vol. 7, pp. 104–113. Schloss Dagstuhl (July 2010)
14. Lopez-Garcia, P., Darmawan, L., Bueno, F., Hermenegildo, M.: Interval-based resource usage verification: formalization and prototype. In: Peña, R., van Eekelen, M., Shkaravska, O. (eds.) FOPARA 2011. LNCS, vol. 7177, pp. 54–71. Springer, Heidelberg (2012). https://doi.org/10.1007/978-3-642-32495-6_4
15. Lopez-Garcia, P., Haemmerlé, R., Klemen, M., Liqat, U., Hermenegildo, M.V.: Towards energy consumption verification via static analysis. In: WS on High Performance Energy Efficient Embedded Systems (HIP3ES) (2015)
16. Lv, M., Guan, N., Reineke, J., Wilhelm, R., Yi, W.: A survey on static cache analysis for real-time systems. LITES **3**(1), 5:1–5:48 (2016)
17. May, D.: The XMOS XS1 architecture (2013). http://www.xmos.com/published/xmos-xs1-architecture
18. Méndez-Lojo, M., Navas, J., Hermenegildo, M.V.: A flexible, (C)LP-based approach to the analysis of object-oriented programs. In: King, A. (ed.) LOPSTR 2007. LNCS, vol. 4915, pp. 154–168. Springer, Heidelberg (2008). https://doi.org/10.1007/978-3-540-78769-3_11
19. Mera, E., López-García, P., Carro, M., Hermenegildo, M.V.: Towards execution time estimation in abstract machine-based languages. In: PPDP 2008, pp. 174–184. ACM Press, July 2008
20. Navas, J., Méndez-Lojo, M., Hermenegildo, M.: Safe upper-bounds inference of energy consumption for Java bytecode applications. In: NASA LFM 2008, pp. 29–32, April 2008
21. Navas, J., Mera, E., López-García, P., Hermenegildo, M.V.: User-definable resource bounds analysis for logic programs. In: Dahl, V., Niemelä, I. (eds.) ICLP 2007. LNCS, vol. 4670, pp. 348–363. Springer, Heidelberg (2007). https://doi.org/10.1007/978-3-540-74610-2_24
22. Pallister, J., Kerrison, S., Morse, J., Eder, K.: Data dependent energy modeling for worst case energy consumption analysis. Technical report, May 2015. http://arxiv.org/abs/1505.03374
23. Serrano, A., Lopez-Garcia, P., Hermenegildo, M.V.: Resource usage analysis of logic programs via abstract interpretation using sized types. TPLP **14**(4–5), 739–754 (2014). ICLP 2014 Special Issue
24. Wagemann, P., Distler, T., Honig, T., Janker, H., Kapitza, R., Schroder-Preikschat, W.: Worst-case energy consumption analysis for energy-constrained embedded systems. In: 2015 27th Euromicro Conference on Real-Time Systems (ECRTS), pp. 105–114, July 2015

25. Watt, D.: Programming XC on XMOS devices. XMOS Limited (2009). http://books.google.co.uk/books?id=81klKQEACAAJ
26. Wilhelm, R., Engblom, J., Ermedahl, A., Holsti, N., Thesing, S., Whalley, D., Bernat, G., Ferdinand, C., Heckmann, R., Mitra, T., Mueller, F., Puaut, I., Puschner, P., Staschulat, J., Stenström, P.: The worst-case execution-time problem - overview of methods and survey of tools. ACM Trans. Embedded Comput. Syst. **7**(3), 1–53 (2008)

CARET Analysis of Multithreaded Programs

Huu-Vu Nguyen[1](✉) and Tayssir Touili[2](✉)

[1] University Paris Diderot and LIPN, Paris, France
nguyen@lipn.univ-paris13.fr
[2] CNRS, LIPN and University Paris 13, Paris, France
touili@lipn.univ-paris13.fr

Abstract. Dynamic Pushdown Networks (DPNs) are a natural model
for multithreaded programs with (recursive) procedure calls and thread
creation. On the other hand, CARET is a temporal logic that allows to
write linear temporal formulas while taking into account the matching
between calls and returns. We consider in this paper the model-checking
problem of DPNs against CARET formulas. We show that this problem
can be effectively solved by a reduction to the emptiness problem of Büchi
Dynamic Pushdown Systems. We then show that CARET model checking is also decidable for DPNs communicating with locks. Our results
can, in particular, be used for the detection of concurrent malware.

1 Introduction

Pushdown Systems (PDSs) are known to be a natural model for sequential programs [18]. Therefore, networks of pushdown systems are a natural model for
concurrent programs where each PDS represents a sequential component of the
system. In this context, Dynamic pushdown Networks (DPNs) [6] were introduced by Bouajjani et al. as a natural model of multithreaded programs with
procedure calls and thread creation. Intuitively, a DPN is a network of pushdown
processes $\{\mathcal{P}_1, ..., \mathcal{P}_n\}$ where each process, represented by a Pushdown system
(PDS), can perform basic pushdown actions, call procedures, as well as spawn
new instances of pushdown processes. A lot of previous researches focused on
investigating automated methods to verify DPNs. In [6,9,14,15], the reachability
analysis of DPNs are considered. While the model-checking problem for DPNs
against double-indexed properties is undecidable, i.e., the properties where the
satisfiability of an atomic proposition depends on control states of two or more
threads [10], it is decidable to model-check DPNs against the linear temporal
logic (LTL) and the computation tree logic (CTL) with single-indexed properties
[19], i.e., properties where the satisfiability of an atomic proposition depends on
control states of only one thread.

CARET is a temporal logic of calls and returns [1]. This logic allows us to
write linear temporal formulas while taking into account the matching between

---

This work was partially funded by the FUI project AiC.

F. Fioravanti and J. P. Gallagher (Eds.): LOPSTR 2017, LNCS 10855, pp. 73–90, 2018.
https://doi.org/10.1007/978-3-319-94460-9_5

calls and returns. CARET is needed to describe several important properties such as malicious behaviors or API usage rules. Thus, to be able to analyse such properties for multithreaded programs, we need to be able to check CARET formulas for DPNs. We tackle this problem in this paper. As LTL is a subclass of CARET, CARET model-checking for DPNs with double-indexed properties is also undecidable. Thus, in this paper, we consider the model-checking problem for DPNs against single-indexed CARET formulas and show that it is decidable. A single-indexed CARET formula is a formula in the form $\bigwedge f_i$ where f_i is a CARET formula over a certain PDS $\mathcal{P}_i$. A DPN satisfies $\bigwedge f_i$ iff all instances of the PDS $\mathcal{P}_i$ created in the network satisfy the subformula f_i.

The model-checking problem of DPNs against single-indexed CARET formulas is non-trivial because the number of instances of pushdown processes in DPNs can be unbounded. It is not sufficient to check if every PDS $\mathcal{P}_i$ satisfies the corresponding formula f_i. Indeed, we need to ensure that all instances of $\mathcal{P}_i$ created during a run of DPN satisfy the formula f_i. Also, it is not correct to check whether all possible instances of $\mathcal{P}_i$ satisfy the formula f_i. Indeed, an instance of $\mathcal{P}_i$ should not be checked if it is not created during the run of DPNs. In this paper, we solve these problems. We show that single-indexed CARET model checking is decidable for DPNs. To this end, we reduce the problem of checking whether Dynamic Pushdown Networks satisfy single-indexed CARET formulas to the membership problem for Büchi Dynamic Pushdown Networks (BDPNs). Finally, we show that single-indexed CARET model checking is decidable for Dynamic Pushdown Networks communicating via nested locks.

Related Work

[2,3,5,7] considered Pushdown networks with communications between processes. However, these works consider only networks with a fixed number of threads. The model-checking problem for pushdown networks where synchronization between threads is ensured by a set of nested locks is considered in [10–12] for single-indexed LTL/CTL and double-indexed LTL. These works do not handle dynamic thread creation.

Multi-pushdown systems were considered in [4,13] to represent multithreaded programs. These systems have only a finite number of stacks, and thus, they cannot handle dynamic thread creation.

Pushdown Networks with dynamic thread creation (DPNs) were introduced in [6]. The reachability problems of DPNs and its extensions are considered in [6,9,14,15,21]. [19] considers the model-checking problem of DPNs against single-indexed LTL and CTL, while [20] investigates the single-indexed LTL model checking problem for DPNs with locks.

[16,17] consider CARET model checking for pushdown systems and its application to malware detection. These works can only handle sequential programs. In this paper, we go one step further and extend these works [16,17] to DPNs and concurrent programs.

2 Linear Temporal Logic of Calls and Returns - CARET

In this section, we recall the definition of CARET [1]. A CARET formula is interpreted on an infinite path where each state on the path is associated with a tag in the set $\{call, ret, int\}$. A *call-state* denotes an invocation to a procedure of a program while the corresponding *ret-state* denotes the *ret* statement of that procedure. A *simple* statement (neither a *call* nor a *ret* statement) is called an *internal* statement and its associated state is called *int-state*.

Let $\omega = s_0 s_1 ...$ be an infinite path where each state on the path is associated with a tag in the set $\{call, ret, int\}$. Over ω, three kinds of successors are defined for every position s_i:

- *global-successor*: The global-successor of s_i is s_{i+1}.
- *abstract-successor*: The abstract-successor of s_i is determined by its associated tag.
  - If s_i is a *call*, the abstract successor of s_i is the matching return point.
  - If s_i is a *int*, the abstract successor of s_i is s_{i+1}.
  - If s_i is a *ret*, the abstract successor of s_i is defined as $\bot$.
- *caller-successor*: The caller-successor of s_i is the most inner unmatched call if there is such a *call*. Otherwise, it is defined as $\bot$.

A *global-path* is obtained by applying repeatedly the global-successor operator. Similarly, an *abstract-path* or a *caller-path* are obtained by repeatedly applying the abstract-successor and caller-successor respectively.

In Fig. 1, from s_4, the global-path is $s_4 s_5 s_6 s_7 s_8 s_9 s_{10}...$, the abstract-path is $s_4 s_5 s_9 s_{10}...$ while the caller-path is $s_4 s_2$. Note that the caller-path is always finite.

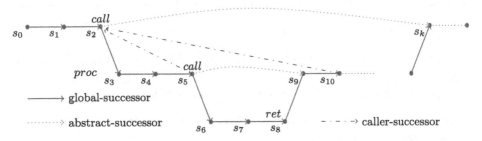

Fig. 1. Three kinds of successors of CARET

Formal Definition. Given a finite set of atomic propositions AP. Let $AP' = AP \cup \{call, ret, int\}$. A CARET formula over AP is defined as follows (where $e \in AP'$):

$$\psi := e \mid \psi \vee \psi \mid \neg\psi \mid X^g\psi \mid X^a\psi \mid X^c\psi \mid \psi U^a\psi \mid \psi U^g\psi \mid \psi U^c\psi$$

Let $\Sigma = 2^{AP} \times \{call, ret, int\}$. Let $\pi = \pi(0)\pi(1)\pi(2)...$ be an ω-word over Σ. Let (π, i) be the suffix of π starting from $\pi(i)$. Let $next_i^g$, $next_i^a$, $next_i^c$ be the global-successor, abstract-successor and caller-successor of $\pi(i)$ respectively. The satisfiability relation is defined inductively as follows:

- $(\pi, i) \vDash e$, where $e \in AP'$, iff $\pi(0) = (Y, d)$ and $e \in Y$ or $e = d$
- $(\pi, i) \vDash \psi_1 \vee \psi_2$ iff $(\pi, i) \vDash \psi_1$ or $(\pi, i) \vDash \psi_2$
- $(\pi, i) \vDash \neg\psi$ iff $(\pi, i) \nvDash \psi$
- $(\pi, i) \vDash X^g\psi$ iff $(\pi, next_i^g) \vDash \psi$
- $(\pi, i) \vDash X^a\psi$ iff $next_i^a \neq \bot$ and $(\pi, next_i^a) \vDash \psi$
- $(\pi, i) \vDash X^c\psi$ iff $next_i^c \neq \bot$ and $(\pi, next_i^c) \vDash \psi$
- $(\pi, i) \vDash \psi_1 U^b \psi_2$ (with $b \in \{g, a, c\}$) iff there exists a sequence of positions $h_0, h_1, ..., h_{k-1}, h_k$ where $h_0 = i$, for every $0 \leq j \leq k - 1 : h_{j+1} = next_{h_j}^b$, $(\pi, h_j) \vDash \psi_1$ and $(\pi, h_k) \vDash \psi_2$

Then, $\pi \vDash \psi$ iff $(\pi, 0) \vDash \psi$. Other CARET operators can be expressed by the above operators: $F^g\psi = true\ U^g\psi$, $G^g\psi = \neg(true\ U^g\neg\psi)$, $F^a\psi = true\ U^a\psi$,...

Closure. Let ψ be a CARET formula over AP. The closure of ψ, denoted $Cl(\psi)$, is the smallest set that contains ψ, $call$, ret and int and satisfies the following properties:

- if $\neg\psi' \in Cl(\psi)$, then $\psi' \in Cl(\psi)$
- if $X^b\psi' \in Cl(\psi)$ (with $b \in \{g, a, c\}$), then $\psi' \in Cl(\psi)$
- if $\psi_1 \vee \psi_2 \in Cl(\psi)$, then $\psi_1 \in Cl(\psi), \psi_2 \in Cl(\psi)$
- if $\psi_1 U^b \psi_2 \in Cl(\psi)$ (with $b \in \{g, a, c\}$), then $\psi_1 \in Cl(\psi), \psi_2 \in Cl(\psi), X^b(\psi_1 U^b \psi_2) \in Cl(\psi)$
- if $\psi' \in Cl(\psi)$, and ψ' is not in the form $\neg\psi''$ then $\neg\psi' \in Cl(\psi)$

Atoms. A set $A \subseteq Cl(\psi)$ is an atom of ψ if it satisfies the following properties:

- $\forall \psi' \in Cl(\psi), \psi' \in A \Leftrightarrow \neg\psi' \notin A$
- $\forall \psi' \vee \psi'' \in Cl(\psi), \psi' \vee \psi'' \in A \Leftrightarrow \psi' \in A$ or $\psi'' \in A$
- $\forall \psi' U^b \psi'' \in Cl(\psi)$, where $b \in \{g, a, c\}, \psi' U^b \psi'' \in A \Leftrightarrow \psi'' \in A$ or ($\psi' \in A$ and $X^b(\psi' U^b \psi'') \in A$)
- A includes exactly one element of the set $\{call, ret, int\}$

Let $Atoms(\psi)$ be the set of atoms of ψ. Let A and A' be two atoms, we define the following predicates:

- $AbsNext(A, A') = true$ iff for every $X^a\phi' \in Cl(\psi) : (X^a\phi' \in A$ iff $\phi' \in A')$.
- $GlNext(A, A') = true$ iff for every $X^g\phi' \in Cl(\psi) : (X^g\phi' \in A$ iff $\phi' \in A')$
- $CallerNext(A, A') = true$ iff for every $X^c\phi' \in Cl(\psi) : (X^c\phi' \in A$ iff $\phi' \in A')$.

We define $NexCallerForms(A)$ (resp. $NexAbsForms(A)$) to be a function which returns the caller-formulas (resp. abstract-formulas) in A. Formally:

- $NexCallerForms(A) = \{X^c\phi' \mid X^c\phi' \in A\}$
- $NexAbsForms(A) = \{X^a\phi' \mid X^a\phi' \in A\}$

3   Dynamic Pushdown Networks (DPNs)

3.1   Definitions

Dynamic Pushdown Networks (DPNs) is a natural model for multithreaded programs [6]. To be able to define CARET formulas over DPNs, we must extend this model to record whether a transition rule corresponds to a *call*, *ret* or a *simple* statement (neither call nor ret).

Definition 1. *A Dynamic Pushdown Network (DPN) $\mathcal{M}$ is a set $\{\mathcal{P}_1, ..., \mathcal{P}_n\}$ s.t. for every $1 \leq i \leq n$, $\mathcal{P}_i = (P_i, \Gamma_i, \Delta_i)$ is a Labelled Dynamic Pushdown System (DPDS), where P_i is a finite set of control locations, $P_i \cap P_j = \emptyset$ for all $j \neq i$, Γ_i is a finite set of stack alphabet, and Δ_i is a finite set of transition rules. Rules of Δ_i are of the following form, where $p, p_1 \in P_i, \gamma, \gamma_1, \gamma_2 \in \Gamma_i, \omega_1 \in \Gamma_i^*$, $d \in \{\square, p_s\omega_s \mid p_s\omega_s \in \bigcup_{1 \leq j \leq n} P_j \times \Gamma_j^*\}$:*

- (r_1) $p\gamma \xrightarrow{\text{call}}_i p_1\gamma_1\gamma_2 \triangleright d$
- (r_2) $p\gamma \xrightarrow{\text{ret}}_i p_1\epsilon \triangleright d$
- (r_3) $p\gamma \xrightarrow{\text{int}}_i p_1\omega_1 \triangleright d$

Intuitively, there are two kinds of transition rules depending on the nature of d. A rule with a suffix of the form $\triangleright \square$ is a nonspawn rule (does not spawn a new process), while a rule with a suffix $\triangleright p_s\omega_s$ describes a spawn rule (a new process is spawned). A nonspawn step describes pushdown operations of one single process in the network. Roughly speaking, a *call* statement is described by a rule in the form $p\gamma \xrightarrow{\text{call}}_i p_1\gamma_1\gamma_2 \triangleright d \in \Delta_i$. This rule usually models a statement of the form $\gamma \xrightarrow{\text{call} \quad \text{proc}} \gamma_2$ where γ is the control point of the program where the function call is made, γ_1 is the entry point of the called procedure *proc*, and γ_2 is the return point of the call; p and p_1 can be used to encode various information, such as the return values of functions, shared data between procedures, etc. A return statement is modeled by a rule (r_2), while a rule (r_3) is used to model a *simple* statement (neither a call nor a return). A spawn step allows in addition the creation of a new process. For instance, a rule of the form $p\gamma \xrightarrow{t}_i p_1\omega_1 \triangleright p_s\omega_s \in \Delta_i$ where $t \in \{call, ret, int\}$ describes that a process $\mathcal{P}_i$ at control location p and having γ on top of the stack can (1) change the control location to p_1 and modify the stack by replacing γ with ω_1 and also (2) create a new instance of a process $\mathcal{P}_j$ $(1 \leq j \leq n)$ starting at $p_s\omega_s$. Note that in this case, if t is call, then ω_1 is $\gamma_1\gamma_2$, and if t is *ret*, then ω_1 is ϵ.

A DPDS $\mathcal{P}_i$ can be seen as a Pushdown System (PDS) if there are no spawn rules in Δ_i. Generally speaking, a DPN consists of a set of PDSs $\{\mathcal{P}_1, ..., \mathcal{P}_n\}$ running in parallel where each PDS can dynamically spawn new instances of PDSs in the set $\{\mathcal{P}_1, ..., \mathcal{P}_n\}$ during the run. An initial local configuration of a newly created instance $p_s\omega_s$ is called a Dynamically Created Local Initial Configuration (DCLIC). For every $i \in \{1...n\}$, let $\mathcal{D}_i = \{p_s\omega_s \in \bigcup_{1 \leq j \leq n} P_j \times \Gamma_j^* \mid p\gamma \xrightarrow{t}_i p_1\omega_1 \triangleright p_s\omega_s \in \Delta_i\}$ be the set of DCLICs that can be created by the DPDS $\mathcal{P}_i$.

A *local configuration* of an instance of a DPDS $\mathcal{P}_i$ is a tuple $p\omega$ where $p \in P_i$ is the control location, $\omega \in \Gamma_i^*$ is the stack content. A *global configuration* of $\mathcal{M}$ is a multiset over $\bigcup_{1 \leq i \leq n} P_i \times \Gamma_i^*$, in which $p\omega \in P_i \times \Gamma_i^*$ is a *local configuration* of an instance of $\mathcal{P}_i$ which is running in parallel in the network $\mathcal{M}$.

A DPDS $\mathcal{P}_i$ defines a transition relation $\Rightarrow_i$ as follows: if $p\gamma \xrightarrow{t}_i p_1\omega_1 \rhd d$ then $p\gamma\omega \Rightarrow_i p_1\omega_1\omega \rhd D$ for every $\omega \in \Gamma_i^*$ where $D = \emptyset$ if $d = \square$, $D = \{p_s\omega_s\}$ if $d = p_s\omega_s$. Let $\Rightarrow_i^*$ be the transitive and reflexive closure of $\Rightarrow_i$, then, for every $p\omega \in P_i \times \Gamma_i^*$:

- $p\omega \Rightarrow_i^* p\omega \rhd \emptyset$
- if $p\omega \Rightarrow_i^* p_1\omega_1 \rhd D_1$ and $p_1\omega_1 \Rightarrow_i^* p_2\omega_2 \rhd D_2$, then, $p\omega \Rightarrow_i^* p_2\omega_2 \rhd D_1 \cup D_2$.

A *local run* of an instance of a DPDS $\mathcal{P}_i$ starting at a local configuration c_0 is a sequence $c_0c_1...$ s.t. for every $x \geq 0$, $c_x \in P_i \times \Gamma_i^*$ is a local configuration of $\mathcal{P}_i$, $c_x \Rightarrow_i c_{x+1} \rhd D$ for some D. A *global run* ρ of $\mathcal{M}$ from a global configuration $\mathcal{G} = \{p_0\omega_0, ..., p_k\omega_k\}$ is a set of local runs (possibly infinite) where each local run describes the execution of one instance of a certain DPDS $\mathcal{P}_i$. Initially, ρ consists of k local runs of k instances starting from $\{p_0\omega_0, ..., p_k\omega_k\}$, when a new instance is created, a new local run of this instance is added to ρ. For example, when a DCLIC c is created by a certain local run of ρ, a new local run that starts at c is added to ρ. Note that from a global configuration, we can obtain a set of global runs because from a local configuration, we can have different local runs.

3.2 Single-Indexed CARET for DPNs

Given a DPN $\mathcal{M} = \{\mathcal{P}_1, ..., \mathcal{P}_n\}$, a single-indexed CARET formula f is a formula in the form $\bigwedge_{i=1}^n f_i$ s.t. for every $1 \leq i \leq n$, f_i is a CARET formula in which the satisfiability of its atomic propositions depends only on the DPDS $\mathcal{P}_i$.

Given a set of atomic propositions AP, let $\lambda : \bigcup_{i=1}^n P_i \to 2^{AP}$ be a labeling function that associates each control location with a set of atomic propositions.

Let $\pi = p_0\omega_0p_1\omega_1....$ be a local run of the DPDS $\mathcal{P}_i$. We associate to each local configuration $p_x\omega_x$ of π a tag t_x in $\{call, int, ret\}$ as follows, where $D = \emptyset$ or $D = \{p_s\omega_s\}$:

- If $p_x\omega_x \Rightarrow_i p_{x+1}\omega_{x+1} \rhd D$ corresponds to a transition rule $p\gamma \xrightarrow{t}_i p_1\omega_1 \rhd d$, then $t_x = t$.

Then, we say that π satisfies f_i iff the ω-word $(\lambda(p_0), t_0)(\lambda(p_1), t_1)...$ satisfies f_i. A local configuration c of $\mathcal{P}_i$ satisfies f_i (denoted $c \vDash f_i$) iff there exists a local run π starting from c such that π satisfies f_i. If D is the set of DCLICs created during the run π, then, we write $c \vDash_D f_i$. A DPN $\mathcal{M}$ satisfies a single-indexed CARET formula f iff there exist a global run ρ s.t. for every $1 \leq i \leq n$, each local run of $\mathcal{P}_i$ in ρ satisfies the formula f_i.

4   Applications

We show in this section how model-checking single-indexed CARET for DPNs is necessary for concurrent malware detection.

Malware detection is nowadays a big challenge. Several malwares are multithreaded programs that involve recursive procedures and dynamic thread creation. Therefore, DPNs can be used to model such programs. We show in what follows how single-indexed CARET for DPNs can describe malicious behaviors of concurrent malwares.

More precisely, we show how this logic can specify email worms. To this aim, let us consider a typical email worm: the worm Bagle. Bagle is a multithreaded email worm. In the main thread, one of the first things the worm does is to register itself into the registry listing to be started at the boot time. Then, it does some different actions to hide itself from users. After this, the malware creates one thread (named *Thread2*) that listens on the port 6777 to receive different commands and also allow the attacker to upload a new file and execute it. This grants the attacker the ability to update new versions for his malware. In addition, the attacker can send a crafted byte sequence to this port to force the malware to kill itself and delete it from the system. Thus, the attacker can remove his malware remotely. In the next step, the malware creates one more thread (named *Thread3*) which contacts a list of websites every 10 min to announce the infection of the current machine. The malware sends the port it is listening to as well as the IP of the infected machine to these sites. At some point in the program, the malware continues to spawn a thread named *Thread4* to search on local drives to look for valid email addresses. In this thread, for each email address found, the malware attaches itself and sends itself to this email address.

Thus, you can see that Bagle is a mutithreaded malware with dynamic thread creation, i.e., the main process can create threads to fulfill various tasks. To model Bagle, DPNs is a good candidate since DPNs allow dynamic thread creation. Let $\mathcal{M} = \{\mathcal{P}_1, \mathcal{P}_2, \mathcal{P}_3, \mathcal{P}_4\}$ be a model of Bagle where $\mathcal{P}_1$ is a PDS that represents the main process of the malware; $\mathcal{P}_2, \mathcal{P}_3, \mathcal{P}_4$ are PDSs that model the code segments corresponding to Thread1, Thread2, Thread3 respectively. Note that $\mathcal{P}_2, \mathcal{P}_3, \mathcal{P}_4$ are designed to execute specific tasks, while $\mathcal{P}_1$ is a main process able to dynamically create an arbitrary number of instances of $\mathcal{P}_2, \mathcal{P}_3, \mathcal{P}_4$ to fulfill tasks in need.

We show now how the malicious behavior of the different threads can be described by a CARET formula. Let us start with the main process. The typical behaviour of this process is to add its own executable name to the registry listing so that it can be started at the boot time. To do this, the malware needs to invoke the API function *GetModuleFileNameA* with 0 and x as parameters. *GetModuleFileNameA* will put the file name of its current executable on the memory address pointed by x. After that, the malware calls the API function *RegSetValueExA* with the same x as parameter. *RegSetValueExA* will use the file name stored at x to add itself into the registry key listing. This malicious behaviour can be specified by CARET as follows:

$\psi_1 = \bigvee_{x \in K} F^g(call(GetModuleFileNameA) \wedge 0x\Gamma^* \wedge F^a(call(RegSetValueExA) \wedge x\Gamma^*))$
where the $\bigvee$ is taken over all possible memory addresses x over domain K.

Note that parameters are passed via the stack in binary programs. For succinctness, we use regular variable expression $x\Gamma^*$ (resp. $0x\Gamma^*$) to describe the requirement that x (resp. $0x$) is on top of the stack. Then, this formula states that there is a call to the API $GetModuleFileNameA$ with 0 and x on the top of the stack (i.e., with 0 and x as parameters), followed by a call to the API $RegSetValueExA$ with x on the top of the stack. Using the operator F^a guarantees that $RegSetValueExA$ is called after $GetModuleFileNameA$ terminates.

Similarly, the malicious behaviors of the Threads 2, 3 and 4 can be described by CARET formulas ψ_2, ψ_3 and ψ_4 respectively.

Thus, the malicious behavior of the concurrent worm Bagle can be described by the single-indexded CARET formula $\psi = \psi_1 \wedge \psi_2 \wedge \psi_3 \wedge \psi_4$.

5   Single-Indexed CARET Model-Checking for DPNs

In this section, we consider the CARET model-checking problem of DPNs. Let $\lambda : \bigcup_{i=1}^n P_i \to 2^{AP}$ be a labeling function that associates each control location with a set of atomic propositions. Let $\mathcal{M} = \{\mathcal{P}_1, ..., \mathcal{P}_n\}$ be a DPN, $f = \bigwedge_{i=1}^n f_i$ be a single-indexed CARET formula.

5.1   Büchi DPNs (BDPNs)

Definition 2. *A Büchi DPDS (BDPDS) is a tuple $\mathcal{BP}_i = (P_i, \Gamma_i, \Delta_i, F_i)$ s.t. $\mathcal{P}_i = (P_i, \Gamma_i, \Delta_i)$ is a DPDS, $F_i \subseteq P_i$ is the set of accepting control locations. A run of a BDPDS is accepted iff it visits infinitely often some control locations in F_i.*

Definition 3. *A Generalized Büchi DPDS (GBDPDS) is a tuple $\mathcal{BP}_i = (P_i, \Gamma_i, \Delta_i, F_i)$, where $\mathcal{P}_i = (P_i, \Gamma_i, \Delta_i)$ is a DPDS and $F_i = \{F_1, ..., F_k\}$ is a set of sets of accepting control locations. A run of a GBDPDS is accepted iff it visits infinitely often some control locations in F_j for every $1 \le j \le k$.*

Given a BDPDS or a GBDPDS $\mathcal{BP}_i = (P_i, \Gamma_i, \Delta_i, F_i)$, let $c \in P_i \times \Gamma_i^*$ be a local configuration of $\mathcal{BP}_i$. Then, let $\mathcal{L}(\mathcal{BP}_i)$ be the set of all pairs $(c, D) \in P_i \times \Gamma_i^* \times 2^{D_i}$ s.t. $\mathcal{BP}_i$ has an accepting run from c and D is the set of DCLICs generated during that run. We get the following properties:

Proposition 1. *Given a GBDPDS $\mathcal{BP}_i$, we can effectively compute a BDPDS $\mathcal{BP'}_i$ s.t. $\mathcal{L}(\mathcal{BP}_i) = \mathcal{L}(\mathcal{BP'}_i)$.*

This result comes from the fact that we can translate a GBDPDS to a corresponding BDPDS by applying the similar approach as the translation from a Generalized Büchi automaton to a corresponding Büchi automaton [8].

Definition 4. *A Büchi Dynamic Pushdown Network (BDPN) is a set* $\{\mathcal{BP}_1, ..., \mathcal{BP}_n\}$ *s.t. for every* $1 \leq i \leq n$, $\mathcal{BP}_i = (P_i, \Gamma_i, \Delta_i, F_i)$ *is a BDPDS. A (global) run* ρ *of a BDPN is accepted iff all local runs in* ρ *are accepting (local) runs.*

Definition 5. *A Generalized Büchi Dynamic Pushdown Network (GBDPN) is a set* $\{\mathcal{BP}_1, ..., \mathcal{BP}_n\}$ *s.t. for every* $1 \leq i \leq n$, $\mathcal{BP}_i = (P_i, \Gamma_i, \Delta_i, F_i)$ *is a GBDPDS. A (global) run* ρ *of a GBDPN is accepted iff all local runs in* ρ *are accepting (local) runs.*

Given a BDPN or a GBDPN $\mathcal{BM} = \{\mathcal{BP}_1, ..., \mathcal{BP}_n\}$, let $\mathcal{L}(\mathcal{BM})$ be the set of all global configurations $\mathcal{G}$ s.t. $\mathcal{BM}$ has an accepting run from $\mathcal{G}$. We get the following properties:

Proposition 2. *Given a GBDPN* $\mathcal{BM}$, *we can effectively compute a BDPN* $\mathcal{BM}'$ *s.t.* $\mathcal{L}(\mathcal{BM}) = \mathcal{L}(\mathcal{BM}')$.

This result is obtained due to the fact that we can translate each GBDPDS in $\mathcal{BM}$ to a corresponding BDPDS in $\mathcal{BM}'$.

Given a BDPN $\mathcal{BM} = \{\mathcal{BP}_1, ..., \mathcal{BP}_n\}$ where $\mathcal{BP}_i = (P_i, \Gamma_i, \Delta_i, F_i)$. Let $I(c)$ be the index i of the local configuration $c \in P_i \times \Gamma_i^*$. Let $\mathcal{D} = \bigcup_{i=1}^n \mathcal{D}_i$. Then, we get the following theorem:

Theorem 1 [19,20]. *The membership problem of a BDPN is decidable in time* $O(\Sigma_{i=1}^n |\Delta_i|.|\Gamma_i|.|P_i|^3.2^{|\mathcal{D}_i|} + \Sigma_{c \in \mathcal{D}}(|c|.|P_{I(c)}|^3.|\Gamma_{I(c)}|.2^{2|\mathcal{D}_{I(c)}|} + |\mathcal{D}|^2.2^{|\mathcal{D}|})$.

Thus, from Proposition 2 and Theorem 1, we get that the membership problem of a GBDPN is decidable.

Theorem 2. *The membership problem of GBDPNs is decidable.*

5.2   From CARET Model Checking of DPNs to the Membership Problem in BDPNs

Given a local run π, let $\vartheta(\pi)$ be the index of the DPDS corresponding to π. Let $\mathcal{G}$ be an initial global configuration of the DPN $\mathcal{M}$, then we say that $\mathcal{G}$ satisfies f iff $\mathcal{M}$ has a global run ρ starting from $\mathcal{G}$ s.t. every local run π in ρ satisfies $f_{\vartheta(\pi)}$. Determining whether $\mathcal{G}$ satisfies f is a non-trivial problem since the number of global runs can be unbounded and the number of local runs of each global run can also be unbounded. Note that it is not sufficient to check whether every pushdown process $\mathcal{P}_i$ satisfies the corresponding CARET formula f_i. Indeed, we need to ensure that all instances of $\mathcal{P}_i$ created during a global run satisfy the formula f_i. Also, it is not correct to check whether all possible instances of $\mathcal{P}_i$ satisfy the formula f_i. Indeed, an instance of $\mathcal{P}_i$ should not be checked if it is not created during a global run. To solve these problems, we reduce the CARET model-checking problem for DPNs to the membership problem for GBDPNs. To do this, we compute a GBDPN $\mathcal{BM} = \{\mathcal{BP}_1, ..., \mathcal{BP}_n\}$ where $\mathcal{BP}_i$ ($i \in \{1..n\}$) is a GBDPDS s.t. (1) the problem of checking whether each instance of $\mathcal{P}_i$ satisfies a CARET formula f_i can be reduced to the membership problem of $\mathcal{BP}_i$; (2) if $\mathcal{P}_i$ creates a new instance of $\mathcal{P}_j$ starting from $p_s\omega_s$, which requires that $p_s\omega_s \vDash f_j$; $\mathcal{BP}_i$ must also create an instance of $\mathcal{BP}_j$ starting from a certain configuration (computed from $p_s\omega_s$) from which $\mathcal{BP}_j$ has an accepting run. In what follows, we present how to compute such GBDPDSs.

Let $Label = \{exit, unexit\}$ (we explain later the need to these labels). Given a DPDS $\mathcal{P}_i$ ($i \in \{1..n\}$), a corresponding CARET formula f_i, we define $Initial_i$ as the set of atoms A ($A \in Atoms(f_i)$) such that $f_i \in A$ and $NextCallerFormulas(A) = \emptyset$. Our goal is that for every $\mathcal{P}_i$ ($i \in \{1..n\}$), we compute a GBDPDS $\mathcal{BP}_i$ s.t. for every $p\omega \in P_i \times \Gamma_i^*$, $p\omega$ satisfies f_i iff there exists an atom A where $A \in Initial_i$ s.t. $\mathcal{BP}_i$ has an accepting run from $(\!(p, A, unexit)\!)\omega$.

GBDPDSs Computation

Let us fix a DPDS $\mathcal{P}_i = (P, \Gamma, \Delta)$ in the DPN $\mathcal{M}$, a CARET formula f_i in $f = \bigwedge_{i=1}^{n} f_i$ corresponding to the DPDS $\mathcal{P}_i$. In this section, we show how to compute such a GBDPDS $\mathcal{BP}_i$ corresponding to $\mathcal{P}_i$. Given a local configuration $p\omega$, let $\delta(p\omega)$ be the index of the DPDS corresponding to $p\omega$. We define $\mathcal{BP}_i = (P', \Gamma', \Delta', F)$ as follows:

- $P' = \{(\!(p, A, l)\!) \mid p \in P, l \in Label, A \in Atoms(f_i) \text{ and } A \cap AP = \lambda(p)\}$ is the finite set of control locations of $\mathcal{BP}_i$
- $\Gamma' = \Gamma \cup (\Gamma \times Atoms(f_i) \times Label)$ is the finite set of stack symbols of $\mathcal{BP}_i$.

The transition relation Δ' of $\mathcal{BP}_i$ is the smallest set of transition rules satisfying the following:

- (α_1)   for   every $p\gamma \xrightarrow{\text{call}}_i q\gamma'\gamma'' \triangleright d$ $\in$ Δ: $(\!(p, A, l)\!)\gamma \longrightarrow_i (\!(q, A', l')\!)\gamma'(\!(\gamma'', A, l)\!) \triangleright d_0 \in \Delta'$ for every $A, A' \in Atoms(f_i)$; $l, l' \in Label$ such that:
  - (β_0) $A \cap \{call, ret, int\} = \{call\}$
  - (β_1) $A \cap AP = \lambda(p)$
  - (β_2) $A' \cap AP = \lambda(q)$
  - (β_3) $GlNext(A, A')$
  - (β_4) $CallerNext(A', A)$
  - (β_5) $l' = unexit$ implies ($l = unexit$ and $NexAbsForms(A) = \emptyset$)
  - (β_6) $d_0 = \square$ if $d = \square$; $d_0 = (\!(p_s, A_0, unexit)\!)\omega_s$ where $A_0 \in Initial_{\delta(p_s\omega_s)}$ if $d = p_s\omega_s$
- (α_2) for every $p\gamma \xrightarrow{\text{ret}}_i q\epsilon \triangleright d \in \Delta$:
  - ($\alpha_{2.1}$) $(\!(p, A, exit)\!)\gamma \longrightarrow_i (\!(q, A', l')\!)\epsilon \triangleright d_0 \in \Delta'$ for every $A, A' \in Atoms$ (f_i); $l, l' \in Label$ such that:
    - (β_0) $A \cap \{call, ret, int\} = \{ret\}$
    - (β_1) $A \cap AP = \lambda(p)$
    - (β_2) $A' \cap AP = \lambda(q)$
    - (β_3) $GlNext(A, A')$
    - (β_4) $NexAbsForms(A) = \emptyset$
    - (β_5) $d_0 = \square$ if $d = \square$; $d_0 = (\!(p_s, A_0, unexit)\!)\omega_s$ where $A_0 \in Initial_{\delta(p_s\omega_s)}$ if $d = p_s\omega_s$

- $(\alpha_{2.2})$ $\langle\!\langle q, A', l'\rangle\!\rangle, \langle\!\langle \gamma_0, A_0, l_0\rangle\!\rangle\rangle \longrightarrow_i \langle\!\langle q, A', l'\rangle\!\rangle\gamma_0 \in \Delta'$ for every $\gamma_0 \in \Gamma, A_0, A' \in Atoms(f_i)$; $l', l_0 \in Label$ such that:
  * (β_6) $AbsNext(A_0, A')$
  * (β_7) $NexCallerForms(A') = NexCallerForms(A_0)$
  * (β_8) $A' \cap AP = \lambda(q)$
  * (β_9) $l_0 = l'$

- (α_3) for every $p\gamma \xrightarrow{int}_i q\omega \rhd d \in \Delta$: $\langle\!\langle p, A, l\rangle\!\rangle\gamma \longrightarrow_i \langle\!\langle q, A', l\rangle\!\rangle\omega \rhd d_0 \in \Delta'$ for every $A, A' \in Atoms(f_i)$, $l \in Label$ such that:
  * (β_0) $A \cap \{call, ret, int\} = \{int\}$
  * (β_1) $A \cap AP = \lambda(p)$
  * (β_2) $A' \cap AP = \lambda(q)$
  * (β_3) $GlNext(A, A')$
  * (β_4) $AbsNext(A, A')$
  * (β_5) $NexCallerForms(A) = NexCallerForms(A')$
  * (β_6) $d_0 = \square$ if $d = \square$; $d_0 = \langle\!\langle p_s, A_0, unexit\rangle\!\rangle\omega_s$ where $A_0 \in Initial_{\delta(p_s\omega_s)}$ if $d = p_s\omega_s$

Let $cl_{U^g}(f_i) = \{\phi_1 U^g \chi_1, ..., \phi_k U^g \chi_k\}$ and $cl_{U^a}(f_i) = \{\xi_1 U^a \tau_1, ..., \xi_{k'} U^a \tau_{k'}\}$ be the set of U^g-formulas and U^a-formulas of $Cl(f_i)$ respectively. The generalized Büchi accepting condition F of $\mathcal{BP}_i$ is defined as: $F = \{F_1\} \cup F_2 \cup F_3$ where

- $F_1 = P \times Atoms(f_i) \times \{unexit\}$
- $F_2 = \{F_1^g, ..., F_k^g\}$ where $F_x^g = \{P \times F_{\phi_x U^g \chi_x} \times Label\}$ where $F_{\phi_x U^g \chi_x} = \{A \in Atoms(f_i) \mid$ if $\phi_x U^g \chi_x \in A$ then $\chi_x \in A\}$ for every $1 \le x \le k$.
- $F_3 = \{F_1^a, ..., F_{k'}^a\}$ where $F_x^a = \{P \times F_{\xi_x U^a \tau_x} \times \{unexit\}\}$ where $F_{\xi_x U^a \tau_x} = \{A \in Atoms(f_i) \mid$ if $\xi_x U^a \tau_x \in A$ then $\tau_x \in A\}$ for every $1 \le x \le k'$.

Given a configuration $p\omega$, let $\mathcal{P}(p\omega)$ be the procedure to which $p\omega$ belongs. For example, in Fig. 2, $\mathcal{P}(p_{x+1}\omega_{x+1}) = proc, ..., \mathcal{P}(p_{y-1}\omega_{y-1}) = proc$. Intuitively, we compute $\mathcal{BP}_i$ as a kind of product of $\mathcal{P}_i$ and f_i which ensures that: for every $p\omega \in P_i \times \Gamma_i^*$, $p\omega$ satisfies f_i iff there exists an atom $A \in Intial_i$ s.t. $\mathcal{BP}_i$ has an accepting run from $\langle\!\langle p, A, unexit\rangle\!\rangle\omega$. To do this, we encode atoms of f_i into control locations of $\mathcal{P}_i$. The form of control locations of $\mathcal{BP}_i$ is $\langle\!\langle p, A, l\rangle\!\rangle$ where A contains all sub formulas of f_i which are satisfied at the configuration $p\omega$, l is a label to determine whether the execution of the procedure of $p\omega$, $\mathcal{P}(p\omega)$, terminates in the path π. A configuration $p\omega$ labeled with $exit$ means that the execution of $\mathcal{P}(p\omega)$ is finished in π, i.e., the run π will run through the procedure $\mathcal{P}(p\omega)$, reaches its ret statement and exits $\mathcal{P}(p\omega)$ after that. On the contrary, $p\omega$ labeled with $unexit$ means that in π, the execution of the procedure $\mathcal{P}(p\omega)$ never terminates, i.e., the run π will be stuck in and never exits the procedure $\mathcal{P}(p\omega)$. Let $\pi = p_0\omega_0 p_1\omega_1...$ be a run of $\mathcal{P}_i$ and $\langle\!\langle p_0, A_0, l_0\rangle\!\rangle\omega_0 \langle\!\langle p_1, A_1, l_1\rangle\!\rangle\omega_1....$ be a corresponding run of $\mathcal{BP}_i$. We give in what follows the intuition behind our construction.

Encoding Atoms to Control Locations. Firstly, we need to ensure that $\mathcal{BP}_i$ has an accepting (local) run from $\langle\!\langle p_x, A_x\rangle\!\rangle\omega_x$ iff $p_x\omega_x$ satisfies ϕ (denoted

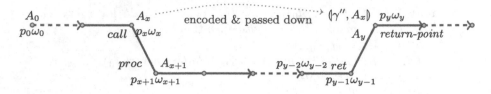

Fig. 2. Case of $X^a\phi' \in A_x$

$p_x\omega_x \vDash \phi$) for every $\phi \in A_x$. To ensure this, in rules (α_1), (α_2) and (α_3), the first class of conditions (β_0) ensures that the tags $\{call, ret, int\}$ assigned to each configuration of the run are guessed correctly. The second class of conditions (β_1) and (β_2) expresses that for every $e \in AP$, $(\pi, x) \vDash e$ iff $e \in \lambda(p_x)$, and the class of conditions (β_3) expresses that $(\pi, x) \vDash X^g\phi'$ iff $(\pi, x + 1) \vDash \phi'$. Now, let us consider the most delicate case where $\phi = X^a\phi' \in A_x$. There are two possibilities:

- $p_x\omega_x \Rightarrow_i p_{x+1}\omega_{x+1} \triangleright d_0$ corresponds to a call statement. Let us consider Fig. 2 to explain this case. Let $p_y\omega_y$ be the abstract-successor of $p_x\omega_x$. $(\pi, x) \vDash X^a\phi'$ iff $(\pi, y) \vDash \phi'$. Thus, we must have $\phi' \in A_y$. This is ensured by rules (α_1) and (α_2): rules (α_1) allow to record $X^a\phi'$ in the return point of the call, and rules (α_2) allow to extract and validate ϕ' when the return-point is reached. In what follows, we show in more details how this works: Let $p_x\gamma \xrightarrow{call}_i p_{x+1}\gamma'\gamma'' \triangleright d$ be the rule associated with the transition $p_x\omega_x \Rightarrow_i p_{x+1}\omega_{x+1} \triangleright d_0$, then we have $\omega_x = \gamma\omega'$ and $\omega_{x+1} = \gamma'\gamma''\omega'$. Let $p_{y-1}\omega_{y-1} \Rightarrow_i p_y\omega_y \triangleright d_0$ be the transition that corresponds to the ret statement of this call. Let then $p_{y-1}\beta \xrightarrow{ret}_i p_y\epsilon \triangleright d \in \Delta$ be the corresponding return rule. Then, we have necessarily $\omega_{y-1} = \beta\gamma''\omega'$, since as explained in Sect. 3.1, γ'' is the return address of the call. After applying this rule, $\omega_y = \gamma''\omega'$. In other words, γ'' will be the topmost stack symbol at the corresponding return point of the call. So, in order to recover ϕ' in A_y, we proceed as follows: At the call $p_x\gamma \xrightarrow{call}_i p_{x+1}\gamma'\gamma'' \triangleright d$, we encode A_x into γ'' by the rule (α_1) stating that $(\!|p_x, A_x, l|\!)\gamma \longrightarrow_i (\!|p_{x+1}, A_{x+1}, l'|\!)\gamma'(\!|\gamma'', A_x, l|\!) \triangleright d_0 \in \Delta'$. This allows to record $X^a\phi'$ in the corresponding return point of the stack. After that, $(\!|\gamma'', A_x, l|\!)$ will be the topmost stack symbol at the corresponding return-point of this call. At the return-point, the condition (β_6) in $(\alpha_{2.2})$ stating that $AbsNext(A_x, A_y)$ and the fact that $\phi = X^a\phi' \in A_x$ imply that $\phi' \in A_y$.
- $p_x\omega_x \Rightarrow_i p_{x+1}\omega_{x+1} \triangleright d_0$ corresponds to a simple statement. Then, the abstract successor of $p_x\omega_x$ is $p_{x+1}\omega_{x+1}$. $(\pi, x) \vDash X^a\phi'$ iff $(\pi, x + 1) \vDash \phi'$. Thus, we must have $\phi' \in A_{x+1}$. This is ensured by condition (β_4) in (α_3) stating that $AbsNext(A_x, A_{x+1}) = true$.

The label l. Now, let us explain how the label l is used in the transition rules to ensure the correctness of the formulas. Note that our explanation above makes implicitly the assumption that along the run π, every call to a procedure *proc* will eventually reach its corresponding return point, i.e., the run π will finally exit *proc*, then, we can encode formulas at the *call* and validate them at its corresponding return-point. However, it might be the case that at a certain point in the procedure *proc*, there will be a loop, and π never exits *proc*. To solve this problem, we annotate the control states by the label $l \in \{exit, unexit\}$ to determine whether π can complete the execution of the procedure $\mathscr{P}(p\omega)$. In the following, we explain three cases corresponding to three kinds of statements:

- Let us consider Fig. 2. $p_x\omega_x \Rightarrow_i p_{x+1}\omega_{x+1} \rhd d_0$ corresponds to a *call* statement. Note that $\mathscr{P}(p_{x+1}\omega_{x+1}) = proc$ in this case. There are two possibilities. If *proc* terminates, then the call at $p_x\omega_x$ will reach its corresponding return-point. In this case, $p_{x+1}\omega_{x+1}$ is labelled by *exit*. If *proc* never terminates, then the call at $p_x\omega_x$ will never reach its corresponding return-point. In this case, $p_{x+1}\omega_{x+1}$ is labelled by *unexit*. If $p_{x+1}\omega_{x+1}$ is labelled by *exit*, then $p_x\omega_x$ can be labelled by *exit* or *unexit*. However, if $p_{x+1}\omega_{x+1}$ is labelled by *unexit*, then $p_x\omega_x$ must be labelled by *unexit*. This is ensured by the condition ($l' = unexit$ implies $l = unexit$) in the rule (α_1). In addition, if $p_{x+1}\omega_{x+1}$ is labelled by *unexit*, then $p_x\omega_x$ never reaches its corresponding return-point. Thus, $p_x\omega_x$ does not satisfy any formula in the form $X^a\phi$. This is ensured by the condition ($l' = unexit$ implies $NexAbsForms(A) = \emptyset$) in the rule ($\alpha_1$).
- Again, let us consider Fig. 2. $p_{y-1}\omega_{y-1} \Rightarrow_i p_y\omega_y \rhd d_0$ corresponds to a *ret* statement. At $p_{y-1}\omega_{y-1}$, we are sure that *proc* will terminate. In this case, $p_{y-1}\omega_{y-1}$ must be always labelled by *exit* and $p_y\omega_y$ can be labelled by *exit* or *unexit*. This is ensured by the rule ($\alpha_{2.1}$). Also, the abstract-successor of $p_{y-1}\omega_{y-1}$ is $\bot$, then, $p_{y-1}\omega_{y-1}$ does not satisfy any formula in the form $X^a\phi$. This is ensured by the condition ($NexAbsForms(A) = \emptyset$) in the rule ($\alpha_{2.1}$).
- Finally, let us consider Fig. 2. $p_{y-2}\omega_{y-2} \Rightarrow_i p_{y-1}\omega_{y-1} \rhd d_0$ corresponds to a *simple statement*. Then, $p_{y-2}\omega_{y-2}$ and $p_{y-1}\omega_{y-1}$ are in the same procedure *proc*. Thus, the labels assigned to $p_{y-2}\omega_{y-2}$ and $p_{y-1}\omega_{y-1}$ should be the same. This is ensured by the transition rule (α_3)

The Accepting Conditions. The generalized Büchi accepting condition F of $\mathcal{BP}_i$ consists of three families of accepting conditions F_1, F_2 and F_3. The first set F_1 guarantees that an accepting run should go infinitely often through the label *unexit*. Each set of F_2 ensures that the liveness requirement ψ_2 in $\psi_1 U^g \psi_2$ is eventually satisfied in $\mathcal{P}$. The idea behind the set F_3 is similar to the set F_2 except that the liveness requirement for a U^a-formula $\phi_1 U^a \phi_2$ is only required on the (unique) infinite abstract path (labelled by *unexit*). With respect to caller-until formulas, note that caller paths are always finite, so we do not need to consider this case in F. The liveness requirements of caller-until formulas are ensured by the condition $NexCallerForms(A) = \emptyset$ since $\pi(0)$ have no caller successors.

Thus, we get the following lemma:

Lemma 1. Given a DPDS $\mathcal{P}_i = (P, \Gamma, \Delta)$, and a CARET formula f_i, we can construct a GBDPDS $\mathcal{BP}_i = (P', \Gamma', \Delta', F)$ such that for every configuration

$p\omega \in P_i \times \Gamma_i^*$, $p\omega \vDash f_i$ iff there exists an atom $A \in Initial_i$ s.t. $\mathcal{BP}_i$ has an accepting run from $(p, A, unexit)\omega$.

Spawning New Instances. Lemma 1 guarantees that the problem of checking whether an instance of $\mathcal{P}_i$ starting from $p\omega$ satisfies f_i can be reduced to the problem of checking if $\mathcal{BP}_i$ has an accepting run from $(p, A, unexit)\omega$ where $A \in Initial_i$. Now, we need to ensure the satisfiability on instances created dynamically. Suppose that $\mathcal{P}_i$ spawns a new instance of $\mathcal{P}_j$ starting from $p_s\omega_s$, this means that we need to guarantee that $p_s\omega_s \vDash f_j$. Note that by applying Lemma 1 for the DPDS $\mathcal{P}_j$, we get that $p_s\omega_s \vDash f_j$ iff there exists an atom $A \in Initial_j$ s.t. $\mathcal{BP}_j$ has an accepting run from $(p_s, A, unexit)\omega_s$. Then, the requirement $p_s\omega_s \vDash f_j$ is ensured by the conditions (β_6) in (α_1), (β_5) in (α_2) and (β_6) in (α_3) stating that for every $p\gamma \xrightarrow{t}_i q\omega \rhd d \in \Delta$ ($t \in \{call, ret, int\}$), we have $(p, A, l)\gamma \longrightarrow_i (q, A', l')\omega \rhd d_0 \in \Delta'$ such that if $d = p_s\omega_s$, then, $d_0 = (p_s, A_0, unexit)\omega_s$ where $A_0 \in Initial_j$ (since $\delta(p_s\omega_s) = j$ in this case).

Thus, we can show that:

Theorem 3. *Given a DPN $\mathcal{M} = \{\mathcal{P}_1, ..., \mathcal{P}_n\}$, a single-indexed CARET formula $f = \bigwedge_{i=1}^n f_i$, we can compute a GBDPN $\mathcal{BM} = \{\mathcal{BP}_1, ..., \mathcal{BP}_n\}$ such that a global configuration $\mathcal{G}$ of $\mathcal{M}$ satisfies f iff $\mathcal{G}' \in \mathcal{L}(\mathcal{BM})$ where $\mathcal{G}'$ is a global configuration of $\mathcal{BM}$ that corresponds to the configuration $\mathcal{G}$.*

6   Single-Indexed CARET Model-Checking for DPNs with Regular Valuations

In this section, we consider the single-indexed CARET model-checking problem for DPNs with regular valuations, in which the set of configurations where an atomic proposition is satisfied is a regular language.

Definition 6. *Let $\mathcal{M} = \{\mathcal{P}_1, ..., \mathcal{P}_n\}$ be a DPN. For every $i \in \{1..n\}$, a set of configurations of a pushdown process $\mathcal{P}_i = (P_i, \Delta_i, \Gamma_i)$ is regular if it can be written as the union of sets of the form E_p, where $p \in P_i$ and $E_p = \{(p, w)|w \in L_p\}$, where L_p is a regular set over Γ_i^*.*

Definition 7. *Let $\mathcal{M} = \{\mathcal{P}_1, ..., \mathcal{P}_n\}$ be a DPN. Let AP be a finite set of atomic propositions. Let $\nu : AP \to 2^{\bigcup_{i=1}^n P_i \times \Gamma_i^*}$ be a valuation. ν is called regular if for every $e \in AP$, $\nu(e)$ is a regular set of configurations.*

Let $\nu : AP \to 2^{\bigcup_{i=1}^n P_i \times \Gamma_i^*}$ be a regular valuation. We define $\lambda_\nu : P \times \Gamma^* \to 2^{AP}$ such that $\lambda_\nu(p\omega) = \{e \in AP \mid p\omega \in \nu(e)\}$. Let $\pi = p_0\omega_0 p_1\omega_1...$ be a local path of $\mathcal{P}_i$. We associate each configuration $p_x\omega_x$ of π with a tag t_x in $\{call, int, ret\}$ as presented in Sect. 3.2. Let f_i be a CARET formula over AP. The satisfiability relation w.r.t. the regular valuation ν is defined as follows:

$$\pi \vDash_\nu f_i \text{ iff } (\lambda_\nu(p_0\omega_0), t_0)(\lambda_\nu(p_1\omega_1), t_1) \cdots \vDash f_i$$

Theorem 4 [19]. *Single-indexed LTL model-checking with regular valuations for DPNs can be reduced to standard LTL model checking for DPNs.*

Given a DPN $\mathcal{M} = \{\mathcal{P}_1, ..., \mathcal{P}_n\}$ and a regular valuation $\nu : AP \rightarrow 2^{\bigcup_{i=1}^{n} P_i \times \Gamma_i^*}$, this result is based on translating every DPDS $\mathcal{P}_i$ ($i \in \{1..n\}$) into a DPDS $\mathcal{P}' = (P_i, \Gamma_i', \Delta_i')$ where the regular valuation requirements are encoded in Γ_i'. The same reduction is still true for single-indexed CARET with regular valuations. For details about this reduction, we refer readers to [19]. We can show that:

Theorem 5. *Single-indexed CARET model-checking with regular valuations for DPNs can be reduced to standard single-indexed CARET model checking for DPNs.*

7 DPNs Communicating via Locks

Dynamic Pushdown Network with Locks (L-DPNs) is a natural formalism for multithreaded programs communicating via locks [14, 20]:

Definition 8. *A Dynamic Pushdown Network with Locks (L-DPN) $\mathcal{M}$ is a set $\{\mathbb{L}, Act, \mathcal{P}_1, ..., \mathcal{P}_n\}$ where $\mathbb{L}$ is a set of locks, $Act = \{acq(l), rel(l), \tau \mid l \in \mathbb{L}\}$ is a set of actions on locks s.t. $acq(l)$ (resp. $rel(l)$) for $l \in \mathbb{L}$ represents an acquisition (resp. release) of the lock l and the action τ describes internal actions (neither acquire nor release locks); for every $1 \le i \le n$, $\mathcal{P}_i = (P_i, \Gamma_i, \Delta_i)$ is a Labelled Dynamic Pushdown System with Locks (L-DPDS), where P_i is a finite set of control locations and $P_i \cap P_j = \emptyset$ for all $j \ne i$, Γ_i is a finite set of stack alphabets, and Δ_i is a finite set of transitions rules. Rules of Δ_i are of the following form, where $a \in Act, p, p_1 \in P_i, \gamma \in \Gamma_i, \omega_1 \in \Gamma_i^*, d \subset \{\Box, p_s\omega_s \mid p_s\omega_s \in \bigcup_{1 \le j \le n} P_j \times \Gamma_j^*\}$:*

- (r_1) $p\gamma \xrightarrow{(a,call)}_i p_1\gamma_1\gamma_2 \triangleright d$
- (r_2) $p\gamma \xrightarrow{(a,ret)}_i p_1\epsilon \triangleright d$
- (r_3) $p\gamma \xrightarrow{(a,int)}_i p_1\omega \triangleright d$

Intuitively, a L-DPN is a DPN where processes communicate via locks. The difference is that each transition rule of L-DPNs is assigned to one additional action $a \in Act$. Depending on the nature of the associated action a, each transition step of L-DPDSs include one additional operation on a given lock l. $acq(l)$ (resp. $rel(l)$) represents an *acquisition* (resp. *release*) of the lock l and the action τ describe internal actions (neither *acquire* nor *release* locks).

A *local configuration* of an instance of a *L-DPDS* $\mathcal{P}_i$ is a tuple $(p\omega, L)$ where $p \in P_i$ is the control location, $\omega \in \Gamma_i^*$ is the stack content and $L \subseteq \mathbb{L}$ is a set of locks owned by the instance. A *global configuration* of $\mathcal{M}$ is a multiset over $\bigcup_{1 \le i \le n} P_i \times \Gamma_i^* \times 2^{\mathbb{L}}$, in which $(p\omega, L) \in P_i \times \Gamma_i^* \times 2^{\mathbb{L}}$ represents the *local configuration* of an instance of a pushdown process $\mathcal{P}_i$ which is running in the network.

A L-DPDS $\mathcal{P}_i$ defines a transition relation $\Rightarrow_i$ as follows where $t \in \{call, ret, int\}$:

- if $p\gamma \xrightarrow{(\tau,t)}_i p_1\omega_1 \rhd d$ then $(p\gamma\omega, L) \Rightarrow_i (p_1\omega_1\omega, L) \rhd D_0$ where $D_0 = \emptyset$ if $d = \square$, $D_0 = \{(p_s\omega_s, \emptyset)\}$ if $d = p_s\omega_s$ for every $\omega \in \Gamma_i^*$, $L \subseteq \mathbb{L}$
- if $p\gamma \xrightarrow{(acq(l),t)}_i p_1\omega_1 \rhd d$ then $(p\gamma\omega, L) \Rightarrow_i (p_1\omega_1\omega, L \cup \{l\}) \rhd D_0$ where $D_0 = \emptyset$ if $d = \square$, $D_0 = \{(p_s\omega_s, \emptyset)\}$ if $d = p_s\omega_s$ for every $\omega \in \Gamma_i^*$, $L \subseteq \mathbb{L}$. This expresses that the current instance can move from $(p\gamma\omega, L)$ to $(p_1\omega_1\omega, L \cup \{l\})$. This ensures that the current instance owns the lock l after the action $acq(l)$.
- if $p\gamma \xrightarrow{(rel(l),t)}_i p_1\omega_1 \rhd d$ then $(p\gamma\omega, L) \Rightarrow_i (p_1\omega_1\omega, L \setminus \{l\}) \rhd D_0$ where $D_0 = \emptyset$ if $d = \square$, $D_0 = \{(p_s\omega_s, \emptyset)\}$ if $d = p_s\omega_s$ for every $\omega \in \Gamma_i^*$, $L \subseteq \mathbb{L}$. This means that the current instance can move from $(p\gamma\omega, L)$ to $(p_1\omega_1\omega, L \setminus \{l\})$. This ensures that the current instance releases the lock l after the action $rel(l)$.

Roughly speaking, if $d = p_s\omega_s$, then the current instance not only does local move but also creates a new instance of the pushdown process $\mathcal{P}_j$ starting at $(p_s\omega_s, \emptyset)$. Note that we suppose that the new instance holds no locks when it is created.

A *local run* of an instance of a L-DPDS $\mathcal{P}_i$ starting at a local configuration c_0 is a sequence $c_0c_1\ldots$ s.t. for every $j \geq 0$, $c_j \in P_i \times \Gamma_i^* \times 2^{\mathbb{L}}$ is a local configuration of $\mathcal{P}_i$, $c_j \Rightarrow_i c_{j+1} \rhd D_0$. The definition of *global run* of a L-DPNs $\mathcal{M}$ is similar to the one for DPNs.

Nested Lock Access. In this work, we suppose that in all local runs, the locks are accessed in a well-nested and no-reentrant manner, i.e. a local run can only release the latest lock it acquired that is not released yet. Indeed, if we allow arbitrary locks, then reachability becomes undecidable [10].

Theorem 6 [20]. *Single-indexed LTL model-checking for L-DPNs can be reduced to single-indexed LTL model checking for DPNs.*

Given a L-DPN $\mathcal{M} = \{\mathbb{L}, Act, \mathcal{P}_1, \ldots, \mathcal{P}_n\}$, this result is based on translating every $\mathcal{P}_i$ ($i \in \{1..n\}$) into a DPDS $\mathcal{P}_i' = (P_i', \Gamma_i, \Delta_i')$ s.t. $\mathcal{P}_i'$ is a kind of product between the DPDS $\mathcal{P}_i$ and the acquisition structure, where an acquisition structure (encoded in control locations of $\mathcal{P}_i'$) stores information about how locks are used such as the number of held locks, the order of acquisition and release of locks. We can compute a DPN $\mathcal{M}' = \{\mathcal{P}_1', \ldots, \mathcal{P}_n'\}$ s.t. the global runs of $\mathcal{M}'$ mimic the global runs of $\mathcal{M}$ and the acquisition structures reflect the lock usages. Thus, the global runs of $\mathcal{M}'$ correspond to global runs of $\mathcal{M}$ in which the locks are accessed in a nested manner. The same reduction is still true for single-indexed CARET formulas. For details of this reduction, we refer readers to [20]. We can show that:

Theorem 7. *Single-indexed CARET model-checking for L-DPNs can be reduced to single-indexed CARET model checking for DPNs.*

References

1. Alur, R., Etessami, K., Madhusudan, P.: A temporal logic of nested calls and returns. In: Jensen, K., Podelski, A. (eds.) TACAS 2004. LNCS, vol. 2988, pp. 467–481. Springer, Heidelberg (2004). https://doi.org/10.1007/978-3-540-24730-2_35

2. Atig, M.F., Bouajjani, A., Touili, T.: On the reachability analysis of acyclic networks of pushdown systems. In: van Breugel, F., Chechik, M. (eds.) CONCUR 2008. LNCS, vol. 5201, pp. 356–371. Springer, Heidelberg (2008). https://doi.org/10.1007/978-3-540-85361-9_29

3. Atig, M.F., Touili, T.: Verifying parallel programs with dynamic communication structures. In: Maneth, S. (ed.) CIAA 2009. LNCS, vol. 5642, pp. 145–154. Springer, Heidelberg (2009). https://doi.org/10.1007/978-3-642-02979-0_18

4. Bansal, K., Demri, S.: Model-checking bounded multi-pushdown systems. In: Bulatov, A.A., Shur, A.M. (eds.) CSR 2013. LNCS, vol. 7913, pp. 405–417. Springer, Heidelberg (2013). https://doi.org/10.1007/978-3-642-38536-0_35

5. Bouajjani, A., Esparza, J., Touili, T.: A generic approach to the static analysis of concurrent programs with procedures. In: POPL 2003 (2003)

6. Bouajjani, A., Müller-Olm, M., Touili, T.: Regular symbolic analysis of dynamic networks of pushdown systems. In: Abadi, M., de Alfaro, L. (eds.) CONCUR 2005. LNCS, vol. 3653, pp. 473–487. Springer, Heidelberg (2005). https://doi.org/10.1007/11539452_36

7. Chaki, S., Clarke, E., Kidd, N., Reps, T., Touili, T.: Verifying concurrent message-passing C programs with recursive calls. In: Hermanns, H., Palsberg, J. (eds.) TACAS 2006. LNCS, vol. 3920, pp. 334–349. Springer, Heidelberg (2006). https://doi.org/10.1007/11691372_22

8. Grumberg, O., Clarke, E.M., Peled, D.A.: Model Checking. MIT Press, Cambridge (1999)

9. Gawlitza, T.M., Lammich, P., Müller-Olm, M., Seidl, H., Wenner, A.: Join-lock-sensitive forward reachability analysis for concurrent programs with dynamic process creation. In: Jhala, R., Schmidt, D. (eds.) VMCAI 2011. LNCS, vol. 6538, pp. 199–213. Springer, Heidelberg (2011). https://doi.org/10.1007/978-3-642-18275-4_15

10. Kahlon, V., Gupta, A.: An automata-theoretic approach for model checking threads for LTL properties. In: LICS 2006 (2006)

11. Kahlon, V., Gupta, A.: On the analysis of interacting pushdown systems. In: POPL 2007 (2007)

12. Kahlon, V., Ivancic, F., Gupta, A.: Reasoning about threads communicating via locks. In: CAV 2005 (2005)

13. La Torre, S., Napoli, M.: A temporal logic for multi-threaded programs. In: Baeten, J.C.M., Ball, T., de Boer, F.S. (eds.) TCS 2012. LNCS, vol. 7604, pp. 225–239. Springer, Heidelberg (2012). https://doi.org/10.1007/978-3-642-33475-7_16

14. Lammich, P., Müller-Olm, M., Wenner, A.: Predecessor sets of dynamic pushdown networks with tree-regular constraints. In: Bouajjani, A., Maler, O. (eds.) CAV 2009. LNCS, vol. 5643, pp. 525–539. Springer, Heidelberg (2009). https://doi.org/10.1007/978-3-642-02658-4_39

15. Lugiez, D.: Forward analysis of dynamic network of pushdown systems is easier without order. Int. J. Found. Comput. Sci. **22**(4), 843–862 (2011)

16. Nguyen, H.-V., Touili, T.: CARET model checking for malware detection. In: SPIN 2017 (2017)

17. Nguyen, H.-V., Touili, T.: CARET model checking for pushdown systems. In: SAC 2017 (2017)
18. Schwoon, S.: Model-checking pushdown systems. Dissertation, Technische Universität München, München (2002)
19. Song, F., Touili, T.: Model checking dynamic pushdown networks. In: Shan, C. (ed.) APLAS 2013. LNCS, vol. 8301, pp. 33–49. Springer, Cham (2013). https://doi.org/10.1007/978-3-319-03542-0_3
20. Song, F., Touili, T.: LTL model-checking for dynamic pushdown networks communicating via locks. CoRR, abs/1611.02528 (2016)
21. Wenner, A.: Weighted dynamic pushdown networks. In: Gordon, A.D. (ed.) ESOP 2010. LNCS, vol. 6012, pp. 590–609. Springer, Heidelberg (2010). https://doi.org/10.1007/978-3-642-11957-6_31

Program Development

Context Generation from Formal Specifications for C Analysis Tools

Michele Alberti[1] and Julien Signoles[2(✉)]

[1] TrustInSoft, Paris, France
michele.alberti@trust-in-soft.com
[2] CEA LIST, Software Reliability and Security Laboratory, 91191 Gif-sur-Yvette
Cedex, France
julien.signoles@cea.fr

Abstract. Analysis tools like abstract interpreters, symbolic execution tools and testing tools usually require a proper context to give useful results when analyzing a particular function. Such a context initializes the function parameters and global variables to comply with function requirements. However it may be error-prone to write it by hand: the handwritten context might contain bugs or not match the intended specification. A more robust approach is to specify the context in a dedicated specification language, and hold the analysis tools to support it properly. This may mean to put significant development efforts for enhancing the tools, something that is often not feasible if ever possible.

This paper presents a way to systematically generate such a context from a formal specification of a C function. This is applied to a subset of the ACSL specification language in order to generate suitable contexts for the abstract interpretation-based value analysis plug-ins of Frama-C, a framework for analysis of code written in C. The idea here presented has been implemented in a new Frama-C plug-in which is currently in use in an operational industrial setting.

Keywords: Formal specification · Code generation · Transformation
Code analysis · Frama-C · ACSL

1 Introduction

Code analysis tools are nowadays effective enough to be able to provide suitable results on real-world code. Nevertheless several of these tools including abstract interpreters, symbolic execution tools, and testing tools must analyze the whole application from the program entry point (the *main* function); or else either they just cannot be executed, or they provide too imprecise results. Unfortunately such an entry point does not necessarily exist, particularly when analyzing libraries.

M. Alberti—This work was done when the first author was at CEA LIST, Software Reliability and Security Laboratory.

F. Fioravanti and J. P. Gallagher (Eds.): LOPSTR 2017, LNCS 10855, pp. 93–111, 2018.
https://doi.org/10.1007/978-3-319-94460-9_6

In such a case, the verification engineer must manually write the context of the analyzed function f as a main function which initializes the parameters of f as well as the necessary global variables. This mandatory initialization step must enforce the function requirements and may restrict the possible input values for the sake of memory footprint and time efficiency of the analysis. This approach is however error-prone: additionally to usual pitfalls of software development (*e.g.* bugs, code maintenance, *etc.*), the handwritten context may not match the function requirements, or be over restrictive. Moreover this kind of shortcomings may be difficult to detect due to the fact that the context is not explicitly the verification objective.

A valid and more robust alternative is to specify such a context in a dedicated specification language, and make the analysis tools handle it properly. This is often an arduous approach as the support for a particular specification language feature may entail a significant development process, something that is often not feasible if ever possible. Also, it requires to do so for every tool.

This paper presents a way to systematically generate an analysis context from a formal specification of a C function. The function requirements as well as the additional restrictions over the input domains are expressed as function preconditions in the ANSI/ISO C Specification Language (in short, ACSL) [2]. This specification S is interpreted as a constraint system, simplified as much as possible, then converted into a C code C which exactly implements the specification S. Indeed not only every possible execution of C satisfies S but conversely, there is an execution of C for every possible input satisfying the constraints expressed by S. We present the formalization of this idea for an expressive subset of ACSL including standard logic operators, integer arithmetic, arrays and pointers, pointer arithmetic, and built-in predicates for the validity and initialization properties of memory location ranges.

We also provide implementation details about our tool, named CfP for *Context from Preconditions*, implemented as a Frama-C plug-in. Frama-C is a code analysis framework for code written in C [12]. Thanks to the aforementioned technique, CfP generates suitable contexts for two abstract interpretation-based value analysis tools, namely the Frama-C plug-in EVA [3] and TIS-Analyzer [9] from the TrustInSoft company. Both tools are actually distinct evolved versions of an older plug-in called Value [6]. In particular, TrustInSoft successfully used CfP on the mbed-TLS library (also known as PolarSSL), an open source implementation of SSL/TLS[1], when building its verification kit [22]. It is worth noting that CfP revealed some mistakes in contexts previously written by hand by expert verification engineers when comparing its results with these pieces of code. Also, CfP generates code as close as possible to human-written code: it is quite readable and follows code patterns that experts of these tools manually write.

Contributions. The contributions of this paper are threefold: **a novel technique to** systematically **generate an analysis context** from a formal specification of a C function, **a precise formalization** of this technique, and a presentation of **a**

---

[1] https://tls.mbed.org/.

tool implementing this technique which is **used in an operational industrial setting**.

Outline. Section 2 presents an overview of our technique through a motivating example. Section 3 details preconditions to constraints conversion, while Sect. 4 explains the C code generation scheme for these latter. Section 5 evaluates our approach and Sect. 6 discusses related work. Section 7 concludes this work by also discussing future work.

2 Overview and Motivating Example

We illustrate our approach on context generation through the function aes_crypt_cbc, a cryptographic utility implemented by the mbed-TLS library. Figure 1 shows its prototype and ACSL preconditions as written by TrustInSoft for its verification kit [22].

```
 1  typedef struct {
 2    int nr;                    /*  number of rounds  */
 3    unsigned long *rk;         /*  AES round keys    */
 4    unsigned long buf[68];     /*  unaligned data    */
 5  } aes_context;
 6
 7  /*@ requires ctx_valid: \valid(ctx);
 8    @ requires ctx_init: \initialized(ctx->buf + (0 .. 63));
 9    @ requires ctx_rk: ctx->rk == ctx->buf;
10    @ requires ctx_nr: ctx->nr == 14;
11    @ requires mode: mode == 0 || mode == 1;
12    @ requires length: 16 <= length <= 16672;
13    @ requires length_mod: length % 16 == 0;
14    @ requires iv_valid: \valid(iv + (0 .. 15));
15    @ requires iv_init: \initialized(iv + (0 .. 15));
16    @ requires input_valid: \valid_read(input + (0 .. length - 1));
17    @ requires input_init: \initialized(input + (0 .. length - 1));
18    @ requires output_valid: \valid(output + (0 .. length - 1)); */
19  int aes_crypt_cbc(aes_context *ctx, int mode, size_t length, unsigned char iv[16],
20                    const unsigned char *input, unsigned char *output);
```

Fig. 1. ACSL preconditions of the mbed-TLS function aes_crypt_cbc.

Specification. The function aes_crypt_cbc provides encryption and decryption of a buffer according to the AES cryptographic standard and the CBC encryption mode. The function takes six parameters. The last two are the input and the output strings. The parameter ctx stores the necessary information to the AES substitution-permutation network, in particular the number of rounds and the round keys defined in a dedicated structure at lines 1–5. The parameter mode indicates whether the function should encrypt or decrypt the input. The parameter length indicates the length of the input string. Finally the parameter iv provides an initialization vector for the output of 16 characters (unsigned char iv[16]). This declared length is actually meaningless for most C tools because an array typed parameter is adjusted to have a pointer type [11, Sect. 6.9.1 and also footnote 79 at p. 71], but CfP nevertheless considers it as part of the specification in order to generate a more precise context.

ACSL annotations are enclosed in /*@ ... */ as a special kind of comments. Therefore they are ignored by any C compiler. A function precondition is introduced by the keyword **requires** right before the function declaration or definition. It must be satisfied at every call site of the given function. Here the function aes_crypt_cbc has 12 precondition clauses, and the whole function precondition is the conjunction of all of them. Clauses may be tagged with names, which are logically meaningless but provide a way to easily refer to and to document specifications. For instance, the first precondition (line 7) is named ctx_valid while the second (line 8) is named ctx_init.

We now detail the meaning of each precondition clause. All pointers must be valid, that is properly allocated, and point to a memory block of appropriate length that the program can safely access either in read-only mode (predicate **\valid_read**), or in read-write mode (predicate **\valid**). That is the purpose of preconditions ctx_valid, iv_valid, input_valid and output_valid: ctx must point to a memory block containing at least a single aes_context struct, iv must be able to contain at least 16 unsigned characters (ranging from 0 to 15), while input and output must be able to contain at least length unsigned characters (ranging from 0 to length − 1). Memory locations, which are read by the function, must be properly initialized. That is the purpose of the precondition clauses ctx_init, iv_init, and input_init which initialize the first 64 cells of ctx->buf as well as every valid cell of iv and input. The specification clause mode specifies that the mode must be either 0 (encryption) or 1 (decryption), while the specification clause length_mod specifies that the length should be a multiple of the block size (*i.e.* 16) as specified in mbed-TLS. The other clauses restrict the perimeter of the analysis in order to make it tractable.

The clause ctx_rk is a standard equality for an AES context, while the clause ctx_nr is true for 256-bit encryption keys. Finally the clause length aims to restrict the analysis to buffers of size from 16 to 16672 unsigned characters.

Context Generation. A naive approach for context generation would consider one precondition clause after the other and directly implement it in C code. However, this would not work, in general, since requirements cannot be treated in any order. In our running example, for instance, variables input and output depends on the variable length: the precondition clauses over this latter must be treated before those over the former, as well as the generated code for these variables must initialize the latter, first, and the former afterwards, to be sound. To solve such problems, one could first record every dependency among the left-values involved in the specification, and then proceed to generate C code accordingly. An approach based only on a dependency graph is nonetheless insufficient for those preconditions that need an inference reasoning in order to be implemented correctly. As an example, treating the precondition /*@**requires** \valid(x+(0..3)) && *(x+4)==1;*/ demands to infer x as an array of 5 elements in order to consider the initialization x[4] = 1; correct.

```
1  int cfp_aes_crypt_cbc(void) {
2    unsigned char *cfp_output, *cfp_input;
3    unsigned char cfp_iv[16];
4    size_t cfp_length;
5    aes_context cfp_ctx;
6    int cfp_disjunction;
7    cfp_length = Frama_C_unsigned_int_interval(16, 16672);
8    if (cfp_length % 16 == 0) {
9      Frama_C_make_unknown((char *)cfp_ctx.buf,256);
10     cfp_ctx.nr = 14;
11     cfp_ctx.rk = cfp_ctx.buf;
12     Frama_C_make_unknown((char *)cfp_iv,16);
13     cfp_input = (unsigned char *)malloc(cfp_length);
14     if (cfp_input != (unsigned char *)0) {
15       Frama_C_make_unknown((char *)cfp_input, cfp_length);
16       cfp_output = (unsigned char *)malloc(cfp_length);
17       if (cfp_output != 0) {
18         cfp_disjunction = Frama_C_int_interval(0,1);
19         if (cfp_disjunction) {
20           int cfp_mode;
21           cfp_mode = 1;
22           aes_crypt_cbc(&cfp_ctx,cfp_mode,cfp_length,cfp_iv,cfp_input,cfp_output);
23         }
24         else {
25           int cfp_mode;
26           cfp_mode = 0;
27           aes_crypt_cbc(&cfp_ctx,cfp_mode,cfp_length,cfp_iv,cfp_input,cfp_output);
28         }
29       }
30     }
31   }
32   return 0;
33 }
```

Fig. 2. Slightly simplified version of the code generated by CfP for the specification in Fig. 1. Compared to the actual version, only a few integer casts have been removed for reasons of brevity.

We now give an overview on how we treat context generation by means of the plug-in CfP of Frama-C. On the aes_crypt_cbc function contract, CfP provides the result shown in Fig. 2 (assuming that the size of unsigned long is 4 bytes[2]).

First note that every execution path ends by a call to the function aes_crypt_cbc. Up to these calls, the code initializes the context variables (prefixed by cfp) in order to satisfy the precondition of this function, while the different paths contribute to cover all the cases of the specification. The initialization code is generated from sets of constraints that are first inferred for every left-value involved in the precondition. While inferring these constraints from the precondition clauses, the implicit dependencies among left-values are made explicit and recorded in a dependency graph. This latter is finally visited to guide the code generation process in order to obtain correct C code.

Let us start detailing the generated code for both preconditions about length (Fig. 1, lines 12–13). First CfP declares a variable cfp_length of the same type as length (line 4). Then it initializes it by means of the Frama-C library function Frama_C_unsigned_int_interval (line 7). It takes two unsigned int arguments and returns a random value comprised between the

---

[2] This kind of system-dependent information is customizable within Frama-C.

two. This allows to fulfill the former requirement and to guarantee that Frama-C-based abstract interpreters will interpret this result with exactly the required interval. Also, it corresponds to the way that expert engineers would write a general context for such analyzers. Finally, the requirement `length % 16 == 0` is implemented by the conditional at line 8.

Lines 9–11 implement the preconditions about `ctx`, a pointer to an `aes_context`. Instead of allocating such a pointer, the generated code just declares a local variable `cfp_ctx` and passes its address to the function calls. This automatically satisfies the precondition on pointer validity. Line 9 initializes the 256 first bytes of the structure field `buf` by using the Frama-C library function `Frama_C_make_unknown`. Assuming that the size of `unsigned long` is 4 bytes, 256 bytes is the size of 64 values of type `unsigned long`. Again, an expert engineer would also use this library function. Lines 10 and 11 initialize the fields `ctx->nr` and `ctx->rk` by single assignments. Here CfP fulfills the equality requirement `ctx->rk == ctx->buf` with respect to `ctx->rk` instead of `ctx->buf` because the latter already refers to a memory buffer.

The requirements on function arguments `iv`, `input`, and `output` are implemented by lines 12–17. Let us just point out how CfP defines the respective variables: while `ctx_iv` is as an array of 16 `unsigned char`, `ctx_input` and `ctx_output` are just pointers to dynamically allocated memory buffers. Indeed, while CfP can infer the exact dimension of the former from the specification, the dimension of these latter depends on the value of `ctx_length`, which is determined only at runtime.

The last part of the generated code (lines 18–29) handles the requirement on `mode`, which is either 0 or 1. Although the generated conditional may seem excessive in the case of these particular values, it is nonetheless required in the general case (for instance, consider the formula `mode == 5 || mode == 7`).

3 Simplifying ACSL Preconditions into State Constraints

This section presents a way to systematically reduce a function precondition to a set of constraints on the function context (*i.e.* function parameters and global variables).

We first introduce an ACSL-inspired specification language on which we shall formalize our solution. Then, we define the notion of state constraint as a form of requirement over a C left-value, which in turn we generate as C code for initializing it. In order to simplify state constraints the most, we make use of symbolic ranges, originally introduced by Blume and Eigenmann [4] for compiler optimization. We finally provide a system of inference rules that formalizes such a simplification process.

3.1 Core Specification Language

In this work we shall consider the specification language in Fig. 3. It is almost a subset of ACSL [2] but for the predicate `defined`, which subsumes the ACSL predicates \initialized and \valid (see below).

Predicates	$P ::=$	$T \text{ cop } T$	term comparison $(\text{cop} \in \{\equiv, \leq, <, \geq, >\})$
		$\mid \text{ defined}(M)$	M is defined
		$\mid P \wedge P \mid P \vee P \mid \neg P$	logic formula
Terms	$T ::=$	z	integer constant $(z \in \mathbb{Z})$
		$\mid M$	memory value
		$\mid T \text{ bop } T$	arithmetic operation $(\text{bop} \in \{+, -, \times, /, \%\})$
Memory Values	$M ::=$	L	left-value
		$\mid M \texttt{ ++ } T$	single displacement
		$\mid M \texttt{ ++ } T \texttt{..} T$	displacement range
Left-Values	$L ::=$	x	C variable
		$\mid \star M$	dereference
Types	$\kappa ::=$	ι	integer
		$\mid \kappa\star$	pointer

Fig. 3. Predicates, terms, and types.

Predicates are logic formulæ defined on top of typed term comparisons and predicates defined. Terms are arithmetic expressions combining integer constants and memory values by means of the classic arithmetic operators. Memory values include left-values, which are C variables and pointer dereferences ($\star$), and memory displacements through the operator (++). In particular, $M \texttt{ ++ } T_1 \texttt{..} T_2$ defines the set of memory values $\{M \texttt{ ++ } T_1, \ldots, M \texttt{ ++ } T_2\}$ and may only appear as the outermost construct in a predicate defined. On integers, $\text{defined}(L)$ holds whenever L is an initialized left-value. On pointers, $\text{defined}(M)$ holds whenever M is a properly allocated and initialized memory region.

Term Typing. Terms of our language are typed. A left-value may take either an integer (ι) or a pointer ($\kappa\star$) type, while memory values are pointers. We omit the typing rules for terms, which are quite standard. Let us just specify that memory values of the form $M \texttt{ ++ } T$ have pointer type, as well as the recursive occurrence M, while T must have integer type. (Memory values $M \texttt{ ++ } T \texttt{..} T$ are typed as set of pointers [2].) Since we do not consider any kind of coercion construct, terms of pointer type cannot appear where integer terms are expected, that is, they cannot appear in arithmetic expressions. It also follows that term comparisons only relate terms of the same type.

Term Normal Forms. For the sake of concision and simplicity, the remainder of this work assumes some simplifications to take place on terms in order to consider term normal forms only. In particular, arithmetic expressions are maximally flattened and factorized (*e.g.* by means of constant folding techniques, *etc.*). We will conveniently write single displacements $M \texttt{ ++ } T$ as $M \texttt{ ++ } T \texttt{..} T$. We also assume memory values with displacement ranges to be either of the form $x \texttt{ ++ } T_1 \texttt{..} T_2$ or $\star L \texttt{ ++ } T_1 \texttt{..} T_2$. To this end, terms of the form $(L \texttt{ ++ } T_1 \texttt{..} T_2) \texttt{ ++ } T_3 \texttt{..} T_4$ simplify into $L \texttt{ ++ } (T_1 + T_3) \texttt{..} (T_2 + T_4)$. Finally, memory values $L \texttt{ ++ } 0 \texttt{..} 0$ normalize to L.

Disjunctive Normal Forms. A precondition is a conjunction of predicate clauses, each one given by an ACSL `requires` (*cf.* example in Fig. 1). As a preliminary step, we shall rewrite this conjunctive clause into its disjunctive normal form $\bigvee_i \bigwedge_j P_{ij}$, where each P_{ij} is a *predicate literal* (or simply *literal*), that is, a predicate without nested logic formulæ. A *negative literal* is either of the form $\neg\text{defined}(M)$ or $\neg(M_1 \equiv M_2)$, with M_1, M_2 pointers, as every other negative literal in the input predicates is translated into a positive literal by applying standard arithmetic and logical laws. A non-negative literal is called a *positive literal.* Most of the rest of this section focuses on positive literals: negative literals and conjunctive clauses are handled in the very end, while disjunctive clauses will be considered when discussing code generation in Sect. 4.

3.2   State Constraints

We are interested in simplifying a predicate literal into a set of constraints over C left-values, called *state constraints.* These are meant to indicate the minimal requirements that the resulting C function context must implement for satisfying the function precondition. In Sect. 4, they will be, in turn, converted into C code.

We intuitively consider a state constraint to represent the domain of definition of a C left-value of the resulting function context state. Since such domains might not be determined in terms of integer constants only, we shall found their definition on the notion of symbolic ranges [4]. As we want to simplify state constraints the most, we define them in terms of the symbolic range algebra proposed by Nazaré et al. [15]. Our definitions are nonetheless significantly different, even though inspired from their work.

Symbolic Expressions. A *symbolic expression* E is defined by the following grammar, where $z \in \mathbb{Z}$, bop $\in \{+, -, \times, /, \%\}$, and max and min are, respectively, the largest and the smallest expression operators. We denote $\mathbb{E}$ the set of symbolic expressions.

$$E ::= z \mid x \mid \star E \mid E \text{ bop } E \mid \max(E, E) \mid \min(E, E).$$

In the rest of this section, we assume a mapping from memory values to their respective symbolic expression, and let the context discriminate the former from the latter.

In Sect. 3.3 we shall simplify symbolic expressions. For this, we need a domain structure. Let us denote $\mathbb{E}_\infty = \mathbb{E} \cup \{-\infty; +\infty\}$ and $\mathbb{Z}_\infty = \mathbb{Z} \cup \{-\infty; +\infty\}$. We define a *valuation of a symbolic expression* E every map $\mathcal{V}(E)$, from $\mathbb{E}_\infty$ to $\mathbb{Z}_\infty$, obtained by substituting every C variable in E with a distinct integer, the symbol $\star$ with a natural number strictly greater than 1 as a multiplicative coefficient, and interpreting the operators $\{\text{bop}, \min, \max\}$ as their respective functions over $\mathbb{Z}_\infty \times \mathbb{Z}_\infty$. If we denote $\leq_\infty$ the standard ordering relation on $\mathbb{Z}_\infty$, then the preorder $\preccurlyeq$ on $\mathbb{E}_\infty$ is defined as follows:

$$E_1 \preccurlyeq E_2 \iff \forall \mathcal{V}, \mathcal{V}(E_1) \leq_\infty \mathcal{V}(E_2).$$

The partial order $\preceq$ over $\mathbb{E}_\infty$ is therefore the one induced from $\preccurlyeq$ by merging in the same equivalence class elements x and y of $\mathbb{E}_\infty$ such that $x \preccurlyeq y$ and $y \preccurlyeq x$. As an example, the elements 0 and $\min(0,0)$ are equivalent.

Lattice of Symbolic Expression Ranges. A *symbolic range* R is a pair of symbolic expressions E_1 and E_2, denoted $[E_1, E_2]$. Otherwise said, a symbolic range is an interval with no guarantee that $E_1 \preceq E_2$. We denote $\mathbb{R}$ the set of symbolic ranges extended with the empty range $\emptyset$ and $\sqsubseteq$ its partial ordering which is the usual partial order over (possibly empty) ranges. Any symbolic range $[E_1, E_2]$ such that $E_2 \prec E_1$ is therefore equivalent to $\emptyset$. Consequently $(\mathbb{R}, \sqsubseteq)$ is a domain. Its infimum is $\emptyset$ while its supremum is $[-\infty, +\infty]$. We denote $\sqcup$ and $\sqcap$ its join and meet operators, respectively. It is worth noting that, given $(E_i)_{1 \le i \le 4}$ four symbolic expressions, the following equations hold:

$$[E_1, E_2] \sqcup [E_3, E_4] = [\min(E_1, E_3), \max(E_2, E_4)]$$
$$[E_1, E_2] \sqcap [E_3, E_4] = [\max(E_1, E_3), \min(E_2, E_4)].$$

In words, $\min$ and $\max$ are compliant with our ordering relations. In Sect. 3.3, when simplifying literals, they will be introduced as soon as incomparable formulæ will be associated to the same left-value, resulting into an unsimplifiable constraint. Also, it is worth noting that $\sqcup$ and $\sqcap$ are, in general, not statically computable operators. To solve this practical issue, when these are not computable on some symbolic expressions, CfP relies on the above equations in order to delay their evaluations at runtime. Eventually, the code generator will convert them into conditionals.

State Constraints as Symbolic Ranges with Runtime Checks. Symbolic ranges capture most minimal requirements over the C left-values of a function precondition: for integer typed left-values, a symbolic range represents the integer variation domain, while for pointer typed left-values, it represents a region of valid offsets. They are commonly used in abstract interpreters for range [8,14] and region analysis [15,19], respectively.

However, some predicate literals cannot be simplified into symbolic ranges, requiring their encoding as *runtime checks*, that is, to be verified at runtime by means of conditionals. We denote $\mathrm{RTC}(T_1 \text{ cop } T_2)$ a runtime check between two terms T_1 and T_2. We then call *state constraint* any pair $C = R \oplus X$ given by a symbolic range R and a set X of runtime checks. We denote $\pi_1(C)$ (resp. $\pi_2(C)$) the first (resp. the second) projection of C, that is, R (resp. X).

3.3   Inferring State Constraints

We now formalize our solution for simplifying a positive literal into a set of state constraints as a system of inference rules. Negative literals, as well as conjunctive clauses, are handled separately at the end of the section.

Simplification Judgments. Simplification rules are given over judgments of the form

$$\Sigma \vdash P \Rightarrow \Sigma',$$

where P is a predicate literal, and Σ, Σ' are maps from left-values to state constraints. Each judgment associates a set of state constraints Σ and a literal P with the result of simplifying P with respect to the left-values appearing in it, that is, an updated map Σ' equal to Σ but for the state constraints on these latter. Figures 4 shows the formalization of the main literal simplifications. This system does not assume the consistency of the precondition: if this is inconsistent, no rule applies and the simplification process fails.

Predicates defined. Figure 4a provides the simplification rules for literal defined. Rules VARIABLE and DEREFERENCE enforce the initialization of a left-value L in terms of the symbolic range $neutral\_ival(\kappa)$. This latter is respectively defined as $\emptyset$, for κ a pointer type, and $[-\infty, +\infty]$, for κ integer type. These are quite common initial approximations when inferring variation domains of either memory or integer values.

Rules RANGE-1 and RANGE-2 enforce the validity of a memory region determined by the displacement range $L ++ (T_1 .. T_2)$. The first premise of these rules established whether L is already enforced in Σ to be an alias of a memory value M, as indicated by the singleton range $[M; M]$. If not, rule RANGE-1 first enforces the initialization of L and the soundness of the displacement bound determined by T_1 and T_2, and then it updates the region of valid offsets pointed to by L to include the range $[0; T_2]$. In practice, predicates $0 \leq T_1 \leq T_2$ are added only if not statically provable. Moreover, note that we do not consider T_1 as the lower bound of the symbolic range, because C memory regions must start at index 0. Rule RANGE-2 handles the case of L alias of M in Σ by enforcing the validity of the memory region determined by M to take into account the displacement range $(T_1 .. T_2)$. In particular, since single displacements only may appear in memory equality predicates (*cf.* rule MEMORY-EQ), M is of the form $L' ++ (T_3 .. T_3)$, and the validity of the alias L within the range $(T_1 .. T_2)$ is obtained by requiring the validity of the displacement range $L' ++ (\min(T_1, T_3) .. \max(T_2, T_3))$.

Rule IDEMPOTENCE is provided only to allow the inference process to progress.

Term Comparison Predicates. Rules in Fig. 4b formalize the simplification of integer term comparison and memory equality predicates. The first two are actually rule schema, as CMP-1 and CMP-2 describe term comparison simplifications over the integer comparison operators $\{\equiv, \leq, \geq\}$. (Strict operators are treated in terms of non-strict ones.) Let us detail rule CMP-1 with respect to a generic operator cop. The rule applies whenever T_1 cop T_2 can be rewritten by means of classic integer arithmetic transformations as L cop T_3, that is, as a left-value in relation cop with an integer term T_3. If so, CMP-1 reduces the symbolic range of L with respect to the one given by $ival(\text{cop}, T_3)$. This latter function takes a comparison operator cop and an integer term T as arguments, and returns as

IDEMPOTENCE
$$\frac{L \in \Sigma}{\Sigma \vdash \mathtt{defined}(L) \Rightarrow \Sigma}$$

VARIABLE
$$\frac{x \notin \Sigma \qquad type(x) = \kappa \qquad \Sigma' = \Sigma \cup \{x \mapsto neutral\_ival(\kappa)\}}{\Sigma \vdash \mathtt{defined}(x) \Rightarrow \Sigma'}$$

DEREFERENCE
$$\frac{\star M \notin \Sigma \qquad \Sigma \vdash \mathtt{defined}(M) \Rightarrow \Sigma' \qquad type(\star M) = \kappa \qquad \Sigma'' = \Sigma' \cup \{\star M \mapsto neutral\_ival(\kappa)\}}{\Sigma \vdash \mathtt{defined}(\star M) \Rightarrow \Sigma''}$$

RANGE-1
$$\frac{\pi_1(\Sigma(L)) \neq [M; M] \qquad \Sigma \vdash \mathtt{defined}(L) \wedge 0 \leq T_1 \leq T_2 \Rightarrow \Sigma' \qquad \Sigma'' = \Sigma' \left[L \leftarrow \pi_1(\Sigma'(L)) \sqcup [0; T_2]\right]}{\Sigma \vdash \mathtt{defined}(L \mathbin{+\!+} (T_1 \mathbin{.\,.} T_2)) \Rightarrow \Sigma''}$$

RANGE-2
$$\frac{\pi_1(\Sigma(L)) = [M; M] \qquad base(M) = L' \qquad offset(M) = T_3 \qquad \Sigma \vdash \mathtt{defined}(L' \mathbin{+\!+} (\min(T_1, T_3) \mathbin{.\,.} \max(T_2, T_3))) \Rightarrow \Sigma'}{\Sigma \vdash \mathtt{defined}(L \mathbin{+\!+} (T_1 \mathbin{.\,.} T_2)) \Rightarrow \Sigma'}$$

(a)-Simplification of literal `defined`.

CMP-1
$$\frac{L \in \{T_1, T_2\} \qquad T_1 \mathop{cop} T_2 \rightsquigarrow L \mathop{cop} T_3 \qquad \Sigma \vdash \mathtt{defined}(L) \wedge \bigwedge_{L' \in T_3} \mathtt{defined}(L') \Rightarrow \Sigma' \qquad \Sigma'' = \Sigma' \left[L \leftarrow \pi_1(\Sigma'(L)) \sqcap ival(\mathop{cop}, T_3)\right]}{\Sigma \vdash T_1 \mathop{cop} T_2 \Rightarrow \Sigma''}$$

CMP-2
$$\frac{\Sigma \vdash \bigwedge_{L \in \{T_1, T_2\}} \mathtt{defined}(L) \Rightarrow \Sigma' \qquad L \in \{T_1, T_2\} \qquad \Sigma'' = \Sigma' \left[L \leftarrow \pi_2(\Sigma'(L)) \cup RTC(T_1 \mathop{cop} T_2)\right]}{\Sigma \vdash T_1 \mathop{cop} T_2 \Rightarrow \Sigma''}$$

MEMORY-EQ
$$\frac{i, j \in \{1, 2\} \wedge i \neq j \qquad base(M_{\{i,j\}}) = L_{\{i,j\}} \qquad offset(M_{\{i,j\}}) = T_{\{i,j\}} \qquad T_3 = T_j + (-T_i) \qquad M' = L_j \mathbin{+\!+} (T_3 \mathbin{.\,.} T_3) \qquad \Sigma \vdash \mathtt{defined}(L_i) \wedge \mathtt{defined}(M') \Rightarrow \Sigma' \qquad \pi_1(\Sigma'(L_i)) \sqsubseteq \pi_1(\Sigma'(L_j)) \qquad \Sigma'' = \Sigma' \left[L_i \leftarrow [M'; M']\right]}{\Sigma \vdash M_1 \equiv M_2 \Rightarrow \Sigma''}$$

(b) Simplification of term comparison and memory equality literals.

NOT-DEFINED
$$\frac{M \notin \Sigma}{\Sigma \vdash \neg \mathtt{defined}(M) \Rightarrow \Sigma}$$

MEMORY-NEQ
$$\frac{\Sigma \vdash \mathtt{defined}(M_1) \wedge \mathtt{defined}(M_2) \Rightarrow \Sigma' \qquad i, j \in \{1, 2\} \wedge i \neq j \qquad base(M_{\{i,j\}}) = L_{\{i,j\}} \qquad [L_i; L_i] \not\sqsubseteq \pi_1(\Sigma'(L_j)) \qquad [L_j; L_j] \not\sqsubseteq \pi_1(\Sigma'(L_i))}{\Sigma \vdash M_1 \not\equiv M_2 \Rightarrow \Sigma'}$$

(c) Simplification of negative literals.

Fig. 4. Simplification of literals into state constraints.

result the symbolic range $[T; T]$ when $\mathtt{cop}$ is $\equiv$, $[-\infty; T]$ (resp. $[T; +\infty]$) when $\mathtt{cop}$ is $\leq$ (resp. $\geq$). Since both L and T_3 are integer typed terms, there is no aliasing issue here. Rule CMP-2 can always be applied, although we normally consider it when CMP-1 cannot. In that case, rule CMP-2 conservatively enforces the validity of the term comparison by means of a runtime check.

Aliasing. Rule MEMORY-EQ handles aliasing between two pointers with single displacement M_1 and M_2. Assuming both of the form $L_{\{i,j\}}$ ++ $T_{\{i,j\}}$, with distinct $i, j \in \{1, 2\}$, a pointer M' is first defined as L_j with single displacement T_3, this latter determined by summing the offsets $-T_i$ and T_j together. Such a pointer is then enforced to be defined, and in the case that the actual region pointed by L_j is established to be larger then the one pointed by L_i, then L_i is considered an alias of M'. Although rather conservative, due to the fact that $\sqsubseteq$ is not statically computable in general, the second to last premise is important for ensuring soundness.

Negative Literals. Figure 4c shows the rules for negative literals. These rules do not simplify literals into state constraints, but rather ensure precondition consistency. For instance, $\neg\mathtt{defined}(x) \wedge x == 0$ is inconsistent as x should be defined with value 0 and undefined at the same time. In such a case, the system must prevent code generation.

Rule NOT-DEFINED just checks that the memory value M does not appear in the map Σ, which suffices to ensure that M is not yet defined.

Rule MEMORY-NEQ applies under the hypothesis that both pointers M_1 and M_2 determine different memory regions. In particular, the two are not aliases whenever each base address of one pointer does not overlap with the memory region of the other.

Conjunctive Clauses. $\bigwedge_i P_i$, on either positive or negative literals P_i, are handled sequentially through the following AND rule. Given the definition of MEMORY-NEQ and NOT-DEFINED, it assumes that negative literals are treated only after the positive ones, by exhaustively applying rule MEMORY-NEQ first, and rule NOT-DEFINED afterwards.

$$
\text{AND} \quad \frac{\Sigma_0 \vdash P_1 \Rightarrow \Sigma_1 \quad \Sigma_1 \vdash P_2 \Rightarrow \Sigma_2 \quad \cdots \quad \Sigma_{n-1} \vdash P_n \Rightarrow \Sigma_n}{\Sigma_0 \vdash \bigwedge_i P_i \Rightarrow \Sigma_n}
$$

Dependency Graph on Memory Values. On a conjunctive clause, the system of inference rules in Fig. 4 not only generates a map Σ, but it also computes a dependency graph $\mathcal{G}$ on memory values. (Considering only the formalization of this section, the memory values of the graph are actually left-values only. However, when considering separately the ACSL predicates \initialized and \valid instead of defined, this is not true anymore.) This graph is necessary for ensuring, first, the soundness of the rule system with respect to mutual dependency on left-values in Σ, and, consequently, for the correct ordering of left-value initializations when generating C code (*cf.* Sect. 4).

Generally speaking, each time a rule that needs inference is used in a state constraint derivation for some left-value L (*e.g.* DEREFERENCE, RANGE-1, CMP-1, *etc.*), edges from L to every other left-value involved in some premise are added to the dependency graph $\mathcal{G}$. Such derivation fails as soon as this latter operation makes the graph $\mathcal{G}$ cyclic.

Example. When applying the inference system on our example in Fig. 1, the final map associates the integer length to $[16, 16672] \oplus \{\mathrm{RTC}(\mathrm{length}\%16 \equiv 0)\}$ and the array input to $[0, \mathrm{length} - 1] \oplus \emptyset$, along with the dependency graph in Fig. 5.

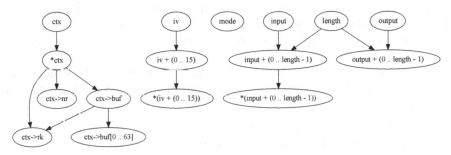

Fig. 5. Dependency graph for the `aes_crypt_cbc` preconditions generated by CfP.

The system of inference rules in Fig. 4 is sound: given a conjunctive clause $\mathcal{C}$, the simplification procedure on $\mathcal{C}$ always terminates, either with Σ or it fails. In the former case, for each left-value L in $\mathcal{C}$, state constraints in Σ satisfy respective literals in $\mathcal{C}$ (that we denote as $\Sigma \models \mathcal{C}$, its formal definition being omitted here).

Theorem 1. *For all conjunctive clause $\mathcal{C}$, either $\emptyset \vdash \mathcal{C} \Rightarrow \Sigma$ and $\Sigma \models \mathcal{C}$, or it fails.*

4   Generating C Code from State Constraints

This section presents the general scheme for implementing preconditions, through state constraints, in a C language enriched with one primitive function for handling ranges. In practice, such primitive is meant to be analyzer-specific so as to characterize state constraints as precisely as possible. As an example, we report on the case of our tool CfP. However, for the sake of conciseness, we do neither detail nor formalize the code generation scheme. We nevertheless believe that the provided explanation should be enough to both understand and implement such a system in a similar setting.

Generating Code from a Conjunctive Clause. Consider a conjunctive clause $\mathcal{C}$ and the pair $(\Sigma, \mathcal{G})$, respectively given by the map of state constraints and the dependency graph of $\mathcal{C}$, inferred by the system of rules in Fig. 4. We shall show the general case of disjunctive normal forms $\bigvee_{i=1}^{n} \mathcal{C}_i$ later on.

To generate semantically correct C code, we topologically iterate over the left-values of $\mathcal{G}$ so as to follow the dependency ordering. For every visited left-value L, we consider its associated state constraint $C = R \oplus X$ in Σ. Then, the symbolic range R is handled by generating statements that initialize L. For most constructs, these statements are actually a single assignment, although a loop over an assignment may be sometimes needed (*e.g.* when initializing a range of array cells). In particular, initializations of left-values L to symbolic ranges $[T_1, T_2]$ are implemented by means of the primitive function $\texttt{make\_range}(\kappa, \overline{T_1}, \overline{T_2})$, where κ is integer or pointer type, and $\overline{T_1}$ (resp. $\overline{T_2}$) are the C translation of T_1 (resp.q T_2). In practice, this function must be provided by the analyzer for which the context is generated, so that, when executed symbolically, the analyzer's abstract state will associate abstract values $[T_1, T_2]$ to respective left-values L. Finally, conditionals are generated to initialize left-values with symbolic expressions involving $\texttt{min}$ and $\texttt{max}$.

Once L has been initialized, the rest of the code is guarded by conditionals generated from runtime checks in X. To resume, the generation scheme for L is the following:

```
1    /* initialization of L from R through assignments */
2    if (/* runtime checks from X */) {
3        /* code for initializing the next left-values */ ...; } }
```

After the initialization of the last left-value, the function under consideration (in our running example, the function $\texttt{aes\_crypt\_cbc}$) is called with the required arguments.

Handling Disjunctions. We rewrite preconditions into disjunctive normal form $\bigvee_{i=1}^{n} \mathcal{C}_i$ as a preliminary step. Then we process each disjunct $\mathcal{C}_i$ independently by applying the inference system in Fig. 4 and the code generation scheme previously described.

We now describe the code generation scheme of such a precondition $\bigvee_{i=1}^{n} \mathcal{C}_i$ given the code fragments for each and every of its disjunct $\mathcal{C}_i$. If $n = 1$, then the code fragment of $\mathcal{C}_1$ is directly generated. Otherwise, an additional variable $\texttt{cfp\_disjunction}$ is generated and initialized to the interval $[1, n]$. Then, a $\texttt{switch}$ construct (or a conditional if $n = 2$) is generated, where each case contains the fragment B_i respective to $\mathcal{C}_i$. To resume, the context is generated as a function including the following code pattern:

```
1    cfp_disjunction = make_range(ι, 1, n);
2    switch (cfp_disjunction) {
3        case 1: { B_1; break; }
4        case 2: { B_2; break; }
5        ...
6        case n: { B_n; break; }
7    }
```

Primitives in CfP. Our tool CfP follows the generation scheme just described. It implements $\texttt{make\_range}$ in terms of the Frama-C built-ins

Frama_C_τ_interval, with τ a C integral type, and Frama_C_make_unknown to handle symbolic ranges for integers and pointers, respectively. These built-ins are properly supported by the two abstract interpretation-based value analysis tools EVA [3] and TIS-Analyzer [9].

5 Implementation and Evaluation

We have implemented our context generation mechanism as a Frama-C plug-in, called CfP for *Context from Preconditions*, written in approximately 3500 lines of OCaml. (Although Frama-C is open source, CfP is not, due to current contractual obligations.) CfP has been successfully used by the company TrustInSoft for its verification kit [22] of the mbed-TLS library, an open source implementation of the SSL/TLS protocol. In this latter use case, CfP is used, among others, to generate contexts for customizing the initialization of structure md5_context needed by functions md5_starts, md5_update and md5_process. This structure is defined as follows.

```
1  typedef struct {
2      unsigned long total[2];      /*!< number of bytes processed  */
3      unsigned long state[4];      /*!< intermediate digest state  */
4      unsigned char buffer[64];    /*!< data block being processed */
5      unsigned char ipad[64];      /*!< HMAC: inner padding        */
6      unsigned char opad[64];      /*!< HMAC: outer padding        */
7  } md5_context;
```

We now evaluate our approach, and in particular CfP, in terms of some quite natural properties, that is, *usefulness*, *efficiency*, and *quality* of the generated contexts.

This work provides a first formal answer to a practical and recurring problem when analyzing single functions. Indeed, the ACSL subset considered is expressive enough for most real-world C programs. Most importantly, CfP enables any tool to support a compelling fragment of ACSL at the minor expense of implementing two Frama-C built-ins, particularly so if compared to the implementation of a native support (if ever possible). Finally, CfP has proved useful in an operational industrial setting in revealing some mistakes in contexts previously written by hand by expert verification engineers. Although we cannot disclose precise data about these latter, CfP revealed, most notably, overlooked cases in disjunctions and led to fix incomplete specifications.

CfP is able to efficiently handle rather complex ACSL preconditions: the generation of real-world contexts (*e.g.* the one of Fig. 2) is usually instantaneous. Although the disjunctive normal form can be exponentially larger than the original precondition formula, such transformation is used in practice [13,18] and leads to better code in terms of readability and tractability by the verification tools. This approach is further justified by the fact that, in practice, just a small number of disjuncts are typically used in manually-written ACSL specifications. Concretely, CfP and its use in combination with TIS-Analyzer or EVA have never suffered from the state-explosion problem or any other unefficiency issue in practice.

Our approach allows to generate contexts which are reasonably readable and follows code patterns that experts of the Frama-C framework use to manually write. In particular, when handling disjunctions, CfP factorizes the generated code for a particular left-value as soon as the rule system infers the very same solution in each conjunctive clause. For instance, in our running example, only the initialization of the variable mode depends on the disjunction mode == 0 || mode == 1. Hence all the other left-values are initialized before considering cfp_disjunction (*cf.* Fig. 2).

We conclude by briefly discussing some current limitations. Our ACSL fragment considers quantifier free predicate formulæ, and no coercion constructs are allowed. Support for casts among integer left-values should be easy to add, whereas treating memory addresses as integers is notoriously difficult. We leave these for future work.

6   Related Work

Similarly to our approach, program synthesis [13, 17, 21] automatically provides program fragments from formal specifications. However, the two approaches have different purposes. Once executed either symbolically or concretely, a synthesized program provides *one* computational state that satisfies the specification, while a context must characterize *all* such states. In particular, not only every state must satisfy the specification but, conversely, this set of states must contain every such possible one.

Some code generators also have to deal with variable dependencies, such as compilers for Lustre-like languages [7]. However, the aims are at odds since our goal is *not* to generate code from a higher language to a lower one to concretely execute it, but to characterize all states represented by a formal specification.

In software testing, contexts are useful for concentrating the testing effort on particular inputs. Most test input generation tools, like CUTE [20] and PathCrawler [5, 10], allow to express contexts as functions which, however, the user must manually write. Some others, like Pex [1], directly compile formal preconditions for runtime checking.

The tool STADY [16] shares some elements of our approach. It instruments C functions with additional code for ensuring pre- and postconditions compliance, allowing monitoring and test generation. However, the tool performs a simple ACSL-to-C translation, it does neither take into account dependencies among C left-values, nor it inferences their domain of definition.

7   Conclusion

This paper has presented a novel technique to automatically generate an analysis context from a formal precondition of a C function. The core of the system has been formalized, while we provide enough details about code generation to allow similar systems to be implemented. Future work includes the formalization of code generation as well as statements and proofs of the fundamental properties of the system as a whole. It also includes evaluating the presented system for different techniques such as symbolic execution or testing tools. A running example from the real world has also illustrated our presentation. The whole system is implemented in the Frama-C plug-in CfP. It generates code as close as possible to human-written code. It is used in an operational industrial setting and already revealed some mistakes in contexts previously written by hand by expert verification engineers.

Acknowledgments. Part of the research work leading to these results has received funding for the S3P project from French DGE and BPIFrance. The authors thank TrustInSoft for the support and, in particular, Pascal Cuoq, Benjamin Monate and Anne Pacalet for providing the initial specification, test cases and insightful comments. Thanks to the anonymous reviewers for many useful suggestions and advice.

A   Response to Reviewer Comments

A.1   Reviewer 1

- The reviewer points out that one important issue has not been addressed in the paper: how our code generation might be tailored for.
  The reviewer is right. While we argue in the introduction that our system may be used for different analysis techniques, this is not demonstrated in the paper since CfP has only been evaluated with 2 different abstract interpreters for the time being. We are however confident about the possible tailoring because the theoretical construction, which is the core of our work, remains the same. Also, adapting the code generator to other settings would not require many efforts, even if we leave it as future work. We have clarified our stance by adding in the Conclusion the following sentence:
  "It [Future work] also includes evaluating the presented system for different techniques such as symbolic execution or testing tools."
- The reviewer assumes we rely implicitly on some formal semantics, and thinks that it would be better to specify them in the paper.
  Indeed, Theorem 1 relies on a formal definition of $\Sigma \models \mathcal{C}$, while we only provide its intuition in the paper. The formal definition has been omitted because we have not enough room to add it and because it does not represent the core of our system. It should be clearer now because we have added ", its formal definition being omitted here" after introducing symbol $\models$.
- The reviewer thinks that work for code generation from executable specification languages should be mentioned as well (notably, Lustre and logic synthesis in hardware).
  We have added a brief comparison with Lustre, but none for logic synthesis in hardware. Indeed our paper already referred to program synthesis, which is closer to our work that logic synthesis in hardware, while still quite different.

A.2   Reviewer 2

- The only reviewer's important comment is about a lack of precision in our sentence "For a 64-bit architecture, 256 bytes is the size of 64 values of type unsigned long.". The reviewer is right. We have rewritten the sentence as follows: "Assuming that the size of unsigned long is 4 bytes, 256 bytes is the size of 64 values of type unsigned long."
  Previously, in the same section, we have also rewritten "(assuming a 64-bit architecture)" by "(assuming that the size of unsigned long is 4 bytes)" and we have added a footnote indicating that this kind of system-dependent information is customizable within Frama-C.
- All the reviewer's minor comments and typos have been addressed.

A.3   Reviewer 3

- The only reviewer's concern is that the paper gives no evidence of generating code from specifications of other functions besides that from the initial motivating example. (S)he has consequently related questions.
  We have extended the first paragraph of Sect. 5 (Implementation and Evaluation) as follows:
  "In this latter use case, CfP is used, among others, to generate contexts for customizing the initialization of structure md5_context needed by functions md5_starts, md5_update and md5_process. This structure is defined as follows.
  <code example added>"
  Also, we have extended the paragraph explaining why DNF explosion is not an issue in practice as follow: "Concretely, CfP and its use in combination with TIS-Analyzer or EVA have never suffered from the state-explosion problem or any other unefficiency issue in practice."

A.4   Other Improvements

- Several minor changes (fixing typos, or using better/more standard math symbols) have been made.

References

1. Barnett, M., Fähndrich, M., de Halleux, P., Logozzo, F., Tillmann, N.: Exploiting the synergy between automated-test-generation and programming-by-contract. In: ICSE 2009 (2009)
2. Baudin, P., Filliâtre, J.-C., Marché, C., Monate, B., Moy, Y., Prevosto, V.: ACSL: ANSI/ISO C Specification Language. http://frama-c.com/acsl.html
3. Blazy, S., Bühler, D., Yakobowski, B.: Structuring abstract interpreters through state and value abstractions. In: Bouajjani, A., Monniaux, D. (eds.) VMCAI 2017. LNCS, vol. 10145, pp. 112–130. Springer, Cham (2017). https://doi.org/10.1007/978-3-319-52234-0_7

4. Blume, W., Eigenmann, R.: Symbolic range propagation. In: IPPS 1995 (1995)
5. Botella, B., Delahaye, M., Ha, S.H.T., Kosmatov, N., Mouy, P., Roger, M., Williams, N.: Automating structural testing of C programs: experience with PathCrawler. In: AST 2009 (2009)
6. Canet, G., Cuoq, P., Monate, B.: A value analysis for C programs. In: SCAM 2009 (2009)
7. Caspi, P., Pilaud, D., Halbwachs, N., Plaice, J.A.: LUSTRE: a declarative language for real-time programming. In: POPL 1987 (1987)
8. Cousot, P., Cousot, R.: Abstract interpretation: a unified lattice model for static analysis of programs by construction or approximation of fixpoints. In: POPL 1977 (1977)
9. Cuoq, P., Rieu-Helft, R.: Result graphs for an abstract interpretation-based static analyzer. In: JFLA 2017 (2017)
10. Delahaye, M., Kosmatov, N.: A late treatment of C precondition in dynamic symbolic execution. In: CSTVA 2013 (2013)
11. ISO. The ANSI C standard (C99). Technical report WG14 N1124, ISO/IEC (1999). http://www.open-std.org/JTC1/SC22/WG14/www/docs/n1124.pdf
12. Kirchner, F., Kosmatov, N., Prevosto, V., Signoles, J., Yakobowski, B.: Frama-C: a software analysis perspective. Form. Asp. Comput. 27(3), 573–609 (2015)
13. Kuncak, V., Mayer, M., Piskac, R., Suter, P.: Complete functional synthesis. In: PLDI 2010 (2010)
14. Logozzo, F., Fähndrich, M.: Pentagons: a weakly relational abstract domain for the efficient validation of array accesses. In: SAC 2008 (2008)
15. Nazaré, H., Maffra, I., Santos, W., Barbosa, L., Gonnord, L., Quintão Pereira, F.M.: Validation of memory accesses through symbolic analyses. SIGPLAN Not. 49(10), 791–809 (2014)
16. Petiot, G., Botella, B., Julliand, J., Kosmatov, N., Signoles, J.: Instrumentation of annotated C programs for test generation. In: SCAM 2014 (2014)
17. Polikarpova, N., Kuraj, I., Solar-Lezama, A.: Program synthesis from polymorphic refinement types. In: PLDI 2016 (2016)
18. Pugh, W.: A practical algorithm for exact array dependence analysis. Commun. ACM 35(8), 102–114 (1992)
19. Rugina, R., Rinard, M.: Symbolic bounds analysis of pointers, array indices, and accessed memory regions. In: PLDI 2000 (2000)
20. Sen, K., Marinov, D., Agha, G.: CUTE: a concolic unit testing engine for C. In: FSE'13 (2005)
21. Solar-Lezama, A., Arnold, G., Tancau, L., Bodik, R., Saraswat, V., Seshia, S.: Sketching stencils. In: PLDI 2007 (2007)
22. TrustInSoft. PolarSSL 1.1.8 verification kit, v1.0. Technical report. http://trust-in-soft.com/polarSSL_demo.pdf

Liveness-Driven Random Program Generation

Gergö Barany[(✉)]

Inria, Paris, France
gergo.barany@inria.fr

Abstract. Randomly generated programs are popular for testing compilers and program analysis tools, with hundreds of bugs in real-world C compilers found by random testing. However, existing random program generators may generate large amounts of dead code (computations whose result is never used). This leaves relatively little code to exercise a target compiler's more complex optimizations.

To address this shortcoming, we introduce liveness-driven random program generation. In this approach the random program is constructed bottom-up, guided by a simultaneous structural data-flow analysis to ensure that the generator never generates dead code.

The algorithm is implemented as a plugin for the Frama-C framework. We evaluate it in comparison to Csmith, the standard random C program generator. Our tool generates programs that compile to more machine code with a more complex instruction mix.

Keywords: Code generation · Random testing · Data-flow analysis
Program optimization

1 Motivation

Optimizing compilers for real-world programming languages are complex pieces of software. Compiler bugs may manifest in several ways: As compiler crashes, missed optimizations, or as silent miscompilations. The third category is especially serious as it may introduce bugs in correct programs. Such wrong-code bugs may invalidate all correctness guarantees provided by source-level verification of safety-critical (and other) software systems.

Two main avenues of work address these problems: compiler verification and compiler testing. Compiler verification has seen much research [4], with Comp-Cert as a prominent example [9]. However, such compilers have not entered the mainstream yet: Compiler verification is difficult and time-consuming, and verified compilers therefore perform fewer optimizations and target fewer CPU architectures than others.

A different approach is to test compilers in a way that instills confidence. Standard compiler test suites exist for exercising C compilers, in particular for testing their conformance to various details of the standard [15,16]. In addition,

© Springer International Publishing AG, part of Springer Nature 2018
F. Fioravanti and J. P. Gallagher (Eds.): LOPSTR 2017, LNCS 10855, pp. 112–127, 2018.
https://doi.org/10.1007/978-3-319-94460-9_7

randomized differential testing has gained prominence in recent years. Compiling many random programs with various compilers and comparing the behaviors of the generated binaries can uncover input programs that cause compiler crashes or miscompilations. The best-known example of this approach is the work of Yang et al. on Csmith [20], a generator of random C programs. Csmith generates programs that are fully self-contained (including all their inputs in initialized global variables) and conform to the C standard by construction. If two compilers produce code that behaves differently for a Csmith-generated program, one of the compilers must contain a miscompilation bug. Testing of C compilers with Csmith has uncovered hundreds of bugs in total, including crashes and miscompilations in every compiler under test. This included bugs in (unverified parts of) the CompCert verified C compiler [20].

This article describes a random generator of C programs developed for a project on finding missed optimizations in C compilers. Inspired by the successes of Csmith, in this project we generate random C programs, compile them using various compilers, then use custom tooling to search for possible optimizations in the resulting binaries. (The details are described in a separate paper [2].)

Starting with Csmith as our program generator, we found early on that it was not an optimal fit for our intended use case: Despite generating realistic-looking programs with complex arithmetic expressions, accesses to global and local variables including through pointers, structures, and arrays, as well as nested loops and branches, it produces large amounts of *dead code* whose results are never used. (See our experiments in Sect. 4.) Dead code elimination, a standard part of every optimizing compiler, can thus remove large parts of the code generated by Csmith, leaving very little relevant code for the remaining more interesting optimizations. Csmith often generate functions of several hundred lines of code that are compiled to ten machine instructions, representing only a small fraction of the computations present on the source code level.

In this paper we address this problem with our new *liveness-driven* random generator `ldrgen`. Our tool uses liveness analysis during program generation to avoid generating dead code. In the following sections we describe liveness-driven program generation; the implementation of our tool as a Frama-C plugin; and its experimental evaluation, showing that `ldrgen` generates programs that compile to a larger amount of code and a more complex instruction mix than programs generated by Csmith.

2   Fully Live Programs

In this section we briefly recall the basics of liveness analysis and then present our novel formulation as a set of structural inference rules.

2.1   Principles of Liveness Analysis

A variable is called *live* at a program point if the value it holds at that point may be read in the future, without an intervening redefinition; otherwise, it is called *dead*. For example, in a code snippet like `x = a + b; x = 0; return x;`, the variable `x` is dead after the first assignment but live after the second one (because it is used in the `return` statement). We can extend the notion of liveness from variables to the assignment statements defining them: An assignment $v = e$ is live iff the variable v is live just after this statement. The first assignment to `x` above is dead, the second one is live. (Unfortunately, some authors use the term *dead code* to refer to *unreachable* code, as in `if (false) x = y`. These concepts are not the same; our use of the terms *live* and *dead* does not refer to reachability.)

Dead assignments without other side effects are useless and can be removed from the program. Even mildly optimizing compilers implement a dead code elimination pass that would completely remove the addition from the first program fragment above. Our goal is to generate only live code, i.e., only code that does *not* contain any such opportunities for dead code elimination.

Liveness analysis is one of the classical data-flow analyses [13]. It is a *backward, may* analysis traditionally performed as backward fixed-point iteration over a program's control-flow graph. A statement S in the control-flow graph has a *live-in* set $S^{\bullet}$ and a *live-out* set S° which capture the sets of live variables before and after execution of S. Every statement S also has a *transfer function* f_S relating these sets. Figure 1 shows the transfer functions for assignments, `if` statements, and `while` loops. Liveness information is noted on the edges of the control flow graph. In the equations, $FV(e)$ denotes the set of all variables in expression e.

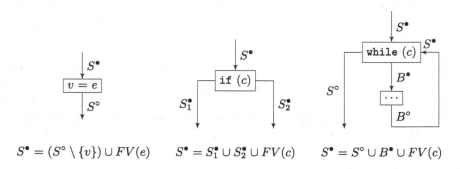

$$S^{\bullet} = (S^{\circ} \setminus \{v\}) \cup FV(e) \qquad S^{\bullet} = S_1^{\bullet} \cup S_2^{\bullet} \cup FV(c) \qquad S^{\bullet} = S^{\circ} \cup B^{\bullet} \cup FV(c)$$

Fig. 1. Liveness transfer functions

The transfer function for an assignment $v = e$ is said to *kill* the variable v and *generate* all the variables in e. The transfer functions for `if` statements and `while` loops kill nothing and generate the variables in their condition c. The live-in set $S^{\bullet}$ of a loop S has a recursive dependency on itself: It is the same as the body's live-out set B°, on which the body's live-in set $B^{\bullet}$ depends. The desired solution for $S^{\bullet}$ is the *least fixed point* of the system of equations, which can be found efficiently by propagating data-flow information backwards around the loop.

2.2   Recognizing Fully Live Programs

We will call a program *fully live* if all of the assignment statements it contains are live. This section develops an inference system characterizing fully live programs.

Figure 2 shows the abstract syntax of our programming language of interest, a subset of C function bodies without declarations. The language contains variables, constants, and all side-effect-free arithmetic and bitwise operators of C. Statements are assignments (the only source of side effects), `return` statements, `if` statements and general `while` loops. In contrast to C's concrete syntax, we view the semicolon ; as a statement separator, not a terminator. For now, the language does not include `for` loops, nor any structures, arrays, or pointers. All variables are considered local.

$$v ::= \mathbf{a} \mid \mathbf{b} \mid \ldots \mid \mathbf{x} \mid \mathbf{y} \mid \ldots \qquad \text{variables}$$
$$n ::= \mathbf{0} \mid \mathbf{1} \mid \ldots \qquad \text{constant literals}$$
$$e ::= v \mid n \mid e + e \mid e - e \mid \ldots \mid e \ll e \mid \ldots \mid -e \mid \,!e \mid \ldots \qquad \text{expressions}$$
$$S ::= v = e \qquad \text{assignment statement}$$
$$\mid \ \mathbf{return}\ v \qquad \text{return statement}$$
$$\mid \ \mathbf{\{\}} \qquad \text{empty block}$$
$$\mid \ S;\ S \qquad \text{sequencing}$$
$$\mid \ \mathbf{if}\ (e)\ S\ \mathbf{else}\ S \qquad \text{conditional branch}$$
$$\mid \ \mathbf{while}\ (e)\ S \qquad \text{loop}$$

Fig. 2. Abstract syntax of a C-like programming language

Figure 3 shows a system of inference rules that characterize fully live programs. In these rules we use a notation similar to Hoare triples. A *liveness triple*

$$\langle S^\bullet \rangle \ S \ \langle S^\circ \rangle$$

means that the variables in the set $S^\bullet$ are live immediately before the statement S (*live in*), and the variables in S° are live immediately after S (*live out*). A program S is fully live iff there is a set of variables $S^\bullet$ such that the liveness triple $\langle S^\bullet \rangle \ S \ \langle \emptyset \rangle$ is derivable in the system.

Intuitively, the system of inference rules encodes two things. First, the rules are an alternative presentation of the transfer functions of liveness analysis. A triple $\langle S^\bullet \rangle \ S \ \langle S^\circ \rangle$ that appears in a valid derivation corresponds to a data-flow equation $S^\bullet = f_S(S^\circ)$ where f_S is the transfer function for the statement S. For example, the transfer function $f_{v=e}$ for an assignment $v = e$ is just $f_{v=e}(S^\circ) = (S^\circ \setminus \{v\}) \cup FV(e)$, as in the side condition of the ASSIGN rule. Similarly, the SEQUENCE rule encodes the composition of transfer functions, and the IF rule encodes the split and join of data-flow information along different program paths.

Second, the other side conditions add a system of constraints to ensure full liveness: Any assignment statement appearing in a fully live program S (i.e., for which a derivation of $\langle S^\bullet \rangle \ S \ \langle \emptyset \rangle$ for some $S^\bullet$ exists) is itself live. This follows

$$\text{RETURN} \; \frac{}{\langle \{v\}\rangle \; \texttt{return } v \; \langle \emptyset \rangle} \qquad \text{SKIP} \; \frac{}{\langle S \rangle \; \{\} \; \langle S \rangle}$$

$$\text{ASSIGN} \; \frac{v \in S^\circ \qquad S^\bullet = (S^\circ \setminus \{v\}) \cup FV(e)}{\langle S^\bullet \rangle \; v = e \; \langle S^\circ \rangle}$$

$$\text{SEQUENCE} \; \frac{\langle S_1^\bullet \rangle \; S_1 \; \langle S_2^\bullet \rangle \qquad \langle S_2^\bullet \rangle \; S_2 \; \langle S_2^\circ \rangle \qquad S_2^\bullet \neq \emptyset}{\langle S_1^\bullet \rangle \; S_1 \; ; \; S_2 \; \langle S_2^\circ \rangle}$$

$$\text{IF} \; \frac{\langle S_1^\bullet \rangle \; S_1 \; \langle S^\circ \rangle \qquad \langle S_2^\bullet \rangle \; S_2 \; \langle S^\circ \rangle \qquad S^\bullet = S_1^\bullet \cup S_2^\bullet \cup FV(c) \qquad S_1 \neq \{\} \vee S_2 \neq \{\}}{\langle S^\bullet \rangle \; \texttt{if } (c) \; S_1 \; \texttt{else } S_2 \; \langle S^\circ \rangle}$$

$$\text{WHILE} \; \frac{\langle B^\bullet \rangle \; B \; \langle B^\circ \rangle \qquad B^\circ = S^\bullet \text{ (minimal)} \qquad S^\bullet = S^\circ \cup B^\bullet \cup FV(c) \qquad S^\circ \neq \emptyset}{\langle S^\bullet \rangle \; \texttt{while } (c) \; B \; \langle S^\circ \rangle}$$

Fig. 3. System of inference rules for fully live programs

directly from the ASSIGN rule's side condition $v \in S^\circ$. For example, a triple of the form

$$\langle S^\bullet \rangle \; \texttt{x = a; x = b} \; \langle S^\circ \rangle$$

can never be derived in the system because the first of the two assignments is dead. The SEQUENCE rule says that to derive this triple, there must be some intermediate set S' of variables such that $\texttt{x} \in S'$ due to ASSIGN on $\texttt{x = a}$ while at the same time $S' = (S \setminus \{\texttt{x}\}) \cup \{\texttt{b}\}$ due to ASSIGN on $\texttt{x = b}$. This is a contradiction, so the derivation attempt must fail.

While the other rules are straight-forward, the WHILE rule deserves some discussion. Unlike the two branches of the if statement, the whole loop's live-out set S° is not identical to the loop body's live-out set B°: Typically there are loop-carried dependences, i.e., cases where a variable is set on one iteration of the loop and its value is read on a later iteration. Such variables are live out of (and live into) the loop body, but if they are no longer used once the loop has terminated, they are not live out of the loop. When performing a derivation in the system, we must guess or calculate the set of these additional variables.

Let f_S denote the liveness transfer function corresponding to the loop body statement S. Then from the liveness triple $\langle B^\bullet \rangle \; S \; \langle B^\circ \rangle$ we have $B^\bullet = f_S(B^\circ)$, and the equation $B^\circ = S^\circ \cup B^\bullet \cup FV(c)$ means that B° is a fixed point of the function $\lambda B. \, (S^\circ \cup f_S(B) \cup FV(c))$. The minimality side condition additionally specifies that we are interested in the *least* fixed point of this function. This least fixed point exists and is unique [13].

In Fig. 4 we illustrate the use of the inference system to prove full liveness of a program taking an input variable n (assumed to be non-negative) and returning the n-th Fibonacci number. We omit some details to focus on the analysis of the

$$\langle\{a,b,n\}\rangle \ n \ = \ n \ - \ 1 \ \langle\{a,b,n\}\rangle$$

$$\frac{\langle\{a,n,t\}\rangle \ b \ = \ t \ \langle\{a,b,n\}\rangle}{\qquad} \qquad \vdots$$

$$\frac{\langle\{b,n,t\}\rangle \ a \ = \ b \ \langle\{a,n,t\}\rangle}{\qquad} \qquad \vdots$$

$$\frac{\langle\{a,b,n\}\rangle \ t \ = \ a \ + \ b \ \langle\{b,n,t\}\rangle}{\langle\{a,b,n\}\rangle \ t \ = \ a \ + \ b; \ a \ = \ b; \ b \ = \ t; \ n \ = \ n \ - \ 1 \ \langle\{a,b,n\}\rangle} \qquad \vdots$$

$$\langle\{a,b,n\}\rangle \ \mathtt{while} \ (n>0) \ \{ \ t=a+b; \ a=b; \ b=t; \ n=n-1 \ \} \ \langle\{a\}\rangle$$

$$\vdots$$

$$\langle\{n\}\rangle \ a=0; b=1; \mathtt{while} \ (n>0) \ \{t=a+b; a=b; b=t; n=n-1\}; \mathtt{return} \, a \ \langle\emptyset\rangle$$

Fig. 4. Example derivation proving full liveness.

loop. Note that only the return variable a is live after the loop. However, the live-out set of the loop's body is $\{a, b, n\}$. This includes the return variable a and the variable n that is used in the loop condition. It also includes the variable b, which is the element computed by fixed point iteration: The value of b at the end of the loop body will be used on the next loop iteration, if any. Conversely, if b were not live at some point in the loop body, our inference system would not allow derivation of a triple for the assignment b = t. Indeed, all assignments in the loop body satisfy the condition that they define variables that are live after the assignment. That is, this program is *fully live* by our definition.

2.3 Limitations of the System

Note that fully live programs may still contain opportunities for simple optimizations that remove code that does not have interesting effects. For example, programs accepted by the inference system above may contain fragments like if (0) { ... } else { ... } where one of the branches of the if statement is unreachable and thus irrelevant; or assignments like y = ...; x = y - y; where the computation for the value of y is irrelevant for x's final value of 0. Our inference rules do not consider the semantics of the code in enough detail to exclude such cases.

Our claims with regards to full liveness are relative to a purely syntactic notion of liveness that does not consider such semantic issues. In particular, we cannot guarantee that the liveness analysis embedded in these rules is equivalent to liveness analysis as performed by any given compiler. Any other analyses or transformations performed by the compiler before liveness analysis may influence the results, typically making the compiler's results more precise than ours.

As our experimental results in Sect. 4 show, our generator performs well nonetheless, so we can leave refinements of the system for future work.

2.4   Generating Fully Live Programs

The inference rules can be translated almost directly into an executable random (or exhaustive) generator of fully live programs. Like traditional liveness analysis, generation proceeds backwards, i.e., in the direction opposite control flow.

The side conditions of the inference rules ensure that a fully live program always ends in a return statement, as no other statement may have an empty live-out set. The generator can thus start by picking a random program variable v and generating a statement **return** v with live-in set $L = \{v\}$. It then iteratively prepends random statements S to the current program fragment and updates the live-in set according to $f_S(L)$. The possibilities for the generation of S are guided by L. In particular, if the generator decides to generate an assignment statement, the target variable v must be an element of L at that point. Conversely, if L ever becomes empty, generation of the current block of code must stop at that point: Any code preceding that point would be dead. Figure 5 shows pseudocode of such a generator in an OCaml-like functional language.

Every statement generation function takes a live variable set L (representing the live-out set S° of the statement S to be generated) and returns a pair of a newly generated statement and an updated live variable set according to the statement's transfer function. We iterate statement generation and collect a list of statements forming a block. In this presentation we omit helper functions such as the ones for generating random variables and expressions.

As before, the handling of loops merits more discussion. Just as the inference system needs a minimal set $B^\bullet$ containing new variables that are live into and out of the loop body, the random generator must synthesize such a set of variables. But here the problem is more difficult: During inference, we can start with an initial live-out set and derive the eventual live-in set by fixed-point iteration. During code generation this is not possible since we cannot analyze the loop body before we have constructed it. Instead, we first generate a random set of newly live variables and let this choice guide generation of the loop's code.

This solution relies on the following observation: The new variables we are interested in are ones that are defined before the loop, may be defined on some loop iteration, and then used on some later iteration. In the example of Fig. 4, this is the case for variable b, which stores the next Fibonacci number for assignment to a on the subsequent iteration. Using the names in the WHILE rule of Fig. 3, the set of these 'new' variables is $B' = B^\circ \backslash (S^\circ \cup FV(c))$. It follows that $B' \subseteq B^\bullet$, i.e., every $b \in B'$ is live into the loop.

To generate a fully live loop, we choose a random set B' of new variables and generate a loop body in a way that ensures that $B^\circ = S^\circ \cup B' \cup FV(c)$ is a least fixed point of the loop. For this we add B' to the live variable set L before generating a loop body block (along with the live variables $FV(c)$ generated by the loop condition). The generated loop body may or may not define or use variables in B', and thus these variables may or may not be live into the generated block. However, we must force them to be used in the loop body and be live into the body: If there were some b in the generated B' that is not live into the loop body, we would violate the condition $B' \subseteq B^\bullet$ established above.

```
let random_statements L code =
    if L ≠ ∅ then
        let (S, L') = random_statement L;
        random_statements L' (S :: code)
    else
        (code, L)

let random_statement L =
    let statement_generator = random_select [assignment; branch; loop];
    statement_generator L

let assignment L =
    let v = random_select L;
    let e = random_expression ();
    ("v = e", (L \ {v}) ∪ FV(e))

let branch L =
    let (t, L₁) = random_statements L [];
    let (f, L₂) = random_statements L [];
    let c = random_expression ();
    ("if (c) t else f", L₁ ∪ L₂ ∪ FV(c))

let loop L =
    (* See main text for explanation. *)
    let c = random_expression ();
    let B' = random_variable_set ();
    let (code, L') = random_statements (L ∪ B' ∪ FV(c)) [];
    let V = {b ∈ B' | b ∉ L' or b not used in S};
    if V ≠ ∅ then
        let e = random_expression_on_variables V;
        let v = random_select L';
        let code' = "v = e" :: code;
        ("while (c) code'", (L' \ {v}) ∪ V ∪ L)
    else
        ("while (c) code", L' ∪ L)

(* Start generation with the terminating return statement. *)
let v = random_variable ()
let (code, L) = random_statements {v} ["return v"]
```

Fig. 5. Pseudocode of a liveness-driven random program generator.

On the other hand, if b were live into the loop body but did not have a use anywhere in the body, then $B^{\bullet}$ would not be minimal and hence B° would not be a least fixed point of the constraint system.

To ensure a correct, minimal solution, we therefore find the set V of all $b \in B'$ that are not in L' or that are in L' but have no use in the generated loop body. We pick a random live variable $v \in L'$ and prepend an assignment v = e to the generated loop body, where e is an expression containing all the variables in V. This final loop body ensures that all variables in B' are live into it and used in it, hence ensuring that $B° = S° \cup B' \cup FV(c)$ is a least fixed point of the loop's liveness constraint system.

A small detail not illustrated in the pseudocode is the case when L' is empty at the beginning of the generated loop body. This can only be the case if the first statement in the body is an assignment of a constant expression (i.e., not using any variables) to some variable v, since such assignments are the only statements that can remove variables from the live variable set without adding any new ones. In this case, we replace this assignment's right-hand side with the expression e generated as above.

3 Implementation

We have implemented the random program generation algorithm sketched above as a plugin for Frama-C [7]. Frama-C is a general, extensible framework for source-level analysis and transformation of C programs. It is written in OCaml and can be extended with plugins written in that language. For this work, we do not need any advanced Frama-C features but benefit from its AST (abstract syntax tree) type definitions, utilities for managing variables and constructing AST fragments, and its pretty-printer for outputting the generated AST as C source code. As these general parts are provided by Frama-C, ldrgen itself can be quite small: It consists of only about 600 lines of generator code, plus some utilities and configuration.

ldrgen is free software, available at https://github.com/gergo-/ldrgen.

3.1 Random Generation

The core of the generator has the same structure as the pseudocode in Fig. 5. After generating an empty function definition and a return statement, it fills in the function's body by generating a fully live sequence of statements as in the pseudocode. Statements are represented by AST fragments; we never need to worry about generating actual C syntax. The current version of ldrgen always generates a single function.

Random expressions are generated by choosing an operator among the arithmetic operators available in C and recursively generating the appropriate number of operand expressions. At this point, C's type system becomes relevant; if needed, we insert type casts to ensure all operands of an operator have the same type. Type casts are also needed in some other cases: Bitwise operators and the modulo operator cannot be applied to floating-point numbers in C, so we insert conversions to integer types in such cases.

Many C operators may invoke undefined behavior when applied to inappropriate values. Two examples are division by zero and signed integer arithmetic overflow. Unlike Csmith in its default mode, ldrgen does not try to guard against such undefined operations, except for two cases that compilers have repeatedly warned us about: We clamp the right-hand-side operands of bit-shift operations to the bit size of the expression on the left-hand-side, and we always generate division and modulo operations of the form $e_1/(e_2+c)$ for some constant c instead of just e_1/e_2. The idea behind this is that e_2+c is less likely to evaluate to zero than a random expression in general. This approach is primitive, but we have found it to work well in practice.

Leaves of expressions are constants or variables. For constant literals we simply generate a random number. For a variable use we either use a previously used variable or generate a new one. Variables generated in this way may be local variables or function parameters. Both can be used in expressions, but we only generate assignments to locals, not to parameters.

Some of the generator's choices are weighted by manually chosen parameters to ensure generation of somewhat more realistic-looking programs. For example, we prefer generation of basic arithmetic operations to bitwise operators. We also ensure that loop and branch conditions are not constant expressions, i.e., that they contain at least one variable. In order to avoid trivial non-termination issues, we also ensure that every loop body's final statement is an assignment to some variable that occurs in the loop condition. If there were no modification of any of these variables at all, a loop once entered could never terminate. Even so, termination is not at all guaranteed.

Bottom-up generation of the function's body may stop if there are no more live variables, or if a user-defined limit is reached. In this latter case, there may remain live local variables at the start of the function's body. Their liveness means that they may be used without being assigned to, so we must ensure that they are initialized. We therefore finalize the function definition by initializing all such live-in variables to constants or to the values of function parameters.

3.2   Configuration

The generator's behavior may be tuned using command-line arguments. These may specify features of the sub-language of C that is used. For example, the user may request the generation of code that only uses integer types, or only floating-point types. They may also specify that no bitwise operations or no divisions should be generated, and whether loops may be generated. Other flags specify structural properties: The maximal number of statements per block, and the maximal nesting depths of statements and expressions.

ldrgen's random generation uses OCaml's standard pseudorandom number generator, which can be seeded with a random seed or with a seed value specified as a command line argument. Invoking a given version of ldrgen with a fixed set of arguments and a fixed seed thus always gives the same reproducible result.

3.3   Extensions to the Basic Model

We describe two extensions to the core language of Fig. 2 that are already implemented in ldrgen: very limited uses of pointers and for loops over arrays.

First, in addition to the arithmetic types used so far, we can generate function parameters of type T * (pointer to T) for some arithmetic type T. A parameter p of such type can be used in generated code as *p. We currently do not generate assignments to such dereferenced pointers, nor any pointer arithmetic.

Second, we want to generate arrays and restricted forms of loops over them in order to exercise loop optimizations such as unrolling or vectorization. For this we generate pointer arguments T *arr which are only used in for loops of the following form:

```
v = ...;
for (unsigned int i = 0; i < N; i++) {
    v = v ∘ f(arr[i]);
}
```

Here, N is a global variable considered to hold the array's size, $f(\texttt{arr[i]})$ is a random expression involving arr[i], and ∘ is a randomly chosen binary arithmetic operator. This loop pattern implements a map-reduce operation, mapping some function f over the array and reducing (folding) the result with ∘. It is currently the only kind of for loop we implement, but this would be easy to generalize.

Similar forms of loops are already generated by Csmith, but there their results are virtually never used. Csmith's loops are therefore completely eliminated by compilers instead of being vectorized. In ldrgen, we choose a loop result variable v that is live after the loop to ensure that it is used, and the loop exposed to the compiler's loop optimizer.

3.4   Future Extensions

In the future, we are planning to extend ldrgen to generate structure types and allow the use of their members.

In the longer term, ldrgen will also be extended to support programs consisting of several random functions which may call each other. We are not planning to support non-structured control flow using goto. The more structured break and continue statements might eventually be supported, but this is not a priority as they complicate the structural liveness analysis.

4   Evaluation

The design goal of ldrgen was to have a random program generator that exposes as much interesting code as possible to all passes of the compiler under test; recall that we found Csmith-generated code to contain much dead code which is never seen by many parts of the compiler because it can be optimized away early on. We will have achieved our goal if, for comparable amounts of generated C code, ldrgen's output results in more, and ideally more varied, assembly code than Csmith's output. We therefore compare the two generators along these

lines. We do not claim superiority to Csmith in any other regard, especially
not concerning its power to find subtle miscompilation bugs. Csmith covers a
larger subset of the C language than `ldrgen` and, in its default mode, carefully
ensures that its output is well-defined according to the C standard. `ldrgen` tries
to guard against oversized shifts and divisions by zero (see Sect. 3.1) but does
not otherwise guarantee well-definedness.

Csmith is designed to run complete, self-contained applications consisting of
several functions, driven by a `main` function. In contrast, `ldrgen` only generates
individual functions without a driver. However, Csmith's many configuration
options allow us to ask it to generate files consisting only a single function
without `main`.[1]

Table 1 presents our experimental results for 1000 programs each generated
by Csmith and `ldrgen`. We investigate three characteristics of the generated
programs: lines of C code, number of instructions in the generated code, and
number of unique opcodes in the generated code. In all cases, the C code was
compiled to x86-64 machine code using GCC 5.4.0 with optimization setting –O3.
For each characteristic, the table shows the total over the 1000 files as well as
the minimum, median, and maximum values. (In cases where the median is not
unique, we chose the arithmetic mean of the two closest values.)

Table 1. Comparison of code generated by Csmith and `ldrgen` in 1000 runs each.

	Generator	Min	Median	Max	Total
Lines of code	Csmith	25	368.5	2953	459021
	ldrgen	12	411.5	1003	389939
Instructions	Csmith	1	15.0	1006	45606
	ldrgen	1	952.5	4420	1063503
Unique opcodes	Csmith	1	8	74	146
	ldrgen	1	95	124	204

Our command line flags for Csmith were chosen in order to generate comparable numbers of lines of C code to `ldrgen`. In fact Table 1 shows that it
generates somewhat more, but these numbers are difficult to compare precisely
because Csmith-generated code tends to contain many initializers for global variables; `ldrgen` does not generate any global variables at all. We believe that the
settings we chose allow a fair comparison of the generators.

Next we compare the number of instructions (executable code only, excluding
static data, assembler directives etc.) emitted by the compiler for the generated
source files. `ldrgen` was designed to increase this number compared to Csmith,
and the table shows that we have succeeded: While on average Csmith's output compiles to a single machine instruction per ten lines of code, `ldrgen`'s

---

[1] The concrete flags we used were `--nomain --float --max-funcs 1 --no-safe`
`-math --max-block-size 8 --concise`.

output has almost three instructions per single line of source code. Overall, ldrgen-generated programs compile to about 20 times as much machine code as Csmith-generated programs of comparable size. We can also see that the distribution for Csmith is highly skewed: The median shows that at least half of the functions generated by Csmith compile to 15 instructions or fewer. This also confirms our initial, more informal observation that Csmith-generated code tends to contain large amounts of dead code. ldrgen manages to generate code with a less skewed distribution, and in particular with generally higher numbers of emitted instructions.

On a side note, we remark that both Csmith and ldrgen sometimes generate functions that compile to a single machine instruction. Inspection showed that this happens in cases where the compiler recognizes that a function ends up in an infinite loop without externally visible side effects. Such functions are then compiled into a single unconditional jump instruction looping back to itself. Many other functions compile to two instructions, typically some simple operation on a function argument or a constant followed by a return. It would be difficult to completely avoid generating infinite loops, but comparatively easy (at least within ldrgen) to avoid generating functions that return after a single operation. For both Csmith and ldrgen, about 10% of all cases fall into one of these trivial categories (with Csmith producing fewer infinite loops).

We analyze the coverage of the instruction set in the generated code by looking at the number of different opcodes generated. Here, too, we see that individual functions generated by ldrgen have a more varied instruction mix than functions generated by Csmith: Even the median for ldrgen is higher than the maximum for Csmith. Totaling over all the machine code in 1000 functions, we see that Csmith-generated code compiles to a mix of 146 different opcodes, while ldrgen-generated code contains 204 different opcodes, an increase in instruction set coverage of 40%. Inspection of the sets of opcodes shows that this difference is almost entirely due to various vector (SIMD) arithmetic instructions generated for ldrgen's code. Compiling to such instructions was the goal of adding for loops over arrays to ldrgen. Manual inspection of some cases shows that such loops are indeed the origin of these instructions. As noted above, such loops are also generated by Csmith, but their results are almost never used, so they do not appear in the compiled code. Disabling generation of for loops in ldrgen brings its total number of unique instructions down to 147, comparable to Csmith.

One of the few opcodes emitted for Csmith-generated code but not for ldrgen are call instructions to memcpy which are sometimes generated by compilers for structure copies. ldrgen currently does not generate structures at all.

Finally, in Table 2 we compare the speed of the two generators. Generating the 1000 files each analyzed above took 871 s with Csmith and 124 s with ldrgen (Csmith backtracks if it finds that it has generated unsafe code). Csmith generates about 527 lines of C code per second, with ldrgen generating 3140 (about 6 × more). With respect to final machine code, Csmith-generated code compiles to about 52 instructions per second of generation time, whereas ldrgen produces 8563 (about 160 ×). These numbers do not include the time taken by

Table 2. Comparison of the time to generate 1000 files.

Generator	Time (sec)	Lines/sec	Instrs/sec
Csmith	871	527	52.4
ldrgen	124	3140	8562.8

the compiler; compiling all 1000 files for each generator takes about 46.6 s for Csmith and 80.3 s for `ldrgen`.

5   Related Work

5.1   Csmith

The best-known random program generator is Csmith [20], based on an earlier system called `randprog` [5,19]. Csmith generates complete, self-contained programs that take all their input from initialized global variables and compute an output consisting of a hash over the values of all global variables at the end of execution. The generator is designed to only generate programs with well-defined semantics: Operations that may be undefined in C, such as overflowing signed integer arithmetic, are guarded by conditionals that exclude undefined cases (these guards can be disabled, and we disabled them for the experiments reported above). Like `ldrgen`, Csmith performs data-flow analysis during generation, although the details differ due to the differing design goals. Csmith's forward analysis computes points-to facts and uses them for safety checks. If the checks fail, Csmith backtracks, deleting code it generated until a safe state is reached again. In contrast, `ldrgen`'s data-flow analysis only deals with liveness, and `ldrgen` never backtracks: Full liveness of variables in loops is ensured by construction. Csmith generates a larger subset of C than current or currently planned versions of `ldrgen`, including unstructured control flow and less restricted use of pointers.

Due to Csmith's forward generation and data-flow analysis, it does not appear possible to directly integrate our backward liveness-driven approach in Csmith. A 'best effort' approach that would not give full liveness guarantees might extend Csmith with a forwards reaching definitions analysis [13]. At each program point, when generating an expression, Csmith could then prefer to use previously defined variables over fresh variables. Alternatively, it might be extended with a mode that computes a function's return value from all otherwise unused variables in the program, artificially making them live.

Csmith has been used to find hundreds of bugs in C compilers when compiling the programs it generates [20]. It has also been used as the basis of mutation-based systems, where Csmith's output was modified using other tools to provoke compiler bugs [8]. The CLsmith tool derived from Csmith has been used to find many bugs in OpenCL compilers [10].

5.2   Other Random Generators

Other notable random generators include Orange3 [12] for C, jsfunfuzz [17] for JavaScript, and efftester [11] for OCaml. Our generator following a system of inference rules is similar to a generator based on Haskell's typing rules [14].

The JTT program generator [21] is aimed at testing compiler optimizations. It uses a model-based approach, with generation guided by test scripts. These scripts contain code templates and temporal logic specifications of the optimizations to be tested. For example, the authors specify opportunities for dead code elimination as cases where a variable is assigned, then assigned again before being used. The test script contains a temporal logic formula expressing this pattern and the test condition that the compiler should eliminate the first assignment. Using this script, JTT generates test programs containing this pattern.

Other work specifically aimed at testing and comparing program verification tools generates code from randomly generated LTL formulae [18]. The generated code is guaranteed to satisfy the specified temporal properties.

5.3   Structural Data-Flow Analysis

Our formulation of liveness analysis as set of structural inference rules is inspired by formulations of interval-based data-flow analysis where reducible programs are decomposed into components called *intervals*, and analysis data is efficiently propagated among the intervals [1,3,6].

6   Conclusions

We presented `ldrgen`, a new generator of random C programs designed for testing C compilers. In contrast to Csmith, the dominant player in this field, `ldrgen` is driven by liveness analysis to avoid generating dead code. We designed an inference system to capture our liveness analysis and implemented its rules as an executable program generation system.

`ldrgen` is implemented as a plugin for the Frama-C framework. Our evaluation of `ldrgen` in comparison to Csmith shows that we have achieved our goal of generating C code that compiles to larger amounts of machine code with a more interesting instruction mix, including many SIMD instructions. We are actively using `ldrgen` in a project on finding missed optimizations in compilers [2]. Because it is able to exercise loop optimizations not usually addressed by Csmith, it may also be useful for finding correctness bugs in these optimizations.

Acknowledgments. The author would like to thank the anonymous reviewers, John Regehr, and Gabriel Scherer for insightful comments on earlier versions of this paper. This research was partially supported by ITEA 3 project no. 14014, ASSUME.

References

1. Allen, F.E.: Control flow analysis. SIGPLAN Not. **5**(7), 1–19 (1970). http://doi.acm.org/10.1145/390013.808479
2. Barany, G.: Finding missed compiler optimizations by differential testing. In: 27th International Conference on Compiler Construction (2018). https://doi.org/10.1145/3178372.3179521
3. Cocke, J.: Global common subexpression elimination. SIGPLAN Not. **5**(7), 20–24 (1970). http://doi.acm.org/10.1145/390013.808480
4. Dave, M.A.: Compiler verification: a bibliography. SIGSOFT Softw. Eng. Notes **28**(6) (2003). http://doi.acm.org/10.1145/966221.966235
5. Eide, E., Regehr, J.: Volatiles are miscompiled, and what to do about it. In: EMSOFT 2008. ACM (2008). http://doi.acm.org/10.1145/1450058.1450093
6. Graham, S.L., Wegman, M.: A fast and usually linear algorithm for global flow analysis. J. ACM **23**(1), 172–202 (1976)
7. Kirchner, F., Kosmatov, N., Prevosto, V., Signoles, J., Yakobowski, B.: Frama-C: a software analysis perspective. Form. Asp. Comp. **27**(3), 573–609 (2015)
8. Le, V., Afshari, M., Su, Z.: Compiler validation via equivalence modulo inputs. In: PLDI 2014. ACM (2014). http://doi.acm.org/10.1145/2594291.2594334
9. Leroy, X.: Formal verification of a realistic compiler. Commun. ACM **52**(7), 107–115 (2009). http://doi.acm.org/10.1145/1538788.1538814
10. Lidbury, C., Lascu, A., Chong, N., Donaldson, A.F.: Many-core compiler fuzzing. In: PLDI 2015, pp. 65–76. ACM (2015)
11. Midtgaard, J., Justesen, M.N., Kasting, P., Nielson, F., Nielson, H.R.: Effect-driven QuickChecking of compilers. Proc. ACM Program. Lang. **1**(ICFP) (2017). http://doi.acm.org/10.1145/3110259
12. Nagai, E., Hashimoto, A., Ishiura, N.: Reinforcing random testing of arithmetic optimization of C compilers by scaling up size and number of expressions. IPSJ Trans. Syst. LSI Des. Methodol. **7**, 91–100 (2014)
13. Nielson, F., Nielson, H.R., Hankin, C.: Principles of Program Analysis. Springer, Heidelberg (1999). https://doi.org/10.1007/978-3-662-03811-6
14. Pałka, M.H., Claessen, K., Russo, A., Hughes, J.: Testing an optimising compiler by generating random lambda terms. In: 6th International Workshop on Automation of Software Test, AST 2011 (2011). http://doi.acm.org/10.1145/1982595.1982615
15. Perennial, Inc.: ACVS ANSI/ISO/FIPS-160 C validation suite. http://www.peren.com/pages/acvs_set.htm
16. Plum Hall, Inc.: The Plum Hall validation suite for C. http://www.plumhall.com/stec.html
17. Ruderman, J.: jsfunfuzz (2015). https://github.com/MozillaSecurity/funfuzz/tree/master/js/jsfunfuzz
18. Steffen, B., Isberner, M., Naujokat, S., Margaria, T., Geske, M.: Property-driven benchmark generation: synthesizing programs of realistic structure. Int. J. Softw. Tools Technol. Transfer **16**(5), 465–479 (2014)
19. Turner, B.: Random C program generator (2007). https://sites.google.com/site/brturn2/randomcprogramgenerator
20. Yang, X., Chen, Y., Eide, E., Regehr, J.: Finding and understanding bugs in C compilers. In: PLDI 2011, pp. 283–294. ACM (2011)
21. Zhao, C., Xue, Y., Tao, Q., Guo, L., Wang, Z.: Automated test program generation for an industrial optimizing compiler. In: ICSE Workshop on Automation of Software Test (2009)

Erlang Code Evolution Control

David Insa, Sergio Pérez, Josep Silva, and Salvador Tamarit[✉]

Universitat Politècnica de València, Camí de Vera s/n, 46022 Valencia, Spain
{dinsa,serperu,jsilva,stamarit}@dsic.upv.es

Abstract. In the software lifecycle, a program can evolve several times for different reasons such as the optimisation of a bottle-neck, the refactoring of an obscure function, etc. These code changes often involve several functions or modules, so it can be difficult to know whether the correct behaviour of the previous releases has been preserved in the new release. Most developers rely on a previously defined test suite to check this behaviour preservation. We propose here an alternative approach to automatically obtain a test suite that specifically focusses on comparing the old and new versions of the code. Our test case generation is directed by: a sophisticated combination of several already existing tools such as TypEr, CutEr, and PropEr; the choice of an expression of interest whose behaviour must be preserved; and the recording of the sequences of values this expression is evaluated to. All the presented work has been implemented in an open-source tool that is publicly available on GitHub.

Keywords: Code evolution control · Automated regression testing
Tracing

1 Introduction

During its useful lifetime, a program might evolve many times. Each evolution is often composed of several changes that produce a new release of the software. There are multiple ways to control that these changes do not modify the behaviour of any part of the program that was already correct. Most of the companies rely on *regression testing* [13,19] to assure that a desired behaviour of the original program is kept in the new release, but there exist other alternatives such as the static inference of the impact of changes [7,9,11,14].

Even when a program is perfectly working and it fulfils all its functional requirements, sometimes we still need to improve parts of it. There are several reasons why a released program needs to be modified. For instance, improving

This work has been partially supported by MINECO/AEI/FEDER (EU) under grant TIN2016-76843-C4-1-R and by the *Generalitat Valenciana* under grant PROMETEO-II/2015/013 (SmartLogic). Salvador Tamarit was partially supported by the *Conselleria de Educación, Investigación, Cultura y Deporte de la Generalitat Valenciana* under grant APOSTD/2016/036.

F. Fioravanti and J. P. Gallagher (Eds.): LOPSTR 2017, LNCS 10855, pp. 128–144, 2018.
https://doi.org/10.1007/978-3-319-94460-9_8

the maintainability or efficiency; or for other reasons such as obfuscation, security improvement, parallelization, distribution, platform changes, and hardware changes, among others. Programmers that want to check whether the semantics of the original program remains unchanged in the new release usually create a test suite. There are several tools that can help in all this process. For instance, Travis CI can be easily integrated in a GitHub repository so that each time a pull request is performed, the test suite is launched. We present here an alternative and complementary approach that creates an automatic test suite to do regression testing. Therefore, our technique can check the evolution of the code even if no test suite has been defined.

In the context of debugging, programmers often use breakpoints to observe the values of an expression during an execution. Unfortunately, this feature is not currently available in testing, even though it would be useful to easily focus the test cases on one specific point without modifying the source code (as it happens when using asserts) or adding more code (as it happens in unit testing). In this paper, we introduce the ability to specify *points of interest* (POI) in the context of testing. A POI can be any expression in the code (e.g., a function call) meaning that we want to check the behaviour of that expression.

In our technique, (1) the programmer identifies a POI, typically a variable[1], and a set of *input functions* whose invocations should evaluate the POI. Then, by using a combination of random test case generation, mutation testing, and concolic testing, (2) the tool automatically generates a test suite that tries to cover all possible paths that reach the POI (trying also to produce execution paths that evaluate the POI several times). Therefore, in our setting, the *input of a test case* (ITC) is defined as a call to an input function with some specific arguments, and the output is the sequence of those values the POI is evaluated to during the execution of the ITC. For the sake of disambiguation, in the rest of the paper we use the term *traces* to refer to these sequences of values. Next, (3) the test suite is used to automatically check whether the behaviour of the program remains unchanged across new versions. This is done by passing each individual test case against the new version, and checking whether the same traces are produced at the POI. Finally, (4) the user is provided with a report about the success or failure of these test cases. When two versions of a program are available at the beginning of the test generation process, we can use both for the generation of ITCs in step (2). In this alternative mode, step (3) is not performed as a separated step but it is integrated in step (2). We named this execution mode the *comparison mode*, and the one that uses only one version the *suite generation mode*. Note that, as it is common in regression testing, both modes only work for deterministic executions. This does not mean that they cannot be used in a program with concurrency or other sources of indeterminism, but POIs not affected by these features should be used in these cases.

---

[1] While our current implementation limits the POI to variables, nothing prevents the technique from accepting any expression as the POI.

We have implemented our approach in a tool named *SecEr* (*Software Evolution Control for Erlang*), which implements both execution modes and is publicly available at: https://github.com/mistupv/secer. Instead of reinventing the wheel, some of the analyses performed by our tool are done by other existing tools such as CutEr [5], a concolic testing tool, to generate an initial set of test cases; TypEr [10], a type inference system for Erlang, to obtain types for the input functions; and PropEr [12], a property-based testing tool, to obtain values of a given type. All the analyses performed by SecEr are transparent to the user. The only task that requires user intervention in our technique is, at each version, selecting the POI that is supposed to produce the same trace. This task is easy when the performed changes are not too aggressive, but it could be more difficult when the similarities between both codes are hard to find. In those cases where the versions are too different, the expression that define the values returned by the main functions can be a good starting point to start checking the behaviour preservation. In case the users need more refined or intricate POIs, they could move them following the control flow backwards on both versions of the code.

Example 1. Consider the real commit in the `string.erl` module of the standard library of the Erlang/OTP whose commit report is available at:

https://github.com/erlang/otp/commit/53288b441ec721ce3bbdcc4ad65b75e11acc5e1b

This change optimizes function `string:tokens/2`. SecEr can automatically check, using the comparison mode, whether this change preserves the original behaviour with a single command. We only need to indicate the two files that must be compared, and a POI for each file. Then, the tool automatically generates test cases that evaluate the POIs, trying to cover as many paths as possible. In this particular example, the POI in both versions is placed in the output of function `string:tokens/2`. SecEr generated 7044 test cases (see Listing 1.8 [6]) that reached these POIs, and it reported that both versions produced the same traces for all test cases.

We can now consider a different scenario and introduce a simple error like, for instance, replacing the expression in line 253 of the new release with the expression `[C | tokens_multiple_2(S, Seps, Toks, [C])]`. In this scenario, SecEr generates 6576 test cases, 5040 of which have a mismatch in their traces (see Listing 1.9 [6]). SecEr stores all the discrepancies found in a file, and it also reports one instance of these failing test cases: ITC `tokens([12,4,5],[2,3,2,5,0,1])`, for which the original program produces the trace `[[[12,4]]]` whereas the new one produces the trace `[[4,[12,4]]]`.

2   A Novel Approach to Automated Regression Testing

Our technique is divided into three sequential phases that are summarized in Figs. 1, 2, and 3. In these figures, the big dark grey areas are used to group several processes with a common objective. The light grey boxes outside these areas represent inputs and the light grey boxes inside these areas represent processes, the white boxes represent intermediate results, and the initial processes of each phase are represented with a thick border box. All these boxes are connected by continuous black arrows (representing the control flow between processes) or by dot-dashed arrows (representing that some data is stored in a database). Finally, there are also parts of these figures contained in light grey boxes with dashed borders. This means that they are only used in the comparison mode. In this case, the process only has two phases instead of three.

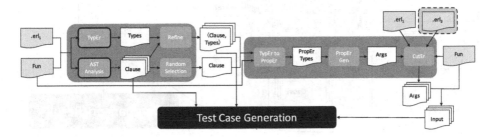

Fig. 1. Type analysis phase

The first phase (Type analysis), depicted in Fig. 1, is in charge of preparing all inputs of the second phase (Test Case Generation). This phase starts by locating in the source code the Erlang module (.erl_1) and an input function (Fun) specified by the user[2] (for instance, function exp in the math module). Then, TypEr is used to obtain the types of the parameters (from now on just *types*) of that function.

It is important to know that, in Erlang, a function is composed of clauses and, when a function is invoked, an internal algorithm traverses all the clauses in order to select the one that will be executed. Unfortunately, TypEr does not provide the individual types of each clause, but global types for the whole function. Therefore, we need to first analyze the AST of the module to identify all the clauses of the input function, and then we refine the types provided by TypEr to determine the specific types of each clause. All these clause types are used in the second phase. In this phase, we use PropEr to instantiate only one of them (e.g., ⟨*Number, Integer*⟩ can be instantiated to ⟨*4.22, 3*⟩ or ⟨*6, 5*⟩). However, PropEr is unable to understand TypEr types, so we have defined a translation process from TypEr types to ProEr types. Finally, CutEr is fed with an initial call (e.g., math:exp(4.22, 3)) and it provides a set of possible arguments (e.g., {⟨*1.5, 6*⟩, ⟨*2, 1*⟩, ⟨*1.33, 4*⟩}). Finally, this set is combined with the function to be called to generate ITCs (e.g., {math:exp(1.5, 6), math:exp(2, 1), math:exp(1.33, 4)}). All this process is explained in detail in Sect. 3.1.

---

[2] We show the process for only one input function. In case the user defined more than one input function, the process described here would be repeated for each of them.

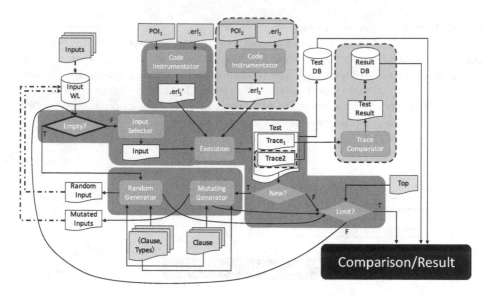

Fig. 2. Test case generation phase

The second phase, shown in Fig. 2, is in charge of generating the test suite. As an initial step, we instrument the program so that its execution records (as a side-effect) the sequence of values produced at the POI (i.e., the traces). Then, we store all ITCs provided by the previous phase onto a working list. Note that it is also possible that the previous phase is unable to provide any ITC due to the limitations of CutEr. In such a case, or when there are no more ITCs left, we randomly generate a new one with PropEr and store it on the working list. Then, each ITC on the working list is executed against the instrumented code, so a trace is produce as a side-effect. The executed ITC and the obtained trace form a new test case, which is a new output of the phase. Moreover, to increase the quality of the test cases produced, whenever a non-previously generated trace is computed, we mutate the ITC that generated that trace to obtain more ITCs. The reason is that a mutation of this ITC will probably generate more ITCs that also evaluate the POI but to different values. This process is repeated until the specified limit of test cases is reached. This phase is slightly modified for the comparison mode where we can directly compare the traces generated by both of them to check discrepancies. Moreover, we only mutate an ITC when the pair of traces generated by both versions has not been obtained before. The entire process is explained in detail in Sects. 3.2 and 3.3.

Finally, the last phase (shown in Fig. 3) checks whether the new version of the code passes the test suite. This suite is only generated in the suite generation mode. In fact, this phase is only applied in this mode. First, the source code of the new release is also instrumented to compute the traces produced at its POI. Then, all the previously generated ITCs are executed and the traces produced are compared with the expected traces.

3   Thorough Description of the Approach

In this section, we describe in more detail the most relevant parts of our approach: the generation of ITCs (Sect. 3.1), the code instrumentation to obtain the traces (Sect. 3.2) and the test case generation (Sect. 3.3).

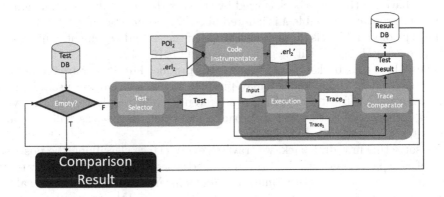

Fig. 3. Comparison phase

3.1   Initial ITC Generation

The process starts from the types inferred by TypEr for the whole input function. This is the first important step to obtain a significant result, because ITCs are generated with the types returned by this process, so the more accurate the types are, the more accurate the ITCs are. TypEr's standard output is an Erlang function type specification returned as a string, which needs to be parsed. For this reason, we have hacked the Erlang module that implements this functionality to obtain the types in a structure, easier to traverse and handle. However, the types returned by TypEr have (in our context) three drawbacks that need to be corrected since they could yield to ITCs that do not match a desired input function.

The first drawback is generated due to the fact that the types provided by TypEr refers to a whole function. We explain the first drawback with an example. Consider a function with two clauses whose headers are g(0,0) and g(1,1). For this function, TypEr infers the function type g(0 | 1, 0 | 1). Thus, the types obtained by TypEr for both parameters are expected to be formed by integers with the values 0 or 1, but the value of each parameter may be any of them in every possible combinations. This means that, if we do not identify the types of each clause, we may generate ITCs that do not match any clause of the function, e.g. g(0,1).

The other two drawbacks are due to the type produced for lists and due to the occurrence of repeated variables. We explain both drawbacks with another example. Consider a function with a single clause whose header is f(A,[A,B]).

For this function, TypEr infers the function type f(1 | 2, [1 | 2 | 5 | 6]). Thus, the type obtained for the second parameter of the f/2 function indicates that the feasible values for this parameter are proper lists with a single constraint: it has to be formed with numbers from the set $\{1, 2, 5, 6\}$. This means that we could build lists of any length, which is our first drawback. If we use these TypEr types, we may generate ITCs that do not match the function, e.g. f(2, [2,1,3,5]).[3] Apart from that, we have another drawback caused by the fact that the value relation generated by the repeated variable A is ignored in the function type. In particular, the actual type of variable A is diluted in the type of the second argument. This could yield to mismatching ITCs if we generate, e.g., f(1, [6,5]).

These three drawbacks show that the types produced by TypEr are too imprecise in our context, because they may produce test cases that are useless (e.g., non-executable). After the TypEr types inference, we can only resolve the type conflict introduced by the first drawback. The other drawbacks will be completely resolved when the ITCs are built.

To solve this first drawback, we traverse every clause classifying the possible types of each parameter with the TypEr deduced types. In this traversal every term is given its own value and every time a variable appears more than once, we calculate its type as the intersection of both the TypEr type and the accumulated type. For instance, in the g/2 example we generate two different types: one for the clause g(0,0) where the only possible value for both parameters is 0, and another one for the clause g(1,1) where the only possible values for both parameters is 1. Furthermore, this transformation is useful not only for functions with multiple clauses, but also with the functions with a single clause like the f/2 function. In this function, we have A = 1 | 2 for the first occurrence, and A = 1 | 2 | 5 | 6 for the second one, obtaining the new accumulated type A = 1 | 2 after applying this solution.

Once we have our refined TypEr types, we rely on PropEr to obtain the input for CutEr. PropEr is a property-based testing framework with a lot of useful underlying functionality. One of them is the value generators, which, given a PropEr type, are able to randomly generate values belonging to such type. Thus, we can use the PropEr generators in our framework to generate values for a given type. However, TypEr and PropEr use slightly different notations for their types, which is reasonable given that their scopes are completely different. Unfortunately, there is no available translator from TypEr types to PropEr types. In our technique, we need such a translator to link the inferred types to the PropEr generators. Therefore, we have built the translator by ourselves. This translation deals with the previously postponed type drawbacks. For that, we use the parameters of the clause in conjunction with their types. To solve the first drawback, each time a list is found during the translation, we traverse its elements and generate a type for each element on the list. Thereby, we synthesize a new type for the list with exactly the same number of elements.

---

[3] Note that having ITCs that do not match with any function clause is not a problem. This scenario is common when TypEr returns the *any* type for some of the function's parameters. However, these ITCs are useless since they will produce an empty trace. This explains our effort to avoid them.

The second drawback is solved by recording the value each variable is assigned to and, whenever a variable already treated is found, the value recorded for its first occurrence is used.

Finally, we can feed CutEr with an initial call by using a randomly selected clause and its values generated by PropEr. CutEr is a concolic testing framework that generates a list of arguments that tries to cover all the execution paths. Unfortunately, this list is internally generated by CutEr but not provided as an output, so we have hacked CutEr to extract all these arguments. Additionally, the execution of CutEr can last too long or even not terminate. For this reason, we run CutEr with a timeout. In the comparison mode, the time assigned to CutEr is equally distributed to generate ITCs of both versions. Finally, by using this slightly modified version of CutEr we are able to generate the initial set of ITCs by mixing the arguments that it provides with the input function.

3.2 Recording the Traces of the Point of Interest

There exist several tools available to trace Erlang executions [2–4,16] (we describe some of them in Sect. 5). However, none of them allows for defining a POI that points to any part of the code. Being able to trace any possible point of interest requires either a code instrumentation, a debugger, or a way to take control of the execution of Erlang. However, using a debugger (e.g., [3]) has the problem that it does not provide a value for the POI when it is inside an expression whose evaluation fails. Therefore, we decided to instrument the code in such a way that, without modifying the semantics of the code, traces are collected as a side effect when the code is executed.

The instrumentation process creates and collects the traces of the POI. To create the traces in an automatic way, we instrument the expression pointed by the POI. To collect the traces, we have several options. For instance, we can store the traces in a file and process it when the execution finishes, but this approach is inefficient. We follow an alternative approach based on message passing. We send messages to a server (which we call the *tracing server*) that is continuously listening for new traces until a message indicating the end of the evaluation is received. This approach is closer to the Erlang's philosophy. Additionally, it is more efficient since the messages are sent asynchronously resulting in an imperceptible overhead in the execution. As a result of the instrumenting process, the transformed code sends to the tracing server the value of the POI each time it is evaluated, and the tracing server stores these values.

In the following, we explain in detail how the communication with the server is placed in the code. This is done by firstly annotating the AST, then obtaining the path from the root to the POI and finally dividing this path in two. In order to do this, the following three steps are applied:

1. We first use the `erl_syntax_lib:annotate_bindings/2` function to annotate the AST of the code. This function annotates each node with two lists of variables: those variables that are being bound and those that were already bound in its subtree.

2. The next step is to find in the code the POI. During the search process, we store the path followed in the AST with tuples of the form (`Node`, `ChildIndex`), where `Node` is the AST node and `ChildIndex` is the index of the node in its parent's children array. When the POI is found, the traversal finishes. Thus, the output of this step is a path in the AST that yields to the POI.

3. The goal of this step is to divide the AST path into two sub-paths (`PathBefore`, `PathAfter`). `PathBefore` yields from the root to the deepest *target expression* (included), and `PathAfter` yields from the first children of the target expression to the POI. We call target expression to those expressions that need a special treatment in the instrumentation. In Erlang, these target expressions are: pattern matchings, list comprehensions, and expressions with clauses (i.e., `case`, `if`, `functions`, ...).

After applying the previous steps we can instrument the POI. Most often, the POI can be easily instrumented by adding a send command to communicate its value to the tracing server. However, when the POI is in the pattern of an expression, this expression needs a special treatment in the instrumentation. Let us show the problem with an example.

Example 2. Consider a POI inside a pattern {1,`POI`,3}. If the execution tries to match it with {2,2,3} nothing should be sent to the tracing server because the POI is never evaluated. Contrarily, if it tries to match the pattern with {1,2,4}, then value 2 must be sent to the tracing server. Note that the matching fails in both cases, but due to the evaluation order, the POI is actually evaluated (and the partial matching succeeds) in the second case. There is an interesting third case, that happens when the `POI` has a value, e.g., 3, and the matching with {1,4,4} is tried. In this case, although the matching at the `POI` fails, we send the value 4 to the tracing server.[4]

We explain now how the actual instrumentation is performed. First, the `PathBefore` path is used to reach the deepest target expression that contains the POI. At this point, five rules (described below) are used to transform the code by using `PathAfter`. Finally, `PathBefore` is traversed backwards to update the AST of the targeted function. The five rules are depicted in Fig. 4. The first four rules are mutually exclusive, and when none of them can be applied, rule (`EXPR`) is applied. Rule (`LEFT_PM`) is fired when the POI is in the pattern of a pattern-matching expression. Rule (`PAT_GEN_LC`) is used to transform a list comprehension when the POI is in the pattern of a generator. Finally, rules (`CLAUSE_PAT`) and (`CLAUSE_GUARD`)[5] transform an expression with clauses when the POI is in the pattern or in the guard of one of its clauses, respectively.

---

[4] We could also send its actual value, i.e., 3. This is just a design decision, but we think that including the value that produced the mismatch could be more useful to find the source of a discrepancy.

[5] Function clauses need an additional transformation that consists in storing all the parameters inside a tuple so that they could be used in the case expressions introduced by these rules.

(LEFT_PM)	p = e ⇒ p = begin np = e, tracer!{add, npoi}, np end
if	$(p = e, \_) = last(PathBefore)$
	$\wedge (\_, pos(p)) = hd(PathAfter)$
where	$(\_, npoi, np) = pfv(p, PathAfter)$

(PAT_GEN_LC)	[e || gg] ⇒ [e || ngg]
if	$([e \parallel gg], \_) = last(PathBefore)$
	$\wedge (\_, pos(p\_gen)) = hd(tl(PathAfter))$
	$\wedge \exists i.\ 1 \leq i \leq length(gg)$ s.t. $gg_i = $ p_gen <- e_gen
where	$(\_, npoi, np\_gen) = pfv(p\_gen,\ tl(PathAfter))$
	$\wedge$ ngg_i = p_gen <- begin tracer!{add, npoi}, [np_gen] end
	$\wedge$ ngg = $gg_1 \ldots gg_{i-1}$, np_gen <- e_gen, ngg_i, $gg_{i+1} \ldots gg_{length(gg)}$

(CLAUSE_PAT)	e ⇒ change_clauses(e, ncls)
if	$(e, \_) = last(PathBefore)$
	$\wedge (\_, pos(p\_c)) = hd(tl(PathAfter))$
	$\wedge \exists i.\ 1 \leq i \leq length(cls)$ s.t. $cls_i = $ p_c when g_c -> b_c
where	$cls = clauses(e)$
	$\wedge (\_, npoi, np\_c) = pfv(p\_c,\ tl(PathAfter))$
	$\wedge$ nb_c = begin tracer!{add, npoi}, case np_c of cls end end
	$\wedge$ ncls_i = np_c when true -> nb_c
	$\wedge$ ncls = $cls_i, \ldots, cls_{i-1}, ncls\_i, cls_{i+1}, \ldots, cls_{length(cls)}$

(CLAUSE_GUARD)	e ⇒ change_clauses(e, ncls)
if	$(e, \_) = last(PathBefore)$
	$\wedge (\_, pos(g\_c)) = hd(tl(PathAfter))$
	$\wedge \exists i.\ 1 \leq i \leq length(cls)$ s.t. $cls_i = $ p_c when g_c -> b_c
where	$cls = clauses(e)$
	$\wedge (poi, \_) = last(PathAfter)$
	$\wedge$ nb_c = begin tracer!{add, poi}, case np_c of cls end end
	$\wedge$ ncl = p_c when true -> nb_c
	$\wedge$ ncls = $cls_i, \ldots, cls_{i-1}, ncl, cls_{i+1}, \ldots, cls_{length(cls)}$

(EXPR)	e ⇒ begin fv = e, tracer!{add, fv}, fv end
otherwise	
where	$(e, \_) = last(PathAfter) \wedge$ fv = $fv()$

Fig. 4. Instrumentation rules for tracing

In the rules, we use the underline symbol (_) to represent a value that is not used. There are several functions used in the rules that need to be introduced. Functions $hd(l)$, $tl(l)$, $length(l)$ and $last(l)$ return the head, the tail, the length, and the last element of the list l, respectively. Function $pos(e)$ returns the index of an expression e on the list of children of its parent. Function $is\_bound(e)$ returns **true** if e is bounded according to the AST binding annotations (see step 1). Function $clauses(e)$ and $change\_clauses(e, clauses)$ obtains and modifies the clauses of e, respectively. Function $fv()$ builds a free variable. Finally, there is a key function named pfv, introduced in Fig. 5, that transforms a pattern so that the constraints after the POI do not inhibit the sending call. This is done by replacing all the terms on the right of the POI with free variables that are built using fv function. Unbound variables on the left and also in the POI are replaced by fresh variables to avoid the shadowing of the original variables. In the pfv function, $children(e)$ and $change\_children(e, children)$ are used to obtain and modify the children of expression e, respectively. In this function, lists are represented with the head-tail notation $(h : t)$.

$$pfv(p,\ path) = \begin{cases} (poi,\ poi',\ p'') & \text{if } path = [(poi, pos)] \\ \quad \text{where } poi' = fv() \wedge p' = fv\_from(pos,\ p) \\ \qquad \wedge\ p'' = p_1' \ldots p_{pos-1}', poi', p_{pos+1}' \ldots p_{length(p)}' \\ (poi,\ poi',\ p''') & \text{otherwise} \\ \quad \text{where } (\_, pos) = hd(path) \wedge p' = fv\_from(pos,\ p) \\ \qquad \wedge\ (poi, poi', p'') = pfv(p_{pos}', tl(path)) \\ \qquad \wedge\ p''' = p_1' \ldots p_{pos-1}', p'', p_{pos+1}' \ldots p_{length(p)}' \end{cases}$$

$$fv\_from(pos,\ p) = \quad p_1' \ldots p_{pos}', fv()_{pos+1} \ldots fv()_{length(p)} \text{ where } (p_1' \ldots p_{pos}', \_) = cv(p_1 \ldots p_{pos},\ [])$$

$$cv(list, map) = \begin{cases} ([], map) & \text{if } list = [] \\ ((fv : p_t'), map') & \text{if } list = (p_h : p_t) \wedge is\_var(p_h) \wedge \neg\ is\_bound(p_h) \\ \quad \text{where } fv = fv() \wedge (p_t', map') = cv(p_t, map \cup \{p_h \mapsto fv\}) \\ ((fv_{map} : p_t'), map') & \text{if } list = (p_h : p_t) \wedge is\_var(p_h) \wedge p_h \mapsto fv_{map} \in map \\ \quad \text{where } (p_t', map') = cv(p_t, map) \\ ((p_h' : p_t'), map'') & \text{otherwise} \\ \quad \text{where } (p_h : p_t) = list \wedge (children_{p_h}', map') = cv(children(p_h), map) \\ \qquad \wedge\ p_h' = change\_children(p_h, children_{p_h}') \\ \qquad \wedge\ (p_t', map'') = cv(p_t, map') \end{cases}$$

Fig. 5. Function pfv

3.3   Generation of New Test Cases Using PropEr and Test Mutation

The test case generation phase uses CutEr whose concolic analyses try to generate 100% branch coverage test cases. Sometimes, these analyses can last too long time. Moreover, even with a 100% branch coverage, frequently the test cases generated by CutEr can be insufficient in our context. For instance, if the expression Z=X-Y is replaced in a new version of the code with Z=X+Y, a single test case that executes both of them with Y=0 cannot detect any difference. Clearly, more values for Y are needed to detect the behaviour change in that expression.

Therefore, to increase the reliability of the test suite when using the suite generation mode, we complement the test cases produced by CutEr with a test mutation technique. Using a mutation technique is much better than using, e.g., the PropEr generator to randomly synthesize new test cases, because random test cases would produce many useless test cases (i.e., test cases that do not execute the POI). In contrast, the use of a test mutation technique increases the probability of generating test cases that execute the POI (because only those test cases that execute the POI are mutated). The function that generates new test cases using mutation is depicted in Fig. 6. The result of the function is a map from the different obtained traces (i.e., the outputs of the test cases) to the set of ITCs that produced them (i.e., the inputs of the test cases). The first call to this function is $tgen(top, cuter\_tests, \emptyset)$, where top is a user-defined limit of the desired number of test cases[6] and *cuter_tests* are the test cases that CutEr generates. Function *tgen* uses the auxiliary functions *proper_gen*, *trace*, and *mut*. The function *proper_gen*() simply calls PropEr to generate a new test case, while function *trace(input)* obtains the corresponding trace when the ITC *input* is executed. The size of a map, *size(map)*, is the total amount of elements stored in all lists that belong to the map. Finally, function *mut(input)* obtains a set of mutations for the ITC *input*, where, for each argument in *input*, a new test case is generated by replacing the argument with a randomly generated value (using PropEr) and leaving the rest of arguments unchanged.

$$
tgen(top, pending, map) =
\begin{cases}
map & \text{if } size(map) \geq top \\
tgen(top, pending', map') & \text{if } size(map) < top \\
& \qquad \wedge\ \exists\ input \in pending \\
& \qquad\qquad \text{s.t. } trace(input) \mapsto \_ \notin map \\
\text{where } pending' = (pending \cup mut(input)) \backslash \{input\} \\
\qquad \wedge\ map' = map \cup \{trace(input) \mapsto \{input\}\} \\
tgen(top, \{proper\_gen()\}, map') & \text{if } size(map) < top \\
& \qquad \wedge\ \nexists\ input \in pending \\
& \qquad\qquad \text{s.t. } trace(input) \mapsto \_ \notin map \\
\text{where } map' = map \\
\qquad \cup\ \{trace(input_p) \mapsto (\{input_p\} \cup inputs_{tp}) \\
\qquad\quad |\ input_p \in pending \wedge trace(input_p) \mapsto inputs_{tp} \in\ map\}
\end{cases}
$$

Fig. 6. Test case generation function

We can define an alternative way to generate tests for the comparison mode. In this scheme, the generated tests are only focused on comparing the differences between two version of the program. This generally yields to better tests for comparison, since some bugs can be explored deeply. For instance, consider that, for a given version of a program, ITCs $f(0,1)$ and $f(0,2)$ produce the same trace, e.g. $[2,3]$. According to the test generation function in Fig. 6, the second generated ITC (e.g., $f(0,2)$) is not further mutated. However, if we used another version of the program and the traces obtained by both ITCs were $[2,3]$ and $[4,5]$, respectively, it would be good to continue mutating the ITC since it is possible that a change in the second parameter reveals new discrepancies between the two versions. Therefore, we do not consider the trace of each individual version to decide whether it should be mutated, but the combination of both of them at the same time. We handle these cases by building a map from a pair of traces to a list of ITCs, instead of from a single trace. For example, the map from the previous example would contain $\langle [2,3], [2,3] \rangle \mapsto [f(0,1)]$ and $\langle [2,3], [4,5] \rangle \mapsto \{f(0,2)\}$ instead of $[2,3] \mapsto \{f(0,1), f(0,2)\}$. Therefore, the key in this new map is different for each ITC so, according to Fig. 6, $f(0,2)$ should be further mutated. In fact, the algorithm to generate traces considering both versions is exactly the same that the one depicted in Fig. 6. The only difference, apart from the change in the map structure, is that the function *trace(input)* is returning here a tuple $\langle trace_{old}(input), trace_{new}(input) \rangle$, where $trace_{old}(input)$

---

[6] In SecEr, a timeout is also used as a way to stop the test case generation.

and $trace_{new}(input)$ are the traces obtained for the ITC *input* using the old and the new version of the code, respectively. Note that in the comparison mode we should obtain a report of the discrepancies during the test generation phase. Obtaining the discrepancies between the traces of both versions is easy using the result of Fig. 6. The following formula calculates them from the map returned by $tgen$.[7]

$$discrepancies(map) = \bigcup\{inputs \mid (\langle t_o, t_n \rangle \mapsto inputs) \in map \text{ s.t. } t_o \neq t_n\}$$

4   The SecEr Tool

SecEr is able to automatically generate a test suite that checks the behaviour of a POI given two versions of the same program. There are two modes of running this tool. The first one allows for generating and storing a test suite of a program that is specific to test a given POI (the suite generation mode). The second one compares the traces of two different versions of a program and reports the discrepancies (the comparison mode).

Listing 1.1. SecEr command format

```
$ ./secer -f FILE -li LINE -var VARIABLE [-oc OCCURRENCE]
          [-f FILE -li LINE -var VARIABLE [-oc OCCURRENCE]]
          [-funs INPUT_FUNCTIONS] -to TIMEOUT
```

Listing 1.1 shows the usage of the SecEr command. If we want to run the command in the suite generation mode, we need to provide the path of the target file (**FILE**), the POI (**LINE**, **VARIABLE**, and **OCCURRENCE**), a list of initial functions (**INPUT_FUNCTIONS**),[8] and a timeout (**TIMEOUT**). If we execute the tool in the comparison mode, the required inputs are slightly different. For each version, we need to specify the path of its file and the details of its POI. Note that both versions use the same input functions. Therefore, these functions need to be exported in both versions of the program for the proper execution of SecEr.

The implementation uses a timeout as a limit to stop generating test cases, while the formalization of the technique uses a number to specify the amount of test cases that must be generated (see variable *top* in Sect. 3.3). This is not a limitation, but a design decision to increase the usability of the tool. The user cannot know a priory how much time it could take to generate an arbitrary number of test cases. Hence, to make the tool predictable and give the user control over the computation time, we use a timeout. Thus, SecEr generates as many test cases as the specified timeout permits.

We have collected some interesting use cases and described how the source of a discrepancy can be spotted using SecEr in them. They are available at [6].

---

[7] According to the definition of function *tgen*, the selection of the ITC that is going to be mutated is completely random. However, in our tool we give more priority to the inputs belonging to *discrepancies(map)* since they are more susceptible of revealing new discrepancies between versions.

[8] The format for this list is [**FUN1/ARITY1**, **FUN2/ARITY2** ...]. If the user does not provide it, all functions exported by the module are used as input functions.

5   Related Work

Automated behavioral testing techniques like Soares et al. [14] and Mongiovi [11] are very similar to our approach, but their techniques are restricted in the kind of changes that can be analyzed (they only focus on refactoring). Contrarily, our approach is independent of the kind (or the cause) of the changes, being able to analyze the effects of any change in the code regardless of its structure.

Automated regression test case generation techniques like Korel and Al-Yami [8] are also very similar to our approach, but they can only generate test cases if they have available both the old and the new releases. Contrarily, in our approach, we can generate test cases with a single release, and reuse the test cases to analyze any new releases by only specifying the points of interest.

Yu et al. [20] presented an approach that combines coverage analysis and delta debugging to locate the sources of the regression faults introduced during some software evolution. Their approach is based on the extraction and analysis of traces. Our approach is also based on traces although not only the goals but also the inputs of this process are slightly different. In particular, we do not require the existence of a test suite (it is automatically generated), while they look for the error sources using a previously defined test suite. Similarly, Zhang et al. [21] use mutation injection and classification to identify commits that introduce faults.

Most of the efforts in regression testing research have been put in the regression testing minimization, selection, and prioritization [19]. In fact, in the particular case of the Erlang language, most of the works in the area are focused on this specific task [1,15,17,18]. We can find other works in Erlang that share similar goals but more focused on checking whether applying a refactoring rule will yield to a semantics-preserving new code [7,9].

With respect to tracing, there are multiple approximations similar to ours. In Erlang's standard libraries, there are implemented two tracing modules. Both are able to trace the function calls and the process related events (spawn, send, receive, etc.). One of these modules is oriented to trace the processes of a single Erlang node [3], allowing for the definition of filters to function calls, e.g., with names of the function to be traced. The second module is oriented to distributed system tracing [4] and the output trace of all the nodes can be formatted in many different ways. Cronqvist [2] presented a tool named redbug where a call stack trace is added to the function call tracing, making possible to trace both the result and the call stack. Till [16] implemented erlyberly, a debugging tool with a Java GUI able to trace the previously defined features (calls, messages, etc.) but also giving the possibility to add breakpoints and trace other features such as exceptions thrown or incomplete calls. All these tools are accurate to trace specific features of the program, but none of them is able to trace the value of an arbitrary point of the program. In our approach, we can trace both the already defined features and also a point of the program regardless of its position.

6   Conclusions

During the lifecycle of any piece of software, different releases may appear, e.g., to correct bugs, to extend the functionality, or to improve the performance. It is of extreme importance to ensure that every new release preserves the correct behaviour of previous releases. Unfortunately, this task is often expensive and time-consuming, because it implies the definition of test cases that must account for the changes introduced in the new release.

In this work, we propose a new approach to automatically check whether the behaviour of certain functionality is preserved among different versions of a program. The approach allows the user to specify a POI that indicates the specific parts of the code that are suspicious or susceptible of presenting discrepancies. Because the POI can be executed several times with a test case, we store the values that the POI takes during the execution. Thus, we can compare all actual evaluations of the POI for each test case.

The technique introduces a new tracing process that allows us to place the POI in patterns, guards, or expressions. For the test case generation, instead of reinventing the wheel, we orchestrate a sophisticated combination of existing tools like CutEr, TypEr, and PropEr. But, we also improve the result produced by the combination of these tools introducing mutation techniques that allow us to find more useful test cases. All the ideas presented have been implemented and made publicly available in a tool called SecEr.

There are several interesting evolutions of this work. We would like to extend our technique to other paradigms. Therefore, we would have to define a generalization of this approach so it could be implemented in other languages. Then, some important features present in most languages (e.g., concurrency) could also be properly traced.

Some extensions to improve the results of the approach can be carried out. Adding some relevant data into the traces, e.g., computation steps, would allow for checking the preservation (or even the improvement) of non-functional properties such as efficiency. In a similar way, allowing for the specification of a list of POIs instead of a single one would enable the tracing of several functionalities in a single run, or the reinforcement of the quality of the test suite. Another way to increase the usefulness of our approach is a special tracing for function calls that would permit to distinguish easier whether an error is due to a discrepancy between either function implementations or calls' arguments. With respect to the mutation technique, we want to find more efficient ways of deciding what should be mutated, e.g., mutate certain elements of a list instead of changing the whole list.

Finally, the user experience can be enriched in several ways. Currently, the approach receives a sequence of functions as input. However, a sequence of concrete calls could be an alternative that could better lead to obscure errors. This alternative also makes it easier to reuse unit test cases building, in this way, a link between unit testing and our approach. Another interesting extension is the implementation of a GUI, which would allow the user to select a POI by just clicking on the source code. We are also interested in investigating whether it is possible to automatically infer POI candidates from the differences between two versions. We could use tools like *diff* to obtain the differences, and either, suggest the inferred candidate POIs to the user, or use them directly without user interaction. Finally, the integration of our tool with control version systems like Git or Subversion would be very beneficial to easily compare code among several versions.

References

1. Bozó, I., Tóth, M., Simos, T.E., Psihoyios, G., Tsitouras, C., Anastassi, Z.: Selecting Erlang test cases using impact analysis. In: AIP Conference Proceedings, vol. 1389, pp. 802–805. AIP (2011)
2. Cronqvist, M.: redbug (2017). https://github.com/massemanet/redbug
3. Ericsson AB: dbg (2017). http://erlang.org/doc/man/dbg.html
4. Ericsson AB: Trace tool builder (2017). http://erlang.org/doc/apps/observer/ttb_ug.html
5. Giantsios, A., Papaspyrou, N., Sagonas, K.: Concolic testing for functional languages. Sci. Comput. Program. **147**, 109–134 (2017). https://doi.org/10.1016/j.scico.2017.04.008
6. Insa, D., Pérez, S., Silva, J., Tamarit, S.: Erlang code evolution control (use cases). CoRR, abs/1802.03998 (2018)
7. Jumpertz, E.: Using QuickCheck and semantic analysis to verify correctness of Erlang refactoring transformations. Master's thesis, Radboud University Nijmegen (2010)
8. Korel, B., Al-Yami, A.M.: Automated regression test generation. ACM SIGSOFT Softw. Eng. Notes **23**(2), 143–152 (1998)
9. Li, H., Thompson, S.: Testing Erlang refactorings with QuickCheck. In: Chitil, O., Horváth, Z., Zsók, V. (eds.) IFL 2007. LNCS, vol. 5083, pp. 19–36. Springer, Heidelberg (2008). https://doi.org/10.1007/978-3-540-85373-2_2
10. Lindahl, T., Sagonas, K.: TypEr: a type annotator of Erlang code. In: Sagonas, K., Armstrong, J. (eds.) Proceedings of the 2005 ACM SIGPLAN Workshop on Erlang, Tallinn, Estonia, 26–28 September 2005, pp. 17–25. ACM (2005). http://doi.acm.org/10.1145/1088361.1088366
11. Mongiovi, M.: Safira: a tool for evaluating behavior preservation. In: Proceedings of the ACM International Conference Companion on Object Oriented Programming Systems Languages and Applications Companion, pp. 213–214. ACM (2011)
12. Papadakis, M., Sagonas, K.: A PropEr integration of types and function specifications with property-based testing. In: Rikitake, K., Stenman, E. (eds.) Proceedings of the 10th ACM SIGPLAN Workshop on Erlang, Tokyo, Japan, 23 September 2011, pp. 39–50. ACM (2011). http://doi.acm.org/10.1145/2034654.2034663
13. Rajal, J.S., Sharma, S.: Article: a review on various techniques for regression testing and test case prioritization. Int. J. Comput. Appl. **116**(16), 8–13 (2015)
14. Soares, G., Gheyi, R., Massoni, T.: Automated behavioral testing of refactoring engines. IEEE Trans. Softw. Eng. **39**(2), 147–162 (2013)
15. Taylor, R., Hall, M., Bogdanov, K., Derrick, J.: Using behaviour inference to optimise regression test sets. In: Nielsen, B., Weise, C. (eds.) ICTSS 2012. LNCS, vol. 7641, pp. 184–199. Springer, Heidelberg (2012). https://doi.org/10.1007/978-3-642-34691-0_14
16. Till, A.: erlyberly (2017). https://github.com/andytill/erlyberly

17. Bozó, I., Tóth, M., Horváth, Z.: Reduction of regression tests for Erlang based on impact analysis (2013)
18. Tóth, M., et al.: Impact analysis of Erlang programs using behaviour dependency graphs. In: Horváth, Z., Plasmeijer, R., Zsók, V. (eds.) CEFP 2009. LNCS, vol. 6299, pp. 372–390. Springer, Heidelberg (2010). https://doi.org/10.1007/978-3-642-17685-2_11
19. Yoo, S., Harman, M.: Regression testing minimization, selection and prioritization: a survey. Softw. Test. Verif. Reliab. **22**(2), 67–120 (2012)
20. Yu, K., Lin, M., Chen, J., Zhang, X.: Practical isolation of failure-inducing changes for debugging regression faults. In: Proceedings of the 27th IEEE/ACM International Conference on Automated Software Engineering, pp. 20–29. ACM (2012)
21. Zhang, L., Zhang, L., Khurshid, S.: Injecting mechanical faults to localize developer faults for evolving software. In: ACM SIGPLAN Notices, vol. 48, pp. 765–784. ACM (2013)

Term Rewriting and CHR

Justifications in Constraint Handling Rules for Logical Retraction in Dynamic Algorithms

Thom Frühwirth[⊠]

Ulm University, Ulm, Germany
`thom.fruehwirth@uni-ulm.de`

Abstract. We present a straightforward source-to-source transformation that introduces justifications for user-defined constraints into the CHR programming language. Then a scheme of two rules suffices to allow for logical retraction (deletion, removal) of constraints during computation. Without the need to recompute from scratch, these rules remove not only the constraint but also undo all consequences of the rule applications that involved the constraint. We prove a confluence result concerning the rule scheme and show its correctness.

When algorithms are written in CHR, constraints represent both data and operations. CHR is already incremental by nature, i.e. constraints can be added at runtime. Logical retraction adds decrementality. Hence any algorithm written in CHR with justifications will become fully dynamic. Operations can be undone and data can be removed at any point in the computation without compromising the correctness of the result.

We present two classical examples of dynamic algorithms, written in our prototype implementation of CHR with justifications that is available online: maintaining the minimum of a changing set of numbers and shortest paths in a graph whose edges change.

1 Introduction

Justifications have their origin in truth maintenance systems (TMS) [McA90] for automated reasoning. In this knowledge representation method, derived information (a formula) is explicitly stored and associated with the information it originates from by means of justifications. This dependency can be used to explain the reason for a conclusion (consequence) by its initial premises. With the help of justifications, conclusions can be withdrawn by retracting their premises. By this *logical retraction*, e.g. default reasoning can be supported and inconsistencies can be repaired by retracting one of the reasons for the inconsistency. An obvious application of justifications are dynamic constraint satisfaction problems (DCSP), in particular over-constrained ones [BM06].

In this work, we extend the applicability of logical retraction to arbitrary algorithms that are expressed in the programming language Constraint Handling

© Springer International Publishing AG, part of Springer Nature 2018
F. Fioravanti and J. P. Gallagher (Eds.): LOPSTR 2017, LNCS 10855, pp. 147–163, 2018.
https://doi.org/10.1007/978-3-319-94460-9_9

Rules (CHR) [Frü09, Frü15, FR18]. To accomplish logical retraction, we have to be aware that CHR constraints can also be deleted by rule applications. These constraints may have to be restored when a premise is retracted. With logical retraction, any algorithm written in CHR will become *fully dynamic*[1].

Minimum Example. Given a multiset of numbers $\mathtt{min}(n_1)$, $\mathtt{min}(n_2)$,..., $\mathtt{min}(n_k)$. The constraint (predicate) $\mathtt{min}(n_i)$ means that the number n_i is a candidate for the minimum value. The following CHR rule filters the candidates.

```
min(N) \ min(M) <=> N=<M | true.
```

The rule consists of a left-hand side, on which a pair of constraints has to be matched, a guard check N=<M that has to be satisfied, and an empty right-hand side denoted by true. In effect, the rule takes two min candidates and removes the one with the larger value (constraints after the \ symbol are deleted). Note that the min constraints behave both as operations (removing other constraints) and as data (being removed).

CHR rules are applied exhaustively. Here the rule keeps on going until only one, thus the smallest value, remains as single min constraint, denoting the current minimum. If another min constraint is added during the computation, it will eventually react with a previous *min* constraint, and the correct current minimum will be computed in the end. Thus the algorithm as implemented in CHR is incremental. It is not decremental, though: We cannot logically retract a *min* candidate. While removing a candidate that is larger than the minimum would be trivial, the retraction of the minimum itself requires to remember all deleted candidates and to find their minimum. With the help of justifications, this logical retraction will be possible automatically.

Contributions and Overview of the Paper. In the next section we recall syntax and operational semantics for CHR. Our contributions are as follows:

- We introduce CHR with justifications (CHR$^{\mathcal{J}}$) in Sect. 3. We enhance standard CHR programs with justifications by a source-to-source program transformation. We show the operational equivalence of rule applications in both settings. Thus CHR$^{\mathcal{J}}$ is a conservative extension of standard CHR.
- We define a scheme of two rules to enable logical retraction of constraints based on justifications in Sect. 4. We show that the rule scheme is confluent with each rule in any given program, independent of the confluence of that program. We prove correctness of logical retraction: the result of a computation with retraction is the same as if the constraint would never have been introduced in the computation.
- We present a proof-of-concept implementation of CHR$^{\mathcal{J}}$ in CHR and Prolog (available online) in Sect. 5. We discuss two classical examples for dynamic algorithms, maintaining the minimum of a changing set of numbers and maintaining shortest paths in a graph whose edges change.

---

[1] Dynamic algorithms for dynamic problems should not be confused with dynamic programming.

The paper ends with discussion of related work in Sect. 6 and with conclusions and directions for future work.

2   Preliminaries

We recall the abstract syntax and the equivalence-based abstract operational semantics of CHR in this section. Upper-case letters stand for (possibly empty) conjunctions of constraints in this paper.

2.1   Abstract Syntax of CHR

Constraints are relations, distinguished predicates of first-order predicate logic. We differentiate between two kinds of constraints: *built-in (pre-defined) constraints* and *user-defined (CHR) constraints* which are defined by the rules in a CHR program.

Definition 1. A *CHR program* is a finite set of rules. A *(generalized) simpagation rule* is of the form

$$r : H_1 \backslash H_2 \Leftrightarrow C | B$$

where r : is an optional *name* (a unique identifier) of a rule. In the rule *head* (left-hand side), H_1 and H_2 are conjunctions of user-defined constraints, the optional *guard* $C|$ is a conjunction of built-in constraints, and the *body* (right-hand side) B is a goal. A *goal* is a conjunction of built-in and user-defined constraints. A *state* is a goal. Conjunctions are understood as *multisets* of their conjuncts.

In the rule, H_1 are called the *kept constraints*, while H_2 are called the *removed constraints*. At least one of H_1 and H_2 must be non-empty. If H_1 is empty, the rule corresponds to a *simplification rule*, also written

$$s : H_2 \Leftrightarrow C | B.$$

If H_2 is empty, the rule corresponds to a *propagation rule*, also written

$$p : H_1 \Rightarrow C | B.$$

In this work, we restrict given CHR programs to rules without built-in constraints in the body except *true* and *false*. This restriction is necessary as long as built-in constraint solvers do not support the removal of built-in constraints.

2.2   Abstract Operational Semantics of CHR

Computations in CHR are sequences of rule applications. The operational semantics of CHR is given by the state transition system. It relies on a structural equivalence between states that abstracts away from technical details in a transition [RBF09, Bet14].

State equivalence treats built-in constraints semantically and user-defined constraints syntactically. Basically, two states are equivalent if their built-in constraints are logically equivalent (imply each other) and their user-defined constraints form syntactically equivalent multisets. For example,

$$X =< Y \wedge Y =< X \wedge c(X,Y) \equiv X = Y \wedge c(X,X) \not\equiv X = Y \wedge c(X,X) \wedge c(X,X).$$

For a state S, the notation S_{bi} denotes the built-in constraints of S and S_{ud} denotes the user-defined constraints of S.

Definition 2 (State Equivalence). Two states $S_1 = (S_{1bi} \wedge S_{1ud})$ and $S_2 = (S_{2bi} \wedge S_{2ud})$ are *equivalent*, written $S_1 \equiv S_2$, if and only if

$$\models \forall(S_{1bi} \rightarrow \exists \bar{y}((S_{1ud} = S_{2ud}) \wedge S_{2bi})) \wedge \forall(S_{2bi} \rightarrow \exists \bar{x}((S_{1ud} = S_{2ud}) \wedge S_{1bi}))$$

with $\bar{x}$ those variables that only occur in S_1 and $\bar{y}$ those variables that only occur in S_2.

Using this state equivalence, the abstract CHR semantics is defined by a single transition (computation step). It defines the application of a rule. Note that CHR is a committed-choice language, i.e. there is no backtracking in the rule applications.

Definition 3 (Transition). Let the rule $(r : H_1 \backslash H_2 \Leftrightarrow C|B)$ be a variant[2] of a rule from a given program $\mathcal{P}$. The *transition (computation step)* $S \mapsto_r T$ is defined as follows, where S is called *source state* and T is called *target state*:

$$\frac{S \equiv (H_1 \wedge H_2 \wedge C \wedge G) \quad (r : H_1 \backslash H_2 \Leftrightarrow C|B) \in \mathcal{P} \quad (H_1 \wedge C \wedge B \wedge G) \equiv T}{S \mapsto_r T}$$

The goal G is called *context* of the rule application. It is left unchanged.

A *computation (derivation)* of a goal S in a program $\mathcal{P}$ is a connected sequence $S_i \mapsto_{r_i} S_{i+1}$ beginning with the *initial state (query)* S_0 that is S and ending in a *final state (answer, result)* or the sequence is *non-terminating (diverging)*. We may drop the reference to the rules r_i to simplify the presentation. The notation $\mapsto^*$ denotes the reflexive and transitive closure of $\mapsto$.

If the source state can be made equivalent to a state that contains the head constraints and the guard built-in constraints of a variant of a rule, then we delete the removed head constraints from the state and add the rule body constraints to it. Any state that is equivalent to this target state is in the transition relation.

The abstract semantics does not account for termination of inconsistent states and propagation rules. From a state with inconsistent built-in constraints, any transition is possible. If a state can fire a propagation rule once, it can do so again and again. This is called trivial non-termination of propagation rules.

Minimum Example, contd. Here is a possible transition from a state $S = (min(0) \wedge min(2) \wedge min(1))$ to a state $T = (min(0) \wedge min(1))$:

$$\frac{S \equiv (min(X) \wedge min(Y) \wedge X \leq Y \wedge (X = 0 \wedge Y = 2 \wedge min(1))) \quad (min(X)\backslash min(Y) \Leftrightarrow X \leq Y|true) \quad (min(X) \wedge X \leq Y \wedge true \wedge (X = 0 \wedge Y = 2 \wedge min(1))) \equiv T}{S \mapsto T}$$

---

[2] A variant (renaming) of an expression is obtained by uniformly replacing its variables by fresh variables.

3   CHR with Justifications (CHR$^{\mathcal{J}}$)

We present a conservative extension of CHR by justifications. If they are not used, programs behave as without them. Justifications annotate atomic CHR constraints. A simple source-to-source transformation extends the rules with justifications.

Definition 4 (CHR Constraints and Initial States with Justifications).
A *justification* f is a unique identifier. Given an atomic CHR constraint G, a *CHR constraint with justifications* is of the form G^F, where F is a set of justifications. An *initial state with justifications* is of the form $\bigwedge_{i=1}^{n} G_i^{\{f_i\}}$ where the f_i are distinct justifications.

We now define a source-to-source translation from rules to rules with justifications. Let *kill* and *rem* (remove) be unary *reserved* CHR constraint symbols. This means they are only allowed to occur in rules as specified in the following.

Definition 5 (Translation to Rules with Justifications). Given a generalized simpagation rule

$$r : \bigwedge_{i=1}^{l} K_i \setminus \bigwedge_{j=1}^{m} R_j \Leftrightarrow C \mid \bigwedge_{k=1}^{n} B_k$$

Its translation to a *simpagation rule with justifications* is of the form

$$rf : \bigwedge_{i=1}^{l} K_i^{F_i} \setminus \bigwedge_{j=1}^{m} R_j^{F_j} \Leftrightarrow C \mid \bigwedge_{j=1}^{m} rem(R_j^{F_j})^F \wedge \bigwedge_{k=1}^{n} B_k^F \text{ where } F = \bigcup_{i=1}^{l} F_i \cup \bigcup_{j=1}^{m} F_j.$$

The translation ensures that the head and the body of a rule mention exactly the same justifications. More precisely, each CHR constraint in the body is annotated with the union of all justifications in the head of the rule, because its creation is caused by all of the head constraints. The constraint *rem/1* (remember removed) stores the constraints removed by the rule together with their justifications.

3.1   Operational Equivalence of Rule Applications

Let $A, B, C \ldots$ be states. For convenience, we will often consider them as multisets of atomic constraints. Then the notation $A - B$ denotes multiset difference, A without B. To avoid clutter, let $A^{\mathcal{J}}, B^{\mathcal{J}}, C^{\mathcal{J}} \ldots$ stand for conjunctions (or corresponding states) whose atomic CHR constraints are annotated with justifications according to the above definition of the rule scheme. Similarly, let $rem(R)^{\mathcal{J}}$ denote a conjunction $\bigwedge_{j=1}^{m} rem(R_j^{F_j})^F$.

We show that rule applications correspond to each other in standard CHR and in CHR$^{\mathcal{J}}$.

Lemma 1 (Equivalence of Program Rules). There is a computation step $S \mapsto_r T$ with simpagation rule

$$r : H_1 \backslash H_2 \Leftrightarrow C | B$$

if and only if there is a computation step with justifications $S^{\mathcal{J}} \mapsto_{rf} T^{\mathcal{J}} \wedge rem(H_2)^{\mathcal{J}}$ with the corresponding simpagation rule with justifications

$$rf : H_1^{\mathcal{J}} \backslash H_2^{\mathcal{J}} \Leftrightarrow C | rem(H_2)^{\mathcal{J}} \wedge B^{\mathcal{J}}.$$

Proof. We compare the two transitions involving rule r and rf, respectively:

$$\frac{(r : H_1 \backslash H_2 \Leftrightarrow C | B)}{S \equiv (H_1 \wedge H_2 \wedge C \wedge G) \quad (H_1 \wedge C \wedge B \wedge G) \equiv T}{S \mapsto_r T}$$

$$\frac{(rf : H_1^{\mathcal{J}} \backslash H_2^{\mathcal{J}} \Leftrightarrow C | rem(H_2)^{\mathcal{J}} \wedge B^{\mathcal{J}})}{S^{\mathcal{J}} \equiv (H_1^{\mathcal{J}} \wedge H_2^{\mathcal{J}} \wedge C \wedge G^{\mathcal{J}}) \quad (H_1^{\mathcal{J}} \wedge C \wedge B^{\mathcal{J}} \wedge G^{\mathcal{J}}) \equiv T^{\mathcal{J}} \wedge rem(H_2)^{\mathcal{J}}}{S^{\mathcal{J}} \mapsto_{rf} T^{\mathcal{J}} \wedge rem(H_2)^{\mathcal{J}}}$$

Given the standard transition with rule r, the corresponding transition with justifications with rule rf is always possible. The rule rf by definition involves the same constraints (up to addition of justifications) as the standard rule r. It does not impose any additional built-in constraints, in particular no constraints on its justifications. The justifications in the rule body are computed as the union of the justifications in the rule head, which is always possible. Furthermore, the *rem* constraints in the rule body are simply added to the target state.

Conversely, given the transition with justifications with rule rf, we can strip away[3] all justifications from it and remove $rem(H_2)^{\mathcal{J}}$ from the rule and the target state to arrive at the standard transition with rule r.   □

Since computations are sequences of connected computation steps, this lemma implies that computations for program rules in CHR and in CHR with justifications correspond to each other. Thus CHR$^{\mathcal{J}}$ is a conservative extension of CHR.

4   Logical Retraction Using Justifications

We use justifications to remove a CHR constraint from a computation without the need to recompute from scratch. This means that all its consequences due to rule applications it was involved in are undone. CHR constraints added by those rules are removed and CHR constraints removed by the rules are re-added. To specify and implement this behavior, we give a scheme of two rules, one for retraction and one for re-adding of constraints. The reserved CHR constraint $kill(f)$ undoes all consequences of the constraint with justification f.

---

[3] For a related strip function, see the proof of Theorem 3.

Definition 6 (Rules for CHR Logical Retraction). For each n-ary CHR constraint symbol c (except the reserved *kill* and *rem*), we add a rule to kill constraints and a rule to revive removed constraints of the form:

$$\text{kill} : kill(f) \setminus G^F \Leftrightarrow f \in F \mid true$$

$$\text{revive} : kill(f) \setminus rem(G^{F_c})^F \Leftrightarrow f \in F \mid G^{F_c},$$

where $G = c(X_1, \ldots, X_n)$, where $X_1, \ldots, X_n$ are different variables.

Note that a constraint may be revived and subsequently killed. This is the case when both F_c and F contain the justification f.

4.1   Confluence of Logical Retraction

Confluence of a program guarantees that any computation starting from a given initial state can always reach equivalent states, no matter which of the applicable rules are applied. There is a decidable, sufficient and necessary syntactic condition to check confluence of terminating programs and to detect rule pairs that lead to non-confluence when applied.

Definition 7 (Confluence). If $A \mapsto^* B$ and $A \mapsto^* C$ then there exist states D_1 and D_2 such that $B \mapsto^* D_1$ and $C \mapsto^* D_2$ where $D_1 \equiv D_2$.

Theorem 1 [Abd97, AFM99]. A terminating CHR program is confluent if and only if all its critical pairs are joinable.

Decidability comes from the fact that there is only a finite number of critical pairs to consider.

Definition 8 (Overlap, Critical Pair). Given two (not necessarily different) simpagation rules whose variables have been renamed apart, $K_1 \setminus R_1 \Leftrightarrow C_1 | B_1$ and $K_2 \setminus R_2 \Leftrightarrow C_2 | B_2$. Let A_1 and A_2 be non-empty conjunctions of constraints taken from $K_1 \wedge R_1$ and $K_2 \wedge R_2$, respectively. An *overlap* of the two rules is the state consisting of the rules heads and guards:

$$((K_1 \wedge R_1) - A_1) \wedge K_2 \wedge R_2 \wedge A_1 = A_2 \wedge C_1 \wedge C_2.$$

The *critical pair* are the two states that come from applying the two rules to the overlap, where $E = (A_1 = A_2 \wedge C_1 \wedge C_2)$:

$$(((K_1 \wedge K_2 \wedge R_2) - A_2) \wedge B_1 \wedge E <> ((K_1 \wedge R_1 \wedge K_2) - A_1) \wedge B_2 \wedge E).$$

Note that the two states in the critical pair differ by $R_2 \wedge B_1$ and $R_1 \wedge B_2$.

A critical pair is *trivially joinable* if its built-in constraints are inconsistent or if both A_1 and A_2 do not contain removed constraints [AFM99].

We are ready to show the confluence of the *kill* and *revive* rules with each other and with each rule in any given program. It is not necessary that the given program is confluent. This means for any given program, the order between applying applicable rules from the program and retracting constraints can be freely interchanged. It does not matter for the result, if we kill a constraint first or if we apply a rule to it and kill it and its consequences later.

Theorem 2 (Confluence of Logical Retraction). Given a CHR program whose rules are translated to rules with justifications together with the *kill* and *revive* rules. We assume there is at most one *kill(f)* constraint for each justification f in any state. Then all critical pairs between the *kill* and *revive* rules and any rule from the program with justifications are joinable.

Proof. There is only one overlap between the *kill* and *revive* rules,

$$\text{kill} : kill(f) \setminus G^F \Leftrightarrow f \in F \mid true$$

$$\text{revive} : kill(f) \setminus rem(G^{F_c})^F \Leftrightarrow f \in F \mid G^{F_c},$$

since G^F cannot have the reserved constraint symbol $rem/1$. The overlap is in the $kill(f)$ constraint. But since it is not removed by any rule, the resulting critical pair is trivially joinable.

By our assumption, the only overlap between two instances of the *kill* rule must have a single $kill(f)$ constraint. Again, since it is not removed, the resulting critical pair is trivially joinable. The same argument applies to the only overlap between two instances of the *revive* rule.

Since the head of a simpagation rule with justifications from the given program

$$rf : K^{\mathcal{J}} \backslash R^{\mathcal{J}} \Leftrightarrow C | rem(R)^{\mathcal{J}} \wedge B^{\mathcal{J}}$$

cannot contain reserved *kill* and *rem* constraints, these program rules cannot have an overlap with the *revive* rule.

But there are overlaps between program rules, say a rule rf, and the *kill* rule. They take the general form:

$$kill(f) \wedge K^{\mathcal{J}} \wedge R^{\mathcal{J}} \wedge G^F = A^F \wedge f \in F \wedge C,$$

where A^F occurs in $K^{\mathcal{J}} \wedge R^{\mathcal{J}}$. This leads to the critical pair

$$(kill(f) \wedge ((K^{\mathcal{J}} \wedge R^{\mathcal{J}}) - G^F) \wedge E) <> (kill(f) \wedge K^{\mathcal{J}} \wedge rem(R)^{\mathcal{J}} \wedge B^{\mathcal{J}} \wedge E),$$

where $E = (G^F = A^F \wedge f \in F \wedge C)$. In the first state of the critical pair, the *kill* rule has been applied and in the second state the rule rf. Note that A^F is atomic since it is equated to G^F in E. Since G^F has been removed in the first state and $G^F = A^F$, rule rf is no longer applicable in that state.

We would like to join these two states. The joinability between a rule rf and the *kill* rule can be visualized by the diagram:

$$kill(f) \wedge K^{\mathcal{J}} \wedge R^{\mathcal{J}} \wedge E$$

$$kill \qquad\qquad\qquad rf$$

$$kill(f) \wedge ((K^{\mathcal{J}} \wedge R^{\mathcal{J}}) - G^F) \wedge E \xleftarrow{\quad revive^*, kill^* \quad}^{*} kill(f) \wedge K^{\mathcal{J}} \wedge rem(R)^{\mathcal{J}} \wedge B^{\mathcal{J}} \wedge E$$

We now explain this joinability result. The states of the critical pair differ. In the first state we have the constraints $R^{\mathcal{J}}$ and have G^F removed from $K^{\mathcal{J}} \wedge R^{\mathcal{J}}$, while in the second state we have the body constraints $rem(R)^{\mathcal{J}} \wedge B^{\mathcal{J}}$ of rule rf instead. Any constraint in $rem(R)^{\mathcal{J}} \wedge B^{\mathcal{J}}$ must include f as justification by definition, because f occurred in the head constraint A^F and E contains $f \in F$.

The goal $rem(R)^{\mathcal{J}}$ contains rem constraints for each removed constraint from $R^{\mathcal{J}}$. But then we can use $kill(f)$ with the *revive* rule to replace all rem constraints by the removed constraints, thus adding $R^{\mathcal{J}}$ back again. Furthermore, we can use $kill(f)$ with the *revive* rule to remove each constraint in $B^{\mathcal{J}}$, as each constraint in $B^{\mathcal{J}}$ contains the justification f. So $rem(R)^{\mathcal{J}} \wedge B^{\mathcal{J}}$ has been removed completely and $R^{\mathcal{J}}$ has been re-added.

The two states may still differ in the occurrence of G^F (which is A^F). In the first state, G^F was removed by the *kill* rule. Now if A^F (G^F) was in $R^{\mathcal{J}}$, it has been revived with $R^{\mathcal{J}}$. But then the *kill* rule is applicable and we can remove A^F again. In the second state, if A^F was in $R^{\mathcal{J}}$ it has been removed together with $R^{\mathcal{J}}$ by application of rule rf. Otherwise, A^F is still contained in $K^{\mathcal{J}}$. But then the *kill* rule is applicable to A^F and removes it from $K^{\mathcal{J}}$. Now A^F (G^F) does not occur in the second state either.

We thus have arrived at the first state of the critical pair. Therefore the critical pair is joinable. □

This means that given a state, if there is a constraint to be retracted, we can either kill it immediately or still apply a rule to it and use the *kill* and *revive* rules afterwards to arrive at the same resulting state.

Note that the confluence between the *kill* and *revive* rules and any rule from the program is independent of the confluence of the rules in the given program.

4.2 Correctness of Logical Retraction

We prove correctness of logical retraction. The result of a computation with retraction is the same as if the retracted constraint would never have been introduced in the computation. We show that given a computation starting from an initial state with a *kill(f)* constraint that ends in a state where the *kill* and *revive* rules are not applicable, i.e. these rules have been applied to exhaustion, then there is a corresponding computation without constraints that contain the justification f.

Theorem 3 (Correctness of Logical Retraction). Given a computation

$$A^{\mathcal{J}} \wedge G^{\{f\}} \wedge kill(f) \mapsto^* B^{\mathcal{J}} \wedge rem(R)^{\mathcal{J}} \wedge kill(f) \not\mapsto_{kill,revive},$$

where f does not occur in $A^{\mathcal{J}}$. Then there is a computation without $G^{\{f\}}$ and $kill(f)$

$$A^{\mathcal{J}} \mapsto^* B^{\mathcal{J}} \wedge rem(R)^{\mathcal{J}}.$$

Proof. We distinguish between transitions that involve the justification f or do not. A rule that applies to constraints that do not contain the justification f

will produce constraints that do not contain the justification. A rule application that involves at least one constraint with a justification f will only produce constraints that contain the justification f.

We now define a mapping from a computation with $G^{\{f\}}$ to a corresponding computation without $G^{\{f\}}$. The mapping essentially strips away constraints that contain the justification f except those that are remembered by *rem* constraints. In this way, the exhaustive application of the *revive* and *kill* rules $kill(f)$ is mimicked.

$$strip(f, A^{\mathcal{J}} \wedge B^{\mathcal{J}}) := strip(f, A^{\mathcal{J}}) \wedge strip(f, B^{\mathcal{J}})$$
$$strip(f, rem(G^{F_1})^{F_2}) := strip(f, G^{F_1}) \text{ if } f \in F_2$$
$$strip(f, G^F) := true \text{ if } G \text{ is an atomic constraint except } rem/1 \text{ and } f \in F$$
$$strip(f, G^F) := G^F \text{ otherwise.}$$

We extend the mapping from states to transitions. We keep the transitions except where the source and target state are equivalent, in that case we replace the transition $\mapsto$ by an equivalence $\equiv$. This happens when a rule is applied that involves the justification f. The mapping is defined in such a way that in this case the source and target state are equivalent. Otherwise a rule that does not involve f has been applied. The mapping ensures in this case that all necessary constraints are in the source and target state, since it keeps all constraints that do not mention the justification f. For a computation step $C^{\mathcal{J}} \mapsto D^{\mathcal{J}}$ we define the mapping as:

$$strip(f, C^{\mathcal{J}} \mapsto_{rf} D^{\mathcal{J}}) := strip(f, C^{\mathcal{J}}) \equiv strip(f, D^{\mathcal{J}}) \text{ if rule } rf \text{ involves } f$$
$$strip(f, C^{\mathcal{J}} \mapsto_{rf} D^{\mathcal{J}}) := strip(f, C^{\mathcal{J}}) \mapsto_{rf} strip(f, D^{\mathcal{J}}) \text{ otherwise.}$$

We next have to show is that the mapping results in correct state equivalences and transitions. If a rule is applied that does not involve justification f, then it is easy to see that the mapping $strip(f, \ldots)$ leaves states and transitions unchanged.

Otherwise the transition is the application of a rule rf from the program, the rule *kill* or the rule *revive* where f is contained in the justifications. Let the context $E^{\mathcal{J}}$ be an arbitrary goal where $f \in \mathcal{J}$. Then we have to compute

$$strip(f, kill(f) \wedge G^F \wedge f \in F \wedge E^{\mathcal{J}} \mapsto_{kill} kill(f) \wedge E^{\mathcal{J}})$$

$$strip(f, kill(f) \wedge rem(G^{F_c})^F \wedge f \in F \wedge E^{\mathcal{J}} \mapsto_{revive} kill(f) \wedge G^{F_c} \wedge E^{\mathcal{J}})$$

$$strip(f, K^{\mathcal{J}} \wedge R^{\mathcal{J}} \wedge C \wedge E^{\mathcal{J}} \mapsto_{rf} K^{\mathcal{J}} \wedge rem(R)^{\mathcal{J}} \wedge B^{\mathcal{J}} \wedge C \wedge E^{\mathcal{J}})$$

and to show that equivalent states are produced in each case. The resulting states are

$$true \wedge true \wedge true \wedge E^{\mathcal{J}'} \equiv true \wedge E^{\mathcal{J}'}$$

$$true \wedge G^{F_c} \wedge true \wedge E^{\mathcal{J}'} \equiv true \wedge G^{F_c} \wedge E^{\mathcal{J}'} \text{ if } f \notin F_c$$

$$true \wedge true \wedge true \wedge E^{\mathcal{J}'} \equiv true \wedge true \wedge E^{\mathcal{J}'} \text{ if } f \in F_c$$

$$K^{\mathcal{J}'} \wedge R^{\mathcal{J}'} \wedge C \wedge E^{\mathcal{J}'} \equiv K^{\mathcal{J}'} \wedge R^{\mathcal{J}'} \wedge C \wedge E^{\mathcal{J}'} \text{ where } f \notin \mathcal{J}',$$

where, given a goal A, the expression $A^{\mathcal{J}'}$ contains all constraints from $A^{\mathcal{J}}$ that do not contain the justification f.

In the end state of the given computation we know that the *revive* and *kill* rules have been applied to exhaustion. Therefore all $rem(G^{F_1})^{F_2}$ where F_2 contains f have been replaced by G^{F_1} by the *revive* rule. Therefore all standard constraints with justification f have been removed by the *kill* rule (including those revived), just as we do in the mapping $strip(f, \ldots)$.

Therefore the end states are indeed equivalent except for the remaining *kill* constraint.   □

5 Implementation

As a proof-of-concept, we implement CHR with justifications (CHR$^{\mathcal{J}}$) in SWI-Prolog using its CHR library. This prototype source-to-source transformation is available online at http://pmx.informatik.uni-ulm.de/chr/translator/. The translated programs can be run in Prolog or online systems like WebCHR.

Constraints with Justifications. CHR constraints annotated by a set of justifications are realized by a binary infix operator ##, where the second argument is a list of justifications:

$C^{\{F_1, F_2, \ldots\}}$ is realized as C ## [F1,F2,...].

For convenience, we add rules that add a new justification to a given constraint C. For each constraint symbol c with arity n there is a rule of the form

addjust @ c(X1,X2,...Xn) <=> c(X1,X2,...Xn) ## [_F].

where the arguments of X1,X2,...Xn are different variables.

Rules with Justifications. A CHR simpagation rule with justifications is realized as follows:

$$rf : \bigwedge_{i=1}^{l} K_i^{F_i} \setminus \bigwedge_{j=1}^{m} R_j^{F_j} \Leftrightarrow C \mid \bigwedge_{j=1}^{m} rem(R_j^{F_j})^F \wedge \bigwedge_{k=1}^{n} B_k^F \text{ where } F = \bigcup_{i=1}^{l} F_i \cup \bigcup_{j=1}^{m} F_j$$

```
rf @ K1 ## FK1,... \ R1 ## FR1,... <=> C |
     union([FK1,...FR1,...],Fs), rem(R1##FR1) ## Fs,...B1 ## Fs,...
```

where the auxiliary predicate union/2 computes the ordered duplicate-free union of a list of lists[4].

---

[4] More precisely, a simplification rule is generated if there are no kept constraints and a propagation rule is generated if there are no removed constraints.

Rules *remove* **and** *revive.* Justifications are realized as *flags* that are initially unbound logical variables. This eases the generation of new unique justifications and their use in killing. Concretely, the reserved constraint *kill(f)* is realized as built-in equality F=r, i.e. the justification variable gets bound. If *kill(f)* occurred in the head of a *kill* or *revive* rule, it is moved to the guard as equality test F==r. Note that we rename rule *kill* to remove in the implementation.

revive : $kill(f) \setminus rem(C^{F_c})^F \Leftrightarrow f \in F \mid C^{F_c}$
kill : $kill(f) \setminus C^F \Leftrightarrow f \in F \mid true$

```
revive @ rem(C##FC) ## Fs <=> member(F,Fs),F==r | C ## FC.
remove @ C ## Fs <=> member(F,Fs),F==r | true.
```

Since rules are tried in program order in the CHR implementation, the constraint C in the second rule is not a reserved rem/1 constraint when the rule is applicable. The check for set membership in the guards is expressed using the standard nondeterministic Prolog built-in predicate member/2.

Logical Retraction with killc/1. We extend the translation to allow for retraction of derived constraints. The constraint killc(C) logically retracts one occurrence of a constraint C. The two rules killc and killr try to find the constraint C. The killr rule applies in the case where constraint C has been removed and is therefore now present in a rem constraint. The associated justifications point to all initial constraints that where involved in producing the constraint C. For retracting the constraint, it is sufficient to remove one of its producers. This introduces a choice which is implemented by the member predicate.

```
killc @  killc(C), C ## Fs <=> member(F,Fs),F=r.
killr @  killc(C), rem(C ## FC) ## _Fs <=> member(F,FC),F=r.
```

Note that in the killr rule, we bind a justification F from FC, because FC contains the justifications of the producers of constraint C, while Fs also contains those that removed it by a rule application.

5.1   Examples

We discuss two classical examples for dynamic algorithms, maintaining the minimum of a changing set of numbers and shortest paths when edges change.

Dynamic Minimum. Translating the minimum rule to one with justifications results in:

```
min(A)##B \ min(C)##D <=> A<C | union([B,D],E), rem(min(C)##D)##E.
```

The following shows an example query and the resulting answer in SWI-Prolog:

```
?- min(1)##[A], min(0)##[B], min(2)##[C].
rem(min(1)##[A])##[A,B], rem(min(2)##[C])##[B,C], min(0)##[B].
```

The constraint min(0) remained. This means that 0 is the minimum. The constraints min(1) and min(2) have been removed and are now remembered. Both have been removed by the constraint with justification B, i.e. min(0).

We now logically retract with killc the constraint min(1) at the end of the query. The killr rule applies and removes rem(min(1)##[A])##[A,B].

```
killr @ killc(C), rem(C ## FC) ## _Fs <=> member(F,FC),F=r.
```

In the rule body, the justification A is bound to r – to no effect, since there are no other constraints with this justification:

```
?- min(1)##[A], min(0)##[B], min(2)##[C], killc(min(1)).
rem(min(2)##[C])##[B,C], min(0)##[B].
```

On the other hand, if we retract the minimum min(0), the killc rule

```
killc @ killc(C), C ## Fs <=> member(F,Fs),F=r
```

applies. It removes min(0)##[B] and binds justification B. The two rem constraints for min(1) and min(2) have justification B as well, so these two constraints are re-introduced by applications of rule revive

```
revive @ rem(C##FC) ## Fs <=> member(F,Fs),F==r | C ## FC.
```

The minimum rule applies to these two revived constraints. Note that min(2) is now removed by min(1) (before it was min(0)). The result is the updated minimum, which of course is 1:

```
?- min(1)##[A], min(0)##[B], min(2)##[C], killc(min(0)).
rem(min(2)##[C])##[A,C], min(1)##[B].
```

Dynamic Shortest Path. Given a graph with directed arcs e(X,Y), we compute the lengths of the shortest paths between all pairs of reachable nodes:

```
% keep shorter of two paths from X to Y
pp @ p(X,Y,L1) \ p(X,Y,L2) <=> L1=<L2 | true.
% edges have a path of unit length
e  @ e(X,Y) ==> p(X,Y,1).
% extend path in front by an edge
ep @ e(X,Y), p(Y,Z,L) ==> L1=:=L+1 | p(X,Z,L1).
```

The corresponding rules in the translated program are:

```
pp@p(A,B,C)##D \ p(A,B,E)##F <=> C=<E |
                        union([D,F],G), rem(p(A,B,E)##F)##G.
e  @e(A,B)##C ==> true | union([C],D), p(A,B,1)##D.
ep@e(A,B)##C,p(B,D,E)##F ==> G is E+1 | union([C,F],H),p(A,D,G)##H.
```

Here is a sample query and its resulting answer.

```
?- e(a,b)##[A], e(b,c)##[B], e(a,c)##[C].
rem(p(a, c, 2)##[A, B])##[A,B,C],
p(a, b, 1)##[A], e(a, b)##[A],
p(b, c, 1)##[B], e(b, c)##[B],
p(a, c, 1)##[C], e(a, c)##[C].
```

We see that a path of length 2 has been removed by the constraint e(a,c)##[C], which produced a shorter path of length one. We next kill this constraint e(a,c).

```
?- e(a,b)##[A], e(b,c)##[B], e(a,c)##[C], kill(e(a,c)).
p(a, b, 1)##[A], e(a, b)##[A],
p(b, c, 1)##[B], e(b, c)##[B],
p(a, c, 2)##[A,B].
```

Its path p(a,c,1) disappears and the removed path p(a,c,2) is re-added. We can see that the justifications of a path contains are those from the edges in that path. The same happens if we logically retract p(a,c,1) instead of e(a,c).

What happens if we remove p(a,c,2) from the initial query? The killr rule applies. Since the path has two justifications, there are two computations generated by the member predicate. In the first one, the constraint e(a,b) disappeared, in the second answer, it is e(b,c). In both cases, the path cannot be computed anymore, i.e. it has been logically retracted.

```
?- e(a,b)##[A], e(b,c)##[B], e(a,c)##[C], kill(p(a,c,2)).
p(b, c, 1)##[B], e(b, c)##[B],
p(a, c, 1)##[C], e(a, c)##[C]
;
p(a, b, 1)##[A], e(a, b)##[A],
p(a, c, 1)##[C], e(a, c)##[C].
```

6   Related Work

The idea of introducing justifications into CHR is not new. The thorough work of Armin Wolf on Adaptive CHR [WGG00] was the first to do so. Different to our work, this technically involved approach requires to store detailed information about the rule instances that have been applied in a derivation in order to undo them. In our approach, we use a straightforward source-to-source transformation and retract constraints one-by-one instead. Adaptive CHR had a low-level implementation in Java [Wol01], while we give an implementation in CHR itself by a straightforward source-to-source transformation that we prove confluent and correct. Moreover we prove confluence of the rule scheme for logical retraction with the rules of the given program. The application of adaptive CHR considered dynamic constraint satisfaction problems (DCSP) only, in particular for the implementation of search strategies [Wol05], while we apply our approach to arbitrary algorithms in order to make them fully dynamic.

The issue of search strategies was further investigated by De Koninck et al. [DKSD08]. They introduce a flexible search framework in $CHR^\vee$ (CHR with disjunction) extended with rule and search branch priorities. In their work, justifications are introduced into the semantics of $CHR^\vee$ to enable dependency-directed backtracking in the form of conflict-directed backjumping. Our work does not need a new semantics for CHR, nor its extension with disjunction, it rather relies on a source-to-source transformation within the standard semantics.

Our work does not have a particular application of justifications in mind, but rather provides the basis for any type of application that requires dynamic algorithms. There are, however, CHR applications that use justifications. The work of Wazny et al. [SSW03] introduced informally a particular kind of justifications into CHR for the specific application of type debugging and reasoning in Haskell. Justifications correspond to program locations in the given Haskell program. Unlike other work, the constraints in the body of CHR rules have given justifications to which justifications from the rule applications are added at runtime. The more recent work of Duck [Duc12] introduces SMCHR, a tight integration of CHR with a Boolean Satisfiability (SAT) solver for quantifier-free formulae including disjunction and negation as logical connectives. It is mentioned without giving further details that for clause generation, SMCHR supports justifications for constraints that include syntactic equality constraints between variables.

7   Conclusions

In this paper, the basic framework for CHR with justifications ($CHR^\mathcal{J}$) has been established and formally analyzed. We defined a straightforward source-to-source program transformation that introduces justifications into CHR as a conservative extension. Justifications enable logical retraction of constraints. If a constraint is retracted, the computation is adapted and continues as if the constraint never was introduced. We proved confluence and correctness of the two-rule scheme that encodes the logical retraction. We presented a prototype implementation that is available online together with two classical examples.

Our approach applies to CHR rules without built-in constraints in the body, because built-in constraint solvers typically do not support removal of constraints. But note that built-in constraints can be re-implemented in CHR. As one reviewer pointed out, CHR systems typically feature a propagation history to avoid the re-application of propagation rules and try to apply rules in the given order. This may lead to adverse effects in our implementation. The reviving of constraints may trigger redundant firings of propagation rules because the propagation history is partially lost then. The order in which constraints are revived may lead to different rule applications and thus to different results if the program is not confluent. We have not observed these effects in our experiments so far.

Future work could investigate three topics: dynamic algorithms, implementation and application domains of CHR with justifications. First, we would like to research how logical as well as classical algorithms implemented in CHR behave when they become dynamic. Second, we would like to improve the implementation, optimize and benchmark it. A first step can be found in the companion paper [Fru17] together with an informal complexity analysis. A formal complexity analysis would clarify the overhead involved in adding justifications. Currently, the entire history of removed constraints is stored. It could suffice to remember only a partial history if only certain constraints can be retracted or if partial recomputation proves to be more efficient for some constraints. A lower-level implementation could benefit from the propagation history of propagation rules. Third, the rule scheme can be extended to support typical application domains of justifications: explanation of derived constraints by justifications (for debugging), detection and repair of inconsistencies (for error diagnosis), and implementing nonmonotonic logical behaviors (e.g. default logic, abduction, defeasible reasoning).

Acknowledgements. We thank Daniel Gall for implementing the online transformation tool for CHR$^{\mathcal{J}}$. We also thank the anonymous reviewers for their helpful suggestions on how to improve the paper.

References

[Abd97] Abdennadher, S.: Operational semantics and confluence of constraint propagation rules. In: Smolka, G. (ed.) CP 1997. LNCS, vol. 1330, pp. 252–266. Springer, Heidelberg (1997). https://doi.org/10.1007/BFb0017444

[AFM99] Abdennadher, S., Frühwirth, T., Meuss, H.: Confluence and semantics of constraint simplification rules. Constraints **4**(2), 133–165 (1999)

[Bet14] Betz, H.: A Unified Analytical Foundation for Constraint Handling Rules. BoD, Norderstedt (2014)

[BM06] Brown, K.N., Miguel, I.: Uncertainty and change. In: Rossi, F., Van Beek, P., Walsh, T. (eds.) Handbook of Constraint Programming, Chap. 21, pp. 731–760. Elsevier, Amsterdam (2006)

[DKSD08] De Koninck, L., Schrijvers, T., Demoen, B.: A flexible search framework for CHR. In: Schrijvers, T., Frühwirth, T. (eds.) Constraint Handling Rules. LNCS (LNAI), vol. 5388, pp. 16–47. Springer, Heidelberg (2008). https://doi.org/10.1007/978-3-540-92243-8_2

[Duc12] Duck, G.J.: SMCHR: Satisfiability modulo constraint handling rules. Theory Pract. Logic Programm. **12**(4–5), 601–618 (2012)

[FR18] Frühwirth, T., Raiser, F. (eds.): Constraint Handling Rules - Compilation, Execution, and Analysis. BOD (2018). ISBN 9783746069050

[Frü09] Frühwirth, T.: Constraint Handling Rules. Cambridge University Press, Cambridge (2009)

[Frü15] Frühwirth, T.: Constraint handling rules - what else? In: Bassiliades, N., Gottlob, G., Sadri, F., Paschke, A., Roman, D. (eds.) RuleML 2015. LNCS, vol. 9202, pp. 13–34. Springer, Cham (2015). https://doi.org/10.1007/978-3-319-21542-6_2

[Fru17] Fruehwirth, T.: Implementation of logical retraction in constraint handling rules with justifications. In: 21st International Conference on Applications of Declarative Programming and Knowledge Management (INAP 2017), September 2017

[McA90]   McAllester, D.A.: Truth maintenance. In: AAAI, vol. 90, pp. 1109–1116 (1990)

[RBF09]   Raiser, F., Betz, H., Frühwirth, T.: Equivalence of CHR states revisited. In: Raiser, F., Sneyers, J. (eds.) CHR 2009, pp. 33–48. Technical report CW 555, Deparment of Computer Science, KU Leuven, July 2009

[SSW03]   Stuckey, P.J., Sulzmann, M., Wazny, J.: Interactive type debugging in Haskell. In: Proceedings of the 2003 ACM SIGPLAN workshop on Haskell, pp. 72–83. ACM (2003)

[WGG00]   Wolf, A., Gruenhagen, T., Geske, U.: On the incremental adaptation of CHR derivations. Appl. Artif. Intell. **14**(4), 389–416 (2000)

[Wol01]   Wolf, A.: Adaptive constraint handling with CHR in Java. In: Walsh, T. (ed.) CP 2001. LNCS, vol. 2239, pp. 256–270. Springer, Heidelberg (2001). https://doi.org/10.1007/3-540-45578-7_18

[Wol05]   Wolf, A.: Intelligent search strategies based on adaptive constraint handling rules. Theory Pract. Logic Program. **5**(4–5), 567–594 (2005)

Confluence and Convergence in Probabilistically Terminating Reduction Systems

Maja H. Kirkeby[✉] and Henning Christiansen

Roskilde University, Roskilde, Denmark
{majaht,henning}@ruc.dk

Abstract. Convergence of an abstract reduction system (ARS) is the property that any derivation from an initial state will end in the same final state, a.k.a. normal form. We generalize this for probabilistic ARS as almost-sure convergence, meaning that the normal form is reached with probability one, even if diverging derivations may exist. We show and exemplify properties that can be used for proving almost-sure convergence of probabilistic ARS, generalizing known results from ARS.

1 Introduction

Probabilistic abstract reduction systems, PARS, are general models of systems that develop over time in discrete steps [7]. In each non-final state, the choice of successor state is governed by a probability distribution, which in turn induces a global, probabilistic behaviour of the system. Probabilities make termination more than a simple yes-no question, and the following criteria have been proposed: *probabilistic termination* – a derivation terminates with some probability > 0 – and *almost-sure termination* – a derivation terminates with probability $= 1$, even if infinite derivations may exist (and whose total probability thus amounts to 0). When considering a PARS as a computational system, almost-sure termination may be the most interesting, and there exist well-established methods for proving this property [6,10].

PARS cover a variety of probabilistic algorithms and programs, scheduling strategies and protocols [5,7,23], and PARS is a well-suited abstraction level for better understanding their termination and correctness properties. Randomized or probabilistic algorithms (e.g., [4,20,21]) come in two groups: Monte Carlo Algorithms that allow a set of alternative outputs (typically only correct with a certain probability or within a certain accuracy), e.g., Karger-Stein's Minimum Cut [18], Monte Carlo integration and Simulated Annealing [19]; and Las Vegas Algorithms, that provide one (correct) output and that may be simpler and on average more efficient than their deterministic counterparts, e.g., Randomized Quicksort [11], checking equivalence of circular lists [17], probabilistic modular

This work is supported by The Danish Council for Independent Research, Natural Sciences, grant no. DFF 4181-00442.

F. Fioravanti and J. P. Gallagher (Eds.): LOPSTR 2017, LNCS 10855, pp. 164–179, 2018.
https://doi.org/10.1007/978-3-319-94460-9_10

GCD [30]. We focus on results that are relevant for the latter kind of systems, and here the property of *convergence* is interesting, as it may be a necessary condition for correctness: a system is convergent if it is guaranteed to terminate with a unique result. We introduce the notion of *almost-sure convergence* for PARS, meaning that a unique result is found with probability $= 1$, although there may be diverging computations; this property is a necessary condition for partial correctness, more precisely a strengthened version of partial correctness where the probability of not getting a result is zero.

The related notion of *confluence* has been extensively studied for ARS, e.g., [3,16], and especially for terminating ones for which confluence implies convergence: a system is confluent if, whenever alternative paths (i.e., repeated reductions; computations) are possible from some state, these paths can be extended to join in a common state. Newman's lemma [22] from 1942 is one of the most central results: in a terminating system, confluence (and thus convergence) can be shown from a simpler property called local confluence. In, e.g., term rewriting [3] and (a subset of) the programming language CHR [1,2], proving local confluence may be reduced to a finite number of cases, described by *critical pairs* (for a definition, see these references), which in some cases may be checked automatically. It is well-known that Newman's lemma does not generalize to non-terminating systems (and thus neither to almost-sure terminating ones); see, e.g., [16].

Probabilistic and almost-sure versions of confluence were introduced concurrently by Frühwirth et al. [12] – in the context of a probabilistic version of CHR – and by Bournez and Kirchner [7] in more generality for PARS. However, the definitions in the latter reference were given indirectly, assuming an insight into Homogeneous Markov Chain Theory, and a number of central properties were listed without hints of proofs.

In the present paper, we consider the important property of almost-sure convergence for PARS and state properties that are relevant for proving it. In contrast to [7], our definitions are self-contained, based on elementary math, and proofs are included. One of our main and novel results is that almost-sure termination together with confluence (in the classical sense) gives almost-sure convergence. Almost-sure convergence and almost-sure termination were introduced in an early 1983 paper [13] for a specific class of probabilistic programs with finite state space, but our generalization to PARS' appears to be new.

In 1991, Curien and Ghelli [9] described a powerful method for proving confluence of non-probabilistic systems, using suitable transformations from the original system into one, known to be confluent. We can show how this result applies to probabilistic systems, and we develop an analogous method for also proving non-confluence.

In Sect. 2, we review definitions for abstract reduction systems and introduce and motivate our choices of definitions for their probabilistic counterparts; a proof that the defined probabilities actually constitute a probability distribution is found in the Appendix. Section 3 formulates and proves important properties, relevant for showing almost-sure convergence of particular systems. Section 4 goes in detail with applications of the transformational approach [9] to (dis-) proving almost-sure convergence, and in Sect. 5 we demonstrate the use of this for a random walk system and Hermans' Ring. We add a few more comments on selected, related work in Sect. 6, and Sect. 7 provides a summary and suggestions for future work.

2   Basic Definitions

The definitions for non-probabilistic systems are standard; see, e.g., [3,16].

Definition 1 (ARS). *An* Abstract Reduction System *is a pair* $R = (A, \rightarrow)$ *where the* reduction $\rightarrow$ *is a binary relation on a countable set* A.

Instead of $(s, t) \in \rightarrow$ we write $s \rightarrow t$ (or $t \leftarrow s$ when convenient), and $s \rightarrow^* t$ denotes the transitive reflexive closure of $\rightarrow$.

In the literature, an ARS is often required to have only finite branching. i.e., for any element s, the set $\{t \mid s \rightarrow t\}$ is finite. We do not require this, as the implicit restriction to countable branching is sufficient for our purposes.

The set of *normal forms* R_{NF} are those $s \in A$ for which there is no $t \in A$ such that $s \rightarrow t$. For given element s, the *normal forms of* s, are defined as the set $R_{NF}(s) = \{t \in R_{NF} \mid s \rightarrow^* t\}$. An element which is not a normal form is said to be *reducible*; i.e., an element s is reducible if and only if $\{s' \mid s \rightarrow s'\} \neq \emptyset$.

A *path* from an element s is a (finite or infinite) sequence of reductions $s \rightarrow s_1 \rightarrow s_2 \rightarrow \cdots$; a finite path $s \rightarrow s_1 \rightarrow s_2 \rightarrow \cdots \rightarrow s_n$ has *length* n $(n \geq 0)$; in particular, we recognize an empty path (of length 0) from a given state to itself. For given elements s and $t \in R_{NF}(s)$, $\Delta(s, t)$ denotes the set of finite paths $s \rightarrow \cdots \rightarrow t$ (including the empty path); $\Delta^\infty(s)$ denotes the set of infinite paths from s. A system is

- *confluent* if for all $s_1 \leftarrow^* s \rightarrow^* s_2$ there is a t such that $s_1 \rightarrow^* t \leftarrow^* s_2$,
- *locally confluent* if for all $s_1 \leftarrow s \rightarrow s_2$ there is a t such that $s_1 \rightarrow^* t \leftarrow^* s_2$,
- *terminating*[1] iff it has no infinite path,
- *convergent* iff it is terminating and confluent, and
- *normalizing*[2] iff every element s has a normal form, i.e., there is an element $t \in R_{NF}$ such that $s \rightarrow^* t$.

Notice that a normalizing system may not be terminating. A fundamental result for ARS is Newman's Lemma: a terminating system is confluent if and only if it is locally confluent.

The following property indicates the complexity of the probability measures that are needed in order to cope with paths in probabilistic abstract reduction systems defined over countable sets.

---

[1] A terminating system is also called *strongly normalizing* elsewhere, e.g., [9].
[2] A normalizing system is also called *weakly normalizing* or *weakly terminating* elsewhere, e.g., [9].

Proposition 1. *Given an ARS as above and given elements s and $t \in R_{NF}(s)$, it holds that $\Delta(s,t)$ is countable, and $\Delta^{\infty}(s)$ may or may not be countable.*

Proof. For the first part, $\Delta(s,t)$ is isomorphic to a subset of $\bigcup_{n=1,2,\ldots} A^n$. A countable union of countable sets is countable, so $\Delta(s,t)$ is countable.

For the second part, consider the ARS $\langle \{0,1\}, \{i \to j \mid i,j \in \{0,1\}\}\rangle$. Each infinite path can be read as a real number in the unit interval, and any such real number can be described by an infinite path. The real numbers are not countable.

This means that we can define discrete and summable probabilities over $\Delta(s,t)$, and – which we will avoid – considering probabilities over the space $\Delta^{\infty}(s)$ requires a more advanced measure.

In the next definition, a path is considered a Markov process/chain, i.e., each reduction step is independent of the previous ones, and thus the probability of a path is defined as a product in the usual way. PARS can be seen as a special case of Homogenous Markov Chains, cf. [7], but for practical reasons it is relevant to introduce them as generalizations of ARS.

Definition 2 (PARS). *A Probabilistic Abstract Reduction System is a pair $R^P = (R, P)$ where $R = (A, \to)$ is an ARS, and for each reducible element $s \in A \setminus R_{NF}$, $P(s \to \cdot)$ is a probability distribution over the reductions from s, i.e., $\sum_{s \to t} P(s \to t) = 1$; it is assumed, that for all s and t, $P(s \to t) > 0$ if and only if $s \to t$.*

The probability of a finite path $s_0 \to s_1 \to \ldots \to s_n$ with $n \geq 0$ is given as

$$P(s_0 \to s_1 \to \ldots \to s_n) = \prod_{i=1}^{n} P(s_{i-1} \to s_i).$$

For any element s and normal form $t \in R_{NF}(s)$, the probability of s reaching t, written $P(s \to^* t)$, is defined as

$$P(s \to^* t) = \sum_{\delta \in \Delta(s,t)} P(\delta);$$

the probability of s not reaching a normal form (or diverging) is defined as

$$P(s \to^{\infty}) = 1 - \sum_{t \in R_{NF}(s)} P(s \to^* t).$$

When referring to confluence, local confluence, termination, and normalization of a PARS, we refer to these properties for the underlying ARS.

Notice that when s is a normal form then $P(s \to^* s) = 1$ since $\Delta(s,t)$ contains only the empty path with probability $\prod_{i=1}^{0} P(s_{i-1} \to s_i) = 1$. It is important that $P(s \to^* t)$ is defined only when t is a normal form of s since otherwise, the defining sum may be ≥ 1, as demonstrated by the following example.

Example 1. Consider the PARS R^P given in Fig. 1(a); formally, $R^P = ((\{0,1\},\{0 \to 1, 1 \to 1\}), P)$ with $P(0 \to 1) = 1$ and $P(1 \to 1) = 1$. An attempt to define $P(0 \to^* 1)$ as in Def. 2, for the reducible element 1, does not lead to a probability, i.e., $P(0 \to^* 1) \not\leq 1$: $P(0 \to^* 1) = P(0 \to 1) + P(0 \to 1 \to 1) + P(0 \to 1 \to 1 \to 1) + \ldots = \infty$.

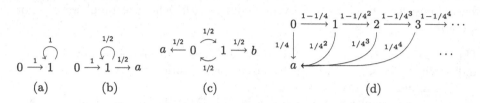

Fig. 1. PARS with different properties, see Table 1.

The following proposition justifies that we refer to P as a probability function.

Proposition 2. *For an arbitrary finite path π, $1 \geq P(\pi) > 0$. For every element s, $P(s \to^* \cdot)$ and $P(s \to^\infty)$ comprise a probability distribution, i.e., $\forall t \in R_{NF}(s): 0 \leq P(s \to^* t) \leq 1; 0 \leq P(s \to^\infty) \leq 1;$ and $\sum_{t \in R_{NF}(s)} P(s \to^* t) + P(s \to^\infty) = 1$.*

Proof. The proofs are simple but lengthy and are given in the Appendix.

Proposition 3 justifies that we refer to $P(s \to^\infty)$ as a probability of divergence.

Proposition 3. *Consider a PARS which has an element s for which $\Delta^\infty(s)$ is countable (finite or infinite). Let $P(s_1 \to s_2 \to \cdots) = \prod_{i=1,2,\ldots} P(s_i \to s_{i+1})$ be the probability of an infinite path then $P(s \to^\infty) = \sum_{\delta \in \Delta^\infty(s)} P(\delta)$ holds.*

Proof. See Appendix.

We can now define *probabilistic* and *almost-surely* (abbreviated "a-s.") versions of important notions for derivation systems. A system is

- *almost-surely convergent* if for all $s_1 \leftarrow^* s \to^* s_2$ there is a normal form $t \in R_{NF}$ such that $s_1 \to^* t \leftarrow^* s_2$ and $P(s_1 \to^* t) = P(s_2 \to^* t) = 1$,
- *locally almost-surely convergent* if for all $s_1 \leftarrow s \to s_2$ there is a $t \in R_{NF}$ such that $s_1 \to^* t \leftarrow^* s_2$ and $P(s_1 \to^* t) = P(s_2 \to^* t) = 1$,
- *almost-surely terminating*[3] iff every element s has $P(s \to^\infty) = 0$, and
- *probabilistically normalizing* iff every element s has a normal form t such that $P(s \to^* t) > 0$.

We have deliberately omitted almost-sure confluence and local confluence [7], since these require a more advanced measure in order to define the probability of visiting a perhaps reducible element.

---

[3] Almost-sure termination is named *probabilistic termination* elsewhere, e.g., [12,28].

Table 1. A property overview of the systems (a)–(d) in Fig. 1 and (d′) with same ARS as (d), but with all probabilities replaced by 1/2.

	(a)	(b)	(c)	(d)	(d′)
Loc. confl.	+	+	+	+	+
Confl.	+	+	−	+	+
Term.	−	−	−	−	−
A-s. loc. conv.	−	+	−	−	+
A-s. conv.	−	+	−	−	+
A-s. term.	−	+	+	−	+

Example 2. The four probabilistic systems in Fig. 1 demonstrate these properties. We notice that (b)–(d) are normalizing in $\{a\}$, $\{a, b\}$ and $\{a\}$, respectively. Furthermore, they are all non-terminating: system (b) and (c) are a-s. terminating, which is neither the case for (a) nor (d); for element 0 in system (d) we have $P(0 \to^\infty) = \prod_{i=1}^{\infty}(1 - (1/4)^i) \approx 0.6885 > 0.$[4] Table 1 summarizes their properties of (almost-sure) (local) confluence; (d′) refers to a PARS with the same underlying ARS as (d) and with all probabilities = 1/2.

System (c) is a probabilistic version of a classical example [15,16] which demonstrates that termination (and not only a-s. termination) is required in order for local confluence to imply confluence. The difference between system (d) and (d′) emphasizes that the choice of probabilities do matter for whether or not different probabilistic properties hold. For any element s in (d′), the probability of reaching the normal form a is $1/2 + 1/2^2 + 1/2^3 + \cdots = 1$.

3   Properties of Probabilistic Abstract Reduction Systems

With a focus on almost-sure convergence, we consider now relevant relationships between the properties of probabilistic and their underlying non-probabilistic systems. Lemmas 1 and 3, below, have previously been suggested by [7] without proofs, and we have chosen to include them as well as their proofs to provide a better understanding of the nature of almost-sure convergence. The most important properties are summarized as follows. For any PARS R^P:

- R^P is normalizing if and only if it is probabilistically normalizing (Lemma 1),
- if R^P is almost-surely terminating then it is normalizing (Lemma 2),
- if R^P is terminating then it is almost-surely terminating (Lemma 3),
- R^P is almost-surely terminating and confluent, if and only if it is almost-surely convergent (Theorem 1).

The following inductive characterization of the probabilities for reaching a given normal form is useful for the proofs that follow.

---

[4] Verified by Mathematica. The exact result is $\left(\frac{1}{4}; \frac{1}{4}\right)_\infty$; see [29] for the definition of this notation.

Proposition 4. *For any reducible element s, the following holds.*

$$\sum_{t \in R_{NF}} P(s \to^* t) = \sum_{s \to s'} \left(P(s \to s') \times \sum_{t \in R_{NF}} P(s' \to^* t) \right)$$

Proof. Any path from s to a normal form t will have the form $s \to s' \to \cdots \to t$, for some direct successor s' of s. The other way round, any normal form for a direct successor s' of s will also be a normal form of s. With this observation, the proposition follows directly from Definition 2 (prob. of path). □

Lemma 1 ([7]). *A PARS is normalizing if and only if it is probabilistically normalizing.*

Proof. Every element s in a normalizing PARS has a normal form t such that $s \to^* t$ and by definition of PARS, $P(s \to^* t) > 0$, which makes it probabilistically normalizing. The other way round, the definition of probabilistic normalizing includes normalization. □

Prob. normalization differs from the other properties in nature (requiring probability > 0 instead of $= 1$), and is the only one which is equivalent to its non-probabilistic counterpart. Thus, the existing results on proving and disproving normalization can be used directly to determine probabilistic normalization. The following lemma is also a consequence of Proposition 7, parts 3 and 5, of [7].

Lemma 2. *If a PARS is almost-surely terminating then it is normalizing.*

Proof. For every element s in a almost-surely terminating system, Proposition 2 gives that $\sum_{t \in R_{NF}} P(s \to^* t) = 1$, and hence s has at least one normal form t such that $P(s \to^* t) > 0$. By Lemma 1, the system is also normalizing. □

The opposite is not the case, as demonstrated by system (d) in Fig. 1; every element has a normal form, but the system is not almost-surely terminating.

Lemma 3 ([7]). *If a PARS is terminating then it is almost-surely terminating.*

Proof. In a terminating PARS, $\Delta^\infty(s) = \emptyset$ for any element s. By Proposition 3 we have $P(s \to^\infty) = 0$. □

The opposite is not the case, as demonstrated by systems (b)–(d) in Fig. 1. The following theorem is a central tool for proving almost-sure convergence.

Theorem 1. *A PARS is almost-surely terminating and confluent if and only if it is almost-surely convergent.*

Thus, to prove almost-sure convergence of a given PARS, one may use the methods of [6,10] to prove almost-sure termination and prove classical confluence – referring to Newman's lemma (cf. our discussion in the Introduction), or using the method of mapping the system into another system, already known to be confluent, as described in Sect. 4, below.

Proof (Theorem 1). We split the proof into smaller parts, referring to properties that are shown below: "if": by Proposition 5 and Lemma 6. "only if": by Lemma 5.

Lemma 4. *A PARS is almost-surely terminating if it is locally almost-surely convergent.*

Proof. Let R^P be a PARS which is locally almost-surely convergent, and consider an arbitrary element s. We must show $P(s \to^\infty) = 0$ or, equivalently, $\sum_{t \in R_{NF}} P(s \to^* t) = 1$.

When s is a normal form, we have $P(s \to^* s) = 1$ and thus the desired property. Assume, now, s is not a normal form. This means that s has at least one direct successor; for any two (perhaps identical) direct successors s', s'', local almost-sure convergence implies a unique normal form $t_{s',s''}$ of s' as well as of s'' with $P(s' \to^* t_{s',s''}) = P(s'' \to^* t_{s',s''}) = 1$. Obviously, this normal form is the same for all such successors and thus a unique normal form of s, so let us call it t_s. We can now use Proposition 4 as follows.

$$\sum_{t \in R_{NF}} P(s \to^* t) = P(s \to^* t_s) = \sum_{s \to s'} \left(P(s \to s') \cdot P(s' \to^* t_s) \right) = \sum_{s \to s'} P(s \to s') = 1.$$

This finishes the proof.

Since almost-sure convergence implies local almost-sure convergence, we obtain the weaker version of the above lemma.

Proposition 5. *A PARS is almost-surely terminating if it is almost-surely convergent.*

The following property for (P)ARS, is used in the proof of Lemma 6, below.

Proposition 6. *A normalizing system is confluent if and only if every element has a unique normal form.*

Proof. "If": By contradiction: Let R^P be a normalizing (P)ARS; assume that every element has a unique normal form and that R^P is not confluent. By non-confluence, there exist $s_1 \leftarrow^* s \to^* s_2$ for which there does not exists a t such that $s_1 \to^* t \leftarrow^* s_2$. However, s has one unique normal form t', i.e., $\{t'\} = R_{NF}(s)$. By definition of normal forms of s, we have that $\forall s': s \to^* s' \Rightarrow R_{NF}(s) \supseteq R_{NF}(s')$. This holds specifically for s_1 and s_2, i.e., $\{t'\} = R_{NF}(s) \supseteq R_{NF}(s_1)$ and $\{t'\} = R_{NF}(s) \supseteq R_{NF}(s_2)$. Since R is normalizing, every element has at least one normal form, i.e., $R_{NF}(s_1) \neq \emptyset$ and $R_{NF}(s_2) \neq \emptyset$, leaving one possibility: $R_{NF}(s_1) = R_{NF}(s_2) = \{t'\}$. From this result we obtain $s \to^* s_1 \to^* t'$ and $s \to^* s_2 \to^* t'$; contradiction. "Only if": This is a known result; see, e.g., [3].

Lemma 5. *If a PARS is almost-surely terminating and confluent then it is almost-surely convergent.*

Proof. Lemma 2 and Proposition 6 ensure that an a-s. terminating system has a unique normal form. A-s. termination also ensures that this unique normal form is reached with probability $= 1$, and thus the system is almost-surely convergent.

Lemma 6. *A PARS is confluent if it is almost-surely convergent.*

Proof. Assume almost-sure convergence, then for each $s_1 \leftarrow^* s \rightarrow^* s_2$ there exists a t (a normal form) such that $s_1 \rightarrow^* t \leftarrow^* s_2$.

4   Showing Probabilistic Confluence by Transformation

The following proposition is a weaker formulation and consequence of Theorem 1; it shows that (dis)proving confluence for almost-surely terminating systems is very relevant when (dis)proving almost-sure convergence.

Proposition 7. *An almost-surely terminating PARS is almost-surely convergent if and only if it is confluent.*

Proof. This is a direct consequence of Theorem 1 (or using Lemmas 5 and 6).

Curien and Ghelli [9] presented a general method for proving confluence by transforming[5] the system of interest (under some restrictions) to a new system which is known to be confluent. We start by repeating their relevant result.

Lemma 7 ([9]). *Given two ARS $R = (A, \rightarrow_R)$ and $R' = (A, \rightarrow_{R'})$ and a mapping $G \colon A \rightarrow A'$, then R is confluent if the following holds.*

(C1) R' is confluent,
(C2) R is normalizing,
(C3) if $s \rightarrow_R t$ then $G(s) \leftrightarrow^*_{R'} G(t)$,
(C4) $\forall t \in R_{NF}$, $G(t) \in R'_{NF}$, and
(C5) $\forall t, u \in R_{NF}$, $G(t) = G(u) \Rightarrow t = u$

We present a version which permits also non-confluence of the transformed system to imply non-confluence of the original system. Notice that (C2)–(C5) is a part of (C2′)–(C5′), and in particular (C4′) requires additionally that only normal forms are mapped to normal forms.

Lemma 8. *Given two ARS $R = (A, \rightarrow_R)$ and $R' = (A, \rightarrow_{R'})$ and a mapping $G \colon A \rightarrow A'$, satisfying*

(C1′) (surjective) $\forall s' \in A', \ \exists s \in A, G(s) = s'$,
(C2′) R and R' are normalizing,
(C3′) if $s \rightarrow_R t$ then $G(s) \leftrightarrow^*_{R'} G(t)$, and
       if $G(s) \leftrightarrow^*_{R'} G(t)$ then $s \leftrightarrow^*_R t$,
(C4′) $\forall t \in R_{NF}$, $G(t) \in R'_{NF}$, and $\forall t' \in R'_{NF}$, $G^{-1}(t') \subseteq R_{NF}$,
(C5′) (injective on normal forms) $\forall t, u \in R_{NF}$, $G(t) = G(u) \Rightarrow t = u$,

---

[5] This is also referred to as interpreting a system elsewhere, e.g., [9].

then R is confluent iff R' is confluent.

Proof. "$\Rightarrow$": follows from Lemma 7.

"$\Leftarrow$": Assume that R is confluent and R' is not confluent, i.e., there exist $s_1' \leftarrow^*_{R'} s' \rightarrow^*_{R'} s_2'$ for which $\nexists t' \in R' : s_1' \rightarrow^*_{R'} t' \leftarrow^*_{R'} s_2'$.

By (C2'): $\exists t_1', t_2' \in R'_{NF} : t_1' \leftarrow^*_{R'} s_1' \leftarrow^*_{R'} s' \rightarrow^*_{R'} s_2' \rightarrow^*_{R'} t_2'$ where $t_1' \neq t_2'$.

By (C1') and (C4'): $\exists t_1, t_2 \in R_{NF} : G(t_1) = t_1' \wedge G(t_2) = t_2'$

By (C5'): $t_1 \neq t_2$

By (C3'): $t_1' \leftrightarrow^*_{R'} t_2' \Rightarrow t_1 \leftrightarrow^*_R t_2$

By confluence of R: $t_1 = t_2$ (contradicts $t_1 \neq t_2$). $\qquad\square$

We summarize the application of the above to probabilistic systems in Theorems 2 and 3.

Theorem 2. *An almost-surely terminating PARS $R^P = ((A, \rightarrow_R), P)$ is almost-surely convergent if there exists an ARS $R' = (A', \rightarrow_{R'})$ and a mapping $G : A \rightarrow A'$ which together with $(A, \rightarrow_R)$ satisfy (C1)–(C5).*

Proof. Since R^P is a-s. terminating, R is normalizing (Lemma 2). So, given an ARS R' and G be a mapping from R to R' satisfying (C1), (C3)–(C5), we can apply Lemma 7 and obtain that R and thereby R^P is confluent. A-s. convergence of R^P follows from Proposition 7 since R^P is confluent and a-s. terminating $\qquad\square$

Example 3. We consider the nonterminating, almost-surely terminating system R^P (below to the left) with the underlying normalizing system R (below, middle), the confluent system R' (below to the right) and the mapping $G(0) = 0, G(a) = a$.

$$R^P : \begin{array}{c} \mathop{\text{\Large $\circlearrowleft$}}\limits^{p} \\ 0 \xrightarrow{\ 1\text{-}p\ } a \end{array} \qquad R : \begin{array}{c} \mathop{\text{\Large $\circlearrowleft$}} \\ 0 \longrightarrow a \end{array} \qquad R' : \ 0 \longrightarrow a$$

The systems R, R' and the mapping G satisfy (C1)–(C5), and therefore we can conclude that R^P is almost-surely convergent.

Theorem 3. *Given an almost-surely terminating PARS $R^P = (R, P)$ with $R = (A, \rightarrow_R)$, an ARS $R' = (A, \rightarrow_{R'})$ and a mapping G from A to A' which together with R satisfy (C1')–(C5'), then system R^P is almost-surely convergent if and only if R' is confluent.*

Proof. Assume notation as above. Since R^P is a-s. terminating, R is normalizing (Lemma 2), thus satisfying the first part of (C2'). So, given an ARS R' and G be a mapping from A to A' which together with R satisfy (C1')–(C5'), we can apply Lemma 7 obtaining that R is confluent iff R' is confluent. Proposition 7 gives that the a-s. terminating R^P is a-s. convergent iff R' is confluent. $\qquad\square$

5   Examples

In the following we show almost-sure convergence in two different cases that exemplifies Theorem 3. We use the existing method for showing almost-sure termination [6,10]: To prove that a PARS $R^P = ((A, \to), P)$ is a-s. terminating, it suffices to show existence of a *Lyapunov ranking function*, i.e., a function $\mathcal{V} : A \to \mathbb{R}^+$ where $\forall s \in A$ there exists an $\epsilon > 0$ so the *inequality of s*, $\mathcal{V}(s) \geq \sum_{s \to s'} P(s \to s') \cdot \mathcal{V}(s') + \epsilon$ holds.

5.1   A Simple, Antisymmetric Random Walk

We consider $R^P = (R, P)$, depicted in Fig. 2(a), a simple positive antisymmetric 1-dimensional random walk. In each step the value n can either increase to $n+1$, $P(n \to n+1) = 1/3$, or decrease to $n-1$ (or if at 0 we "decrease" to the normal form a instead), $P(n \to n-1) = P(0 \to a) = 2/3$. Formally, the underlying system $R = (A, \to)$ is defined by $A = \mathbb{N} \uplus \{a\}$ and $\to = \{0 \to a\} \uplus \{n \to n' \mid n, n' \in \mathbb{N}, n' = n+1 \vee n' = n-1\}$.

We start by showing R^P a-s. terminating, i.e., that a Lyapunov ranking function exists: let the function $\mathcal{V}$ be defined as follows.

$$\mathcal{V}(s) = \begin{cases} s+2, & \text{if } s \in \mathbb{N} \\ 1, & \text{if } s = a \end{cases}$$

This function is a Lyapunov ranking since the inequality (see above) holds for all elements $s \in A$; we divide into three cases $s > 0$, $s = 0$, and $s = a$:

$\mathcal{V}(s) > \frac{1}{3} \cdot \mathcal{V}(s+1) + \frac{2}{3} \cdot \mathcal{V}(s-1) \Leftrightarrow s+2 > \frac{1}{3} \cdot (s+3) + \frac{2}{3} \cdot (s+1) \quad (= s + \frac{5}{3})$

$\mathcal{V}(0) > \frac{1}{3} \cdot \mathcal{V}(1) + \frac{2}{3} \cdot \mathcal{V}(a) \qquad \Leftrightarrow 2 > \frac{1}{3} \cdot 3 + \frac{2}{3} \cdot 1$, and

$\mathcal{V}(a) > 0 \qquad\qquad\qquad\qquad\quad \Leftrightarrow 1 > 0.$

Since R^P is a-s. terminating, it suffice to define $R' = (\{\mathsf{number}, a\}, \mathsf{number} \to a)$, see Fig. 2(c), and the mapping $G : \mathbb{N} \uplus \{a\} \to \{\mathsf{number}, a\}$.

$$G(s) = \begin{cases} \mathsf{number}, & \text{if } s \in \mathbb{N} \\ a, & \text{otherwise}. \end{cases}$$

Because R^P is a-s. terminating, R' is (trivially) a confluent system, and the mapping G satisfies (C1')–(C5') then R^P is a-s. convergent (by Theorem 3).

5.2   Herman's Self-stabilizing Ring

Herman's Ring [14] is an algorithm for self-stabilizing n identical processors connected in an uni-directed ring, indexed 1 to n. Each process can hold one or zero tokens, and for each time-step, each process either keeps its token or passes it to its left neighbour (-1) with probability 1/2 of each event. When a process keeps its token and receives another, both tokens are eliminated.

Herman showed that for an initial state with an odd number of tokens, the system will reach a stable state with one token with probability $=1$. This system is not almost-sure convergent, but proving it for a similar system can be a part of showing that Herman's Ring with 3 processes either will stabilize with 1 token

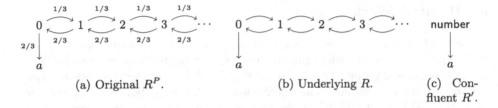

(a) Original R^P.

(b) Underlying R.

(c) Confluent R'.

Fig. 2. Random walk (1 Dimension)

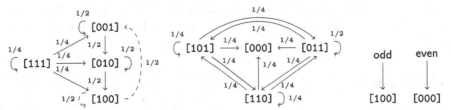

(a) Original R^P (both dashed and solid edges) and the almost-surely terminating R'^P (without the dashed edges).

(b) Confluent R''.

Fig. 3. Herman's self-stabilizing Ring

with probability $= 1$ or 0 tokens with probability $= 1$. We use a boolean array to represent whether each process holds a token (1 indicates a token) and is defined as in Fig. 3(a), where both dashed and solid edges indicate reductions.

Since [000] is a normal form and $\{[100], [010], [001]\}$ is the set of successor-states of each of [100], [010] and [001], then we can prove stabilization of R^P by showing almost-sure convergence for a slightly altered system R'^P, i.e., the system in Fig. 3(a) consisting of the solid edges only.

To show almost-sure convergence of R'^P, we prove almost-sure termination by showing the existence of a Lyapunov ranking function, namely $\mathcal{V}([b_1\ b_2\ b_3]) = 2^2 \cdot (b_1 + b_2 + b_3) + b_1 \cdot 2^0 + b_2 \cdot 2^1 + b_3 \cdot 2^2$, which decreases, firstly, with the reduction of tokens and, secondly, by position of the tokens. The only two states where $\mathcal{V}$ increases in a direct successor are [110] and [101] where the inequality of [110] reduces to $11 > 9 + \frac{1}{2}$ and that of [101] to $14 > 9 + \frac{1}{2}$ showing R^P to be a-s. terminating.

We provide, now, a mapping G from the elements of the underlying system into the elements of a trivially confluent system, i.e., R'' in Fig. 3(b):

$$G([100]) = [100] \qquad G([000]) = [000]$$
$$G([111]) = G([001]) = G([010]) = \text{odd}$$
$$G([011]) = G([101]) = G([110]) = \text{even}$$

The R^P is a-s. term., R'' is confluent and G satisfy (C1')–(C5'), then (by Theorem 3) R^P is a-s. convergent.

6   Related Work

We see our work as a succession of the earlier work by Bournez and Kirchner [7], with explicit and simple definitions (instead of referring to Homogeneous Markov Chain theory) and proofs of central properties, and showing novel properties that are important for showing (non-) convergence. Our work borrows inspirations from the result of [12,27,28], given specifically for probabilistic extensions of the programming languages CHR. A notion of so-called nondeterministic PARS have been introduced, e.g., [6,10], in which the choice of probability distribution for next reduction is nondeterministic; these are not covered by our results.

PARS can be implemented directly in Sato's PRISM System [24,25], which is a probabilistic version of Prolog, and recent progress for nonterminating programs [26] may be useful convergence considerations.

7   Conclusion

We have considered almost-sure convergence – and how to prove it – for probabilistic abstract reduction systems. Our motivation is the application of such systems as computational systems having a deterministic input-output relationship, and therefore almost-sure termination is of special importance. We have provided properties that are useful when showing almost-sure (non-) convergence by consequence of other probabilistic and "classic" properties and by transformation. We plan to generalize these results to almost-sure convergence modulo equivalence relevant for some Monte-Carlo Algorithms, that produces several correct answers (e.g. Simulated Annealing), and thereby continuing the work we have started for (non-probabilistic) CHR [8].

A   Selected Proofs

Proposition 2. *For an arbitrary finite path π, $1 \geq P(\pi) > 0$. For every element s, $P(s \rightarrow^* \cdot)$ and $P(s \rightarrow^\infty)$ comprise a probability distribution, i.e., $\forall t \in R_{NF}(s): 0 \leq P(s \rightarrow^* t) \leq 1; 0 \leq P(s \rightarrow^\infty) \leq 1;$ and $\sum_{t \in R_{NF}(s)} P(s \rightarrow^* t) + P(s \rightarrow^\infty) = 1$.*

Proof. Part one follows by Definition 2. Part two is shown by defining a sequence of distributions $P^{(n)}$, $n \in \mathbb{N}$, only containing paths up to length n, and show that it converges to P. Let $\Delta^{(n)}(s,t)$ be the subset of $\Delta(s,t)$ with paths of length n or less, and $\Delta^{(n)}(s,\sharp)$ be the set of paths of length n, starting in s and ending in a reducible element.

We can now define $P^{(n)}$ over $\{\Delta^{(n)}(s,t) \mid t \in R_{NF}(s)\} \uplus \{\Delta^{(n)}(s,\sharp)\}$ as follows:

$$P^{(n)}(s \rightarrow^* t) = \sum_{\delta \in \Delta^{(n)}(s,t)} P(\delta), \quad \text{and} \tag{1}$$

$$P^{(n)}(s \rightarrow^\infty) = \sum_{\pi \in \Delta^{(n)}(s,\sharp)} P(\pi). \tag{2}$$

First, we prove by induction that $P^{(n)}$ is a distribution for all n. The $P^{(0)}$ is a distribution because: [(i)] If s is irreducible, $P^{(0)}(s \to^* s) = 1$ (the empty-path); and $P^{(0)}(s \to^\infty) = 0$ (a sum of zero elements). [(ii)] If s is reducible, $P^{(0)}(s \to^* s) = 0$; and $P^{(0)}(s \to^\infty) = \sum_{s \to t} P(s \to t) = 1$ by Definition 2.

The inductive step: The sets $\Delta^{(n+1)}(s,t), t \in R_{NF}(s)$, and $\Delta^{(n+1)}(s, \natural)$ can be constructed by, for each path in $\Delta^{(n)}(s, \natural)$, create its possible extensions by one reduction. When an extension leads to a normal form t, it is added to $\Delta^{(n)}(s,t)$. Otherwise, i.e., if the new path leads to a reducible, it is included in $\Delta^{(n+1)}(s, \natural)$. Formally, for any normal form t of s, we write:

$$\Delta^{(n+1)}(s,t) = \{(s \to \cdots \to u \to t) \mid (s \to \cdots \to u) \in \Delta^{(n)}(s, \natural),\, u \to t\} \uplus \Delta^{(n)}(s,t)$$
$$\Delta^{(n+1)}(s, \natural) = \{(s \to \cdots \to u \to v) \mid (s \to \cdots \to u) \in \Delta^{(n)}(s, \natural),\, u \to v,\, u \notin R_{NF}(s)\}$$

We show that for a given s, the probability mass added to the $\Delta^{(\cdot)}(s,t)$ sets is equal to the probability mass removed from $\Delta^{(\cdot)}(s, \natural)$ as follows (where $\delta_{su} = (s \to \cdots \to u)$).

$$\sum_{t \in R_{NF}(s)} P^{(n+1)}(s \to^* t) + P^{(n+1)}(s \to^\infty) = \sum_{\substack{t \in R_{NF}(s) \\ \delta \in \Delta^{(n+1)}(s,t)}} P^{(n+1)}(\delta) + P^{(n+1)}(s \to^\infty)$$

$$= \sum_{\substack{t \in R_{NF}(s) \\ \delta_{st} \in \Delta^{(n)}(s,t)}} P^{(n)}(\delta) + \sum_{\substack{\delta_{su} \in \Delta^{(n)}(s, \natural), \\ u \to v, v \in R_{NF}(s)}} P^{(n)}(\delta)P(u \to v) + \sum_{\substack{\delta_{su} \in \Delta^{(n)}(s, \natural), \\ u \to v, v \notin R_{NF}(s)}} P^{(n)}(\delta)P(u \to v)$$

$$= \sum_{t \in R_{NF}(s)} P^{(n)}(s \to^* t) + \sum_{\substack{\delta_{su} \in \Delta^{(n)}(s, \natural), \\ u \to v}} P^{(n)}(\delta)P(u \to v) = \sum_{t \in R_{NF}(s)} P^{(n)}(s \to^* t) + \sum_{\delta_{su} \in \Delta^{(n)}(s, \natural)} P^{(n)}(\delta)\left(\sum_{u \to v} P(u \to v)\right)$$

$$= \sum_{t \in R_{NF}(s)} P^{(n)}(s \to^* t) + P^{(n)}(s \to^\infty) = 1$$

Thus, for given s, $P^{(n+1)}$ defines a probability distribution. Notice also that the equations above indicate that $P^{(n+1)}(s \to^* t) \geq P^{(n)}(s \to^* t)$, for all $t \in R_{NF}(s)$.

Finally, for any s and $t \in R_{NF}(s)$, $\lim_{n \to \infty} \Delta^{(n)}(s,t) = \Delta(s,t)$, we get (as we consider increasing sequences of real numbers in a closed interval) $\lim_{n \to \infty} P^{(n)}(s \to^* t) = P(s \to^* t)$, and as a consequence of this, $\lim_{n \to \infty} P^{(n)}(s \to^\infty) = P(s \to^\infty)$. This finishes the proof.

Proposition 3. *Consider a PARS which has an element s for which $\Delta^\infty(s)$ is countable (finite or infinite). Let $P(s_1 \to s_2 \to \cdots) = \prod_{i=1,2,\ldots} P(s_i \to s_{i+1})$ be the probability of an infinite path then $P(s \to^\infty) = \sum_{\delta \in \Delta^\infty(s)} P(\delta)$ holds.*

Proof. We assume the characterization in the proof of Proposition 2 above, of P by the limits of the functions $P^{(n)}(s \to^* t)$ and $P^{(n)}(s \to^\infty)$ given by equations (1) and (2). When $\Delta^\infty(s)$ is countable, $\lim_{n \to \infty} P^{(n)}(s \to^\infty) = \sum_{\delta \in \Delta^\infty(s)} P(\delta)$.

References

1. Abdennadher, S.: Operational semantics and confluence of constraint propagation rules. In: Smolka, G. (ed.) CP 1997. LNCS, vol. 1330, pp. 252–266. Springer, Heidelberg (1997). https://doi.org/10.1007/BFb0017444
2. Abdennadher, S., Frühwirth, T., Meuss, H.: On confluence of constraint handling rules. In: Freuder, E.C. (ed.) CP 1996. LNCS, vol. 1118, pp. 1–15. Springer, Heidelberg (1996). https://doi.org/10.1007/3-540-61551-2_62
3. Baader, F., Nipkow, T.: Term Rewriting and All That. Cambridge University Press, Cambridge (1999)
4. Babai, L.: Monte-Carlo algorithms in graph isomorphism testing. Université de Montréal Technical report, DMS, vol. 79, pp. 1–33 (1979)
5. Baier, C., Katoen, J.-P.: Principles of Model Checking, vol. 950. MIT Press (2008)
6. Bournez, O., Garnier, F.: Proving positive almost sure termination under strategies. In: Pfenning, F. (ed.) RTA 2006. LNCS, vol. 4098, pp. 357–371. Springer, Heidelberg (2006). https://doi.org/10.1007/11805618_27
7. Bournez, O., Kirchner, C.: Probabilistic rewrite strategies. applications to ELAN. In: Tison, S. (ed.) RTA 2002. LNCS, vol. 2378, pp. 252–266. Springer, Heidelberg (2002). https://doi.org/10.1007/3-540-45610-4_18
8. Christiansen, H., Kirkeby, M.H.: On proving confluence modulo equivalence for Constraint Handling Rules. Formal Aspects Comput. **29**(1), 57–95 (2017)
9. Curien, P.-L., Ghelli, G.: On confluence for weakly normalizing systems. In: RTA-1991, pp. 215–225 (1991)
10. Fioriti, L.M.F., Hermanns, H.: Probabilistic termination: soundness, completeness, and compositionality. In: POPL 2015, pp. 489–501 (2015)
11. Donald Frazer, W., McKellar, A.C.: Samplesort: a sampling approach to minimal storage tree sorting. J. ACM **17**(3), 496–507 (1970)
12. Frühwirth, T.W., Di Pierro, A., Wiklicky, H.: Probabilistic constraint handling rules. Electr. Notes Theor. Comput. Sci. **76**, 115–130 (2002)
13. Hart, S., Sharir, M., Pnueli, A.: Termination of probabilistic concurrent program. ACM Trans. Program. Lang. Syst. **5**(3), 356–380 (1983)
14. Herman, T.: Probabilistic self-stabilization. Inf. Process. Letters **35**(2), 63–67 (1990)
15. Roger Hindley, J.: An abstract Church-Rosser theorem. II: applications. J. Symb. Log. **39**(1), 1–21 (1974)
16. Huet, G.P.: Confluent reductions: abstract properties and applications to term rewriting systems: Abstract properties and applications to term rewriting systems. J. ACM **27**(4), 797–821 (1980)
17. Itai, A.: A randomized algorithm for checking equivalence of circular lists. Inf. Process. Lett. **9**(3), 118–121 (1979)
18. Karger, D.R., Stein, C.: A new approach to the minimum cut problem. J. ACM **43**(4), 601–640 (1996)
19. Kirkpatrick, S., Gelatt Jr., D., Vecchi, M.P.: Optimization by simulated annealing. Science **220**(4598), 671–680 (1983)
20. Maffioli, E., Speranza, M.G., Vercellis, C.: Randomized algorithms: an annotated bibliography. Ann. Oper. Res. **1**(3), 331–345 (1984)
21. Motwani, R., Raghavan, P.: Randomized Algorithms. Cambridge University Press, New York (1995)
22. Newman, M.H.A.: On theories with a combinatorial definition of "equivalence". Ann. Math. **43**(2), 223–243 (1942)

23. Rabin, M.O.: The choice coordination problem. Acta Informatica **17**(2), 121–134 (1982)
24. Sato, T.: A statistical learning method for logic programs with distribution semantics. ICLP **1995**, 715–729 (1995)
25. Sato, T.: A glimpse of symbolic-statistical modeling by PRISM. J. Intell. Inf. Syst. **31**(2), 161–176 (2008)
26. Sato, T., Meyer, P.J.: Infinite probability computation by cyclic explanation graphs. TPLP **14**(6), 909–937 (2014)
27. Sneyers, J., Meert, W., Vennekens, J., Kameya, Y., Sato, T.: CHR(PRISM)-based probabilistic logic learning. In: TPLP, vol. 10(4–6) (2010)
28. Sneyers, J., De Schreye, D.: Probabilistic termination of CHRiSM programs. In: Vidal, G. (ed.) LOPSTR 2011. LNCS, vol. 7225, pp. 221–236. Springer, Heidelberg (2012). https://doi.org/10.1007/978-3-642-32211-2_15
29. Weisstein, E.W.: q-Pochhammer Symbol. MathWorld - A Wolfram Web Resource (2017)
30. Zippel, R.: Probabilistic algorithms for sparse polynomials. In: Ng, E.W. (ed.) Symbolic and Algebraic Computation. LNCS, vol. 72, pp. 216–226. Springer, Heidelberg (1979). https://doi.org/10.1007/3-540-09519-5_73

Analysis of Rewriting-Based Systems as First-Order Theories

Salvador Lucas[(⊠)]

DSIC, Universitat Politècnica de València, Valencia, Spain
slucas@dsic.upv.es

Abstract. Computational systems based on a first-order language that can be given a *canonical model* which captures provability in the corresponding calculus can often be seen as first-order theories $\mathcal{S}$, and computational properties of such systems can be formulated as first-order sentences φ that hold in such a canonical model of $\mathcal{S}$. In this setting, standard results regarding the *preservation* of satisfiability of different classes of first-order sentences yield a number of interesting applications in program analysis. In particular, properties expressed as existentially quantified boolean combinations of atoms (for instance, a set of *unification problems*) can then be *disproved* by just finding an *arbitrary* model of the considered theory plus the *negation* of such a sentence. We show that rewriting-based systems fit into this approach. Many computational properties (e.g., infeasibility and non-joinability of critical pairs in (conditional) rewriting, non-loopingness, or the secure access to protected pages of a web site) can be investigated in this way. Interestingly, this semantic approach succeeds when specific techniques developed to deal with the aforementioned problems fail.

Keywords: Logical models · Program analysis
Rewriting-based systems

1 Introduction

First-Order Logic is an appropriate language to express the semantics of computational systems and also the (claimed) properties of such computational systems [5]. In this paper we explore some new uses of first-order logic in program analysis. After providing a generic approach where we consider arbitrary first-order theories, we apply our results to *rewriting-based systems*, including Term Rewriting Systems (TRSs, [2]), *Conditional* TRSs (CTRSs, [3,11,28]), *Membership Equational Programs* [26], and more general rewriting-based formalisms [4,15,27]. The insertion of a 'rewriting-based system' $\mathcal{R}$ into First-Order Logic is made as a *Horn theory* $\overline{\mathcal{R}}$, i.e., a set of universally quantified implications $A_1 \wedge \cdots \wedge A_n \Rightarrow B$ for some $n \geq 0$, where A_i, $1 \leq i \leq n$ and B are

---

Partially supported by the EU (FEDER), Spanish MINECO project TIN2015-69175-C4-1-R and GV project PROMETEOII/2015/013.

F. Fioravanti and J. P. Gallagher (Eds.): LOPSTR 2017, LNCS 10855, pp. 180–197, 2018.
https://doi.org/10.1007/978-3-319-94460-9_11

atoms with predicate symbols $\to$, $\to^*$, etc. Such a *Horn theory* is obtained from the *operational semantics* of the considered rewriting-based system $\mathcal{R}$, which is usually given by means of some *inference rules*.

Example 1. Consider the following CTRS $\mathcal{R}$:

$$\mathsf{b} \to \mathsf{a} \tag{1}$$

$$\mathsf{a} \to \mathsf{b} \Leftarrow \mathsf{c} \to \mathsf{b} \tag{2}$$

Its associated Horn theory $\overline{\mathcal{R}}$ (using predicate symbols $\to$ and $\to^*$) is:

$$(\forall x)\, x \to^* x \tag{3}$$

$$(\forall x, y, z)\, x \to y \land y \to^* z \Rightarrow x \to^* z \tag{4}$$

$$\mathsf{b} \to \mathsf{a} \tag{5}$$

$$\mathsf{c} \to^* \mathsf{b} \Rightarrow \mathsf{a} \to \mathsf{b} \tag{6}$$

Sentence (3) corresponds to *reflexivity* of the rewrite relation $\to^*$ and (4) describes how the one-step rewrite relation $\to$ contributes to the rewrite relation $\to^*$. Finally, (5) and (6) describe rules (1) and (2).

In this setting, our approach goes back to Floyd, Hoare, and Manna's early work on proving program properties using first-order logic: we can use logical formulas to describe the execution of a program and then other formulas describe the property of interest [5, Chap. 10]. However, the natural idea of using the notion of *logical consequence* $\overline{\mathcal{R}} \models \varphi$ (i.e., that φ is satisfied in *every* model of $\overline{\mathcal{R}}$) as a formal definition of "*system* $\mathcal{R}$ *has property* φ" may fail to work.

Example 2 (Continuing Example 1). Note that a does *not* rewrite into b because the conditional part of rule (2) cannot be satisfied: c cannot be rewritten into b. We are tempted to formalize this as follows: $\overline{\mathcal{R}} \models \neg(\mathsf{a} \to \mathsf{b})$ holds, i.e., every model of $\overline{\mathcal{R}}$ satisfies $\neg(\mathsf{a} \to \mathsf{b})$. However, an interpretation of symbols a and b as 0, with $\to$ and $\to^*$ interpreted as the *equality* satisfies (3)–(6) (i.e., it is a model of $\overline{\mathcal{R}}$), but $\neg(\mathsf{a} \to \mathsf{b})$ does *not* hold. Thus, $\overline{\mathcal{R}} \models \neg(\mathsf{a} \to \mathsf{b})$ does *not* hold!

This 'mismatch' between the expressivity of pure first-order logic and the intended meaning of logic sentences referred to the *computational logic* describing a given computational system is usually avoided by the assumption that sentences expressing program properties should be *checked* with respect to a given *canonical model* only [6, Chap. 4]. For instance, the problem in Example 2 disappears if we assume that $\neg(\mathsf{a} \to \mathsf{b})$ must hold in the *least Herbrand model* $\mathcal{H}_{\mathcal{R}}$ of $\overline{\mathcal{R}}$ only. In $\mathcal{H}_{\mathcal{R}}$, $\to$ and $\to^*$ are interpreted precisely as the sets $(\to)^{\mathcal{H}_{\mathcal{R}}}$ and $(\to^*)^{\mathcal{H}_{\mathcal{R}}}$ of pairs (s, t) of ground terms s and t such that $s \to_{\mathcal{R}} t$ and $s \to^*_{\mathcal{R}} t$, respectively. Then, we indeed have $\mathcal{H}_{\mathcal{R}} \models \neg(\mathsf{a} \to \mathsf{b})$, which is agreed to be the *intended meaning* of the logic expression $\neg(\mathsf{a} \to \mathsf{b})$.

In general, the (standard) least Herbrand model $\mathcal{H}$ of a first-order theory is not computable[1]. Thus, the practical verification of properties φ as satisfiability in $\mathcal{H}$, i.e., $\mathcal{H} \models \varphi$, can be unfeasible. In this paper we show that the

---

[1] For instance, given terms s and t, $s \to^*_{\mathcal{R}} t$ is undecidable (Post's correspondence problem is a particular case). Hence, $\mathcal{H}_{\mathcal{R}} \models s \to^* t$ is undecidable.

class of properties φ which can be written as the *existential closure of a positive boolean combination of atoms* can be *disproved* (with regard to the least Herbrand model of the first-order theory $\mathcal{S}$) by showing the satisfiability of $\neg\varphi$ in an *arbitrary* model $\mathcal{A}$ of $\mathcal{S}$, i.e., by proving $\mathcal{A} \models \neg\varphi$. Dealing with rewriting-based systems $\mathcal{R}$ with Horn theories $\overline{\mathcal{R}}$, a number of interesting properties (some of them already considered in the literature) can be expressed and disproved in this way. Examples are given in Table 1, where s and t denote *ground terms*, and $s_1, \ldots, s_n, t_1, \ldots, t_n$, denote arbitrary terms with variables in $\boldsymbol{x}$, and $\unrhd$ is the *subterm relation*.

Table 1. Some properties about rewriting-based systems

Property	φ
*Reach*able	$s \to^* t$
*Feas*ible	$(\exists\boldsymbol{x})s_1 \to^* t_1 \wedge \cdots \wedge s_n \to^* t_n$
*Join*able	$(\exists x)\ s \to^* x \wedge t \to^* x$
*Red*ucible	$(\exists x)\ t \to x$
*Conv*ertible	$s \to t \vee t \to s$
*Cycl*ing term	$(\exists x)\ t \to x \wedge x \to^* t$
*Cycl*ing system	$(\exists x, y)\ x \to y \wedge y \to^* x$
*Loop*ing term	$(\exists x, y)\ t \to x \wedge x \to^* y \wedge y \unrhd t$
*Loop*ing system	$(\exists x, y, z)\ x \to y \wedge y \to^* z \wedge z \unrhd x$
*Unif*iable	$(\exists\boldsymbol{x})\ s_1 = t_1 \wedge \cdots \wedge s_n = t_n$

Example 3 (Continuing Example 2). The fact that a rewrites into b (i.e., a $\to_\mathcal{R}$ b) can be *disproved* if there is a model $\mathcal{A}$ of (3)–(6) satisfying $\neg$(a $\to$ b). The interpretation $\mathcal{A}$ with domain $\mathbb{N}$, interpreting both a and c as 1, b as 2, $\to$ as $>_\mathbb{N}$ and $\to^*$ as $\geq_\mathbb{N}$ is a model of $\{(3)$–$(6)\} \cup \{\neg$(a $\to$ b)$\}$. This proves that a $\not\to_\mathcal{R}$ b.

After some preliminaries, Sect. 3 presents the main results of the paper which are formulated in a standard first-order logic framework [17,25]. Sections 4 and 5 explain their use in a rewriting setting. By lack of space we mainly focus on CTRSs but other rewriting-based and computational systems could be treated in this way. Section 6 discusses some related work. Section 7 concludes.

2   Preliminaries

A *signature with predicates*[2] Ω is a pair $\Omega = (\mathcal{F}, \Pi)$, where $\mathcal{F}$ is a set of function symbols $\mathcal{F} = \{f, g, \ldots\}$ and Π is a set of *predicate symbols* $\Pi = \{P, Q, \ldots\}$ with $\mathcal{F} \cap \Pi = \emptyset$. An *arity* mapping $ar : \mathcal{F} \cup \Pi \to \mathbb{N}$ fixes the number of arguments for each symbol. First-order terms t and formulas φ are built from these symbols

---

[2] We follow the terminology and notation in [15].

(and an infinite set $\mathcal{X}$ of variable symbols $\mathcal{X} = \{x, y, z, \ldots\}$, which is disjoint from $\mathcal{F} \cup \Pi$) in the usual way. Equations $s = t$ for terms s and t can also be used as *atoms* if necessary, even without any equality symbol in Π. The set of terms is denoted as $\mathcal{T}(\mathcal{F}, \mathcal{X})$; the set of *ground* terms, i.e., terms *without variables*, is denoted as $\mathcal{T}(\mathcal{F})$. The set of (first-order) formulas is denoted as $Form_{\mathcal{F}, \Pi}$.

An Ω-structure $\mathcal{A}$ for a signature with predicates Ω is an interpretation of the function and predicate symbols in Ω as mappings $f^{\mathcal{A}}, g^{\mathcal{A}}, \ldots$ and relations $P^{\mathcal{A}}, Q^{\mathcal{A}}, \ldots$ on a given set (carrier) $dom(\mathcal{A})$, often denoted $\mathcal{A}$ as well. The equality symbol has a *fixed* interpretation as the identity relation $\{(a, a) \mid a \in \mathcal{A}\}$ on $\mathcal{A}$. An Ω-homomorphism between Ω-structures $\mathcal{A}$ and $\mathcal{A}'$ is a mapping $h : dom(\mathcal{A}) \rightarrow dom(\mathcal{A}')$ such that (i) for each k-ary symbols $f \in \mathcal{F}$, and $a_1, \ldots, a_k \in dom(\mathcal{A})$, $h(f^{\mathcal{A}}(a_1, \ldots, a_k)) = f^{\mathcal{A}'}(h(a_1), \ldots, h(a_k))$ and (ii) for each n-ary predicate symbols $P \in \Pi$ and $a_1, \ldots, a_n \in dom(\mathcal{A})$, if $(a_1, \ldots, a_n) \in P^{\mathcal{A}}$, then $(h(a_1), \ldots, h(a_n)) \in P^{\mathcal{A}'}$ [17, Sect. 1.2]. Given a *valuation mapping* $\alpha :$ $\mathcal{X} \rightarrow \mathcal{A}$, the evaluation mapping $[\_]_{\mathcal{A}}^{\alpha} : \mathcal{T}(\mathcal{F}, \mathcal{X}) \rightarrow \mathcal{A}$ is given by $[t]_{\mathcal{A}}^{\alpha} = \alpha(t)$ if $t \in \mathcal{X}$ and $[t]_{\mathcal{A}}^{\alpha} = f^{\mathcal{A}}([t_1]_{\mathcal{A}}^{\alpha}, \ldots, [t_k]_{\mathcal{A}}^{\alpha})$ if $t = f(t_1, \ldots, t_k)$ (if $k = 0$, then t is just a constant symbol f). Finally, $[\_]_{\mathcal{A}}^{\alpha} : Form_{\mathcal{F}, \Pi} \rightarrow Bool$ is given by:

1. $[P(t_1, \ldots, t_n)]_{\mathcal{A}}^{\alpha} = true$ (with $P \in \Pi$) if and only if $([t_1]_{\mathcal{A}}^{\alpha}, \ldots, [t_n]_{\mathcal{A}}^{\alpha}) \in P^{\mathcal{A}}$;
2. $[\neg \phi]_{\mathcal{A}}^{\alpha} = true$ if and only if $[\phi]_{\mathcal{A}}^{\alpha} = false$;
3. $[\phi \wedge \psi]_{\mathcal{A}}^{\alpha} = true$ if and only if $[\phi]_{\mathcal{A}}^{\alpha} = true$ and $[\psi]_{\mathcal{A}}^{\alpha} = true$;
4. $[\phi \vee \psi]_{\mathcal{A}}^{\alpha} = true$ if and only if $[\phi]_{\mathcal{A}}^{\alpha} = true$ or $[\psi]_{\mathcal{A}}^{\alpha} = true$;
5. $[(\forall x) \phi]_{\mathcal{A}}^{\alpha} = true$ if and only if for all $a \in \mathcal{A}$, $[\phi]_{\mathcal{A}}^{\alpha[x \mapsto a]} = true$; and
6. $[(\exists x) \phi]_{\mathcal{A}}^{\alpha} = true$ if and only if there is $a \in \mathcal{A}$, such that $[\phi]_{\mathcal{A}}^{\alpha[x \mapsto a]} = true$.

A valuation $\alpha \in \mathcal{X} \rightarrow \mathcal{A}$ *satisfies* a formula φ in $\mathcal{A}$ (written $\mathcal{A} \models \varphi [\alpha]$) if $[\varphi]_{\mathcal{A}}^{\alpha} = true$. A model for a *theory* $\mathcal{S}$, i.e., a set of *sentences* (which are formulas whose variables are all *quantified*), is just a structure that makes them all true, written $\mathcal{A} \models \mathcal{S}$, see [17]. Let $Mod(\mathcal{S})$ be the class of structures $\mathcal{A}$ which are models of $\mathcal{S}$. A sentence φ is a logical consequence of a theory $\mathcal{S}$ (written $\mathcal{S} \models \varphi$) if for all $\mathcal{A} \in Mod(\mathcal{S})$, $\mathcal{A} \models \varphi$. If φ can be *proved* from $\mathcal{S}$ by using an appropriate calculus (e.g., the axiomatic calculus by Hilbert [25, Sect. 2.3], or Gentzen's natural deduction, see [29]), we write $\mathcal{S} \vdash \varphi$.

3 Existentially Closed Boolean Combinations of Atoms

Every set $\mathcal{S}$ of ground atoms has an *initial model*.

Theorem 1 [17, Theorem 1.5.2]. *Let Ω be a first-order signature and $\mathcal{S}$ be a set of ground atoms. Then, there is a structure $\mathcal{I}_{\mathcal{S}}$ such that*

1. *$\mathcal{I}_{\mathcal{S}} \models \mathcal{S}$,*
2. *every element of $dom(\mathcal{I}_{\mathcal{S}})$ is of the form $t^{\mathcal{I}_{\mathcal{S}}}$ for some ground term t,*
3. *if $\mathcal{A}$ is an Ω-structure and $\mathcal{A} \models \mathcal{S}$, then there is a unique homomorphism $h : \mathcal{I}_{\mathcal{S}} \rightarrow \mathcal{A}$.*

Actually, the *initial structure* $\mathcal{I}_S$ (or just $\mathcal{I}$, if S is understood from the context) which is mentioned in Theorem 1, and also in some of the results below, consists of the usual *Herbrand Domain* of ground terms modulo the equivalence $\sim$ generated by the equations in S [17, Lemma 1.5.1]: For each ground term $t \in \mathcal{T}(\mathcal{F})$, let $t^\sim$ be the equivalence class of t under $\sim$. Then,

1. For each constant $c \in \mathcal{F}$, we let $c^\mathcal{I} = c^\sim$.
2. For each function symbol $f \in \mathcal{F}$ of arity k, define $f^\mathcal{I}$ by $f^\mathcal{I}(t_1^\sim, \ldots, t_k^\sim) = f(t_1, \ldots, t_k)^\sim$.
3. For each predicate symbol $P \in \Omega$ of arity n, define $P^\mathcal{I}$ as the set $\{(t_1^\sim, \ldots, t_n^\sim) \mid P(t_1, \ldots, t_n) \in S\}$.

If S contains no equation, then $\mathcal{I}$ is the *Least Herbrand Model* of S [17]. A *positive boolean combination of atoms* is a formula

$$\bigvee_{i=1}^{m} \bigwedge_{j=1}^{n_i} A_{ij} \tag{7}$$

where $m \geq 0$, $n_i \geq 0$ for all $1 \leq i \leq m$, and A_{ij} are atoms for all $1 \leq i \leq m$ and $1 \leq j \leq n_i$ (cf. [17, Sect. 2.4]); if $m = 0$, then (7) is equivalent to *false*. Satisfiability of the *existential closure* of formulas (7), i.e., formulas of the form

$$(\exists x_1) \cdots (\exists x_k) \bigvee_{i=1}^{m} \bigwedge_{j=1}^{n_i} A_{ij} \tag{8}$$

where $x_1, \ldots, x_k$ for some $k \geq 0$ are the variables occurring in the atoms A_{ij} for all $1 \leq i \leq m$ and $1 \leq j \leq n_i$, is *preserved* under homomorphism, i.e., the following holds:

Theorem 2 [17, cf. Theorem 2.4.3(a)]. *Let Ω be a signature with predicates and A_{ij} be atoms for all $1 \leq i \leq m$ and $1 \leq j \leq n_i$ with variables $x_1, \ldots, x_k$. Let $\mathcal{A}$ and $\mathcal{A}'$ be Ω-structures such that there is an Ω-homomorphism from $\mathcal{A}$ to $\mathcal{A}'$. Then,*

$$\mathcal{A} \models (\exists x_1) \cdots (\exists x_k) \bigvee_{i=1}^{m} \bigwedge_{j=1}^{n_i} A_{ij} \implies \mathcal{A}' \models (\exists x_1) \cdots (\exists x_k) \bigvee_{i=1}^{m} \bigwedge_{j=1}^{n_i} A_{ij} \tag{9}$$

Our main result is just a combination of the two previous results. If S is a set of ground atoms, then it is satisfiable in the initial model $\mathcal{I}_S$ of S (i.e., $\mathcal{I}_S \models S$ holds) and for all models $\mathcal{A}$ of S there is a homomorphism $h : \mathcal{I}_S \to \mathcal{A}$ (Theorem 1). By Theorem 2, if $\mathcal{I}_S$ satisfies a formula φ of the form (8), then for all such models $\mathcal{A}$ of S (for which we have a homomorphism $h : \mathcal{I}_S \to \mathcal{A}$) we have $\mathcal{A} \models \varphi$. Thus, φ is a logical consequence of S: $S \models \varphi$.

Corollary 1. *Let Ω be a first-order signature, S be a set of ground atoms, and A_{ij} be atoms for all $1 \leq i \leq m$ and $1 \leq j \leq n_i$ with variables $x_1, \ldots, x_k$. Then,*

$$\mathcal{I}_S \models (\exists x_1) \cdots (\exists x_k) \bigvee_{i=1}^{m} \bigwedge_{j=1}^{n_i} A_{ij} \implies S \models (\exists x_1) \cdots (\exists x_k) \bigvee_{i=1}^{m} \bigwedge_{j=1}^{n_i} A_{ij} \tag{10}$$

Corollary 1 does not hold for universally quantified formulas or when negated atoms are present (stronger requirements on the homomorphisms are required, see [17, Theorems 2.4.1 and 2.4.3(b, c)]).

Example 4. Let $S = \{\mathsf{P}(\mathsf{a})\}$ and $\varphi = (\forall x)\mathsf{P}(x)$, which clearly holds in the least Herbrand model of S. The structure $\mathcal{A}$ with domain $\mathbb{N}$ that interprets a as 0 and P as $\{0\}$ is a model of S but $\mathcal{A} \models \varphi$ does not hold. Thus, $S \models \varphi$ does *not* hold.

Add a new constant symbol b to the previous signature and consider $\varphi' = (\exists x)\neg\mathsf{P}(x)$. Clearly, $\mathcal{I}_S \models \varphi'$ holds. The structure $\mathcal{A}'$ over $\{0\}$, interpreting both a and b as 0 and P again as $\{0\}$, is a model of S, but $\mathcal{A}' \models \varphi'$ does *not* hold.

Now consider a set S_0 of first-order sentences (i.e., a first-order theory) and let S be the set of ground atoms obtained as the *deductive closure* of S_0, i.e., the set of *atoms* $P(t_1, \ldots, t_n)$ for each n-ary predicate symbol P and ground terms $t_1, \ldots, t_n$, such that $S_0 \vdash P(t_1, \ldots, t_n)$. By construction, every model $\mathcal{A}$ of S_0 is also a model of S. By Theorem 1, there is a homomorphism h from $\mathcal{I}_S$ to $\mathcal{A}$. By Theorem 2, if $\mathcal{A} \models \neg\varphi$ holds and φ is the existential closure of a positive boolean combination of atoms, then $\mathcal{I}_S \models \neg\varphi$ holds, which we often read: S_0 *lacks property* φ. Accordingly, the following result is the basis of the practical applications discussed in the following sections.

Corollary 2 (Semantic criterion). *Let S_0 be a first-order theory and S be the set of its ground atomic consequences, φ be the existential closure of a positive boolean combination of atoms, and $\mathcal{A}$ be a structure. If $\mathcal{A} \models S_0 \cup \{\neg\varphi\}$, then $\mathcal{I}_S \models \neg\varphi$.*

Using Corollary 2 only makes sense if S_0 is *consistent* (otherwise, $\mathcal{A} \models S_0$ never holds, [17, Sect. 2.3]) and the set $\mathcal{T}(\mathcal{F})$ of ground terms is *not* empty (i.e., $\mathcal{F}$ contains at least a constant symbol, which can be a *dummy* one). Otherwise, the domain of $\mathcal{I}_S$ is empty and every existentially closed formula φ is trivially *false* in $\mathcal{I}_S$. In the following, we use S (rather than S_0) to refer the considered first-order theory.

Remark 1 (Many-sorted signatures). Corollaries 1 and 2 easily generalize to many-sorted signatures: each variable x of sort s_i is given an atom $S_i(x)$ which is added as a new conjunction to the matrix formula (7) [36]. In Sect. 5.6 we use this without further formalization (but see [15]).

Models $\mathcal{A}$ to be used in Corollary 2 can be automatically generated from the (many-sorted) first-order theory S and sentence φ at stake by using a tool like AGES [16] which implements the methodology described in [19]. Models displayed in the examples of this paper have been automatically generated by AGES.

Case Study: Unsolvable Unification (φ_{Unif}). Two expressions e and e' (terms or atoms) unify iff there is a substitution σ (which is called a *unifier*) which make them *syntactically equal*. A *unification problem* is usually represented as $e =^? e'$ and said to be *solvable* if such a unifier exists. Similarly, a set of unification problems $U = \{e_i =^? e'_i \mid 1 \leq i \leq n\}$ is solvable iff there is a substitution σ which is a unifier of $e_i =^? e'_i$ for all $1 \leq i \leq n$. We can use Corollary 2 together with φ_{Unif} (see Table 1) to show that a set of unification problems among terms $s_1 =^? t_1, \ldots, s_n =^? t_n$ is *unsolvable*. In this case, S consists of the equality axioms only (see, e.g., [25, Proposition 2.25]).

$$
(Rf) \quad \frac{}{x \to^* x} \qquad (C)_{f,i} \quad \frac{x_i \to y_i}{f(x_1, \ldots, x_i, \ldots, x_k) \to f(x_1, \ldots, y_i, \ldots, x_k)}
$$
$$
\text{for all } f \in \mathcal{F} \text{ and } 1 \leq i \leq k = arity(f)
$$

$$
(T) \quad \frac{x \to y \quad y \to^* z}{x \to^* z} \qquad (Rl)_\alpha \quad \frac{s_1 \to^* t_1 \quad \cdots \quad s_n \to^* t_n}{\ell \to r}
$$
$$
\text{for } \alpha : \ell \to r \Leftarrow s_1 \to t_1, \ldots, s_n \to t_n \in \mathcal{R}
$$

Fig. 1. Inference rules for conditional rewriting with a CTRS $\mathcal{R}$ with signature $\mathcal{F}$

Example 5. Consider a first-order signature with constant symbols a and b. In order to prove that there is no unifier for $U = \{x =^? \mathsf{a}, x =^? \mathsf{b}\}$, we try to find a model of $\{\neg\varphi_{Unif}\}$, where φ_{Unif} is $(\exists x)\ x = \mathsf{a} \wedge x = \mathsf{b}$. The structure $\mathcal{A}$ with domain $\mathcal{A} = \{-1, 0, 1\}$ and interpretation for symbols given by $\mathsf{a}^{\mathcal{A}} = 0$, $\mathsf{b}^{\mathcal{A}} = 1$, and $=^{\mathcal{A}}$ the equality on $\mathcal{A}$ shows unsolvability of U.

If we consider a set of equations E together with the usual equality axioms, then the interpretation of φ_{Unif} would be E-unification and we could use Corollary 2 to disprove the E-unification of terms or finite sets of pairs of terms.

4   Conditional Rewrite Systems as Horn Theories

A CTRS is a pair $\mathcal{R} = (\mathcal{F}, R)$ where $\mathcal{F}$ is a signature of function symbols and R is a set of conditional rules $\ell \to r \Leftarrow c$ where ℓ and r are terms and c is the *conditional part* of the rule consisting of sequences $s_1 \approx t_1, \ldots, s_n \approx t_n$ of expressions $s_i \approx t_i$, usually interpreted as *reachability* or *joinability* problems after an appropriate instantiation with a substitution σ, i.e., for all i, $1 \leq i \leq n$, $\sigma(s_i) \to^*_{\mathcal{R}} \sigma(t_i)$ (for the *rewriting semantics*); or $\sigma(s_i) \downarrow_{\mathcal{R}} \sigma(t_i)$ (for the joinability semantics) [3,11,28]. In the following we focus on the reachability semantics for CTRSs[3]. We write $s \to^*_{\mathcal{R}} t$ for terms s and t iff there is a proof tree for $s \to^* t$ using $\mathcal{R}$ in the inference system of Fig. 1 (and similarly for one-step rewriting steps $s \to_{\mathcal{R}} t$ regarding *proofs* of the goal $s \to t$) [20].

---

[3] Note that the joinability semantics can be rephrased into a reachability semantics: a joinability condition $s \downarrow t$ is equivalent to a reachability condition $s \to^* x, t \to^* x$ if x is a fresh variable not occurring elsewhere in the rule.

Remark 2. Schematic rules $\frac{B_1 \ \cdots \ B_n}{A}$ actually denote *instances* $\frac{\sigma(B_1) \ \cdots \ \sigma(B_n)}{\sigma(A)}$ by a substitution σ [31]. For instance, $(Rl)_\alpha$ in Fig. 1 establishes that, for all substitutions σ, $\sigma(\ell)$ rewrites into $\sigma(r)$ whenever $\sigma(s_i) \to^* \sigma(t_i)$ for $1 \leq i \leq n$.

In the logic of CTRSs, with binary *predicates* $\to$ and $\to^*$, the *Horn theory* $\overline{\mathcal{R}}$ for a CTRS $\mathcal{R}$ is obtained from the inference rules in Fig. 1 (for the *reachability semantics of conditions*) by *specializing* $(C)_{f,i}$ for each $f \in \mathcal{F}$ and $1 \leq i \leq ar(f)$, and $(Rl)_\alpha$ for all $\alpha : \ell \to r \Leftarrow c \in R$. Inference rules $\frac{B_1 \ \cdots \ B_n}{A}$ become universally quantified *implications* $B_1 \wedge \cdots \wedge B_n \Rightarrow A$ [22, Sect. 2].

Example 6. For the following CTRS $\mathcal{R}$ [14, p. 46]:

$$\mathsf{a} \to \mathsf{b} \tag{11}$$

$$\mathsf{f}(\mathsf{a}) \to \mathsf{b} \tag{12}$$

$$\mathsf{g}(x) \to \mathsf{g}(\mathsf{a}) \Leftarrow \mathsf{f}(x) \to x \tag{13}$$

We have the following Horn theory $\overline{\mathcal{R}}$:

$$(\forall x) \ x \to^* x \tag{14}$$

$$(\forall x, y, z) \ (x \to y \wedge y \to^* z \Rightarrow x \to^* z) \tag{15}$$

$$(\forall x, y) \ (x \to y \Rightarrow \mathsf{f}(x) \to \mathsf{f}(y)) \tag{16}$$

$$(\forall x, y) \ (x \to y \Rightarrow \mathsf{g}(x) \to \mathsf{g}(y)) \tag{17}$$

$$\mathsf{a} \to \mathsf{b} \tag{18}$$

$$\mathsf{f}(\mathsf{a}) \to \mathsf{b} \tag{19}$$

$$(\forall x) \ (\mathsf{f}(x) \to^* x \Rightarrow \mathsf{g}(x) \to \mathsf{g}(\mathsf{a})) \tag{20}$$

5   Application to (Conditional) Term Rewriting

Most sentences in Table 1 are particular cases of (8) when the language of the logic of CTRSs is used. Some of the problems represented by these formulas have been investigated in the literature. In the following, we consider them and show that our results are useful to improve or complement the already developed proof methods for these analysis problems.

5.1   Infeasible Conditional Critical Pairs (φ_{Feas})

In the literature about *confluence* of conditional rewriting, the so-called *infeasible* Conditional Critical Pairs (CCPs) for a CTRS $\mathcal{R}$ are those critical pairs $s \downarrow t \Leftarrow c$ whose *conditional parts* c are *infeasible*, i.e., there is no substitution σ such that for all i, $1 \leq i \leq n$, we have $\sigma(s_i) \to_{\mathcal{R}}^* \sigma(t_i)$ (for the *rewriting semantics*; or $\sigma(s_i) \downarrow_{\mathcal{R}} \sigma(t_i)$ for the joinability semantics) [28, Definition 7.1.8]. Detecting infeasible CCPs is important in proofs of confluence of CTRSs [3,28,33,34].

Although infeasibility of CCPs is undecidable, recent tools developed to prove confluence of CTRSs (e.g., [32]) implement a number of sufficient criteria to prove infeasibility of CCPs [33,34]. Infeasibility of CCPs with respect to a CTRS $\mathcal{R}$ can be investigated using φ_{Feas}, i.e., $(\exists x)\, s_1 \to^* t_1 \wedge \cdots \wedge s_n \to^* t_n$ (see Table 1) together with Corollary 2.

Example 7. The following CTRS [33, Example 5.1]

$$0 \leq x \to \text{true} \qquad \text{s}(x) > 0 \to \text{true} \qquad x - 0 \to x$$
$$\text{s}(x) \leq \text{s}(y) \to x \leq y \quad \text{s}(x) > \text{s}(y) \to x > y \quad 0 - x \to 0 \quad \text{s}(x) - \text{s}(y) \to x - y$$

$$x \div y \to \langle 0, y \rangle \Leftarrow y > x \to \text{true}$$
$$x \div y \to \langle \text{s}(q), r \rangle \Leftarrow y \leq x \to \text{true}, (x - y) \div x \to \langle y, z \rangle$$

has the following conditional critical pair:

$$\langle 0, x \rangle \downarrow \langle \text{s}(y), z \rangle \Leftarrow x \leq w \to \text{true}, (w - x) \div x \to \langle y, z \rangle, x > w \to \text{true}$$

The structure $\mathcal{A}$ below provides a model of $\overline{\mathcal{R}} \cup \{\neg \varphi_{Feas}\}$ where φ_{Feas} is

$$(\exists w, x, y, z)\, (x \leq w \to^* \text{true}, (w - x) \div x \to^* \langle y, z \rangle, x > w \to^* \text{true}) \qquad (21)$$

The domain of $\mathcal{A}$ is the set of natural numbers $\mathbb{N}$. Function symbols are interpreted as follows:

$$\text{true}^{\mathcal{A}} = 1 \qquad\qquad 0^{\mathcal{A}} = 0 \qquad\qquad \text{s}^{\mathcal{A}}(x) = x + 1$$

$$x \leq^{\mathcal{A}} y = \begin{cases} 1 \text{ if } y \geq_{\mathbb{N}} x \\ 0 \text{ otherwise} \end{cases} \qquad x >^{\mathcal{A}} y = \begin{cases} 1 \text{ if } x >_{\mathbb{N}} y \\ 0 \text{ otherwise} \end{cases} \qquad x \div^{\mathcal{A}} y = 1$$

$$x -^{\mathcal{A}} y = \begin{cases} x -_{\mathbb{N}} y \text{ if } x \geq_{\mathbb{N}} y \\ 0 \quad \text{otherwise} \end{cases} \qquad \langle x, y \rangle^{\mathcal{A}} = 1$$

Predicate symbols $\to$ and $\to^*$ are interpreted as follows:

$$x \to y \Leftrightarrow x =_{\mathbb{N}} y \qquad x \to^* y \Leftrightarrow x \geq_{\mathbb{N}} y$$

Thus, the critical pair is infeasible. In [33, Example 5.1] this is proved by using the theorem prover Waldmeister [12].

Example 8. The following CTRS $\mathcal{R}$ [34, Example 23]

$$g(x) \to f(x, x) \tag{22}$$
$$g(x) \to g(x) \Leftarrow g(x) \to f(\text{a}, \text{b}) \tag{23}$$

has a conditional critical pair $f(x, x) \downarrow g(x) \Leftarrow g(x) \to f(\text{a}, \text{b})$. The following structure $\mathcal{A}$ over the finite domain $\{0, 1\}$:

$$\text{a}^{\mathcal{A}} = 1 \qquad \text{b}^{\mathcal{A}} = \text{c}^{\mathcal{A}} = 0 \qquad f^{\mathcal{A}}(x, y) = \begin{cases} x - y + 1 \text{ if } x \geq y \\ y - x + 1 \text{ otherwise} \end{cases}$$
$$g^{\mathcal{A}}(x) = 1 \qquad x \to^{\mathcal{A}} y \Leftrightarrow x = y \qquad x\, (\to^*)^{\mathcal{A}} y \Leftrightarrow x \geq y$$

is a model $\overline{\mathcal{R}} \cup \{\neg \varphi_{Feas}\}$ for φ_{Feas} given by $(\exists x)\, g(x) \to^* f(\text{a}, \text{b})$. Thus, the critical pair is infeasible. In [34, Example 23] this is proved by using unification tests together with a transformation. It is discussed that the alternative tree automata techniques investigated in the paper do *not* work for this example.

5.2   Infeasible Rules (φ_{Feas})

The infeasibility of the *conditional part* c of a conditional rule $\ell \to r \Leftarrow c$ with respect to a given CTRS is also important to prove other computational properties of such systems. In particular, proving the infeasibility of the *conditional dependency pairs* which are used to characterize termination properties of CTRSs [21] is useful in (automated) proofs of such termination properties [24].

Example 9. A CTRS $\mathcal{R}$ is *operationally terminating* iff no term t has an infinite proof tree using the inference system in Fig. 1 [20]. According to [21,24], a formal proof of operational termination of $\mathcal{R}$ in Example 6 is easily obtained if the following *conditional dependency pair* (which is just a conditional rule):

$$G(x) \to G(a) \Leftarrow f(x) \to x \tag{24}$$

(where G is a new function symbol) is proved *infeasible* with respect to reductions with $\mathcal{R}$. The following structure $\mathcal{A}$ over $\mathbb{N} - \{0\}$:

$$a^{\mathcal{A}} = 1 \qquad\qquad b^{\mathcal{A}} = 2 \qquad f^{\mathcal{A}}(x) = x + 1 \qquad g^{\mathcal{A}}(x) = 1$$
$$x \to^{\mathcal{A}} y \Leftrightarrow x \leq y \qquad x\,(\to^{*})^{\mathcal{A}}\,y \Leftrightarrow x \leq y$$

is a model of $\overline{\mathcal{R}} \cup \{\neg\varphi_{Feas}\}$, where $\overline{\mathcal{R}}$ is in Example 6 and φ_{Feas} is $(\exists x)\,f(x) \to^{*} x$. Thus, rule (24) is proved $\mathcal{R}$-infeasible and $\mathcal{R}$ operationally terminating.

Example 10. Consider the following CTRS $\mathcal{R}$ [34, Example 17]:

$$h(x) \to a \tag{25}$$
$$g(x) \to x \tag{26}$$
$$g(x) \to a \Leftarrow h(x) \to b \tag{27}$$
$$c \to c \tag{28}$$

The following structure $\mathcal{A}$ over $\mathbb{N}$:

$$a^{\mathcal{A}} = 0 \qquad\qquad b^{\mathcal{A}} = c^{\mathcal{A}} = 1 \qquad g^{\mathcal{A}}(x) = x + 2 \qquad h^{\mathcal{A}}(x) = 0$$
$$x \to^{\mathcal{A}} y \Leftrightarrow x \geq y \qquad x\,(\to^{*})^{\mathcal{A}}\,y \Leftrightarrow x \geq y$$

is a model of $\overline{\mathcal{R}} \cup \{\neg\varphi_{Feas}\}$ where φ_{Feas} is $(\exists x)\,h(x) \to^{*} b$. Therefore, rule (27) is proved $\mathcal{R}$-infeasible. In [34, Example 17] this is proved by using tree automata techniques. It is also shown that the alternative technique investigated in the paper (the use of unification tests) does *not* work in this case.

5.3   Non-joinability of Critical Pairs (φ_{Join})

The analysis of *confluence* often relies on checking for *joinability* of the components s and t of a *critical pair* $s \downarrow t$ obtained from the rules of the (C)TRS $\mathcal{R}$, i.e., we look for a term u such that $s \to^{*}_{\mathcal{R}} u$ and $t \to^{*}_{\mathcal{R}} u$. The problem of *disproving* joinability of *ground* terms has been investigated for TRSs, as an interesting contribution to the development of methods for (automatically) proving *non-confluence* of TRSs [1].

Actually, proving *non-joinability* of (ground) terms can be seen as a particular case of *infeasibility*: given ground terms s and t, we prove that $(\exists x)(s \to^* x \wedge t \to^* x)$ does *not* hold. In this way, we use our technique to check non-joinability of ground terms in CTRSs, something which is also considered in [34].

Example 11. The following CTRS $\mathcal{R}$ [34, Example 3]

$$f(x) \to a \Leftarrow x \to a \tag{29}$$

$$f(x) \to b \Leftarrow x \to b \tag{30}$$

has a conditional critical pair $a \downarrow b \Leftarrow x \to a, x \to b$, which is both *non-joinable* and *infeasible*. For non-joinability, consider the structure $\mathcal{A}$ over $\{0, 1\}$:

$$a^{\mathcal{A}} = 0 \qquad b^{\mathcal{A}} = 1 \qquad f^{\mathcal{A}}(x) = x$$
$$x \to^{\mathcal{A}} y \Leftrightarrow x = y \qquad x (\to^*)^{\mathcal{A}} y \Leftrightarrow x = y$$

which is a model $\overline{\mathcal{R}} \cup \{\neg \varphi_{Join}\}$ for φ_{Join} given by $(\exists x)\, a \to^* x \wedge b \to^* x$. Thus, the critical pair is non-joinable. In [34, Example 3] this is proved by an unification test. For infeasibility, consider the structure $\mathcal{A}$ over $\mathbb{N}$:

$$a^{\mathcal{A}} = 1 \qquad b^{\mathcal{A}} = 0 \qquad f^{\mathcal{A}}(x) = x$$
$$x \to^{\mathcal{A}} y \Leftrightarrow x = y \qquad x (\to^*)^{\mathcal{A}} y \Leftrightarrow x = y$$

which is a model $\overline{\mathcal{R}} \cup \{\neg \varphi_{Feas}\}$ for φ_{Feas} given by $(\exists x)\, x \to^* a \wedge x \to^* b$. Thus, the critical pair is infeasible. In [34, Example 3] this is not actually proved but the authors argue that the unification test does not work.

5.4   Irreducible Terms (φ_{Red})

It is well-known that, in sharp contrast to unconditional rewriting, for CTRSs $\mathcal{R}$ it is *not* decidable whether a given term t is (one-step) reducible. In Example 3, we already exemplified the use of our technique to check whether a given reduction step $s \to t$ for ground terms s and t is *not* possible. In general, with φ_{Red}, i.e., $(\exists x)\, t \to x$, and Corollary 2 we can prove that a given ground term t is *irreducible*. In the following example we show an interesting variant.

Example 12. Consider the following CTRS $\mathcal{R}$ [23, Example 13]:

$$a \to b \tag{31}$$

$$b \to a \tag{32}$$

$$f(x) \to x \Leftarrow c \to d, a \to c \tag{33}$$

Note that every term $f(t)$ is *irreducible at the root*. We can prove this claim with a slight variant of φ_{Red}: $(\exists x, y)\, f(x) \overset{\Lambda}{\to} y$, which claims for the existence of a *root-reducible* instance $f(t)$ of $f(x)$. The new predicate $\overset{\Lambda}{\to}$ has a slightly different

Horn theory $H_{\underset{\mathcal{R}}{\Lambda}}$ where reductions with $\xrightarrow{\Lambda}_{\mathcal{R}}$ are *not* propagated below the root of terms: for each rule $\ell \to r \Leftarrow s_1 \to t_1, \ldots, s_n \to t_n$, we have a sentence:

$$(\forall x_1, \ldots, x_k)\ s_1 \to^* t_1 \wedge \cdots \wedge s_n \to^* t_n \Rightarrow \ell \xrightarrow{\Lambda} r \tag{34}$$

in $H_{\underset{\mathcal{R}}{\Lambda}}$ (where $x_1, \ldots, x_k$ are the variables occurring in the rule) and nothing else. Note that the conditions in the rules are evaluated with $\to^*_{\mathcal{R}}$ rather than with $\xrightarrow{\Lambda}^*_{\mathcal{R}}$. For this reason, no definition of the reflexive and transitive closure of $\xrightarrow{\Lambda}$ is given. Thus, the Horn theory $\overline{\mathcal{R}} \cup H_{\underset{\mathcal{R}}{\Lambda}}$ we have to deal with is

$$(\forall x) x \to^* x \tag{35}$$
$$(\forall x, y, z)(x \to y \wedge y \to^* z \Rightarrow x \to^* z) \tag{36}$$
$$(\forall x, y)(x \to y \Rightarrow \mathsf{f}(x) \to \mathsf{f}(y)) \tag{37}$$
$$\mathsf{a} \to \mathsf{b} \tag{38}$$
$$\mathsf{b} \to \mathsf{a} \tag{39}$$
$$(\forall x)\ \mathsf{c} \to^* \mathsf{d} \wedge \mathsf{a} \to^* \mathsf{c} \Rightarrow \mathsf{f}(x) \to x \tag{40}$$
$$\mathsf{a} \xrightarrow{\Lambda} \mathsf{b} \tag{41}$$
$$\mathsf{b} \xrightarrow{\Lambda} \mathsf{a} \tag{42}$$
$$(\forall x)\ \mathsf{c} \to^* \mathsf{d} \wedge \mathsf{a} \to^* \mathsf{c} \Rightarrow \mathsf{f}(x) \xrightarrow{\Lambda} x \tag{43}$$

with $\overline{\mathcal{R}} = \{(35)$–$(40)\}$ and $H_{\underset{\mathcal{R}}{\Lambda}} = \{(41)$–$(43)\}$. The following structure $\mathcal{A}$ over $\{-1, 0, 1\}$ is a model of $\overline{\mathcal{R}} \cup H_{\underset{\mathcal{R}}{\Lambda}} \cup \{\neg \varphi_{RRed}\}$ where φ_{RRed} is $(\exists x, y)\ \mathsf{f}(x) \xrightarrow{\Lambda} y$:

$$\mathsf{a}^{\mathcal{A}} = \mathsf{b}^{\mathcal{A}} = -1 \qquad \mathsf{c}^{\mathcal{A}} = 0 \qquad \mathsf{d}^{\mathcal{A}} = 1 \qquad \mathsf{f}^{\mathcal{A}}(x) = 1$$
$$x \to^{\mathcal{A}} y \Leftrightarrow x \geq y \quad x\ (\to^*)^{\mathcal{A}}\ y \Leftrightarrow x \geq y \quad x (\xrightarrow{\Lambda})^{\mathcal{A}} y \Leftrightarrow 5x + y \leq 1$$

This proves that for all ground terms t, $\mathsf{f}(t)$ is irreducible at the root.

5.5 Non-cycling/looping Terms and Systems ($\varphi_{Cycl}/\varphi_{Loop}$)

A term t *loops* (with respect to a CTRS $\mathcal{R}$) if there is a rewrite sequence $t = t_1 \to_{\mathcal{R}} \cdots \to_{\mathcal{R}} t_n$ for some $n > 1$ such that t is a (non-necessarily strict) subterm of t_n, written $t_n \unrhd t$ (cf., [10, Definition 3]). We say that a CTRS is non-looping if no term loops. We can prove *non-loopingness* of terms t or CTRSs $\mathcal{R}$ by using φ_{Loopt} and φ_{Loop} in Table 1 if the considered Horn theory is the union of $\overline{\mathcal{R}}$ and the Horn theory $H_{\unrhd}$ describing the subterm relation $\unrhd$:

$$(\forall x)\ x \unrhd x \tag{44}$$
$$(\forall x, y, z)\ x \unrhd y \wedge y \unrhd z \Rightarrow x \unrhd z \tag{45}$$
$$(\forall x_1, \ldots, x_k)\ f(x_1, \ldots, x_k) \unrhd x_i \tag{46}$$
$$\text{for each } f \in \mathcal{F} \text{ and } 1 \leq i \leq k$$

Example 13. Consider the two rules TRS $\mathcal{R} = \{a \to c(b), b \to c(b)\}$. We can prove a non-looping. The Horn theory $\overline{\mathcal{R}} \cup H_{\unrhd}$ is the following

$$(\forall x) \; x \to^* x \tag{47}$$

$$(\forall x, y, z) \; (x \to y \wedge y \to^* z \Rightarrow x \to^* z) \tag{48}$$

$$(\forall x, y) \; (x \to y \Rightarrow c(x) \to c(y)) \tag{49}$$

$$a \to c(b) \tag{50}$$

$$b \to c(b) \tag{51}$$

$$(\forall x) \; x \unrhd x \tag{52}$$

$$(\forall x, y, z) \; x \unrhd y \wedge y \unrhd z \Rightarrow x \unrhd z \tag{53}$$

$$(\forall x) \; c(x) \unrhd x \tag{54}$$

The following structure over $\mathbb{N} \cup \{-1\}$:

$$a^{\mathcal{A}} = -1 \qquad\qquad b^{\mathcal{A}} = 1 \qquad c^{\mathcal{A}}(x) = x$$
$$x \to^{\mathcal{A}} y \Leftrightarrow x \leq 1 \wedge y \geq 1 \quad x \; (\to^*)^{\mathcal{A}} y \Leftrightarrow x \leq y \quad x \unrhd^{\mathcal{A}} y \Leftrightarrow x \leq y$$

is a model of $\overline{\mathcal{R}} \cup H_{\unrhd} \cup \{\neg\varphi_{Loopt}\}$ where φ_{Loopt} is $(\exists x, y) \; a \to x \wedge x \to^* y \wedge y \unrhd a$. Therefore, a is non-looping. On the other hand, although b is a looping term, we can also prove that it is *non-cycling*. Actually, we can prove that $\mathcal{R}$ itself is non-cycling with the following structure over $\mathbb{N} \cup \{-1\}$

$$a^{\mathcal{A}} = -1 \qquad\qquad b^{\mathcal{A}} = -1 \qquad c^{\mathcal{A}}(x) = 2x + 2$$
$$x \to^{\mathcal{A}} y \Leftrightarrow x < y \quad x \; (\to^*)^{\mathcal{A}} y \Leftrightarrow x \leq y$$

which is a model of $\overline{\mathcal{R}} \cup \{\neg\varphi_{Cycl}\}$ where φ_{Cycl} is $(\exists x, y) \; x \to y \wedge y \to^* x$.

5.6   Secure Access to Web Sites

The *order-sorted* specification in Fig. 2 provides a partial representation of the structure and connectivity of the web site of the 1st International Workshop on Automated Specification and Verification of Web Sites, WWV'05[4]. Web pages are modeled as terms $p(u)$ of sort WPage where u represents the *user* browsing page p. The sort of u is used to allow/disallow the access to some web pages. Registered and eventual users are given sorts RegUsr and EvUsr, respectively (subsorts of Usr). Transitions among web pages are modeled as rewrite rules. Browsing the web site is modeled as *rewriting* in the corresponding OS-TRS $\mathcal{R}$. For this reason, the specification is given as a Maude module whose syntax is hopefully self-explanatory [7]. Our goal is verifying that *no* eventual *user can submit*. Thus, we formulate the property we want to *avoid*:

$$(\exists u : EvUsr) \; wwv05(u) \to^* submit(u) \tag{55}$$

---

[4] http://users.dsic.upv.es/workshops/wwv05/.

```
mod WWV05-WEBSITE is
  sorts EvUsr RegUsr Usr WPage . subsorts RegUsr EvUsr < Usr .
  ops login register sbmlink submission submit vlogin wwv05 : Usr -> WPage .
  op good  : -> RegUsr .
  op maybe : -> EvUsr .
  var R : RegUsr . var U : Usr .
  rl wwv05(U) => submission(U) .
  rl submission(U) => sbmlink(U) .
  rl sbmlink(U) => login(U) .
  rl sbmlink(U) => register(U) .
  rl login(U) => vlogin(U) .
  rl vlogin(R) => submit(R) .
endm
```

Fig. 2. Maude specification of part of the WWV05 web site

The following structure $\mathcal{A}$ with $\mathcal{A}_{\text{EvUsr}} = \{1\}$, $\mathcal{A}_{\text{RegUsr}} = \{0\}$, $\mathcal{A}_{\text{Usr}} = \mathbb{N}$, $\mathcal{A}_{\text{WPage}} = \mathbb{N} \cup \{-1\}$; function symbols interpreted by $\text{good}^{\mathcal{A}} = 0$, $\text{maybe}^{\mathcal{A}} = 1$, $\text{login}^{\mathcal{A}}(x) = 7x + 2$, $\text{register}^{\mathcal{A}}(x) = 8x + 2$, $\text{sbmlink}^{\mathcal{A}}(x) = 7x + 1$, $\text{submission}^{\mathcal{A}}(x) = 6x$, $\text{submit}^{\mathcal{A}}(x) = 4$ $\text{vlogin}^{\mathcal{A}}(x) = 8x + 3$, $\text{wwv05}^{\mathcal{A}}(x) = 6x - 1$; and predicate symbols interpreted by $x \to^{\mathcal{A}} y \Leftrightarrow y > x$ and $x(\to^*)^{\mathcal{A}} y \Leftrightarrow y \geq x$ is a model of $\overline{\mathcal{R}} \cup \{\neg(\exists u : \text{EvUsr}) \text{ wwv05}(u) \to^* \text{submit}(u)\}$, thus proving the desired security property. This crucially depends on the type RegUsr of variable R controling the 'identity' of any user reaching the web page submit.

6   Related Work

The so-called *first-order theory of rewriting* (*FOThR* in the following) uses a restricted first-order language (without constant or function symbols, and with only two predicate symbols $\to$ and $\to^*$). The predicate symbols are by definition *interpreted* on an *intended model* [9]: the least Herbrand model $\mathcal{H}_{\mathcal{R}}$ (see Sect. 1). *FOThR* is often used to express and verify properties of TRSs. For instance, confluence can be expressed as follows:

$$(\forall x, y, z) \ (x \to^* y \wedge x \to^* z \Rightarrow (\exists u)(y \to^* u \wedge z \to^* u)) \tag{56}$$

Given a TRS $\mathcal{R}$ and a formula φ in the language of *FOThR*, $\mathcal{H}_{\mathcal{R}} \models \varphi$ (i.e., the satisfiability of φ in $\mathcal{H}_{\mathcal{R}}$) actually *means* that the property expressed by φ *holds* for the TRS $\mathcal{R}$. For instance $\mathcal{H}_{\mathcal{R}} \models$ (57) means '$\mathcal{R}$ is ground confluent'. And $\neg(\mathcal{H}_{\mathcal{R}} \models$ (57)), which is equivalent to $\mathcal{H}_{\mathcal{R}} \models \neg$(57), means '$\mathcal{R}$ is *not* ground confluent'. Decision algorithms for these properties exist for restricted classes of TRSs $\mathcal{R}$ like left-linear right-ground TRSs, where variables are allowed in the left-hand side of the rules (without repeated occurrences of the same variable) but disallowed in the right-hand side [30]. However, a simple fragment of *FOThR* like the *First-Order Theory of One-Step Rewriting*, where only a single predicate symbol $\to$ representing one-step rewritings with $\mathcal{R}$ is allowed, has been proved undecidable even for *linear* TRSs [35].

In a different approach, Gallagher and Rosendahl use Horn clauses to encode TRSs and then investigate reachability issues [13]. Their approach, however, is quite different from ours. As explained in Sect. 4, our starting point is not just a TRS but the *inference rules* associated to the TRS in a given computational logic which can be different for the *same* TRS. In this way, we make explicit not only the rules of the TRS but also the description of the considered operational semantics (and possibly other relations). Such a semantic description is implicit (and therefore *fixed*) in their encoding. Also, we view rewrite rules $\ell \rightarrow r$ just as *atoms* for a binary predicate $\rightarrow$, whereas they translate each rewrite rule into several Horn clauses which flatten the original terms to simulate pattern matching [13, Sect. 3]. Furthermore, we do not restrict the attention to TRSs.

In contrast to *FOThR*, we use the full expressive power of first-order logic to represent sophisticated rewrite theories where sorts, conditional rules and equations, membership predicates, etc., are allowed. We do not impose any restriction on the class of rewrite systems we can deal with. In contrast to *FOThR*, where function symbols are not allowed in formulas, we can use sentences involving arbitrary terms. Also in contrast to *FOThR*, with a single allowed model $\mathcal{H}_\mathcal{R}$, we permit the *arbitrary interpretation* of the underlying first-order logic language for proving properties. As a consequence of this, though, we also need to impose restrictions to the shape of first-order sentences (8) we can deal with. The application of this approach to well-known problems in rewriting leads to new methods which show their usefulness with regard to existing ones. In contrast to *FOThR*, though, sentences like (56) do not fit format (8) considered in this paper. But most sentences in Table 1 cannot be expressed in *FOThR* either, as they involve specific *terms* with or without variables.

Other approaches like the ITP tool, *a theorem prover that can be used to prove properties of membership equational specifications* [8] work like the ones using *FOThR*: the tool can be used to verify properties *with respect to ITP-models* which are actually special versions of the Herbrand model of the underlying theory. Then, one may have similar decidability problems as discussed for *FOThR*.

7   Conclusions

We have presented a semantic approach to prove properties of computational systems whose semantics can be given as a first-order theory $\mathcal{S}$. Provided that a program property can be expressed as a first-order sentence φ which is the existential closure of a positive boolean combination of atoms, the *satisfaction* of the negation $\neg\varphi$ of this sentence by an arbitrary model $\mathcal{A}$ of $\mathcal{S}$ implies that $\neg\varphi$ holds in the standard Herbrand model of $\mathcal{S}$. As usual, we can think of this fact as $\mathcal{S}$ actually *lacking* the property expressed by φ.

We have explained how to apply this simple technique to deal with rewriting-based computational systems, in particular with (possibly sorted) conditional rewrite systems. We have considered a number of properties that have been investigated in the literature (infeasibility of conditional critical pairs and rules, non-joinability of ground terms, non-loopingness, nonreachability, etc.).

Quite surprisingly, we could handle many specific examples coming from papers developing specific techniques to deal with these problems with our semantic approach (Corollary 2). In particular, we could deal with all the examples solved in [33,34] (some of them reported in our examples above; note that these papers explore several *alternative* methods and, as reported by the authors, some of them *fail* in specific examples which then require a different approach). We also dealt with all Aoto's examples in [1] in combination with his *usable rules* refinement (see also [18]). Furthermore, these examples were all handled by using our tool AGES for the automatic generation of models of Order-Sorted First-Order Theories.

Acknowledgements. I thank María Alpuente and José Meseguer for many fruitful discussions. I also thank the anonymous referees for their comments.

References

1. Aoto, T.: Disproving confluence of term rewriting systems by interpretation and ordering. In: Fontaine, P., Ringeissen, C., Schmidt, R.A. (eds.) FroCoS 2013. LNCS (LNAI), vol. 8152, pp. 311–326. Springer, Heidelberg (2013). https://doi.org/10. 1007/978-3-642-40885-4_22
2. Baader, F., Nipkow, T.: Term Rewriting and All That. Cambridge University Press, Cambridge (1998)
3. Bergstra, J.A., Klop, J.W.: Conditional rewrite rules: confluence and termination. J. Comput. Syst. Sci. **32**, 323–362 (1986)
4. Bruni, R., Meseguer, J.: Semantic foundations for generalized rewrite theories. Theor. Comput. Sci. **351**(1), 386–414 (2006)
5. Chang, C.L., Lee, R.C.: Symbolic Logic and Mechanical Theorem Proving. Academic Press, New York (1973)
6. Clark, K.L.: Predicate logic as a computational formalism. Ph.D. thesis, Research Monograph 79/59 TOC, Department of Computing, Imperial College of Science, and Technology, University of London, December 1979
7. Clavel, M., Durán, F., Eker, S., Lincoln, P., Martí-Oliet, N., Meseguer, J., Talcott, C.: All About Maude - A High-Performance Logical Framework. LNCS, vol. 4350. Springer, Heidelberg (2007). https://doi.org/10.1007/978-3-540-71999-1
8. Clavel, M., Palomino, M., Riesco, A.: Introducing the ITP tool: a tutorial. J. Univ. Comput. Sci. **12**(11), 1618–1650 (2006)
9. Dauchet, M., Tison, S.: The theory of ground rewrite systems is decidable. In: Proceedings of LICS 1990, pp. 242–248. IEEE Press (1990)
10. Dershowitz, N.: Termination of rewriting. J. Symb. Comput. **3**, 69–115 (1987)
11. Dershowitz, N., Okada, M.: A rationale for conditional equational programming. Theor. Comput. Sci. **75**, 111–138 (1990)
12. Gaillourdet, J.-M., Hillenbrand, T., Löchner, B., Spies, H.: The new WALDMEISTER loop at work. In: Baader, F. (ed.) CADE 2003. LNCS (LNAI), vol. 2741, pp. 317–321. Springer, Heidelberg (2003). https://doi.org/10.1007/978-3-540-45085-6_27
13. Gallagher, J.P., Rosendahl, M.: Approximating term rewriting systems: a horn clause specification and its implementation. In: Cervesato, I., Veith, H., Voronkov, A. (eds.) LPAR 2008. LNCS (LNAI), vol. 5330, pp. 682–696. Springer, Heidelberg (2008). https://doi.org/10.1007/978-3-540-89439-1_47

14. Giesl, J., Arts, T.: Verification of Erlang processes by dependency pairs. Appl. Algebra Eng. Commun. Comput. **12**, 39–72 (2001)
15. Goguen, J.A., Meseguer, J.: Models and equality for logical programming. In: Ehrig, H., Kowalski, R., Levi, G., Montanari, U. (eds.) TAPSOFT 1987. LNCS, vol. 250, pp. 1–22. Springer, Heidelberg (1987). https://doi.org/10.1007/BFb0014969
16. Gutiérrez, R., Lucas, S., Reinoso, P.: A tool for the automatic generation of logical models of order-sorted first-order theories. In: Proceedings of PROLE 2016, pp. 215–230 (2016). Tool http://zenon.dsic.upv.es/ages/
17. Hodges, W.: A Shorter Model Theory. Cambridge University Press, Cambridge (1997)
18. Lucas, S., Gutiérrez, R.: A semantic criterion for proving infeasibility in conditional rewriting. In: Proceedings of IWC 2017, pp. 15–20 (2017)
19. Lucas, S., Gutiérrez, R.: Automatic synthesis of logical models for order-sorted first-order theories. J. Autom. Reason. **60**(4), 465–501 (2018)
20. Lucas, S., Marché, C., Meseguer, J.: Operational termination of conditional term rewriting systems. Inf. Process. Lett. **95**, 446–453 (2005)
21. Lucas, S., Meseguer, J.: Dependency pairs for proving termination properties of conditional term rewriting systems. J. Log. Algebraic Methods Program. **86**, 236–268 (2017)
22. Lucas, S., Meseguer, J.: Models for logics and conditional constraints in automated proofs of termination. In: Aranda-Corral, G.A., Calmet, J., Martín-Mateos, F.J. (eds.) AISC 2014. LNCS (LNAI), vol. 8884, pp. 9–20. Springer, Cham (2014). https://doi.org/10.1007/978-3-319-13770-4_3
23. Lucas, S., Meseguer, J.: Normal forms and normal theories in conditional rewriting. J. Log. Algebraic Methods Program. **85**(1), 67–97 (2016)
24. Lucas, S., Meseguer, J., Gutiérrez, R.: Extending the 2D dependency pair framework for conditional term rewriting systems. In: Proietti, M., Seki, H. (eds.) LOPSTR 2014. LNCS, vol. 8981, pp. 113–130. Springer, Cham (2015). https://doi.org/10.1007/978-3-319-17822-6_7
25. Mendelson, E.: Introduction to Mathematical Logic, 4th edn. Chapman & Hall, Boca Raton (1997)
26. Meseguer, J.: Membership algebra as a logical framework for equational specification. In: Presicce, F.P. (ed.) WADT 1997. LNCS, vol. 1376, pp. 18–61. Springer, Heidelberg (1998). https://doi.org/10.1007/3-540-64299-4_26
27. Meseguer, J.: Twenty years of rewriting logic. J. Logic Algebraic Program. **81**, 721–781 (2012)
28. Ohlebusch, E.: Advanced Topics in Term Rewriting. Springer, New York (2002). https://doi.org/10.1007/978-1-4757-3661-8
29. Prawitz, D.: Natural Deduction: A Proof-Theoretical Study. Dover, Mineola (2006)
30. Rapp, F., Middeldorp, A.: Automating the first-order theory of rewriting for left-linear right-ground rewrite systems. In: Proceedings of FSCD 2016, LIPIcs, vol. 52, pp. 36:1–36:12 (2016). Article No. 36
31. Smullyan, R.M.: Theory of Formal Systems. Princeton University Press, Princeton (1961)
32. Sternagel, T., Middeldorp, A.: Conditional confluence (system description). In: Dowek, G. (ed.) RTA 2014. LNCS, vol. 8560, pp. 456–465. Springer, Cham (2014). https://doi.org/10.1007/978-3-319-08918-8_31
33. Sternagel, T., Middeldorp, A.: Infefasible conditional critical pairs. In: Proceedings of IWC 2015, pp. 13–18 (2015)

34. Sternagel, C., Sternagel, T.: Certifying confluence of almost orthogonal CTRSs via exact tree automata completion. In: Proceedings of FSCD 2016, LIPIcs, vol. 52, pp. 85:1–85:16 (2016). Article No. 85
35. Treinen, R.: The first-order theory of linear one-step rewriting is undecidable. Theor. Comput. Sci. **208**, 179–190 (1998)
36. Wang, H.: Logic of many-sorted theories. J. Symb. Logic **17**(2), 105–116 (1952)

Theory

A Constructor-Based Reachability Logic for Rewrite Theories

Stephen Skeirik[✉], Andrei Stefanescu, and José Meseguer

University of Illinois at Urbana-Champaign, Champaign, USA
{skeirik2,stefane1,meseguer}@illinois.edu

Abstract. Reachability logic has been applied to $\mathbb{K}$ rewrite-rule-based language definitions as a *language-generic* logic of programs. To be able to verify not just code but also *distributed system designs*, a new *rewrite-theory-generic* reachability logic is presented and proved sound for a wide class of rewrite theories. *Constructor-based* semantic unification, matching, and satisfiability procedures greatly increase the range of decidable background theories that can be used in reachability logic proofs. New methods for proving invariants of possibly never terminating distributed systems are developed, and experiments with a prototype implementation illustrating the new proof methods are presented.

Keywords: Program verification · Rewriting logic · Reachability logic

1 Introduction

The main applications of reachability logic to date have been as a *language-generic* logic of programs [14,15]. In these applications, a $\mathbb{K}$ specification of a language's operational semantics by means of rewrite rules is assumed as the language's "golden semantic standard," and a correct-by-construction reachability logic for a language so defined is automatically obtained [15]. This method has been effective in proving reachability properties for a wide range of programs.

Although the foundations of reachability logic are very general [14,15], the existing theory does not provide straightforward answers to the following questions: (1) Could a reachability logic be developed to verify not just conventional programs, but also *distributed system designs and algorithms* formalized as *rewrite theories* in rewriting logic [8]? (2) If so, what would be the most natural way to conceive such a *rewrite-theory-generic* logic? A satisfactory answer to questions (1)–(2) would move the verification game from the level of verifying *code* to that of verifying *both code and distributed system designs*. Since the cost of design errors can be several orders of magnitude higher than that of coding errors, answering questions (1) and (2) is of practical software engineering interest.

Although a first step towards a reachability logic for rewrite theories has been taken in [6], as explained in Sect. 7 and below, that first step still leaves several

F. Fioravanti and J. P. Gallagher (Eds.): LOPSTR 2017, LNCS 10855, pp. 201–217, 2018.
https://doi.org/10.1007/978-3-319-94460-9_12

important questions open. The most burning one is how to prove *invariants*. Since they are the most basic safety properties, support for proving invariants is a *sine qua non* requirement. As explained below, a serious obstacle is what we call the *invariant paradox*: we cannot verify in this manner *any* invariants of a never-terminating system such as, for example, a mutual exclusion protocol.

A second open question is how to best take advantage of the wealth of equational reasoning techniques such as matching, unification, and narrowing modulo an equational theory (Σ, E), and of recent results on decidable satisfiability of quantifier-free formulas in initial algebras, e.g., [9] to *automate* as much as possible reachability logic deduction. In this regard, the very general foundations of reachability logic—which assume any Σ-algebra $\mathcal{A}$ with a first-order-definable transition relation—provide no help at all for automation. As shown in this work and its prototype implementation, if we assume instead that the model in question is the *initial model* $\mathcal{T}_\mathcal{R}$ of a rewrite theory $\mathcal{R}$ satisfying reasonable assumptions, large parts of the verification effort can be automated.

A third important issue is *simplicity*. Reachability logic has eight inference rules [14, 15]. Could a reachability logic for rewrite theories be simpler? This work tackles head on these three open questions to provide a general reachability logic and a prototype implementation suitable for reasoning about properties of *both* distributed systems and programs based on their rewriting logic semantics.

Rewriting Logic in a Nutshell. A distributed system can be designed and modeled as a *rewrite theory* $\mathcal{R} = (\Sigma, E, R)$ [8] in the following way: (i) the distributed system's *states* are modeled as elements of the initial algebra $T_{\Sigma/E}$ associated to the equational theory (Σ, E) with function symbols Σ and equations E; and (ii) the system's *concurrent transitions* are modeled by rewrite rules R, which are applied *modulo E*. Let us consider the QLOCK [5] mutual exclusion protocol, explained in detail in Sect. 2. QLOCK allows an unbounded number of processes, which can be identified by numbers. Such processes can be in one of three states: "normal" (doing their own thing), "waiting" for a resource, and "critical," i.e., using the resource. Waiting processes enqueue their identifier at the end of a waiting queue and can become critical when their name appears at the head of the queue. A QLOCK state can be represented as a tuple $< n \mid w \mid c \mid q >$ where n, resp. w, resp. c, denotes the set of identifiers for normal, resp. waiting, resp. critical processes, and q is the waiting queue. QLOCK can be modeled as a rewrite theory $\mathcal{R} = (\Sigma, E, R)$, where E includes axioms such as associativity-commutativity of multiset union, list associativity, and identity axioms for $\emptyset$ and *nil*. QLOCK's behavior is specified by five rewrite rules R. Rule *w2c* below specifies a waiting process i becoming critical

$$w2c : < n \mid w\ i \mid c \mid i; q > \rightarrow < n \mid w \mid c\ i \mid i; q > .$$

Reachability Logic in a Nutshell. A reachability logic formula has the form $A \rightarrow^{\circledast} B$, with A and B state predicates (see Sect. 3). Assume for simplicity that $vars(A) \cap vars(B) = \emptyset$. Such a formula is then interpreted in the initial model $\mathcal{T}_\mathcal{R}$ of a rewrite theory $\mathcal{R} = (\Sigma, E, R)$, whose states are E-equivalence classes $[u]$ of ground Σ-terms, and where a state transition $[u] \rightarrow_\mathcal{R} [v]$ holds iff

$\mathcal{R} \vdash u \rightarrow v$ according to the rewriting logic inference system [8] (computation = deduction). As a first approximation, $A \rightarrow^{\circledast} B$ is a Hoare logic *partial correctness* assertion of the form $\{A\}\mathcal{R}\{B\}$, but with the slight twist that B need not hold of a terminating state, but just *somewhere along the way*. To be fully precise, $A \rightarrow^{\circledast} B$ holds in $\mathcal{T}_{\mathcal{R}}$ iff for each state $[u_0]$ satisfying A and each terminating sequence $[u_0] \rightarrow_{\mathcal{R}} [u_1] \ldots \rightarrow_{\mathcal{R}} [u_{n-1}] \rightarrow_{\mathcal{R}} [u_n]$ there is a j, $0 \leq j \leq n$ such that $[u_j]$ satisfies B. A key question is how to choose a good language of state predicates like A and B. Here is where the potential for increasing the logic's automation resides. We call our proposed logic *constructor-based*, because our choice is to make A and B positive (only $\vee$ and $\wedge$) combinations of what we call *constructor patterns* of the form $u \mid \varphi$, where u is a *constructor* term[1] and φ a quantifier-free (QF) Σ-formula. The state predicate $u \mid \varphi$ holds for a state $[u']$ iff there is a ground substitution ρ such that $[u'] = [u\rho]$ and $E \models \varphi\rho$.

The Invariant Paradox. How can we *prove invariants* in such a reachability logic? For example, mutual exclusion for QLOCK? Paradoxically, we cannot! This is because QLOCK, like many other protocols, *never terminates*, that is, has no terminating sequences whatsoever. And this has the ludicrous trivial consequence that QLOCK's initial model $\mathcal{T}_{\mathcal{R}}$ vacuously satisfies *all* reachability formulas $A \rightarrow^{\circledast} B$. This of course means that it is in fact *impossible* to prove any invariants using reachability logic in the initial model $\mathcal{T}_{\mathcal{R}}$. But it does *not* mean that it is impossible using *some other* initial model. In Sect. 4.1 we give a systematic solution to this paradox by means of a *simple theory transformation* allowing us to prove any invariant in the original initial model $\mathcal{T}_{\mathcal{R}}$ by proving an equivalent reachability formula in the initial model of the transformed theory.

Our Contributions. Section 2 gathers preliminaries. The main theoretical contributions of a *simple* semantics and inference system for a rewrite-theory-generic reachability logic with just *two* inference rules and its soundness are developed in Sects. 4 and 5. A systematic methodology to prove *invariants* by means of reachability formulas is developed in Sect. 4.1. The goal of increasing the logic's potential for automation by making it constructor-based is advanced in Sects. 3–5. A proof of concept of the entire approach is given by means of a Maude-based prototype implementation and a suite of experiments verifying various properties of distributed system designs in Sect. 6. Related work and conclusions are discussed in Sect. 7. Proofs can be found in [13].

2   Many-Sorted Algebra and Rewriting Logic

We present some preliminaries on many-sorted algebra and rewriting logic. For a more general treatment using order-sorted algebra see [13]. Readers familiar with many-sorted logic may go directly to Definition 1. We assume familiarity with the following basic concepts and notation that are explained in full detail in, e.g., [10]: (i) *many-sorted (MS) signature* as a pair $\Sigma = (S, \Sigma)$ with S a set of *sorts*

---

[1] That is, a term in a subsignature $\Omega \subseteq \Sigma$ such that each ground Σ-term is equal modulo E to a ground Ω-term.

and Σ an $S^* \times S$-indexed family $\Sigma = \{\Sigma_{w,s}\}_{(w,s)\in S^* \times S}$ of function symbols, where $f \in \Sigma_{s_1\ldots s_n,s}$ is displayed as $f : s_1 \ldots s_n \to s$; (ii) Σ-algebra A as a pair $A = (A, {}_{-A})$ with $A = \{A_s\}_{s\in S}$ an S-indexed family of sets, and ${}_{-A}$ a mapping interpreting each $f : s_1 \ldots s_n \to s$ as a function in the set $[A_{s_1} \times \ldots \times A_{s_n} \to A_s]$. (iii) Σ-*homomorphism* $h : A \to B$ as an S-indexed family of functions $h = \{h_s : A_s \to B_s\}_{s\in S}$ preserving the operations in Σ; (iv) the term Σ-algebra T_Σ and its initiality in the category **MSAlg**$_\Sigma$ of Σ-algebras when Σ is unambiguous.

An S-sorted set $X = \{X_s\}_{s\in S}$ of *variables*, satisfies $s \neq s' \Rightarrow X_s \cap X_{s'} = \emptyset$, and the variables in X are always assumed *disjoint* from all constants in Σ. The Σ-*term algebra* on variables X, $T_\Sigma(X)$, is the *initial algebra* for the signature $\Sigma(X)$ obtained by adding to Σ the variables X *as extra constants*. Since a $\Sigma(X)$-algebra is just a pair (A, α), with A a Σ-algebra, and α an *interpretation of the constants* in X, i.e., an S-sorted function $\alpha \in [X \to A]$, the $\Sigma(X)$-initiality of $T_\Sigma(X)$ means that for each $A \in$ **MSAlg**$_\Sigma$ and $\alpha \in [X \to A]$, there exists a unique Σ-homomorphism, ${}_{-}\alpha : T_\Sigma(X) \to A$ extending α, i.e., such that for each $s \in S$ and $x \in X_s$ we have $x\alpha_s = \alpha_s(x)$. In particular, when $A = T_\Sigma(Y)$, an interpretation of the constants in X, i.e., an S-sorted function $\sigma \in [X \to T_\Sigma(Y)]$ is called a *substitution*, and its unique homomorphic extension ${}_{-}\sigma : T_\Sigma(X) \to T_\Sigma(Y)$ is also called a substitution. Define $dom(\sigma) = \{x \in X \mid x \neq x\sigma\}$, and $ran(\sigma) = \bigcup_{x \in dom(\sigma)} vars(x\sigma)$. Given variables Z, the substitution $\sigma|_Z$ agrees with σ on Z and is the identity elsewhere.

We also assume familiarity with many-sorted first-order logic including: (i) the first-order language of Σ-*formulas* for Σ a signature (in our case Σ has only function symbols and the $=$ predicate); (ii) given a Σ-algebra A, a formula $\varphi \in Form(\Sigma)$, and an assignment $\alpha \in [Y \to A]$, with $Y = fvars(\varphi)$ the free variables of φ, the *satisfaction relation* $A, \alpha \models \varphi$ (iii) the notions of a formula $\varphi \in Form(\Sigma)$ being *valid*, denoted $A \models \varphi$, resp. *satisfiable* in a Σ-algebra A. For a subsignature $\Omega \subseteq \Sigma$ and $A \in$ **MSAlg**$_\Sigma$, the *reduct* $A|_\Omega \in$ **MSAlg**$_\Omega$ agrees with A in the interpretation of all sorts and operations in Ω and discards everything in $\Sigma \setminus \Omega$. If $\varphi \in Form(\Omega)$ we have the equivalence $A \models \varphi \Leftrightarrow A|_\Omega \models \varphi$.

An MS *equational theory* is a pair $T = (\Sigma, E)$, with E a set of (possibly conditional) Σ-equations. **MSAlg**$_{(\Sigma,E)}$ denotes the full subcategory of **MSAlg**$_\Sigma$ with objects those $A \in$ **MSAlg**$_\Sigma$ such that $A \models E$, called the (Σ, E)-*algebras*. **MSAlg**$_{(\Sigma,E)}$ has an *initial algebra* $T_{\Sigma/E}$ [10]. The inference system in [10] is *sound and complete* for MS equational deduction, i.e., for any MS equational theory (Σ, E), and Σ-equation $u = v$ we have an equivalence $E \vdash u = v \Leftrightarrow E \models u = v$. For the sake of simpler inference we assume *non-empty sorts*, i.e., $\forall s \in S\ T_\Sigma, s \neq \emptyset$. Deducibility $E \vdash u = v$ is abbreviated as $u =_E v$, called E-*equality*. An E-*unifier* of a system of Σ-equations, i.e., a conjunction $\phi = u_1 = v_1 \wedge \ldots \wedge u_n = v_n$ of Σ-equations is a substitution σ such that $u_i\sigma =_E v_i\sigma$, $1 \leq i \leq n$. An E-*unification algorithm* for (Σ, E) is an algorithm generating a *complete set* of E-unifiers $Unif_E(\phi)$ for any system of Σ equations ϕ, where "complete" means that for any E-unifier σ of ϕ there is a $\tau \in Unif_E(\phi)$ and a substitution ρ such that $\sigma =_E (\tau\rho)|_{dom(\sigma)\cup dom(\tau)}$, where $=_E$ here means that for any variable x we have $x\sigma =_E x(\tau\rho)|_{dom(\sigma)\cup dom(\tau)}$. The algorithm is *finitary* if it always terminates with a *finite set* $Unif_E(\phi)$ for any ϕ.

We recall some basic concepts about *rewriting logic*. The survey in [8] gives a fuller account. A rewrite theory $\mathcal{R}$ axiomatizes a *distributed system*, so that concurrent computation is modeled as concurrent rewriting with the rules of $\mathcal{R}$ *modulo* the equations of $\mathcal{R}$. Recall also the following notation from [3]: (i) positions in a term viewed as a tree are marked by strings $p \in \mathbb{N}^*$ specifying a path from the root, (ii) $t|_p$ denotes the subterm of term t at position p, and (iii) $t[u]_p$ denotes the result of *replacing* subterm $t|_p$ at position p by u.

Definition 1. *A rewrite theory is a 3-tuple $\mathcal{R} = (\Sigma, E \cup B, R)$ with $(\Sigma, E \cup B)$ an MS equational theory and R a set of conditional Σ-rewrite rules $l \to r$ if ϕ, with $l, r \in T_\Sigma(X)_s$ for some $s \in S$, and ϕ a quantifier-free Σ-formula. We further assume that: (1) Each equation $u = v \in B$ is regular, i.e., $vars(u) = vars(v)$, and linear, i.e., there are no repeated variables in either u or v. (2) The equations E, when oriented as conditional rewrite rules $\vec{E} = \{u \to v$ if $\psi \mid u = v$ if $\psi \in E\}$, are convergent modulo B, i.e., strictly coherent, confluent, and operationally terminating as rewrite rules modulo B [7]. (3) The rules R are ground coherent with the equations E modulo B [4].*

Conditions (1)–(2) ensure that the initial algebra $T_{\Sigma/E\cup B}$ is isomorphic to the *canonical term algebra* $C_{\Sigma/E,B}$, whose elements are B-equivalence classes of $\vec{E}, B$-irreducible ground Σ-terms. Define the *one-step R, B-rewrite relation* $t \to_{R,B} t'$ between ground terms as follows. For $t, t' \in T_{\Sigma,s}$, $s \in S$, $t \to_{R,B} t'$ holds iff there is a rewrite rule $l \to r$ if $\phi \in R$, a ground substitution $\sigma \in [Y \to T_\Sigma]$ with Y the rule's variables, and a term position p in t such that $t|_p =_B l\sigma$, $t' = t[r\sigma]_p$, and $E \cup B \models \phi\sigma$. In the context of (1)–(2), condition (3) ensures that "computing $\vec{E}, B$-canonical forms before performing R, B-rewriting" is a *complete* strategy. That is, if $t \to_{R,B} t'$ and $u = t!_{E,B}$, i.e., $t \to^*_{\vec{E},B} u$ with u in $\vec{E}, B$-canonical form (abbreviated in what follows to $u = t!$), then there exists a u' such that $u \to_{R,B} u'$ and $t'! =_B u'!$. Note that $vars(r) \subseteq vars(l)$ *is nowhere assumed* for rules $l \to r$ if $\phi \in R$. This means that $\mathcal{R}$ can specify an *open system*, in the sense of [11], that interacts with an external, non-deterministic environment such as, for example, a thermostat.

Conditions (1)–(3) allow a simple description of the *initial reachability model* $T_{\mathcal{R}}$ [8] of $\mathcal{R}$ as the *canonical reachability model* $C_{\mathcal{R}}$ whose states belong to the canonical term algebra $C_{\Sigma/E,B}$, and the one-step transition relation $[u] \to_{\mathcal{R}} [v]$ holds iff $u \to_{R,B} u'$ and $[u'!] = [v]$. Furthermore, if $u \to_{R,B} u'$ has been performed with a rewrite rule $l \to r$ if $\phi \in R$ and a ground substitution $\sigma \in [Y \to T_\Sigma]$, then, assuming B-equality is decidable, checking whether condition $E \cup B \models \phi\sigma$ holds is *decidable* by reducing the terms in $\phi\sigma$ to $\vec{E}, B$-canonical form.

A Running Example. Consider the following rewrite theory $\mathcal{R} = (\Sigma, E \cup B, R)$ modeling a dynamic version of the QLOCK mutual exclusion protocol [5], where (Σ, B) defines the protocol's states, involving natural numbers, lists, and multi-sets over natural numbers. Σ has sorts $S = \{Nat, List, MSet, Conf, State, Pred\}$

with subsorts[2] $Nat < List$ and $Nat < MSet$ and operators $F = \{0 : \rightarrow Nat, \, s\_ : Nat \rightarrow Nat, \, \emptyset : \rightarrow MSet, \, nil : \rightarrow List, \, \_\_ : MSet \, MSet \rightarrow MSet, \, \_;\_ : List \, List \rightarrow List, dupl : MSet \rightarrow Pred, tt : \rightarrow Pred, < \_ > : Conf \rightarrow State, \_|\_|\_|\_ : MSet \, MSet \, MSet \, List \rightarrow Conf\}$, where underscores denote operator argument placement. The axioms B are the associativity-commutativity of the multiset union $\_\_$ with identity $\emptyset$, and the associativity of list concatenation $\_;\_$ with identity nil. The only equation in E is $dupl(s\,i\,i) = tt$. It defines the $dupl$ predicate by detecting a duplicated element i in the multiset $s\,i\,i$ (s could be empty). $States$ of QLOCK are B-equivalence classes of ground terms of sort $State$.

QLOCK [5] is a mutual exclusion protocol where the number of processes is unbounded. Furthermore, in the $dynamic$ version of QLOCK presented below, such a number can grow or shrink. Each process is identified by a number. The system configuration has three sets of processes (normal, waiting, and critical) plus a waiting queue. To ensure mutual exclusion, a normal process must first register its name at the end of the waiting queue. When its name appears at the front of the queue, it is allowed to enter the critical section. The first three rewrite rules in R below specify how a $normal$ process i first transitions to a $waiting$ process, then to a $critical$ process, and back to normal. The last two rules in R specify how a process can dynamically join or exit the system.

$$
\begin{array}{rcccccl}
n2w : & <\,n\,i\ |\ w & |\ c & |\ q & > \ \rightarrow\ <\,n & |\ w\,i\ |\ c & |\ q\,;\,i\,> \\
w2c : & <\,n & |\ w\,i\ |\ c & |\ i\,;\,q\,> & \rightarrow\ <\,n & |\ w & |\ c\,i\ |\ i\,;\,q\,> \\
c2n : & <\,n & |\ w & |\ c\,i\ |\ i\,;\,q\,> & \rightarrow\ <\,n\,i & |\ w & |\ c & |\ q\ > \\
join : & <\,n & |\ w & |\ c & |\ q\ > \ \rightarrow\ <\,n\,i & |\ w & |\ c & |\ q\ > \ if\ \phi \\
exit : & <\,n\,i\ |\ w & |\ c & |\ q & > \ \rightarrow\ <\,n & |\ w & |\ c & |\ q\ >
\end{array}
$$

where $\phi \equiv dupl(n\,i\,w\,c) \neq tt$, i is a number, n, w, and c are, respectively, normal, waiting, and critical process identifier sets, and q is a queue of process identifiers. It is easy to check that $\mathcal{R} = (\Sigma, E \cup B, R)$ satisfies requirements (1)–(3). Note that $join$ makes QLOCK an $open$ system in the sense explained above.

3   Constrained Constructor Pattern Predicates

Given an MS equational theory $(\Sigma, E \cup B)$, the $atomic\ state\ predicates$ appearing in the constructor-based reachability logic formulas of Sect. 4 will be pairs $u \mid \varphi$, called $constrained\ constructor\ patterns$, with u a term in a subsignature $\Omega \subseteq \Sigma$ of constructors, and φ a quantifier-free Σ-formula. Intuitively, $u \mid \varphi$ is a pattern describing the set of states that are $E_\Omega \cup B_\Omega$-equal to ground terms of the form $u\rho$ for ρ a ground constructor substitution such that $E \cup B \models \varphi\rho$. Therefore, $u \mid \varphi$ can be used as a $symbolic\ description$ of a, typically infinite, $set\ of\ states$ in the canonical reachability model $\mathcal{C}_\mathcal{R}$ of a rewrite theory $\mathcal{R}$.

---

[2] As pointed out at the beginning of Sect. 2, [13] treats the more general $order\text{-}sorted$ case, where sorts form a poset $(S, \leq)$ with $s \leq s'$ interpreted as set containment $A_s \subseteq A_{s'}$ in a Σ-algebra A.

Often, the signature Σ on which $T_{\Sigma/E\cup B}$ is defined has a natural decomposition as a disjoint union $\Sigma = \Omega \uplus \Delta$, where the elements of the canonical term algebra $C_{\Sigma/E,B}$ are Ω-terms, whereas the function symbols $f \in \Delta$ are viewed as *defined functions* which are *evaluated away* by $\vec{E}, B$-simplification. Ω (with same poset of sorts as Σ) is then called a *constructor subsignature* of Σ.

A *decomposition* of a MS equational theory $(\Sigma, E \cup B)$ is a triple $(\Sigma, B, \vec{E})$ such that the rules $\vec{E}$ are convergent modulo B. $(\Sigma, B, \vec{E})$ is called *sufficiently complete* with respect to the *constructor subsignature* Ω iff for each $t \in T_\Sigma$ we have: (i) $t!_{\vec{E},B} \in T_\Omega$, and (ii) if $u \in T_\Omega$ and $u =_B v$, then $v \in T_\Omega$. This ensures that for each $[u]_B \in C_{\Sigma/E,B}$ we have $[u]_B \subseteq T_\Omega$. Sufficient completeness is closely related to the notion of a *protecting* inclusion of decompositions.

Definition 2. *Let* $(\Sigma_0, E_0 \cup B_0) \subseteq (\Sigma, E \cup B)$ *be a theory inclusion such that* $(\Sigma_0, B_0, \vec{E_0})$ *and* $(\Sigma, B, \vec{E})$ *are respective decompositions of* $(\Sigma_0, E_0 \cup B_0)$ *and* $(\Sigma, E \cup B)$. *We then say that the decomposition* $(\Sigma, B, \vec{E})$ *protects* $(\Sigma_0, B_0, \vec{E_0})$ *iff (i) for all* $t, t' \in T_{\Sigma_0}(X)$ *we have: (i)* $t =_{B_0} t' \Leftrightarrow t =_B t'$, *(ii)* $t = t!_{\vec{E_0},B_0} \Leftrightarrow t = t!_{\vec{E},B}$, *and (iii)* $C_{\Sigma_0/E_0,B_0} = C_{\Sigma/E,B}|_{\Sigma_0}$.

$(\Omega, B_\Omega, \vec{E_\Omega})$ *is a constructor decomposition of* $(\Sigma, B, \vec{E})$ *iff (i)* $(\Sigma, B, \vec{E})$ *protects* $(\Omega, B_\Omega, \vec{E_\Omega})$, *and (ii)* $(\Sigma, B, \vec{E})$ *is sufficiently complete with respect to the constructor subsignature* Ω. *Furthermore,* Ω *is called a subsignature of free constructors modulo* B_Ω *iff* $E_\Omega = \emptyset$, *so that* $C_{\Omega/E_\Omega,B_\Omega} = T_{\Omega/B_\Omega}$.

We are now ready to define constrained constructor pattern predicates.

Definition 3. *Let* $(\Omega, B_\Omega, \vec{E_\Omega})$ *be a constructor decomposition of* $(\Sigma, B, \vec{E})$. *A constrained constructor pattern is an expression* $u \mid \varphi$ *with* $u \in T_\Omega(X)$ *and* φ *a QF* Σ*-formula. The set* $PatPred(\Omega, \Sigma)$ *of constrained constructor pattern predicates contains* $\bot$ *and the set of constrained constructor patterns, and is closed under disjunction* $(\vee)$ *and conjunction* $(\wedge)$. *Capital letters* $A, B, \ldots, P, Q, \ldots$ *range over* $PatPred(\Omega, \Sigma)$. *The semantics of a constrained constructor pattern predicate* A *is a subset* $[\![A]\!] \subseteq C_{\Sigma/E,B}$ *defined inductively as follows:*

1. $[\![\bot]\!] = \emptyset$
2. $[\![u \mid \varphi]\!] = \{[(u\rho)!]_{B_\Omega} \in C_{\Sigma/E,B} \mid \rho \in [X \to T_\Omega] \wedge E \cup B \models \varphi\rho\}$.
3. $[\![A \vee B]\!] = [\![A]\!] \cup [\![B]\!]$
4. $[\![A \wedge B]\!] = [\![A]\!] \cap [\![B]\!]$.

Note that for any constructor pattern predicate A, if σ is a (sort-preserving) bijective renaming of variables we always have $[\![A]\!] = [\![A\sigma]\!]$. Given constructor patterns $u \mid \varphi$ and $v \mid \psi$ with $vars(u \mid \varphi) \cap vars(v \mid \psi) = \emptyset$, we say that $u \mid \varphi$ *subsumes* $v \mid \psi$ iff there is a substitution α such that: (i) $v =_{E_\Omega \cup B_\Omega} u\alpha$, and (ii) $\mathcal{T}_{E \cup B} \models \psi \Rightarrow (\varphi\alpha)$. It then follows easily from the above definition of $[\![u \mid \varphi]\!]$ that if $u \mid \varphi$ subsumes $v \mid \psi$, then $[\![v \mid \psi]\!] \subseteq [\![u \mid \varphi]\!]$. Likewise, $\bigvee_{i \in I} u_i \mid \varphi_i$ *subsumes* $v \mid \psi$ iff there is a $k \in I$ such that $u_k \mid \varphi_k$ subsumes $v \mid \psi$.

Pattern Predicate Example. Letting n, w, c be multisets of process identifiers and q be an associative list of process identifiers, recall that QLOCK states have the form $< n \mid w \mid c \mid q >$. From the five rewrite rules defining QLOCK, it is easy to prove that if $< n \mid w \mid c \mid q > \rightarrow^* < n' \mid w' \mid c' \mid q' >$ and $n\,w\,c$ is a set (has no repeated elements), then $n'\,w'\,c'$ is also a set. Of course, it seems very reasonable to assume that these process identifier multisets are, in fact, sets, since otherwise we could, for example, have a process i which is *both* waiting and critical at the *same* time. We can rule out such ambiguous states by means of the pattern predicate $< n \mid w \mid c \mid q > \mid dupl(n\ w\ c) \neq tt$.

If $E_\Omega \cup B_\Omega$ has a finitary unification algorithm, any constrained constructor pattern predicate A is semantically equivalent to a finite disjunction $\bigvee_i u_i \mid \varphi_i$ of constrained constructor patterns. This is because: (i) by (3)–(4) in Definition 3 we may assume A in disjunctive normal form; and (ii) it is easy to check that $[\![(u \mid \varphi) \wedge (v \mid \phi)]\!] = \bigcup_{\alpha \in Unif_{E_\Omega \cup B_\Omega}(u,v)} [\![u\alpha \mid (\varphi \wedge \phi)\alpha]\!]$, were we assume that $vars(u \mid \varphi) \cap vars(v \mid \psi) = \emptyset$, and that all variables in $ran(\alpha)$ are *fresh*. Pattern intersection can also be defined when $u \mid \varphi$ and $v \mid \phi$ share *parameters* $Y = vars(u \mid \varphi) \cap vars(v \mid \phi) = vars(u) \cap vars(v)$. [13] defines in detail the notions of *parametric intersection* $[\![u \mid \varphi]\!] \cap_Y [\![v \mid \phi]\!]$ and of *parametric subsumption* $v \mid \phi \subseteq_Y u \mid \varphi$ of patterns. These notions are very useful to reason about *parameterized* invariants and co-invariants (see Sect. 4.1 and [13]).

4 Constructor-Based Reachability Logic

The constructor-based reachability logic we define is a logic to reason about reachability properties of the canonical reachability model $\mathcal{C}_\mathcal{R}$ of a topmost rewrite theory $\mathcal{R}$ where "topmost" intuitively means all rewrites must occur at the top of the term.[3] Many rewrite theories of interest, including those specifying distributed object-oriented systems or the semantics of (possibly concurrent) programming languages, can be easily made topmost by a theory transformation (see, e.g., [16]). Formally, we require $\mathcal{R} = (\Sigma, E \cup B, R)$, besides satisfying the requirements in Definition 1, also satisfies:

1. $(\Sigma, E \cup B)$ has a sort *State*, a decomposition $(\Sigma, B, \vec{E})$, and a constructor decomposition $(\Omega, B_\Omega, \vec{E_\Omega})$ where: (i) $\forall u \in T_\Omega(X)_{State}, vars(u) = vars(u!)$; (ii) B_Ω are linear and regular with a finitary $E_\Omega \cup B_\Omega$-unification algorithm.
2. Rules in R have the form $l \rightarrow r$ if φ with $l \in T_\Omega(X)$. Furthermore, they are *topmost* in the sense that: (i) for all such rules, l and r have sort *State*, and (ii) for any $u \in T_\Omega(X)_{State}$ and any non-empty position p in u, $u|_p \notin T_\Omega(X)_{State}$.

Requirements (1)–(2) ensure that in the canonical reachability model $\mathcal{C}_\mathcal{R}$ if $[u] \rightarrow_\mathcal{R} [v]$ holds, then the R, B-rewrite $u \rightarrow_{R,B} u'$ such that $[u'] = [v]$ *happens at the top* of u, i.e., uses a rewrite rule $l \rightarrow r$ if $\varphi \in R$ and a ground substitution $\sigma \in [Y \rightarrow T_\Omega]$, with Y the rule's variables, such that $u =_{B_\Omega} l\sigma$ and $u' = r\sigma$.

---

[3] Topmost theories have reachability completeness for narrowing [16]. Our inference system uses narrowing to symbolically compute successor states in $\mathcal{C}_\mathcal{R}$.

We are now ready to define the formulas of our constructor-based reachability logic for $\mathcal{R}$ satisfying above requirements (1)–(2). Let $PatPred(\Omega, \Sigma)_{State}$ denote the subset of $PatPred(\Omega, \Sigma)$ determined by those pattern predicates A such that, for all atomic constrained constructor predicates $u \mid \varphi$ appearing in A, u has sort $State$. Reachability logic formulas then have the form: $A \to^{\circledast} B$, with $A, B \in PatPred(\Omega, \Sigma)_{State}$. The *parameters* Y of $A \to^{\circledast} B$ are the variables in the set $Y = vars(A) \cap vars(B)$, and $A \to^{\circledast} B$ is called *unparameterized* iff $Y = \emptyset$.

The reachability logic in [14,15] is based on *terminating* sequences of state transitions; when there are no terminating states, *all* reachability formulas are *vacuously true*. Our purpose is to extend the logic in order to verify properties of general distributed systems specified as rewrite theories $\mathcal{R}$ which *may never terminate*. For this, as explained in Sect. 4.1, we *generalize* the all-paths satisfaction relation in [15], which for a theory $\mathcal{R}$ we denote by $\mathcal{R} \models^{\forall} A \to^{\circledast} B$, to a *relativized* satisfaction relation $\mathcal{R} \models^{\forall}_{T} A \to^{\circledast} B$, where T is a constrained pattern predicate such that $\llbracket T \rrbracket$ is a set of terminating states. That is, let $Term_{\mathcal{R}} = \{[u] \in \mathcal{C}_{\mathcal{R}, State} \mid (\not\exists [v]) \, [u] \to_{\mathcal{R}} [v]\}$. We then require $\llbracket T \rrbracket \subseteq Term_{\mathcal{R}}$. The standard relation $\mathcal{R} \models^{\forall} A \to^{\circledast} B$ is then recovered as the special case where $\llbracket T \rrbracket = Term_{\mathcal{R}}$. Call $[u] \to^{*}_{\mathcal{R}} [v]$ a *T-terminating sequence* iff $[v] \in \llbracket T \rrbracket$.

Definition 4. *Given T with $\llbracket T \rrbracket \subseteq Term_{\mathcal{R}}$, the* all-paths satisfaction relation *$\mathcal{R} \models^{\forall}_{T} u \mid \varphi \to^{\circledast} \bigvee_{j \in J} v_j \mid \phi_j$ asserts the satisfaction of the formula $u \mid \varphi \to^{\circledast} \bigvee_{j \in J} v_j \mid \phi_j$ in the canonical reachability model $\mathcal{C}_{\mathcal{R}}$ of a rewrite theory $\mathcal{R}$ satisfying topmost requirements (1)–(2). It is defined as follows:*

For $u \mid \varphi \to^{\circledast} \bigvee_{j \in J} v_j \mid \phi_j$ unparameterized, $\mathcal{R} \models^{\forall}_{T} u \mid \varphi \to^{\circledast} \bigvee_{j \in J} v_j \mid \phi_j$ holds iff for each T-terminating sequence $[u_0] \to_{\mathcal{R}} [u_1] \ldots [u_{n-1}] \to_{\mathcal{R}} [u_n]$ with $[u_0] \in \llbracket u \mid \varphi \rrbracket$ there exist k, $0 \leq k \leq n$ and $j \in J$ such that $[u_k] \in \llbracket v_j \mid \phi_j \rrbracket$. For $u \mid \varphi \to^{\circledast} \bigvee_{j \in J} v_j \mid \phi_j$ with parameters Y, $\mathcal{R} \models^{\forall}_{T} u \mid \varphi \to^{\circledast} \bigvee_{j \in J} v_j \mid \phi_j$ holds if $\mathcal{R} \models^{\forall}_{T} (u \mid \varphi)\rho \to^{\circledast} (\bigvee_{j \in J} v_j \mid \phi_j)\rho$ holds for each $\rho \in [Y \to T_{\Omega}]$.

Since a constrained pattern predicate is equivalent to a disjunction of atomic ones, we can define satisfaction on general reachability logic formulas as follows: $\mathcal{R} \models^{\forall}_{T} \bigvee_{1 \leq i \leq n} u_i \mid \varphi_i \to^{\circledast} A$ iff $\bigwedge_{1 \leq i \leq n} \mathcal{R} \models^{\forall}_{T} u_i \mid \varphi_i \to^{\circledast} A$, assuming same parameters $Y_i = vars(u_i \mid \varphi_i) \cap vars(A)$, i.e., $Y_i = Y_{i'}$ for $1 \leq i < i' \leq n$.

$\mathcal{R} \models^{\forall}_{T} A \to^{\circledast} B$ is a *partial correctness assertion*: If state $[u]$ satisfies "precondition" A, then "postcondition" B is satisfied *somewhere* along *each* T-terminating sequences from $[u]$, generalizing a Hoare formula $\{A\}\mathcal{R}\{B\}$ [13].

Recall that rewrite rules $l \to r$ if ϕ are assumed to have $l \in T_{\Omega}(X)$. For symbolic reasoning purposes it will be very useful to also require that $r \in T_{\Omega}(X)$. This can be achieved by a theory transformation $\mathcal{R} \mapsto \hat{\mathcal{R}}$. Stated formally, if $\mathcal{R} = (\Sigma, E \cup B, R)$, then $\hat{\mathcal{R}} = (\Sigma, E \cup B, \hat{R})$, where the rules $\hat{R}$ are obtained from the rules R by transforming each $l \to r$ if ϕ in R into the rule $l \to r'$ if $\phi \wedge \hat{\theta}$, where: (i) r' is the Ω-abstraction of r obtained by replacing each length-minimal position p of r such that $t|_p \notin T_{\Omega}(X)$ by a fresh variable x_p whose sort is the least sort of $t|_p$, (ii) $\hat{\theta} = \bigwedge_{p \in P} x_p = t_p$, where P is the set of all length-minimal positions in r such that $t|_p \notin T_{\Omega}(X)$.

The key semantic property about this transformation is:

Lemma 1. *The canonical reachability models $\mathcal{C_R}$ and $\mathcal{C_{\hat{R}}}$ are identical.*

4.1 Invariants, Co-Invariants, and Never-Terminating Systems

The notion of an *invariant* applies to any transition system $\mathcal{S} = (S, \rightarrow_{\mathcal{S}})$ with states S and *transition relation* $\rightarrow_{\mathcal{S}} \subseteq S \times S$. The set $Reach(S_0)$ of states *reachable* from $S_0 \subseteq S$ is defined as $Reach(S_0) = \{s \in S \mid (\exists s_0 \in S_0)\ s_0 \rightarrow^*_{\mathcal{S}} s\}$, where $\rightarrow^*_{\mathcal{S}}$ denotes the reflexive-transitive closure of $\rightarrow_{\mathcal{S}}$. An invariant about $\mathcal{S}$ with initial states S_0 can be specified in two ways: (i) by a "good" property $P \subseteq S$, the *invariant*, that *always holds* from S_0, i.e., such that $Reach(S_0) \subseteq P$, or (ii) as a "bad" property $Q \subseteq S$, the *co-invariant*, that *never holds* from S_0, i.e., such that $Reach(S_0) \cap Q = \emptyset$. Obviously, P is an invariant iff $S \setminus P$ is a co-invariant.

Suppose we have specified a distributed system by a topmost rewrite theory $\mathcal{R}$, and constrained pattern predicates S_0 and P, and we want to prove that $[\![P]\!]$ is an *invariant* of the system $(\mathcal{C}_{\mathcal{R},State}, \rightarrow_{\mathcal{R}})$ from $[\![S_0]\!]$. Can we specify such invariant or co-invariant by means of *reachability formulas* and use the inference system of Sect. 5 to try to prove such formulas?

The answer to the above question is not obvious. Suppose $\mathcal{R}$ specifies a *never-terminating system*, i.e., $Term_{\mathcal{R}} = \emptyset$. For example, QLOCK and other mutual exclusion protocols are never-terminating. Then, no reachability formula can characterize and invariant holding by means of the satisfaction relation $\mathcal{R} \models^{\forall}_T A \rightarrow^{\circledast} B$. The reason for this impossibility is that, since $Term_{\mathcal{R}} = \emptyset$, $\mathcal{R} \models^{\forall}_T A \rightarrow^{\circledast} B$ holds vacuously for *all* reachability formulas $A \rightarrow^{\circledast} B$.

Is then reachability logic useless to prove invariants? Definitely *not*. We need to first perform a simple *theory transformation*. Call an invariant *specifiable by constrained pattern predicates* S_0 and P if $[\![P]\!]$ is an *invariant* of $(\mathcal{C}_{\mathcal{R},State}, \rightarrow_{\mathcal{R}})$ from $[\![S_0]\!]$. To ease the exposition, we explain the transformation for the case where Ω has a single state constructor operator, say, $\langle \_, \ldots, \_ \rangle : s_1, \ldots, s_n \rightarrow State$. The extension to several such operators is straightforward. The theory transformation is of the form $\mathcal{R} \mapsto \mathcal{R}_{stop}$, where $\mathcal{R}_{stop}$ is obtained from $\mathcal{R}$ by just adding: (1) a new state constructor operator $[\_, \ldots, \_] : s_1, \ldots, s_n \rightarrow State$ to Ω, and (2) a new rewrite rule $stop : \langle x_1{:}s_1, \ldots, x_n{:}s_n \rangle \rightarrow [x_1{:}s_1, \ldots, x_n{:}s_n]$ to R. Also, let $[\,]$ denote the pattern predicate $[x_1{:}s_1, \ldots, x_n{:}s_n] \mid \top$. Likewise, for any atomic constrained pattern predicate $B = \langle u_1, \ldots, u_n \rangle \mid \varphi$ we define the pattern predicate $[B] = [u_1, \ldots, u_n] \mid \varphi$ and extend this notation to any union Q of atomic predicates. Since $\langle \_, \ldots, \_ \rangle : s_1, \ldots, s_n \rightarrow State$ is the only state constructor, we can assume without loss of generality that any atomic constrained pattern predicate in $\mathcal{R}$ is semantically equivalent to one of the form $\langle u_1, \ldots, u_n \rangle \mid \varphi$. Likewise, any pattern predicate will be semantically equivalent to a union of atomic predicates of such form, called in *standard form*.

Theorem 1. *For $S_0, P \in PatPred(\Omega, \Sigma)$ constrained pattern predicates in standard form with $vars(S_0) \cap vars(P) = \emptyset$, $[\![P]\!]$ is an invariant of $(\mathcal{C}_{\mathcal{R},State}, \rightarrow_{\mathcal{R}})$ from $[\![S_0]\!]$ iff $\mathcal{R}_{stop} \models^{\forall}_{[\,]} S_0 \rightarrow^{\circledast} [P]$.*

The notion of a *parametric invariant* can be reduced to the unparameterized one: if $Y = vars(S_0) \cap vars(P)$, then $[\![P]\!]$ is an *invariant* of $(\mathcal{C}_{\mathcal{R},State}, \to_{\mathcal{R}})$ from $[\![S_0]\!]$ *with parameters* Y iff $\mathcal{R}_{stop} \models^{\vee}_{[]} S_0 \to^{\circledast} [P]$. That is, iff $[\![P\rho]\!]$ is an (unparameterized) invariant of $(\mathcal{C}_{\mathcal{R},State}, \to_{\mathcal{R}})$ from $[\![S_0\rho]\!]$ for each $\rho \in [Y \to T_\Omega]$. In this way, Theorem 1 extends to parametric invariants.

Specifying Invariants for QLOCK. Consider the QLOCK specification from Sects. 2 and 3. QLOCK is *never* terminating. However, we can apply the theory transformation in Theorem 1 by adding an operator $[\_] : Conf \to State$ and a rule $stop : < t > \to [t]$ for $t{:}Conf$. Define the set of initial states by the pattern predicate $S_0 = < n' \mid \emptyset \mid \emptyset \mid nil > \mid dupl(n') \neq tt$. Since QLOCK states have the form $< n \mid w \mid c \mid q >$, mutual exclusion means $|c| \leq 1$, which is expressible by the pattern predicate $< n \mid w \mid i \mid i ; q > \vee < n \mid w \mid \emptyset \mid q >$. But we need also to ensure our multisets are actually *sets*. Thus, the pattern predicate $P = (< n \mid w \mid i \mid i ; q > \mid dupl(n \ w \ i) \neq tt) \vee (< n \mid w \mid \emptyset \mid q > \mid dupl(n \ w) \neq tt)$ specifies mutual exclusion. By Theorem 1, QLOCK ensures mutual exclusion from $[\![S_0]\!]$ iff $\mathcal{R}_{stop} \models^{\vee}_{[]} S_0 \to^{\circledast} [P]$.

The following easy corollary can be very helpful in proving invariants. It can, for example, be applied to prove the mutual exclusion of QLOCK.

Corollary 1. *Let* $S_0, P \in PatPred(\Omega, \Sigma)$ *be constrained pattern predicates in standard form with* $vars(S_0) \cap vars(P) = \emptyset$. $[\![P]\!]$ *is an invariant of* $(\mathcal{C}_{\mathcal{R},State}, \to_{\mathcal{R}})$ *from* $[\![S_0]\!]$ *if: (i)* $S_0 \subseteq P$, *and (ii)* $\mathcal{R}_{stop} \models^{\vee}_{[]} P \to^{\circledast} [P\sigma]$, *where* σ *is a sort-preserving bijective renaming of variables such that* $vars(P) \cap vars(P\sigma) = \emptyset$.

Corollary 1 can be extended to parametric invariants (see [13]). The treatment of co-invariants is similar and can also be found in [13].

5   A Sound Inference System

We present our inference system for all-path reachability for any $\mathcal{R}$ satisfying topmost requirements (1)–(2), with rules $R = \{l_j \to r_j \text{ if } \phi_j\}_{j \in J}$ such that $l_j, r_j \in T_\Omega(X)$, $j \in J$. *Variables of rules in* R *are always assumed disjoint from variables in reachability formulas*; this can be ensured by renaming. The inference system has two proof rules. The STEP$^\vee$ + SUBSUMPTION proof rule allows taking one step of (symbolic) rewriting along all paths according to the rules in $\mathcal{R}$. The AXIOM proof rule allows the use of a trusted reachability formula to summarize multiple rewrite steps, and thus to handle repetitive behavior.

These proof rules derive sequents of the form $[\mathcal{A}, \mathcal{C}] \vdash_T u \mid \varphi \longrightarrow^{\circledast} \bigvee_i v_i \mid \psi_i$, where $\mathcal{A}$ and $\mathcal{C}$ are finite sets of reachability formulas and T a pattern predicate defining a set of T-terminating ground states. Formulas in $\mathcal{A}$ are called *axioms* and those in $\mathcal{C}$ are called *circularities*. We furthermore assume that in all reachability formulas $u \mid \varphi \longrightarrow^{\circledast} \bigvee_i v_i \mid \psi_i$ we have $vars(\psi_i) \subseteq vars(v_i) \cup vars(u \mid \varphi)$ for each i. According to the implicit quantification of the semantic relation $\models^{\vee}_T$ this means that any variable in ψ_i is either universally quantified and comes from the precondition $u \mid \varphi$, or is existentially quantified and comes from v_i only. This property is an invariant preserved by the two inference rules.

Proofs always begin with a set $\mathcal{C}$ of formulas that we want to *simultaneously* prove, so that the proof effort only succeeds if *all* formulas in $\mathcal{C}$ are eventually proved. $\mathcal{C}$ contains the main properties we want to prove as well as any auxiliary lemmas that may be needed to carry out the proof. The initial set of goals we want to prove is $[\emptyset, \mathcal{C}] \vdash_T \mathcal{C}$, which is a shorthand for the set of goals $\{[\emptyset, \mathcal{C}] \vdash_T u \mid \varphi \longrightarrow^{\circledast} \bigvee_i v_i \mid \psi_i \mid (u \mid \varphi \longrightarrow^{\circledast} \bigvee_i v_i \mid \psi_i) \in \mathcal{C}\}$. Thus, we start *without any axioms* $\mathcal{A}$, but we shall be able to use the formulas in $\mathcal{C}$ as axioms in their own derivation *after* taking at least on step with the rewrite rules in $\mathcal{R}$.

A very useful feature is that sequents $[\emptyset, \mathcal{C}] \vdash_T u \mid \varphi \longrightarrow^{\circledast} \bigvee_i v_i \mid \psi_i$, whose formulas $\mathcal{C}$ have been *postulated* (as the conjectures to be proved), are transformed by $\text{STEP}^{\forall} + \text{SUBSUMPTION}$ into sequents of the form $[\mathcal{C}, \emptyset] \vdash_T u' \mid \varphi' \longrightarrow^{\circledast} \bigvee_i v_i' \mid \psi_i'$, where now the formulas in $\mathcal{C}$ *can be assumed valid*, and can be used in derivations with the AXIOM rule.

Verifying QLOCK's Mutual Exclusion. By Corollary 1, QLOCK's mutual exclusion can be verified by: (i) using pattern subsumption to check the trivial inclusion $[\![S_0]\!] \subseteq [\![P]\!]$, and (ii) proving $\mathcal{R}_{stop} \models_{[]}^{\forall} P\sigma \rightarrow^{\circledast} [P]$, where σ is a sort-preserving bijective renaming of variables such that $vars(P) \cap vars(P\sigma) = \emptyset$. But, since for QLOCK, P is a disjunction, in our inference system this means proving from $\mathcal{R}_{stop}$ that $[\emptyset, \mathcal{C}] \vdash_{[]} \mathcal{C}$, where $\mathcal{C}$ are the conjectures:

$$< n' \mid w' \mid i' \mid i' \; ; \; q' > \mid \varphi' \rightarrow^{\circledast} [< n \mid w \mid i \mid i \; ; \; q > \mid \varphi \lor < n \mid w \mid \emptyset \mid q > \mid \psi]$$

$$< n' \mid w' \mid \emptyset \mid q' > \mid \psi' \rightarrow^{\circledast} [< n \mid w \mid i \mid i \; ; \; q > \mid \varphi \lor < n \mid w \mid \emptyset \mid q > \mid \psi].$$

where $\varphi \equiv dupl(n \; w \; i) \neq tt$, $\psi \equiv dupl(n \; w) \neq tt$, and φ', ψ' are their obvious renamings.

Before explaining the $\text{STEP}^{\forall} + \text{SUBSUMPTION}$ proof rule we introduce some notational conventions. Assume T is the pattern predicate $T = \bigvee_j t_j \mid \chi_j$, with $vars(\chi_j) \subseteq vars(t_j)$, and let $R = \{l_j \rightarrow r_j \text{ if } \phi_j\}_{j \in J}$, we then define:

$$\text{MATCH}(u, \{v_i\}_{i \in I}) \subseteq \{(i, \beta) \mid \beta \in [vars(v_i) \setminus vars(u) \rightarrow T_{\Omega}(X)] \text{ s.t. } u =_{E_{\Omega} \cup B_{\Omega}} v_i\beta\}$$

a *complete* set of (parameter-preserving) $E_{\Omega} \cup B_{\Omega}$-matches of u against the v_i,

$$\text{UNIFY}(u \mid \varphi', R) \equiv \{(j, \alpha) \mid \alpha \in \text{Unif}_{E_{\Omega} \cup B_{\Omega}}(u, l_j) \text{ and } (\varphi' \land \phi_j)\alpha \text{ satisfiable in } T_{\Sigma/E \cup B}\}$$

a complete set of $E_{\Omega} \cup B_{\Omega}$-unifiers of a pattern $u \mid \varphi'$ with the lefthand-sides of the rules in R with satisfiable associated constraints.[4] Consider now the rule:

---

[4] In the current prototype implementation (see Sect. 6), variant satisfiability makes constraint checking decidable. Future versions will only assume $\vec{E}$ convergent modulo B for the equational part $E \cup B$ of $\mathcal{R}$, so that satisfiability of such constraints will in general be undecidable. Unifiers whose associated constraints cannot be proved unsatisfiable will then be included in $\text{UNIFY}(u \mid \varphi', R)$ as a safe over-approximation. The same approach will apply to the, in general undecidable, checking of satisfiability/validity for other constraints involved in the application of the $\text{STEP}^{\forall} + \text{SUBSUMPTION}$ or AXIOM rules below: they will be either over-approximated, or will become proof obligations to be discharged by an inductive theorem prover.

Step$^\forall$ + Subsumption

$$\frac{\bigwedge_{(j,\alpha)\in\text{UNIFY}(u|\varphi',\ R)} [\mathcal{A}\cup\mathcal{C},\ \emptyset]\ \vdash_T\ (r_j\mid\varphi'\wedge\phi_j)\alpha\longrightarrow^\circledast\bigvee_i(v_i\mid\psi_i)\alpha}{[\mathcal{A},\ \mathcal{C}]\ \vdash_T\ u\mid\varphi\longrightarrow^\circledast\bigvee_i v_i\mid\psi_i}$$

where $\varphi'\equiv\varphi\wedge\bigwedge_{(i,\beta)\in\text{MATCH}(u,\ \{v_i\})}\neg(\psi_i\beta)$. This inference rule allows us to take one step with the rules in $\mathcal{R}$. Intuitively, $u\mid\varphi'$ characterizes the states satisfying $u\mid\varphi$ that are not subsumed by any $v_i\mid\psi_i$; that is, states in the lefthand side of the current goal that have not yet reached the righthand side. Note that, according to Definition 4, $u\mid\varphi\longrightarrow^\circledast\bigvee_i v_i\mid\psi_i$ is semantically valid iff $u\mid\varphi'\longrightarrow^\circledast\bigvee_i v_i\mid\psi_i$ is valid. Thus, this inference rule only unifies $u\mid\varphi'$ with the lefthand sides of rules in R. We impose on this inference rule a side condition that $\bigvee_{j,\gamma\in Unif_{E_\Omega\cup B_\Omega}(u,t_j)}(\varphi'\wedge\chi_j)\gamma$ is unsatisfiable in $\mathcal{T}_{\Sigma/E\cup B}$, where $T=\bigvee_j t_j\mid\chi_j$ is the pattern predicate characterizing the chosen T-terminating states. This condition ensures that any state in $u\mid\varphi'$ has an $\mathcal{R}$-successor. Thus, a state in $u\mid\varphi'$ reaches on all T-terminating paths a state in $\bigvee_i v_i\mid\psi_i$ if all its successors do so. Each $\mathcal{R}$-successor is covered by one of $(r_j\mid\varphi'\wedge\phi_j)\alpha$. As an optimization, we check that $(\varphi'\wedge\phi_j)\alpha$ is satisfiable and we drop the ones which are not. Finally, we also assume that $vars((u\mid\varphi)\alpha)\cap vars((\bigvee_i v_i\mid\psi_i)\alpha)=vars((r_j\mid\varphi'\wedge\phi_j)\alpha)\cap vars((\bigvee_i v_i\mid\psi_i)\alpha)$. This parameter preservation condition ensures correct implicit quantification. Note that formulas in $\mathcal{C}$ are added to $\mathcal{A}$, so that from now on they can be used by Axiom. By using $E_\Omega\cup B_\Omega$-unification, this inference rule performs narrowing of $u\mid\varphi'$ with rules R [16].

Axiom

$$\frac{\bigwedge_j[\{u'\mid\varphi'\longrightarrow^\circledast\bigvee_j v'_j\mid\psi'_j\}\cup\mathcal{A},\ \emptyset]\ \vdash_T\ v'_j\alpha\mid\varphi\wedge\psi'_j\alpha\longrightarrow^\circledast\bigvee_i v_i\mid\psi_i}{[\{u'\mid\varphi'\longrightarrow^\circledast\bigvee_j v'_j\mid\psi'_j\}\cup\mathcal{A},\ \emptyset]\ \vdash_T\ u\mid\varphi\longrightarrow^\circledast\bigvee_i v_i\mid\psi_i}$$

if $\exists\alpha$ such that $u=_{E_\Omega\cup B_\Omega}u'\alpha$ and $\mathcal{T}_{\Sigma/E\cup B}\models\varphi\Rightarrow\varphi'\alpha$. This inference rule allows us to use a trusted formula in $\mathcal{A}$ to summarize multiple transition steps. This is similar to how several transition steps would apply to a ground term, except that for ground terms we would check that $\varphi'\alpha$ is valid, whereas here we check that the condition φ implies $\varphi'\alpha$. Since φ is stronger than $\varphi'\alpha$, we add φ to $(v'_j\mid\psi'_j)\alpha$ (the result of using axiom $u'\mid\varphi'\longrightarrow^\circledast\bigvee_j v'_j\mid\psi'_j$). We assume that $u\mid\varphi\longrightarrow^\circledast\bigvee_i v_i\mid\psi_i$ and $u'\mid\varphi'\longrightarrow^\circledast\bigvee_j v'_j\mid\psi'_j$ do not share variables, which can always be guaranteed by renaming. For correct implicit quantification, as in Step$^\forall$ + Subsumption, we assume for each j the parameter preservation condition $vars(u\mid\varphi)\cap vars(\bigvee_i v_i\mid\psi_i)=vars(v'_j\alpha\mid\varphi\wedge\psi'_j\alpha)\cap vars(\bigvee_i v_i\mid\psi_i)$. On a practical note, in order to be able to find the α, our implementation requires that $vars(\varphi')\subseteq vars(u')$, so that all the variables in $vars(\varphi')$ are matched.

The soundness of STEP$^\forall$ + SUBSUMPTION plus AXIOM is now the theorem:

Theorem 2 *(Soundness). Let $\mathcal{R}$ be a rewrite theory, and $\mathcal{C}$ a finite set of reachability formulas. If $\mathcal{R}$ proves $[\emptyset, \mathcal{C}] \vdash_T \mathcal{C}$ then $\mathcal{R} \models_T^\forall \mathcal{C}$.*

Investigating completeness of the logic is left as future work.

6   Prototype Implementation and Experiments

We have implemented the reachability logic proof system in Maude [1]. Our prototype takes as input (i) a rewrite theory $\mathcal{R} = (\Sigma, E \cup B, R, \phi)$ and (ii) a set of reachability formulas $\mathcal{C} = \{A_i \to^\circledast B_i\}_{i \in I}$ to be simultaneously proved.

To mechanize the two proof rules we use a finitary B-unification algorithm as well as an SMT solver to discharge $E \cup B$ constraints. For SMT solving we use variant satisfiability [9,12], which allows us to handle any rewrite theory $\mathcal{R} = (\Sigma, E \cup B, R)$ satisfying topmost requirements (1)–(2) and such that the equational theory $(\Sigma, E \cup B)$ has a convergent decomposition satisfying the finite variant property [2] and protects a constructor subtheory which we assume consists only of commutative and/or AC and/or identity axioms B_Ω. Thus, both validity and satisfiability of QF formulas in the initial algebra $\mathcal{T}_{\Sigma/E \cup B}$ are decidable [9]. Future implementations will support more general rewrite theories, add other decision procedures, and use an inductive theorem prover backend.

We have verified properties for a suite of examples of rewrite theories specifying distributed systems such as communication or mutual exclusion protocols and real-time systems. Table 1 summarizes these experiments. For further details plus runnable code see http://maude.cs.illinois.edu/tools/rltool/.

Table 1. Examples verified in the prototype implementation

Example	Description of the system/property
Choice	Nondeterministically throws away elements from a multiset/eventually only one element left
Comm. Protocol 1	Simple communication protocol/received data is always a prefix of the data to be sent
Comm. Protocol 2	Fault-tolerant communication protocol/all data is eventually received in-order
Dijkstra	Dijkstra's mutual exclusion alg./mutual exclusion
Fixed-size token ring	2-Token ring mutual exclusion alg./mutual exclusion
QLOCK	QLOCK mutual exclusion alg./mutual exclusion
Readers/writers	Readers-writers mutual exclusion alg./mutual exclusion
Lamport's bakery	Unbounded Lamport's bakery/mutual exclusion
Thermostat	Open system that dynamically responds to temperature/temperature remains in preset bounds

$$T_1 \equiv \left\{ \frac{}{\begin{array}{c} [\mathcal{C}, \emptyset] \vdash_{\square} [n^3 \mid w^3 \mid \emptyset \mid q^3] \mid dupl(n'' \, w' \, p) \neq tt \wedge \\ dupl(n^3 \, w^3) \neq tt \rightarrow^{\circledast} [P_1] \vee [P_2] \end{array}} \; sub(P_1, \alpha) \right.$$

$$T_2 \equiv \left\{ \frac{}{\begin{array}{c} [\mathcal{C}, \emptyset] \vdash_{\square} [n^3 \mid w^3 \mid i^3 \mid i^3; q^3] \mid dupl(n'' \, w' \, p) \neq tt \wedge \\ dupl(n^3 \, w^3 \, i^3) \neq tt \rightarrow^{\circledast} [P_1] \vee [P_2] \end{array}} \; sub(P_2, \alpha) \right.$$

$$\frac{\begin{array}{cc} T_1 & T_2 \end{array}}{\cdots \; [\mathcal{C}, \emptyset] \vdash_{\square} <n'' \mid w' \; p \mid \emptyset \mid q' > \mid dupl(n'' \, w' \, p) \neq tt \; \cdots} \; axiom(G_2, \alpha)$$
$$\frac{\rightarrow^{\circledast} [P_1] \vee [P_2]}{\begin{array}{c} [\emptyset, \mathcal{C}] \vdash_{\square} <n' \mid w' \mid \emptyset \mid q' > \mid dupl(n' \, w') \neq tt \\ \rightarrow^{\circledast} [P_1] \vee [P_2] \end{array}} \; step(n2w, \theta)$$

Fig. 1. Partial proof tree for QLOCK

To illustrate how the tool works in practice, Fig. 1 shows a partial derivation of a sequent. Recall that for QLOCK we had to prove $[\emptyset, \mathcal{C}] \vdash_{\square} \mathcal{C}$, where $\mathcal{C}$ was two already-discussed reachability formulas $G_i \equiv P_i' \rightarrow [P_1] \vee [P_2]$ for $i \in \{1, 2\}$ with respective preconditions the renamed disjuncts P_i', $1 \leq i \leq 2$ in invariant $P_1 \vee P_2$, and postcondition $[P_1] \vee [P_2]$, where $P_1 \equiv < n \mid w \mid i \mid i \; ; \; q > \mid dupl(n \, w \, i) \neq tt$ and $P_2 \equiv < n \mid w \mid \emptyset \mid q > \mid dupl(n \, w) \neq tt$. Now, consider $[\emptyset, \mathcal{C}] \vdash_{\square} P_2' \rightarrow^{\circledast} [P]$. In the proof fragment below, the initial sequent must apply the step rule. The result of $step(n2w, \theta)$ is the goal resulting from unifying the head of the sequent with the lefthand side of the rule $n2w$ using the unifier $\theta = \{n \mapsto n'' p, w \mapsto w', c \mapsto \emptyset, q \mapsto q'\}$. The next inference $axiom(G_2, \alpha)$ applies axiom G_2 using the substitution $\alpha \supseteq \{n \mapsto n^3, w \mapsto w^3, i \mapsto i^3, q \mapsto q^3\}$. Since G_2 has two constrained patterns in its succedent, we derive two new goals, represented by proof trees T_1 and T_2. In either case, we can immediately subsume by noting that our reachability formula's antecedent is an instance of either $[P_1]$ or $[P_2]$ using substitution α, thus terminating the proof.

7   Related Work and Conclusions

This work extends reachability logic [14,15] to a rewrite-theory-generic logic to reason about *both* distributed system designs and programs. This extension is non-trivial. It requires: (i) relativizing terminating sequences to a chosen subset $[\![T]\!]$ of terminating states; (ii) solving the "invariant paradox," to reason about invariants and co-invariants and characterizing them by reachability formulas through a theory transformation; and (iii) making it possible to achieve higher levels of automation by systematically basing the state predicates on positive Boolean combination of patterns of the form $u \mid \varphi$ with u a constructor term.

In contrast, standard reachability logic [14,15] uses matching logic, which assumes a first-order model $\mathcal{M}$ and its satisfaction relation $\mathcal{M} \models \varphi$ in its reachability logic proof system. As discusses in Sect. 3, we choose $\mathcal{T}_{\Sigma/E \cup B}$ as the model and $\rightarrow_{\mathcal{R}}$ for transitions, rather than some general $\mathcal{M}$ and systematically exploit the isomorphism $T_{\Sigma/E\cup B}|_{\Omega} \cong T_{\Omega/E_{\Omega}\cup B_{\Omega}}$, allowing us to use unification, matching, narrowing, and satisfiability procedures based on the typically much simpler initial algebra of constructors $T_{\Omega/E_{\Omega}\cup B_{\Omega}}$. This has the advantage that we can explicitly give the complete details of our inference rules (e.g. how STEP$^{\forall}$ + SUBSUMPTION checks the subsumption, or ensures that states have at least a successor), instead of relying on a general satisfaction relation $\models$ on some $\mathcal{M}$. The result is a simpler logic with only two rules (versus eight in [14,15]).

We agree with the work in [6] on the common goal of making reachability logic rewrite-theory-generic, but differ on the methods used. Main differences include: (1) [6] does not give an inference system but a verification algorithm. (2) the theories used in [6] assume restrictions like those in [11] for "rewriting modulo SMT," which limit the class of equational theories. (3) Matching is used in [6] instead of unification. Thus, unless a formula has been sufficiently instantiated, no matching rule may exist, whereas unification with some rule is always possible in our case. (4) No method for proving invariants is given in [6].

In conclusion, the goal of making reachability logic a rewrite-theory-generic verification logic has been advanced. Feasibility has been validated with a prototype and a suite of examples. Building a robust and highly effective reachability logic tool for rewrite theories is a more ambitious future goal.

Acknowledgements. Partially supported by NSF Grant CNS 14-09416.

References

1. Clavel, M., et al.: All About Maude - A High-Performance Logical Framework. LNCS, vol. 4350. Springer, Heidelberg (2007). https://doi.org/10.1007/978-3-540-71999-1
2. Comon-Lundh, H., Delaune, S.: The finite variant property: how to get rid of some algebraic properties. In: Giesl, J. (ed.) RTA 2005. LNCS, vol. 3467, pp. 294–307. Springer, Heidelberg (2005). https://doi.org/10.1007/978-3-540-32033-3_22
3. Dershowitz, N., Jouannaud, J.-P.: Rewrite systems. In: Handbook of Theoretical Computer Science, vol. B, pp. 243–320. North-Holland (1990)
4. Durán, F., Meseguer, J.: On the Church-Rosser and coherence properties of conditional order-sorted rewrite theories. J. Log. Algebr. Program. **81**(7–8), 816–850 (2012)
5. Futatsugi, K.: Fostering proof scores in CafeOBJ. In: Dong, J.S., Zhu, H. (eds.) ICFEM 2010. LNCS, vol. 6447, pp. 1–20. Springer, Heidelberg (2010). https://doi.org/10.1007/978-3-642-16901-4_1
6. Lucanu, D., Rusu, V., Arusoaie, A., Nowak, D.: Verifying reachability-logic properties on rewriting-logic specifications. In: Martí-Oliet, N., Ölveczky, P.C., Talcott, C. (eds.) Logic, Rewriting, and Concurrency. LNCS, vol. 9200, pp. 451–474. Springer, Cham (2015). https://doi.org/10.1007/978-3-319-23165-5_21
7. Lucas, S., Meseguer, J.: Normal forms and normal theories in conditional rewriting. J. Log. Algebr. Meth. Program. **85**(1), 67–97 (2016)
8. Meseguer, J.: Twenty years of rewriting logic. J. Algebr. Logic Program. **81**, 721–781 (2012)

9. Meseguer, J.: Variant-based satisfiability in initial algebras. In: Artho, C., Ölveczky, P.C. (eds.) FTSCS 2015. CCIS, vol. 596, pp. 3–34. Springer, Cham (2016). https://doi.org/10.1007/978-3-319-29510-7_1

10. Meseguer, J., Goguen, J.: Initiality, induction and computability. In: Algebraic Methods in Semantics, pp. 459–541. Cambridge UP (1985)

11. Rocha, C., Meseguer, J., Muñoz, C.: Rewriting modulo SMT and open system analysis. J. Logic Algebr. Methods Program. **86**, 269–297 (2017)

12. Skeirik, S., Meseguer, J.: Metalevel algorithms for variant satisfiability. In: Lucanu, D. (ed.) WRLA 2016. LNCS, vol. 9942, pp. 167–184. Springer, Cham (2016). https://doi.org/10.1007/978-3-319-44802-2_10

13. Skeirik, S., Stefanescu, A., Meseguer, J.: A constructor-based reachability logic for rewrite theories. Technical report. http://hdl.handle.net/2142/95770

14. Ştefănescu, A., et al.: All-path reachability logic. In: Dowek, G. (ed.) RTA 2014. LNCS, vol. 8560, pp. 425–440. Springer, Cham (2014). https://doi.org/10.1007/978-3-319-08918-8_29

15. Stefanescu, A., Park, D., Yuwen, S., Li, Y., Rosu, G.: Semantics-based program verifiers for all languages. In: Proceedings of the OOPSLA 2016, pp. 74–91. ACM (2016)

16. Thati, P., Meseguer, J.: Symbolic reachability analysis using narrowing and its application to the verification of cryptographic protocols. J. High.-Order Symb. Comput. **20**(1–2), 123–160 (2007)

Fuzzy Unification and Generalization of First-Order Terms over Similar Signatures

Hassan Aït-Kaci[1($\boxtimes$)] and Gabriella Pasi[2]

[1] HAK Language Technologies, Surrey, BC, Canada
hak@acm.org
[2] Universitá de Milano-Bicocca, Milan, Italy
pasi@disco.unimib.it

Abstract. Unification and generalization are operations on two terms computing respectively their greatest lower bound and least upper bound when the terms are quasi-ordered by subsumption up to variable renaming (*i.e.*, $t_1 \preceq t_2$ iff $t_1 = t_2\sigma$ for some variable substitution σ). When term signatures are such that distinct functor symbols may be related with a fuzzy equivalence (called a *similarity*), these operations can be formally extended to tolerate mismatches on functor names and/or arity or argument order. We reformulate and extend previous work with a declarative approach defining unification and generalization as sets of axioms and rules forming a complete constraint-normalization proof system. These include the Reynolds-Plotkin term-generalization procedures, Maria Sessa's "weak" unification with partially fuzzy signatures and its corresponding generalization, as well as novel extensions of such operations to fully fuzzy signatures (*i.e.*, similar functors with possibly different arities). One advantage of this approach is that it requires no modification of the conventional data structures for terms and substitutions. This and the fact that these declarative specifications are efficiently executable conditional Horn-clauses offers great practical potential for fuzzy information-handling applications.

1 Subsumption Lattice

The first-order term ($\mathcal{FOT}$) was introduced as a data structure in software programming by the Prolog (https://en.wikipedia.org/wiki/Prolog) language. Just like the S-expression for LISP, the $\mathcal{FOT}$ is Prolog's universal data structure. Using formal algebra notation, we write $\mathcal{T}_{\Sigma,\mathcal{V}}$ for the set of $\mathcal{FOT}$s on an operator signature $\Sigma \stackrel{\text{def}}{=} \bigcup_{n\geq 0} \Sigma_n$ where Σ_n is a set of operator symbols of n arguments

---

This article appears in the pre-proceedings of LOPSTR 2017 with the title "*Lattice Operations on Terms over Similar Signatures.*" Its new title is technically more accurate. All proofs and more examples can be found in a more detailed paper [2]. This work is part of a wider study [3].

© Springer International Publishing AG, part of Springer Nature 2018
F. Fioravanti and J. P. Gallagher (Eds.): LOPSTR 2017, LNCS 10855, pp. 218–234, 2018.
https://doi.org/10.1007/978-3-319-94460-9_13

$\Sigma_n \overset{\text{def}}{=} \{f \,|\, \mathbf{arity}(f) = n, n \in \mathbb{N}\}$, and $\mathcal{V}$ is a set of variables.[1] We shall designate an element f in Σ as a *functor*, with $\mathbf{arity}(f)$ denoting its number of arguments.[2] This set $\mathcal{T}_{\Sigma,\mathcal{V}}$ can then be defined inductively as:

$$\mathcal{T}_{\Sigma,\mathcal{V}} \overset{\text{def}}{=} \mathcal{V} \cup \{f(t_1,\ldots,t_n) \,|\, f \in \Sigma_n, \ t_i \in \mathcal{T}_{\Sigma,\mathcal{V}}, \ 0 \le i \le n, \ n \ge 0\}.$$

We write c instead of $c()$ for a constant $c \in \Sigma_0$. Also, when the set Σ of functor symbols and the set $\mathcal{V}$ of variables are implicit from the context, we simply write $\mathcal{T}$ instead of $\mathcal{T}_{\Sigma,\mathcal{V}}$. The set $\mathbf{var}(t)$ of variables occurring in a $\mathcal{FOT}$ $t \in \mathcal{T}$ is defined as:

$$\mathbf{var}(t) \overset{\text{def}}{=} \begin{cases} \{X\} & \text{if } t = X \in \mathcal{V} \\ \bigcup_{i=1}^{n} \mathbf{var}(t_n) & \text{if } t = f(t_1,\ldots,t_n). \end{cases}$$

The lattice-theoretic properties of $\mathcal{FOT}$s as data structures were first exposed and studied by Reynolds (in [16]) and Plotkin (in [14,15]). They noted that the set $\mathcal{T}$ is ordered by term subsumption (denoted as '$\preceq$'); *viz.*, $t \preceq t'$ (and we say: "t *subsumes* t'") iff there exists a variable substitution $\sigma : \mathbf{var}(t') \to \mathcal{T}$ such that $t'\sigma = t$. Two $\mathcal{FOT}$s t and t' are considered "*equal up to variable renaming*" (denoted as $t \simeq t'$) whenever both $t \preceq t'$ and $t' \preceq t$. Then, the set of first-order terms modulo variable renaming, when lifted with a bottom element $\bot$ standing for "*no term*" (*i.e.*, the set $\mathcal{T}_{/\simeq} \cup \{\bot\}$) has a lattice structure for subsumption. It has a top element $\top = \mathcal{V}$ (indeed, since any variable in $\mathcal{V}$ can be substituted for any term, $\mathcal{V}$ is therefore the class of any variable modulo renaming). Unification corresponds to its greatest lower bound (**glb**) operation. The dual operation, generalization of two terms, yields a term that is their least upper bound (**lub**) for subsumption. This can be summarized as the lattice diagram shown in Fig. 1. In this diagram, given a pair of terms $\langle t_1, t_2 \rangle$, the pair of substitutions $\langle \sigma_1, \sigma_2 \rangle$ are their respective most general generalizers, and the substitution σ is the pair's most general unifier (**mgu**). We formalize next these lattice operations on $\mathcal{FOT}$s as declarative constraint normalization rules.

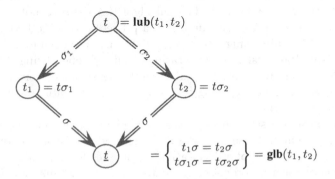

Fig. 1. Subsumption lattice operations

---

[1] We shall use Prolog's convention of writing variables with capitalized symbols.
[2] When $\mathbf{arity}(f) = n$, this is often denoted by writing f/n.

(1) **TERM DECOMPOSITION**:

$$\frac{E \cup \{f(s_1, \ldots, s_n) \doteq f(t_1, \ldots, t_n)\}}{E \cup \{s_1 \doteq t_1, \ldots, s_n \doteq t_n\}} \, [n \geq 0]$$

(2) **VARIABLE ERASURE**:

$$\frac{E \cup \{X \doteq X\}}{E}$$

(3) **VARIABLE ELIMINATION**:

$$\frac{E \cup \{X \doteq t\}}{E[X \leftarrow t] \cup \{X \doteq t\}} \begin{bmatrix} X \notin \mathbf{var}(t) \\ X \text{ occurs in } E \end{bmatrix}$$

(4) **EQUATION ORIENTATION**:

$$\frac{E \cup \{t \doteq X\}}{E \cup \{X \doteq t\}} \, [t \notin \mathcal{V}]$$

Fig. 2. Herbrand-Martelli-Montanari unification rules

1.1 Unification Rules

n Fig. 2, we give the set of equation normalization rules that we shall call Herbrand-Martelli-Montanari [8,13]. Each rule is *provably correct* in that it is a solution-preserving transformation of a set of equations. We can use these rules to unify two $\mathcal{FOT}$s t_1 and t_2. We start with the singleton set of equations $E \stackrel{\text{def}}{=} \{t_1 \doteq t_2\}$, and apply any applicable rule in any order until none applies. This always terminates into a finite set of equations E'. If all the equations in E' are of the form $X \doteq t$ with X occurring nowhere else in E', then this is a most general unifying substitution (up to consistent variable renaming) $\sigma \stackrel{\text{def}}{=} \{t/X \mid X \doteq t \in E'\}$ solving the original equation (*i.e.*, $t_1\sigma = t_2\sigma$); otherwise, there is no solution—*i.e.*, $\mathbf{glb}(t_1, t_2) = \bot$. In these rules, we check for circular terms ("*occurs-check*" is side condition: $X \notin \mathbf{var}(t)$ of Rule **VARIABLE ELIMINATION**). We could do without it, technically, so that these same rules without this "occurs-check" would perform rational term unification [9].

1.2 Generalization Rules

In 1970, John Reynolds and Gordon Plotkin published each an article, in the same volume [15,16], giving two identical algorithms (up to notation) for the generalization of two $\mathcal{FOT}$s. Each describes a procedural method computing the most specific $\mathcal{FOT}$ subsuming two given $\mathcal{FOT}$s in finitely many steps by comparing them simultaneously, and generating a pair of generalizing substitutions from a fresh variable wherever they disagree being scanned from left to right, each time replacing the disagreeing terms by the new variable everywhere they both occur in each term.

Next, we present a set of declarative normalization rules for generalization which are equivalent to these procedural algorithms. As far as we know, this is the first such presentation of a declarative set of rules for generalization besides its more general form as order-sorted feature term generalization in [5]. The advantage of specifying this operation in this manner rather than procedurally as done originally by Reynolds and Plotkin is that each rule or axiom relates a pair of prior substitutions to a pair of posterior substitutions based only on local syntactic-pattern properties of the terms to generalize, and this without resorting to side-effects on global structures. In this way, the terms and sub-stitutions involved are derived as solutions of logical syntactic constraints. In addition, correctness of the so-specified operation is made much easier to establish since we only need to prove each rule's correctness independently of that of the others. Finally, the rules also provide an effective means for the derivation of an operational semantics for the so-specified operation by constraint solving, without need for control specification as any applicable rule may be invoked in any order.[3]

Definition 1 (Generalization Judgement). *A generalization judgement is an expression of the form:*

$$\begin{pmatrix} \sigma_1 \\ \sigma_2 \end{pmatrix} \vdash \begin{pmatrix} t_1 \\ t_2 \end{pmatrix} t \begin{pmatrix} \theta_1 \\ \theta_2 \end{pmatrix} \tag{1}$$

where $\sigma_i : \boldsymbol{var}(t_i) \to \mathcal{T}$ and $\theta_i : \boldsymbol{var}(t) \to \mathcal{T}$ $(i = 1, 2)$ are substitutions, and $t \in \mathcal{T}$ and $t_i \in \mathcal{T}$ $(i = 1, 2)$ are $\mathcal{FOT}$s.

Definition 2 (Generalization Judgement Validity). *A generalization judgement such as (1) is said to be* valid *whenever $t_i \sigma_i = t \theta_i$, for $i = 1, 2$.*

Contrary to other normalization rules in this document which are expressed as conditional rewrite rules whereby a prior form (the "numerator") is related to a posterior form (the "denominator"), these normalization rules are more naturally rendered as (conditional) Horn clauses of judgements. This is as convenient as rewrite rules since a Prolog-like operational semantics can then readily provide an effective interpretation. This operational semantics is efficient because it does not need backtracking as long as the complete set of conditions of a ruleset covers all but mutually exclusive syntactic patterns. Thus, a generalization rule is of the form:

$$\frac{[\phi]}{J_1 \quad \dots \quad J_n} \tag{2}$$
$$\overline{\hspace{2em} J \hspace{2em}}$$

where ϕ is a side meta-condition, and $J, J_1, \dots, J_n$ are judgements, and it reads, *"whenever the side condition ϕ holds, if all the n antecedent judgements J_n are valid, then the consequent judgement J is also valid."* Such a generalization rule without a specified antecedent (a "numerator") is called a *"generalization axiom."* Such an axiom is said to be valid iff its consequent (the "denominator") is valid whenever its optional side condition holds. It is equivalent to a rule where the only antecedent is the trivial generalization judgement **TRUE**.

Definition 3 (Generalization Rule Correctness). *A conditional Horn rule such as Rule (2) is correct iff J_k is a valid judgement for all $k = 1, \dots, n$ implies that J is a valid judgement, whenever the side condition ϕ holds.*

---

[3] Such as the Herbrand-Martelli-Montanari unification rules *w.r.t.* to Robinson's procedural unification algorithm.

Given t_1 and t_2 two $\mathcal{FOT}$s having no variable in common, in order to find the most specific term t and most general substitutions σ_i, $i = 1, 2$, such that $t\sigma_i = t_i$, $i = 1, 2$, one needs to establish the generalization judgement:

$$\begin{pmatrix} \emptyset \\ \emptyset \end{pmatrix} \vdash \begin{pmatrix} t_1 \\ t_2 \end{pmatrix} t \begin{pmatrix} \sigma_1 \\ \sigma_2 \end{pmatrix}. \tag{3}$$

In other words, this expresses the upper half of Fig. 1 whereby $t = \mathbf{lub}(t_1, t_2)$, with most general substitutions σ_1 and σ_2. We give a complete set of normalization axioms and rule for generalization for all syntactic patterns in Fig. 3. Rule "**EQUAL FUNCTORS**" uses an "*unapply*" operation ('$\uparrow$') on a pair of terms (t_1, t_2) given a pair of substitutions (σ_1, σ_2). It may be conceived as (and in fact is) the result of simultaneously "*unapplying*" σ_i from t_i into a common variable X only if such X is bound to t_i by σ_i, for $i = 1, 2$. If there is no such a variable, it is the identity. Formally, this is defined as:

$$\begin{pmatrix} t_1 \\ t_2 \end{pmatrix} \uparrow \begin{pmatrix} \sigma_1 \\ \sigma_2 \end{pmatrix} \overset{\text{def}}{=} \begin{cases} \begin{pmatrix} X \\ X \end{pmatrix} & \text{if } t_i = X\sigma_i, \text{ for } i = 1, 2; \\ \begin{pmatrix} t_1 \\ t_2 \end{pmatrix} & \text{otherwise.} \end{cases} \tag{4}$$

(5) **EQUAL VARIABLES** :

$$\begin{pmatrix} \sigma_1 \\ \sigma_2 \end{pmatrix} \vdash \begin{pmatrix} X \\ X \end{pmatrix} X \begin{pmatrix} \sigma_1 \\ \sigma_2 \end{pmatrix}$$

(6) **VARIABLE-TERM** :

$$[t_1 \in \mathcal{V} \text{ or } t_2 \in \mathcal{V}; \ t_1 \neq t_2; \ X \text{ is new}]$$

$$\begin{pmatrix} \sigma_1 \\ \sigma_2 \end{pmatrix} \vdash \begin{pmatrix} t_1 \\ t_2 \end{pmatrix} X \begin{pmatrix} \sigma_1\{t_1/X\} \\ \sigma_2\{t_2/X\} \end{pmatrix}$$

(7) **UNEQUAL FUNCTORS** :

$$[m \geq 0, n \geq 0; \ m \neq n \text{ or } f \neq g; \ X \text{ is new}]$$

$$\begin{pmatrix} \sigma_1 \\ \sigma_2 \end{pmatrix} \vdash \begin{pmatrix} f(s_1, \ldots, s_m) \\ g(t_1, \ldots, t_n) \end{pmatrix} X \begin{pmatrix} \sigma_1\{f(s_1, \ldots, s_m)/X\} \\ \sigma_2\{g(t_1, \ldots, t_n)/X\} \end{pmatrix}$$

(8) **EQUAL FUNCTORS** :

$$[n \geq 0]$$

$$\frac{\begin{pmatrix} \sigma_1 \\ \sigma_2 \end{pmatrix} \vdash \begin{pmatrix} s_1 \\ t_1 \end{pmatrix} \uparrow \begin{pmatrix} \sigma_1 \\ \sigma_2 \end{pmatrix} u_1 \begin{pmatrix} \sigma_1^1 \\ \sigma_2^1 \end{pmatrix} \quad \cdots \quad \begin{pmatrix} \sigma_1^{n-1} \\ \sigma_2^{n-1} \end{pmatrix} \vdash \begin{pmatrix} s_n \\ t_n \end{pmatrix} \uparrow \begin{pmatrix} \sigma_1^{n-1} \\ \sigma_2^{n-1} \end{pmatrix} u_n \begin{pmatrix} \sigma_1^n \\ \sigma_2^n \end{pmatrix}}{\begin{pmatrix} \sigma_1 \\ \sigma_2 \end{pmatrix} \vdash \begin{pmatrix} f(s_1, \ldots, s_n) \\ f(t_1, \ldots, t_n) \end{pmatrix} f(u_1, \ldots, u_n) \begin{pmatrix} \sigma_1^n \\ \sigma_2^n \end{pmatrix}}$$

Fig. 3. Generalization axioms and rule

Note also that Rule "**EQUAL FUNCTORS**" is defined for $n \geq 0$. For $n = 0$ (for any constant c), it becomes the following axiom:

$$\begin{pmatrix} \sigma_1 \\ \sigma_2 \end{pmatrix} \vdash \begin{pmatrix} c \\ c \end{pmatrix} c \begin{pmatrix} \sigma_1 \\ \sigma_2 \end{pmatrix}. \tag{5}$$

Theorem 1. *The axioms and the rule of Fig. 3 are correct.*

In particular, with empty prior substitutions, we obtain the following corollary.

Corollary 1 ($\mathcal{FOT}$ Generalization). *Whenever the judgement* $\begin{pmatrix} \emptyset \\ \emptyset \end{pmatrix} \vdash \begin{pmatrix} t_1 \\ t_2 \end{pmatrix} t \begin{pmatrix} \sigma_1 \\ \sigma_2 \end{pmatrix}$ *is valid, then* $t\sigma_i = t_i$, *for* $i = 1, 2$.

2   Fuzzy Lattice Operations

2.1   Fuzzy Unification

A fuzzy unification operation on $\mathcal{FOT}$s, dubbed *"weak unification,"* was proposed by Maria Sessa in [17]. It normalizes equations between conventional $\mathcal{FOT}$s modulo a similarity relation $\sim$ over functor symbols. This similarity relation is then homomorphically extended to one over all $\mathcal{FOT}$s. It is: (1) the (crisp) identity relation on variables (*i.e.*, $X \sim_1 X$, for any X in $\mathcal{V}$); otherwise, (2) zero when either of the two terms is a variable (*i.e.*, $X \sim_0 t$ and $t \sim_0 X$, for any $X \neq t$ in $\mathcal{V}$); otherwise (3):

$$f(s_1, \ldots, s_n) \sim_{(\alpha \wedge \bigwedge_{i=1}^n \alpha_i)} g(t_1, \ldots, t_n) \text{ if } f \sim_\alpha g \text{ and } s_i \sim_{\alpha_i} t_i, \quad i = 1, \ldots, n$$

where $\alpha \in [0, 1]$ and $\alpha_i \in [0, 1]$ ($i = 1, \ldots, n$) denote the *unification degrees* to which each corresponding equation holds.[4]

In Fig. 4, we provide a set of declarative rewrite rules equivalent to Sessa's case-based "weak unification algorithm" [17]. To simplify the presentation of these rules while remaining faithful to Sessa's weak unification algorithm, it is assumed for now that functor symbols f/m and g/n of different arities $m \neq n$ are never similar. This is without any loss of generality since Sessa's weak unification fails on term structures of different arities.[5] Later, we will relax this and allow functors of different arities to be similar.

The rules of Fig. 4 transform E_α a finite conjunctive set E of equations among $\mathcal{FOT}$s along with an associated truth value, or *"unification degree,"* $\alpha \in [0, 1]$, into $E'_{\alpha'}$ another set of equations E' with truth value $\alpha' \in [0, \alpha]$. Given to solve a fuzzy unification equation $s \doteq t$ between two $\mathcal{FOT}$s s and t, form the set $\{s \doteq t\}_1$ (*i.e.*, with unification degree 1), and apply any applicable rules in Fig. 4 until either the unification degree of the set of equations is 0 (in which case there is no solution to the original equation, not even a fuzzy one), or the final resulting set E_α is a solution with truth value α in the form of a variable substitution $\sigma \stackrel{\text{def}}{=} \{X/t \mid X \doteq t \in E\}$ such that $s\sigma \sim_\alpha t\sigma$.

From our perspective, a fuzzy unification operation ought to be able to fuzzify *full $\mathcal{FOT}$* unification: whether (1) functor symbol mismatch, and/or (2) arity

---

[4] The $\wedge$ operation used by Sessa in this expression is min; but other interpretations are possible [3,7].

[5] See Case (2) of the weak unification algorithm given in [17], Page 413.

(9) FUZZY TERM DECOMPOSITION:

$$\frac{(E \cup \{f(s_1,\ldots,s_n) \doteq g(t_1,\ldots,t_n)\})_\alpha}{(E \cup \{s_1 \doteq t_1,\ldots,s_n \doteq t_n\})_{\alpha \wedge \beta}} \begin{bmatrix} f \sim_\beta g \\ n \geq 0 \end{bmatrix}$$

(11) VARIABLE ELIMINATION:

$$\frac{(E \cup \{X \doteq t\})_\alpha}{(E[X \leftarrow t] \cup \{X \doteq t\})_\alpha} \begin{bmatrix} X \notin \mathbf{var}(t) \\ X \text{ occurs in } E \end{bmatrix}$$

(10) VARIABLE ERASURE:

$$\frac{(E \cup \{X \doteq X\})_\alpha}{E_\alpha}$$

(12) EQUATION ORIENTATION:

$$\frac{(E \cup \{t \doteq X\})_\alpha}{(E \cup \{X \doteq t\})_\alpha} [t \notin \mathcal{V}]$$

Fig. 4. Normalization rules corresponding to Maria Sessa's "weak unification"

mismatch, and/or (3) in which order subterms correspond. Sessa's fuzzification of unification as weak unification misses on the last two items. This is unfortunate as this can turn out to be quite useful. In real life, there is indeed no such guarantee that argument positions of different functors match similar information in data and knowledge bases, hence the need for alignment [12].

Still, it has several qualities:

- *It is simple*—specified as a straightforward extension of crisp unification: only one rule (Rule "FUZZY TERM DECOMPOSITION") may alter the fuzziness of an equation set by tolerating similar functors.
- *It is conservative*—neither $\mathcal{FOT}$s nor $\mathcal{FOT}$ substitutions *per se* need be fuzzified; so conventional crisp representations and operations can be used; if restricted to only 0 or 1 truth values, it is equivalent to crisp $\mathcal{FOT}$ unification.

We now give an extension of Sessa's weak unification which can tolerate such fuzzy similarity among functors of different arities. Given a similarity relation $\sim$ on a ranked signature $\Sigma \overset{\text{def}}{=} \Sigma_{n \geq 0}$, $\sim: \Sigma^2 \to [0, 1]$ which, unlike M. Sessa's equal-arity condition, now allows mismatches of similar symbols with distinct arities or equal arities but different argument orders. Namely,

- it admits that $(\sim \cap \Sigma_m \times \Sigma_n) \neq \emptyset$ for some $m \geq 0$, $n \geq 0$, such that $m \neq n$;
- for each pair of functors $\langle f, g \rangle \in \Sigma^2$, such that $f \in \Sigma_m$ and $g \in \Sigma_n$, with $0 \leq m \leq n$, and $f \sim_\alpha g$, ($\alpha \in (0, 1]$), there exists an injective (*i.e.*, one-to-one) mapping $p : \{1, \ldots, m\} \to \{1, \ldots, n\}$ associating each of the m argument positions of f to a unique position among the n arguments of g (which is denoted as $f \sim_\alpha^p g$).

Note that in the above, m and n are such that $0 \leq m \leq n$; so the one-to-one argument-position mapping goes from the lesser set to the larger set. There is no loss of generality with this assumption as this will be taken into account in the normalization rules.

Example 1. [Similar functors with different arities] Consider *person*/3, a functor of arity 3, and *individual*/4, a functor of arity 4 with:

- similarity truth value of .9; *i.e.*, `person`/3 $\sim_{.9}$ `individual`/4; and,
- one-to-one position mapping $p : \{1, 2, 3\} \rightarrow \{1, 2, 3, 4\}$:

$$\text{from } person/3 \text{ to } individual/4 \text{ with } p : \{1 \rightarrow 1, 2 \rightarrow 3, 3 \rightarrow 4\}$$

so that:

$$person(Name, SSN, Address) \sim_{.9}^{p} individual(Name, DoB, SSN, Address)$$

writing $f \sim_{\alpha}^{p} g$ a similarity relation between a functor f and a functor g of truth value α and f-to-g argument-position mapping p; in our example, $person \sim_{.9}^{\{1 \rightarrow 1, 2 \rightarrow 3, 3 \rightarrow 4\}}$ *individual*.

With this kind of specification, we can tolerate not only fuzzy mismatching of terms with distinct functors `person` and `individual`, but also up to a correspondence of argument positions from `person` to *individual* specified as p, all with a truth value of .9.

Starting with the Herbrand-Martelli-Montanari ruleset of Fig. 2, fuzziness is introduced by relaxing "**TERM DECOMPOSITION**" to make it also tolerate possible arity or argument-order mismatch in two structures being unified. In other words, the given functor similarity relation $\sim$ is adjoined a position mapping from argument positions of a functor f to those of a functor g when $f \neq g$ and $f \sim_{\alpha} g$ with $\alpha \in (0, 1]$. This is then taken into account in tolerating a fuzzy mismatch between two term structures $s = f(s_1, \ldots, s_m)$ and $t = g(t_1, \ldots, t_n)$. This may involve a mismatch between the terms' functor symbols (f and g), their arities (m and n), subterm orders, or a combination. We first reorient all such equations by flipping sides so that the left-hand side is the one with lesser or equal arity. In this manner, assuming $f \sim_{\beta}^{p} g$ and $0 \leq \alpha, \beta \leq 1$, an equation of the form: $\left\{f(s_1, \ldots, s_m) \doteq g(t_1, \ldots, t_n)\right\}_{\alpha}$ for $0 \leq m \leq n$ acquires its truth value $\alpha \wedge \beta$ due to functor and arity mismatch when equated. A fully fuzzified term-decomposition rule should proceed with replacing such a fuzzy structure equation with the following conjunction of fuzzy equations between subterms at corresponding indices given by the one-to-one argument mapping $p : \{1, \ldots, m\} \rightarrow \{1, \ldots, n\}$: $\left\{s_1 \doteq t_{p(1)}, \ldots, s_m \doteq t_{p(m)}, \ldots\right\}_{\alpha \wedge \beta}$. Note that all the subterms in the right-hand side term that are arguments at indices which are not p-images are ignored as they have no counterparts in the left-hand side. These terms are simply dropped as part of the fuzzy approximative unification. This generic rule is shown in Fig. 5 along with another rule needed to make it fully effective: a rule reorienting a term equation into one with a lesser-arity term on the left.

Theorem 2. *The fuzzy unification rules of Fig. 4 where Rule "**FUZZY TERM DECOMPOSITION**" is replaced by the rules of Fig. 5 are correct.*

In other words, applying this modified ruleset to $E_1 \stackrel{\text{def}}{=} \{s \doteq t\}_1$, an equation set of truth value 1 (in any order as long as a rule applies and its truth value is not zero) always terminates. And when the final equation set is a substitution σ, it is a fuzzy solution with truth value α such that $s\sigma \sim_{\alpha} t\sigma$.

(13) **GENERIC WEAK TERM DECOMPOSITION** :

$$\left[0 \le m \le n;\ f \sim_\beta^p g\right]$$

$$\frac{(E \cup \{f(s_1,\ldots,s_m) \doteq g(t_1,\ldots,t_n)\})_\alpha}{(E \cup \{s_1 \doteq t_{p(1)},\ldots,s_m \doteq t_{p(m)}\})_{\alpha \wedge \beta}}$$

(14) **FUZZY EQUATION REORIENTATION** :

$$[0 \le n < m]$$

$$\frac{(E \cup \{f(s_1,\ldots,s_m) \doteq g(t_1,\ldots,t_n)\})_\alpha}{(E \cup \{g(t_1,\ldots,t_n) \doteq f(s_1,\ldots,s_m)\})_\alpha}$$

Fig. 5. Generic fuzzification of $\mathcal{FOT}$ unification's decomposition rule

Example 2. [$\mathcal{FOT}$ **fuzzy unification with similar functors of different arities**]
Let us take a functor signature such that: $\{a,b,c,d\} \subseteq \Sigma_0$, $\{f,g,\ell\} \subseteq \Sigma_2$, $\{h\} \subseteq \Sigma_3$; and let us further assume that the only non-zero similarities argument mappings among these functors are:

- $a \sim_{.7} b$,
- $c \sim_{.6} d$,
- $f \sim_{.9}^{\{1 \to 2, 2 \to 1\}} g$ and $g \sim_{.9}^{\{1 \to 2, 2 \to 1\}} f$,
- $\ell \sim_{.8}^{\{1 \to 2, 2 \to 3\}} h$.

Let us consider the fuzzy equation set $\{\mathbf{t_1} \doteq \mathbf{t_2}\}_1$:

$$\{h(X, g(Y,b), f(Y,c)) \doteq \ell(f(a,Z), g(d,c))\}_1 \tag{6}$$

and let us apply the rules of Fig. 4 with rule **WEAK TERM DECOMPOSITION** is replaced by the rules of Fig. 5:

- apply Rule **FUZZY EQUATION REORIENTATION** with $\alpha = 1$ since **arity**$(\ell) <$ **arity**(h):
$$\{\ell(f(a,Z), g(d,c)) \doteq h(X, g(Y,b), f(Y,c))\}_1\ ;$$

- apply Rule **GENERIC WEAK TERM DECOMPOSITION** to:
$$\ell(f(a,Z), g(d,c)) \doteq h(X, g(Y,b), f(Y,c))$$

with $\alpha = 1$ and $\beta = .8$ since $\ell \sim_{.8}^{\{1 \to 2, 2 \to 3\}} h$, to obtain:
$$\{f(a,Z) \doteq g(Y,b), g(d,c) \doteq f(Y,c)\}_{.8}\ ;$$

- apply Rule **GENERIC WEAK TERM DECOMPOSITION** to $f(a,Z) \doteq g(Y,b)$ with $\alpha = .8$ and $\beta = .9$ since $f \sim_{.9}^{\{1 \to 2, 2 \to 1\}} g$, to obtain:
$$\{a \doteq b, Z \doteq Y, g(d,c) \doteq f(Y,c)\}_{.8}\ ;$$

- apply Rule **GENERIC WEAK TERM DECOMPOSITION** to $a \doteq b$ with $\alpha = .8$ and $\beta = .7$ since $a \sim_{.7} b$, to obtain:
$$\{Z \doteq Y, g(d,c) \doteq f(Y,c)\}_{.7}\ ;$$

- apply Rule **GENERIC WEAK TERM DECOMPOSITION** to $g(d, c) \doteq f(Y, c)$ with $\alpha = .7$ and $\beta = .9$ since $f \sim_{.9}^{\{1 \to 2, 2 \to 1\}} g$, to obtain:

$$\{Z \doteq Y, d \doteq c, c \doteq Y\}_{.7};$$

- apply Rule **GENERIC WEAK TERM DECOMPOSITION** to $d \doteq c$ with $\alpha = .7$ and $\beta = .6$ since $d \sim_{.6} c$, to obtain:

$$\{Z \doteq Y, c \doteq Y\}_{.6};$$

- apply Rule **EQUATION ORIENTATION** to $c \doteq Y$ with $\alpha = .6$, to obtain:

$$\{Z \doteq Y, Y \doteq c\}_{.6}.$$

- apply Rule **VARIABLE ELIMINATION** to $Y \doteq c$ with $\alpha = .6$, to obtain:

$$\{Z \doteq c, Y \doteq c\}_{.6}.$$

This last equation set is in normal form with truth value .6 and defines the substitution $\sigma = \{c/Z, c/Y\}$ so that:

$$\mathbf{t}_1\sigma = h(X, g(Y, b), f(Y, c))\,\{c/Z, c/Y\} \sim_{.6} \mathbf{t}_2\sigma = \ell(f(a, Z), g(d, c))\,\{c/Z, c/Y\}, \tag{7}$$

that is:

$$\mathbf{t}_1\sigma = h(X, g(c, b), f(c, c)) \sim_{.6} \mathbf{t}_2\sigma = \ell(f(a, c), g(d, c)). \tag{8}$$

Example 3. [The same fuzzy unification with more expressive symbols] Let us give more expressive names to functors of Example 2 in the context of, say, a gift-shop Prolog database which describes various configurations for multi-item gift boxes or bags containing such items as flowers, sweets, *etc.*, which can be already joined as pairs or not joined as loose couples.

- $a \stackrel{\text{def}}{=} \textit{violet}$,
- $b \stackrel{\text{def}}{=} \textit{lilac}$,
- $c \stackrel{\text{def}}{=} \textit{chocolate}$,
- $d \stackrel{\text{def}}{=} \textit{candy}$,
- $f \stackrel{\text{def}}{=} \textit{pair}$,
- $g \stackrel{\text{def}}{=} \textit{couple}$,
- $\ell \stackrel{\text{def}}{=} \textit{small-gift-bag}$,
- $h \stackrel{\text{def}}{=} \textit{small-gift-box}$,

with the following similarity degrees and argument mappings,:

- $\textit{violet} \sim_{.7} \textit{lilac}$,
- $\textit{chocolate} \sim_{.6} \textit{candy}$,
- $\textit{pair} \sim_{.9} \textit{couple}$,
- $\textit{pair} \sim_{.9}^{\{1 \to 2, 2 \to 1\}} \textit{couple}$ and $\textit{couple} \sim_{.9}^{\{1 \to 2, 2 \to 1\}} \textit{pair}$,
- $\textit{small-gift-bag} \sim_{.8}^{\{1 \to 2, 2 \to 3\}} \textit{small-gift-box}$.

With these functors Eq. (6) now reads:

$$\text{(t}_1)\quad \begin{array}{ll} \textit{small-gift-box (} & X \\ & \textit{, couple}(Y, \textit{lilac}) \\ & \textit{, pair}(Y, \textit{chocolate}) \\ &) \end{array}$$

$$\doteq$$

$$\text{(t}_2)\quad \begin{array}{ll} \textit{small-gift-bag (} & \textit{pair}(\textit{violet}, Z) \\ & \textit{, couple}(\textit{candy}, \textit{chocolate}) \\ &) \end{array}$$

With the new functor symbols, the substitution $\sigma = \{\textit{chocolate}/Z, \textit{chocolate}/Y\}$ obtained after normalization yields the fuzzy solution:

$$\text{(t}_1\sigma)\quad \begin{array}{ll} \textit{small-gift-box (} & X \\ & \textit{, couple}(\textit{chocolate}, \textit{lilac}) \\ & \textit{, pair}(\textit{chocolate}, \textit{chocolate}) \\ &) \end{array}$$

$$\sim_{.6}$$

$$\text{(t}_2\sigma)\quad \begin{array}{ll} \textit{small-gift-bag (} & \textit{pair}(\textit{violet}, \textit{chocolate}) \\ & \textit{, couple}(\textit{candy}, \textit{chocolate}) \\ &) \end{array}$$

with truth value .6 capturing the unification degree to which σ solves the original equation.

Rule GENERIC WEAK TERM DECOMPOSITION is a very general rule for normalizing fuzzy equations over $\mathcal{FOT}$ structures. It has the following convenient properties:

1. it accounts for fuzzy mismatches of similar functors of possibly different arity or order of arguments;
2. when restricted to tolerating only similar equal-arity functors with matching argument positions, it reduces to Sessa's weak unification's WEAK TERM DECOMPOSITION rule;
3. when truth values are further restricted to be in $\{0, 1\}$, it reduces to Herbrand-Martelli-Montanari's TERM DECOMPOSITION rule;
4. it requires no alteration of the standard notions of $\mathcal{FOT}$s and $\mathcal{FOT}$ substitutions: similarity among $\mathcal{FOT}$s is derived from that of signature symbols;
5. finally, and most importantly, it keeps fuzzy unification in the same complexity class as crisp unification: that of Union-Find [11,18].[6]

As a result, it is more general than all other extant approaches we know which propose a fuzzy $\mathcal{FOT}$ unification operation. The same will be established for the

---

[6] Quasi-linear; *i.e.*, linear with a log...log coefficient [1].

fuzzification of the dual operation: first a limited *"functor-weak"* $\mathcal{FOT}$ generalization corresponding to the dual operation of Sessa's "weak" unification, then to a more expressive *"functor/arity-weak"* $\mathcal{FOT}$ generalization corresponding to our extension of Sessa's unification to functor/arity weak unification.

2.2 Fuzzy Generalization

Let t_1 and t_2 be two $\mathcal{FOT}$s in $\mathcal{T}$ to generalize. We shall use the following notation for a fuzzy generalization judgement:

$$\binom{\sigma_1}{\sigma_2}_\alpha \vdash \binom{t_1}{t_2} t \binom{\theta_1}{\theta_2}_\beta \tag{9}$$

given:

- $\sigma_i : \mathbf{var}(t_i) \to \mathcal{T}$ $(i = 1, 2)$: two prior substitutions with prior truth value α,
- t_i $(i = 1, 2)$: two prior $\mathcal{FOT}$s,
- t: a posterior $\mathcal{FOT}$,
- $\theta_i : \mathbf{var}(t) \to \mathcal{T}$ $(i = 1, 2)$: two posterior substitutions with truth value β.

Definition 4 (Fuzzy Generalization Judgement Validity). *A fuzzy generalization judgement such as (9) is* valid *whenever* $0 \leq \beta \leq \alpha \leq 1$ *and* $t_i \sigma_i \sim_\beta t \theta_i$ *for* $i = 1, 2$.

Definition 5 (Fuzzy Generalization Rule Correctness). *A fuzzy generalization rule is* correct *iff, whenever the side condition holds, if all the fuzzy generalization judgements making up its antecedent are valid, then necessarily the generalization judgement in its consequent is valid.*

In Fig. 6, we give a fuzzy version of the generalization rules of Fig. 3. As was the case in Sessa's weak unification, we assume as well (for now) that we are only given a similarity relation $\sim \in \Sigma \times \Sigma \to [0, 1]$ on the signature $\Sigma = \cup_{n \geq 0} \Sigma_n$ such that for all $m \geq 0$ and $n \geq 0$, $m \neq n$ implies $\sim \cap \Sigma_m \times \Sigma_n = \emptyset$ (*i.e.*, if functors f and g have different arities, then $f \not\sim g$).

Rule **SIMILAR FUNCTORS** uses a *"fuzzy unapply"* operation ('$\uparrow_\alpha$') on a pair of terms (t_1, t_2) given a pair of substitutions (σ_1, σ_2) and a truth value α. It is the result of *"unapplying"* σ_i from t_i into a common variable, if any, whenever it is bound by σ_1 to a term t_1' and by σ_2 to a term t_2' which are respectively α-similar to t_i for $i = 1, 2$. It is defined as:

$$\binom{t_1}{t_2} \uparrow_\alpha \binom{\sigma_1}{\sigma_2} \;\stackrel{\text{def}}{=}\; \begin{cases} \binom{X}{X} & \text{if } t_i \sim_\alpha X\sigma_i \text{ for } i = 1, 2; \\[2mm] \binom{t_1}{t_2} & \text{otherwise.} \end{cases} \tag{10}$$

Theorem 3. *The fuzzy generalization rules of Fig. 6 are correct.*

(15) **FUZZY EQUAL VARIABLES** :

$$\begin{pmatrix} \sigma_1 \\ \sigma_2 \end{pmatrix}_\alpha \vdash \begin{pmatrix} X \\ X \end{pmatrix} X \begin{pmatrix} \sigma_1 \\ \sigma_2 \end{pmatrix}_\alpha$$

(16) **FUZZY VARIABLE-TERM** :

$$[t_1 \in \mathcal{V} \text{ or } t_2 \in \mathcal{V}; \ t_1 \neq t_2; \ X \text{ is new}]$$

$$\begin{pmatrix} \sigma_1 \\ \sigma_2 \end{pmatrix}_\alpha \vdash \begin{pmatrix} t_1 \\ t_2 \end{pmatrix} X \begin{pmatrix} \sigma_1\{t_1/X\} \\ \sigma_2\{t_2/X\} \end{pmatrix}_\alpha$$

(17) **DISSIMILAR FUNCTORS** :

$$[f \not\sim g; \ m \geq 0, n \geq 0; \ X \text{ is new}]$$

$$\begin{pmatrix} \sigma_1 \\ \sigma_2 \end{pmatrix}_\alpha \vdash \begin{pmatrix} f(s_1,\ldots,s_m) \\ g(t_1,\ldots,t_n) \end{pmatrix} X \begin{pmatrix} \sigma_1\{f(s_1,\ldots,s_m)/X\} \\ \sigma_2\{g(t_1,\ldots,t_n)/X\} \end{pmatrix}_\alpha$$

(18) **SIMILAR FUNCTORS** :

$$\left[f \sim_\beta g; \ n \geq 0; \ \alpha_0 \stackrel{\text{def}}{=} \alpha \wedge \beta \right]$$

$$\frac{\begin{pmatrix} \sigma_1 \\ \sigma_2 \end{pmatrix}_{\alpha_0} \vdash \begin{pmatrix} s_1 \\ t_1 \end{pmatrix} \uparrow_{\alpha_0} \begin{pmatrix} \sigma_1^1 \\ \sigma_2^1 \end{pmatrix} u_1 \begin{pmatrix} \sigma_1^1 \\ \sigma_2^1 \end{pmatrix}_{\alpha_1} \cdots \begin{pmatrix} \sigma_1^{n-1} \\ \sigma_2^{n-1} \end{pmatrix}_{\alpha_{n-1}} \vdash \begin{pmatrix} s_n \\ t_n \end{pmatrix} \uparrow_{\alpha_{n-1}} \begin{pmatrix} \sigma_1^{n-1} \\ \sigma_2^{n-1} \end{pmatrix} u_n \begin{pmatrix} \sigma_1^n \\ \sigma_2^n \end{pmatrix}_{\alpha_n}}{\begin{pmatrix} \sigma_1 \\ \sigma_2 \end{pmatrix}_\alpha \vdash \begin{pmatrix} f(s_1,\ldots,s_n) \\ g(t_1,\ldots,t_n) \end{pmatrix} f(u_1,\ldots,u_n) \begin{pmatrix} \sigma_1^n \\ \sigma_2^n \end{pmatrix}_{\alpha_n}}$$

Fig. 6. Functor-weak generalization axioms and rule

Example 4. [$\mathcal{FOT}$ **fuzzy generalization**] Let us apply the fuzzy generalization axioms and rules of Fig. 6 to:

$$\mathbf{t}_1 \stackrel{\text{def}}{=} h(f(a, X_1), g(X_1, b), f(Y_1, Y_1)),$$
$$\mathbf{t}_2 \stackrel{\text{def}}{=} h(X_2, X_2, g(c, d)).$$

- Let us find term t, substitutions $\sigma_i : \mathbf{var}(t) \to \mathbf{var}(\mathbf{t}_i)$ ($i = 1, 2$), and truth value $\alpha \in [0, 1]$ such that $t\sigma_1 \sim_\alpha h(f(a, X_1), g(X_1, b), f(Y_1, Y_1))$ and $t\sigma_2 \sim_\alpha h(X_2, X_2, g(c, d))$; that is, solve the following fuzzy generalization constraint problem:

$$\begin{pmatrix} \emptyset \\ \emptyset \end{pmatrix}_1 \vdash \begin{pmatrix} h(f(a, X_1), g(X_1, b), f(Y_1, Y_1)) \\ h(X_2, X_2, g(c, d)) \end{pmatrix} t \begin{pmatrix} \sigma_1 \\ \sigma_2 \end{pmatrix}_\alpha.$$

- By Rule **SIMILAR FUNCTORS**, we must have $t = h(u_1, u_2, u_3)$ since:

$$\begin{pmatrix} \emptyset \\ \emptyset \end{pmatrix}_1 \vdash \begin{pmatrix} h(f(a, X_1), g(X_1, b), f(Y_1, Y_1)) \\ h(X_2, X_2, g(c, d)) \end{pmatrix} h(u_1, u_2, u_3) \begin{pmatrix} \sigma_1 \\ \sigma_2 \end{pmatrix}_\alpha$$

where:

- u_1 is the fuzzy generalization of $\begin{pmatrix} f(a, X_1) \\ X_2 \end{pmatrix} \uparrow_1 \begin{pmatrix} \emptyset \\ \emptyset \end{pmatrix}$; that is, of $f(a, X_1)$ and X_2; and by Rule **FUZZY VARIABLE-TERM**:

$$\begin{pmatrix} \emptyset \\ \emptyset \end{pmatrix}_1 \vdash \begin{pmatrix} f(a, X_1) \\ X_2 \end{pmatrix} X \begin{pmatrix} \{f(a, X_1)/X\} \\ \{X_2/X\} \end{pmatrix}_1$$

and so $u_1 = X$; u_2 is the fuzzy generalization of $\begin{pmatrix} g(X_1, b) \\ X_2 \end{pmatrix} \uparrow_1 \begin{pmatrix} \{f(a, X_1)/X\} \\ \{X_2/X\} \end{pmatrix}$; that is, of $g(X_1, b)$ and X_2; and by Rule **FUZZY VARIABLE-TERM**:

$$\begin{pmatrix} \{f(a, X_1)/X\} \\ \{X_2/X\} \end{pmatrix}_1 \vdash \begin{pmatrix} g(X_1, b) \\ X_2 \end{pmatrix} Y \begin{pmatrix} \{\ldots, g(X_1, b)/Y\} \\ \{\ldots, X_2/Y\} \end{pmatrix}_1$$

and so $u_2 = Y$;

- $u_3 = f(v_1, v_2)$ is the fuzzy generalization of

$$\begin{pmatrix} f(Y_1, Y_1) \\ g(c, d) \end{pmatrix} \uparrow_{.9} \begin{pmatrix} \{f(a, X_1)/X, g(X_1, b)/Y\} \\ \{X_2/X, X_2/Y\} \end{pmatrix};$$

that is, of $f(Y_1, Y_1)$ and $g(c, d)$ with truth value .9, because of Rule **SIMILAR FUNCTORS** and $f \sim_{.9} g$, and:

* v_1 is the fuzzy generalization of

$$\begin{pmatrix} \{f(a, X_1)/X, g(X_1, b)/Y\} \\ \{X_2/X, X_2/Y\} \end{pmatrix} \uparrow_{.9} \begin{pmatrix} Y_1 \\ c \end{pmatrix};$$

that is, of Y_1 and c; and by Rule **FUZZY VARIABLE-TERM**:

$$\begin{pmatrix} \{f(a, X_1)/X, g(X_1, b)/Y\} \\ \{X_2/X, X_2/Y\} \end{pmatrix}_{.9} \vdash \begin{pmatrix} Y_1 \\ c \end{pmatrix} Z \begin{pmatrix} \{\ldots, Y_1/Z\} \\ \{\ldots, c/Z\} \end{pmatrix}_{.9}$$

that is, $v_1 = Z$;

* v_2 is the fuzzy generalization of

$$\begin{pmatrix} Y_1 \\ d \end{pmatrix} \uparrow_{.9} \begin{pmatrix} \{f(a, X_1)/X, g(X_1, b)/Y, Y_1/Z\} \\ \{X_2/X, X_2/Y, c/Z\} \end{pmatrix};$$

that is, of Y_1 and d; and by Rule **FUZZY VARIABLE-TERM**:

$$\begin{pmatrix} \{f(a, X_1)/X, g(X_1, b)/Y, Y_1/Z\} \\ \{X_2/X, X_2/Y, c/Z\} \end{pmatrix}_{.9} \vdash \begin{pmatrix} Y_1 \\ d \end{pmatrix} U \begin{pmatrix} \{\ldots, Y_1/U\} \\ \{\ldots, d/U\} \end{pmatrix}_{.9}$$

that is, $v_2 = U$;
in other words, $u_3 = f(Z, U)$ since:

$$\begin{pmatrix} \{f(a, X_1)/X, g(X_1, b)/Y\} \\ \{X_2/X, X_2/Y\} \end{pmatrix}_1 \vdash \begin{pmatrix} f(Y_1, Y_1) \\ g(c, d) \end{pmatrix} f(Z, U) \begin{pmatrix} \{\ldots, Y_1/Z, Y_1/U\} \\ \{\ldots, c/Z, d/U\} \end{pmatrix}_{.9}$$

and so:

$$\begin{pmatrix} \emptyset \\ \emptyset \end{pmatrix}_1 \vdash \begin{pmatrix} t_1 \\ t_2 \end{pmatrix} h(X, Y, f(Z, U)) \begin{pmatrix} \{f(a, X_1)/X, g(X_1, b)/Y, Y_1/Z, Y_1/U\} \\ \{X_2/X, X_2/Y, c/Z, d/U\} \end{pmatrix}_{.9}.$$

In Fig. 7, we give a fuzzy version of the generalization rules taking into account mismatches not only in functors, but also in arities; *i.e.*, number and/or order of arguments. Unlike Sessa's unification, we now assume that we are not only given a similarity relation $\sim \in \Sigma \times \Sigma \to [0, 1]$ on the signature $\Sigma = \cup_{n \geq 0} \Sigma_n$, but also that functors of different arities may be similar with some non-zero truth value as specified by an one-to-one argument-position mapping for each pair of so-similar functors associating to each argument position of the functor of least arity a distinct argument position of the functor of larger arity. The only rule among those of Fig. 6 that differs is the last one (**SIMILAR FUNCTORS**) which is now a pair of rules called **FUNCTOR/ARITY SIMILARITY LEFT** and **FUNCTOR/ARITY SIMILARITY RIGHT** to account for similar functors's argument positions depending which side has less arguments. If the arities are the same, the two rules are equivalent.

Theorem 4. *The fuzzy generalization rules of Fig. 6 where Rule "SIMILAR FUNCTORS" is replaced with the rules in Fig. 7 are correct.*

(19) **FUNCTOR/ARITY SIMILARITY LEFT** :

$$\left[f \sim_\beta^p g;\ 0 \le m \le n;\ \alpha_0 \overset{\text{def}}{=} \alpha \wedge \beta\right]$$

$$\frac{\begin{pmatrix}\sigma_1\\\sigma_2\end{pmatrix}_{\alpha_0} \vdash \begin{pmatrix}s_1\\t_{p(1)}\end{pmatrix} \uparrow_{\alpha_0} \begin{pmatrix}\sigma_1\\\sigma_2\end{pmatrix} u_1 \begin{pmatrix}\sigma_1^1\\\sigma_2^1\end{pmatrix}_{\alpha_1} \cdots \begin{pmatrix}\sigma_1^{m-1}\\\sigma_2^{m-1}\end{pmatrix}_{\alpha_{m-1}} \vdash \begin{pmatrix}s_m\\t_{p(m)}\end{pmatrix} \uparrow_{\alpha_{m-1}} \begin{pmatrix}\sigma_1^{m-1}\\\sigma_2^{m-1}\end{pmatrix} u_m \begin{pmatrix}\sigma_1^m\\\sigma_2^m\end{pmatrix}_{\alpha_m}}{\begin{pmatrix}\sigma_1\\\sigma_2\end{pmatrix}_\alpha \vdash \begin{pmatrix}f(s_1,\ldots,s_m)\\g(t_1,\ldots,t_n)\end{pmatrix} f(u_1,\ldots,u_m) \begin{pmatrix}\sigma_1^m\\\sigma_2^m\end{pmatrix}_{\alpha_m}}$$

(20) **FUNCTOR/ARITY SIMILARITY RIGHT** :

$$\left[g \sim_\beta^p f;\ 0 \le n \le m;\ \alpha_0 \overset{\text{def}}{=} \alpha \wedge \beta\right]$$

$$\frac{\begin{pmatrix}\sigma_1\\\sigma_2\end{pmatrix}_{\alpha_0} \vdash \begin{pmatrix}s_{p(1)}\\t_1\end{pmatrix} \uparrow_{\alpha_0} \begin{pmatrix}\sigma_1\\\sigma_2\end{pmatrix} u_1 \begin{pmatrix}\sigma_1^1\\\sigma_2^1\end{pmatrix}_{\alpha_1} \cdots \begin{pmatrix}\sigma_1^{n-1}\\\sigma_2^{n-1}\end{pmatrix}_{\alpha_{n-1}} \vdash \begin{pmatrix}s_{p(n)}\\t_n\end{pmatrix} \uparrow_{\alpha_{n-1}} \begin{pmatrix}\sigma_1^{n-1}\\\sigma_2^{n-1}\end{pmatrix} u_n \begin{pmatrix}\sigma_1^n\\\sigma_2^n\end{pmatrix}_{\alpha_n}}{\begin{pmatrix}\sigma_1\\\sigma_2\end{pmatrix}_\alpha \vdash \begin{pmatrix}f(s_1,\ldots,s_m)\\g(t_1,\ldots,t_n)\end{pmatrix} g(u_1,\ldots,u_n) \begin{pmatrix}\sigma_1^n\\\sigma_2^n\end{pmatrix}_{\alpha_n}}$$

Fig. 7. Functor/arity-weak generalization axioms and rule

3   Conclusion

We have summarized the principal results regarding the derivation of fuzzy lattice operations for the data structure known as first-order term. This is achieved by means of syntax-driven constraint normalization rules for both unification and generalization. These operations are then extended to enable arbitrary mismatch between similar terms whether functor-based, arity-based (number and order), or combinations. The resulting lattice operations are in the same class of complexity as their crisp versions, of which they are conservative extensions—namely that of Union/Find. All these details, along with proofs and examples, are to be found in [2].

As for future work, there are several avenues to explore. The most immediate concerns implementation of such operations in the form of public libraries to complement extant tools for first-order terms and substitutions [10]. This is eased by the fact that the fuzzy lattice operations do no require altering these conventional first-order structures. There are several other disciplines where this technology has potential for fuzzifying applications wherever $\mathcal{FOT}$s are used for their lattice-theoretic properties such as linguistics and learning. Finally, most promising is using this work's approach to more generic and more expressive knowledge structures for applications such as Fuzzy Information Retrieval [6]. We are currently developing the same formal construction for fuzzy lattice operations over order-sorted feature ($\mathcal{OSF}$) graphs [4]. Encouraging initial results are being reported in [3].

References

1. Aho, A., Hopcroft, J., Ullmann, J.: The Design and Analysis of Computer Algorithms. Addison-Wesley, Reading (1974)
2. Aït-Kaci, H., Pasi, G.: Fuzzy lattice operations on first-order terms over signatures with similar constructors. Journal Submission Preprint (2017). http://hassan-ait-kaci.net/pdf/fuzfotlat-preprint.pdf
3. Aït-Kaci, H., Pasi, G.: Fuzzy lattice-theoretic operations over data and knowledge structures. Technical report, HAK Language Technologies (2017, in preparation). http://hassan-ait-kaci.net/pdf/fuzlatopdks.pdf
4. Aït-Kaci, H., Podelski, A., Goldstein, S.C.: Order-sorted feature theory unification. J. Logic Program. **30**(2), 99–124 (1997). http://www.hassan-ait-kaci.net/pdf/osf-theory-unification.pdf
5. Aït-Kaci, H., Podelski, A., Goldstein, S.C.: Order-sorted feature theory unification. J. Logic Program. **30**(2), 99–124 (1997). www.hassan-ait-kaci.net/pdf/ecml01.pdf
6. Baziz, M., Boughanem, M., Pasi, G., Prade, H.: A fuzzy set approach to concept-based information retrieval. In: Montseny, E., Sobrevilla, P. (eds.) Proceedings of the Joint 4th Conference of the European Society for Fuzzy Logic and Technology, Barcelona, Spain, pp. 1287–1292, 7–9 September 2005. https://www.irit.fr/publis/ADRIA/BougPetal001a.pdf
7. Dubois, D., Prade, H.: Fuzzy sets and systems: theory and applications. In: Ames, W.F. (ed.) Mathematics in Science and Engineering, Georgia Institute of Technology, vol. 144. Academic Press (1980). ftp://ftp.micronet-rostov.ru/linux-support/books/computer%20science/Fuzzy%20systems/Fuzzy%20Sets%20And%20Systems%20Theory%20And%20Applications%20-%20Didier%20Dubois%20,%20Henri%20Prade.pdf
8. Herbrand, J.: Recherches sur la théorie de la démonstration. Ph.D. thesis, Faculté des sciences de l'université de Paris, Paris, France (1930)
9. Jaffar, J.: Efficient unification over infinite terms. New Gener. Comput. **2**(3), 207–219 (1984). https://link.springer.com/article/10.1007/BF03037057
10. Julián-Iranzo, P., Rubio-Manzano, C.: A similarity-based WAM for Bousi Prolog. In: Cabestany, J., Sandoval, F., Prieto, A., Corchado, J.M. (eds.) IWANN 2009. LNCS, vol. 5517, pp. 245–252. Springer, Heidelberg (2009). https://doi.org/10.1007/978-3-642-02478-8_31
11. Knight, K.: Unification: a multidisciplinary survey. ACM Comput. Surv. **21**(1), 93–124 (1989). http://citeseerx.ist.psu.edu/viewdoc/download;jsessionid=92AF7CA745E2C0B8EB619F09FFB5D3CA?doi=10.1.1.64.8967&rep=rep1&type=pdf
12. Lacoste-Julien, S., Palla, K., Davies, A., Kasneci, G., Graepel, T., Ghahramani, Z.: SiGMa: simple greedy matching for aligning large knowledge bases. In: Proceedings of the 19th ACM International Conference on Knowledge Discovery and Data Mining (SIGKDD 2013), Chicago, IL, USA, pp. 572–580. ACM, New York, 11–14 August 2013. http://snap.stanford.edu/social2012/papers/lacostejulien-palla-etal.pdf; see also https://arxiv.org/pdf/1207.4525.pdf
13. Martelli, A., Montanari, U.: An efficient unification algorithm. ACM Trans. Program. Lang. Syst. **4**(2), 258–282 (1982). http://moscova.inria.fr/levy/courses/X/IF/03/pi/levy2/martelli-montanari.pdf
14. Plotkin, G.D.: Lattice theoretic properties of subsumption. Technical Memo MIP-R-77, Department of Machine Intelligence and Perception, University of Edinburgh, Edinburgh, Scotland, UK, June 1970

15. Plotkin, G.D.: A note on inductive generalization. In: Metzer, B., Michie, D. (eds.) Machine Intelligence, Chap. 8, vol. 5, pp. 154–163. Edinburgh University Press, Edinburgh (UK) (1970), http://homepages.inf.ed.ac.uk/gdp/publications/MI5_note_ind_gen.pdf

16. Reynolds, J.C.: Transformational systems and the algebraic nature of atomic formulas. In: Metzer, B., Michie, D. (eds.) Machine Intelligence, Chap. 7, vol. 5, pp. 135–151. Edinburgh University Press, Edinburgh (1970). http://www.cs.cmu.edu/afs/cs/user/jcr/ftp/transysalg.pdf

17. Sessa, M.I.: Approximate reasoning by similarity-based SLD resolution. Theor. Comput. Sci. **275**, 389–426 (2002). http://www.sciencedirect.com/science/article/pii/S0304397501001888

18. Wayne, K.: Union-find. Tutorial lecture slides based on book "Algorithm Design" by Jon Kleinberg and Éva Tardos. Addison-Wesley (2015). https://www.cs.princeton.edu/wayne/kleinberg-tardos/pdf/UnionFind.pdf

Nominal C-Unification

Mauricio Ayala-Rincón[1]([⊠]), Washington de Carvalho-Segundo[1]([⊠]),
Maribel Fernández[2]([⊠]), and Daniele Nantes-Sobrinho[1]([⊠])

[1] Depts. de Matemática e Ciência da Computação,
Universidade de Brasília, Brasília, Brazil
{ayala,dnantes}@unb.br, wtonribeiro@gmail.com
[2] Department of Informatics, King's College London, London, UK
maribel.fernandez@kcl.ac.uk

Abstract. Nominal unification is an extension of first-order unification that takes into account the α-equivalence relation generated by binding operators, following the nominal approach. We propose a sound and complete procedure for nominal unification with commutative operators, or nominal C-unification for short, which has been formalised in Coq. The procedure transforms nominal C-unification problems into simpler (finite families) of *fixed point* constraints, whose solutions can be generated by algebraic techniques on combinatorics of permutations.

1   Introduction

Unification, where the goal is to solve equations between first-order terms, is a key notion in logic programming systems, type inference algorithms, protocol analysis tools, theorem provers, etc. Solutions to unification problems are represented by substitutions that map variables $(X, Y, \dots)$ to terms.

When terms include binding operators, a more general notion of unification is needed: unification modulo α-equivalence. In this paper, we follow the nominal approach to the specification of binding operators [20,26,30], where the syntax of terms includes, in addition to variables, also *atoms* $(a, b, \dots)$, which can be abstracted, and α-equivalence is axiomatised by means of a *freshness relation* $a\#t$ and *name-swappings* $(a\ b)$. For example, the first-order logic formula $\forall a.a \geq 0$ can be written as a nominal term $\forall([a]geq(a,0))$, using function symbols $\forall$ and geq and an abstracted atom a. Nominal unification [30] is the problem of solving equations between nominal terms modulo α-equivalence; it is a decidable problem and efficient nominal unification algorithms are available [9,11,24], that compute solutions consisting of *freshness contexts* (containing freshness constraints of the form $a\#X$) and substitutions.

In many applications, operators obey equational axioms. Nominal reasoning and unification have been extended to deal with equational theories presented by rewrite rules (see, e.g., [5,17,18]) or defined by equational axioms (see, e.g., [14,

Work supported by the Brazilian agencies FAPDF (DE 193.001.369/2016), CAPES (Proc. 88881.132034/2016-01, 2nd author) and CNPq (PQ 307009/2013, 1st author).

F. Fioravanti and J. P. Gallagher (Eds.): LOPSTR 2017, LNCS 10855, pp. 235–251, 2018.
https://doi.org/10.1007/978-3-319-94460-9_14

19]). The case of associative and commutative nominal theories was considered in [3], where a parametric $\{\alpha, AC\}$-equivalence relation was formalised in Coq. However, only equational deduction was considered (not unification). In this paper, we study nominal C-unification.

Contributions: We present a nominal C-unification algorithm, based on a set of *simplification rules*. The algorithm transforms a given *nominal C-unification problem* $\langle \Delta, Q \rangle$, where Δ is a freshness context and Q a set of freshness constraints and equations, respectively of the form $a\#_?s$ and $s \approx_? t$, into a finite set of triples of the form $\langle \nabla, \sigma, P \rangle$, consisting of a freshness context ∇, a substitution σ and a set of fixed point equations (for short, FP equations) P of the form $\pi.X \approx_? X$. The simplifications are based on a set of deduction rules for freshness and α-C-equivalence (denoted as $\approx_{\{\alpha,C\}}$).

The role of FP equations in nominal C-unification is tricky: while in standard nominal unification [30], solving a FP equation of the form $(a\ b).X \approx_? X$ reduces to checking whether the constraints $a\#X, b\#X$ (a and b fresh in X) are satisfied, and in this case the solution is the *identity* substitution, in nominal C-unification, for $*$ and $+$ commutative operators, one can have additional combinatory solutions of the form $\{X/a+b\}, \{X/(a+b)*\dots*(a+b)\}, \{X/f(a)+f(b)\}$, etc. We show that in general there is no finitary representation of solutions using only freshness contexts and substitutions, hence a nominal C-unification problem may have a potentially infinite set of independent most general unifiers (unlike standard C-unification, which is well-known to be finitary).

We adapt the proof of NP-completeness of syntactic C-unification to show that nominal C-unification is NP-complete as well. Soundness and completeness of the simplification rules were formalised in Coq. The formalisation, an extended version of the paper with all proof details and an OCaml implementation are available at http://ayala.mat.unb.br/publications.html.

Related work: To generate the set of combinatorial solutions for FP equations we can use an enumeration procedure given in [4], which is based on the combinatorics of permutations. By combining the simplification and enumeration methods, we obtain a nominal C-unification procedure in two phases: a *simplification phase*, described in this paper, which outputs a finite set of most general solutions that may include FP constraints, and a *generation phase*, which eliminates the FP constraints according to [4].

Several extensions of the nominal unification algorithm have been defined, in addition to the equational extensions already mentioned.

An algorithm for nominal unification of higher-order expressions with recursive *let* was proposed in [23]; as in the case of nominal C-unification, FP equations are obtained in the process. Using the techniques in [4], it is possible to proceed further and generate the combinatorial solutions of FP equations.

Recently, Aoto and Kikuchi [1] proposed a rule-based procedure for nominal equivariant unification [13], an extension of nominal unification that is useful in confluence analysis of nominal rewriting systems [2,16].

Furthermore, several formalisations and implementations of the nominal unification algorithm are available. For example, formalisations of its soundness and completeness were developed by Urban et al [29,30], Ayala-Rincón et al [6], and Kumar and Norrish [22] using, respectively, the proof assistants Isabelle/HOL, PVS and HOL4. An implementation in Maude using term graphs [10] is also available. Urban and Cheney used a nominal unification algorithm to develop a Prolog-like language called α-Prolog [12]. Our formalisation of nominal C-unification is based on the formalisation of equivalence modulo $\{\alpha, AC\}$ presented in [3]. The representations of permutations and terms are similar, but here we deal also with substitutions and unification rules, and prove soundness and completeness of the unification algorithm.

Reasoning modulo equational theories (but without considering the nominal approach to deal with α-equivalence) has been subject of formalisations. For instance, Nipkow [25] presented a set of Isabelle/HOL tactics for reasoning modulo A, C and AC; Braibant and Pous [8] designed a plugin for Coq, with an underlying AC-matching algorithm, that extends the system tactic `rewrite` to deal with AC function symbols; also, Contejean [15] formalised in Coq the correction of an AC-matching algorithm implemented in CiME.

Syntactic unification with commutative operators is an NP-complete problem and its solutions can be finitely generated [21,28]. Since C-unification problems are a particular case of nominal C-unification problems, our simplification algorithm, checked in Coq, is also a formalisation of the C-unification algorithm.

Organisation: Section 2 presents basic concepts and notations. Section 3 introduces the formalised equational and freshness inference rules for nominal C-unification, and briefly discusses NP-completeness; Sect. 4 shows that a single FP equation can have infinite independent solutions; Sect. 5 shortly discusses the formalisation in Coq and Sect. 6 concludes and proposes future work.

2   Background

Consider countable disjoint sets of variables $\mathcal{X} := \{X, Y, Z, \cdots\}$ and atoms $\mathcal{A} := \{a, b, c, \cdots\}$. A *permutation* π is a bijection on $\mathcal{A}$ with a finite *domain*, where the domain (i.e., the *support*) of π is the set $dom(\pi) := \{a \in \mathcal{A} \mid \pi \cdot a \neq a\}$. The inverse of π is denoted by π^{-1}. Permutations can be represented by lists of *swappings*, which are pairs of different atoms $(a\, b)$; hence a *permutation* π is a finite list of the form $(a_1\, b_1) :: \ldots :: (a_n\, b_n) :: nil$, where the empty list nil corresponds to the identity permutation; concatenation is denoted by $\oplus$ and, when no confusion may arise, $::$ and nil are omitted. We follow Gabbay's permutative convention: Atoms differ on their names, so for atoms a and b the expression $a \neq b$ is redundant. Also, $(a\, b)$ and $(b\, a)$ have identical *action*: they exchange a and b; thus, they represent the same swapping.

We will assume as in [3] countable sets of function symbols with different equational properties such as associativity, commutativity, idempotence, etc. Function symbols have superscripts that indicate their equational properties;

thus, f_k^C will denote the kth function symbol that is commutative and $f_j^\emptyset$ the jth function symbol without any equational property.

Nominal terms are generated by the following grammar:

$$s, t := \langle\rangle \mid \bar{a} \mid [a]t \mid \langle s, t \rangle \mid f_k^E t \mid \pi.X$$

$\langle\rangle$ denotes the *unit* (that is the empty tuple), $\bar{a}$ denotes an *atom term*, $[a]t$ denotes an *abstraction* of the atom a over the term t, $\langle s, t \rangle$ denotes a *pair*, $f_k^E t$ the *application* of f_k^E to t and, $\pi.X$ a *moderated variable* or *suspension*. Suspensions of the form $nil.X$ will be represented just by X.

The set of variables occurring in a term t will be denoted as $Var(t)$. This notation extends to a set S of terms in the natural way: $Var(S) = \bigcup_{t \in S} Var(t)$. As usual, $|\_|$ will be used to denote the cardinality of sets as well as to denote the size or number of symbols occurring in a given term.

Definition 1 (Permutation action). *The action of a permutation on atoms is defined as: $nil \cdot a := a$; $(b\,c) :: \pi \cdot a := \pi \cdot a$; and, $(b\,c) :: \pi \cdot b := \pi \cdot c$. The action of a permutation on terms is defined recursively as:*

$$
\begin{aligned}
\pi \cdot \langle\rangle &:= \langle\rangle & \pi \cdot \langle u, v \rangle &:= \langle \pi \cdot u, \pi \cdot v \rangle & \pi \cdot f_k^E t &:= f_k^E (\pi \cdot t) \\
\pi \cdot \bar{a} &:= \overline{\pi \cdot a} & \pi \cdot ([a]t) &:= [\pi \cdot a](\pi \cdot t) & \pi \cdot (\pi'.X) &:= (\pi' \oplus \pi).X
\end{aligned}
$$

Notice that according to the definition of the action of a permutation over atoms, the composition of permutations π and π', usually denoted as $\pi \circ \pi'$, corresponds to the append $\pi' \oplus \pi$. Also notice that $\pi' \oplus \pi \cdot t = \pi \cdot (\pi' \cdot t)$. The *difference set* between two permutations π and π' is the set of atoms where the action of π and π' differs: $ds(\pi, \pi') := \{a \in \mathcal{A} \mid \pi \cdot a \neq \pi' \cdot a\}$.

A *substitution* σ is a mapping from variables to terms such that its *domain*, $dom(\sigma) := \{X \mid X \neq X\sigma\}$, is finite. For $X \in dom(\sigma)$, $X\sigma$ is called the *image* of X. Define the *image* of σ as $im(\sigma) := \{X\sigma \mid X \in dom(\sigma)\}$. Let $dom(\sigma) = \{X_1, \cdots, X_n\}$, then σ can be represented as a set of *bindings* in the form $\{X_1/t_1, \cdots, X_n/t_n\}$, where $X_i\sigma = t_i$, for $1 \leq i \leq n$.

Definition 2 (Substitution action). *The action of a substitution σ on a term t, denoted $t\sigma$, is defined recursively as follows:*

$$
\begin{aligned}
\langle\rangle\sigma &:= \langle\rangle & \bar{a}\sigma &:= \bar{a} & (f_k^E t)\sigma &:= f_k^E t\sigma \\
\langle s, t \rangle\sigma &:= \langle s\sigma, t\sigma \rangle & ([a]t)\sigma &:= [a]t\sigma & (\pi.X)\sigma &:= \pi \cdot X\sigma
\end{aligned}
$$

The following result can be proved by induction on the structure of terms.

Lemma 1 (Substitutions and Permutations Commute). $(\pi \cdot t)\sigma = \pi \cdot (t\sigma)$

The inference rules defining freshness and α-equivalence are given in Figs. 1 and 2. The symbols ∇ and Δ are used to denote *freshness contexts* that are sets of constraints of the form $a\#X$, meaning that the atom a is fresh in X. The domain of a freshness context $dom(\nabla)$ is the set of atoms appearing in it; $\nabla|_X$ denotes the restriction of ∇ to the freshness constraints on X: $\{a\#X \mid a\#X \in \nabla\}$. The

$$\frac{}{\nabla \vdash a \# \langle \rangle}\,(\#\langle \rangle) \quad \frac{}{\nabla \vdash a \# \overline{b}}\,(\#\,\mathbf{atom}) \quad \frac{\nabla \vdash a \# t}{\nabla \vdash a \# f_k^E\, t}\,(\#\,\mathbf{app}) \quad \frac{}{\nabla \vdash a \# [a]t}\,(\#\,\mathbf{a[a]})$$

$$\frac{\nabla \vdash a \# t}{\nabla \vdash a \# [b]t}\,(\#\,\mathbf{a[b]}) \quad \frac{(\pi^{-1} \cdot a \# X) \in \nabla}{\nabla \vdash a \# \pi.X}\,(\#\,\mathbf{var}) \quad \frac{\nabla \vdash a \# s \quad \nabla \vdash a \# t}{\nabla \vdash a \# \langle s,t \rangle}\,(\#\,\mathbf{pair})$$

Fig. 1. Rules for the freshness relation

$$\frac{}{\nabla \vdash \langle \rangle \approx_\alpha \langle \rangle}\,(\approx_\alpha \langle \rangle) \quad \frac{}{\nabla \vdash \overline{a} \approx_\alpha \overline{a}}\,(\approx_\alpha \mathbf{atom}) \quad \frac{\nabla \vdash s \approx_\alpha t}{\nabla \vdash f_k^E\, s \approx_\alpha f_k^E\, t}\,(\approx_\alpha \mathbf{app})$$

$$\frac{\nabla \vdash s \approx_\alpha t}{\nabla \vdash [a]s \approx_\alpha [a]t}\,(\approx_\alpha [\mathbf{aa}]) \quad \frac{\nabla \vdash s \approx_\alpha (a\,b)\cdot t \quad \nabla \vdash a \# t}{\nabla \vdash [a]s \approx_\alpha [b]t}\,(\approx_\alpha [\mathbf{ab}])$$

$$\frac{ds(\pi,\pi')\# X \subseteq \nabla}{\nabla \vdash \pi.X \approx_\alpha \pi'.X}\,(\approx_\alpha \mathbf{var}) \quad \frac{\nabla \vdash s_0 \approx_\alpha t_0 \quad \nabla \vdash s_1 \approx_\alpha t_1}{\nabla \vdash \langle s_0,s_1 \rangle \approx_\alpha \langle t_0,t_1 \rangle}\,(\approx_\alpha \mathbf{pair})$$

Fig. 2. Rules for the relation $\approx_\alpha$

rules in Fig. 1 are used to check if an atom a is fresh in a nominal term t under a freshness context ∇, also denoted as $\nabla \vdash a\#t$. The rules in Fig. 2 are used to check if two nominal terms s and t are α-equivalent under some freshness context ∇, written as $\nabla \vdash s \approx_\alpha t$. These rules use the inference system for freshness constraints: specifically freshness constraints are used in rule $(\approx_\alpha [\mathbf{ab}])$.

Example 1. Let $\sigma = \{X/[a]a\}$. Verify that $\langle (a\,b).X, f(e) \rangle \sigma \approx_\alpha \langle X, f(e) \rangle \sigma$.

By $dom(\pi)\#X$ and $ds(\pi,\pi')\#X$ we abbreviate the sets $\{a\#X \mid a \in dom(\pi)\}$ and $\{a\#X \mid a \in ds(\pi,\pi')\}$, respectively.

Key properties of the nominal freshness and α-equivalence relations have been extensively explored in previous works [3,6,29,30].

2.1 The Relation $\approx_{\{\alpha,C\}}$ as an Extension of $\approx_\alpha$

In [3], the relation $\approx_\alpha$ was extended to deal with associative and commutative theories. Here we will consider α-equivalence modulo commutativity, denoted as $\approx_{\{\alpha,C\}}$. This means that some function symbols in our syntax are commutative, and therefore the rule for function application $(\approx_\alpha \mathbf{app})$ in Fig. 2 should be replaced by the rules in Fig. 3.

The following properties for $\approx_{\{\alpha,C\}}$ were formalised as simple adaptations of the formalisations given in [3] for $\approx_\alpha$.

Lemma 2 (Inversion). *The inference rules of $\approx_{\{\alpha,C\}}$ are invertible.*

This means, for instance, that for rules $(\approx_\alpha [\mathbf{ab}])$ one has $\nabla \vdash [a]s \approx_{\{\alpha,C\}} [b]t$ implies $\nabla \vdash s \approx_{\{\alpha,C\}} (a\,b)\cdot t$ and $\nabla \vdash a\#t$; and for $(\approx_{\{\alpha,C\}} \mathbf{app})$,

$$\frac{\nabla \vdash s \approx_{\{\alpha,C\}} t}{\nabla \vdash f_k^E \, s \approx_{\{\alpha,C\}} f_k^E \, t} \, , \quad E \neq C \text{ or both } s \text{ and } t \text{ are not pairs} \quad (\approx_{\{\alpha,\mathbf{C}\}} \mathbf{app})$$

$$\frac{\nabla \vdash s_0 \approx_{\{\alpha,C\}} t_i, \quad \nabla \vdash s_1 \approx_{\{\alpha,C\}} t_{(i+1) \, mod \, 2}}{\nabla \vdash f_k^C \, \langle s_0, s_1 \rangle \approx_{\{\alpha,C\}} f_k^C \, \langle t_0, t_1 \rangle} \, , \quad i = 0, 1 \quad (\approx_{\{\alpha,\mathbf{C}\}} \mathbf{C})$$

Fig. 3. Additional rules for $\{\alpha, C\}$-equivalence

$\nabla \vdash f_k^C \, \langle s_0, s_1 \rangle \approx_{\{\alpha,C\}} f_k^C \, \langle t_0, t_1 \rangle$ implies $\nabla \vdash s_0 \approx_{\{\alpha,C\}} t_0$ and $\nabla \vdash s_1 \approx_{\{\alpha,C\}} t_1$, or $\nabla \vdash s_0 \approx_{\{\alpha,C\}} t_1$ and $\nabla \vdash s_1 \approx_{\{\alpha,C\}} t_0$.

Lemma 3 (Freshness preservation). *If $\nabla \vdash a \# s$ and $\nabla \vdash s \approx_{\{\alpha,C\}} t$ then $\nabla \vdash a \# t$.*

Lemma 4 (Intermediate transitivity for $\approx_{\{\alpha,C\}}$ with $\approx_\alpha$). *If $\nabla \vdash s \approx_{\{\alpha,C\}} t$ and $\nabla \vdash t \approx_\alpha u$ then $\nabla \vdash s \approx_{\{\alpha,C\}} u$.*

Lemma 5 (Equivariance). $\nabla \vdash \pi \cdot s \approx_{\{\alpha,C\}} \pi \cdot t$ *whenever* $\nabla \vdash s \approx_{\{\alpha,C\}} t$.

Lemma 6 (Equivalence). $\_ \vdash \_ \approx_{\{\alpha,C\}} \_$ *is an equivalence relation.*

Remark 1. According to the grammar for nominal terms, function symbols have no fixed arity: any function symbol can apply to any term. Despite this, in the syntax of our Coq formalisation commutative symbols apply only to tuples.

3   A Nominal C-Unification Algorithm

Inference rules are given that transform a nominal C-unification problem into a finite family of problems that consist exclusively of FP equations of the form $\pi.X \approx_? X$, together with a substitution and a set of freshness constraints.

Definition 3 (Unification problem). *A unification problem is a pair $\langle \nabla, P \rangle$, where ∇ is a freshness context and P is a finite set of equations and freshness constraints of the form $s \approx_? t$ and $a \# ? s$, respectively, where $\approx_?$ is symmetric, s and t are terms and a is an atom. Nominal terms in the equations preserve the syntactic restriction that commutative symbols are only applied to tuples.*

Given $\langle \nabla, P \rangle$, by $P_\approx, P_\#, P_{\mathrm{fp}_\approx}$ and $P_{\mathrm{nfp}_\approx}$ we will resp. denote the sets of equations, freshness constraints, FP and non FP equations in the set P.

Example 2. Given the nominal unification problem $\mathcal{P} = \langle \emptyset, \{[a][b]X \approx_? [b][a]X\} \rangle$, the standard unification algorithm [30] reduces it to $\langle \emptyset, \{X \approx_? (a\,b).X\} \rangle$, which gives the solution $\langle \{a\#X, b\#X\}, id \rangle$. However, we will see that infinite independent solutions are feasible when there is at least a commutative operator.

We design a nominal C-unification algorithm using one set of transformation rules to deal with equations (Fig. 4) and another set of rules to deal with freshness constraints and contexts (Fig. 5). These rules act over triples of the form $\langle \nabla, \sigma, P \rangle$, where σ is a substitution. The triple that will be associated by default with a unification problem $\langle \nabla, P \rangle$ is $\langle \nabla, id, P \rangle$. We will use calligraphic uppercase letters (e.g., $\mathcal{P}, \mathcal{Q}, \mathcal{R}$, etc) to denote triples.

Remark 2. Let ∇ and ∇' be freshness contexts and σ and σ' be substitutions.

- $\nabla' \vdash \nabla\sigma$ denotes that $\nabla' \vdash a \# X\sigma$ holds for each $(a\#X) \in \nabla$, and
- $\nabla \vdash \sigma \approx \sigma'$ that $\nabla \vdash X\sigma \approx_{\{a,C\}} X\sigma'$ for all X (in $dom(\sigma) \cup dom(\sigma')$).

Definition 4 (Solution for a triple or problem). *A solution for a triple $\mathcal{P} = \langle \Delta, \delta, P \rangle$ is a pair $\langle \nabla, \sigma \rangle$, where the following conditions are satisfied:*

1. $\nabla \vdash \Delta\sigma$;
2. $\nabla \vdash a \# t\sigma$, *if* $a\#_? t \in P$;
3. $\nabla \vdash s\sigma \approx_{\{a,C\}} t\sigma$, *if* $s \approx_? t \in P$;
4. *there is a substitution λ such that* $\nabla \vdash \delta\lambda \approx \sigma$.

A solution for a unification problem $\langle \Delta, P \rangle$ is a solution for the associated triple $\langle \Delta, id, P \rangle$. The solution set for a problem or triple $\mathcal{P}$ is denoted by $\mathcal{U}_C(\mathcal{P})$.

Definition 5 (More general solution and complete set of solutions). *For $\langle \nabla, \sigma \rangle$ and $\langle \nabla', \sigma' \rangle$ in $\mathcal{U}_C(\mathcal{P})$, we say that $\langle \nabla, \sigma \rangle$ is more general than $\langle \nabla', \sigma' \rangle$, denoted $\langle \nabla, \sigma \rangle \preccurlyeq \langle \nabla', \sigma' \rangle$, if there exists a substitution λ satisfying $\nabla' \vdash \sigma\lambda \approx \sigma'$ and $\nabla' \vdash \nabla\lambda$. A subset $\mathcal{V}$ of $\mathcal{U}_C(\mathcal{P})$ is said to be a complete set of solutions of $\mathcal{P}$ if for all $\langle \nabla', \sigma' \rangle \in \mathcal{U}_C(\mathcal{P})$, there exists $\langle \nabla, \sigma \rangle$ in $\mathcal{V}$ such that $\langle \nabla, \sigma \rangle \preccurlyeq \langle \nabla', \sigma' \rangle$.*

We will denote the set of variables occurring in the set P of a problem $\langle \Delta, P \rangle$ or triple $\mathcal{P} = \langle \nabla, \sigma, P \rangle$ as $Var(P)$. We also will write $Var(\mathcal{P})$ to denote this set.

The unification algorithm proceeds by simplification. Derivation with rules of Figs. 4 and 5 is respectively denoted by $\Rightarrow_\approx$ and $\Rightarrow_\#$. Thus, $\langle \nabla, \sigma, P \rangle \Rightarrow_\approx \langle \nabla, \sigma', P' \rangle$ means that the second triple is obtained from the first one by application of one rule. We will use the standard rewriting nomenclature, e.g., we will say that $\mathcal{P}$ is a *normal form* or *irreducible* by $\Rightarrow_\approx$, denoted by $\Rightarrow_\approx$-*nf*, whenever there is no $\mathcal{Q}$ such that $\mathcal{P} \Rightarrow_\approx \mathcal{Q}$; $\Rightarrow_\approx^*$ and $\Rightarrow_\approx^+$ denote respectively derivations in zero or more and one or more applications of the rules in Fig. 4.

The only rule that can generate branches is $(\approx_? \mathbf{C})$, which is an abbreviation for two rules providing the different forms in which one can relate the arguments s and t in an equation $f_k^C s \approx_? f_k^C t$ for a commutative function symbol (s, t are tuples, by the syntactic restriction in Definition 3): either $\langle s_0, s_1 \rangle \approx_? \langle t_0, t_1 \rangle$ or $\langle s_0, s_1 \rangle \approx_? \langle t_1, t_0 \rangle$.

The syntactic restriction on arguments of commutative symbols being only tuples, is not crucial since any equation of the form $f_k^C \pi.X \approx_? t$ can be translated into an equation of form $f_k^C \langle \pi.X_1, \pi.X_2 \rangle \approx_? t$, where X_1 and X_2 are new variables and ∇ is extended to ∇' in such a way that both X_1 and X_2 inherit all freshness constraints of X in ∇: $\nabla' = \nabla \cup \{a\#X_i \mid i = 1, 2, \text{ and } a\#X \in \nabla\}$.

$$\frac{\langle \nabla, \sigma, P \uplus \{s \approx_? s\}\rangle}{\langle \nabla, \sigma, P\rangle} \; (\approx_? \; \mathbf{refl}) \qquad \frac{\langle \nabla, \sigma, P \uplus \{\langle s_1, t_1\rangle \approx_? \langle s_2, t_2\rangle\}\rangle}{\langle \nabla, \sigma, P \cup \{s_1 \approx_? s_2, t_1 \approx_? t_2\}\rangle} \; (\approx_? \; \mathbf{pair})$$

$$\frac{\langle \nabla, \sigma, P \uplus \{f_k^E \, s \approx_? f_k^E \, t\}\rangle}{\langle \nabla, \sigma, P \cup \{s \approx_? t\}\rangle}, \text{ if } E \neq C \; (\approx_? \; \mathbf{app})$$

$$\frac{\langle \nabla, \sigma, P \uplus \{f_k^C \, s \approx_? f_k^C \, t\}\rangle}{\langle \nabla, \sigma, P \cup \{s \approx_? v\}\rangle}, \left\{ \begin{array}{l} \text{where } s = \langle s_0, s_1\rangle \text{ and } t = \langle t_0, t_1\rangle \\ v = \langle t_i, t_{(i+1) \bmod 2}\rangle, i = 0, 1 \end{array} \right\} (\approx_? \; \mathbf{C})$$

$$\frac{\langle \nabla, \sigma, P \uplus \{[a]s \approx_? [a]t\}\rangle}{\langle \nabla, \sigma, P \cup \{s \approx_? t\}\rangle} \; (\approx_? \; [\mathbf{aa}]) \qquad \frac{\langle \nabla, \sigma, P \uplus \{[a]s \approx_? [b]t\}\rangle}{\langle \nabla, \sigma, P \cup \{s \approx_? (a\,b)\,t, a\#_?t\}\rangle} \; (\approx_? \; [\mathbf{ab}])$$

$$\frac{\langle \nabla, \sigma, P \uplus \{\pi.X \approx_? t\}\rangle \; \text{let } \sigma' := \sigma\{X/\pi^{-1} \cdot t\}}{\left\langle \nabla, \sigma', P\{X/\pi^{-1} \cdot t\} \; \cup \bigcup\limits_{\substack{Y \in dom(\sigma'), \\ a\#Y \in \nabla}} \{a\#_?Y\sigma'\} \right\rangle}, \text{ if } X \notin Var(t) \; (\approx_? \; \mathbf{inst})$$

$$\frac{\langle \nabla, \sigma, P \uplus \{\pi.X \approx_? \pi'.X\}\rangle}{\langle \nabla, \sigma, P \cup \{\pi \oplus (\pi')^{-1}.X \approx_? X\}\rangle}, \text{ if } \pi' \neq nil \; (\approx_? \; \mathbf{inv})$$

Fig. 4. Reduction rules for equational problems

In the rule ($\approx_?$ **inst**) the inclusion of new constraints in the problem, given in $\bigcup\limits_{\substack{Y \in dom(\sigma'), \\ a\#Y \in \nabla}} \{a\#_?Y\sigma'\}$ is necessary to guarantee that the new substitution σ' is *compatible* with the freshness context ∇.

Examples 3, 4 and 5 are running examples of the C-unification procedure. A graphic representation of the derivation tree for these examples, generated using the OCaml implementation, is depicted in the extended version of this paper.

Example 3. Let $*^1$ be a commutative function symbol. Below, we show how the problem $\mathcal{P} = \langle \emptyset, \{[e](a\,b).X * Y \approx_? [f](a\,c)(c\,d).X * Y\}\rangle$ reduces (via rules

$$\frac{\langle \nabla, \sigma, P \uplus \{a\#_?\langle\rangle\}\rangle}{\langle \nabla, \sigma, P\rangle} \; (\#_?\langle\rangle) \qquad \frac{\langle \nabla, \sigma, P \uplus \{a\#_?\bar{b}\}\rangle}{\langle \nabla, \sigma, P\rangle} \; (\#_?\mathbf{a\bar{b}})$$

$$\frac{\langle \nabla, \sigma, P \uplus \{a\#_?f\,t\}\rangle}{\langle \nabla, \sigma, P \cup \{a\#_?t\}\rangle} \; (\#_?\mathbf{app}) \qquad \frac{\langle \nabla, \sigma, P \uplus \{a\#_?[a]t\}\rangle}{\langle \nabla, \sigma, P\rangle} \; (\#_?\mathbf{a[a]})$$

$$\frac{\langle \nabla, \sigma, P \uplus \{a\#_?[b]t\}\rangle}{\langle \nabla, \sigma, P \cup \{a\#_?t\}\rangle} \; (\#_?\mathbf{a[b]}) \qquad \frac{\langle \nabla, \sigma, P \uplus \{a\#_?\pi.X\}\rangle}{\langle \{(\pi^{-1} \cdot a)\#X\} \cup \nabla, \sigma, P\rangle} \; (\#_?\mathbf{var})$$

$$\frac{\langle \nabla, \sigma, P \uplus \{a\#_?\langle s, t\rangle\}\rangle}{\langle \nabla, \sigma, P \cup \{a\#_?s, a\#_?t\}\rangle} \; (\#_?\mathbf{pair})$$

Fig. 5. Reduction rules for freshness problems

---

[1] Infix notation is adopted for commutative symbols: $s * t$ abbreviates $*\langle s, t\rangle$.

in Figs. 4 and 5). Application of rule ($\approx_?$ **C**) gives two branches that reduce into two FP problems: $\mathcal{Q}_1$ and $\mathcal{Q}_2$. Highlighted terms show where the rules are applied. For brevity, let $\pi_1 = (a\,c)(c\,d)(e\,f)$, $\pi_2 = (a\,b)(e\,f)(c\,d)(a\,c)$, $\pi_3 = (a\,c)(c\,d)(e\,f)(a\,b)$ and $\sigma = \{X/(e\,f)(a\,b).Y\}$.

$\langle \emptyset, id, \{\ [e](a\,b).X * Y \approx_? [f](a\,c)(c\,d).X * Y\ \}\rangle$ $\Rightarrow_{(\approx_?[\mathbf{ab}])}$

$\langle \emptyset, id, \{\ (a\,b).X * Y \approx_? \pi_1.X * (e\,f).Y\ ,\ e\#_?(a\,c)(c\,d).X * Y\}\rangle \Rightarrow_{(\approx_?\mathbf{C})}$

branch 1: $\langle \emptyset, id, \{\ (a\,b).X \approx_? \pi_1.X\ ,\ Y \approx_? (e\,f).Y\ ,\ e\#_?(a\,c)(c\,d).X * Y\}\rangle$

$\Rightarrow_{(\approx_?\mathbf{inv})}(2\times)$ $\langle \emptyset, id, \{(a\,b)[\pi_1]^{-1}.X \approx_? X,\ [(e\,f)]^{-1}.Y \approx_? Y,\ e\#_?(a\,c)(c\,d).X * Y\ \}\rangle$

$\Rightarrow_{(\#_?\mathbf{app}),}$ $\langle \emptyset, id, \{\pi_2.X \approx_? X, (e\,f).Y \approx_? Y,\ e\#_?(a\,c)(c\,d).X\ ,\ e\#_?Y\ \}\rangle$
$\quad(\#_?\mathbf{pair})$

$\Rightarrow_{(\#_?\mathbf{var})}(2\times)$ $\langle \{e\#X, e\#Y\}, id, \{\pi_2.X \approx_? X, (e\,f).Y \approx_? Y\}\rangle = \mathcal{Q}_1$

branch 2: $\langle \emptyset, id, \{\ (a\,b).X \approx_? (e\,f).Y\ ,\ Y \approx_? \pi_1.X,\ e\#_?(a\,c)(c\,d).X * Y\}\rangle$

$\Rightarrow_{(\approx_?\mathbf{inst})}$ $\langle \emptyset, \sigma, \{\ Y \approx_? (a\,c)(c\,d)(e\,f)(e\,f)[(a\,b)]^{-1}.Y\ , e\#_?\pi_1[(a\,b)]^{-1}.Y * Y\}\rangle$

$\Rightarrow_{(\approx_?\mathbf{inv})}$ $\langle \emptyset, \sigma, \{[(a\,c)(c\,d)(a\,b)]^{-1}.Y \approx_? Y,\ e\#_?\pi_3.Y * Y\ \}\rangle$

$\Rightarrow_{(\#_?\mathbf{app}),}$ $\langle \emptyset, \sigma, \{(a\,b)(c\,d)(a\,c).Y \approx_? Y,\ e\#_?\pi_3.Y\ ,\ e\#_?Y\ \}\rangle$
$\quad(\#_?\mathbf{pair})$

$\Rightarrow_{(\#_?\mathbf{var})}(2\times)$ $\langle \{e\#Y, f\#Y\}, \sigma, \{(a\,b)(c\,d)(a\,c).Y \approx_? Y\}\rangle = \mathcal{Q}_2$

Definition 6 (Set of $\Rightarrow_\approx$ and $\Rightarrow_\#$-normal forms). *We denote by $\mathcal{P}_{\Rightarrow_\approx}$ (resp. $\mathcal{P}_{\Rightarrow_\#}$) the set of normal forms of $\mathcal{P}$ with respect to $\Rightarrow_\approx$ (resp. $\Rightarrow_\#$).*

Definition 7 (Fail and success for $\Rightarrow_\approx$). *Let $\mathcal{P}$ be a triple, such that the rules in Fig. 4 give rise to a normal form $\langle \nabla, \sigma, P\rangle$. The rules in Fig. 4 are said to fail if P contains non FP equations. Otherwise $\langle \nabla, \sigma, P\rangle$ is called a successful triple regarding $\Rightarrow_\approx$ (i.e., in a successful triple, P consists only of FP equations and, possibly, freshness constraints).*

The rules in Fig. 5 will only be applied to successful triples regarding $\Rightarrow_\approx$.

Definition 8 (Fail and success for $\Rightarrow_\#$). *Let $\mathcal{Q} = \langle \nabla, \sigma, Q\rangle$ be a successful triple regarding $\Rightarrow_\approx$, and $\mathcal{Q}' = \langle \nabla', \sigma, Q'\rangle$ its normal form via rules in Fig. 5, that is $\mathcal{Q} \Rightarrow_\#^* \mathcal{Q}'$ and $\mathcal{Q}'$ is in $\mathcal{Q}_{\Rightarrow_\#}$. If Q' contains freshness constraints it is said that $\Rightarrow_\#$ fails for $\mathcal{Q}$; otherwise, $\mathcal{Q}'$ will be called a successful triple for $\Rightarrow_\#$.*

Remark 3. Since in a successful triple regarding $\Rightarrow_\approx$, $\mathcal{Q}$, one has only FP equations and $\Rightarrow_\#$ acts only over freshness constraints, Q' in the definition above contains only FP equations and freshness constraints. Also, by a simple case analysis on t one can check that any triple with freshness constraints $a\#_?t$ is reducible by $\Rightarrow_\#$, except when $t \equiv \bar{a}$. Hence the freshness constraints in Q' would be only of the form $a\#_?\bar{a}$.

The relation $\Rightarrow_\approx$, starts from a triple with the identity substitution and always maintains a triple $\langle \nabla, \sigma', P'\rangle$ in which the substitution σ' does not affect the current problem P'. The same happens for $\Rightarrow_\#$ since the substitution does not change with this relation. This motivates the next definition and lemma.

Definition 9 (Valid triple). $\mathcal{P} = \langle \nabla, \sigma, P \rangle$ is valid *if* $im(\sigma) \cap dom(\sigma) = \emptyset$ *and* $dom(\sigma) \cap Var(P) = \emptyset$.

Remark 4. A substitution σ in a valid triple $\mathcal{P}$ is *idempotent*, that is, $\sigma\sigma = \sigma$.

Lemma 7 is proved by case analysis on the rules used by $\Rightarrow_{\approx}$ and $\Rightarrow_{\#}$.

Lemma 7 (Preservation of valid triples). *If* $\mathcal{P} = \langle \nabla, \sigma, P \rangle$ *is valid and* $\mathcal{P} \Rightarrow_{\approx} \cup \Rightarrow_{\#} \mathcal{P}' = \langle \nabla', \sigma', P' \rangle$, *then* $\mathcal{P}'$ *is also valid.*

From now on, we consider only valid triples.

Lemma 8 (Termination of $\Rightarrow_{\approx}$ and $\Rightarrow_{\#}$). *There is no infinite chain of reductions* $\Rightarrow_{\approx}$ *(or* $\Rightarrow_{\#}$*) starting from an arbitrary triple* $\mathcal{P} = \langle \nabla, \sigma, P \rangle$.

Proof. – The proof for $\Rightarrow_{\approx}$ is by well-founded induction on $\mathcal{P}$ using the measure $\|\mathcal{P}\| = \langle |Var(P_{\approx})|, \|P\|, |P_{nfp_{\approx}}| \rangle$ with a lexicographic ordering, where $\|P\| = \sum_{s \approx_? t \in P_{\approx}} |s| + |t| + \sum_{a \#_? u \in P_{\#}} |u|$. Note that this measure decreases after each step $\langle \nabla, \sigma, P \rangle \Rightarrow_{\approx} \langle \nabla, \sigma', P' \rangle$: for ($\approx_?$ **inst**), $|Var(P_{\approx})| > |Var(P'_{\approx})|$; for ($\approx_?$ **refl**), ($\approx_?$ **pair**), ($\approx_?$ **app**), ($\approx_?$ **[aa]**), ($\approx_?$ **[ab]**) and ($\approx_?$ **C**), $|Var(P_{\approx})| \geq |Var(P'_{\approx})|$, but $\|P\| > \|P'\|$; and, for ($\approx_?$ **inv**), both $|Var(P_{\approx})| = |Var(P' \approx)|$ and $\|P\| = \|P'\|$, but $|P_{nfp_{\approx}}| > |P'_{nfp_{\approx}}|$.
 – The proof for $\Rightarrow_{\#}$ is by induction on $\mathcal{P}$ using as measure $\|P_{\#}\|$. It can be checked that this measure decreases after each step: $\langle \nabla, \sigma, P \rangle \Rightarrow_{\#} \langle \nabla, \sigma', P' \rangle$.

To solve a unification problem, $\langle \nabla, P \rangle$, one builds the derivation tree for $\Rightarrow_{\approx}$, labelling the root node with $\langle \nabla, id, P \rangle$. This tree has leaves labelled with $\Rightarrow_{\approx}$-nf's that are either failing or successful triples. Then, the tree is extended by building $\Rightarrow_{\#}$-derivations starting from all successful leaves. The extended tree will include failing leaves and successful leaves. The successful leaves will be labelled by triples $\mathcal{P}'$ in which the problem P' consists only of FP equations. Since $\Rightarrow_{\approx}$ and $\Rightarrow_{\#}$ are both terminating (Lemma 8), the process described above must be also terminating.

Definition 10 (Derivation tree for $\langle \Delta, P \rangle$). *A derivation tree for the unification problem* $\langle \Delta, P \rangle$, *denoted as* $\mathcal{T}_{\langle \Delta, P \rangle}$, *is a tree with root label* $\mathcal{P} = \langle \Delta, id, P \rangle$ *built in two stages:*

- *Initially, a tree is built, whose branches end in leaf nodes labelled with the triples in* $P_{\Rightarrow_{\approx}}$. *The labels in each path from the root to a leaf correspond to a* $\Rightarrow_{\approx}$*-derivation.*
- *Further, for each leaf labelled with a successful triple* Q *in* $P_{\Rightarrow_{\approx}}$, *the tree is extended with a path to a new leaf that is labelled with a* $\bar{Q} \in Q_{\Rightarrow_{\#}}$. *The labels in the extended path from the node with label* Q *to the new leaf correspond to a* $\Rightarrow_{\#}$*-derivation.*

Remark 5. For $\langle \Delta, P \rangle$, all labels in the nodes of $\mathcal{T}_{\langle \Delta, P \rangle}$ are *valid* by Lemma 7.

The next lemma is proved by case analysis on elements of $\mathcal{P}_{\Rightarrow_{\approx}}$ and $\mathcal{P}_{\Rightarrow_{\#}}$.

Lemma 9 (Characterisation of leaves of $\mathcal{T}_{\langle \Delta, P \rangle}$). *Let $\langle \Delta, P \rangle$ be a unification problem. If $\mathcal{P}' = \langle \nabla, \sigma', P' \rangle$ is the label of a leaf in $\mathcal{T}_{\langle \Delta, P \rangle}$, then P' can be partitioned as follows: $P' = P'' \cup P_{\perp}$, where P'' is the set of all FP equations in P' and $P_{\perp} = P' - P''$. If $P_{\perp} \neq \emptyset$ then $\mathcal{U}_C(\mathcal{P}') = \emptyset$.*

The next definition is motivated by the previous characterisation of the labels of leaves in derivation trees.

Definition 11 (Successful leaves). *Let $\langle \Delta, P \rangle$ be a unification problem. A leaf in $\mathcal{T}_{\langle \Delta, P \rangle}$ that is labelled with a triple of the form $\mathcal{Q} = \langle \nabla, \sigma, Q \rangle$, where Q consists only of FP equations, is called a* successful leaf *of $\mathcal{T}_{\langle \Delta, P \rangle}$. In this case $\mathcal{Q}$ is called a* successful triple *of $\mathcal{T}_{\langle \Delta, P \rangle}$. The sets of successful leaves and triples of $\mathcal{T}_{\langle \Delta, P \rangle}$ are denoted respectively by $SL(\mathcal{T}_{\langle \Delta, P \rangle})$ and $ST(\mathcal{T}_{\langle \Delta, P \rangle})$.*

The soundness theorem states that successful leaves of $\mathcal{T}_{\langle \Delta, P \rangle}$ produce *correct* solutions. The proof is by induction on the number of steps of $\Rightarrow_{\approx}$ and $\Rightarrow_{\#}$ and uses Lemma 9 and auxiliary results on the *preservation of solutions* by $\Rightarrow_{\approx}$ and $\Rightarrow_{\#}$. Proving preservation of solutions for rules ($\approx_? [\mathbf{ab}]$) and ($\approx_?$ **inst**) is not straightforward and uses Lemmas 1, 2, 3 and 5 to check that the four conditions of Definition 4 are valid before, if one supposes their validity after the rule application.

Theorem 1 (Soundness of $\mathcal{T}_{\langle \Delta, P \rangle}$). *$\mathcal{T}_{\langle \Delta, P \rangle}$ is correct, i.e., if $\mathcal{P}' = \langle \nabla, \sigma, P' \rangle$ is the label of a leaf in $\mathcal{T}_{\langle \Delta, P \rangle}$, then 1. $\mathcal{U}_C(\mathcal{P}') \subseteq \mathcal{U}_C(\langle \Delta, id, P \rangle)$, and 2. if P' contains non FP equations or freshness constraints then $\mathcal{U}_C(\mathcal{P}') = \emptyset$.*

The completeness theorem guarantees that the set of successful triples provides a complete set of solutions. Its proof uses case analysis on the rules of the relations $\Rightarrow_{\approx}$ and $\Rightarrow_{\#}$ by an argumentation similar to the one used for Theorem 1. For $\Rightarrow_{\#}$ one has indeed equivalence: $\mathcal{P} \Rightarrow_{\#} \mathcal{P}'$, implies $\mathcal{U}_C(\mathcal{P}) = \mathcal{U}_C(\mathcal{P}')$. The same is true for all rules of the relation $\Rightarrow_{\approx}$ except the branching rule ($\approx_? \mathbf{C}$), for which it is necessary to prove that all solutions of a triple reduced by ($\approx_? \mathbf{C}$) must belong to the set of solutions of one of its children triples.

Theorem 2 (Completeness of $\mathcal{T}_{\langle \Delta, P \rangle}$). *Let $\langle \Delta, P \rangle$ and $\mathcal{T}_{\langle \Delta, P \rangle}$ be a unification problem and its derivation tree. Then $\mathcal{U}_C(\langle \Delta, id, P \rangle) = \bigcup_{\mathcal{Q} \in ST(\mathcal{T}_{\langle \Delta, P \rangle})} \mathcal{U}_C(\mathcal{Q})$.*

Corollary 1 (Generality of successful triples). *Let $\mathcal{P} = \langle \Delta, P \rangle$ be a unification problem and $\langle \nabla'', \sigma' \rangle \in \mathcal{U}_C(\mathcal{P})$. Then there exists a successful triple $\mathcal{Q} \in ST(\mathcal{T}_{\langle \Delta, P \rangle})$ where $\mathcal{Q} = \langle \nabla, \sigma, Q \rangle$ such that $\langle \nabla'', \sigma' \rangle \in \mathcal{U}_C(\mathcal{Q})$, and hence, $\nabla'' \vdash \nabla \sigma'$ and there exists λ such that $\nabla'' \vdash \sigma \lambda \approx \sigma'$.*

Proof. By Theorem 2, $\mathcal{U}_C(\mathcal{P}) = \bigcup_{\mathcal{P}' \in ST(\mathcal{T}_{\langle \Delta, P \rangle})} \mathcal{U}_C(\mathcal{P}')$. Then there exists $\mathcal{Q} \in ST(\mathcal{T}_{\langle \Delta, P \rangle})$ such that $\langle \nabla'', \sigma' \rangle \in \mathcal{U}_C(\mathcal{Q})$. Suppose $\mathcal{Q} = \langle \nabla, \sigma, Q \rangle$. Then by the first and fourth conditions of the definition of solution (Definition 4) we have that $\nabla'' \vdash \nabla \sigma'$ and there exists λ such that $\nabla'' \vdash \sigma \lambda \approx \sigma'$.

Remark 6. The nominal C-unification problem is to decide, for a given $\mathcal{P}$, if $\mathcal{U}_C(\mathcal{P})$ is non empty; that is, whether $\mathcal{P}$ has nominal C-unifiers. To prove that this problem is in NP, a non-deterministic procedure using the reduction rules in the same order as in Definition 10 is designed. In this procedure, whenever rule $(\approx_? \mathbf{C})$ applies, only one of the two possible branches is guessed. In this manner, if the derivation tree has a successful leaf, this procedure will guess a path to the successful leaf, answering positively to the decision problem. According to the measures used in the proof of termination (Lemma 8), reduction with both the relations $\Rightarrow_\approx$ and $\Rightarrow_\#$ is polynomially bound, which implies that this non-deterministic procedure is polynomially bound.

To prove NP-completeness, one can polynomially reduce the well-known NP-complete positive 1-in-3-SAT problem into nominal C-unification, as done in [7] for the C-unification problem. An instance of the positive 1-in-3-SAT problem consists of a set of clauses $\mathcal{C} = \{\mathcal{C}_i | 1 \leq i \leq n\}$, where each $\mathcal{C}_i$ is a disjunction of three propositional variables, say $\mathcal{C}_i = p_i \vee q_i \vee r_i$. A solution of $\mathcal{C}$ is a valuation with exactly one variable true in each clause. The proposed reduction of $\mathcal{C}$ into a nominal C-unification problem would require just a commutative function symbol, say $\oplus$, two atoms, say a and b, a variable for each clause $\mathcal{C}_i$, say Y_i, and a variable for each propositional variable p in $\mathcal{C}$, say X_p. Instantiating X_p as $\overline{a}$ or $\overline{b}$, would be interpreted as evaluating p as true or false, respectively. Each clause $\mathcal{C}_i = p_i \vee q_i \vee r_i$ in $\mathcal{C}$ is translated into an equation E_i of the form $((X_{p_i} \oplus X_{q_i}) \oplus X_{r_i}) \oplus Y_i \approx_? ((\overline{b} \oplus \overline{b}) \oplus \overline{a}) \oplus ((\overline{b} \oplus \overline{a}) \oplus \overline{b})$. The nominal C-unification problem for $\mathcal{C}$ is given by $\mathcal{P}_\mathcal{C} = \langle \emptyset, \{E_i | 1 \leq i \leq n\}\rangle$. Simplifying $\mathcal{P}_\mathcal{C}$ would not introduce freshness constraints since the problem does not include abstractions. Thus, to conclude it is only necessary to check that $\langle \emptyset, \sigma \rangle$ is a solution for $\mathcal{P}_\mathcal{C}$ if and only if σ instantiates exactly one of the variables X_{p_i}, X_{q_i} and X_{r_i} in each equation with $\overline{a}$ and the other two with $\overline{b}$, which means that $\mathcal{C}$ has a solution.

4   Generation of Solutions for Successful Leaves of $\mathcal{T}_{\langle \Delta, P \rangle}$

To build solutions for a successful leaf $\mathcal{P} = \langle \nabla, \sigma, P \rangle$ in the derivation tree of a given unification problem, we will select and combine solutions generated for FP equations $\pi.X \approx_? X$, for each $X \in Var(P)$. We introduce the notion of *pseudo-cycle of a permutation*, in order to provide precise conditions to build terms t by combining the atoms in $dom(\pi)$, such that $\pi \cdot t \approx_{\{\alpha, C\}} t$. For convenience, we use the algebraic cycle representation of permutations. Thus, instead of sequences of swappings, permutations in nominal terms will be read as products of disjoint cycles [27].

Example 4. (Continuing Example 3) The permutations $(a\,b) :: (e\,f) :: (c\,d) :: (a\,c) :: nil$ and $(a\,b) :: (c\,d) :: (a\,c) :: nil$ are respectively represented as the product of permutation cycles $(a\,b\,c\,d)(e\,f)$ and $(a\,b\,c\,d)(e)(f)$.

Permutation cycles of length one are omitted. In general the cyclic representation of a permutation consists of the product of all its cycles.

Let π be a permutation with $dom(\pi) = n$. Given $a \in dom(\pi)$ the elements of the sequence $a, \pi(a), \pi^2(a), \ldots$ cannot be all distinct. Taking the first $k \leq n$, such that $\pi^k(a) = a$, we have the k-cycle $(a\ \pi(a)\ \ldots \pi^{k-1}(a))$, where $\pi^{j+1}(a)$ is the *successor* of $\pi^j(a)$. For the 4-cycle in the permutation $(a\,b\,c\,d)\,(e\,f)$, the 4-cycles generated by a, b, c and d are the same: $(a\,b\,c\,d) = (b\,c\,d\,a) = (c\,d\,a\,b) = (d\,a\,b\,c)$.

Definition 12 establishes the notion of a *pseudo-cycle w.r.t. a k-cycle κ*. Intuitively, given a k-cycle κ and a commutative function symbol $*$, a pseudo-cycle w.r.t κ, $(A_0 \ldots A_l)$, is a cycle whose elements are either atom terms built from the atoms in κ or terms of the form $A_i' * A_j'$, for A_i', A_j' elements of a pseudo-cycle w.r.t κ.

Definition 12 (Pseudo-cycle). *Let $\kappa = (a_0\ a_1\ \ldots\ a_{k-1})$ be a k-cycle of a permutation π. A pseudo-cycle w.r.t. κ is inductively defined as follows:*

1. *$\overline{\kappa} = (\overline{a_0} \cdots \overline{a_{k-1}})$ is a pseudo-cycle w.r.t. κ, called* trivial pseudo-cycle *of κ.*
2. *$\kappa' = (A_0 \ldots A_{k'-1})$ is a pseudo-cycle w.r.t. κ, if the following conditions are simultaneously satisfied:*
   (a) *each element of κ' is of the form $B_i * B_j$, where $*$ is a commutative function symbol in the signature, and B_i, B_j are different elements of κ'', a pseudo-cycle w.r.t. κ. κ' will be called a* first-instance pseudo-cycle *of κ'' w.r.t. κ.*
   (b) *$A_i \not\approx_{\alpha,C} A_j$ for $i \neq j$, $0 \leq i, j \leq k' - 1$;*
   (c) *for each $0 \leq i < k' - 1$, $\kappa \cdot A_i \approx_{\{\alpha,C\}} A_{(i+1) \bmod k'}$.*

The *length* of the pseudo-cycle κ, denoted by $|\kappa|$, consists of the number of elements in κ. A pseudo-cycle of length one will be called *unitary*.

Example 5. A (Continuing Example 2) The unitary pseudo-cycles of $\kappa = (a\,b)$ are of the form $(\overline{a} * \overline{b})$ for $*$ any commutative symbol in the signature. These pseudo-cycles are the basis for a more elaborated construction used to build infinite independent solutions for the leaf $\langle \emptyset, id, \{X \approx_? (a\,b).X\}\rangle$. Examples of these solutions are: $\langle \emptyset, \{X/\overline{a}*\overline{b}\}\rangle$, $\langle \emptyset, \{X/(\overline{a}*\overline{a})*(\overline{b}*\overline{b})\}\rangle$, $\langle \emptyset, \{X/(\overline{a}*\overline{b})*(\overline{a}*\overline{b})\}\rangle$, $\langle \emptyset, \{X/((\overline{a}*\overline{a})*\overline{a})*((\overline{b}*\overline{b})*\overline{b})\}\rangle$, $\langle \emptyset, \{X/(\overline{a}*(\overline{a}*\overline{a}))*(\overline{b}*(\overline{b}*\overline{b}))\}\rangle$, etc.

B (Continuing Examples 3 and 4) In $\mathcal{Q}_1$ and $\mathcal{Q}_2$ we have the occurrences of the 4-cycle $\kappa = (a\,b\,c\,d)$. Suppose $*, \oplus, +$ are commutative operators in the signature. The following are pseudo-cycles w.r.t. κ: $\overline{\kappa} = (\overline{a}\ \overline{b}\ \overline{c}\ \overline{d})$; $\kappa_1 = ((\overline{a}*\overline{b})\ (\overline{b}*\overline{c})\ (\overline{c}*\overline{d})\ (\overline{d}*\overline{a}))$; $\kappa_2 = ((\overline{a}\oplus\overline{c})\ (\overline{b}\oplus\overline{d}))$; $\kappa_{11} = (((\overline{a}*\overline{b})+(\overline{b}*\overline{c}))\ ((\overline{b}*\overline{c})+(\overline{c}*\overline{d}))((\overline{c}*\overline{d})+(\overline{d}*\overline{a}))\ ((\overline{d}*\overline{a})+(\overline{a}*\overline{b})))$; $\kappa_{12} = (((\overline{a}*\overline{b})*(\overline{c}*\overline{d}))\ ((\overline{b}*\overline{c})*(\overline{d}*\overline{a})))$; $\kappa_{21} = (((\overline{a}\oplus\overline{c})*(\overline{b}\oplus\overline{d})))$; $\kappa_{121} = (((\overline{a}*\overline{b})*(\overline{c}*\overline{d}))*((\overline{b}*\overline{c})*(\overline{d}*\overline{a})))$. κ_1 and κ_2 are first-instance pseudo-cycles of $\overline{\kappa}$, and κ_{11} and κ_{12} of κ_1 and κ_{21} of κ_2. Notice that, $|\overline{\kappa}| = |\kappa_1| = |\kappa_{11}| = 4$, $|\kappa_{12}| = 2$, and $|\kappa_{21}| = |\kappa_{121}| = 1$. Also, κ_1 corresponds to $((\overline{a}*\overline{d})\ (\overline{b}*\overline{a})\ (\overline{c}*\overline{b})\ (\overline{d}*\overline{c}))$, a first-instance pseudo-cycle of $\overline{\kappa}$. Finally, observe that for the elements of the unitary pseudo-cycles κ_{21} and κ_{121}, say $s = (\overline{a} \oplus \overline{c}) * (\overline{b} \oplus \overline{d})$ and $t = ((\overline{a} * \overline{b}) * (\overline{c} * \overline{d})) * ((\overline{b} * \overline{c}) * (\overline{d} * \overline{a}))$, $\{X/s\}$ and $\{X/t\}$ (resp. $\{Y/s\}$ and $\{Y/t\}$) are solutions of the FP equation $(a\,b\,c\,d)(e\,f).X \approx_? X$ (resp. $(a\,b\,c\,d).Y \approx_? Y$).

Let κ be a pseudo-cycle. Notice that only item 2 of Definition 12 may build a first-instance pseudo-cycle κ' w.r.t. κ with fewer elements. If $|\kappa'| < |\kappa|$ then, due to algebraic properties of cycles and commutativity of the operator applied $(*)$, one must have that $|\kappa'| = |\kappa|/2$. Thus, unitary pseudo-cycles can only be generated from cycles of length a power of two. This is the intuition behind the next theorem, proved by induction on the size of the cycle κ.

Theorem 3. *A pseudo-cycle κ generates unitary pseudo-cycles iff $|\kappa|$ is a power of two.*

Notice that, according to item 2.c of Definition 12, if $\kappa' = (A_0 \ldots A_{k'-1})$ is a pseudo-cycle w.r.t. π then $\pi \cdot A_{k'-1} \approx_{\{\alpha, C\}} A_0$; particularly, if $k' = 1$ then $\pi \cdot A_0 \approx_{\{\alpha, C\}} A_0$. Below, given $\mathcal{P} = \langle \emptyset, \{\pi.X \approx_? X\} \rangle$ a FP equational problem, we call a *combinatory solution* of $\mathcal{P}$, a substitution $\{X/t\}$, such that $\pi \cdot t \approx_C t$, and t contains only atoms from π and commutative function symbols, built as unary pseudo-cycles w.r.t. κ a cycle in π.

The next theorem is proved by contradiction, supposing that κ has an odd factor and using Theorem 3.

Theorem 4. *Let $\mathcal{P} = \langle \emptyset, \{\pi.X \approx_? X\} \rangle$ be a FP problem. $\mathcal{P}$ has a combinatory solution iff there exists a unitary pseudo-cycle κ w.r.t. π.*

Remark 7. Since one can generate infinitely many unitary pseudo-cycles from a given 2^n-cycle κ in π, $n \in \mathbb{N}$, there exist infinite independent solutions for the FP problem $\langle \emptyset, \{\pi.X \approx_? X\} \rangle$.

General solutions for FP problems. To compute the set of solutions for a FP equation, we use a method described in [4], which is based on the computation of unitary *extended pseudo-cycles* (epc). We refer to [4] for the definition of extended pseudo-cycles and an algorithm to enumerate all the solutions of a successful leaf in the derivation tree.

Pseudo-cycles are built just from atom terms in $dom(\pi)$ and commutative function symbols, while epc's consider all nominal syntactic elements including new variables, and also non commutative function symbols. The soundness and completeness of the generator of solutions described in [4] relies on the properties of pseudo-cycles described above, in particular the fact that only unitary pseudo-cycles generate solutions.

5   Formal Proofs

In the Coq formalisation, nominal terms are specified inductively, which permits to use induction to formalise properties of terms (to check nominal α-equality modulo C we use the rules given in [3]; see Fig. 3). The relations $\Rightarrow_{\#}$ and $\Rightarrow_{\approx}$ are inductivelty specified, as propositions from problems to problems, resp. as fresh_sys and equ_sys, and normal forms and their reflexive-transitive closures are specified using abstract relations as shown below.

Definition NF $(T{:}\text{Type})\ (R{:}T{\rightarrow}T{\rightarrow}\text{Prop})\ (s{:}T) := \forall\ t,\ \neg\ R\ s\ t.$

Inductive **tr_clos** $(T{:}\text{Type})\ (R{:}T{\rightarrow}T{\rightarrow}\text{Prop}) : T{\rightarrow}T{\rightarrow}\text{Prop} :=$
| tr_rf : $\forall\ s$, **tr_clos** $T\ R\ s\ s$
| tr_os : $\forall\ s\ t,\ R\ s\ t \rightarrow$ **tr_clos** $T\ R\ s\ t$
| tr_ms : $\forall\ s\ t\ u,\ R\ s\ t \rightarrow$ **tr_clos** $T\ R\ t\ u \rightarrow$ **tr_clos** $T\ R\ s\ u$

A unification step, unif_step, is a reduction step either with the relation equ_sys or with the relation fresh_sys, the latter restricted to FP problems; and a leaf is a normal form for this relation.

Inductive **unif_step** : Triple $\rightarrow$ Triple $\rightarrow$ Prop :=
| equ_unif_step : $\forall\ T\ T'$, **equ_sys** $T\ T' \rightarrow$ **unif_step** $T\ T'$
| fresh_unif_step : $\forall\ T\ T'$, fixpoint_Problem (equ_proj (snd T)) $\rightarrow$
$\qquad\qquad\qquad\qquad$ **fresh_sys** $T\ T' \rightarrow$ **unif_step** $T\ T'$.

Definition leaf $(T :$ Triple$) :=$ NF _ **unif_step** T .

Unification paths are derivations with the relation unif_step to a leaf:

Definition unif_path $(T\ T' :$ Triple$) :=$ **tr_clos** _ **unif_step** $T\ T' \wedge$ leaf T'.

Soundness is specified as the Theorem below, which reads: for any unification problem T that reduces into a problem T' with the relation unif_path, and such that S1 is a solution of T', S1 is also a solution of T.

Theorem c_unif_path_soundness : $\forall\ T\ T'\ Sl$,
$\qquad$ valid_triple $T \rightarrow$ unif_path $T\ T' \rightarrow$ sol_c $Sl\ T' \rightarrow$ sol_c $Sl\ T$.

The formalisation of soundness is given in a theory that consists of 902 lines or 35 KB. This theory also includes lemmas that characterise successful leaves and their solutions. The theorem uses three auxiliary lemmas, also proved by induction. A lemma expresses preservation of the set of solutions of unification problems under reduction by the relation $\Rightarrow_{\#}$:

Lemma fresh_sys_compl : $\forall\ T\ T'\ Sl$, **fresh_sys** $T\ T' \rightarrow$ (sol_c $Sl\ T \leftrightarrow$ sol_c $Sl\ T'$) .

Another lemma, the longer one, states that the solutions of a unification problem obtained from a given problem through application of the relation $\Rightarrow_{\approx}$ are solutions of the given problem:

Lemma equ_sol_preserv : $\forall\ T\ T'\ Sl$, valid_triple $T \rightarrow$
$\qquad\qquad\qquad$ **equ_sys** $T\ T' \rightarrow$ sol_c $Sl\ T' \rightarrow$ sol_c $Sl\ T$.

Finally, the last auxiliary lemma applied to prove soundness states that solutions are preserved in each unification step:

Lemma unif_step_preserv : $\forall\ T\ T'\ Sl$,
$\qquad$ valid_triple $T \rightarrow$ **unif_step** $T\ T' \rightarrow$ sol_c $Sl\ T' \rightarrow$ sol_c $Sl\ T$.

Since except ($\approx_{\{\alpha,\mathbf{C}\}}$ $\mathbf{C}$) unification rules are invertible, the formalisation of the proof of completeness is shorter, consisting only of 351 lines or 13 KB. The additional element to be considered is the nondeterminism of ($\approx_{\{\alpha,\mathbf{C}\}}$ $\mathbf{C}$), indeed implemented as two rules. The key theorem states that Sl is a solution for T iff there exists a unification path form T to some T' with solution Sl.

Theorem unif_path_compl : $\forall$ T Sl,
  valid_triple T $\to$ (sol_c Sl T $\leftrightarrow$ $\exists$ T', unif_path T T' $\wedge$ sol_c Sl T').

Excluding formalisation of nominal terms and E-equivalence, subject of [3], the whole theory consists of theories Completeness, Soundness, Termination, C-Unif, Substs, Problems and C-Equiv, which consist of 5474 lines or 204 KB.

6   Conclusions and Future Work

A Coq formalisation of a sound and complete nominal C-unification algorithm was obtained by combining $\Rightarrow_\approx$- and $\Rightarrow_\#$-reduction. The algorithm builds finite derivation trees, such that the leaves, which may contain FP equations, represent a complete set of unifiers. We have shown that nominal C-unification is infinitary and NP-complete. An OCaml implementation of the simplification phase has been developed, which outputs derivation trees. Extensions to deal with different equational theories will be considered in future work.

References

1. Aoto, T., Kikuchi, K.: A rule-based procedure for equivariant nominal unification. In: Pre-proceeding of Higher-Order Rewriting (HOR), pp. 1–5 (2016)
2. Aoto, T., Kikuchi, K.: Nominal confluence tool. In: Olivetti, N., Tiwari, A. (eds.) IJCAR 2016. LNCS (LNAI), vol. 9706, pp. 173–182. Springer, Cham (2016). https://doi.org/10.1007/978-3-319-40229-1_12
3. Ayala-Rincón, M., Carvalho-Segundo, W., Fernández, M., Nantes-Sobrinho, D.: A formalisation of nominal equivalence with associative-commutative function symbols. ENTCS **332**, 21–38 (2017)
4. Ayala-Rincón, M., de Carvalho-Segundo, W., Fernández, M., Nantes-Sobrinho, D.: On solving nominal fixpoint equations. In: Dixon, C., Finger, M. (eds.) FroCoS 2017. LNCS (LNAI), vol. 10483, pp. 209–226. Springer, Cham (2017)
5. Ayala-Rincón, M., Fernández, M., Nantes-Sobrinho, D.: Nominal narrowing. In: Proceedings of the 1st International Conference on Formal Structures for Computation and Deduction (FSCD). LIPIcs, vol. 52, pp. 11:1–11:17 (2016)
6. Ayala-Rincón, M., Fernández, M., Rocha-oliveira, A.C.: Completeness in PVS of a nominal unification algorithm. ENTCS **323**, 57–74 (2016)
7. Baader, F., Nipkow, T.: Term Rewriting and All That. Cambridge UP, New York (1998)
8. Braibant, T., Pous, D.: Tactics for reasoning modulo AC in Coq. In: Jouannaud, J.-P., Shao, Z. (eds.) CPP 2011. LNCS, vol. 7086, pp. 167–182. Springer, Heidelberg (2011)
9. Calvès, C.F.: Complexity and implementation of nominal algorithms. Ph.D Thesis, King's College London (2010)
10. Calvès, C.F., Fernández, M.: Implementing nominal unification. ENTCS **176**(1), 25–37 (2007)
11. Calvès, C., Fernández, M.: The first-order nominal link. In: Alpuente, M. (ed.) LOPSTR 2010. LNCS, vol. 6564, pp. 234–248. Springer, Heidelberg (2011)
12. Cheney, J.: αProlog Users Guide & Language Reference Version 0.3 DRAFT (2003)
13. Cheney, J.: Equivariant unification. J. Autom. Reasoning **45**(3), 267–300 (2010)

14. Clouston, R.A., Pitts, A.M.: Nominal equational logic. ENTCS **172**, 223–257 (2007)
15. Contejean, E.: A certified AC matching algorithm. In: van Oostrom, V. (ed.) RTA 2004. LNCS, vol. 3091, pp. 70–84. Springer, Heidelberg (2004)
16. Fernández, M., Gabbay, M.J.: Nominal rewriting. Inf. Comput. **205**(6), 917–965 (2007)
17. Fernández, M., Gabbay, M.J.: Closed nominal rewriting and efficiently computable nominal algebra equality. In: Proceedings of the 5th International Workshop on Logical Frameworks and Meta-languages: Theory and Practice (LFMTP). EPTCS, vol. 34, pp. 37–51 (2010)
18. Fernández, M., Gabbay, M.J., Mackie, I.: Nominal rewriting systems. In: Proceedings of the 6th International Conference on Principles and Practice of Declarative Programming (PPDP), pp. 108–119. ACM Press (2004)
19. Gabbay, M.J., Mathijssen, A.: Nominal (Universal) algebra: equational logic with names and binding. J. Logic Comput. **19**(6), 1455–1508 (2009)
20. Gabbay, M.J., Pitts, A.M.: A new approach to abstract syntax with variable binding. Formal Aspects Comput. **13**(3–5), 341–363 (2002)
21. Kapur, D., Narendran, P.: Matching unification and complexity. SIGSAM Bull. **21**(4), 6–9 (1987)
22. Kumar, R., Norrish, M.: (Nominal) Unification by recursive descent with triangular substitutions. In: Kaufmann, M., Paulson, L.C. (eds.) ITP 2010. LNCS, vol. 6172, pp. 51–66. Springer, Heidelberg (2010)
23. Schmidt-Schauß, M., Kutsia, T., Levy, J., Villaret, M.: Nominal unification of higher order expressions with recursive let. In: Hermenegildo, M.V., Lopez-Garcia, P. (eds.) LOPSTR 2016. LNCS, vol. 10184, pp. 328–344. Springer, Cham (2017)
24. Levy, J., Villaret, M.: An efficient nominal unification algorithm. In: Proceedings of the 21st International Conference on Rewriting Techniques and Applications (RTA). LIPIcs, vol. 6, pp. 209–226 (2010)
25. Nipkow, T.: Equational reasoning in Isabelle. Sci. Comput. Program. **12**(2), 123–149 (1989)
26. Pitts, A.M.: Nominal Sets: Names and Symmetry in Computer Science. Cambridge UP, Cambridge (2013)
27. Sagan, B.E.: The Symmetric Group: Representations, Combinatorial Algorithms, and Symmetric Functions, 2nd edn. Springer, New York (2001)
28. Siekmann, J.: Unification of commutative terms. In: Ng, E.W. (ed.) Symbolic and Algebraic Computation. LNCS, vol. 72, pp. 22–29. Springer, Heidelberg (1979). https://doi.org/10.1007/3-540-09519-5_53
29. Urban, C.: Nominal unification revisited. In: Proceedings of the 24th International Workshop on Unification (UNIF). EPTCS, vol. 42, pp. 1–11 (2010)
30. Urban, C., Pitts, A.M., Gabbay, M.J.: Nominal unification. Theor. Comput. Sci. **323**(1–3), 473–497 (2004)

On Uniquely Closable and Uniquely Typable Skeletons of Lambda Terms

Olivier Bodini[1] and Paul Tarau[2(✉)]

[1] Laboratoire d'Informatique de Paris-Nord, UMR CNRS 7030, Paris, France
`olivier.bodini@lipn.univ-paris13.fr`
[2] Department of Computer Science and Engineering, University of North Texas,
Denton, USA
`paul.tarau@unt.edu`

Abstract. Uniquely closable skeletons of lambda terms are Motzkin-trees that predetermine the unique closed lambda term that can be obtained by labeling their leaves with de Bruijn indices. Likewise, uniquely typable skeletons of closed lambda terms predetermine the unique simply-typed lambda term that can be obtained by labeling their leaves with de Bruijn indices.

We derive, through a sequence of logic program transformations, efficient code for their combinatorial generation and study their statistical properties.

As a result, we obtain context-free grammars describing closable and uniquely closable skeletons of lambda terms, opening the door for their in-depth study with tools from analytic combinatorics.

Our empirical study of the more difficult case of (uniquely) typable terms reveals some interesting open problems about their density and asymptotic behavior.

As a connection between the two classes of terms, we also show that uniquely typable closed lambda term skeletons of size $3n + 1$ are in a bijection with binary trees of size n.

Keywords: Deriving efficient logic programs
Logic programming and computational mathematics
Combinatorics of lambda terms · Inferring simple types
Uniquely closable lambda term skeletons
Uniquely typable lambda term skeletons

1 Introduction

Lambda calculus [1] has been, together with Turing machines and combinators a key foundational framework describing the essence of universal computations on which computers and their smaller siblings help running our everyday digital lives.

Lambda calculus has started being used as an actual programming language construct in early functional languages like LISP and is prevalent in this role

© Springer International Publishing AG, part of Springer Nature 2018
F. Fioravanti and J. P. Gallagher (Eds.): LOPSTR 2017, LNCS 10855, pp. 252–268, 2018.
https://doi.org/10.1007/978-3-319-94460-9_15

in modern functional languages like Haskell, ML and F#. In the last few years it has also made it as an actual language construct in virtually all widely used programming languages ranging from C++, C# and Java to Python, Javascript, Ruby and Scala.

Computation in the lambda calculus operate on *lambda terms*, an amazingly simple data structure, conveniently seen, in *de Bruijn notation* [2], as trees made of unary and binary nodes with leaves labeled with integers indicating their way up to their lambda binders, as described by the following Haskell data type declaration:

```
data DeBruijnTerm =
  DeBruijnIndex Integer |
  Lambda DeBruijnTerm |
  Application DeBruijnTerm DeBruijnTerm
```

When computations are triggered via binary application nodes, lambda binders on their left side direct substitutions of terms on their right side to the leaf nodes the binders cover.

When every de Bruijn index has a lambda binder a term is called *closed*. Among closed lambda terms, *simply typed lambda terms* stand out as a model of well-behaved computations that mimic the semantics of mathematical functions operating on sets.

The study of combinatorial properties of lambda terms has theoretical ramifications ranging from their connection to proofs in intuitionistic logic via the Curry-Howard correspondence [3] and their role as a foundation of Turing-complete as well as expressive but terminating computations in the case of simply typed lambda terms [4]. At the same time, lambda terms are used in the internal representations of compilers for functional programming languages and proof assistants, for which the generation of large random lambda terms helps with automated testing [5].

This paper focuses on binary-unary trees that are obtained from lambda terms in de Bruijn form, represented as trees, by erasing the de Bruijn indices labeling variables at their leaves. Such "skeletons" of the lambda terms turn out to predetermine some non-trivial properties the lambda terms they host, e.g., if such terms are closed or simply-typed. Of particular interest are the cases when unique such terms exist.

Our declarative meta-language is Prolog, which turns out to provide everything we need: easy combinatorial generation via backtracking over the set of all answers, specified as a Definite Clause Grammar (DCG) that enforces size constraints and allows placing more complex constraints at points in the code where they ensure the earliest possible pruning of the search space.

Our meta-language also facilitates program transformations that allow us to derive step-by-step faster programs as well as simpler expressions of the underlying combinatorial mechanisms, e.g., a context-free grammar in the case of uniquely closable skeletons, that in turn makes them amenable to study with powerful techniques from analytical combinatorics.

The paper is organized as follows. Section 2 describes generators for closed lambda terms and their Motzkin-tree skeletons. Section 3 introduces closable skeletons and studies their statistical properties. Section 4 derives algorithms (including a CF-grammar) for efficient generation of uniquely closable skeletons. Section 5 discusses typable and untypable closed skeletons. Section 6 introduces uniquely typable closed skeletons, studies the special case of uniquely closable and uniquely typable skeletons and establishes their connection to members of the Catalan family of combinatorial objects. Section 7 overviews related work and Sect. 8 concludes the paper.

The paper is structured as a literate Prolog program to facilitate an easily replicable, concise and declarative expression of our concepts and algorithms.

The code extracted from the paper, tested with SWI-Prolog [6] version 7.5.3, is available at: http://www.cse.unt.edu/~tarau/research/2017/uct.pro.

2   Closed Lambda Terms and their Motzkin-Tree Skeletons

A *Motzkin tree* (also called binary-unary tree) is a rooted ordered tree built from binary nodes, unary nodes and leaf nodes. Thus the set of Motzkin trees can be seen as the free algebra generated by the constructors v/0, l/1 and a/2.

We define lambda terms in de Bruijn form [2] as the free algebra generated by the constructors l/1, and a/2 and leaves labeled with natural numbers wrapped with the constructor v/1.

A lambda term in de Bruijn form is *closed* if for each of its de Bruijn indices it exists a lambda binder to which it points, on the path to the root of the tree representing the term. They are counted by sequence **A135501** in [7].

The predicate closedTerm/2 specifies an all-terms generator, which, given a natural number N backtracks one member X at a time, over the set of terms of size N.

```
closedTerm(N,X):-closedTerm(X,0,N,0).

closedTerm(v(I),V)-->{V>0,V1 is V-1,between(0,V1,I)}.
closedTerm(l(A),V)-->l,{succ(V,NewV)},closedTerm(A,NewV).
closedTerm(a(A,B),V)-->a,closedTerm(A,V),closedTerm(B,V).
```

The *size definition* is expressed by the work of the predicates l/1, consuming *1* size unit for each *lambda binder* and a/2 consuming *2* size units for each a/2 *application* constructor and *0* units for variables v/1. The initial term which is just a unique variable has size *0*.

Given that the number of leaves in a Motzkin tree is the number of binary nodes +*1*, it follows that:

Proposition 1. *The set of terms of size n for the size definition* {application=2, lambda=1, variable=0} *is equal to the set of terms of size $n+1$ for the size definition* {application=1, lambda=1, variable=1}.

Thus our size definition gives the sequence **A135501** of counts, first introduced in [8], shifted by one. For instance, the term $l(a(v(0), v(0)))$ will have size $3 = 1 + 2$ with our definition, which corresponds to size $4 = 1 + 1 + 1 + 1$ using the size definition of [8].

Our size definition is implemented as

```
l(SX,X):-succ(X,SX). % true if SX>0 and X is SX-1
a-->l,l.
```

with Prolog's DCG notation controlling the consumption of size units from N to 0.

The predicate `toMotSkel/2` computes the Motzkin skeleton of a term.

```
toMotSkel(v(_),v).
toMotSkel(l(X),l(Y)):-toMotSkel(X,Y).
toMotSkel(a(X,Y),a(A,B)):-toMotSkel(X,A),toMotSkel(Y,B).
```

The predicate `motSkel/2` generates Motzkin trees X of size N, using the same size definition as the lambda terms for which they serve as skeletons.

```
motSkel(N,X):-motSkel(X,N,0).

motSkel(v)-->[].
motSkel(l(X))-->l,motSkel(X).
motSkel(a(X,Y))-->a,motSkel(X),motSkel(Y).
```

3   Closable and Unclosable Skeletons

We call a Motzkin tree *closable* if it is the skeleton of at least one closed lambda term.

The predicate `isClosable/1` tests if it exists a closed lambda term having X as its skeleton. For each lambda binder it increments a count V (starting at 0), and ensures that it is strictly positive for all leaf nodes.

```
isClosable(X):-isClosable(X,0).

isClosable(v,V):-V>0.
isClosable(l(A),V):-succ(V,NewV),isClosable(A,NewV).
isClosable(a(A,B),V):-isClosable(A,V),isClosable(B,V).
```

We define generators for closable and unclosable skeletons by filtering the stream of answers of the Motzkin tree generator `motSkel/2` with the predicate `isClosable/1` and its negation.

```
closableSkel(N,X):-motSkel(N,X),isClosable(X).

unClosableSkel(N,X):-motSkel(N,X),not(isClosable(X)).
```

In Fig. 1 we show 3 closable and 3 unclosable Motzkin skeletons.

Next, we derive the predicate `quickClosableSkel/2` that generates closable skeletons about 3 times faster by testing directly that lambda binders are available at each leaf node, resulting in earlier pruning of those that do not satisfy this constraint.

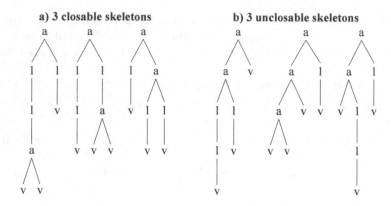

Fig. 1. Closable vs. unclosable skeletons of size 7

```
quickClosableSkel(N,X):-quickClosableSkel(X,0,N,0).

quickClosableSkel(v,V)-->{V>0}.
quickClosableSkel(l(A),V)-->l,{succ(V,NewV)},quickClosableSkel(A,NewV).
quickClosableSkel(a(A,B),V)-->a,
  quickClosableSkel(A,V),
  quickClosableSkel(B,V).
```

One step further, we can derive a grammar generating closable skeletons, by observing that they require at least one lambda (1/1 constructor) on each path, with Motzkin trees below the 1/1 constructor, as generated by the predicate motSkel/3 introduced in Sect. 2. Thus, the following holds:

Proposition 2. *A Motzkin tree is a skeleton of a closed lambda term if and only if it exists at least one lambda binder on each path from the leaf to the root.*

The predicate closable/2, implementing the corresponding CF-grammar as a generator, runs about 3 times as fast as closableSkel/2.

```
closable(N,X):-closable(X,N,0).

closable(l(Z))-->l,motSkel(Z).
closable(a(X,Y))-->a,closable(X),closable(Y).
```

By entering this grammar as input to Maciej Bendkowski's Boltzmann sampler generator [9] we have obtained a Haskell program generating uniformly random closable skeletons of one hundred thousand nodes in a few seconds. The probability to pick 1/1 and enter a Motzkin subtree instead of an a/2 constructor was 0.8730398709632761. The threshold within the Motzkin subtree to pick a leaf was 0.3341408333975344, then 0.667473848839429 for a unary constructor, over which a binary constructor was picked.

We observe that there are slightly more unclosable Motzkin trees than closable ones as size grows:

closable: $0,1,1,2,5,11,26,65,163,417,1086,2858,7599,20391,55127,150028,410719,\ ...$

unclosable: $1,0,1,2,4,10,25,62,160,418,1102,2940,7912,21444,58507,160544,442748,\ ...$

Let us denote by $M(z) = \sum m_n z^n$ the ordinary generating function for Motzkin trees (m_n is the number of Motzkin trees of size n). It is well known [10] that $M(z)$ follows the algebraic functional equation $M = z + zM + zM^2$ which can be obtained directly from the symbolic method and we get $M(z) = \frac{1-z-\sqrt{-3z^2-2z+1}}{2z}$. From this, we obtain the classical result that asymptotically the number m_n of Motzkin trees of size n is equivalent to $\frac{\sqrt{3}}{2\sqrt{\pi}}3^n n^{-3/2}$.

Now, following the proposition 1 (and the predicate `closable/2` providing the corresponding grammar definition), we can deduce that the ordinary generating function $C(z)$ for closable lambda terms satisfies $C(z) = zC(z)^2 + zM(z)$. Indeed, a closable term has either an application at the root followed by two sub-closable terms (which gives rise to $zC(z)^2$), either an abstraction at the root followed by a term (which gives rise to $zM(z)$). Consequently, $C(z) = \frac{1-\sqrt{2z\sqrt{-3z^2-2z+1}+2z^2-2z+1}}{2z}$. Now, we are in the framework of the Flajolet-Odlysko transfer theorems [11] which gives directly the asymptotics of the number c_n of closable skeletons: $c_n \sim \frac{\sqrt{15}}{10\sqrt{\pi}}3^n n^{-3/2}$. By dividing c_n with m_n we obtain:

Proposition 3. *When n tends to the infinity, the proportion of closable lambda term skeletons tends to* $\dfrac{1}{\sqrt{5}} \doteq 44.7\%$.

It is possible to calculate very efficiently the coefficients c_n. For that purpose, from the equation $C(z) = zC(z)^2 + zM(z)$, an easy calculation gives that $C(z)$ satisfies the algebraic equation $z^2 C(z)^4 - 2zC(z)^3 + (-z^2 + z + 1)C(z)^2 + (z - 1)C(z) + z^2$. Thus, dealing with classical tools (in order to pass from an algebraic equation into a holonomic one), we can deduce a linear differential equation from it:

$$
\begin{aligned}
0 = {}& -208z^6 - 168z^5 + 12z^4 + 94z^3 - 42z^2 + 6z \\
&+ \left(-16z^6 + 24z^5 + 36z^4 - 92z^3 + 60z^2 - 12z\right)C(z) \\
&+ \left(768z^9 - 480z^8 - 1088z^7 - 64z^6 + 216z^5 + 44z^4 + 30z^3 - 54z^2 + 18z - 2\right)\tfrac{\mathrm{d}}{\mathrm{d}z}C(z) \\
&+ \left(384z^{10} - 32z^9 - 368z^8 - 56z^7 - 4z^6 + 110z^5 - 21z^4 - 21z^3 + 9z^2 - z\right)\tfrac{\mathrm{d}^2}{\mathrm{d}z^2}C(z)
\end{aligned}
$$

with the initial condition $C(0) = 0$. Now, extracting a relation on the coefficients from this holonomic equation, we obtain the following P-recurrence for the coefficient c_n:

$$
\begin{aligned}
&\left(384n^2 + 384n\right)c_n \\
&+ \left(-32n^2 - 512n - 480\right)c_{n+1} \\
&+ \left(-368n^2 - 2192n - 2928\right)c_{n+2}
\end{aligned}
$$

$$+ \left(-56n^2 - 344n - 504\right) c_{n+3}$$
$$+ \left(-4n^2 + 188n + 852\right) c_{n+4}$$
$$+ \left(110n^2 + 1034n + 2328\right) c_{n+5}$$
$$+ \left(-21n^2 - 201n - 390\right) c_{n+6}$$
$$+ \left(-21n^2 - 327n - 1272\right) c_{n+7}$$
$$+ \left(9n^2 + 153n + 648\right) c_{n+8}$$
$$+ \left(-n^2 - 19n - 90\right) c_{n+9} = 0$$

with the initial conditions $c_0 = 0, c_1 = 0, c_2 = 1, c_3 = 1, c_4 = 2, c_5 = 5, c_6 = 11, c_7 = 26, c_8 = 65$.

Note that by a guess-and-prove approach, we can a little simplify the recurrence into:

$$\left(1200n^5 + 18480n^4 + 90816n^3 + 161088n^2 + 87552n\right) c_n$$
$$+ \left(800n^5 + 13520n^4 + 79024n^3 + 202312n^2 + 231768n + 95760\right) c_{n+1}$$
$$+ \left(-100n^5 - 1840n^4 - 12848n^3 - 38792n^2 - 44100n - 9576\right) c_{n+2}$$
$$+ \left(-100n^5 - 1990n^4 - 14648n^3 - 48254n^2 - 66276n - 23940\right) c_{n+3}$$
$$\left(-225n^5 - 4815n^4 - 38883n^3 - 147519n^2 - 260286n - 167580\right) c_{n+4}$$
$$+ \left(150n^5 + 3435n^4 + 29817n^3 + 120441n^2 + 218739n + 131670\right) c_{n+5}$$
$$+ \left(-25n^5 - 610n^4 - 5642n^3 - 24128n^2 - 45405n - 26334\right) c_{n+6} = 0$$

with the initial conditions $c_0 = 0, c_1 = 0, c_2 = 1, c_3 = 1, c_4 = 2, c_5 = 5$.

This recurrence is extremely efficient in order to calculate the coefficient c_n.

Alternatively, the expansion into Taylor series of $C(z)$ gives $z^2 + z^3 + 2z^4 + 5z^5 + 11z^6 + 26z^7 + 65z^8 + 163z^9 + 417z^{10} + 1086z^{11} + 2858z^{12} + 7599z^{13} + 20391z^{14} + 55127z^{15}...$ with its coefficients matching the number of terms of sizes given by the exponents, corresponding to the number of solutions of the predicate `closableSkel/2`.

4   Uniquely Closable Skeletons

We call a skeleton *uniquely closable* if it exists exactly one closed lambda term having it as its skeleton.

Proposition 4. *A skeleton is uniquely closable if and only if exactly one lambda binder is available above each of its leaf nodes.*

Proof. Note that if more than one were available for any leaf v, one could choose more then one de Bruijn index at the corresponding leaf v/1 of a lambda term, resulting in more than one possible lambda terms having the given skeleton.

The predicate `uniquelyClosable1/2` derived from `quickClosableSkel1/2` ensures that for each leaf v/0 exactly one lambda binder is available.

```
uniquelyClosable1(N,X):-uniquelyClosable1(X,0,N,0).

uniquelyClosable1(v,1)-->[].
uniquelyClosable1(l(A),V)-->l,{succ(V,NewV)},uniquelyClosable1(A,NewV).
uniquelyClosable1(a(A,B),V)-->a,uniquelyClosable1(A,V),
  uniquelyClosable1(B,V).
```

As a skeleton is uniquely closable if on any path from a leaf to the root there's exactly one l/1 constructor, we derive the predicate uniquelyClosable2/2 that marks subtrees below a lambda 11/1 constructor to ensure no other l/1 constructor is used in them.

```
uniquelyClosable2(N,X):-uniquelyClosable2(X,hasNoLambda,N,0).

uniquelyClosable2(v,hasOneLambda)-->[].
uniquelyClosable2(l(A),hasNoLambda)-->l,
  uniquelyClosable2(A,hasOneLambda).
uniquelyClosable2(a(A,B),Has)-->a,uniquelyClosable2(A,Has),
  uniquelyClosable2(B,Has).
```

By specializing with respect to having or not having a lambda binder above, we obtain uniquelyClosable/2 which mimics a context-free grammar generating all uniquely closable skeletons of a given size.

```
uniquelyClosable(N,X):-uniquelyClosable(X,N,0).

uniquelyClosable(l(A))-->l,closedAbove(A).
uniquelyClosable(a(A,B))-->a,uniquelyClosable(A),uniquelyClosable(B).

closedAbove(v)-->[].
closedAbove(a(A,B))-->a,closedAbove(A),closedAbove(B).
```

In fact, if one wants to only count the number of solutions, the actual term (argument 1) can be omitted, resulting in the even faster predicate uniquelyClosableCount/1.

```
uniquelyClosableCount(N):-uniquelyClosableCount(N,0).

uniquelyClosableCount-->l,closedAboveCount.
uniquelyClosableCount-->a,uniquelyClosableCount,uniquelyClosableCount.

closedAboveCount-->[].
closedAboveCount-->a,closedAboveCount,closedAboveCount.
```

This sequence of program transformations results in code running an order of magnitude faster, with all counts up to size 30, shown in Fig. 2, obtained in less than a minute. Figure 2 shows the growths of the set of uniquely closable skeletons.

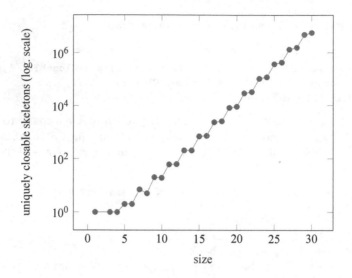

Fig. 2. Uniquely closable skeletons by increasing sizes

If expressed as a Haskell data type, the grammar describing the set of closable skeletons becomes:

```
data UniquelyClosable =  L ClosedAbove
  | A UniquelyClosable UniquelyClosable deriving(Eq,Show,Read)

data ClosedAbove = V | B ClosedAbove ClosedAbove deriving(Eq,Show,Read)
```

With this notation, a skeleton, with the constructor B used for binary trees not containing an L constructor, is A (A (L V) (L V)) (L (B (B V V) V)).

One can transliterate the Prolog DCG grammar into Haskell by using list comprehensions to mimic backtracking as follows.

```
genA 0 = []
genA n | n>0 =
  [L x | x <- genB (n-1)] ++
  [A x y | k <- [0..n-2], x <- genA k,  y <- genA (n-2-k)]

genB 0 = [V]
genB n | n>0 = [B a b | k <- [0..n-2], a <- genB k, b <- genB (n-2-k)]
```

By entering the equivalent of this data type definition as input to Maciej Bendkowski's Boltzmann sampler generator [9] we have obtained a Haskell program generating uniformly random terms of one hundred thousand nodes in a few seconds. The probability threshold for a unary constructor was below 0.5001253328728457 and then, once having entered a closed above subtree, it was 0.5001253328728457 to stop at a leaf rather than continuing with a binary node.

Let us denote by $B(z)$ the ordinary generating function for binary trees. The series $B(z)$ follows the algebraic functional equation $B = z + zB^2$ and consequently $B(z) = \frac{1 - \sqrt{-4z^2 + 1}}{2z}$.

The ordinary generating function $U(z)$ for uniquely closable lambda terms satisfies $U(z) = zU(z)^2 + zB(z)$. Indeed, a uniquely closable term has either an application at the root followed by two sub uniquely closable terms (which gives rise to $zC(z)^2$), either an abstraction at the root followed by a term with no abstraction (which gives rise to $zB(z)$). Consequently, $U(z) = \frac{1 - \sqrt{2z\sqrt{-4z^2+1} - 2z+1}}{2z}$. We are again in the framework of the Flajolet-Odlysko transfer theorems [11] which gives directly the asymptotics of the number u_n of uniquely closable terms: $u_n \sim \frac{2^{1/4+n}}{4\Gamma(3/4)n^{5/4}}$.

We can follow the same approach that for $C(z)$ to calculate quickly the coefficients u_n. In particular, $U(z)$ satisfies the algebraic equation $z^2U(z)^4 - 2zU(z)^3 + (z+1)U(z)^2 - U(z) + z^2 = 0$. From which we deduce a linear differential equation:

$$
\begin{aligned}
0 = &- 128z^5 - 40z^4 + 52z^3 + 18z^2 - 6z + (16z^5 + 56z^4 - 20z^3 - 20z^2 + 8z - 2)U(z) \\
&+ (512z^8 - 512z^7 - 320z^6 + 96z^5 + 144z^4 + 16z^3 - 24z^2 - 6z + 2)(\tfrac{d}{dz}U(z)) \\
&+ (256z^9 - 128z^8 - 128z^7 - 32z^6 + 64z^5 + 24z^4 - 16z^3 - 2z^2 + z)(\tfrac{d^2}{dz^2}U(z))
\end{aligned}
$$

with the initial condition $U(0) = 0$.

Thus, we can efficiently compute the coefficient u_n using the P-recurrence:

$$
\begin{aligned}
&(256n^2 + 256n)\,u_n + \qquad (-128n^2 - 640n - 512)\,u_{n+1} \\
&+ (-128n^2 - 704n - 880)\,u_{n+2} + (-32n^2 - 64n + 152)\,u_{n+3} \\
&+ (64n^2 + 592n + 1324)\,u_{n+4} + (24n^2 + 232n + 540)\,u_{n+5} \\
&+ (-16n^2 - 200n - 616)\,u_{n+6} \\
&+ (-2n^2 - 32n - 128)\,u_{n+7} + (n^2 + 17n + 72)\,u_{n+8} = 0
\end{aligned}
$$

with the initial conditions $u_0 = 0, u_1 = 0, u_2 = 1, u_3 = 0, u_4 = 1, u_5 = 1, u_6 = 2, u_7 = 2$.

The Taylor series expansion of $U(z)$ gives $z^2 + z^4 + z^5 + 2z^6 + 2z^7 + 7z^8 + 5z^9 + 20z^{10} + 19z^{11} + 60z^{12} + 62z^{13} + 202z^{14} + 202z^{15}...$ with coefficients of z matching the number of solutions of the predicate uniquelyClosable/2 for sizes given by the exponents of z.

Let us notice that the polynomial factor in the asymptotics is not in $n^{-3/2}$ as it is universal for tree-like structures. Here we have an interesting polynomial factor in $n^{-5/4}$ which appears when two square-root singularities coalesce. This fact has a positive effect on the performance of the Boltzmann random sampling.

5   Typable and Untypable Closable Skeletons

Let us denote $x : T$ the fact that x has type T. In the simply typed lambda calculus, given a context (a set of *variable:type* pairs), types are inferred using the following rules:

1. if $x : T$ in a context then $x : T$
2. term constants (if part of the language) have appropriate base type
3. if in a context, x has type S and an expression e has type T, then in the same context, with the binding of x removed from the context, $\lambda x.e$ has type $S \rightarrow T$
4. if in a context the term e has type $S \rightarrow T$ and the term f has type S then the application of e to f has type T.

We call a Motzkin skeleton *typable* if it exists at least one simply-typed closed lambda term having it as its skeleton. An *untypable* skeleton is a closable skeleton for which no such term exists.

We will follow the interleaving of term generation, checking for closedness and type inference steps shown in [12], but split it into a two stage program, with the first stage generating code to be executed, via Prolog's metacall by the second, while also ensuring that the terms generated by the second stage are closed.

The predicate `genSkelEqs/4` generates type unification equations, that, if satisfied by a closed lambda term, ensure that the term is simply-typable.

```
genSkelEqs(N,X,T,Eqs):-genSkelEqs(X,T,[],Eqs,true,N,0).

genSkelEqs(v,V,Vs,(el(V,Vs),Es),Es)-->{Vs=[_|_]}.
genSkelEqs(l(A),(S->T),Vs,Es1,Es2)-->l,genSkelEqs(A,T,[S|Vs],Es1,Es2).
genSkelEqs(a(A,B),T,Vs,Es1,Es3)-->a,genSkelEqs(A,(S->T),Vs,Es1,Es2),
  genSkelEqs(B,S,Vs,Es2,Es3).

el(V,Vs):-member(V0,Vs),unify_with_occurs_check(V0,V).
```

Note that each lambda binder adds a new type variable to the list (starting empty at the root) on the way down to a leaf node. A term is then closed if the list of those variables `Vs` is not empty at each leaf node.

Thus, to generate the typable terms, one simply *executes the equations* Eqs, as shown by the predicate `typableClosedTerm/2`.

```
typableClosedTerm(N,Term):-genSkelEqs(N,Term,_,Eqs),Eqs.
```

The predicate `typableSkel/2` generates skeletons that are typable by running the same equations Eqs and ensuring they have *at least one solution* using the Prolog built-in `once/1`. The predicate `untypableSkel/2` succeeds, when the negation of these equations succeeds, indicating that no simply-typed lambda term exists having the given skeleton. Clearly, this is much faster than naively generating all the closed lambda terms and then finding their distinct skeletons.

```
typableSkel(N,Skel):-genSkelEqs(N,Skel,_,Eqs),once(Eqs).
untypableSkel(N,Skel):-genSkelEqs(N,Skel,_,Eqs),not(Eqs).
```

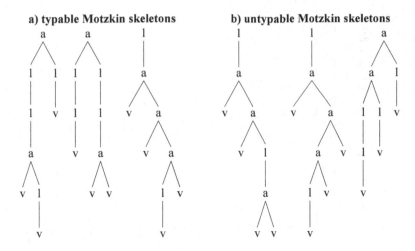

Fig. 3. Typable vs. untypable skeletons of size 8

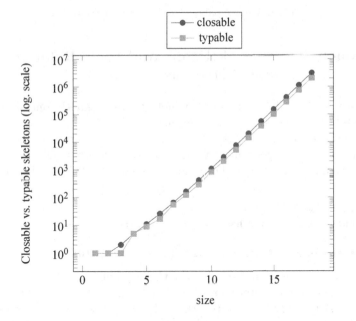

Fig. 4. Closable skeletons vs. typable skeletons by increasing sizes

In Fig. 3 we show 3 typable and 3 untypable Motzkin skeletons.

An interesting question arises at this point about the relative density of closable and typable skeletons. Figure 4, shows how many typable skeletons are among the closable skeletons for sizes up to 18. We leave as an *open problem* finding out the asymptotic behavior of the relative density of the typable skeletons in the set of closable ones.

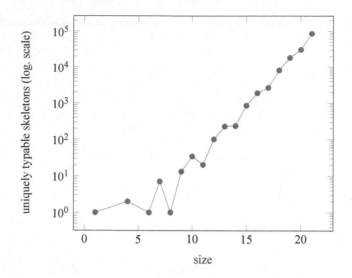

Fig. 5. Uniquely typable skeletons by increasing sizes

6 Uniquely Typable Skeletons and their Relation to Uniquely Closable Skeletons

A *uniquely typable skeleton* is one for which it exists exactly one simply-typed closed lambda term having it as a skeleton.

The predicate `uniquelyTypableSkel/2` generates unification equations for which, with the use of the built-in `findnsols/4`, it ensures efficiently that they have unique solutions. Figure 5 shows the counts of the skeletons it generates up to size **21**.

```
uniquelyTypableSkel(N,Skel):-
  genSkelEqs(N,Skel,_,Eqs),has_unique_answer(Eqs).
```

```
has_unique_answer(G):-findnsols(2,G,G,Sols),!,Sols=[G].
```

The natural question arises at this point: are there (uniquely) typable skeletons among the set of uniquely closable ones? The predicate `uniquelyTypableSkel/2` generates them by filtering the answer stream of `uniquelyClosable/2` with the predicate `isUniquelyTypableSkel/1`.

```
uniquelyClosableTypable(N,X):-
  uniquelyClosable(N,X),isUniquelyTypableSkel(X).
```

```
isUniquelyTypableSkel(X):-skelType(X,_).
```

The predicate isUniquelyTypableSkel/2 works by trying to infer the simple type of a uniquely typable lambda term corresponding to the skeleton. Note that this is a specialization of a general type inferencer to the case when exactly one type variable is available for each leaf node.

```
skelType(X,T):-skelType(X,T,[]).

skelType(v,V,[V0]):-unify_with_occurs_check(V,V0).
skelType(l(A),(S->T),Vs):-skelType(A,T,[S|Vs]).
skelType(a(A,B),T,Vs):-skelType(A,(S->T),Vs),skelType(B,S,Vs).
```

Proposition 5. *Uniquely closable typable skeletons of size $3n+1$ are in bijection with Catalan objects (binary trees) of size n.*

Proof. We will exhibit a simple bijection to binary trees. We want to show that terminal subtrees must be of the form $l(v(0))$. As there's a unique lambda above each leaf, closing it, the leaf should be (in de Bruijn notation), $v(0)$ pointing to the first and only lambda above it. Assume a terminal node of the form $a(v(0),v(0))$. Then the two leaves must share a lambda binder resulting in a circular term when unifying their types (i.e., as in the case of the well-known term $\omega = l(a(v(0),v(0))))$ and thus it could not be typable.

The following two trees illustrate the shape of such skeletons and their bijection to binary trees. Note that the skeleton is mapped into a binary tree simply by replacing its terminal subtrees of the form $l(v)$ with a leaf node v.

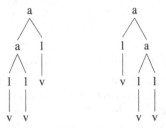

In this case, terms of size $3n + 1 = 7 = 2 + 2 + 1 + 1 + 1 + 0 + 0 + 0$ are mapped to binary trees of size $n = 2 = 1 + 1 + 0 + 0 + 0$ (with a/2 nodes there counted as 1 and v/0 nodes as 0) after replacing $l(v)$ nodes with v nodes.

As a consequence, *each uniquely closable term that is typable is uniquely typable*, as identity functions of the form $l(v(0))$ would correspond to the end of each path from the root to a leaf in a lambda term having this skeleton. This tells us that there are no "interesting" uniquely closable terms that are typable. However, as there are normalizable terms that are not simply typed, an interesting *open problem* is to find out if uniquely closable terms, other than those ending with $l(v(0))$ are (weakly) normalizable.

7   Related work

The classic reference for lambda calculus is [1]. Various instances of typed lambda calculi are overviewed in [4].

The first paper where de Bruijn indices are used in counting lambda terms is [8], which also uses a size definition equivalent to ours (but shifted by 1). The idea of using Boltzmann samplers for lambda terms was first introduced in [13].

The combinatorics and asymptotic behavior of various classes of lambda terms are extensively studied in [14,15]. However, the concepts of closable and typable skeletons of lambda terms and their uniquely closable and typable variants are new and have not been studied previously. The second author has used extensively Prolog as a meta-language for the study of combinatorial and computational properties of lambda terms in papers like [12,16] covering different families of terms and properties, but not in combination with the precise analytic methods as developed in this paper.

It has been a long tradition in logic programming to use step-by-step program transformations to derive semantically simpler as well as more efficient code, going back as far as [17], that we have informally followed. In [18] a general constraint logic programming framework is defined for size-constrained generation of data structures as well as a program-transformation mechanism. By contrast, we have not needed to use constraint solvers in our code as our derivation steps allowed us to place constraints explicitly at the exact program points where they were needed, for both the case of closable and typable skeletons. Keeping our programs close to Horn Clause Prolog has helped deriving CF-grammars for closable and uniquely closable skeletons and has enabled the use of tools from analytic combinatorics to fully understand their asymptotic behavior.

8   Conclusion

We have used simple program transformations to derive more efficient or conceptually simpler logic programs in the process of attempting to state, empirically study and solve some interesting problems related to the combinatorics of lambda terms. Several open problems have also been generated in the process with interesting implications on better understanding structural properties of the notoriously hard set of simply-typed lambda terms.

The lambda term skeletons introduced in the paper involve abstraction mechanisms that "forget" properties of the difficult class of simply-typed closed lambda terms to reveal classes of terms that are easier to grasp with analytic tools. In the case of the combinatorially simpler set of closed lambda terms, we have found that interesting subclasses of their skeletons turn out to be easier to handle. The case of uniquely closable terms turned out to be covered by a context free grammar, after several program transformation steps, and thus amenable to study analytically.

The focus on uniquely closable and uniquely typable Motzkin-tree skeletons of lambda terms, as well as their relations, has shown that closability and typability are properties that *predetermine* which lambda terms in de Bruijn notation can have such Motzkin trees as skeletons. Our analytic and experimental study has shown exponential growth for each of these families and suggests possible uses as positive or negative lemmas for all-term and random lambda term generation in dynamic programming algorithms.

Last but not least, we have shown that a language as simple as side-effect-free Prolog, with limited use of impure features and meta-programming, can handle elegantly complex combinatorial generation problems, when the synergy between sound unification, backtracking and DCGs is put at work.

Acknowledgement. This research has been supported by NSF grant 1423324.

We thank the anonymous reviewers of LOPSTR'17 for their careful reading and valuable suggestions, Maciej Bendkowski for salient comments on an earlier draft of this paper and the participants of the 10th Workshop on Computational Logic and Applications (https://cla.tcs.uj.edu.pl) for enlightening discussions on the combinatorics of lambda terms.

References

1. Barendregt, H.P.: The Lambda Calculus Its Syntax and Semantics. Revised edn. vol. 103. North Holland (1984)
2. de Bruijn, N.G.: Lambda calculus notation with nameless dummies, a tool for automatic formula manipulation, with application to the Church-Rosser theorem. Indagationes Mathematicae **34**, 381–392 (1972)
3. Howard, W.: The formulae-as-types notion of construction. In: Seldin, J., Hindley, J. (eds.) To H.B. Curry: Essays on Combinatory Logic, Lambda Calculus and Formalism, pp. 479–490. Academic Press, London (1980)
4. Barendregt, H.P.: Lambda calculi with types. In: Handbook of Logic in Computer Science, vol. 2. Oxford University Press, Oxford (1991)
5. Palka, M.H., Claessen, K., Russo, A., Hughes, J.: Testing an optimising compiler by generating random lambda terms. In: Proceedings of the 6th International Workshop on Automation of Software Test, AST 2011, New York, NY, USA, pp. 91–97. ACM (2011)
6. Wielemaker, J., Schrijvers, T., Triska, M., Lager, T.: SWI-prolog. Theory Pract. Logic Program. **12**, 67–96 (2012)
7. Sloane, N.J.A.: The on-line encyclopedia of integer sequences (2017). https://oeis org/
8. Lescanne, P.: On counting untyped lambda terms. Theor. Comput. Sci. **474**, 80–97 (2013)
9. Bendkowski, M.: Boltzmann-brain (2017). Software (Haskell stack module). https://github.com/maciej-bendkowski/boltzmann-brain
10. Flajolet, P., Sedgewick, R.: Analytic Combinatorics, 1st edn. Cambridge University Press, New York (2009)
11. Flajolet, P., Odlyzko, A.: Singularity analysis of generating functions. SIAM J. Discrete Math. **3**(2), 216–240 (1990)
12. Tarau, P.: On a uniform representation of combinators, arithmetic, lambda terms and types. In: Albert, E. (ed.) Proceedings of the 17th International ACM SIGPLAN Symposium on Principles and Practice of Declarative Programming, PPDP 2015, New York, NY, USA, pp. 244–255. ACM (2015)
13. Grygiel, K., Lescanne, P.: Counting and generating terms in the binary lambda calculus. J. Funct. Program. **25**, e24 (2015)
14. Grygiel, K., Lescanne, P.: Counting and generating lambda terms. J. Funct. Program. **23**(5), 594–628 (2013)
15. Bodini, O., Gardy, D., Jacquot, A.: Asymptotics and random sampling for BCI and BCK lambda terms. Theor. Comput. Sci. **502**, 227–238 (2013)

16. Bendkowski, M., Grygiel, K., Tarau, P.: Boltzmann samplers for closed simply-typed lambda terms. In: Lierler, Y., Taha, W. (eds.) PADL 2017. LNCS, vol. 10137, pp. 120–135. Springer, Cham (2017). https://doi.org/10.1007/978-3-319-51676-9_8
17. Pettorossi, A., Proietti, M.: Transformation of logic programs: foundations and techniques. J. Logic Program. **19**, 261–320 (1994)
18. Fioravanti, F., Proietti, M., Senni, V.: Efficient generation of test data structures using constraint logic programming and program transformation. J. Logic Comput. **25**(6), 1263–1283 (2015)

Verification

A Certified Reference Validation Mechanism for the Permission Model of Android

Gustavo Betarte[1], Juan Campo[1], Felipe Gorostiaga[2], and Carlos Luna[1(✉)]

[1] InCo, Facultad de Ingeniería, Universidad de la República, Montevideo, Uruguay
{gustun,jdcampo,cluna}@fing.edu.uy
[2] IMDEA Software Institute, Madrid, Spain
felipe.gorostiaga@imdea.org

Abstract. Android embodies security mechanisms at both OS and application level. In this platform application security is built primarily upon a system of permissions which specify restrictions on the operations a particular process can perform. The critical role of these security mechanisms makes them a prime target for (formal) verification. We present an idealized model of a reference monitor of the novel mechanisms of Android 6 (and further), where it is possible to grant permissions at run time. Using the programming language of the proof-assistant Coq we have developed a functional implementation of the reference validation mechanism and certified its correctness with respect to the specified reference monitor. Several properties concerning the permission model of Android 6 and its security mechanisms have been formally formulated and proved. Applying the program extraction mechanism provided by Coq we have also derived a certified Haskell prototype of the reference validation mechanism.

1 Introduction

The Android [21] platform for mobile devices captures more than 85% of the total market-share [16]. Mobile devices allow people to develop multiple tasks in different areas, regrettably, the benefits of using them are counteracted by increasing security risks.

Android embodies security mechanisms at both OS and application level. Application security is built primarily upon a system of permissions, which specify restrictions on the operations a particular process can perform. Permissions in Android are basically tags that developers declare in their applications, more precisely in the so-called application *manifest*, to gain access to sensitive resources. On all versions of Android an application must declare both the normal and the dangerous permissions it needs in its application manifest. However, the effect

Partially funded by project ANII-FCE_1_2014_1_103803: Mecanismos autónomos de seguridad certificados para sistemas computacionales móviles, Uruguay, and by the EU H2020 project Elastest under num. 731535.

© Springer International Publishing AG, part of Springer Nature 2018
F. Fioravanti and J. P. Gallagher (Eds.): LOPSTR 2017, LNCS 10855, pp. 271–288, 2018.
https://doi.org/10.1007/978-3-319-94460-9_16

of that declaration is different depending on the system version and the application's target SDK level [3]. In particular, if a device is running Android 6 (Marshmallow) and the application's target SDK is 23 or higher the application has to list the permissions in the manifest, and it must request each dangerous permission it needs while the application is running. The user can grant or deny each permission, and the application can continue to run with limited capabilities even if the user denies a permission request. This modification of the access control and decision process, on the one side, streamlines the application install process, since the user does not need to grant permissions when he/she installs or updates an application. On the other hand, as users can revoke the (previously granted) permissions at any time, the application needs to check whether it has the corresponding privileges every time it attempts to access a resource on the device [3]. The important and critical role of these security mechanisms makes them a prime target for (formal) verification.

Security models play an important role in the design and evaluation of security mechanisms of systems. Their importance was already pointed out in 1972 in the Anderson report [1], where the concept of *reference monitor* was first introduced. This concept defines the design requirements for implementing what is called a *reference validation mechanism*, which shall be responsible for enforcing the access control policy of a system. The work presented here is concerned with the formal analysis and verification of properties performed on an idealized model that abstracts away the specifics of any particular implementation, and yet provides a realistic setting in which to explore the issues that pertain to the realm of (critical) security mechanisms of Android.

Contributions. In [9,10], we have presented a formal specification of an idealized formulation of the permission model of version 5 of Android. Here we present an enriched version of that model which can be used to perform a formal analysis of the novel mechanisms of Android 6, which make it possible to grant permissions at run time. Furthermore, using the programming language of Coq [24] we have developed an executable (functional) specification of the reference validation mechanism and it has been proved that those functions conform to the axiomatic specification as specified in the model. Additionally, and using the program extraction mechanism provided by Coq, we have derived a certified Haskell prototype of the reference validation mechanism. Several properties concerning the security model of Android 6 have been formally formulated and proved.

Organization of the Paper. Section 2 reviews the security mechanisms of Android. Section 3 describes the formal axiomatic specification of the Android security system and discusses some of the verified properties. Section 4 presents a functional (operational) semantics of the specified reference monitor and outlines its proof of correctness. This section also discusses security properties satisfied by the certified implementation of the security mechanisms. Section 5 considers related work and finally, Sect. 6 concludes with a summary of our contributions and directions for future work. The full formalization may be obtained from [17] and verified using the Coq proof assistant.

2   Android's Security Model

The architecture of Android takes the form of a software stack which comprises an OS, a run-time environment, middleware, services and libraries, and applications. An Android application is built up from *components*. A component is a basic unit that provides a particular functionality and that can be run by any other application with the right permissions. There exist four types of components [2]: (i) *activity*, which is essentially a user interface of the application; (ii) *service*, a component that executes in background without providing an interface to the user; (iii) *content provider*, a component intended to share information among applications; and (iv) *broadcast receiver*, a component whose objective is to receive messages, sent either by the system or an application, and trigger the corresponding actions. Activities, services and broadcast receivers are activated by a special kind of message called *intent*. An intent makes it possible for different components to interact at runtime. An intent filter specifies the types of intents that a component receiver can respond to [2].

Applications usually need to use system resources to execute properly. Since applications run inside sandboxes, this entails the existence of a decision procedure (a reference validation mechanism) that guarantees the authorized access to those resources. Decisions are made by following security policies using a simple notion of permission. Every permission is identified by a name/text, has a protection level and may belong to a permission group. There exist two principal classes of permissions: the ones defined by the application, for the sake of self-protection; and those predefined by Android, which are intended to protect access to resources and services of the system. An application declares –in an XML file called `AndroidManifest`– the set of permissions it needs to acquire further capacities than the default ones. When an action involving permissions is required, the system determines which permissions every application has and either allows or denies its execution.

Depending on the protection level of the permission, the system defines the corresponding decision procedure [4]. There are four classes of permission levels: (i) *Normal*, assigned to low risk permissions that grant access to isolated characteristics; (ii) *Dangerous*, permissions of this level are those that provide access to private data or control over the device. From version 6 of Android dangerous permissions are not granted at installation time; (iii) *Signature*, a permission of this level is granted only if the application that requires it and the application that defined it are both signed with the same certificate; and (iv) *Signature/System*, this level is assigned to permissions that regulate the access to critical system resources or services. Additionally, an application can also declare the permissions that are needed to access it. A running application may ask the user to grant it dangerous permission groups and ungrouped permissions, who in turn can accept or decline this request.

If the execution of an action requires for an application to have certain permission the system will first make sure that this holds by means of the following rules: (i) the application must declare the permission as used in its manifest; (ii) if the permission is of level *Normal*, then the application does have it;

(iii) if the permission is of level *Dangerous* and belongs to a permission group, such group must have been granted to the application; (iv) if the permission is of level *Dangerous* but is ungrouped, then it must have been individually granted to the application; (v) if the permission is of level *Signature*, then both the involved application and the one that declares it must have been signed with the same certificate; (vi) lastly, if the permission is of level *Signature/System*, then the involved application must have been signed with either the same certificate as the one who declares it or the certificate of the device manufacturer. Otherwise, an error is thrown and the action is not executed.

Android provides two mechanisms by which an application can delegate its own permissions to another one. These mechanisms are called *pending intents* and *URI permissions*. An intent may be defined by a developer to perform a particular action. A `PendingIntent` is an object which is associated to the action, a reference that might be used by another application to execute that action. The *URI permissions* mechanism can be used by an application that has read/write access to a *content provider* to delegate those permissions to another application.

3   Formalization of the Permission Model

In this section we provide a short account of the axiomatic semantics of the Android security system and discuss some of the verified security properties.

Formal Language Used. The `Coq` proof assistant provides a (dependently typed) functional programming language and a reasoning framework based on higher order logic to perform proofs of (complex) specifications and programs. `Coq` allows the definition of objects (sets, lists, streams, functions, programs), the writing of formulas (using basic predicates, logical connectives and quantifiers), and the construction of proofs. The type of propositions is called *Prop*. The `Coq` environment provides program extraction towards languages like Ocaml and Haskell for execution of (certified) algorithms [18,19].

In this work, enumerated types and sum types are defined using Haskell-like notation; for example, $option\ T \stackrel{\text{def}}{=} None \mid Some\ (t : T)$. Record types are of the form $\{l_1 : T_1, \ldots, l_n : T_n\}$, whereas their elements are of the form $\{t_1, \ldots, t_n\}$. Field selection is written as $r.l_i$. We also use $\{T\}$ to denote the set of elements of type T. Finally, the symbol $\times$ defines tuples, and *nat* is the datatype of natural numbers. We omit `Coq` code for reasons of clarity; this code is available in [17].

3.1   Model States

The Android security model we have developed has been formalized as an abstract state machine. In this model, states (`AndroidST`) are modelled as 12-tuples that respectively store data about the applications installed, their permissions and the running instances of components; the formal definition appears in Fig. 1.

```
OpTy         ::= read | write | rw
PermLvl      ::= Dangerous | Normal | Signature | Signature/System
Perm         ::= PermId × option PermGroup × PermLvl
InstApps     ::= {AppId}
PermsGr      ::= {AppId × PermGroup}
AppPS        ::= {AppId × PermId}
CompInstance ::= iComp × Comp
CompInsRun   ::= {CompInstance}
DelPPerms    ::= {AppId × ContProv × Uri × OpTy}
DelTPerms    ::= {iComp × ContProv × Uri × OpTy}
ARVS         ::= {AppId × Res × Val}
Intents      ::= {iComp × Intent}
Manifest     ::= {Comp} × option nat × option nat × {PermId} × {Perm} × option PermId
Manifests    ::= {AppId × Manifest}
Certs        ::= {AppId × Cert}
AppDefPS     ::= {AppId × Perm}
SysImage     ::= {SysImgApp}

AndroidST    ::= InstApps × PermsGr × AppPS × CompInsRun × DelPPerms × DelTPerms ×
                 ARVS × Intents × Manifests × Certs × AppDefPS × SysImage
```

Fig. 1. Android state

The type PermId represents the set of permissions identifiers; PermGroup, the set of permission groups identifiers; Comp, the application components whose code will run on the system; AppId represents the set of application identifiers; iComp is the set of identifiers of running instances of application components; ContProv is a subset of Comp, a special type of component that allows sharing resources among different applications; a member of the type Uri is a particular uri (uniform resources identifier); the type Res represents the set of resources an application can have (through its *content providers*, members of ContProv); the type Val is the set of possible values that can be written on resources; an intent –i.e. a member of type Intent– represents the intention of a running component instance to start or communicate with other applications; a member of SysImgApp is a special kind of applications which are deployed along with the OS itself and has certain privileges, like being impossible to uninstall.

The first component of a state records the identifiers (AppId) of the applications installed by the user. The second and third components of the state keep track, respectively, of the permission groups (PermGroup) and ungrouped permissions granted to each application present in the system, both the ones installed by the user and the system applications. The fourth component of the state stores the set of running component instances (CompInstance), while the components DelPPerms and DelTPerms store the information concerning permanent and temporary permissions delegations, respectively[1]. The seventh and eight components of the state store respectively the values (Val) of resources (Res) of applications and the set of intents (Intent) sent by running instances of components (iComp) not yet processed. The four last components of the state record information that represents the manifests of the applications installed by

---

[1] A permanent delegated permission represents that an app has delegated permission to perform an operation on the resource identified by an URI. A temporary delegated permission refers to a permission that has been delegated to a component instance.

the user, the certificates (Cert) with which they were signed and the set of permissions they define. The last component of the state stores the set of (native) applications installed in the Android system image, information that is relevant when granting permissions of level *Signature/System*.

A manifest (Manifest) is modelled as a 6-tuple that respectively declare application components (set of components, of type Comp, included in the application); optionally, the minimum version of the Android SDK required to run the application; optionally, the version of the Android SDK targeted on development; the set of permissions it may need to run at its maximum capability; the set of permissions it declares; and the permission required to interact with its components, if any. Application components are all denoted by a component identifier. A content provider (ContProv), in addition, encompasses a mapping to the managed resources from the URIs assigned to them for external access. While the components constitute the static building blocks of an application, all runtime operations are initiated by component instances, which are represented in our model as members of an abstract type.

We define a notion of valid state, through the predicate *valid_state* on the elements of type AndroidST, that captures several well-formedness conditions.

3.2   Action Semantics

The axiomatic semantics of the Android security system is modeled by defining a set of actions, and providing their semantics as state transformers. Table 1 summarises a subset of the actions specified in our model, which provide coverage to the different functionalities of the Android security model.

The behaviour of actions (of type Action) is specified by a precondition *Pre* and by a postcondition *Post* of respective types: Pre : AndroidST $\rightarrow$ Action $\rightarrow$ *Prop*, and $Post$: AndroidST $\rightarrow$ Action $\rightarrow$ AndroidST $\rightarrow$ *Prop*. For instance, the axiomatic semantics of the `install` action is given by:

$$Pre(s, \texttt{install}\ app\ m\ c\ lRes) \overset{\text{def}}{=}$$
$$\neg isAppInstalled(app, s)\ \wedge\ \neg has\_duplicates\_cmp(m)\ \wedge$$
$$\forall c : \mathsf{Comp}, c \in cmp(m)\ \rightarrow\ c \notin cmpInState(s)\ \wedge$$
$$\neg hasDuplicates\_perm(m)\ \wedge\ authPerms(m, s)\ \wedge$$
$$\forall c : \mathsf{Comp}, c \in cmp(m)\ \rightarrow\ cmpDeclareIntentFilterCorrectly(c)$$

$$Post(s, \texttt{install}\ app\ m\ c\ lRes, s') \overset{\text{def}}{=}$$
$$addManifest(m, app, s, s')\ \wedge\ addCert(c, app, s, s')\ \wedge$$
$$addDefPerms(app, m, s, s')\ \wedge\ addApp(app, s, s')\ \wedge$$
$$addRes(app, lRes, s, s')\ \wedge\ initializePermLists(app, s, s')\ \wedge$$
$$sameOtherFields\_install(s, s')$$

The precondition of action `install` *app m c lRes* in a state *s* requires that the application is not already installed, and that no system application has its same identifier ($\neg isAppInstalled(app, s)$). The identifiers of the components listed in its manifest ($c \in cmp(m)$) must be different from each other ($\neg has\_duplicates\_cmp(m)$), and also different from those of the components already present in the device ($c \notin cmpInState(s)$). The permissions defined by the application to be installed must be different from each other ($\neg hasDuplicates\_perm(m)$) as well as different from those defined by other applications ($authPerms(m, s)$). Finally, the intent filters of its components ($c \in cmp(m)$) must be well-defined, that is the specified types of intents must match ($cmpDeclareIntentFilterCorrectly(c)$).

The postcondition of action `install` *app m c lRes*, with initial state s and final state s', specifies that its manifest (m), the certificate with which it was signed (c) and the permissions it defines that are not system permissions must be added to the state bound to the application identifier (predicates $addManifest, addCert$, and $addDefPerms$); which in turn must be included in the list of installed applications ($addApp(app, s, s')$). The application resources are initialized with the initial value $initVal$ ($addRes(app, lRes, s, s')$), while the lists of permission and permission groups granted to the application are initialized as empty ($initializePermLists(app, s, s')$). The rest of the system components remain unchanged ($sameOtherFields\_install(s, s')$).

3.3   Executions

There can be attempts to execute an action on a state that does not verify the precondition of that action. In the presence of one such situation the system answers with a corresponding error code (of type $ErrorCode$).

Executing an action a over a valid state s produces a new state s' and a corresponding answer r (denoted $s \xrightarrow{a/r} s'$), where the relation between the former state and the new one is given by the postcondition relation $Post$.

$$\frac{valid\_state(s) \;\; Pre(s,a) \;\; Post(s,a,s')}{s \xrightarrow{a/ok} s'} \qquad \frac{valid\_state(s) \;\; ErrorMsg(s,a,ec)}{s \xrightarrow{a/error(ec)} s}$$

Whenever an action occurs for which the precondition holds, the valid state may change in such a way that the action postcondition is established. The notation $s \xrightarrow{a/ok} s'$ may be read as *the execution of the action a in a valid state s results in a new state s'*. However, if the precondition is not satisfied, then the valid state s remains unchanged and the system answer is the error message determined by a relation $ErrorMsg$[2]. Formally, the possible answers of the system are defined by the type $Response \stackrel{def}{=} ok \mid error$ ($ec : ErrorCode$), where ok is the answer resulting from a successful execution of an action. One-step execution with error management preserves valid states.

Lemma 1 (Validity is invariant).

$\forall\ (s\ s' : \mathsf{AndroidST})(a : \mathsf{Action})(r : Response),\ s \xrightarrow{a/r} s' \rightarrow valid\_state(s')$

The results presented in this work are obtained from valid states of the system.

---

[2] Given a state s, an action a and an error code ec, $ErrorMsg(s, a, ec)$ holds iff *error ec* is an acceptable response when the execution of a is requested on state s.

Table 1. Actions

install *app m c lRes*	Install application with id *app*, whose manifest is *m*, is signed with certificate *c* and its resources list is *lRes*
uninstall *app*	Uninstall the application with id *app*
grant *p app*	Grant the permission *p* to the application *app*
revoke *p app*	Remove the permission *p* from the application *app*
grantPermGroup *g app*	Grant the permission group *g* to the application *app*
revokePermGroup *g app*	Remove the permission group *g* from the application *app*
hasPermission *p app*	Check if the application *app* has the permission *p*
read *ic cp u*	The running comp. *ic* reads the resource corresponding to URI *u* from content provider *cp*
write *ic cp u val*	The running comp. *ic* writes value *val* on the resource corresponding to URI *u* from content provider *cp*
startActivity *i ic*	The running comp. *ic* asks to start an activity specified by the intent *i*
startActivityRes *i n ic*	The running comp. *ic* asks to start an activity specified by the intent *i*, and expects as return a token *n*
startService *i ic*	The running comp. *ic* asks to start a service specified by the intent *i*
sendBroadcast *i ic p*	The running comp. *ic* sends the intent *i* as broadcast, specifying that only those components who have the permission *p* can receive it
sendOrdBroadcast *i ic p*	The running comp. *ic* sends the intent *i* as an ordered broadcast, specifying that only those components who have the permission *p* can receive it
sendSBroadcast *i ic*	The running comp. *ic* sends the intent *i* as a sticky broadcast
resolveIntent *i app*	Application *app* makes the intent *i* explicit
receiveIntent *i ic app*	Application *app* receives the intent *i*, sent by the running comp. *ic*
stop *ic*	The running comp. *ic* finishes its execution
grantP *ic cp app u pt*	The running comp. *ic* delegates permanent permissions to application *app*. This delegation enables *app* to perform operation *pt* on the resource assigned to URI *u* from content provider *cp*
revokeDel *ic cp u pt*	The running comp. *ic* revokes delegated permissions on URI *u* from content provider *cp* to perform operation *pt*
call *ic sac*	The running comp. *ic* makes the API call *sac*

3.4   Reasoning over the Specified Reference Monitor

In this section we present and discuss some relevant properties that can be established concerning the Android Marshmallow security framework. In particular, we shall focus on vulnerabilities that if exploited would allow violations to the intended security policy. The helper functions and predicates used to define the properties and lemmas discussed in this paper are presented and described in Table 2. The full formal definition of the lemmas as well as those of other security properties that were formally analyzed can be found in [17], along with their corresponding proofs. We also include an informal description of each property, in italics.

The first property presents a controversial characteristic of Android's new permission system. For example, as the dangerous permissions READ_CONTACTS (required for reading the contact list) and WRITE_CONTACTS (required for writing the contact list) both belong to the permission group CONTACTS, none of them can be individually granted. Instead, the application must be granted the permission group CONTACTS, giving it the right to both reading and writing the user's contact list. This violates the intended least privilege security policy claimed by the designers of the platform.

Property 1 (No fine control over grouped permissions).
$\forall(s, s' : \mathsf{AndroidST})(p : \mathsf{Perm})(g : \mathsf{PermGroup})(app : \mathsf{AppId}),$
$permissionIsGrouped(p) \rightarrow \neg s \xrightarrow{grant\ p\ app/ok} s'$

Android's permission system is not granular enough for granting a proper subset of the set of permissions that belong to a group.

The next property formalizes another weak point in the specification of Android's new permission system: in a valid state an application may have the right of writing the contact list (WRITE_CONTACTS) even if this permission was never individually granted.

Property 2 (Implicit individual permission granting).
$\exists(s : \mathsf{AndroidST})(p : \mathsf{Perm})(app : \mathsf{AppId}), valid\_state(s) \wedge$
$getPermissionLevel(p) = dangerous \wedge p \notin getGrantedPermsApp(app, s) \wedge$
$p \notin getDefPermsApp(app, s) \wedge appHasPermission(app, p, s)$

Applications may obtain permissions that were never granted to them individually.

In Android 6 an application that wishes to send information through the network must have the permission INTERNET but, since this permission is of level *normal*, any application that lists it as used in its manifest file has the right to access the network in an implicit and irrevocable way. Once again, this has been criticized due to the potential information leakage it allows. The following property formally generalizes this situation and embodies a reasonable argument to roll back this security issue introduced in Android Marshmallow.

Table 2. Helper functions and predicates

Function/Predicate	Description
$appHasPermission(app, p, s)$	holds iff app is considered to have permission p on state s
$canGrant(cp, u, s)$	holds iff the content provider cp allows the delegation of permissions over the resource at URI u on state s
$canStart(c', c, s)$	holds if the app containing component c' (installed in s) has the required permissions to create a new running instance of c
$cmpProtectedByPerm(c)$	returns the permission by which the component c is protected
$componentIsExported(c)$	holds iff the component c is exported and can be accessed from other applications
$existsRes(cp, u, s)$	holds iff the URI u belongs to the content provider cp on s
$getAppFromCmp(c, s)$	given a component c on s, returns the app to which it belongs
$getAppRequestedPerms(m)$	given the manifest m of an app, returns the set of permissions it uses
$getDefPermsApp(app, s)$	returns the set of permissions defined by app on state s
$getGrantedPermsApp(app, s)$	returns the set of individual permissions granted to app on s
$getInstalledApps(s)$	returns the set of identifiers of the applications installed on s
$getManifestForApp(app, s)$	returns the manifest of application app on state s
$getPermissionId(p)$	returns the identifier of permission p
$getPermissionLevel(p)$	returns the permission level of permission p
$getRunningComponents(s)$	returns the set of pairs consisting of a running instance id, and its associated component currently running on state s
$inApp(c, app, s)$	holds iff the component c belongs to application app on state s
$permissionIsGrouped(p)$	holds iff permission p belongs to any permission group
$permissionRequiredRead(c)$	returns the permission required for reading the component
$permSACs(p, sac)$	holds iff permission p is required for performing the system call sac (of type $SACall$)

Property 3 (Internet access implicitly and irrevocably allowed).
$\forall(s : \mathsf{AndroidST})(sac : SACall)(c : \mathsf{Comp})(ic : \mathsf{iComp})(p : \mathsf{Perm}),$
$valid\_state(s) \rightarrow permSAC(p, sac) \rightarrow$
$getPermissionLevel(p) = normal \rightarrow getPermissionId(p) \in$
$getAppRequestedPerms(getManifestForApp(getAppFromCmp(c, s), s)) \rightarrow$
$(ic, c) \in getRunningComponents(s) \rightarrow s \xrightarrow{call\ ic\ sac/ok} s$

If the execution of an Android API call only requires permissions of level normal,
it is enough for an application to list them as used on its manifest file to be
allowed to perform such call.

4   A Certified Reference Validation Mechanism

The implementation of the Android security system that we have developed
consists of a set of Coq functions such that for every predicate involved in the
axiomatic specification of action execution there exists a function which stands
for the functional counterpart of that predicate. In this section we show how the
correctness of the implementation is certified by a formal proof that establishes
its soundness with respect to the inductive (axiomatic) semantics of the Android
security mechanisms.

The execution of an action has been implemented as a *step* function that
given a system state s and an action a invokes the function that implements
the execution of a in s and returns an object *res* of type $Result \stackrel{\text{def}}{=} \{resp :$
$Response, st : \mathsf{AndroidST}\}$, where *res.resp* is either an error code *ec*, if the precondition of the actions does not hold in state s, or otherwise the value *ok*, and
the state *res.st* represents the execution effect. The *step* function acts basically
as an action dispatcher[3]. Figure 2, which shows the structure of the dispatcher,
details the branch corresponding to the dispatching of action `install`, which is
the action we shall use along this section to illustrate the working of the implementation. The functions invoked in the branches, like *install_safe*, are state
transformers whose definition follows this pattern: first it is checked whether the
precondition of the action is satisfied in state s, and then, if that is the case,
the function that implements the execution of the action is invoked. Otherwise,
the state s, unchanged, is returned along with an appropriate response specifying an error code which describes the failure. In this figure we also describe the
function that implements the execution of the `install` action. The Coq code
of this function, together with that of the remaining functions, can be found
in [17][4]. The function *install_pre* is defined as the nested validation of each of
the properties of the precondition, specifying which error to throw when one of
them doesn't hold. The function *install_post* implements the expected behavior
of the *install* action: the identifier of the application is prepended to the list of
installed applications, both the list of granted permission and the list of granted
permission groups are initialized as empty for it, its resource list is added to the

---

[3] Mechanism to trigger actions, on a state, according to the type of event considered.
[4] We omit here the formal definition of these functions due to space constraints.

system, and its manifest, certificate and defined permissions are included in the system state[5].

Definition $step(s, a)$:=
   match a **with**
      | ... ⇒ ...
      | **install** $app\ m\ c\ lRes$ ⇒ $install\_safe(app, m, c, lRes, s)$
      | ... ⇒ ...
  end.

Definition $install\_safe(app, m, c, lRes, s)$: $Result$:=
   match $install\_pre(app, m, c, lRes, s)$ **with**
      | $Some\ ec$ ⇒ $\{error(ec), s\}$
      | $None$ ⇒ $\{ok, install\_post(app, m, c, lRes, s)\}$
  end.

Fig. 2. The *step* function and execution of `install` action

4.1 Correctness of the Implementation

We proceed now to outline the proof that the functional implementation of the security mechanisms of Android correctly implements the axiomatic model. This property has been formally stated as the following correctness theorem which in turn was verified using Coq [17].

Theorem 1 (Correctness of the reference validation mechanism).
$\forall\ (s : \mathsf{AndroidST})\ (a : \mathsf{Action}), valid\_state(s) \rightarrow s \xrightarrow{a/step(s,a).resp} step(s, a).st$

The proof of this theorem follows by, in the first place, performing a case analysis on $Pre(s, a)$ (this predicate is decidable) and then in the case that $Pre(s, a)$ applying Lemma 2; otherwise applying Lemma 4.

Lemma 2 (Correctness of valid execution).
$\forall\ (s : \mathsf{AndroidST})\ (a : \mathsf{Action}), valid\_state(s) \rightarrow Pre(s, a) \rightarrow$
$s \xrightarrow{a/ok} step(s, a).st \wedge step(s, a).resp = ok$

The proof of Lemma 2 proceeds by applying functional induction on *step(s, a)* and then by providing the corresponding proof of soundness of the function that implements the execution of each action. Thus, in the case of the action `install` we have stated and proved Lemma 3. This lemma, in turn, follows by performing a case analysis on the result of applying the function *install_pre* on s and the action: if the result is an error code then the thesis follows by contradiction. Otherwise, it follows by the correctness of the function *install_post*.

Lemma 3 (Correctness of `install` execution).
$\forall\ (s : \mathsf{AndroidST})\ (app : \mathsf{App})\ (m : \mathsf{Manifest})\ (c : \mathsf{Cert})\ (lRes : list\ \mathsf{Res}),$
$valid\_state(s) \rightarrow Pre(s, \mathbf{install}\ app\ m\ c\ lRes) \rightarrow$
$Post(s, \mathbf{install}\ app\ m\ c\ lRes, install\_post(app, m, c, lRes, s))$

---

[5] We implement the sets in the model with lists of Coq.

As to Lemma 4, the proof also proceeds by first applying functional induction on *step(s, a)*. Then, for each action *a*, it is shown that if $\neg Pre(s, a)$ the execution of the function that implements that action yields the values returned by the branch corresponding to the case that the function that validates the precondition of the action *a* in state *s* fails, i.e., an error code *ec* and the (unchanged) state *s*.

Lemma 4 (Correctness of error execution).

$\forall$ $(s : \text{AndroidST})$ $(a : \text{Action})$, $valid\_state(s) \rightarrow \neg Pre(s, a) \rightarrow \exists (ec : ErrorCode)$,
$step(s, a).st = s \land step(s, a).resp = error(ec) \land ErrorMsg(s, a, ec)$

4.2 Reasoning over the Certified Reference Validation Mechanism

We have modeled the execution of the permission validation mechanism during a session of the system as a function that implements the execution of a list of actions starting in an (initial) system state. The output of the execution, a trace, is the corresponding sequence of states.

> **Function** *trace* $(s : \text{AndroidST})$ $(actions : list \text{ Action})$: $list \text{ AndroidST}$:=
>   **match** *actions* **with**
> | *nil* $\Rightarrow$ *nil*
> | *action* :: *rest* $\Rightarrow$ **let** $s' := (step\ s\ action).st$ **in** $s' :: trace\ s'\ rest$
> **end.**

We have stated and proved several security properties over the function *trace*. In what follows *s*, *initstate*, *sndstate* and *laststate* stand for variables of type AndroidST, *p* is a variable of type Perm, *app* and *app'* of type AppId and *l* of type *list* Action. We present first a property that formally states that in version 6 of the OS for an application to have a non-grouped dangerous permission it must be explicitly granted to it.

Property 4 (Dangerous permissions must be explicitly granted).
$valid\_state(initState) \rightarrow app \in getInstalledApps(initState) \rightarrow$
$getPermissionLevel(p) = dangerous \rightarrow permissionIsGrouped(p) = None \rightarrow$
$appHasPermission(app, p, lastState) \rightarrow$
$\neg appHasPermission(app, p, initState) \rightarrow \textbf{\textit{uninstall}}\ app \notin l \rightarrow$
$last(trace(initState, l), initState) = lastState \rightarrow \textbf{\textit{grant}}\ p\ app \in l$

A non-grouped dangerous permission can only be explicitly granted to an application.

The following property refers to the revocation of permissions and how to obtain them again.

Property 5 (Revoked permissions must be regranted).
$valid\_state(initState) \rightarrow getPermissionLevel(p) = dangerous \rightarrow$
$permissionIsGrouped(p) = None \rightarrow$
$p \notin getDefPermsForApp(app, initState) \rightarrow$

$step(initState, \textbf{revoke } p \ app).st = sndState \rightarrow$
$step(initState, \textbf{revoke } p \ app)).resp = ok \rightarrow$
$\textbf{uninstall } app \notin l \rightarrow \textbf{grant } p \ app \notin l \rightarrow$
$last(trace(sndState, l), sndState) = lastState \rightarrow$
$\neg appHasPermission(app, p, lastState)$

If an application used to have a permission that was later revoked, only regranting it will allow the application to have it again.

Certain assertions on which a developer could rely in previous versions of Android OS do not hold in its latest version. The following property states that a running component may have the right of starting another one on a certain state, but may not be able to do so at a later time.

Property 6 (The right to start an external component is revocable).
$\forall (c : \textsf{Comp}) \ (act : \textsf{Activity}) \ valid\_state(initState) \rightarrow$
$getPermissionLevel(p) = dangerous \rightarrow permissionIsGrouped(p) = None \rightarrow$
$app \neq app' \rightarrow p \notin getDefPermsApp(app, initState) \rightarrow$
$inApp(c, app, initState) \rightarrow$
$inApp(act, app', initState) \rightarrow cmpProtectedByPerm(act) = Some \ p \rightarrow$
$canStart(c, act, initState) \rightarrow \exists (l : list \ \textsf{Action}), \textbf{uninstall } app \notin l \wedge$
$\textbf{uninstall } app' \notin l \wedge \neg canStart(c, act, last(trace(initState, l), initState))$

A running component may have the right of starting another one on a certain state, but may not be able to do so at a later time.

When an application *app* is granted a permission *p* to access certain resource, it is also given the right to delegate this ability to another application, say *app'*, to access that same resource on its behalf. However, if *p* is revoked from the application *app*, the permission delegations are not invalidated and thus the application *app'* may still be able to access the resource. This property is a proof that the current specification allows a behavior which is arguably against the user's will.

Property 7 (Delegated permissions are not recursively revoked).
$\forall (ic, ic' : \textsf{iComp}) \ (c, c' : \textsf{Comp}) \ (u : uri) \ (cp : CProvider),$
$valid\_state(s) \rightarrow step(s, \textbf{grant } p \ app).resp = ok \rightarrow$
$getAppFromCmp(c, s) = app \rightarrow getAppFromCmp(c', s) = app' \rightarrow$
$(ic, c) \in getRunningComponents(s) \rightarrow$
$(ic', c') \in getRunningComponents(s) \rightarrow$
$canGrant(cp, u, s) \rightarrow existsRes(cp, u, s) \rightarrow componentIsExported(cp) \rightarrow$
$permissionRequiredRead(cp) = Some \ p \rightarrow$
let $opsResult := trace(s, [\textbf{grant } p \ app, \textbf{grantP } ic \ cp \ app' \ u \ Read,$
$\textbf{revoke } p \ app]$ in $step(last(opsResult, s), \textbf{read } ic' \ cp \ u).resp = ok$

In Android 6 if a permission p is revoked for an application app not necessarily shall it be revoked for the applications to which app delegated p.

5   Related Work

Several analyses have been carried out concerning the security of the Android system [5,11,12,14,15,20]. Few works, however, pay attention to the formal aspects of the permission enforcing framework. In particular, Shin et al. [22,23] build a formal framework that represents the Android permission system, which is developed in Coq, as we do. However, that work does not consider several aspects of the platform covered in our model, namely, the different types of components, the interaction between a running instance and the system, the R/W operation on a content provider, the semantics of the permission delegation mechanism and novel aspects of the security model, such as the management of runtime permissions.

Moving away from OS verification, many works have addressed the problem of relating inductively defined relations and executable functions, in particular in the context of programming language semantics. For instance, Tollitte et al. [25] show how to extract a functional implementation from an inductive specification in the Coq proof assistant. Similar approaches exist for Isabelle, see e.g. [8]. Earlier, alternative approaches such as [6,7] aim to provide reasoning principles for executable specifications. An alternative approach is presented in [13], where the verification of properties of imperative programs is performed using techniques based on the specialization of constrained logic programs. In our case, given that Coq provides a reasoning framework based on higher order logic to perform proofs of specifications and programs and a functional programming language, we are able to develop independently the specification of the reference monitor and the implementation of the validation mechanism. More specifically, in this work we present a model of a reference monitor and demonstrate properties which shall hold for every correct implementation of the model. Then, using the programming language of Coq we have developed a functional implementation of the reference validation mechanism and proved its correctness with respect to the specified reference monitor. Applying the program extraction mechanism provided by Coq we have also derived a certified Haskell prototype of the reference validation mechanism, which can be used to conduct verification activities on actual (real) implementations of the platform.

The results presented in this paper extend the ones reported in [9,10]. We have enriched the (formal) model presented in [9,10] so as to consider, in particular, the run time requesting/granting of permissions behavior introduced in Android Marshmallow. We also consider in this work execution error management and we have developed a certified monitor of the security model. Finally, several new properties concerning the security model of Android 6 (and further) have been formally formulated and proved.

6   Conclusion and Future Work

We have presented the development of an exhaustive formal specification of the Android security model that includes elements and properties that have been partially analyzed in previous work. We have enhanced the model considered in [9,10] with an explicit treatment of errors and with the latest version of the security mechanisms of the platform, which makes it possible to grant permissions at run time. We also present the formalization of security properties concerning the Android permission mechanisms that have not previously been formally verified and proved.

Using the programming language of the proof-assistant Coq we have defined a functional implementation of the reference validation mechanism, certified its correctness with respect to the axiomatic specification of the reference monitor and derived a certified Haskell prototype (CertAndroidSec) applying the program extraction mechanism provided by the proof assistant. The full certified code is available in [17].

The formal development is about 21k LOC of Coq, including proofs, and constitutes a suitable basis for reasoning about Android's permission model and security mechanisms.

One important goal of our work is to help to increase the level of reliability on the security of the Android platform by providing certified guarantees that the specified security mechanisms effectively allow to enforce the expected security policies. The use of idealized models and certified prototypes is a good step forward but no doubt the definitive step is to be able to provide similar guarantees concerning actual implementations of the platform. We plan to use the certified extracted algorithm, CertAndroidSec, as a testing oracle and also to conduct verification activities on actual implementations of the platform. In particular, we are investigating the use of that algorithm to compare the results of executing an action on a real Android platform and executing that same action on the correct program. This would allow us to monitor the actions performed in a real system and assessing whether the intended security policy is actually enforced by the particular implementation of the platform.

On the other hand, we are interested in to gain confidence in whether actual implementations of the platform conform with the abstract reference monitor, using lightweight verification techniques such as model-based testing (MBT) [26]. In general, MBT methods generate abstract test cases by performing different static analyzes of a (formal) model (of a given program). Those test cases are later refined to the level of the program; the program is run on these refined test cases; the outputs are collected and abstracted away on the model; and, finally, the model, the abstract test cases and the abstracted outputs are used to decide whether the program has errors or not. In the last step we plan to use CertAndroidSec instead of the Coq axiomatic specification. In effect, as CertAndroidSec is a certified prototype it behaves as prescribed by the Coq specification. Furthermore, as CertAndroidSec is a program it can be easily run on the abstract test cases, thus greatly simplifying this step.

References

1. Anderson, J.P.: Computer Security technology planning study. Technical report, Deputy for Command and Management System, USA (1972)

2. Android Developers: Application Fundamentals. http://developer.android.com/guide/components/fundamentals.html. Accessed Feb 2018

3. Android Developers: Requesting Permissions at Run Time. https://developer.android.com/intl/es/training/permissions/requesting.html. Accessed Feb 2018

4. Android Developers: R.styleable. http://developer.android.com/reference/android/R.styleable.html. Accessed Feb 2018

5. Armando, A., Carbone, R., Costa, G., Merlo, A.: Android permissions unleashed. In: Fournet, C., Hicks, M., Viganò, L. (eds.) IEEE 28th Computer Security Foundations Symposium, pp. 320–333. IEEE Computer Society (2015)

6. Balaa, A., Bertot, Y.: Fix-point equations for well-founded recursion in type theory. In: Aagaard, M., Harrison, J. (eds.) TPHOLs 2000. LNCS, vol. 1869, pp. 1–16. Springer, Heidelberg (2000). https://doi.org/10.1007/3-540-44659-1_1

7. Barthe, G., Forest, J., Pichardie, D., Rusu, V.: Defining and reasoning about recursive functions: a practical tool for the Coq proof assistant. In: Hagiya, M., Wadler, P. (eds.) FLOPS 2006. LNCS, vol. 3945, pp. 114–129. Springer, Heidelberg (2006). https://doi.org/10.1007/11737414_9

8. Berghofer, S., Bulwahn, L., Haftmann, F.: Turning inductive into equational specifications. In: Berghofer, S., Nipkow, T., Urban, C., Wenzel, M. (eds.) TPHOLs 2009. LNCS, vol. 5674, pp. 131–146. Springer, Heidelberg (2009). https://doi.org/10.1007/978-3-642-03359-9_11

9. Betarte, G., Campo, J.D., Luna, C., Romano, A.: Verifying Android's permission model. In: Leucker, M., Rueda, C., Valencia, F.D. (eds.) ICTAC 2015. LNCS, vol. 9399, pp. 485–504. Springer, Cham (2015). https://doi.org/10.1007/978-3-319-25150-9_28

10. Betarte, G., Campo, J.D., Luna, C., Romano, A.: Formal analysis of Android's permission-based security model. Sci. Ann. Comp. Sci. 26(1), 27–68 (2016)

11. Bugliesi, M., Calzavara, S., Spanò, A.: Lintent: towards security type-checking of Android applications. In: Beyer, D., Boreale, M. (eds.) FMOODS/FORTE 2013. LNCS, vol. 7892, pp. 289–304. Springer, Heidelberg (2013). https://doi.org/10.1007/978-3-642-38592-6_20

12. Conti, M., Nguyen, V.T.N., Crispo, B.: CRePE: context-related policy enforcement for Android. In: Burmester, M., Tsudik, G., Magliveras, S., Ilić, I. (eds.) ISC 2010. LNCS, vol. 6531, pp. 331–345. Springer, Heidelberg (2011). https://doi.org/10.1007/978-3-642-18178-8_29

13. De Angelis, E., Fioravanti, F., Pettorossi, A., Proietti, M.: Program verification via iterated specialization. Sci. Comput. Program. 95, 149–175 (2014)

14. Felt, A., Wang, H., Moshchuk, A., Hanna, S., Chin, E.: Permission re-delegation: attacks and defenses. In: USENIX Security Symposium. USENIX Association (2011)

15. Fragkaki, E., Bauer, L., Jia, L., Swasey, D.: Modeling and enhancing Android's permission system. In: Foresti, S., Yung, M., Martinelli, F. (eds.) ESORICS 2012. LNCS, vol. 7459, pp. 1–18. Springer, Heidelberg (2012). https://doi.org/10.1007/978-3-642-33167-1_1

16. Gartner: Gartner says worldwide sales of smartphones grew 9 percent in first quarter of 2017. Technical report. Gartner Inc. (2017)

17. GSI: Formal verification of the security model of Android: Coq code. http://www.fing.edu.uy/inco/grupos/gsi/documentos/proyectos/Android6-Coq-model.tar.gz. Accessed Feb 2018

18. Letouzey, P.: Programmation fonctionnelle certifiée - L'extraction de programmes dans l'assistant Coq. Ph.D. thesis, Université Paris-Sud, July 2004

19. Letouzey, P.: A new extraction for Coq. In: Geuvers, H., Wiedijk, F. (eds.) TYPES 2002. LNCS, vol. 2646, pp. 200–219. Springer, Heidelberg (2003). https://doi.org/10.1007/3-540-39185-1_12

20. Nauman, M., Khan, S., Zhang, X.: Apex: extending android permission model and enforcement with user-defined runtime constraints. In: Proceedings of ASIACCS 2010 (2011)

21. Open Handset Alliance: Android project. https://source.android.com/. Accessed Feb 2018

22. Shin, W., Kiyomoto, S., Fukushima, K., Tanaka, T.: A formal model to analyze the permission authorization and enforcement in the android framework. In: SocialCom 2010, pp. 944–951. IEEE Computer Society, Washington, DC (2010)

23. Shin, W., Kiyomoto, S., Fukushima, K., Tanaka, T.: A first step towards automated permission-enforcement analysis of the android framework. In: SAM 2010, pp. 323–329. CSREA Press (2010)

24. The Coq Team: The Coq Proof Assistant Reference Manual - Version V8.6 (2016)

25. Tollitte, P.-N., Delahaye, D., Dubois, C.: Producing certified functional code from inductive specifications. In: Hawblitzel, C., Miller, D. (eds.) CPP 2012. LNCS, vol. 7679, pp. 76–91. Springer, Heidelberg (2012). https://doi.org/10.1007/978-3-642-35308-6_9

26. Utting, M., Legeard, B.: Practical Model-Based Testing: A Tools Approach. Morgan Kaufmann Publishers Inc., San Francisco (2006)

Predicate Pairing with Abstraction for Relational Verification

Emanuele De Angelis[1]([⊠]), Fabio Fioravanti[1]([⊠]), Alberto Pettorossi[2,3]([⊠]), and Maurizio Proietti[3]([⊠])

[1] DEC, University 'G. d'Annunzio', Chieti-Pescara, Italy
{emanuele.deangelis,fabio.fioravanti}@unich.it
[2] DICII, University of Rome 'Tor Vergata', Rome, Italy
pettorossi@info.uniroma2.it
[3] IASI-CNR, Rome, Italy
maurizio.proietti@iasi.cnr.it

Abstract. Relational verification is a technique that aims at proving properties that relate two different program fragments, or two different program runs. It has been shown that constrained Horn clauses (CHCs) can effectively be used for relational verification by applying a CHC transformation, called *Predicate Pairing*, which allows the CHC solver to infer relations among arguments of different predicates. In this paper we study how the effects of the Predicate Pairing transformation can be enhanced by using various abstract domains based on Linear Arithmetic (i.e., the domain of convex polyhedra and some of its subdomains) during the transformation. After presenting an algorithm for Predicate Pairing with abstraction, we report on the experiments we have performed on over a hundred relational verification problems by using various abstract domains. The experiments have been performed by using the VeriMAP verification system, together with the Parma Polyhedra Library (PPL) and the Z3 solver for CHCs.

1 Introduction

Relational program properties are properties that relate two different programs or two executions of the same program. Relational properties that have been studied in the literature include program equivalence, non-interference for software security, and relative correctness [4,5,22].

Recent papers have advocated the use of *Constrained Horn Clauses* (CHCs) for the verification of relational program properties [12,18,27]. As suggested in these papers a verification problem is first translated into a set of Horn clauses with constraints in a suitable domain (usually, Linear Arithmetic), and then the satisfiability of that set of clauses is verified by using an SMT solver for Horn clauses, called here a CHC solver, such as Z3 [15] or Eldarica [19].

This work has been partially funded by INdAM-GNCS (Italy). E. De Angelis, F. Fioravanti, and A. Pettorossi are research associates at IASI-CNR, Rome, Italy.

© Springer International Publishing AG, part of Springer Nature 2018
F. Fioravanti and J. P. Gallagher (Eds.): LOPSTR 2017, LNCS 10855, pp. 289–305, 2018.
https://doi.org/10.1007/978-3-319-94460-9_17

The main difficulty encountered by CHC solvers when verifying relational properties is that these solvers find models of *single* predicates expressed in terms of Linear Arithmetic constraints, whereas the proof of relational properties often requires the discovery of relations among arguments of *two* (*or more*) distinct predicates. To mitigate this difficulty, *Predicate Pairing* transforms a set of clauses defining two predicates, say p and q, into a new set of clauses defining a new predicate, say r, equivalent to the conjunction of p and q [12]. Thus, when the CHC solver finds a model for the predicate r, it discovers relations among the arguments of p and q.

In the approach presented in this paper we use Predicate Pairing together with *Abstraction*, which is a technique often used in program analysis and transformation. It consists in mapping the concrete semantics of a program into an abstract domain, where some program properties can more easily be verified [6]. In the context of relational verification, Predicate Pairing combined with a basic form of abstraction has been introduced in a previous paper [12]. In that paper, in fact, Predicate Pairing is performed by introducing new definitions whose bodies are made out of two atoms together with equalities between some arguments of these predicates, and these equality constraints can be viewed as an abstraction into the domain of equalities.

Abstraction is also used by CHC *Specialization*, which is another transformation technique that has been proposed to increase the effectiveness of CHC solvers [8, 20]. Given a set of clauses, CHC Specialization propagates constraints through the clauses, and since this propagation often causes strengthening of the constraints, it may be the case that, if we first specialize a given set of clauses, the task of CHC solving is made easier. However, the impact of the specialization process very much depends on the choices of the particular *abstract domain* and associated *widening operator*, which are used when the specialized predicates are introduced or manipulated.

In this paper we address the problem of evaluating various combinations of (i) Predicate Pairing, (ii) Abstraction, and (iii) Specialization for the specific objective of verifying relational properties of programs. In order to do so, we have introduced a general algorithm for Predicate Pairing that is parametric with respect to the abstract constraint domain that is used. This domain is taken to be a subdomain of Linear Arithmetic, such as *Convex Polyhedra, Boxes, Bounded Differences*, and *Octagons* [2, 3, 7, 26]. Our parametric Abstraction-based Predicate Pairing algorithm, called the APP strategy, generalizes the one that makes use of equalities between variables that has been used in a previous paper of ours [12]. We have also considered a CHC Specialization algorithm, called the ASp strategy, that is parametric with respect to the abstract constraint domain that is used, and can be viewed as a particular instance of the APP strategy. Finally, we have performed various sets of experiments by applying different sequences of the APP and ASp strategies to sets of CHCs encoding relational properties of imperative programs. In these experiments we have varied the abstract constraint domains that the strategies use and we have explored the relative merits of these different domains when verifying relational properties.

The lesson we learned from our experiments is that the strategies achieving the best results use constraint domains, such as Bounded Differences or Octagons, in which one can express relations between variables, without requiring more precise domains, such as Convex Polyhedra. Moreover, Abstraction-based Predicate Pairing essentially incorporates the effect of CHC Specialization, and thus extra specializations steps (before or after Abstraction-based Predicate Pairing) are not cost-effective.

The paper is organized as follows. In Sect. 2 we present an introductory example showing the usefulness of abstraction. Then, in Sect. 3 we present the various abstract constraint domains, such as Convex Polyhedra, Boxes, Bounded Differences, and Octagons, and the operations defined on them. In Sect. 4 we present the APP and ASp strategies, and we prove that they preserve satisfiability (and unsatisfiability). In Sect. 5 we briefly describe the implementation of our verification method based on: (i) the VeriMAP transformation and verification system, (ii) the Parma Polyhedra Library for constraint manipulation [3], and (iii) the Z3 solver for CHC satisfiability. We also report on the experiments we performed on more that one hundred verification problems. Finally, in Sect. 6, we discuss the related work on program transformation and verification.

2   An Introductory Example

In this section we present our running example concerning the problem of proving the equivalence of two imperative programs. CHC solvers, like Z3 [15], which are based on Linear Arithmetic are not able to prove that equivalence starting from its direct encoding in CHC. However, we will show that if we pre-process that encoding by the Predicate Pairing strategy which uses a suitable abstract constraint domain, then the Z3 solver is able to make that proof.

Let us consider the programs $P1$ and $P2$ shown in Fig. 1, where program $P2$ is obtained from program $P1$ by applying a compiler optimization technique, called *software pipelining*. Software pipelining takes as input a program with a loop and produces in output a program with a new loop whose instructions are taken from different iterations of the original loop. Combined with other program transformations, software pipelining may allow more parallelism during program execution, and indeed, it can produce loops whose instructions have no read/write dependencies and thus can be executed in parallel. For example, in program $P2$, derived by pipelining from program $P1$, the dependency on x in the instructions of the loop in $P2$ can be removed by: (i) introducing a fresh variable u initialized to x, and (ii) replacing x by u on the right-hand side of the assignments within the loop. After this replacement we get the instructions 'u = x; y = y+u; a = a+1; x = u+a', and we can safely execute in parallel the instruction 'y = y+u' and the sequence of instructions 'a = a+1; x = u+a'.

$P1:$

```
while (a < b) {
    x = x+a;
    y = y+x;
    a = a+1;
}
```

$P2:$

```
if (a < b) {
    x = x+a;
    while (a < b-1) {
        y = y+x;
        a = a+1;
        x = x+a;
    }
    y = y+x;
    a = a+1;
}
```

Fig. 1. The input program $P1$ and the output program $P2$ obtained from $P1$ by applying software pipelining.

The equivalence of programs $P1$ and $P2$ with respect to the output value of x, can be expressed by the following clause F:

$$F: \; false \leftarrow X1 \neq X2, \; whl1(A, B, X, Y, A1, B1, X1, Y1),$$
$$ifte(A, B, X, Y, A2, B2, X2, Y2)$$

where: (i) predicates $whl1$ and $ifte$ represent the input/output relation of programs $P1$ and $P2$, respectively, (ii) A, B, X, Y and $A1, B1, X1, Y1$ represent the values of the variables a, b, x, y at the beginning and at the end, respectively, of the execution of program $P1$, and similarly, (iii) A, B, X, Y and $A2, B2, X2, Y2$ represent the values of a, b, x, y at the beginning and at the end, respectively, of the execution of program $P2$. The clauses defining $whl1$ and $ifte$, as well as the predicate $whl2$ on which $ifte$ depends, are reported below. (The non-expert reader may find the description of the technique for constructing clauses starting from imperative programs in a previous paper of ours [13].) Note that predicates $whl1$ and $whl2$ correspond to the while-loops of programs $P1$ and $P2$, respectively. Note also that strict inequalities occurring in programs (such as a < b in program $P1$) are represented by using non-strict inequalities in clauses (see, for instance, $A \leq B-1$ in clause 2).

1. $whl1(A, B, X, Y, A, B, X, Y) \leftarrow A \geq B$
2. $whl1(A, B, X, Y, A2, B2, X2, Y2) \leftarrow A \leq B-1, A1 = A+1, X1 = X+A,$
   $\qquad\qquad Y1 = X1+X, whl1(A1, B, X1, Y1, A2, B2, X2, Y2)$
3. $ifte(A, B, X, Y, A, B, X, Y) \leftarrow A \geq B$
4. $ifte(A, B, X, Y, A2, B2, X2, Y2) \leftarrow A \leq B-1, X1 = X+A,$
   $\qquad\qquad whl2(A, B, X1, Y, A2, B2, X2, Y2)$
5. $whl2(A, B, X, Y, A2, B, X, Y2) \leftarrow A \geq B-1, A2 = A+1, Y2 = Y+X$
6. $whl2(A, B, X, Y, A2, B2, X2, Y2) \leftarrow A \leq B-2, A1 = A+1, X1 = A1+1,$
   $\qquad\qquad Y1 = Y+X, whl2(A1, B, X1, Y1, A2, B2, X2, Y2)$

Let P be the set of clauses $\{1, \ldots, 6\}$. By proving the satisfiability of $P \cup \{F\}$, we prove that programs $P1$ and $P2$ produce identical values for x as output, when provided with the same input values. Unfortunately, CHC solvers, like Z3, based on Linear Arithmetic cannot prove the satisfiability of $P \cup \{F\}$. This inability is due to the fact that the solver computes models of *single* predicates expressed in terms of *linear* constraints among their arguments, while *non-linear* constraints among the arguments of each predicate *whl1* and *ifte* need be discovered to prove that the conjunction of the two atoms in the body of clause F implies $X1 = X2$. In particular, the solver has to discover that the *whl1* and *ifte* atoms imply $X1 = X + (B^2 - A^2 - B + A)/2$ and $X1 = X + (B^2 - A^2 - B + A)/2$, respectively.

The Predicate Pairing strategy we have introduced in a previous paper [12] may help in overcoming this difficulty. By Predicate Pairing we may introduce new predicates defined in terms of two (or more) atoms, together with suitable *linear* constraints among their arguments. Then, CHC solvers based on Linear Arithmetic may be able to infer relations among arguments of the new predicates that correspond to conjunctions of predicates before Predicate Pairing.

However, the efficacy of the Predicate Pairing strategy crucially depends on the choice of the constraints that are added when introducing new predicates. The original Predicate Pairing strategy [12] adds equalities between arguments. In Sect. 4 we extend that strategy so as to be parametric with respect to the domain of constraints used, and in Sect. 5 we evaluate in an experimental way the effect of varying the choice of that domain for relational verification.

In Sect. 4, after presenting our extended Predicate Pairing transformation strategy, we complete our running example and we show that the transformation strategy that uses the constraint domain of Bounded Differences is able to prove the equivalence property.

3   Constrained Horn Clauses over Numerical Domains

Let us first recall the basic notions about: (i) some abstract domains used in static program analysis based on abstract interpretation [6], and (ii) constrained Horn clauses (CHCs).

We consider the abstract constraint domain of *Convex (Closed) Polyhedra* [2, 3, 7, 26], CP for short, over the n-dimensional real space $\mathbb{R}^n$. The *atomic constraints* of the CP domain are of the form $a_1 x_1 + \ldots + a_n x_n \leq a$, where the a_i's are coefficients in $\mathbb{R}$ and the x's are variables ranging over $\mathbb{R}$. A *constraint* c is either *true*, or *false*, or an atomic constraint, or a conjunction of constraints.

Given a formula Γ, by $\forall(F)$ and $\exists(F)$ we denote its universal and existential closure, respectively. By $vars(F)$ we denote the set of variables occurring in F. A constraint c is said to be *satisfiable* if CP $\models \exists(c)$. Given two constraints c and d, we say that c *entails* d, and we write $c \sqsubseteq d$, if CP $\models \forall(c \rightarrow d)$. We say that c and d are *equivalent* if $c \sqsubseteq d$ and $d \sqsubseteq c$.

We also consider the following abstract constraint domains, namely: (i) *Univ*, (ii) *Boxes*, (iii) *Bounded Differences*, and (iv) *Octagons*, which are all subdomains of *Convex Polyhedra* in the sense that they are defined by putting restrictions on the form of the polyhedra associated with the atomic constraints. These abstract domains have all *true* and *false* as constraints and are closed under conjunction.

The constraints of the domain Univ are *true* and *false* only, and in the n-dimensional case *true* denotes the whole space $\mathbb{R}^n$ and *false* denotes the empty set on n-tuples of reals. The atomic constraints of Boxes are inequalities of the form $x \leq a$, where $a \in \mathbb{R}$. The atomic constraints of Bounded Differences are inequalities of the form $a_1 x_1 + a_2 x_2 \leq a$, where $a \in \mathbb{R}$, $a_i \in \{-1, 0, 1\}$, for $i = 1, 2$, and a_1 is different from a_2. The atomic constraints of Octagons are inequalities of the form $a_1 x_1 + a_2 x_2 \leq a$, where $a \in \mathbb{R}$ and $a_i \in \{-1, 0, 1\}$, for $i = 1, 2$.

Each abstract constraint domain $D \subseteq CP$ is endowed with some operators that we now define. (Details and examples of these operators can be found in [2, 3, 7, 26].) Let c and d be two constraints in D, or D-constraints.

The *least upper bound* operator is a function $\sqcup : D \times D \rightarrow D$ such that (i) $c \sqsubseteq c \sqcup d$, (ii) $d \sqsubseteq c \sqcup d$ and (iii) for all D-constraints e, if $c \sqsubseteq e$ and $d \sqsubseteq e$, then $c \sqcup d \sqsubseteq e$.

A *widening operator* is a function $\nabla : D \times D \rightarrow D$ such that (i) $c \sqsubseteq c \nabla d$, (ii) $d \sqsubseteq c \nabla d$, and (iii) for all chains $y_0 \sqsubseteq y_1 \sqsubseteq \ldots$, the chain $x_0 \sqsubseteq x_1 \sqsubseteq \ldots$, where $x_0 = y_0$ and, for $i > 0$, $x_{i+1} = x_i \nabla y_{i+1}$, has finitely many distinct elements (modulo equivalence in Linear Arithmetic).

The *abstraction operator* for a subdomain D of CP, is a function $\alpha : CP \rightarrow D$ such that (i) $c \sqsubseteq \alpha(c)$, and (ii) for all D-constraints e, if $c \sqsubseteq e$, then $\alpha(c) \sqsubseteq e$.

The *projection* of a D-constraint c onto a set X of variables, denoted $c \Downarrow X$, is a D-constraint c', with variables in X, which is equivalent to $\exists Y.c$, where $Y = vars(c) - X$. Clearly, $c \sqsubseteq c'$.

An *atom* is a formula of the form $p(X_1, \ldots, X_m)$, where p is a predicate symbol different from '$\leq$' and $X_1, \ldots, X_m$ are distinct variables. A *constrained Horn clause* (or simply, a *clause*, or a *CHC*) is an implication of the form $A \leftarrow c, G$ (comma denotes conjunction), where the conclusion (or *head*) A is either an atom or *false*, the premise (or *body*) is the conjunction of a constraint c and a (possibly empty) conjunction G of atoms. The empty conjunction is identified with *true*. We also assume that two atoms in the body of a clause do not share any variable. Note that, for reasons of simplicity, we wrote the clauses of the example in Sect. 2 in a form which does not comply with the syntax defined in this section. However, they can be rewritten into a compliant form by applying the following transformations: (i) the removal of multiple occurrences of variables in (conjunctions of) atoms in favor of equalities, (ii) the replacement of equalities by conjunctions of inequalities, and (iii) the split of clause F into two clauses where the disequality $X1 \neq X2$ has been replaced by the inequalities $X1 \leq X2 - 1$ and $X1 \geq X2 + 1$, respectively.

A set S of CHCs is said to be *satisfiable* if $S \cup CP$ has a model, or equivalently, $S \cup CP \not\models false$.

4   Predicate Pairing with Abstraction

In this section we present an algorithm for transforming CHCs, called *Abstraction-based Predicate Pairing* (or *APP strategy*, for short), which combines Predicate Pairing [12] with abstraction operators acting on a given constraint domain (see Fig. 2). The APP transformation strategy preserves satisfiability of clauses and has the objective of increasing the effectiveness of the satisfiability check that is performed by the subsequent application of a CHC solver.

The APP transformation strategy tuples together two or more predicates into a single new predicate which is equivalent to their conjunction. As discussed in Sect. 2, the addition of suitable constraints among the variables of the predicates paired together (or tupled together, if more than two), may ease the discovery of the relations existing among the arguments of the individual predicates. The APP strategy is parametric with respect to: (i) the abstract constraint domain which is considered, and (ii) a *Partition* operator that determines, for a given a clause, the atoms to be tupled together by splitting the conjunction G of atoms in the body of the clause into n (≥ 1) subconjunctions $G_1, \ldots, G_n$. By choosing the abstract constraint domain and the Partition operator in suitable ways, we can derive a wide range of transformations, and among these, the Predicate Pairing strategy introduced in a previous paper [12], *Linearization* [10], and CHC Specialization [8, 20].

In particular, the Predicate Pairing strategy is derived as follows. The constraint domain is the set of equalities between variables (thus, a subdomain of the Bounded Differences domain). For defining the Partition operator, suppose that the goal of the strategy is to pair two predicates q and r defined by two disjoint sets of clauses Q and R, respectively. Then, for a clause $H \leftarrow c, Q_1, \ldots, Q_m, R_1, \ldots, R_n$, with $m \leq n$, where $Q_1, \ldots, Q_m$ are atoms defined by clauses in Q and $R_1, \ldots, R_n$ are atoms defined by clauses in R, the Partition operator returns the partition $(Q_1, R_1), \ldots, (Q_m, R_m), (R_{m+1}), \ldots, (R_n)$, and similarly for the case $m \geq n$ (more sophisticated ways of choosing (Q_i, R_j) pairs have been proposed [14]).

A CHC Specialization strategy with Abstraction, which we call *ASp strategy*, can be derived by instantiating the APP strategy as we now specify. The ASp strategy is obtained by using the Partition operator that, given a conjunction of atoms $A_1, \ldots, A_n$ in the body of a clause, returns n subconjunctions, each consisting of a single atom A_i, with $i \in \{1, \ldots, n\}$ (that is, Predicate Pairing is not performed). In Sect. 5 we will show the effects of using ASp, together with APP, with different abstract constraint domains.

The APP strategy is realized by performing a sequence of applications of the well-known *unfold/fold rules* [17]. In order to be self-contained, now we present the version of the Unfolding rule used in this paper. The other rules will be presented when describing the APP strategy.
Unfolding Rule. Let P be a set of clauses and C be a clause of the form $H \leftarrow c, L, A, R$, where A is an atom and L and R are (possibly empty) conjunctions of atoms. Let us consider the set $\{A \leftarrow c_i, B_i \mid i = 1, \ldots, m\}$ made out of all the clauses in P whose head is A (after renaming). By unfolding C w.r.t. A using P, we derive the set of clauses $\{(H \leftarrow c, c_i, L, B_i, R) \mid i = 1, \ldots, m\}$.

The APP strategy constructs a tree *Defs* of clauses whose head is either *false* or a new predicate, that is, a predicate not occurring in the input set P of clauses. Clauses with new head predicates are called *definitions*. A definition D is said to be a *child* of a definition C, and equivalently, C is said to be the *parent* of D, if D is introduced to fold a clause derived by unfolding from clause C. The *ancestor* relation on *Defs* is the *reflexive transitive* closure of the parent relation.

Input: A set $P \cup \{C\}$ of clauses where C is a clause whose head is *false*.
Output: A set *TransfCls* of clauses.

INITIALIZATION: $InCls := \{C\}$; *Defs* is the tree made out of the root clause C only;
TransfCls $:= P$;
while there is a clause C in *InCls* of the form $H \leftarrow c, B$ *do*

- UNFOLDING: From clause C derive a set $U(C)$ of clauses by unfolding C with respect to each atom occurring in its body using P;

- CLAUSE DELETION: Remove from $U(C)$ all clauses with an unsatisfiable constraint;

- DEFINITION & FOLDING:
  for every clause $E \in U(C)$ of the form $H \leftarrow d, G$ *do*
    Partition the conjunction G into $n \, (\geq 1)$ subconjunctions $G_1, \ldots, G_n$;
    for $i = 1, \ldots, n$ *do*
        $d_i := \alpha(d) \Downarrow V_i$, where V_i is the set of variables in G_i;
        if in *Defs* there is no clause $newp_i(V_i) \leftarrow e_i, G_i$ such that $d_i \sqsubseteq e_i$ *then*
            if in *Defs* there is an ancestor clause of C of the form $newq(V_i) \leftarrow f_i, G_i$
            then $D_i := (newp_i(V_i) \leftarrow a_i, G_i)$, where $a_i = f_i \nabla (f_i \sqcup d_i)$
            else $D_i := (newp_i(V_i) \leftarrow d_i, G_i)$;
            $InCls := InCls \cup \{D_i\}$;   add D_i as a child of C in *Defs*;
        end-for;
        TransfCls $:=$ *TransfCls* $\cup \{H \leftarrow d, newp_1(V_1), \ldots, newp_n(V_n)\}$;
    end-for;
  $InCls := InCls - \{C\}$;
end-while

Fig. 2. The APP transformation strategy.

Note that, by construction, every constraint, either a_i or d_i, occurring in a new definition D_i introduced during the DEFINITION & FOLDING phase (see Fig. 2), belongs to the abstract constraint domain.

Let us now prove the termination and soundness of the strategy. A Partition operator is said to be *bounded* if there exists a positive integer k such that, for any clause C, the operator splits the body of C into the subconjunctions $G_1, \ldots, G_n$, where, for $i = 1, \ldots, n$, the number of atoms in G_i is at most k. For instance, $k \leq 2$ is a bound for the Partition operators described above.

Theorem 1 (Termination and Soundness of Predicate Pairing with Abstraction). *Let the set $P \cup \{C\}$ of clauses be the input of the APP strategy. Suppose that APP uses a bounded Partition operator. Then, the strategy terminates and returns a set TransfCls of clauses such that $P \cup \{C\}$ is satisfiable iff TransfCls is satisfiable.*

Proof (Sketch). Since the Partition operator is bounded and, by definition, no sequence of applications of the widening operator ∇ can generate infinitely many distinct constraints (modulo equivalence), the set of new predicate definitions that can be introduced by the APP strategy is finite. Thus, the number of executions of the *while* loop of the strategy is also finite, and hence APP terminates.

To show the soundness of APP we first recall the following result (see Theorem 2 in [12], which is a consequence of a well-known result by Etalle and Gabbrielli [17]): Suppose that from a set *Cls* of clauses we derive a new set *TransfCls* of clauses by a sequence of applications of the unfold/fold rules, such that every definition used for folding is unfolded during that sequence. Then *Cls* is satisfiable iff *TransfCls* is satisfiable. Now, by taking *Cls* to be the set $P \cup \{C\}$ of clauses that are an input of APP, the thesis follows from the fact that every clause added to *Defs* (and hence to *InCls*) is eventually unfolded.   □

Let us see the APP strategy in action on the example of Sect. 2. As already mentioned, the disequality $X1 \neq X2$ is viewed as a disjunction of two inequalities, and hence clause F is split into two clauses, say $F1$ and $F2$, containing the two disjuncts. For reasons of space we only prove the satisfiability of the set $P \cup \{F1\}$, where $F1$ is the following clause:

$$F1: \mathit{false} \leftarrow X1 \leq X2-1, \ \mathit{whl1}(A, B, X, Y, A1, B1, X1, Y1),$$
$$\mathit{ifte}(A, B, X, Y, A2, B2, X2, Y2)$$

The satisfiability of $P \cup \{F1, F2\}$ can be proved by applying the strategy twice. For the application of the APP strategy we use the Bounded Differences domain, or *BDS*, for short.

After the INITIALIZATION step, the APP strategy selects $F1$ from *InCls* and applies the UNFOLDING step. The unfolding of *whl1* and *ifte* occurring in the body of $F1$ mimics the execution of the *while* loop of program P1 and the *if-then-else* of program P2. By unfolding we get four clauses, three of which have unsatisfiable constraints and are removed by the subsequent CLAUSE DELETION step. The only clause with a satisfiable constraint is the following one (up to equivalence in Linear Arithmetic and variable renaming):

7. $\mathit{false} \leftarrow X2 \leq X4-1, A1 \leq B1, A1 = A3+1, Y1 = Y3+X1, B1 = B3, X1 = X3,$
    $\mathit{whl1}(A1, B1, X1, Y1, A2, B2, X2, Y2),$
    $\mathit{whl2}(A3, B3, X3, Y3, A4, B4, X4, Y4).$

Then the DEFINITION & FOLDING step adds the following new definition to *Defs* and to *InCls*:

8. $pp(A1, B1, X1, Y1, A2, B2, X2, Y2, A3, B3, X3, Y3, A4, B4, X4, Y4) \leftarrow$
    $X2 \leq X4-1, \ A1 \leq B1, \ A1 = A3+1, \ B1 = B3, \ X1 = X3,$
    $\mathit{whl1}(A1, B1, X1, Y1, A2, B2, X2, Y2),$
    $\mathit{whl2}(A3, B3, X3, Y3, A4, B4, X4, Y4).$

The body of clause 8 consists of the conjunction of the two atoms occurring in the body of clause 7 together with the constraints obtained from the constraints of clause 7 by applying the abstraction operator α for BDS (the projection is the identity in this case, because the variables occurring in the constraints are a subset of the variables in the atoms). The operator α drops the constraint $Y1 = Y3+X1$ whose least overapproximation in BDS is *true*. By folding clause 7 using definition 8 we get the following clause, which is then added to *TranfCls*:

9. $false \leftarrow X2 \leq X4-1, A1 \leq B1, A1 = A3+1, Y1 = Y3+X1, B1 = B3, X1 = X3,$
$\qquad pp(A1, B1, X1, Y1, A2, B2, X2, Y2, A3, B3, X3, Y3, A4, B4, X4, Y4).$

Now, the APP strategy performs a second iteration of the *while* loop to process definition 8 in *InDefs*. By UNFOLDING and CLAUSE DELETION we have that the constraints occurring in definition 8 are preserved. Hence, we get a clause that can be folded again using definition 8, thereby deriving:

10. $pp(A1, B1, X1, Y1, A2, B2, X2, Y2, A3, B3, X3, Y3, A4, B4, X4, Y4) \leftarrow$
$\qquad X2 \leq X4-1, \ A1 \leq B1, \ A1 = A3+1, \ B1 = B3, \ X1 = X3, \ A5 \leq B1,$
$\qquad A5 = A1+1, \ X5 = X1+A1, \ Y5 = Y1+X5, \ X6 = X5, \ Y6 = Y3+X1,$
$\qquad pp(A5, B1, X5, Y5, A2, B2, X2, Y2, A1, B3, X6, Y6, A4, B4, X4, Y4).$

Since there are no more clauses to be processed in *InCls*, the final set of clauses is *TransfCls* = {9,10}. The satisfiability of *TransfCls* is trivial, and is easily checked by Z3, because it contains no constrained facts (that is, clauses with only constraints in their body), and hence a model is obtained by taking *pp* to be *false*.

Note that the widening and least upper bound operators were not used in our running example, but widening is needed, in general, to guarantee the termination of APP (see Theorem 1).

Note also that the abstract constraint domain used by APP is crucial for deriving clauses without constrained facts. Indeed, if in our running example we use the domain Univ, instead of BDS, then the body of the new definition introduced after unfolding consists of the conjunction of the two *whl*1 and *whl*2 atoms without any constraint, as the abstraction operator for Univ maps every satisfiable constraint to *true*. Then, by unfolding this new definition, we get a constrained fact derived from the constrained facts of *whl*1 and *whl*2 (i.e., clauses 1 and 5 of Sect. 2).

5   Experimental Evaluation

In this section we present the results of the experiments we have performed by applying in various ways both the APP strategy and its instance, the ASp strategy. These results illustrate the role of abstract constraint domains considered when applying those strategies, and they also show the usefulness of the APP strategy for improving the performance of the CHC solvers when checking satisfiability of clauses.

We have implemented the APP and the ASp strategies using the VeriMAP transformation system [9] and the Parma Polyhedra Library (PPL) [3], and we have used the Z3 solver [15] for checking satisfiability of the clauses generated by those strategies. The verification process is depicted in Fig. 3 and can be described as follows. The clauses encoding a verification problem are given

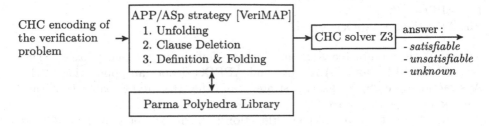

Fig. 3. The verification process.

as input to the VeriMAP system which applies to them a (possibly empty) sequence of APP (or ASp) strategies, using a specific constraint domain. When applying these strategies the constraints in the domain abstract are manipulated using the Parma Polyhedra Library. The resulting clauses, if produced within a specified timeout, will be passed in input to the Z3 solver to test their satisfiability.

Implementation of the APP and ASp Strategies. We have ported the VeriMAP system from SICStus Prolog 3.12.5 to SWI-Prolog 7.4.2 and we have extended its transformation engine so to use the abstract constraint domains and the associated operations provided by the Parma Polyhedra Library 1.2.

The domains we have considered are: (i) *Univ*, (ii) *Boxes*, (iii) *Bounded Differences* (also called Bounded Difference Shapes, and denoted BDS, for short), (iv) *Octagons* (also called Octagonal Shapes, and denoted OS, for short), and (v) *Convex Polyhedra*, together with the operations of projection, least upper bound, widening, emptiness check, and inclusion check (these two kinds of checks correspond to satisfiability and entailment, respectively). In particular, we have considered the following two variants of the Convex Polyhedra domain: (1) the one with the widening operator of Halbwachs [7], and (2) the one with the widening operator of Bagnara et al. [2]. These variants will be denoted by CP-H and CP-B, respectively. Since VeriMAP natively represents constraints using the syntax of the Constraint Logic Programming (CLP), when implementing the APP strategy, we have used the translation from PPL polyhedra to CLP constraints, and vice versa.

Benchmark Suite. We have considered a benchmark suite consisting of 136 verification problems, for a total number of 1655 input constrained Horn clauses. Each problem consists in the verification of a relational property, such as equivalence, monotonicity, injectivity, functional dependency, loop optimization, and non-interference [4,5,10,12,18].

Experiments. We have performed the following six sets of experiments E0–E5 (see the corresponding six frames in Table 1):

E0: Z3
E1: ASp(X); Z3
E2: ASp(X); APP(X); Z3
E3: ASp(X); APP(X); ASp(X); Z3

E4: APP(X); Z3
E5: APP(Univ); ASp(X); Z3

where: (i) the parameter X is an abstract domain in the set {Boxes, BDS, OS, CP-H, CP-B} and (ii) ASp(X) and APP(X) denote an application of the Abstraction-based Specialization strategy and the Abstraction-based Predicate Pairing strategy, respectively, by using the abstract domain X.

When trying to solve a single verification problem, we set a timeout of 300 s for each application of the APP(X) strategy or of the ASp(X) strategy or of the Z3 solver.

Here is an explanation of the experiments E0, E1 with X = OS, and E2 with X = OS. The explanation of the other experiments is similar.

Experiment E0 (see Frame E0 in Table 1) consists in performing a run of Z3 directly on the clauses that encode each verification problem. Z3 solves (either positively or negatively) 28 problems (see Column *SolProbls*) out of the total 136 verification problems, by providing the answer (either '*satisfiable*' or '*unsatisfiable*', respectively) within the timeout in an average time of 2.36 s (see Column *Avg Time2*) per solved problem.

Experiment E1 with X = OS (see line OS of Frame E1 in Table 1) consists in applying the ASp(OS) strategy on the clauses that encode each of the 136 verification problems, and then running Z3. From a total of 1655 input clauses these 136 applications of ASp(OS) produce a total of 3540 output clauses (see Column *OutCls*) with a size increase of about $2.14 (\approx 3540/1655)$ times (see Column *SizeRatio*), in an average time of 0.73 s per problem (see Column *Avg Time1*). Then, on the 3540 output clauses we run Z3 that solves 28 problems with an average time of 4.10 s per solved problem.

Experiment E2 with X = OS (see line OS of Frame E2 in Table 1) consists in applying the ASp(OS) strategy on the input clauses, exactly as in Experiment E1, then applying the APP(OS) strategy, which produces a total of 20361 output clauses, and finally running Z3. Note that for two problems APP(OS) is unable to produce the output clauses within the timeout (see Column *OutProbls* where the entry is 134, instead of 136).

When trying to solve a verification problem among the 136 problems of a given experiment, it may be the case that the ASp(X) strategy, or the APP(X) strategy, does not complete its execution within the timeout. In that case we say that the verification problem is *aborted* and the input clauses encoding that problem are not taken into account when computing the size ratios of Column *SizeRatio*. Similarly, the time taken for any aborted verification problem is not taken into account when computing the average times of Column *Avg Time1*.

In all our experiments we have used as constraint solver Z3 4.5.0 with the Duality fixed-point engine [24] on an Intel Xeon CPU E5-2640 2.00 GHz processor with 64 GB of memory under the GNU/Linux 64 bit operating system CentOS 7.

Discussion of the Results. Let us now comment on the experimental results presented in Table 1. First we observe that various combinations of the ASp and APP strategies (or the APP strategy alone) significantly increase the number

Table 1. Column *Exp* reports the set of experiments considered in each frame. Every line in each frame reports the results of a single experiment which consists of 136 verification problems. The abstract domain used in an experiment is shown in Column *Domain* X. Columns *OutProbls* and *OutCls* report the number of non-aborted verification problems and the total number of their output clauses, respectively. Column *SizeRatio* reports the value *OutCls* divided by the total number of input clauses of the non-aborted verification problems. Column *Avg Time*1 reports the time taken to produce the clauses of Column *OutCls* divided by the value *OutProbls*. Columns *SolProbls* and *Avg Time*2 report the number of (non-aborted) verification problems solved by Z3 and the average time taken by Z3 per solved problem. The times are the CPU seconds spent in user mode.

Exp	VeriMAP					Z3	
	Domain X	*OutProbls*	*OutCls*	*SizeRatio*	*Avg Time*1	*SolProbls*	*Avg Time*2
E0	—	—	—	—	—	28	2.36
E1	Boxes	136	3111	1.88	0.67	29	3.15
	BDS	136	2629	1.59	0.66	28	3.79
	OS	136	3540	2.14	0.73	28	4.10
	CP-H	136	3021	1.83	0.66	34	3.95
	CP-B	136	3633	2.20	0.69	36	10.14
E2	Boxes	134	27753	17.10	2.52	73	2.20
	BDS	136	12793	7.73	3.26	119	3.69
	OS	134	20361	12.44	5.23	121	3.90
	CP-H	135	16193	9.84	3.74	113	0.93
	CP-B	127	12554	8.06	3.51	114	3.65
E3	Boxes	134	45970	28.32	5.09	77	3.54
	BDS	136	26683	16.12	6.56	121	3.80
	OS	134	36871	22.52	10.21	119	3.06
	CP-H	135	31521	19.16	7.66	115	2.05
	CP-B	127	25495	16.37	8.10	112	1.27
E4	Boxes	136	20296	12.26	2.27	78	2.01
	BDS	136	8630	5.21	1.38	121	2.45
	OS	135	13762	8.37	2.97	120	1.77
	CP-H	135	13823	8.40	2.59	110	1.57
	CP-B	131	11718	7.35	2.22	113	2.19
E5	Boxes	136	19932	12.04	2.94	74	3.07
	BDS	136	8387	5.07	2.17	120	1.63
	OS	135	14065	8.55	3.64	118	1.39
	CP-H	135	14111	8.58	3.29	112	1.44
	CP-B	129	9831	6.24	3.12	113	2.05

of problems that Z3 solves. Indeed, while Z3 alone solves 28 problems only (see Frame E0), suitable combinations of the ASp and APP strategies (or APP alone) allow Z3 to solve over 120 problems (see Frames E2–E5).

However, the increase of efficacy in proving the desired properties is mainly due to the APP strategy, rather then the ASp strategy. Indeed, Frame E1 shows that the use of ASp alone makes just a marginal increase in the number of problems solved by Z3 (from the 28 solved problems, as shown in Frame E0, to a maximum of 36 solved problems, as shown in Frame E1). Moreover, by combining the ASp and APP strategies (see Frames E2 and E3, Column *SolProbls*) we get results which are not significantly better than the ones obtained by using the APP strategy alone (see Frame E4, Column *SolProbls*).

The comparison between Frames E4 and E5 (Columns for Z3) tells us that the effect of the APP(X) strategy, for a given abstract domain X, can also be obtained in two steps: (i) first, by applying APP(Univ), and (ii) then, by applying ASp(X). Recall that the abstraction operator for the Univ domain maps any satisfiable constraint to *true*, and hence APP(Univ) does not add any constraint when new definitions are introduced. In other terms, APP(Univ); ASp(X) separates Predicate Pairing from constraint addition using domain X, whereas APP(X) does the two transformations at the same time.

Let us now analyze our results from the perspective of the constraint domain X used in ASp(X) and APP(X). The use of the Boxes domain, that is, interval constraints on single real variables, is not very effective. Indeed, in Frames E2–E5 we see that Boxes allows the solution of at most 78 problems (see Frame E4, line 'Boxes'), while the other domains enable Z3 to solve at least 110 problems (see Frame E4, line 'CP-H'). The poor performance of Boxes with respect to those of the other domains can be explained by the fact that constraints in Boxes are not expressive enough to represent relations among program variables. Hence, they are of little help for proving relational properties. Note, however, that if precision is increased, from BDS and OS to Convex Polyhedra (CP-H or CP-B), the efficacy of the verification process decreases. For instance, Frame E4 shows that APP(BDS) and APP(OS) allow Z3 to solve 121 and 120 problems, respectively, while APP(CP-H) and APP(CP-B) allow Z3 to solve at most 113 problems. We would also like to point out that the sets of problems solved with two different abstract domains are not always comparable. For instance, in Frame E2 the set of 119 problems solved with BDS is not a subset of the 121 problems solved with OS. In particular, two problems were solved by using BDS and not by using OS.

Finally, we would like to comment on the computational performances of the transformations. Some combinations of ASp and APP significantly increase the number of output clauses (see, in particular, the increase of over 28 times shown in Frame E3, line 'Boxes', Column *SizeRatio*) and are costly (see, for instance, the average time of 10.21 s in Frame E3, line 'OS', Column *AvgTime1*). This is mainly due to the fact that ASp may introduce several specialized versions for the same predicate occurring in the original set of clauses. However, if we consider the APP(BDS) strategy, without previous or subsequent applications of ASp (see Frame E4), then the increase of the number of output clauses is limited to about 5 times and the average transformation time is only 1.38 s, and hence much lower than the average solving time taken by Z3.

6 Related Work and Conclusions

We have proposed various ways of combining transformation and abstraction techniques for constrained Horn clauses with the goal of verifying relational properties of imperative programs. To this aim we have presented two algorithms, the Predicate Pairing and Specialization algorithms, which are parameterized with respect to a given abstract constraint domain and its operators. Then we have presented an extensive experimental evaluation of CHC satisfiability problems encoding relational verification problems. Our experiments show that suitable combinations of transformations and abstraction dramatically increase the effectiveness of the Z3 solver on the given benchmark. The most effective techniques combine Predicate Pairing and Abstraction based on Bounded Differences or Octagons [2,26], that is, constraint domains that are quite simple, but expressive enough to capture the relations between predicate arguments.

Relational verification has been extensively studied, and still receives much attention as a relevant problem in the field of software engineering [4,12,18,22,27]. In particular, during the software development process it may be helpful to prove that the semantics of a new program version has some specified relation with the semantics of an old version.

Among the various methods to prove relational properties, those by Mordvinov and Fedyunkovich [27] and by Felsing et al. [18] are the most closely related to ours. The method proposed in the former paper [27] introduces the notion of CHC product (somewhat related to Predicate Pairing), that is, a CHC transformation that synchronizes computations to improve the effectiveness of the CHC satisfiability checks. The latter method proposed by Felsing et al. [18] presents proof rules for relations between imperative programs that are translated into constrained Horn clauses. The satisfiability of these clauses, which entails the relation of interest, is then checked by state-of-the-art CHC solvers.

The Predicate Pairing technique we present in this paper is a descendant of well-known techniques for logic program transformation, such as *Tupling* [29] and *Conjunctive Partial Deduction* [16], which derive new predicates defined in terms of conjunctions of atoms. The goal of these techniques is to derive efficient logic programs by: (i) avoiding multiple traversals of data structures and repeated evaluations of predicate calls, and (ii) producing specialized program versions that take into account partial information on the input values. An integration of Conjunctive Partial Deduction and abstract interpretation, called *Abstract Conjunctive Partial Deduction*, has also been presented in the literature [23]. Recent work has shown that the extension of these transformation techniques to constrained Horn clauses can play a significant role in improving the effectiveness of CHC solvers for proving properties of imperative programs, and in particular for verifying relational properties [11,12].

The CHC Specialization strategy we consider in this paper is a variant of specialization techniques for (constraint) logic programs which have been proposed to support program verification [1,8,10,13,20,21,25,28]. However, these techniques are focused on the verification of partial or total correctness of single programs, and not on the relational verification.

Acknowledgements. We thank the anonymous referees for their constructive comments.

References

1. Albert, E., Gómez-Zamalloa, M., Hubert, L., Puebla, G.: Verification of Java Bytecode using analysis and transformation of logic programs. In: Hanus, M. (ed.) PADL 2007. LNCS, vol. 4354, pp. 124–139. Springer, Heidelberg (2007). https://doi.org/10.1007/978-3-540-69611-7_8
2. Bagnara, R., Hill, P.M., Ricci, E., Zaffanella, E.: Precise widening operators for convex polyhedra. Sci. Comput. Program. **58**(1), 28–56 (2005)
3. Bagnara, R., Hill, P.M., Zaffanella, E.: The Parma Polyhedra Library: Toward a complete set of numerical abstractions for the analysis and verification of hardware and software systems. Sci. Comput. Program. **72**(1–2), 3–21 (2008)
4. Barthe, G., Crespo, J.M., Kunz, C.: Relational verification using product programs. In: Butler, M., Schulte, W. (eds.) FM 2011. LNCS, vol. 6664, pp. 200–214. Springer, Heidelberg (2011). https://doi.org/10.1007/978-3-642-21437-0_17
5. Benton, N.: Simple relational correctness proofs for static analyses and program transformations. In: Proceedings of POPL 2004, pp. 14–25. ACM (2004)
6. Cousot, P., Cousot, R.: Abstract interpretation: A unified lattice model for static analysis of programs by construction of approximation of fixpoints. In: Proceedings of POPL 1977, pp. 238–252. ACM (1977)
7. Cousot, P., Halbwachs, N.: Automatic discovery of linear restraints among variables of a program. In: Proceedings of POPL 1978, pp. 84–96. ACM (1978)
8. De Angelis, E., Fioravanti, F., Pettorossi, A., Proietti, M.: Program verification via iterated specialization. Sci. Comput. Program. **95**(Part 2), 149–175 (2014)
9. De Angelis, E., Fioravanti, F., Pettorossi, A., Proietti, M.: VeriMAP: a tool for verifying programs through transformations. In: Ábrahám, E., Havelund, K. (eds.) TACAS 2014. LNCS, vol. 8413, pp. 568–574. Springer, Heidelberg (2014). https://doi.org/10.1007/978-3-642-54862-8_47
10. De Angelis, E., Fioravanti, F., Pettorossi, A., Proietti, M.: Proving correctness of imperative programs by linearizing constrained Horn clauses. Theory Pract. Logic Program. **15**(4–5), 635–650 (2015)
11. De Angelis, E., Fioravanti, F., Pettorossi, A., Proietti, M.: A rule-based verification strategy for array manipulating programs. Fundamenta Informaticae **140**(3–4), 329–355 (2015)
12. De Angelis, E., Fioravanti, F., Pettorossi, A., Proietti, M.: Relational verification through Horn clause transformation. In: Rival, X. (ed.) SAS 2016. LNCS, vol. 9837, pp. 147–169. Springer, Heidelberg (2016). https://doi.org/10.1007/978-3-662-53413-7_8
13. De Angelis, E., Fioravanti, F., Pettorossi, A., Proietti, M.: Semantics-based generation of verification conditions by program specialization. Sci. Comput. Program. **147**, 78–108 (2017)

14. De Angelis, E., Fioravanti, F., Pettorossi, A., Proietti, M.: Predicate pairing for program verification. Theory Pract. Logic Program., 1–41 (2017). https://doi.org/10.1017/S1471068417000497

15. de Moura, L., Bjørner, N.: Z3: An efficient SMT solver. In: Ramakrishnan, C.R., Rehof, J. (eds.) TACAS 2008. LNCS, vol. 4963, pp. 337–340. Springer, Heidelberg (2008). https://doi.org/10.1007/978-3-540-78800-3_24

16. De Schreye, D., Glück, R., Jørgensen, J., Leuschel, M., Martens, B., Sørensen, M.H.: Conjunctive partial deduction: Foundations, control, algorithms, and experiments. J. Logic Program. **41**(2–3), 231–277 (1999)

17. Etalle, S., Gabbrielli, M.: Transformations of CLP modules. Theoret. Comput. Sci. **166**, 101–146 (1996)

18. Felsing, D., Grebing, S., Klebanov, V., Rümmer, P., Ulbrich, M.: Automating regression verification. In: Proceedings of ASE 2014, pp. 349–360. ACM (2014)

19. Hojjat, H., Konečný, F., Garnier, F., Iosif, R., Kuncak, V., Rümmer, P.: A verification toolkit for numerical transition systems. In: Giannakopoulou, D., Méry, D. (eds.) FM 2012. LNCS, vol. 7436, pp. 247–251. Springer, Heidelberg (2012). https://doi.org/10.1007/978-3-642-32759-9_21

20. Kafle, B., Gallagher, J.P.: Constraint specialisation in Horn clause verification. Sci. Comput. Program. **137**, 125–140 (2017)

21. Kafle, B., Gallagher, J.P.: Horn clause verification with convex polyhedral abstraction and tree automata-based refinement. Comput. Lang. Syst. Struct. **47**, 2–18 (2017)

22. Lahiri, S.K., McMillan, K.L., Sharma, R., Hawblitzel, C.: Differential assertion checking. In: Proceedings of ESEC/FSE 2013, pp. 345–355. ACM (2013)

23. Leuschel, M.: A framework for the integration of partial evaluation and abstract interpretation of logic programs. ACM TOPLAS **26**(3), 413–463 (2004)

24. McMillan, K.L., Rybalchenko, A.: Solving constrained Horn clauses using interpolation. MSR Technical Report 2013-6, Microsoft Report (2013)

25. Méndez-Lojo, M., Navas, J., Hermenegildo, M.V.: A flexible, (C)LP-based approach to the analysis of object oriented programs. In: King, A. (ed.) LOPSTR 2007. LNCS, vol. 4915, pp. 154–168. Springer, Heidelberg (2008). https://doi.org/10.1007/978-3-540-78769-3_11

26. Miné, A.: The octagon abstract domain. Higher-Order Symbolic Comput. **19**(1), 31–100 (2006)

27. Mordvinov, D., Fedyukovich, G.: Synchronizing constrained Horn clauses. In: Proceedings of LPAR 2017. EPiC Series in Computing, vol. 46, pp. 338–355. EasyChair (2017)

28. Peralta, J.C., Gallagher, J.P., Sağlam, H.: Analysis of imperative programs through analysis of constraint logic programs. In: Levi, G. (ed.) SAS 1998. LNCS, vol. 1503, pp. 246–261. Springer, Heidelberg (1998). https://doi.org/10.1007/3-540-49727-7_15

29. Pettorossi, A., Proietti, M.: Transformation of logic programs: foundations and techniques. J. Logic Program. **19**(20), 261–320 (1994)

Variant-Based Decidable Satisfiability in Initial Algebras with Predicates

Raúl Gutiérrez[1]([✉]) [iD] and José Meseguer[2]

[1] Universitat Politècnica de València, Valencia, Spain
rgutierrez@dsic.upv.es
[2] University of Illinois at Urbana-Champaign, Champaign, USA

Abstract. Decision procedures can be either *theory-specific*, e.g., Presburger arithmetic, or *theory-generic*, applying to an infinite number of user-definable theories. Variant satisfiability is a theory-generic procedure for quantifier-free satisfiability in the initial algebra of an order-sorted equational theory $(\Sigma, E \cup B)$ under two conditions: (i) $E \cup B$ has the *finite variant property* and B has a finitary unification algorithm; and (ii) $(\Sigma, E \cup B)$ protects a constructor subtheory $(\Omega, E_\Omega \cup B_\Omega)$ that is OS-*compact*. These conditions apply to many user-definable theories, but have a main limitation: they apply well to *data structures*, but often do *not* hold for user-definable *predicates* on such data structures. We present a theory-generic satisfiability decision procedure, and a prototype implementation, extending variant-based satisfiability to initial algebras with user-definable predicates under fairly general conditions.

Keywords: Finite variant property (fvp) · OS-compactness
User-definable predicates · Decidable validity and satisfiability
in initial algebras

1 Introduction

Some of the most important recent advances in software verification are due to the systematic use of decision procedures in both model checkers and theorem provers. However, a key limitation in exploiting the power of such decision procedures is their current *lack of extensibility*. The present situation is as follows. Suppose a system has been formally specified as a theory T about which we want to verify some properties, say $\varphi_1, \ldots, \varphi_n$, using some model checker or theorem prover that relies on an SMT solver for its decision procedures. This limits *a priori* the decidable subtheory $T_0 \subseteq T$ that can be handled by the SMT

Partially supported by NSF Grant CNS 14-09416, NRL under contract number N00173-17-1-G002, the EU (FEDER), Spanish MINECO project TIN2015-69175-C4-1-R and GV project PROMETEOII/2015/013. Raúl Gutiérrez was also supported by INCIBE program "Ayudas para la excelencia de los equipos de investigación avanzada en ciberseguridad".

F. Fioravanti and J. P. Gallagher (Eds.): LOPSTR 2017, LNCS 10855, pp. 306–322, 2018.
https://doi.org/10.1007/978-3-319-94460-9_18

solver. Specifically, the SMT solver will typically support a fixed set $Q_1, \ldots, Q_k$ of decidable theories, so that, using a theory combination method such as Nelson and Oppen [25], or Shostak [26], T_0 must be a finite combination of the decidable theories $Q_1, \ldots, Q_k$ supported by the SMT solver.

In non-toy applications it is unrealistic to expect that the entire specification T of a software system will be decidable. Obviously, the bigger the decidable subtheory $T_0 \subseteq T$, the higher the levels of automation and the greater the chances of scaling up the verification effort. With *theory-specific* procedures for, say, $Q_1, \ldots, Q_k$, the decidable fragment T_0 of T is a priori bounded. One promising way to extend the decidable fragment T_0 is to develop *theory-generic* satisfiability procedures. These are procedures that make decidable not a single theory Q, but an *infinite class* of *user-specifiable* theories. Therefore, an SMT solver supporting both theory-specific and theory-generic decision procedures becomes *user-extensible* and can carve out a potentially much bigger Decidable Fragment T_0 of the given system specification T.

Variant-based satisfiability [21] is a recent theory-generic decision procedure applying to the following, easily user-specifiable infinite class of equational theories $(\Sigma, E \cup B)$: (i) Σ is an order-sorted [15] signature of function symbols, supporting types, subtypes, and subtype polymorphisms; (ii) $E \cup B$ has the *finite variant property* [9] and B has a finitary unification algorithm; and (iii) $(\Sigma, E \cup B)$ protects a constructor subtheory $(\Omega, E_\Omega \cup B_\Omega)$ that is OS-*compact* [21]. The procedure can then decide satisfiability in the initial algebra $T_{\Sigma/E \cup B}$, that is, in the *algebraic data type* specified by $(\Sigma, E \cup B)$. These conditions apply to many user-definable theories, but have a main limitation: they apply well to *data structures*, but often do *not* hold for user-definable *predicates*.

The notions of variant and of OS-compactness mentioned above are defined in detail in Sect. 2. Here we give some key intuitions. Given Σ-equations $E \cup B$ such that the equations E oriented as left-to-right rewrite rules are confluent and terminating modulo the equational axioms B, a *variant* of a Σ-term t is a pair (u, θ) where θ is a substitution, and u is the canonical form of the term instance $t\theta$ by the rewrite rules E modulo B. Intuitively, the variants of t are the fully simplified *patterns* to which the instances of t can reduce. Some simplified instances are of course more general (as patterns) than others. $E \cup B$ has the *finite variant property* (FVP) if any Σ-term t has a *finite* set of most general variants. For example, the addition equations $E = \{x + 0 = x, x + s(y) = s(x + y)\}$ are *not* FVP, since $(x+y, id)$, $(s(x+y_1), \{y \mapsto s(y_1)\})$, $(s(s(x+y_2)), \{y \mapsto s(s(y_2))\})$, $\ldots$, $(s^n(x+y_n), \{y \mapsto s^n(y_n)\})$, $\ldots$, are all *incomparable* variants of $x+y$. Instead, the Boolean equations $G = \{x \vee \top = \top, x \vee \bot = x, x \wedge \top = x, x \wedge \bot = \bot\}$ *are* FVP. For example, the most general variants of $x \vee y$ are: $(x \vee y, id)$, $(x, \{y \mapsto \bot\})$, and $(\top, \{y \mapsto \top\})$. Assuming for simplicity that all sorts in a theory $(\Omega, E_\Omega \cup B_\Omega)$ have an infinite number of ground terms of that sort which are all different modulo the equations $E_\Omega \cup B_\Omega$, then OS-compactness of $(\Omega, E_\Omega \cup B_\Omega)$ means that any conjunction of disequalities $\bigwedge_{1 \leq i \leq n} u_i \neq v_i$ such that $E_\Omega \cup B_\Omega \vdash u_i = v_i$, $1 \leq i \leq n$, is *satisfiable* in the initial algebra $T_{\Omega/E_\Omega \cup B_\Omega}$, obtaining a decision procedure. For example, $(\{0, s\}, \varnothing)$ is OS-compact, where $\{0, s\}$ are the usual natural number constructors. Thus, $s(x) \neq s(y) \wedge 0 \neq y$ *is* satisfiable in $T_{\{0,s\}}$.

The key reason why user-definable predicates present a serious obstacle is the following. Variant satisfiability works by *reducing* satisfiability in the initial algebra $T_{\Sigma/E\cup B}$ to satisfiability in the much simpler algebra of constructors $T_{\Omega/E_\Omega\cup B_\Omega}$. In many applications $E_\Omega = \varnothing$, and if the axioms B_Ω are any combination of associativity, commutativity and identity axioms, except associativity without commutativity, then (Ω, B_Ω) is an OS-compact theory [21], making satisfiability in T_{Ω/B_Ω} and therefore in $T_{\Sigma/E\cup B}$ decidable. We can equationally specify a predicate p with sorts $A_1, \ldots, A_n$ in a *positive* way as a function $p : A_1, \ldots, A_n \to Pred$, where the sort $Pred$ of predicates contains a "true" constant tt, so that $p(u_1, \ldots, u_n)$ not holding for concrete ground arguments $u_1, \ldots, u_n$ is expressed as the *disequality* $p(u_1, \ldots, u_n) \neq tt$. But $p(u_1, \ldots, u_n) \neq tt$ means that p must be a *constructor* of sort $Pred$ in Ω, and that the equations defining p must belong to E_Ω, making $E_\Omega \neq \varnothing$ and ruling out the case when $T_{\Omega/E_\Omega\cup B_\Omega} = T_{\Omega/B_\Omega}$ is decidable by OS-compactness.

This work extends variant-based satisfiability to initial algebras with user-definable predicates under fairly general conditions using two key ideas: (i) characterizing the cases when $p(u_1, \ldots, u_n) \neq tt$ by means of *constrained patterns*; and (ii) eliminating all occurrences of disequalities of the form $p(v_1, \ldots, v_n) \neq tt$ in a quantifier-free (QF) formula by means of such patterns. In this way, the QF satisfiability problem can be reduced to formulas involving only *non-predicate* constructors, for which OS-compactness holds in many applications. More generally, if some predicates fall within the OS-compact fragment, they can be kept.

Preliminaries are in Sect. 2. Constructor variants and OS-compactness in Sect. 3. The satisfiability decision procedure is defined and proved correct in Sect. 4, and its prototype implementation is described in Sect. 5. Related work and conclusions are discussed in Sect. 6. All proofs can be found in [16].

2   Many-Sorted Logic, Rewriting, and Variants

We present some preliminaries on many-sorted (MS) logic, rewriting and finite variant and variant unification notions needed in the paper. For a more general treatment using order-sorted (OS) logic see [16].

We assume familiarity with the following basic concepts and notation that are explained in full detail in, e.g., [23]: (i) *many-sorted (MS) signature* as a pair $\Sigma = (S, \Sigma)$ with S a set of *sorts* and Σ an $S^* \times S$-indexed family $\Sigma = \{\Sigma_{w,s}\}_{(w,s)\in S^*\times S}$ of function symbols, where $f \in \Sigma_{s_1\ldots s_n,s}$ is displayed as $f : s_1 \ldots s_n \to s$; (ii) Σ-*algebra* A as a pair $A = (A, \_A)$ with $A = \{A_s\}_{s\in S}$ an S-indexed family of sets, and $\_A$ a mapping interpreting each $f : s_1 \ldots s_n \to s$ as a function in the set $[A_{s_1} \times \ldots \times A_{s_n} \to A_s]$. (iii) Σ-*homomorphism* $h : A \to B$ as an S-indexed family of functions $h = \{h_s : A_s \to B_s\}_{s\in S}$ preserving the operations in Σ; (iv) the Σ-algebra T_Σ and its initiality in the category $\mathbf{MSAlg}_\Sigma$ of Σ-algebras when Σ is unambiguous.

An S-sorted set $X = \{X_s\}_{s\in S}$ of *variables*, satisfies $s \neq s' \Rightarrow X_s \cap X_{s'} = \varnothing$, and the variables in X are always assumed *disjoint* from all constants in Σ. The Σ-*term algebra* on variables X, $T_\Sigma(X)$, is the *initial algebra* for the signature

$\Sigma(X)$ obtained by adding to Σ the variables X *as extra constants.* Since a $\Sigma(X)$-algebra is just a pair (A, α), with A a Σ-algebra, and α an *interpretation of the constants* in X, i.e., an S-sorted function $\alpha \in [X \rightarrow A]$, the $\Sigma(X)$-initiality of $T_\Sigma(X)$ means that for each $A \in \mathbf{MSAlg}_\Sigma$ and $\alpha \in [X \rightarrow A]$, there exists a unique Σ-homomorphism, $\_\alpha : T_\Sigma(X) \rightarrow A$ extending α, i.e., such that for each $s \in S$ and $x \in X_s$ we have $x\alpha_s = \alpha_s(x)$. In particular, when $A = T_\Sigma(Y)$, an interpretation of the constants in X, i.e., an S-sorted function $\sigma \in [X \rightarrow T_\Sigma(Y)]$ is called a *substitution*, and its unique homomorphic extension $\_\sigma : T_\Sigma(X) \rightarrow T_\Sigma(Y)$ is also called a substitution. Define $dom(\sigma) = \{x \in X \mid x \neq x\sigma\}$, and $ran(\sigma) = \bigcup_{x \in dom(\sigma)} vars(x\sigma)$. Given variables Z, the substitution $\sigma|_Z$ agrees with σ on Z and is the identity elsewhere.

We also assume familiarity with many-sorted first-order logic including: (i) the first-order language of Σ-*formulas* for Σ a signature (in our case Σ has only function symbols and the $=$ predicate); (ii) given a Σ-algebra A, a formula $\varphi \in Form(\Sigma)$, and an assignment $\alpha \in [Y \rightarrow A]$, with $Y = fvars(\varphi)$ the free variables of φ, the *satisfaction relation* $A, \alpha \models \varphi$; (iii) the notions of a formula $\varphi \in Form(\Sigma)$ being *valid*, denoted $A \models \varphi$, resp. *satisfiable*, in a Σ-algebra A. For a subsignature $\Omega \subseteq \Sigma$ and $A \in \mathbf{MSAlg}_\Sigma$, the *reduct* $A|_\Omega \in \mathbf{MSAlg}_\Omega$ agrees with A in the interpretation of all sorts and operations in Ω and discards everything in $\Sigma \setminus \Omega$. If $\varphi \in Form(\Omega)$ we have the equivalence $A \models \varphi \Leftrightarrow A|_\Omega \models \varphi$.

An MS *equational theory* is a pair $T = (\Sigma, E)$, with E a set of Σ-equations. $\mathbf{MSAlg}_{(\Sigma, E)}$ denotes the full subcategory of $\mathbf{MSAlg}_\Sigma$ with objects those $A \in \mathbf{MSAlg}_\Sigma$ such that $A \models E$, called the (Σ, E)-*algebras.* $\mathbf{MSAlg}_{(\Sigma, E)}$ has an *initial algebra* $T_{\Sigma/E}$ [23]. The inference system in [23] is *sound and complete* for MS equational deduction, i.e., for any MS equational theory (Σ, E), and Σ-equation $u = v$ we have an equivalence $E \vdash u = v \Leftrightarrow E \models u = v$. For the sake of simpler inference we assume *non-empty sorts*, i.e., $\forall s \subset S$, $T_{\Sigma, s} \neq \emptyset$. Deducibility $E \vdash u = v$ is abbreviated as $u =_E v$.

In the above notions there is only an *apparent* lack of predicate symbols: full many-sorted first-order logic can be *reduced* to many-sorted algebra and the above language of equational formulas. The reduction is achieved as follows. A many-sorted first-order (MS-FO) signature, is a pair (Σ, Π) with Σ a MS signature with set of sorts S, and Π an S^*-indexed set $\Pi = \{\Pi_w\}_{w \in S^*}$ of *predicate symbols.* We associate to a MS-FO signature (Σ, Π) a MS signature $(\Sigma \cup \Pi)$ by adding to Σ a new sort $Pred$ with a constant tt and viewing each $p \in \Pi_w$ as a function symbol $p : s_1 \ldots s_n \rightarrow Pred$. The reduction at the model level is now very simple: each $(\Sigma \cup \Pi)$-algebra A defines a (Σ, Π)-model A° with Σ-algebra structure $A|_\Sigma$ and having for each $p \in \Pi_w$ the predicate interpretation $A^\circ_p = A^{-1}_{p:w \rightarrow Pred}(tt)$. The reduction at the formula level is also quite simple: we map a (Σ, Π)-formula φ to an equational formula $\widetilde{\varphi}$, called its *equational version*, by just replacing each atom $p(t_1, \ldots, t_n)$ by the equational atom $p(t_1, \ldots, t_n) = tt$. The *correctness* of this reduction is just the easy to check equivalence: $A^\circ \models \varphi \Leftrightarrow A \models \widetilde{\varphi}$. A MS-FO *theory* is just a pair $((\Sigma, \Pi), \Gamma)$, with (Σ, Π) a MS-FO signature and Γ a set of (Σ, Π)-formulas. Call $((\Sigma, \Pi), \Gamma)$ *equational* iff

$(\Sigma \cup \Pi, \widetilde{\Gamma})$ is a many-sorted equational theory. By the above equivalence and the completeness of many-sorted equational logic such theories allow a sound and complete use of equational deduction also with predicate atoms. Note that if $((\Sigma, \Pi), \Gamma)$ is equational, it is a very simple type of theory in many-sorted Horn Logic with Equality and therefore has an initial model $T_{(\Sigma,\Pi),\Gamma}$ [14]. A useful, easy to check fact is that we have an identity: $T^{\circ}_{\Sigma \cup \Pi/\widetilde{\Gamma}} = T_{(\Sigma,\Pi),\Gamma}$.

Recall the notation for term positions, subterms, and term replacement from [10]: (i) positions in a term viewed as a tree are marked by strings $p \in \mathbb{N}^*$ specifying a path from the root, (ii) $t|_p$ denotes the subterm of term t at position p, and (iii) $t[u]_p$ denotes the result of *replacing* subterm $t|_p$ at position p by u.

Definition 1. *A rewrite theory is a triple $\mathcal{R} = (\Sigma, B, R)$ with (Σ, B) a MS equational theory and R a set of Σ-rewrite rules, i.e., sequents $l \to r$, with $l, r \in T_{\Sigma}(X)_s$ for some $s \in S$. In what follows it is always assumed that: (1) For each $l \to r \in R$, $l \notin X$ and $vars(r) \subseteq vars(l)$. (2) Each equation $u = v \in B$ is regular, i.e., $vars(u) = vars(v)$, and linear, i.e., there are no repeated variables in either u or v. The one-step R, B-rewrite relation $t \to_{R,B} t'$, holds between $t, t' \in T_{\Sigma}(X)_s$, $s \in S$, iff there is a rewrite rule $l \to r \in R$, a substitution $\sigma \in [X \to T_{\Sigma}(X)]$, and a term position p in t such that $t|_p =_B l\sigma$, and $t' = t[r\sigma]_p$.*

$\mathcal{R}$ is called: (i) terminating iff the relation $\to_{R,B}$ is well-founded; (ii) strictly B-coherent [22] iff whenever $u \to_{R,B} v$ and $u =_B u'$ there is a v' such that $u' \to_{R,B} v'$ and $v =_B v'$; (iii) confluent iff $u \to^*_{R,B} v_1$ and $u \to^*_{R,B} v_2$ imply that there are w_1, w_2 such that $v_1 \to^*_{R,B} w_1$, $v_2 \to^*_{R,B} w_2$, and $w_1 =_B w_2$ (where $\to^*_{R,B}$ denotes the reflexive-transitive closure of $\to_{R,B}$); and (iv) convergent if (i)–(iii) hold. If $\mathcal{R}$ is convergent, for each Σ-term t there is a term u such that $t \to^*_{R,B} u$ and ($\not\exists v$) $u \to_{R,B} v$. We then write $u = t!_{R,B}$ and $t \to^!_{R,B} t!_{R,B}$, and call $t!_{R,B}$ the R, B-normal form of t, which, by confluence, is unique up to B-equality.

Given a set E of Σ-equations, let $R(E) = \{u \to v \mid u = v \in E\}$. A *decomposition* of a MS equational theory (Σ, E) is a convergent rewrite theory $\mathcal{R} = (\Sigma, B, R)$ such that $E = E_0 \uplus B$ and $R = R(E_0)$. The key property of a decomposition is the following:

Theorem 1 *(Church-Rosser Theorem)* [17,22]. *Let $\mathcal{R} = (\Sigma, B, R)$ be a decomposition of (Σ, E). Then we have an equivalence:*

$$E \vdash u = v \quad \Leftrightarrow \quad u!_{R,B} =_B v!_{R,B}.$$

If $\mathcal{R} = (\Sigma, B, R)$ is a decomposition of (Σ, E), and X an S-sorted set of variables, the *canonical term algebra* $C_{\mathcal{R}}(X)$ has $C_{\mathcal{R}}(X)_s = \{[t!_{R,B}]_B \mid t \in T_{\Sigma}(X)_s\}$, and interprets each $f : s_1 \ldots s_n \to s$ as the function $C_{\mathcal{R}}(X)_f : ([u_1]_B, \ldots, [u_n]_B) \mapsto [f(u_1, \ldots, u_n)!_{R,B}]_B$. By the Church-Rosser Theorem we then have an isomorphism $h : T_{\Sigma/E}(X) \cong C_{\mathcal{R}}(X)$, where $h : [t]_E \mapsto [t!_{R,B}]_B$. In particular, when X is the empty family of variables, the canonical term algebra $C_{\mathcal{R}}$ is an initial algebra, and is the most intuitive possible model for $T_{\Sigma/E}$ as an algebra of *values* computed by R, B-simplification.

Quite often, the signature Σ on which $T_{\Sigma/E}$ is defined has a natural decomposition as a disjoint union $\Sigma = \Omega \uplus \Delta$, where the elements of $C_\mathcal{R}$, that is, the *values* computed by R, B-simplification, are Ω-terms, whereas the function symbols $f \in \Delta$ are viewed as *defined functions* which are *evaluated away* by R, B-simplification. Ω (with same poset of sorts as Σ) is then called a *constructor subsignature* of Σ. Call a decomposition $\mathcal{R} = (\Sigma, B, R)$ of (Σ, E) *sufficiently complete* with respect to the *constructor subsignature* Ω iff for each $t \in T_\Sigma$ we have: (i) $t!_{R,B} \in T_\Omega$, and (ii) if $u \in T_\Omega$ and $u =_B v$, then $v \in T_\Omega$. This ensures that for each $[u]_B \in C_\mathcal{R}$ we have $[u]_B \subseteq T_\Omega$. We will give several examples of decompositions $\Sigma = \Omega \uplus \Delta$ into constructors and defined functions.

As we can see in the following definition, sufficient completeness is closely related to the notion of a *protecting* theory inclusion.

Definition 2. *An equational theory (Σ, E) protects another theory (Ω, E_Ω) iff $(\Omega, E_\Omega) \subseteq (\Sigma, E)$ and the unique Ω-homomorphism $h : T_{\Omega/E_\Omega} \to T_{\Sigma/E}|_\Omega$ is an isomorphism $h : T_{\Omega/E_\Omega} \cong T_{\Sigma/E}|_\Omega$. A decomposition $\mathcal{R} = (\Sigma, B, R)$ protects another decomposition $\mathcal{R}_0 = (\Sigma_0, B_0, R_0)$ iff $\mathcal{R}_0 \subseteq \mathcal{R}$, i.e., $\Sigma_0 \subseteq \Sigma$, $B_0 \subseteq B$, and $R_0 \subseteq R$, and for all $t, t' \in T_{\Sigma_0}(X)$ we have: (i) $t =_{B_0} t' \Leftrightarrow t =_B t'$, (ii) $t = t!_{R_0, B_0} \Leftrightarrow t = t!_{R,B}$, and (iii) $C_{\mathcal{R}_0} = C_\mathcal{R}|_{\Sigma_0}$.*

$\mathcal{R}_\Omega = (\Omega, B_\Omega, R_\Omega)$ is a constructor decomposition *of $\mathcal{R} = (\Sigma, B, R)$ iff $\mathcal{R}$ protects $\mathcal{R}_\Omega$ and, Σ and Ω have the same poset of sorts, so that by (iii) above $\mathcal{R}$ is sufficiently complete with respect to Ω. Furthermore, Ω is called a subsignature of* free constructors modulo B_Ω *iff $R_\Omega = \varnothing$, so that $C_{\mathcal{R}_\Omega} = T_{\Omega/B_\Omega}$.*

The case where all constructor terms are in R, B-normal form is captured by Ω being a subsignature of free constructors modulo B_Ω. Note also that conditions (i) and (ii) are, so called, "no confusion" conditions, and for protecting extensions (iii) is a "no junk" condition, that is, $\mathcal{R}$ does not add new data to $C_{\mathcal{R}_0}$.

Given a MS equational theory (Σ, E) and a conjunction of Σ-equations $\phi = u_1 = v_1 \wedge \ldots \wedge u_n = v_n$, an *E-unifier* of ϕ is a substitution σ such that $u_i \sigma =_E v_i \sigma$, $1 \le i \le n$. An *E-unification algorithm* for (Σ, E) is an algorithm generating for each system of Σ-equations ϕ and finite set of variables $W \supseteq vars(\phi)$ a *complete set* of E-unifiers $Unif_E^W(\phi)$ where each $\tau \in Unif_E^W(\phi)$ is assumed idempotent and with $dom(\tau) = vars(\phi)$, and is "away from W" in the sense that $ran(\tau) \cap W = \varnothing$. The set $Unif_E^W(\phi)$ is called "complete" in the precise sense that for any *E-unifier* σ of ϕ there is a $\tau \in Unif_E(\phi)$ and a substitution ρ such that $\sigma|_W =_E (\tau\rho)|_W$, where, by definition, $\alpha =_E \beta$ means $(\forall x \in X)\ \alpha(x) =_E \beta(x)$ for substitutions α, β. Such an algorithm is called *finitary* if it always terminates with a *finite set* $Unif_E^W(\phi)$ for any ϕ.

The notion of *variant* answers, in a sense, two questions: (i) how can we best describe symbolically the elements of $C_\mathcal{R}(X)$ that are *reduced substitution instances* of a *pattern term* t? and (ii) given an original pattern t, how many other patterns do we need to describe the reduced instances of t in $C_\mathcal{R}(X)$?

Definition 3. *Given a decomposition $\mathcal{R} = (\Sigma, B, R)$ of a MS equational theory (Σ, E) and a Σ-term t, a variant[1] [9, 13] of t is a pair (u, θ) such that: (i) $u =_B (t\theta)!_{R,B}$, (ii) $dom(\theta) \subseteq vars(t)$, and (iii) $\theta = \theta!_{R,B}$, that is, $\theta(x) = \theta(x)!_{R,B}$ for all variables x. (u, θ) is called a ground variant iff, furthermore, $u \in T_\Sigma$. Given variants (u, θ) and (v, γ) of t, (u, θ) is called more general than (v, γ), denoted $(u, \theta) \sqsupseteq_B (v, \gamma)$, iff there is a substitution ρ such that: (i) $(\theta\rho)|_{vars(t)} =_B \gamma$, and (ii) $u\rho =_B v$. Let $[\![t]\!]_{R,B} = \{(u_i, \theta_i) \mid i \in I\}$ denote a complete set of variants of t, that is, a set of variants such that for any variant (v, γ) of t there is an $i \in I$, such that $(u_i, \theta_i) \sqsupseteq_B (v, \gamma)$.*

A decomposition $\mathcal{R} = (\Sigma, B, R)$ of (Σ, E) has the finite variant property *[9] (FVP) iff for each Σ-term t there is a finite complete set of variants $[\![t]\!]_{R,B} = \{(u_1, \theta_1), \ldots, (u_n, \theta_n)\}$. If B has a finitary B-unification algorithm the relation $(u, \alpha) \sqsupseteq_B (v, \beta)$ is decidable by B-matching. Under this assumption on B, if $\mathcal{R} = (\Sigma, B, R)$ is FVP, $[\![t]\!]_{R,B}$ can be chosen to be not only complete, but also a set of* most general variants, *in the sense that for $1 \leq i < j \leq n$, $(u_i, \theta_i) \not\sqsupseteq_B (u_j, \theta_j) \wedge (u_j, \theta_j) \not\sqsupseteq_B (u_i, \theta_i)$. Also, given any finite set of variables $W \supseteq vars(t)$ we can always choose $[\![t]\!]_{R,B}$ to be of the form $[\![t]\!]_{R,B}^W$, where each $(u_i, \theta_i) \in [\![t]\!]_{R,B}^W$ has θ_i idempotent with $dom(\theta_i) = vars(t)$, and "away from W," in the sense that $ran(\theta_i) \cap W = \varnothing$.*

If B has a finitary unification algorithm, the *folding variant narrowing* strategy described in [13] provides an effective method to generate $[\![t]\!]_{R,B}$. Furthermore, folding variant narrowing *terminates* for each input $t \in T_\Sigma(X)$ with a finite set $[\![t]\!]_{R,B}$ iff $\mathcal{R}$ has FVP [13].

Two example theories, one FVP and another not FVP, were given in the Introduction. Many other examples are given in [21]. The following will be used as a running example of an FVP theory:

Example 1. (Sets of Natural Numbers). Let $NatSet = (\Sigma, B, R)$ be the following equational theory. Σ has sorts Nat and $NatSet$, subsort inclusion[2] $Nat < NatSet$, and decomposes as $\Sigma = \Omega_c \uplus \Delta$, where the constructors Ω_c include the following operators: 0 and 1 of sort Nat, $\_+\_ : Nat\,Nat \to Nat$ (addition), $\varnothing$ of sort $NatSet$ and $\_,\_ : NatSet\,NatSet \to NatSet$ (set union). B decomposes as $B = B_{\Omega_c} \uplus B_\Delta$. The axioms B_{Ω_c} include: (i) the associativity and commutativity of $\_ + \_$ with identity 0, the associativity and commutativity of $\_,\_$. R decomposes as $R = R_{\Omega_c} \uplus R_\Delta$. The rules R_{Ω_c} include: (i) an identity rule for union $NS, \varnothing \to NS$; and (ii) idempotency rules for union $NS, NS \to NS$, and $NS, NS, NS' \to NS, NS'$. The signature Δ of defined functions has operators $max : Nat\,Nat \to Nat$, $min : Nat\,Nat \to Nat$, and $\_ \dot- \_ : Nat\,Nat \to Nat$, for the maximum, minimum and "monus" (subtraction) functions. The axioms B_Δ are the commutativity

---

[1] For a discussion of similar but not exactly equivalent versions of the variant notion see [6]. Here we follow the shaper formulation in [13], rather than the one in [9], because it is technically essential for some results to hold [6].

[2] As pointed out at the beginning of Sect. 2, [16] treats the more general *order-sorted* case, where sorts form a poset $(S, \leq)$ with $s \leq s'$ interpreted as set containment $A_s \subseteq A_{s'}$ in a Σ-algebra A. All results in this paper hold in the order-sorted case.

of the *max* and *min* functions. The rules R_Δ for the defined functions are: $max(N, N + M) \rightarrow N + M$, $min(N, N + M) \rightarrow N$, $N \dot{-} (N + M) \rightarrow 0$, and $(N + M) \dot{-} N \rightarrow M$, where N and M have sort *Nat*.

FVP is a *semi-decidable* property [6], which can be easily verified (when it holds) by checking (using folding variant narrowing supported by Maude 2.7) that for each function symbol $f : s_1 \ldots s_n \rightarrow s$ the term $f(x_1, \ldots, x_n)$, with x_i of sort s_i, $1 \leqslant i \leqslant n$, has a finite number of most general variants. Given an FVP decomposition $\mathcal{R}$ its *variant complexity* is the total number n of variants for all such $f(x_1, \ldots, x_n)$, provided f has some associated rules of the form $f(t_1, \ldots, t_n) \rightarrow t'$. This gives a *rough* measure of how costly it is to perform variant computations *relative* to the cost of performing B-unification. For example, the variant complexity of *NatSet* above is 16.

To be able to express systems of equations, say, $u_1 = v_1 \wedge \ldots \wedge u_n = v_n$, as *terms*, we can extend an MS signature Σ with sorts S to an OS signature $\Sigma^\wedge$ by: (1) adding to S fresh new sorts *Lit* and *Conj* with a subsort inclusion $Lit < Conj$; (2) adding a binary conjunction operator $\_\wedge\_ : Lit \; Conj \rightarrow Conj$; and (3) adding for each $s \in S$ binary operators $\_ = \_ : s \; s \rightarrow Lit$ and $\_ \neq \_ : s \; s \rightarrow Lit$.

Variant-based unification goes back to [13]. The paper [21] gives a more precise characterization using $\Sigma^\wedge$-terms as follows. If $\mathcal{R} = (\Sigma, B, R)$ is an FVP decomposition of (Σ, E) and B has a finitary B-unification algorithm, given a system of Σ-equations ϕ with variables W, folding variant narrowing computes a *finite* set $VarUnif_E^W(\phi)$ of E-unifiers away from W that is *complete* in the strong sense that if α is an R, B-normalized E-unifier of ϕ there exists $\theta \in VarUnif_E^W(\phi)$ and an R, B-*normalized* ρ such that $\alpha|_W =_B (\theta\rho)|_W$.

3   Constructor Variants and OS-Compactness

We gather some technical notions and results needed for the inductive satisfiability procedure given in Sect. 4.

The notion of *constructor variant* is used to answer the question: what variants of t cover as instances modulo B_Ω all canonical forms of all ground instances of t? The following lemma (stated and proved at the more general order-sorted level in [16], but stated here for the MS case for simplicity) gives a precise answer under reasonable assumptions. For more on constructor variants see [16,21,27].

Lemma 1. *Let* $\mathcal{R} = (\Sigma, B, R)$ *be an FVP decomposition of* (Σ, E) *protecting a constructor decomposition* $\mathcal{R}_\Omega = (\Omega, B_\Omega, R_\Omega)$. *Assume that: (i)* $\Sigma = \Omega \cup \Delta$ *with* $\Omega \cap \Delta = \varnothing$; *(ii)* B *has a finitary* B-unification algorithm and $B = B_\Omega \uplus B_\Delta$, *with* B_Ω Ω-equations and if $u = v \in B_\Delta$, u, v *are non-variable* Δ-terms. *Call* $[\![t]\!]_{R,B}^\Omega = \{(v, \theta) \in [\![t]\!]_{R,B} \mid v \in T_\Omega(X)\}$ *the set of constructor variants of* t. *If* $[u] \in \mathcal{C}_{\mathcal{R}_\Omega}$ *is of the form* $u =_B (t\gamma)!_{R,B}$, *then there is* $(v, \theta) \in [\![t]\!]_{R,B}^\Omega$ *and a normalized ground substitution* τ *such that* $u =_B v\tau$.

We finally need the notion of an order-sorted OS-*compact* equational OS-FO theory $((\Sigma, \Pi), \Gamma)$, generalizing the compactness notion in [8]. The notion is the *same* (but called MS-compactness) for the special case of MS theories treated in the preliminaries to simplify the exposition. It is stated here in the more general OS case because the satisfiability algorithm in Sect. 4 works for the more general OS case, and the paper's examples are in fact OS theories.

Given a OS equational theory (Σ, E), call a Σ-equality $u = v$ *E-trivial* iff $u =_E v$, and call a Σ-disequality $u \neq v$, denoting the negated atom $\neg(u = v)$, *E-consistent* iff $u \neq_E v$. Likewise, call a conjunction $\bigwedge D$ of Σ-disequalities *E-consistent* iff each $u \neq v$ in D is so. Call a sort $s \in S$ *finite* in both (Σ, E) and $T_{\Sigma/E}$ iff $T_{\Sigma/E,s}$ is a finite set, and *infinite* otherwise.

Definition 4. *An equational OS-FO theory* $((\Sigma, \Pi), \Gamma)$ *is called* OS-compact *iff: (i) for each sort s in Σ we can effectively determine whether s is finite or infinite in* $T_{\Sigma \cup \Pi / \tilde{\Gamma}, s}$*, and, if finite, can effectively compute a representative ground term* $rep([u]) \in [u]$ *for each* $[u] \in T_{\Sigma \cup \Pi / \tilde{\Gamma}, s}$*; (ii)* $=_{\tilde{\Gamma}}$ *is decidable and $\tilde{\Gamma}$ has a finitary unification algorithm; and (iii) any finite conjunction $\bigwedge D$ of negated (Σ, Π)-atoms whose variables all have infinite sorts and such that $\bigwedge \tilde{D}$ is $\tilde{\Gamma}$-consistent is satisfiable in* $T_{\Sigma, \Pi, \Gamma}$*.*

Call an OS theory (Σ, E) OS-compact *iff OS-FO theory $((\Sigma, \varnothing), E)$ is OS-compact.*

The key theorem, generalizing a similar one in [8] is the following:

Theorem 2 ([21]). *If $((\Sigma, \Pi), \Gamma)$ is an* OS-compact *theory, then satisfiability of $QF (\Sigma, \Pi)$-formulas in $T_{\Sigma, \Pi, \Gamma}$ is decidable.*

The following OS-compactness results are proved in detail in [21]: (i) a free constructor decomposition modulo axioms $\mathcal{R}_\Omega = (\Omega, B_\Omega, \varnothing)$ for B_Ω any combination of associativity, commutativity and identity axioms, except associativity without commutativity, is OS-compact; and (ii) the constructor decompositions for parameterized modules for lists, compact lists, multisets, sets, and hereditarily finite (HF) sets are all *OS-compact-preserving*, in the sense that if the actual parameter has an OS-compact constructor decomposition, then the corresponding instantiation of the parameterized constructor decomposition is OS-compact.

Example 2. The constructor decomposition $\mathcal{R}_{\Omega_c} = (\Omega, B_{\Omega_c}, R_{\Omega_c})$ for the *NatSet* theory in Example 1 is OS-compact. This follows from the fact that *NatSet* is just the instantiation of the constructor decomposition for the parameterized module of (finite) sets in [21] to the natural numbers with 0, 1, and $\_ + \_$, which is itself a theory of free constructors modulo associativity, commutativity and identity 0 for $\_ + \_$ and therefore OS-compact by (i), so that, by (ii), $\mathcal{R}_{\Omega_c} = (\Omega, B_{\Omega_c}, R_{\Omega_c})$ is also OS-compact.

4   QF Satisfiability in Initial Algebras with Predicates

The known variant-based quantifier-free (QF) satisfiability and validity results [21] apply to the initial algebra $T_{\Sigma/E}$ of an equational theory (Σ, E) such that

(1) $\mathcal{R} = (\Sigma, B, R)$ is a FVP variant-decomposition, (2) $\mathcal{R}$ protects a constructor decomposition $\mathcal{R}_\Omega = (\Omega, B_\Omega, R_\Omega)$ and (3): (i) B has a finitary unification algorithm; and (ii) the equational theory of $\mathcal{R}_\Omega = (\Omega, B_\Omega, R_\Omega)$ is OS-compact.

Example 3. QF validity and satisfiability in the initial algebra $T_{\Sigma/E}$ for (Σ, E) the theory with the *NatSet* FVP variant-decomposition $\mathcal{R} = (\Sigma, B, R)$ in Example 1 are decidable because its axioms B have a finitary unification algorithm and, as explained in Example 2, its constructor decomposition $\mathcal{R}_\Omega = (\Omega, B_\Omega, R_\Omega)$ is OS-compact.

The decidable inductive validity and satisfiability results in [21] apply indeed to many *data structures* of interest, which may obey structural axioms B such as commutativity, associativity-commutativity, or identity. Many useful examples are given in [21], and a prototype Maude implementation is presented in [27]. There is, however, a main limitation about the range of examples to which these results apply, which this work directly addresses. The limitation comes from the introduction of *user-definable predicates*. Recall that we represent a predicate p with sorts $s_1, \ldots, s_n$ as a function $p : s_1, \ldots, s_n \to Pred$ defined in the *positive* case by confluent and terminating equations $p(u_1^i, \ldots, u_n^i) = tt$, $1 \leq i \leq k$. The key problem with such predicates p is that, except in trivial cases, there are typically ground terms $p(v_1, \ldots, v_n)$ for which the predicate does *not* hold. This means that p must be a *constructor* operator of sort *Pred* which is *not* a free constructor modulo the axioms B_Ω. This makes proving OS-compactness for a constructor decomposition $\mathcal{R}_\Omega = (\Omega, B_\Omega, R_\Omega)$ including user-definable predicates a non-trivial case-by-case task. For example, the proofs of OS-compactness for the set containment predicate $\_ \subseteq \_$ in the parameterized module of finite sets and for other such predicates in other FVP parameterized modules in [21] all required non-trivial analyses. Furthermore, OS-compactness may fail for some $\mathcal{R}_\Omega$ precisely because of predicates (see Example 4 below).

Example 4. Consider the following extension by predicates *NatSetPreds* of the *NatSet* theory in Example 1. Its constructor signature $\Omega = \Omega_c \uplus \Omega_\Pi$ adds the subsignature Ω_Π containing the sort *Pred*, a constant tt of sort *Pred*, the subset containment predicate $\_ \subseteq \_ : NatSet\ NatSet \to Pred$, the strict order predicate $\_ > \_ : Nat\ Nat \to Pred$, the "sort predicate" $\_{:}Nat : NatSet \to Pred$, characterizing when a set of natural numbers is a natural, and the even and odd predicates *even, odd* $: NatSet \to Pred$, defined by the rules R_Π: $\varnothing \subseteq NS \to tt$, $NS \subseteq NS \to tt$, $NS \subseteq NS, NS' \to tt$, $N + M + 1 > N \to tt$, $N{:}Nat \to tt$, $even(N + N) \to tt$ and $odd(N + N + 1) \to tt$, where NS and NS' have sort *NatSet*, and N and M have sort *Nat*. *NatSetPreds* is FVP, but its constructor decomposition $\mathcal{R}_\Omega = (\Omega_c \uplus \Omega_\Pi, B_{\Omega_c}, R_{\Omega_c} \uplus R_\Pi)$ is *not* OS-compact, since the negation of the trichotomy law $N > M \vee M > N \vee N = M$ is the B_{Ω_c}-consistent but *unsatisfiable* conjunction $N > M \neq tt \wedge M > N \neq tt \wedge N \neq M$.

The goal of this work is to provide a decision procedure for validity and satisfiability of QF formulas in the initial algebra of an FVP theory $\mathcal{R}$ that may contain user-definable predicates and protects a constructor decomposition $\mathcal{R}_\Omega$

that need not be OS-compact, under the following reasonable assumptions: (1) $\mathcal{R} = (\Delta \uplus \Omega_c \uplus \Omega_\Pi, B_\Delta \uplus B_{\Omega_c}, R_\Delta \uplus R_{\Omega_c} \uplus R_\Pi)$ protects $\mathcal{R}_\Omega = (\Omega_c \uplus \Omega_\Pi, B_{\Omega_c}, R_{\Omega_c} \uplus R_\Pi)$, where Ω_Π consists only of predicates, and R_Π consists of rules of the form $p(u_1^i, \ldots, u_n^i) \to tt$, $1 \leqslant i \leqslant k_p$, defining each $p \in \Omega_\Pi$; furthermore, $\mathcal{R}_\Omega$ satisfies conditions (i)–(ii) in Lemma 1; (2) $\mathcal{R}_{\Omega_c} = (\Omega_c, B_{\Omega_c}, R_{\Omega_c})$ is OS-compact, its finite sorts (if any) are different from $Pred$, and is the constructor decomposition of $(\Delta \uplus \Omega_c, B_\Delta \uplus B_{\Omega_c}, R_\Delta \uplus R_{\Omega_c})$; and (3) each $p \in \Omega_\Pi$ has an associated set of *negative constrained patterns* of the form:

$$\bigwedge_{1 \leqslant l \leqslant n_j} w^j{}_l \neq w'^j{}_l \Rightarrow p(v^j{}_1, \ldots, v^j{}_n) \neq tt, \quad 1 \leqslant j \leqslant m_p$$

with the v_i^j, $w^j{}_l$ and $w'^j{}_l$ Ω_c-terms with variables in $Y_j = vars(p(v^j{}_1, \ldots, v^j{}_n))$. These negative constrained patterns are interpreted as meaning that the following *semantic equivalences* are valid in $\mathcal{C}_\mathcal{R}$ for each $p \in \Omega_\Pi$, where $\rho_j \in \{\rho \in [Y_j \to T_{\Omega_c}] \mid \rho = \rho!_{R,B}\}$, $B = B_\Delta \uplus B_{\Omega_c}$, and $R = R_\Delta \uplus R_{\Omega_c} \uplus R_\Pi$:

$$[p(v^j{}_1, \ldots, v^j{}_n)\rho_j] \in \mathcal{C}_\mathcal{R} \Leftrightarrow \bigwedge_{1 \leqslant l \leqslant n_j} (w^j{}_l \neq w'^j{}_l)\rho_j \wedge \bigwedge_{1 \leqslant i \leqslant n} v^j{}_i \rho_j =_B (v^j{}_i \rho_j)!_{R,B}$$

$$[p(t_1, \ldots, t_n)] \in \mathcal{C}_\mathcal{R} \Leftrightarrow \exists j \exists \rho_j \, [p(t_1, \ldots, t_n)] = [p(v^j{}_1, \ldots, v^j{}_n)\rho_j]$$
$$\wedge \bigwedge_{1 \leqslant l \leqslant n_j} (w^j{}_l \neq w'^j{}_l)\rho_j$$

The first equivalence means that any instance of a negative predicate pattern by a normalized ground substitution ρ_j satisfying its constraint where the predicate's arguments are normalized is itself normalized, so that $\mathcal{C}_\mathcal{R} \models p(v^j{}_1, \ldots, v^j{}_n)\rho_j \neq tt$. It can be automatically checked by computing the non-identity variants (u, α) of the pattern term $p(v^j{}_1, \ldots, v^j{}_n)$ such that $v^j{}_i \alpha =_B (v^j{}_i \alpha)!_{R,B}$, $1 \leqslant i \leqslant n$, and then checking that all associated substitutions α for such variants invalidate the pattern's constraint. The second equivalence means that $[p(t_1, \ldots, t_n)] \in \mathcal{C}_\mathcal{R}$ iff $[p(t_1, \ldots, t_n)]$ instantiates a negative pattern satisfying its constraint. Its proof requires a case analysis showing that for each $p \in \Omega_\Pi$ each ground instance $p(x_1, \ldots x_n)\theta$, $\theta(x_i) =_B \theta(x_i)!_{R,B}$, $1 \leqslant i \leqslant n$, is either reducible to tt or irreducible and an instance of a constrained pattern.

Example 5. The module *NatSetPreds* from Example 4 satisfies above assumptions (1)–(3). Indeed, (1), including conditions (i)–(ii) in Lemma 1, follows easily from its definition and that of *NatSet*, and (2) also follows easily from the definition of *NatSet* and the remarks in Example 2. This leaves us with condition (3), where the negative constrained patterns for $\Omega_\Pi = \{\_ \subseteq \_, \_ > \_, even, odd, \_:Nat\}$ are the following:

$-\ (NS, NS') \neq NS' \Rightarrow NS \subseteq NS' \neq tt.$
$-\ N > N + M \neq tt$

- $even(N + N + 1) \neq tt$, $even(\emptyset) \neq tt$, $(N \neq NS \wedge NS \neq \emptyset) \Rightarrow even(N, NS) \neq tt$
- $odd(N + N) \neq tt$, $odd(\emptyset) \neq tt$, $(N \neq NS \wedge NS \neq \emptyset) \Rightarrow odd(N, NS) \neq tt$
- $\emptyset{:}Nat \neq tt$, $(N \neq NS \wedge NS \neq \emptyset) \Rightarrow (N, NS){:}Nat \neq tt$.

where N and M have sort Nat, and NS and NS' sort $NatSet$. The first equivalence can be automatically checked as explained above. For example, the non-identity variants of $NS \subseteq NS'$ are $(tt, \{NS \mapsto \emptyset\})$, $(tt, \{NS \mapsto NS'\})$, and $(tt, \{NS' \mapsto NS, NS''\})$. Their substitutions all leave the instances of NS and NS' irreducible, and violate the constraint $(NS, NS') \neq NS'$. The second equivalence is proved in [16].

The Inductive Satisfiability Decision Procedure. Assume $\mathcal{R}$ satisfies conditions (1)–(3) above and let $\Sigma = \Delta \uplus \Omega_c \uplus \Omega_\Pi$, and E be the axioms B plus the equations associated with the rules R in $\mathcal{R}$. Given a QF Σ-formula φ the procedure decides if φ is satisfiable in $\mathcal{C}_\mathcal{R}$. We can reduce the inductive validity decision problem of whether $\mathcal{C}_\mathcal{R} \models \varphi$ to deciding whether $\neg\varphi$ is unsatisfiable in $\mathcal{C}_\mathcal{R}$. Since any QF Σ-formula φ can be put in disjunctive normal form, a disjunction is satisfiable in $\mathcal{C}_\mathcal{R}$ iff one of the disjuncts is, and all predicates have been turned into functions of sort $Pred$, it is enough to decide the satisfiability of a conjunction of Σ-literals of the form $\bigwedge G \wedge \bigwedge D$, where the G are equations and the D are disequations. The procedure performs the following steps:

1. **Unification.** Satisfiability of the conjunction $\bigwedge G \wedge \bigwedge D$ is replaced by satisfiability for some conjunction in the set $\{(\bigwedge D\alpha)!_{R,B} \mid \alpha \in VarUnif_E(\bigwedge G)\}$, discarding any obviously unsatisfiable $(\bigwedge D\alpha)!_{R,B}$ in such a set.

2. **Π-Elimination.** After Step (1), each conjunction is a conjunction of disequalities $\bigwedge D'$. If $\bigwedge D'$ is a $\Delta \uplus \Omega_c$-formula, we go directly to Step (3); otherwise $\bigwedge D'$ has the form $\bigwedge D' = \bigwedge D_1 \wedge p(t_1, \ldots, t_n) \neq tt \wedge \bigwedge D_2$, where $p \in \Omega_\Pi$ and D_1 and/or D_2 may be empty conjunctions. We then replace $\bigwedge D'$ by all not obviously unsatisfiable conjunctions of the form:

$$(\bigwedge D_1 \wedge \bigwedge_{1 \le l \le n_j} w^j{}_l \neq w'^j{}_l \wedge \bigwedge D_2)\theta\alpha$$

where $1 \le j \le m_p$, $W = vars(\bigwedge D')$, $(p(t'_1, \ldots, t'_n), \theta) \in [\![p(t_1, \ldots, t_n)]\!]^{W,\Omega}_{R,B}$, and α is a *disjoint B_{Ω_c}*-unifier of the equation $p(t'_1, \ldots, t'_n) = p(v^1{}_1, \ldots, v^j{}_n)$ (i.e., sides are renamed to *share no variables* and $ran(\alpha) \cap (W \cup ran(\theta)) = \emptyset$). We use the negative constrained patterns of p and the constructor variants of $p(t_1, \ldots, t_n)$ to *eliminate* the disequality $p(t_1, \ldots, t_n) \neq tt$. If for some $p' \in \Omega_\Pi$ some disequality remains in $(\bigwedge D_1 \wedge \bigwedge D_2)\theta\alpha$, we iterate Step 2.

3. **Computation of $\Omega_c^\wedge$-Variants and Elimination of Finite Sorts.** For $\bigwedge D'$ a $\Delta \uplus \Omega_c$-conjunction of disequalities, viewed as a $(\Delta \uplus \Omega_c)^\wedge$-term its constructor $\Omega_c^\wedge$-variants are of the form $(\bigwedge D'', \gamma)$, with $\bigwedge D''$ an Ω_c-conjunction of disequalities. The variables of $\bigwedge D''$ are then $Y_{fin} \uplus Y_\infty$, with Y_{fin} the variables whose sorts are finite, and Y_∞ the variables with infinite sorts. Compute

all normalized ground substitution τ of the variables Y_{fin} obtained by: (i) independently choosing for each variable $y \in Y_{fin}$ a canonical representative for the sort of y in all possible ways, and (ii) checking that for the τ so chosen $\bigwedge D'' \tau$ is normalized, keeping τ if this holds and discarding it otherwise. Then $\bigwedge D'$ is satisfiable in $\mathcal{C}_\mathcal{R}$ iff some $\bigwedge D'' \tau$ so obtained is B_{Ω_c}-consistent for some $\Omega_c^\wedge$-variant $(\bigwedge D'', \gamma)$ of $\bigwedge D'$.

Example 6. We can illustrate the use of the above decision procedure by proving the validity of the QF formula $odd(N) = tt \Leftrightarrow even(N) \neq tt$ in the initial algebra $\mathcal{C}_\mathcal{R}$ of *NatSetPreds*. That is, we need to show that its negation $(odd(N) = tt \wedge even(N) = tt) \vee (odd(N) \neq tt \wedge even(N) \neq tt)$ is unsatisfiable in $\mathcal{C}_\mathcal{R}$. Applying the **Unification** step to the first disjunct $odd(N) = tt \wedge even(N) = tt$ no variant unifiers are found, making this disjunct unsatisfiable. Applying the Π-**Elimination** step to the first disequality in the second disjunct $odd(N) \neq tt \wedge even(N) \neq tt$, since the only constructor variant of $odd(N)$ different from tt is the identity variant, and the only disjoint B_{Ω_c}-unifier of $odd(N)$ with the negative patterns for *odd* is $\{N \mapsto M + M\}$ for the (renamed) unconstrained negative pattern $odd(M + M) \neq tt$, we get the disequality $even(M + M) \neq tt$, whose normal form $tt \neq tt$ is unsatisfiable.

Theorem 3. *For FVP* $\mathcal{R} = (\Delta \uplus \Omega_c \uplus \Omega_\Pi, B_\Delta \uplus B_{\Omega_c}, R_\Delta \uplus R_{\Omega_c} \uplus R_\Pi)$ *protecting* $\mathcal{R}_\Omega = (\Omega_c \uplus \Omega_\Pi, B_{\Omega_c}, R_{\Omega_c} \uplus R_\Pi)$ *and satisfying above conditions (1)–(3), the above procedure correctly decides the satisfiability of a QF Σ-formula φ in the canonical term algebra $\mathcal{C}_\mathcal{R}$.*

Sort Predicates for Recursive Data Structures. Theorem 3 can be used to add sort predicates to (non-circular) recursive data structures, which can be axiomatized as the elements of an initial algebra T_Ω on a many-sorted signature of free constructors Ω. For example, lists can be so axiomatized with Ω consisting of just two sorts, *Elt*, viewed as a parametric sort of list elements, and *List*, a constant *nil* of sort *List*, and a "cons" constructor $\_;\_: Elt\ List \rightarrow List$.

In general, however, adding to such data structures defined functions corresponding to "selectors" that can extract the constituent parts of each data structure cannot be done in a satisfactory way if we remain within a many-sorted setting. For example, for lists we would like to have selectors *head* and *tail* (the usual *car* and *cdr* in Lisp notation). For *head* the natural equation is $head(x; l) = x$. Likewise, the natural equation for *tail* is $tail(x; l) = l$. But this leaves open the problem of how to define $head(nil)$, for which no satisfactory solution exists. Meseguer and Goguen proposed a simple solution to this "constructor-selector" problem using initial order-sorted algebras in [24]. The key idea is the following. For each non-constant constructor symbol, say $c : A_1 \ldots A_n \rightarrow B$, $n \geqslant 1$, we introduce a subsort $B_c < B$ and give the tighter typing $c : A_1 \ldots A_n \rightarrow B_c$. The selector problem is now easily solved by associating to each non-constant constructor c selector functions $sel_i^c : B_c \rightarrow A_i$, $1 \leqslant i \leqslant n$, defined by the equations $sel_i^c(c(x_1, \ldots, x_n)) = x_i$, $1 \leqslant i \leqslant n$. Outside the subsort B_c the selectors sel_i^c are actually undefined. For the above example of lists this just means adding a subsort $List_{-;-} < List$, where $List_{-;-}$ is usually written as $NeList$ (non-empty lists), and tightening the typing of "cons" to $_-;_- : Elt\ List \rightarrow NeList$. In this way the *head* and *tail* selectors have typings $head : NeList \rightarrow Elt$ and $tail : NeList \rightarrow List$, again with equations $head(x; l) = x$ and $tail(x; l) = l$, with x of sort Elt and l of sort $List$.

We have just described a general theory transformation $\Omega \mapsto (\widetilde{\Omega} \uplus \Delta, E_\Delta)$ from any MS signature Ω to an OS theory with selectors Δ. Due to space limitations, the following key facts are discussed in detail in [16]: (1) $(\widetilde{\Omega} \uplus \Delta, \varnothing, R(E_\Delta))$ is FVP with $(\widetilde{\Omega}, \varnothing, \varnothing)$ as its constructor decomposition. (2) To increase expressiveness, we can define for each subsort B_c associated with a constructor c a corresponding equationally-defined sort predicate $_-:B_c$, thus obtaining a decomposition $(\widetilde{\Omega} \uplus \Pi \uplus \Delta, \varnothing, R(E_\Delta) \uplus R(E_\Pi))$ that is also FVP. (3) Each sort predicate $_-:B_c$ has an associated set of *negative patterns*, so that our variant satisfiability algorithm makes satisfiability of QF formulas in the initial algebra $T_{\widetilde{\Omega} \uplus \Pi \uplus \Delta / E_\Delta \uplus E_\Pi}$ *decidable*.

Example 7. (Lists of Naturals with Sort Predicates). We can instantiate the above order-sorted theory of lists with selectors *head* and *tail* by instantiating the parameter sort Elt to a sort Nat with constant 0, subsort $NzNat < Nat$, and unary constructor $s : Nat \rightarrow NzNat$ with selector $p : NzNat \rightarrow Nat$ satisfying the equation $p(s(n)) = n$. We then extend this specification with sort predicates $_- : NzNat : Nat \rightarrow Pred$ and $_- : NeList : List \rightarrow Pred$, defined by equations $n':NzNat = tt$ and $l':NeList = tt$, with n' of sort $NzNat$ and l' of sort $NeList$. Their corresponding negative patterns are: $0:NzNat \neq tt$ and $nil:NeList \neq tt$.

One advantage of adding these sort predicates is that some properties not expressible as QF formulas become QF-expressible. For example, to state that every number is either 0 or a non-zero number (resp. every list is either *nil* or a non-empty list) we need the formula $n = 0 \vee (\exists n')\ n = n'$ (resp. $l = nil \vee (\exists l')\ l = l'$), where n has sort Nat and n' sort $NzNat$ (resp. l has sort $List$ and l' sort $NeList$). But with sort predicates this can be expressed by means of the QF formula $n = 0 \vee n:NzNat = tt$ (resp. $l = nil \vee l:NeList = tt$).

5   Implementation

We have implemented the variant satisfiability decision procedure of Sect. 4 in a new prototype tool (see http://users.dsic.upv.es/~rgutierrez/var-pred/). The implementation consists of 11 new Maude modules (from 17 in total), 2345 new lines of code, and uses the Maude's META-LEVEL to carry out the procedure in a reflective way. The three steps of the variant satisfiability procedure are implemented using Maude's META-LEVEL functions. Let us illustrate *NatSetPreds*.

Example 8. We can prove the inductive validity of the formula N - M = 0 $\Leftrightarrow$ (M > N = tt $\vee$ N = M), where N - M denotes N "monus" M, by showing that each conjunction in its negation, (N - M = 0 $\wedge$ M > N $\neq$ tt $\wedge$ N $\neq$ M) $\vee$ (N - M $\neq$ 0 $\wedge$ M > N = tt) $\vee$ (N - M $\neq$ 0 $\wedge$ N = M) is unsatisfiable. For the first conjunct the algorithm's three steps are as follows. After the **unification** step, we obtain (V2 + V3) > V2 $\neq$ tt $\land$ V2 $\neq$ V2 + V3, where V2 and V3 are variables of sort Natural. Applying the Π-**elimination** step, we obtain: V4 $\neq$ V4 + 0, where V4 is a variable of sort Natural. After normalization, the formula becomes B_{Ω_c}-inconsistent and therefore unsatisfiable. The other two conjuncts are likewise unsatisfiable.

For a more detailed discussion of the implementation see [16].

6   Related Work and Conclusions

The original paper proposing the concepts of variant and FVP is [9]. FVP ideas have been further advanced in [4,6,7,13]. Variant satisfiability has been studied in [21,27]. In relation to that work, the main contribution of this paper is the extension of variant satisfiability to handle user-definable predicates.

As mentioned in the Introduction, satisfiability decision procedures can be either theory-specific or theory-generic. These two classes of procedures complement each other: theory specific ones are more efficient; but theory-generic ones are user-definable and can substantially increase the range of SMT solvers. On theory-specific decision procedures advanced textbooks include, e.g., [5,18], and work on data type satisfiability includes, e.g., [3,11,28]. In relation to theory-specific work, what the results in this paper provide is a *generic algorithm* for a wide class of user-definable data types *with user-definable predicates*.

Other theory-generic satisfiability approaches include: (i) the superposition-based one, e.g., [1,2,19,20,29], where it is proved that a superposition theorem proving inference system terminates for a given first-order theory together with any given set of ground clauses representing a satisfiability problem; and (ii) that of decidable theories defined by means of formulas with triggers [12], that allows a user to define a new theory with decidable QF satisfiability by axiomatizing it according to some requirements, and then making an SMT solver extensible by such a user-defined theory. While not directly comparable to the present one, these approaches (discussed in considerably greater detail in [21]) can be seen as complementary ones, further enlarging the repertoire of theory-generic satisfiability methods.

In conclusion, the present work has extended variant satisfiability to support initial algebras specified by FVP theories with user-definable predicates under fairly general conditions. Since such predicates are often needed in specifications, this substantially enlarges the scope of variant-based initial satisfiability algorithms. The most obvious next step is to combine the original variant satisfiability algorithm defined in [21] and implemented in [27] with the present one. To simplify both the exposition and the prototype implementation, a few simplifying assumptions, such as the assumption that the signature Ω of constructors and that Δ of defined functions share no subsort-overloaded symbols, have been made. For both greater efficiency and wider applicability, the combined generic algorithm will drop such assumptions and will use constructor unification [21,27].

References

1. Armando, A., Bonacina, M.P., Ranise, S., Schulz, S.: New results on rewrite-based satisfiability procedures. TOCL **10**(1), 4 (2009)
2. Armando, A., Ranise, S., Rusinowitch, M.: A rewriting approach to satisfiability procedures. I&C **183**(2), 140–164 (2003)
3. Barrett, C., Shikanian, I., Tinelli, C.: An abstract decision procedure for satisfiability in the theory of inductive data types. JSAT **3**, 21–46 (2007)
4. Bouchard, C., Gero, K.A., Lynch, C., Narendran, P.: On forward closure and the finite variant property. In: Fontaine, P., Ringeissen, C., Schmidt, R.A. (eds.) FroCoS 2013. LNCS (LNAI), vol. 8152, pp. 327–342. Springer, Heidelberg (2013). https://doi.org/10.1007/978-3-642-40885-4_23
5. Bradley, A.R., Manna, Z.: The Calculus of Computation - Decision Procedures with Applications to Verification. Springer, Heidelberg (2007). https://doi.org/10.1007/978-3-540-74113-8
6. Cholewa, A., Meseguer, J., Escobar, S.: Variants of variants and the finite variant property. Technical report, CS Dept. University of Illinois at Urbana-Champaign (2014). http://hdl.handle.net/2142/47117
7. Ciobaca., S.: Verification of composition of security protocols with applications to electronic voting. Ph.D. thesis, ENS Cachan (2011)
8. Comon, H.: Complete axiomatizations of some quotient term algebras. TCS **118**(2), 167–191 (1993)
9. Comon-Lundh, H., Delaune, S.: The finite variant property: how to get rid of some algebraic properties. In: Giesl, J. (ed.) RTA 2005. LNCS, vol. 3467, pp. 294–307. Springer, Heidelberg (2005). https://doi.org/10.1007/978-3-540-32033-3_22
10. Dershowitz, N., Jouannaud, J.P.: Rewrite systems. In: Handbook of Theoretical Computer Science, North-Holland, vol. B, pp. 243–320 (1990)
11. Dovier, A., Piazza, C., Rossi, G.: A uniform approach to constraint-solving for lists, multisets, compact lists, and sets. TOCL **9**(3), 15 (2008)
12. Dross, C., Conchon, S., Kanig, J., Paskevich, A.: Adding decision procedures to SMT solvers using axioms with triggers. JAR **56**(4), 387–457 (2016)
13. Escobar, S., Sasse, R., Meseguer, J.: Folding variant narrowing and optimal variant termination. JALP **81**, 898–928 (2012)
14. Goguen, J.A., Meseguer, J.: Models and equality for logical programming. In: Ehrig, H., Kowalski, R., Levi, G., Montanari, U. (eds.) TAPSOFT 1987. LNCS, vol. 250, pp. 1–22. Springer, Heidelberg (1987). https://doi.org/10.1007/BFb0014969
15. Goguen, J., Meseguer, J.: Order-sorted algebra I: equational deduction for multiple inheritance, overloading, exceptions and partial operations. TCS **105**, 217–273 (1992)
16. Gutiérrez, R., Meseguer, J.: Variant satisfiability in initial algebras with predicates. Technical report, CS Department, University of Illinois at Urbana-Champaign (2018). http://hdl.handle.net/2142/99039
17. Jouannaud, J.P., Kirchner, H.: Completion of a set of rules modulo a set of equations. SICOMP **15**, 1155–1194 (1986)
18. Kroening, D., Strichman, O.: Decision Procedures - An algorithmic point of view. Texts in TCS. An EATCS Series. Springer, Heidelberg (2008). https://doi.org/10.1007/978-3-540-74105-3
19. Lynch, C., Morawska, B.: Automatic decidability. In: Proceedings of LICS 2002, p. 7. IEEE Computer Society (2002)

20. Lynch, C., Tran, D.-K.: Automatic decidability and combinability revisited. In: Pfenning, F. (ed.) CADE 2007. LNCS (LNAI), vol. 4603, pp. 328–344. Springer, Heidelberg (2007). https://doi.org/10.1007/978-3-540-73595-3_22
21. Meseguer, J.: Variant-based satisfiability in initial algebras. SCP **154**, 3–41 (2018)
22. Meseguer, J.: Strict coherence of conditional rewriting modulo axioms. TCS **672**, 1–35 (2017)
23. Meseguer, J., Goguen, J.: Initiality, induction and computability. In: Algebraic Methods in Semantics, Cambridge, pp. 459–541 (1985)
24. Meseguer, J., Goguen, J.: Order-sorted algebra solves the constructor-selector, multiple representation and coercion problems. I&C **103**(1), 114–158 (1993)
25. Nelson, G., Oppen, D.C.: Simplification by cooperating decision procedures. TOPLAS **1**(2), 245–257 (1979)
26. Shostak, R.E.: Deciding combinations of theories. J. ACM **31**(1), 1–12 (1984)
27. Skeirik, S., Meseguer, J.: Metalevel algorithms for variant satisfiability. In: Lucanu, D. (ed.) WRLA 2016. LNCS, vol. 9942, pp. 167–184. Springer, Cham (2016). https://doi.org/10.1007/978-3-319-44802-2_10
28. Stump, A., Barrett, C.W., Dill, D.L., Levitt, J.R.: A decision procedure for an extensional theory of arrays. In: Proceedings of LICS 2001, pp. 29–37. IEEE (2001)
29. Tushkanova, E., Giorgetti, A., Ringeissen, C., Kouchnarenko, O.: A rule-based system for automatic decidability and combinability. SCP **99**, 3–23 (2015)

Combining Static and Dynamic Contract Checking for Curry

Michael Hanus[(✉)] [iD]

Institut für Informatik, CAU Kiel, 24098 Kiel, Germany
mh@informatik.uni-kiel.de

Abstract. Static type systems are usually not sufficient to express all requirements on function calls. Hence, contracts with pre- and postconditions can be used to express more complex constraints on operations. Contracts can be checked at run time to ensure that operations are only invoked with reasonable arguments and return intended results. Although such dynamic contract checking provides more reliable program execution, it requires execution time and could lead to program crashes that might be detected with more advanced methods at compile time. To improve this situation for declarative languages, we present an approach to combine static and dynamic contract checking for the functional logic language Curry. Based on a formal model of contract checking for functional logic programming, we propose an automatic method to verify contracts at compile time. If a contract is successfully verified, dynamic checking of it can be omitted. This method decreases execution time without degrading reliable program execution. In the best case, when all contracts are statically verified, it provides trust in the software since crashes due to contract violations cannot occur during program execution.

1 Introduction

Static types, provided by the programmer or inferred by the compiler, are useful to detect specific classes of run-time errors at compile time. This is expressed by Milner [23] as "well-typed expressions do not go wrong." However, not all requirements on operations can be expressed by standard static type systems. Hence, one can either refine the type system, e.g., use a dependently typed programming language and a more sophisticated programming discipline [28], or add contracts with pre- and postconditions to operations. In this paper, we follow the latter approach since it provides a smooth integration into existing software development processes. For instance, consider the well-known factorial function:

```
fac n = if n==0 then 1
                else n * fac (n-1)
```

The research described in this paper has been partially supported by the German Federal Ministry of Education and Research (BMBF) under Grant No. 01IH15006B.

F. Fioravanti and J. P. Gallagher (Eds.): LOPSTR 2017, LNCS 10855, pp. 323–340, 2018.
https://doi.org/10.1007/978-3-319-94460-9_19

Although `fac` is intended to work on non-negative natural numbers, standard static type systems cannot express this constraint so that

```
fac :: Int  →  Int
```

is provided or inferred as the static type of `fac`.[1] Although this type avoids the application of `fac` on characters or strings, it allows to apply `fac` on negative numbers which results in an infinite loop.

A *precondition* is a Boolean expression to restrict the applicability of an operation. Following the notation proposed in [6], a precondition for an operation f is a Boolean operation with name f'pre. For instance, a precondition for `fac` is

```
fac'pre n = n >= 0
```

To use a precondition for checking `fac` invocations at run time, a preprocessor could transform each call to `fac` by attaching an additional test whether the precondition is satisfied (see [6]). After this transformation, an application to `fac` to a negative number results in a run-time error (contract violation) instead of an infinite loop.

Unfortunately, run-time contract checking requires additional execution time so that it is often turned off, in particular, in production systems. To improve this situation for declarative languages, we propose to reduce the number of contract checks by (automatically) verifying them at compile time. Since we do not expect to verify all of them at compile time, our approach can be seen as a compromise between a full static verification, e.g., with proof assistants like Agda, Coq, or Isabelle, which is time-consuming and difficult, and a full dynamic checking, which might be inefficient.

For instance, one can verify (e.g., with an SMT solver [12]) that the precondition for the recursive call of `fac` is always satisfied provided that `fac` is called with a satisfied precondition. Hence, we can omit the precondition checking for recursive calls so that $n - 1$ precondition checks are avoided when we evaluate `fac` n.

In the following, we make this idea more precise for the functional logic language Curry [21], briefly reviewed in the next section, so that the same ideas can also be applied to purely functional as well as logic languages. After discussing contracts for Curry in Sect. 3, we define a formal model of contract checking for Curry in Sect. 4. This is the basis to extract proof obligations for contracts at compile time. If these proof obligations can be verified, the corresponding dynamic checks can be omitted. Some examples for contract verification are shown in Sect. 5 before we discuss the current implementation and first benchmark results, which are quite encouraging. Due to lack of space, the proofs are omitted (they are available in a long version of this paper).

2   Functional Logic Programming and Curry

Functional logic languages combine the most important features of functional and logic programming in a single language (see [17] for a recent survey).

---

[1] The inferred type depends on the underlying static type system. For instance, Haskell infers a more general overloaded type.

In particular, the functional logic language Curry [21] conceptually extends Haskell with common features of logic programming, i.e., non-determinism, free variables, and constraint solving. Since we discuss our methods in the context of functional logic programming, we briefly review those elements of functional logic languages and Curry that are necessary to understand the contents of this paper. More details can be found in surveys on functional logic programming [17] and in the language report [21].

The syntax of Curry is close to Haskell [25]. In addition to Haskell, Curry applies rules with overlapping left-hand sides in a (don't know) non-deterministic manner (where Haskell always selects the first matching rule) and allows *free (logic) variables* in conditions and right-hand sides of rules. These variables must be explicitly declared unless they are anonymous. Function calls can contain free variables, in particular, variables without a value at call time. These calls are evaluated lazily where free variables as demanded arguments are non-deterministically instantiated [2].

Example 1. The following simple program shows the functional and logic features of Curry. It defines an operation "++" to concatenate two lists, which is identical to the Haskell encoding. The operation `ins` inserts an element at some (unspecified) position in a list:

```
(++)   :: [a]  →  [a]  →  [a]          ins :: a  →  [a]  →  [a]
[]        ++ ys = ys                    ins x ys      = x : ys
(x:xs) ++ ys = x : (xs ++ ys)          ins x (y:ys) = y : ins x ys
```

Note that `ins` is a *non-deterministic operation* since it might deliver more than one result for a given argument, e.g., the evaluation of `ins 0 [1,2]` yields the values `[0,1,2]`, `[1,0,2]`, and `[1,2,0]`. Non-deterministic operations, which are interpreted as mappings from values into sets of values [15], are an important feature of contemporary functional logic languages. Hence, there is also a predefined *choice* operation:

```
x ? _  = x
_ ? y = y
```

Thus, "0 ? 1" evaluates to 0 and 1 with the value non-deterministically chosen.

Non-deterministic operations can be used as any other operation. For instance, exploiting `ins`, we can define an operation `perm` that returns an arbitrary permutation of a list:

```
perm []      = []
perm (x:xs) = ins x (perm xs)
```

Non-deterministic operations are quite expressive since they can be used to completely eliminate logic variables in functional logic programs. Actually, it has been shown that non-deterministic operations and logic variables have the same expressive power [4,11]. For instance, a Boolean logic variable can be replaced by the non-deterministic *generator* operation for Booleans defined by

```
aBool = False ? True
```

This equivalence can be exploited when Curry is implemented by translation into a target language without support for non-determinism and logic variables. For instance, KiCS2 [9] compiles Curry into Haskell by adding a mechanism to handle non-deterministic computations. In our case, we exploit this fact by simply ignoring logic variables since they are considered as syntactic sugar for non-deterministic value generators.

Curry has many additional features not described here, like monadic I/O [31] for declarative input/output, set functions [5] to encapsulate non-deterministic search, functional patterns [3] and default rules [7] to specify complex transformations in a high-level manner, and a hierarchical module system together with a package manager[2] that provides access to dozens of packages with hundreds of modules.

Due to the complexity of the source language, compilers or analysis and optimization tools often use an intermediate language where the syntactic sugar of the source language has been eliminated and the pattern matching strategy is explicit. This intermediate language, called FlatCurry, has also been used to specify the operational semantics of Curry programs [1]. Since we will use FlatCurry as the basis for verifying contracts, we sketch the structure of FlatCurry and its semantics.

$$
\begin{array}{llll}
P & ::= & D_1 \ldots D_m & \text{(program)} \\
D & ::= & f(x_1, \ldots, x_n) = e & \text{(function definition)} \\
e & ::= & x & \text{(variable)} \\
  & \mid & c(e_1, \ldots, e_n) & \text{(constructor call)} \\
  & \mid & f(e_1, \ldots, e_n) & \text{(function call)} \\
  & \mid & case\ e\ of\ \{p_1 \to e_1; \ldots; p_n \to e_n\} & \text{(case expression)} \\
  & \mid & e_1\ or\ e_2 & \text{(disjunction)} \\
  & \mid & let\ \{x_1 = e_1; \ldots; x_n = e_n\}\ in\ e & \text{(let binding)} \\
p & ::= & c(x_1, \ldots, x_n) & \text{(pattern)}
\end{array}
$$

Fig. 1. Syntax of the intermediate language FlatCurry

The abstract syntax of FlatCurry is summarized in Fig. 1. In contrast to some other presentations (e.g., [1,17]), we omit the difference between rigid and flexible case expressions since we do not consider residuation (which becomes less important in practice and is also omitted in newer implementations of Curry [9]). A FlatCurry program consists of a sequence of function definitions, where each function is defined by a single rule. Patterns in source programs are compiled into case expressions and overlapping rules are joined by explicit disjunctions. For instance, the non-deterministic insert operation ins is represented in FlatCurry as

$$\text{ins}(x, xs) = (x : xs)\ or\ (case\ xs\ of\ \{y : ys \to y : \text{ins}(x, ys)\})$$

---

[2] http://curry-language.org/tools/cpm.

The semantics of FlatCurry programs is defined in [1] as an extension of Launchbury's natural semantics for lazy evaluation [22]. For this purpose, we consider only *normalized* FlatCurry programs, i.e., programs where the arguments of constructor and function calls and the discriminating argument of case expressions are always variables. Any FlatCurry program can be normalized by introducing new variables by let expressions [1]. For instance, the expression "$y : \text{ins}(x, ys)$" is normalized into "$let \ \{z = \text{ins}(x, ys)\} \ in \ y : z$." In the following, we assume that all FlatCurry programs are normalized.

In order to model sharing, which is important for lazy evaluation and also semantically relevant in case of non-deterministic operations [15], variables are interpreted as references into a heap where new let bindings are stored and function calls are updated with their evaluated results. To be more precise, a *heap*, denoted by Γ, Δ, or Θ, is a partial mapping from variables to expressions. The *empty heap* is denoted by $[]$. $\Gamma[x \mapsto e]$ denotes a heap Γ' with $\Gamma'(x) = e$ and $\Gamma'(y) = \Gamma(y)$ for all $x \neq y$.

Val	$\Gamma : v \Downarrow \Gamma : v$ where v is constructor-rooted
VarExp	$\dfrac{\Gamma : e \Downarrow \Delta : v}{\Gamma[x \mapsto e] : x \Downarrow \Delta[x \mapsto v] : v}$
Fun	$\dfrac{\Gamma : \rho(e) \Downarrow \Delta : v}{\Gamma : f(\overline{x_n}) \Downarrow \Delta : v}$ where $f(\overline{y_n}) = e \in P$ and $\rho = \{\overline{y_n \mapsto x_n}\}$
Let	$\dfrac{\Gamma[\overline{y_k \mapsto \rho(e_k)}] : \rho(e) \Downarrow \Delta : v}{\Gamma : let \ \{\overline{x_k = e_k}\} \ in \ e \Downarrow \Delta : v}$ where $\rho = \{\overline{x_k \mapsto y_k}\}$ and $\overline{y_k}$ are fresh variables
Or	$\dfrac{\Gamma : e_i \Downarrow \Delta : v}{\Gamma : e_1 \ or \ e_2 \Downarrow \Delta : v}$ where $i \subset \{1, 2\}$
Select	$\dfrac{\Gamma : x \Downarrow \Delta : c(\overline{y_n}) \quad \Delta : \rho(e_i) \Downarrow \Theta : v}{\Gamma : case \ x \ of \ \{\overline{p_k \to e_k}\} \Downarrow \Theta : v}$ where $p_i = c(\overline{x_n})$ and $\rho = \{\overline{x_n \mapsto y_n}\}$

Fig. 2. Natural semantics of normalized FlatCurry programs

Using heap structures, one can provide a high-level description of the operational behavior of FlatCurry programs in natural semantics style. The semantics uses judgements of the form "$\Gamma : e \Downarrow \Delta : v$" with the meaning that in the context of heap Γ the expression e evaluates to value (head normal form) v and produces a modified heap Δ. Figure 2 shows the rules defining this semantics w.r.t. a given normalized FlatCurry program P ($\overline{o_k}$ denotes a sequence of objects $o_1, \ldots, o_k$).

Constructor-rooted expressions (i.e., head normal forms) are just returned by rule Val. Rule VarExp retrieves a binding for a variable from the heap and evaluates it. In order to avoid the re-evaluation of the same expression, VarExp updates the heap with the computed value, which models sharing. In contrast to the original rules [1], **VarExp** removes the binding from the heap. On the one hand, this allows the detection of simple loops ("black holes") as in functional programming. On the other hand, it is crucial in combination with non-determinism to avoid the binding of a variable to different values in the same derivation (see [8] for a detailed discussion on this issue). Rule **Fun** unfolds function calls by evaluating the right-hand side after binding the formal parameters to the actual ones. **Let** introduces new bindings in the heap and renames the variables in the expressions with the fresh names introduced in the heap. **Or** non-deterministically evaluates one of its arguments. Finally, rule **Select** deals with *case* expressions. When the discriminating argument of *case* evaluates to a constructor-rooted term, **Select** evaluates the corresponding branch of the *case* expression.

FlatCurry and its operational semantics has been used for various language-oriented tools, like compilers, partial evaluators, or debugging and profiling tools (see [17] for references). We use it in this paper to define a formal model of contract checking and extract proof obligations for contracts from programs.

3   Contracts

The use of contracts even in declarative programming languages has been motivated in Sect. 1. Contracts in the form of pre- and postconditions as well as specifications have been introduced into functional logic programming in [6]. Contracts and specifications for some operation are operations with the same name and a specific suffix. If f is an operation of type $\tau \to \tau'$, then a *specification* for f is an operation f'`spec` of type $\tau \to \tau'$, a *precondition* for f is an operation f'`pre` of type $\tau \to$ `Bool`, and a *postcondition* for f is an operation f'`post` of type $\tau \to \tau' \to$ `Bool`.

Intuitively, an operation and its specification should be equivalent operations. For instance, a specification of non-deterministic list insertion could be stated with a single rule containing a functional pattern [3] as follows:

```
ins'spec :: a  → [a]  → [a]
ins'spec x (xs ++ ys) = xs ++ [x] ++ ys
```

A precondition should be satisfied if an operation is invoked, and a postcondition is a relation between input and output values which should be satisfied when an operation yields some result. We have already seen a precondition for the factorial function in Sect. 1. A postcondition for `fac` could state that the result is always positive:

```
fac'post n f = f > 0
```

This postcondition ensures that the precondition of nested `fac` applications always holds, like in the expression `fac (fac 3)`. If an operation has no postcondition but a specification, the latter can be used as a postcondition. For instance, a postcondition derived from the specification for `ins` is

```
ins'post :: a  → [a]  → [a]  → Bool
ins'post x ys zs = zs 'valueOf' ins'spec x ys
```

This postcondition states that the value zs computed by ins is in the set of all values computed by ins'spec (where f_S denotes the set function of f, see [5]).

Antoy and Hanus [6] describe a tool which transforms programs containing contracts and specifications into programs where these contracts and specifications are dynamically checked. This tool is available in recent distributions of the Curry implementations PAKCS [19] and KiCS2 [9] as a preprocessor so that the transformation can be automatically performed when Curry programs are compiled. Furthermore, the property-based testing tool CurryCheck [18] automatically tests contracts and specifications with generated input data.

Although these dynamic and static testing tools provide some confidence in the software under development, a static *verification* of contracts is preferable since it holds for all input values, i.e., it is ensured that violations of verified contracts cannot occur at run time so that their run-time tests can be omitted. As a first step towards this objective, we specify the operational meaning of contract checking by extending the semantics of Fig. 2. Since pre- and postconditions are checked before and after a function invocation, respectively, it is sufficient to extend rule **Fun**. Assume that function f has a precondition f'pre and a postcondition f'post (if some of them is not present, we assume that they are defined as predicates which always return True). Then we replace rule **Fun** by the extended rule **FunCheck**:

$$\frac{\Gamma : f'\text{pre}(\overline{x_n}) \Downarrow \Gamma' : \text{True} \quad \Gamma' : \rho(e) \Downarrow \Delta' : v \quad \Delta' : f'\text{post}(\overline{x_n}, v) \Downarrow \Delta : \text{True}}{\Gamma : f(\overline{x_n}) \Downarrow \Delta : v}$$

where $f(\overline{y_n}) = e \in P$ and $\rho = \{\overline{y_n \mapsto x_n}\}$. For the sake of readability, we omit the normalization of the postcondition in the premise, which can be added by an introduction of a *let* binding for v. The reporting of contract violations can be specified by the following rules:

$$\frac{\Gamma : f'\text{pre}(\overline{x_n}) \Downarrow \Gamma' : \text{False}}{\Gamma : f(\overline{x_n}) \Downarrow \text{<<precondition of } f \text{ violated>>}}$$

$$\frac{\Gamma : f'\text{pre}(\overline{x_n}) \Downarrow \Gamma' : \text{True} \quad \Gamma' : \rho(e) \Downarrow \Delta' : v \quad \Delta' : f'\text{post}(\overline{x_n}, v) \Downarrow \Delta : \text{False}}{\Gamma : f(\overline{x_n}) \Downarrow \text{<<postcondition of } f \text{ violated>>}}$$

Note that we specified *eager* contract checking, i.e., pre- and postconditions are immediately and completely evaluated. Although this is often intended, there are cases where eager contract checking might influence the execution behavior of a program, e.g., if the evaluation of a pre- or postcondition requires to evaluate more than demanded by the original program. To avoid this problem, Chitil et al. [10] proposed *lazy* contract checking where contract arguments are not evaluated but the checks are performed when the demanded arguments become evaluated by the application program. Lazy contract checking could have the problem that the occurrence of contract violations depend on the demand of evaluation so that they are detected "too late." Since there seems to be no ideal solution to this problem, we simply stick to eager contract checking.

4   Contract Verification

In order to statically verify contracts, we have to extract some proof obligation from the program and contracts. For instance, consider the factorial function and its precondition, as shown in Sect. 1. The normalized FlatCurry representation of the factorial function is

```
fac(n) = let { x = 0 ; y = n==x }
           in case y of True   → 1
                        False  → let { n1 = n - 1 ; f = fac(n1) }
                                 in n * f
```

Now consider the call `fac(n)`. Since we assume that the precondition holds when an operation is invoked, we know that $n \geq 0$ holds before the case expression is evaluated. If the `False` branch of the case expression is selected, we know that $n = 0$ has the value `False`. Altogether, we know that $n \geq 0 \wedge \neg(n = 0)$ holds when the right-hand side of the `False` branch is evaluated. Since this implies that $n > 0$ and, thus, $(n - 1) \geq 0$ holds (in integer arithmetic), we know that the precondition of the recursive call to `fac` always holds. Hence, its check can be omitted at run time.

This example shows that we have to collect in expressions (the rules' right-hand sides) properties that are ensured to be valid when we reach particular points. For this purpose, we define an *assertion-collecting semantics*. It is oriented towards the concrete semantics shown before but has the following differences:

1. We compute with symbolic values instead of concrete ones.
2. We collect properties that are known to be valid (also called *assertions* in the following).
3. Instead of evaluating functions, we collect their pre- and postconditions.

This semantics uses judgements of the form "$\Gamma : C \mid z \leftarrow e \Downarrow D$" where Γ is a heap, z is a (result) variable, e is an expression, and C and D are *assertions*, i.e., Boolean formulas over the program signature. Intuitively, this judgement means that if e is evaluated to z in the context Γ where C holds, then D holds after the evaluation.

Figure 3 shows the rules defining the assertion-collecting semantics. Rule *Val* immediately returns the collected assertions. Since this semantics is intended to compute with symbolic values, there might be variables without a binding to a concrete value. Hence, *Val* also returns such unbound variables. Rule *VarExp* behaves similarly to rule **VarExp** of the concrete semantics and returns the assertions collected during the evaluation of the expression. Note that the assertion-collecting semantics does not really evaluate expressions since it should always return the collected assertions in a finite amount of time. For the same reason, rule *Fun* does not invoke the function in order to evaluate its right-hand side. Instead, the pre- and postcondition information is added to the collected assertions since they must hold if the function returns some value. The notation $f'\text{pre}(\overline{x_n})$ and $f'\text{post}(\overline{x_n}, z)$ in the assertion means that the logical formulas

$$Val \qquad \Gamma : C \mid z \leftarrow v \Downarrow C \wedge z = v \qquad \begin{array}{l} \text{where } v \text{ is constructor-rooted or} \\ v \text{ is a variable not bound in } \Gamma \end{array}$$

$$VarExp \qquad \frac{\Gamma : C \mid z \leftarrow e \Downarrow D}{\Gamma[x \mapsto e] : C \mid z \leftarrow x \Downarrow D}$$

$$Fun \qquad \Gamma : C \mid z \leftarrow f(\overline{x_n}) \Downarrow C \wedge f' \, \mathtt{pre}(\overline{x_n}) \wedge f' \, \mathtt{post}(\overline{x_n}, z)$$

$$Let \qquad \frac{\Gamma[\overline{y_k \mapsto \rho(e_k)}] : C \mid z \leftarrow \rho(e) \Downarrow D}{\Gamma : C \mid z \leftarrow let \, \{\overline{x_k = e_k}\} \, in \, e \Downarrow D} \qquad \begin{array}{l} \text{where } \rho = \{\overline{x_k \mapsto y_k}\} \\ \text{and } \overline{y_k} \text{ are fresh variables} \end{array}$$

$$Or \qquad \frac{\Gamma : C \mid z \leftarrow e_1 \Downarrow D_1 \qquad \Gamma : C \mid z \leftarrow e_2 \Downarrow D_2}{\Gamma : C \mid z \leftarrow e_1 \, or \, e_2 \Downarrow D_1 \vee D_2}$$

$$Select \qquad \frac{\Gamma : C \mid x \leftarrow x \Downarrow D \quad \Gamma : D_1 \mid z \leftarrow e_1 \Downarrow E_1 \, \ldots \, \Gamma : D_k \mid z \leftarrow e_k \Downarrow E_k}{\Gamma : C \mid z \leftarrow case \, x \, of \, \{\overline{p_k \rightarrow e_k}\} \Downarrow E_1 \vee \ldots \vee E_k}$$
$$\text{where } D_i = D \wedge x = p_i \, (i = 1, \ldots, k)$$

Fig. 3. Assertion-collecting semantics

corresponding to the pre- and postcondition are added as an assertion. These formulas might be simplified by replacing occurrences of operations defined in the program by their definitions. Rule *Let* adds the let bindings to the heap, similarly to the concrete semantics, before evaluating the argument expression. Rules *Or* and *Select* collect all information derived from alternative computations, instead of the non-deterministic concrete semantics. Rule *Select* also collects inside each branch the condition that must hold in the selected branch, which is important to get precise proof obligations. To avoid the renaming of local variables in different branches, we implicitly assume that all local variables are unique in a normalized function definition.

In contrast to the concrete semantics, the assertion-collecting semantics is deterministic, i.e., for each heap Γ, assertion C, variable z, and expression e, there is a unique (up to variable renamings in let bindings) proof tree and assertion D so that the judgement "$\Gamma : C \mid z \leftarrow e \Downarrow D$" is derivable.

The assertion-collecting semantics allows to extract proof obligations to verify contracts. For instance, to verify that a postcondition $f'\mathtt{post}$ for some function f defined by $f(\overline{x_n}) = e$ holds, one derives a judgement (where z is a new variable)

$$[] : f'\mathtt{pre}(\overline{x_n}) \mid z \leftarrow e \Downarrow C$$

and proves that C implies $f'\mathtt{post}(\overline{x_n}, z)$.

As an example, consider the non-deterministic operation

```
coin = 1 or 2
```

and its postcondition

```
coin'post z = z > 0
```

(the precondition is simply `True`). We derive for the right-hand side of `coin` the following proof tree:

$$Or \cfrac{Val \cfrac{}{[] : true \mid z \leftarrow 1 \Downarrow z = 1} \qquad \cfrac{}{[] : true \mid z \leftarrow 2 \Downarrow z = 2} \; Val}{[] : true \mid z \leftarrow 1 \; or \; 2 \Downarrow z = 1 \vee z = 2}$$

Since $z = 1 \vee z = 2$ implies $z > 0$, the postcondition of `coin` is always satisfied.

If we construct the proof tree for the right-hand side e of the factorial function, we derive the following judgement:

$$[] : n \geq 0 \mid z \leftarrow e \Downarrow (n \geq 0 \wedge y = true \wedge z = 1) \vee (n \geq 0 \wedge y = false)$$

Since there is no condition on the result variable z in the second argument of the disjunction, this assertion does not imply the postcondition $z > 0$. The reason is that the recursive call to `fac` is not considered in the proof tree since it does not occur at the top level. Note that rule *Fun* only adds the contract information of top-level operations but no contracts of operations occurring in arguments. Due to the lazy evaluation strategy, one does not know at compile time whether some argument expression is evaluated. Hence, it would not be correct to add the contract information of nested arguments. For instance, consider the operations

```
const x y = y        f x | x>0 = 0              g x = const (f x) 42
                     f'post x z = x>0
```

If e denotes the right-hand side of `g` (in normalized FlatCurry form), then we can derive with the inference rules of Fig. 3 the judgement

$$[] : true \mid z \leftarrow e \Downarrow true$$

If we change rule *Fun* so that the contracts of argument calls are also added to the returned assertion, then we could derive

$$[] : true \mid z \leftarrow e \Downarrow x > 0$$

This postcondition is clearly wrong since (`g 0`) successfully evaluates to 42.

Nevertheless, we can improve our semantics in cases where it is ensured that arguments are evaluated. For instance, primitive operations, like `+`, `*`, or `==`, evaluate their arguments. Thus, we add the following rule (and restrict rule *Fun* to exclude these operations):

$$PrimOp \; \cfrac{\Gamma : C \mid x \leftarrow x \Downarrow D \quad \Gamma : D \mid y \leftarrow y \Downarrow E}{\Gamma : C \mid z \leftarrow x \oplus y \Downarrow E \wedge z = x \oplus y} \quad \text{where } \oplus \in \{==, +, -, *, \ldots\}$$

Since primitive operations are often known to the underlying verifier, we also collect the information about the call of the primitive operation. In a similar way, one can also improve user-defined functions if some argument is known to be demanded, a property which can be approximated at compile time by a demand analysis [16].

If we construct a proof tree for the factorial function with these refined inference rules, we obtain the following (simplified) assertion:

$$(n \geq 0 \wedge n = 0 \wedge z = 1) \vee (n \geq 0 \wedge n \neq 0 \wedge n1 \geq 0 \wedge f > 0 \wedge z = n * f)$$

Since this assertion implies $z > 0$, the postcondition `fac'post` holds so that its checking can be omitted at run time.

Proof obligations for preconditions can also be extracted from the proof tree. For this purpose, one has to consider occurrences of operations with non-trivial preconditions. If such an operation occurs as a top-level expression or in a let binding associated to a top-level expression and the assertion before this expression implies the precondition, then one can omit the precondition checking for this call. For instance, consider again the proof tree for the right-hand side of the factorial function which contains the following (simplified) judgement:

$$[] : n \geq 0 \wedge n \neq 0 \mid z \leftarrow \text{let } \{n1 = n - 1; f = \text{fac } n1\} \text{ in } n * f \Downarrow \ldots$$

Since $n \geq 0 \wedge n \neq 0 \wedge n1 = n - 1$ implies $n1 \geq 0$, the precondition holds so that its check can be omitted for this recursive call.

The correctness of our approach relies on the following relation between the concrete and the assertion-collecting semantics:

Theorem 1. *If* $\Gamma : e \Downarrow \Gamma' : v$ *is a valid judgement,* z *a variable, and* C *an assertion such that* $\widehat{\Gamma} \Rightarrow C$ *is valid, then there is a valid judgement* $\Gamma : C \mid z \leftarrow e \Downarrow D$ *with* $(\widehat{\Gamma'} \wedge z = v) \Rightarrow D$.

Here, $\widehat{\Gamma}$ denotes the representation of heap information as a logic formula, i.e.,

$$\widehat{\Gamma} = \bigwedge \{x = e \mid x \mapsto e \subset \Gamma, \ e \text{ constructor-rooted or a variable}\}$$

The proof is by induction on the height of the proof tree and requires some technical lemmas which we omit here due to lack of space.

5 More Examples

There are various recursively defined operations with pre- and postconditions that can be verified similarly to `fac` as shown above. For instance, the postcondition and the preconditions for both recursive calls to `fib` in

```
fib x | x == 0    = 0
      | x == 1    = 1
      | otherwise = fib (x-1) + fib (x-2)

fib'pre n = n >= 0
fib'post n f = f >= 0
```

can be verified with a similar reasoning. SMT solvers like Z3 [12] provide good reasoning on integer theories. This can be successfully applied to verify more complex postconditions. For instance, consider the function which sums up all natural numbers:

```
sum n = if n==0 then 0
                else n + sum (n-1)
```

The precondition requires that the argument must be non-negative, and the postcondition specifies the correctness of this function by Gauss' formula:

```
sum'pre n    = n>=0
sum'post n f = f == n * (n+1) 'div' 2
```

Our method allows a fully automatic verification of this postcondition.

The precondition on the operation `take` defined by

```
take 0 xs              = []
take n (x:xs) | n>0 = x : take (n-1) xs

take'pre n xs = n >= 0
```

can be verified similarly to `fac` or `fib` since the list structures are not relevant here. On the other hand, the verification of the precondition of the recursive call of the function `last` defined by

```
last [x]      = x
last (_:x:xs) = last (x:xs)

last'pre xs = not (null xs)
```

requires the verification of the implication

$$not\ (null\ xs) \wedge xs = (y{:}ys) \wedge ys = (z{:}zs) \Rightarrow not\ (null\ (z{:}zs))$$

This can be proved by evaluating the right-hand side to *true*. Hence, a reasonable verification strategy includes the simplification of proof obligations by symbolic evaluation before passing them to the external verifier.[3]

A more involved operation is the list index operator which selects the nth element of a list:

```
nth (x:xs) n | n==0 = x
             | n>0  = nth xs (n-1)

nth'pre xs n = n >= 0 && length (take (n+1) xs) == n+1
```

The precondition ensures that the element to be selected always exists since the selected position is not negative and not larger than the length of the list. The use of the operation `take` (instead of the simpler condition `length xs > n`) is important to allow the application of `nth` also to infinite lists. To verify that the precondition holds for the recursive call, one has to verify that

$$n \geq 0 \wedge length\ (take\ (n+1)\ xs) = n+1 \wedge xs = (y{:}ys) \wedge n \neq 0 \wedge n > 0$$

---

[3] Since Curry programs might contain non-terminating operations, one has to be careful when simplifying expressions. In order to ensure the termination of the simplification process, one can either limit the number of simplification steps or use only operations for simplification that are known to be terminating. Since the latter property can be approximated by various program analysis techniques, the Curry program analyzer CASS [20] contains such an analysis.

implies

$$(n - 1) \geq 0 \ \wedge \ length \ (take \ ((n - 1) + 1) \ ys) = (n - 1) + 1$$

The proof of the first conjunct uses reasoning on integer arithmetic as in the previous examples. The second conjunct can also be proved by SMT solvers when the rules of the operations `length` and `take` are axiomatized as logic formulas.

6 Implementation and Benchmarks

We implemented static contract verification as a fully automatic tool which tries to verify contracts at compile time and, in case of a successful verification, removes their run-time checking from the generated code. The complete compilation chain with this tool is as follows:

1. The Curry preprocessor performs a source-level transformation to add contracts as run-time checks, as sketched in Sect. 3 and described in [6].
2. The preprocessed program is compiled with the standard Curry front end into an intermediate FlatCurry program.
3. For each contract, the contract verifier extracts the proof obligation as described in Sect. 4.
4. Each proof obligation is translated into SMT-LIB format and sent to an SMT solver (here: Z3 [12]).
5. If the proof shows the validity of the contract, its check is removed from the FlatCurry program.

This general approach can be refined. For instance, if a pre- or postcondition is a conjunction of formulas, each conjunct can separately be verified and possibly removed. This allows to make dynamic contract checking more efficient even if the complete contract cannot be verified.

Although our tool is a prototype, we applied it to some initial benchmarks in order to get an idea about the efficiency improvement by static contract verification. For this purpose, we compared the execution time of the program with and without static contract checking. Note that in case of preconditions, only verified preconditions for recursive calls can be omitted so that the operations can safely be invoked as before.

For the benchmarks, we used the Curry implementation KiCS2 (Version 0.6.0) [9] with the Glasgow Haskell Compiler (GHC 7.10.3, option -O2) as its back end on a Linux machine (Debian 8.9) with an Intel Core i7-4790 (3.60 GHz) processor and 8 GiB of memory. Table 1 shows the execution times (in seconds, where "0.00" means less than 10 ms) of executing a program with the given main expression. Column "dynamic" denotes purely dynamic contract checking and column "static+dynamic" denotes the combination of static and dynamic contract checking as described in this paper. The column "speedup" is the ratio of the previous columns (where a lower bound is given if the execution time of the optimized program is below 10 ms).

Table 1. Benchmarks comparing dynamic and static contract checking

Expression	Dynamic	static+dynamic	Speedup
`fac 20`	0.00	0.00	n.a.
`sum 1000000`	0.99	0.19	5.10
`fib 35`	1.95	0.60	3.23
`last [1..20000000]`	0.63	0.35	1.78
`take 200000 [1..]`	0.31	0.19	1.68
`nth [1..] 50000`	26.33	0.01	2633
`allNats 200000`	0.27	0.19	1.40
`init [1..10000]`	2.78	0.00	>277
`[1..20000] ++ [1..1000]`	4.21	0.00	>420
`nrev [1..1000]`	3.50	0.00	>349
`rev [1..10000]`	1.88	0.00	>188

Many of the programs that we tested are already discussed in this paper. `allNats` produces (non-deterministically) some natural number between 0 and the given argument, where the precondition requires that the argument must be non-negative. `init` removes the last element of a list, where the precondition requires that the list is non-empty and the postcondition states that the length of the output list is decremented by one. The list concatenation (`++`) has a postcondition which states that the length of the output list is the sum of the lengths of the input lists. `nrev` and `rev` are naive and linear list reverse operations, respectively, where their postconditions require that the input and output lists are of identical length.

As expected, the benchmarks show that static contract checking has a positive impact on the execution time. If contracts are complex, e.g., require recursive computations on arguments, as in `nth`, `init`, "`++`", or `rev`, static contract checking can improve the execution times by orders of magnitudes. Even if the improvement is small or not measurable (e.g., `fac`), static contract verification is useful since any verified contract increases the confidence in the correctness of the software and contributes to a more reliable software product.

7   Related Work

As contract checking is an important contribution to obtain more reliable software, techniques for it have been extensively explored. Mostly related to our approach is the work of Stulova et al. [27] on reducing run-time checks of assertions by static analysis in logic programs. Although the objectives of this and our work are similar, the techniques and underlying programming languages are different. For instance, Curry with its demand-driven evaluation strategy prevents the construction of static call graphs that are often used to analyze the data flow as in logic programming. The latter is used by Stulova et al. where assertions are verified by static analysis methods. Hence, the extensive set of benchmarks presented in their work is related to typical abstract domains used in logic programming, like modes or regular types. There are also approaches to approximate argument/result size relations in logic programs, e.g., [26], which might be used to verify assertions related to the size of data. In contrast to these fixpoint-based approaches, we simply collect assertions from program expressions and use symbolic reasoning, e.g., integer arithmetic with user-defined functions, to solve them. SMT solvers are well suited for this purpose and we showed that they can be successfully applied to verify complex assertions (see example nth above).

Static contract checking has also been explored in purely functional languages. [32] presents a method for static contract checking in Haskell by a program transformation and symbolic execution. Since an external verifier is not used, the approach is more limited. SMT solvers for static contract checking are also used in [24]. Similarly to our work, abstract assertions are collected and solved by an SMT solver in order to verify contracts. However, we consider a non-strict non-deterministic language which requires a different reasoning compared to the strict functional language used there. Another approach is the extension of the type system to express contracts as specific types. Dependent types are quite powerful since they allow to express size or shape constraints on data in the language of types. Although this supports the development of programs together with their correctness proofs [28], programming in such a language could be challenging if the proofs are difficult to construct. Therefore, we prefer a more practical method by checking properties which cannot be statically proved at run time. One can also express contracts as refinement types as in LiquidHaskell [29,30]. Similarly to our approach, LiquidHaskell uses an external SMT solver to verify contracts. Hence, LiquidHaskell can verify quite complex assertions, as shown by various case studies in [29]. Nevertheless, there might be assertions that cannot be verified in this way so that a combination of static and dynamic checking is preferable in practice.

An alternative approach to make dynamic contract checking more efficient has been proposed in [13] where assertions are checked in parallel to the application program. Thus, one can exploit the power of multi-core computers for assertion checking by running the main program and the contract checker on different cores.

8   Conclusions

In this paper we proposed a framework to combine static and dynamic contract checking. Contracts are useful to make software more reliable, e.g., avoid invoking operations with unintended arguments. Since checking all contracts at run time increases the overall execution time, we presented a method to verify contracts in Curry at compile time by using an external SMT solver. Of course, this might not be successful in all cases so that unverified contracts are still required to be checked at run time. Nevertheless, our initial experiments show the advantages of this technique, in particular, to reduce dynamic contract checking for recursive calls. Since we developed this framework for Curry, a language combining functional and logic programming features, the same techniques can be applied to purely functional or purely logic languages.

We do not expect that all contracts can be statically verified. Apart from the complexity of some contracts, preconditions of operations of the API of some libraries or packages cannot be checked since their use is unknown at compile time. However, one could provide two versions of such operations, one with a dynamic precondition check and one ("unsafe") without this check. Whenever one can verify that the precondition is satisfied at the call site, one can invoke the version without the precondition check. If all versions with precondition checks become dead code in a complete application, one has a high confidence in the quality of the entire application.

For future work, we will improve our tool in order to test the effectiveness of our approach on larger examples. This might provide also insights how to improve this approach in practice, e.g., how to use demand information to generate more precise proof obligations. If the contract verifier finds counter-examples to some proof obligation, one could also analyze these in order to check whether they show an actual contract violation. Furthermore, it might also be interesting to improve the power of static contract checking by integrating abstract interpretation techniques, like [14,27].

Acknowledgments. The author is grateful to John Gallagher, Grigore Rosu, and the anonymous reviewers for their helpful comments to improve the paper.

References

1. Albert, E., Hanus, M., Huch, F., Oliver, J., Vidal, G.: Operational semantics for declarative multi-paradigm languages. J. Symb. Comput. **40**(1), 795–829 (2005)
2. Antoy, S., Echahed, R., Hanus, M.: A needed narrowing strategy. J. ACM **47**(4), 776–822 (2000)
3. Antoy, S., Hanus, M.: Declarative programming with function patterns. In: Hill, P.M. (ed.) LOPSTR 2005. LNCS, vol. 3901, pp. 6–22. Springer, Heidelberg (2006). https://doi.org/10.1007/11680093_2
4. Antoy, S., Hanus, M.: Overlapping rules and logic variables in functional logic programs. In: Etalle, S., Truszczyński, M. (eds.) ICLP 2006. LNCS, vol. 4079, pp. 87–101. Springer, Heidelberg (2006). https://doi.org/10.1007/11799573_9
5. Antoy, S., Hanus, M.: Set functions for functional logic programming. In: Proceedings of the 11th ACM SIGPLAN International Conference on Principles and Practice of Declarative Programming (PPDP 2009), pp. 73–82. ACM Press (2009)
6. Antoy, S., Hanus, M.: Contracts and specifications for functional logic programming. In: Russo, C., Zhou, N.-F. (eds.) PADL 2012. LNCS, vol. 7149, pp. 33–47. Springer, Heidelberg (2012). https://doi.org/10.1007/978-3-642-27694-1_4
7. Antoy, S., Hanus, M.: Default rules for Curry. Theory Pract. Log. Program. **17**(2), 121–147 (2017)
8. Braßel, B.: Implementing functional logic programs by translation into purely functional programs. Ph.D. thesis, Christian-Albrechts-Universität zu Kiel (2011)

9. Braßel, B., Hanus, M., Peemöller, B., Reck, F.: KiCS2: a new compiler from Curry to Haskell. In: Kuchen, H. (ed.) WFLP 2011. LNCS, vol. 6816, pp. 1–18. Springer, Heidelberg (2011). https://doi.org/10.1007/978-3-642-22531-4_1

10. Chitil, O., McNeill, D., Runciman, C.: Lazy assertions. In: Trinder, P., Michaelson, G.J., Peña, R. (eds.) IFL 2003. LNCS, vol. 3145, pp. 1–19. Springer, Heidelberg (2004). https://doi.org/10.1007/978-3-540-27861-0_1

11. de Dios Castro, J., López-Fraguas, F.J.: Extra variables can be eliminated from functional logic programs. Electron. Notes Theor. Comput. Sci. **188**, 3–19 (2007)

12. de Moura, L., Bjørner, N.: Z3: an efficient SMT solver. In: Ramakrishnan, C.R., Rehof, J. (eds.) TACAS 2008. LNCS, vol. 4963, pp. 337–340. Springer, Heidelberg (2008). https://doi.org/10.1007/978-3-540-78800-3_24

13. Dimoulas, C., Pucella, R., Felleisen, M.: Future contracts. In: Proceedings of the 11th ACM SIGPLAN International Conference on Principles and Practice of Declarative Programming (PPDP 2009), pp. 195–206. ACM Press (2009)

14. Fähndrich, M., Logozzo, F.: Static contract checking with abstract interpretation. In: Beckert, B., Marché, C. (eds.) FoVeOOS 2010. LNCS, vol. 6528, pp. 10–30. Springer, Heidelberg (2011). https://doi.org/10.1007/978-3-642-18070-5_2

15. González-Moreno, J.C., Hortalá-González, M.T., López-Fraguas, F.J., Rodríguez-Artalejo, M.: An approach to declarative programming based on a rewriting logic. J. Log. Program. **40**, 47–87 (1999)

16. Hanus, M.: Improving lazy non-deterministic computations by demand analysis. In: Technical Communications of the 28th International Conference on Logic Programming. Leibniz International Proceedings in Informatics (LIPIcs), vol. 17, pp. 130–143 (2012)

17. Hanus, M.: Functional logic programming: from theory to Curry. In: Voronkov, A., Weidenbach, C. (eds.) Programming Logics. LNCS, vol. 7797, pp. 123–168. Springer, Heidelberg (2013). https://doi.org/10.1007/978-3-642-37651-1_6

18. Hanus, M.: CurryCheck: checking properties of Curry programs. In: Hermenegildo, M.V., Lopez-Garcia, P. (eds.) LOPSTR 2016. LNCS, vol. 10184, pp. 222–239. Springer, Cham (2017). https://doi.org/10.1007/978-3-319-63139-4_13

19. Hanus, M., Antoy, S., Braßel, B., Engelke, M., Höppner, K., Koj, J., Niederau, P., Sadre, R., Steiner, F.: PAKCS: The Portland Aachen Kiel Curry System (2016). http://www.informatik.uni-kiel.de/~pakcs/

20. Hanus, M., Skrlac, F.: A modular and generic analysis server system for functional logic programs. In: Proceedings of the ACM SIGPLAN 2014 Workshop on Partial Evaluation and Program Manipulation (PEPM 2014), pp. 181–188. ACM Press (2014)

21. Hanus, M. (ed.): Curry: an integrated functional logic language (vers. 0.9.0) (2016). http://www.curry-language.org

22. Launchbury, J.: A natural semantics for lazy evaluation. In: Proceedings of the 20th ACM Symposium on Principles of Programming Languages (POPL 1993), pp. 144–154. ACM Press (1993)

23. Milner, R.: A theory of type polymorphism in programming. J. Comput. Syst. Sci. **17**, 348–375 (1978)

24. Nguyen, P.C., Tobin-Hochstadt, S., Van Horn, D.: Soft contract verification. In: Proceedings of the 19th ACM SIGPLAN International Conference on Functional Programming (ICFP 2014), pp. 139–152. ACM Press (2014)

25. Peyton Jones, S. (ed.): Haskell 98 Language and Libraries—The Revised Report. Cambridge University Press, Cambridge (2003)

26. Serrano, A., López-García, P., Bueno, F., Hermenegildo, M.V.: Sized type analysis for logic programs. Theory Pract. Log. Program. **13**(4–5–Online–Supplement), 1–15 (2013)
27. Stulova, N., Morales, J.F., Hermenegildo, M.: Reducing the overhead of assertion run-time checks via static analysis. In: Proceedings of the 18th International Symposium on Principles and Practice of Declarative Programming (PPDP 2016), pp. 90–103. ACM Press (2016)
28. Stump, A.: Verified Functional Programming in Agda. ACM and Morgan & Claypool, New York (2016)
29. Vazou, N., Seidel, E.L., Jhala, R.: LiquidHaskell: experience with refinement types in the real world. In: Proceedings of the 2014 ACM SIGPLAN Symposium on Haskell, pp. 39–51. ACM Press (2014)
30. Vazou, N., Seidel, E.L., Jhala, R., Peyton Jones, S.: Refinement types for Haskell. In: Proceedings of the 19th ACM SIGPLAN International Conference on Functional Programming (ICFP), pp. 269–282. ACM Press (2014)
31. Wadler, P.: How to declare an imperative. ACM Comput. Surv. **29**(3), 240–263 (1997)
32. Xu, D.N., Peyton Jones, S.L., Claessen, K.: Static contract checking for Haskell. In: Proceedings of the 36th ACM Symposium on Principles of Programming Languages (POPL 2009), pp. 41–52 (2009)

Author Index

Printed in the United States
By Bookmasters